Windows 3.1: A Developer's Guide

2nd Edition

Windows 3.1: A Developer's Guide

2nd Edition

Features in-depth
coverage of
Windows' most
advanced and
powerful features.

Includes 12
complete
applications,
including Colonel
Special Edition.

Jeffrey M. Richter

M&T Books
A Division of M & T Publishing, Inc.
411 Borel Avenue, Suite 100
San Mateo, CA 94402

Library of Congress Cataloging-in-Publication Data

Richter, Jeffrey
    Windows 3.1: a developer's guide / Jeffrey M. Richter.—2nd ed.
        p. cm.
    Includes index.
    ISBN 1-55851-276-4
    1. Windows (Computer programs) 2. Microsoft Windows (Computer program) I. Title
QA76.76.W56R55   1992   92-16517
005.4'3--dc20   CIP

Project Editor: Sarah Wadsworth   **Cover Design:** Lauren Smith Design
Copy Editor: Laura Moorhead   **Production Supervisor:** Cindy Williams

95   94   93 92   4 3 2 1

This book is dedicated to Donna Murray
for all of the great times that we spent together over the past years.

Contents

WHY THIS BOOK IS FOR YOU 1

CHAPTER 1: ANATOMY OF A WINDOW 3

Registering a Window Class 3
Class Types 4
    System Global Classes 4
    Application Global Classes 4
    Application Local Classes 5
    Window Classes with the Same Name 5
The Parts of a Window Class 6
How Windows Stores Window Classes Internally 8
Creating and Destroying Window Instances 12
Window Styles 14
    How Windows Stores Window Instances Internally 16
Window Properties 20
Window Messages 22
    Kinds of Messages 23
    Class-Defined Integer Messages 24
    System-Global String Messages 25
Sneaking a Peek at Windows 25
    Voyeur's Initialization 27
    Initializing the Statistics Dialog Box 29
    Peering into Windows 32
    Updating the Dialog Box 35
    Freezing the Dialog-Box Information 37
    Drawing a Frame Around the Window 38
    Setting the Class and Window Information 40
    Filling the Style List Boxes 42

v

CHAPTER 2: SUBCLASSING AND SUPERCLASSING
    WINDOWS 63
How Window Subclassing Works 63
Limitations Imposed by Window Subclassing 68
The Program Manager Restore Program 68
    How PM Restore Works 69
    The *WinMain* Function 70
    Changing Program Manager's Menus 73
A Word About Procedural Instances 75
    The *PMSubClass* Function and Message Trapping 80
    The *AnyAppsRunning* Function 84
    Running PM Restore 84
How Window Superclassing Works 93
An Example of Window Superclassing 99
The Window Superclassing Package: SUPERCLS.C 99
The Application Program: NOALPHA.C 105
    Initializing the Application 105
    The Superclass Window Procedure 106
    The Dialog-Box Function 108

CHAPTER 3: DIALOG-BOX TECHNIQUES 125
The *SetWindowPos* Dialog Box 127
The Options Dialog Box 131
    Designing the Dialog Box 132
    The Dialog-Box Function 133
    The *ShowArea* Function 135
Modalless Dialog Boxes 138
    Working with Modalless Dialog Boxes 139
    How Modalless Dialog Boxes Work 142
Dynamic Dialog Boxes 144
    Building the Dialog-Box Template 149
Managing the Dialog Templates Memory Block 153
Mode-Select Dialog Boxes 154
    Approach 1: Modeless dialog box in a modal dialog box 156
    Approach 2: Using the *SetParent* function 157
    Final Approach: The brute force method 161

CHAPTER 4: DESIGNING CUSTOM CHILD CONTROLS....213

Rules for Designing Custom Child Controls....................................214
Implementing a Meter Control..218
    Designing the Meter Programmer's Interface.........................219
    Implementing the Meter Control Code...............................221
    Special Messages for Child Controls................................224
    Painting the Meter Control 226
A Homespun Spin Button...236
    Designing the Spin Button Programmer's Interface..................237
    Implementing the Spin Button Code 239
    Painting the Spin Button Control.................................240
    Changing a Value with the Spin Button............................242
    Scrolling the Spin Button..245
Integrating Custom Child Controls with Microsoft's Dialog Editor.........255
    Preparing the Dialog Editor 255
    Adding the Dialog Editor Support Functions to Custom Controls.....257
    The Class*Info* Function...259
    The Class*Style* and Class*DlgFn* Functions 262
    The Class*Flags* Function 270
Using Custom Controls in an Application 285

CHAPTER 5: SETTING UP PRINTERS 295

How Windows Manages Printers...295
    Printer Device Drivers 302
    The *DEVMODE* Structure and Printer Environments 306
    Printer Environments 312
    The*ExtDeviceMode* Function 314
    Sending Output to a Printer 319
    Getting Printer-Specific Information 320
    Printer Driver Caveats 322
The Print and Print Setup Common Dialog Boxes...........................323
Printer Setup Demonstration Application 331

CHAPTER 6: TASKS AND QUEUES...........................341

Tasks and Their Handles 341
    Looking Toward the Future 348

Application Queues 348
The System and Application Queues 351

CHAPTER 7: HOOKS **363**
Hook Basics...365
Removing a Filter Function from the Chain 373
    The *WH_CALLWNDPROC* and *WH_GETMESSAGE* Hooks...................373
    The *WH_KEYBOARD* Hook...375
    The *WH_MOUSE* Hook..377
    The *WH_HARDWARE* Hook 379
    The *WH_SYSMSGFILTER* and *WH_MSGFILTER* Hooks.....................380
    The *WH_JOURNALRECORD* and *WH_JOURNALPLAYBACK* Hooks....384
    The *WH_SHELL* Hook 390
    The *WH_CBT* Hook...391
    The *WH_DEBUG* Hook...396
The Screen-Blanker Utility 398
The Echo Application (a Macro Recorder) 415
    Recording and Playing Events..415
    Requesting Help...418

CHAPTER 8: MDI APPLICATION TECHNIQUES **437**
MDI Application Basics..437
The MDI Sample Application 444
Closing MDI Child Windows...445
Eating Mouse Messages 450
Status Bars..454
Menu Option Help..457
Custom Tiling...471
Implementing a Ribbon 477
Closing an MDI Application 482

CHAPTER 9: IMPLEMENTING DRAG-AND-DROP...........**541**
Becoming a Dropfile Client 546
How it Works..547
BurnIt...550
Becoming a Dropfile Server..558

Sample Dropfile Server 563
Other Uses for Drag-and-Drop 576
Where Do We Go From Here? 577

CHAPTER 10: INSTALLING COMMERCIAL
APPLICATIONS **579**
Designing a Setup Program 579
Microsoft's Setup Program Support 582
Version Control 587
Putting Version Control and Decompression Together 602
Special Considerations for Setup Programs 611
The Setup Application 616
The SETUP.INF File 616
The *[App]* section 621
The *[Disks]* section 622
The *[SrcDirs]* section 622
The *[DstDirs]* section 622
The *[Files]* section 623
The *[PM Info]* section 623
The *[End]* section 624
Dynamic Data Exchange With Program Manager 631
Sending Commands to Program Manager 634
Terminating the DDE Conversation 636

APPENDIX A: DETERMINING THE STACK SIZE
REQUIRED BY AN APPLICATION **693**

APPENDIX B: ACCESSING CLASS AND WINDOW
EXTRA BYTES **697**

APPENDIX C: THE BUILTINS.JMR FILE **701**

INDEX **703**

Acknowledgements

I would like to thank the following people, for without their assistance, you would be staring at the palm of your hand right now:

To Susan Ramee for her unending help and assistance. It is not possible to thank you enough for putting up with me during the marathon writing and coding sessions. Your contribution to this project can be seen throughout each and every page. Between reading every chapter, making comments and suggestions, creating the figures, and designing the best icons ever seen, may you never get stung by that pesky Budgie, Budgie Bee.

To (Aunt) Donna Murray for her help in the first edition of this book: proofreading every chapter, making suggestions, discussing various implementations for the sample applications, and playing that popular all new game, "Stump the Author." Aren't you tired of eating spaghetti?

To my parents, Arlene and Sylvan, who bought me my first computer (a TRS-80 Model 1). They were afraid that I would use the computer for a week and then toss it in the closet next to the chemistry set. I will never be able to thank you enough for all the love and support you have given me over the years.

To Jim Harkins and Carlos Richardson, mere bytes, words, and double-words cannot express how grateful I am to both of you for helping me by going above and beyond the duty of ordinary mortals. We'll see who beats who the next time we play the virtual-reality game!

To Dan Horn at Borland International for keeping me up-to-date with new versions of the Borland C++ compiler.

To Sarah "Here's the FedEx number again" Wadsworth and Laura "Somebody might notice" Moorhead at M&T Books for investing their time and effort in my book.

To Elvira Peretsman for her assistance with the original creation of the MDI Sample Application and for always brightening my every day with a new wardrobe.

Preface

It wasn't until the introduction of Microsoft Windows Version 3.0 on May 22, 1990, that graphical computing finally took the IBM-PC family of computers by storm. There are many reasons for Windows 3.0's success: the improved interface, the improved memory management, and the abundance of applications being developed and distributed for Windows. While it's true that Windows 3.0 sports some impressive technical features, I believe that Windows owes most of its success to the third-party companies that have devoted their time and money into producing Windows applications. After all, people don't buy operating environments; they buy applications that help them do their work more efficiently.

Microsoft, realizing this itself, set up a "Microsoft Windows Pre-release" program. This program was designed to allow serious Windows developers the ability to design and use Windows 3.0 about a full year before its commercial release. This meant that a large number of commercial applications were able to be announced on the same day as the Windows 3.0 announcement. Without these third-party products available, Microsoft Windows would not be in as much demand as it is today.

If you thought the pre-release program for Windows 3.0 was impressive, it was nothing compared to the program for Windows 3.1. For its beta, Microsoft had over ten thousand testers. Many of these testers were companies that had already been shipping Windows versions of their products. When Windows 3.1 was finally announced, vendors already had updated copies of their products ready to go out the door.

At this stage of the game, many companies are abandoning their product's DOS counterparts and are focusing their development efforts on Windows exclusively. And because Windows 3.1 now includes the Multimedia extensions and support for pen recognition, new types of applications can be written. These relatively new technologies will bring computers to people who have never used a computer before.

In addition, Microsoft is working on Windows-NT and Windows-32. Windows-NT is coined the "portable version of Windows." This version runs on computers that do not use Intel-based microprocessors. By Microsoft endowing Windows with the capability of running on different hardware platforms, the potential market of customers becomes much greater.

Special versions of Windows are also being created to run on home appliances. That's right, in just a few years, you'll be using Windows to program your VCR, compact disk player, television set, microwave oven, and so on. With all these enhancements to Windows, there should be no question in your mind—Learn Windows today! The need for Windows developers is growing exponentially every day.

This book is for the experienced Windows developer who wants to gain insight into some of this complicated environment's most powerful features. Almost every chapter contains at least one programming example that demonstrates the concepts presented. Some of these programs are complete applications that may be used unmodified, while others show how to combine various Windows features to produce a result greater than the sum of its parts. Many of the applications contain code sections or modules that isolate some of the more fundamental concepts. These isolated sections are usually general enough so that they may be included in your own Windows application without any modifications. All of the explanations and source code examples are geared toward designing and implementing applications that will someday become commercial products.

It is much easier to write a Windows application than it is to write a great Windows application. The great applications are the ones that pay strict attention to detail and are tested thoroughly. Below is a short checklist of things to verify when creating your application:

1. Test it under the most common screen resolutions. Problems are most notable when dialog boxes appear. Text is often clipped or wrapped to another line. I find it is best to design dialog boxes using the lowest resolution that you ever expect a user to have.

2. Test it in color and monochrome. Many applications use hard-coded colors or choose default colors for certain things. In monochrome, this often leads to items not being distinguishable from one another. It would not be

good, for example, if a word processing program painted its text black on top of a black background.

3. Test your application using only a keyboard. While it's true that almost every Windows user will have a mouse or similar pointing device, some users prefer to use the keyboard. This issue actually extends to several different situations. For example, make sure that nmemonic keys in menus are unique.

4. For dialog boxes, test the tabbing order for controls. This is so often overlooked. It drives me up the wall when I am using an application's dialog box and press tab to go to the next control and instead, I am placed in some other control.

5. Again for dialog boxes, test the nmemonic keys. Make sure that none are duplicated and that selecting a nmemonic actually takes you to the right control.

6. Follow Windows' style guidelines. There are two good reasons why.
   A. Users expect your application to work this way and find it easier to use.
   B. Windows is designed by Microsoft to work this way, making it easier for you to write your application.
   I have seen a couple of companies invest enormous amounts of both time and money so that their applications have a different "look and feel." What ends up happening is that subtle bugs are introduced into the applications that often require hacking the code just to get it right.

7. Test your application with end users. If there is a bug, the users will find it. It is often difficult for developers to find their own bugs. End users, on the other hand, come up with ways to use your software that you never imagined. Unfortunately, it's difficult to find beta testers that actually report errors when they find them. Many of them assume that they are just not doing something right and don't want to appear stupid by calling for help.

I think that we, as developers, should try much harder to open the doors of communication with users.

I apologize for going off on some kind of rampage, but I do get awfully passionate about this kind of thing. Anyway, when designing a Windows application, it is extremely important to pay attention to small details like the previous items. These concepts are stressed throughout this book.

Tools Necessary to Compile the Sample Source Code Examples

All of the sample applications presented throughout the book were compiled using the Borland C++ compiler (Version 3.1) and tested using Windows 3.0 and 3.1 (except for the hook and drag-and-drop applications that require 3.1). While all of the programs were developed using the Borland compiler, they should compile cleanly using any other company's C/C++ compiler.

I use several conventions in my code that make it much easier for you to follow and understand. These conventions are explained as follows:

1. All of the variable names use standard Hungarian notation.

2. All global variables are prefixed with a single underscore character. This helps to make understanding a function easier because any variable not preceded by an underscore is either a parameter to the function or an *auto* or *static* local variable.

3. When a function is declared, a space appears immediately before the opening parenthesis. For example:

```
int FunctionName (int nX, int nY) { }
                 ^ space character
```

However, when calls to this function are made, the space is not used. For example:

```
nZ = FunctionName(nX, nY);
                  ^ no space character
```

The reason for this is so that you can locate a function declaration in a source module very easily. By requesting that your program editor search for: "FunctionName " (notice the trailing space), the editor will find the function itself instead of calls to this function.

4. Windows 3.1 offers a new header file, WINDOWSX.H. This file contains a number of macros to make writing Windows applications easier and faster. Mostly, these macros help by performing any necessary casting so that you don't have to sprinkle casts throughout your code. I have used many of these macros in my own code. There is also a set of macros called message crackers. I have only used these macros in the sample MDI application because the other applications are easier to understand without the crackers.

I have mixed feelings about the message crackers. If you are developing a complex window procedure, I highly recommend using them. But if your window procedure is simple, keep it that way by not using the message crackers. However, Microsoft claims that porting an application from 16-bit Windows to Win-32 will be much simpler if you use message crackers. The choice is yours.

Why this Book is for You

This book is for the Windows developer who wants to explore this intricate operating environment in detail. While there are many books about Microsoft Windows programming, most of them simply discuss the basic features, capabilities, and resources that Windows offers. This book covers some of the more advanced and powerful features of Windows that get little or no mention in other Windows books. It also demonstrates how to combine the basic Windows building blocks to create complete applications.

With each topic presented, insights into Windows' inner workings are discussed, followed by sample source code demonstrating the implementation details. Having this understanding will help you to better exploit the facilities offered by Windows, making your applications more robust and efficient. The goal of this book is to give you the tools and knowledge necessary to develop professional Windows applications.

CHAPTER 1

Anatomy of a Window

The window class, which controls a window's appearance and behavior, plays a central role in Windows programming. It must be explicitly defined before any windows can be created.

The process of defining a class in Windows is called *registering the class*. Registering a class does not create any windows. However, once the class is defined any number of windows can be created.

Applications may register many window classes. Windows maintains knowledge of these classes until all instances of the registering application terminate or the class is explicitly unregistered.

Registering a Window Class

To create a window class, you must write a window procedure, initialize a *WNDCLASS* structure, and call the *RegisterClass* function. The most important members of the *WNDCLASS* structure are:

- *lpszClassName*. The name given to the class.
- *lpfnWndProc*. The address of the procedure that performs operations for windows of the class.
- *hInstance*. The handle or owner of the application or dynamic link library (DLL) that registered the class.

The remaining members of the *WNDCLASS* structure define default attributes for windows of the class.

When a window class is no longer needed, the *UnregisterClass* function can be called to remove the class from memory. All windows must be destroyed before their class is unregistered. Windows automatically unregisters window classes when the owning application or DLL terminates.

Class Types

There are three types of window classes: system global, application global, and application local.

System Global Classes

System global classes are only registered by Windows when you start up the environment; an application cannot register system global classes. Windows defines all the window procedures for these classes internally, initializes the *WNDCLASS* structure for each of them, and calls *RegisterClass*—all before the shell application (usually Program Manager) appears on the screen. System global classes are unregistered only when Windows terminates. This means that all these classes are available the entire time Windows is running.

To use these system global classes, call *CreateWindow* or *CreateWindowEx* and pass it the class name of the type of window you wish to create. Below is a list of the system global classes you can use in your applications:

BUTTON	COMBOBOX	EDIT	LISTBOX
MDICLIENT	SCROLLBAR	STATIC	

Although these classes are frequently referred to as *child controls*, they are no different from classes that you register yourself, except that they are available to all applications.

Windows also registers a number of window classes that are used implicitly by applications. Windows automatically creates instances of these window classes as needed. For example, when you call the *DialogBox* or *CreateDialog* function, Windows creates a dialog-box window and all the child controls are created as children of this window. Windows also creates a caption window when your application is minimized. The text that appears below your application's icon is painted in a caption window that Windows created implicitly when the application was minimized.

Application Global Classes

Application global classes are registered by an application or, more often, a DLL. DLLs usually include class registration in their initialization code and unregister the classes at termination. This means that window classes registered in DLLs are only available while the DLL is running.

Once a class is registered, any application can create windows of that class. Custom controls that you create yourself should be registered as application global classes. For example, you might design a window class called SPIN for use in two applications. By registering the class in a DLL as application global, you can ensure that both applications can create windows of the SPIN class.

To register a class as application global, include the *CS_GLOBALCLASS* style flag when initializing the *style* member of the *WNDCLASS* structure.

Application Local Classes

Application local classes are registered by your application for its sole use. Applications cannot create windows based on application local classes registered by other applications. These classes are available from the time they are registered to the time they are unregistered, or until all instances of the registering application terminate.

A class is registered as application local by default; the *CS_GLOBALCLASS* flag is omitted when the style member of the *WNDCLASS* structure is initialized.

Window Classes with the Same Name

It's possible for different applications to register window classes with the same name. When an application is creating a window, Windows first tries to match the class name specified with local window classes registered by the same application. If a matching application local class cannot be found, Windows searches for an application global class with the same name. Finally, if a matching application global class cannot be found, Windows searches the system global window classes.

Because Windows uses this order to locate classes, defining an application local class called EDIT would cause all EDIT windows subsequently created by your application (including those in your dialog-box templates) to be of the application local class and not of the Windows system global class. This scheme also allows two applications to register SPIN classes and be guaranteed that windows created in each application are based on their respective SPIN classes.

The following table summarizes the results of calling *RegisterClass* when an application attempts to register a window class having the same name as a previously registered class.

How the class was previously registered:				
Application wants to register the new class as:	System Global	Application Global	Application Local, same application	Application Local, different application
Application Global	Successful	Failure	Failure	Successful
Application Local	Successful	Failure	Failure	Successful

It would be logical to assume that an application local class could override an application global class. However, Windows does not allow this, as it would break compatibility with previous versions of Windows.

The Parts of a Window Class

The first step in registering a window class is to initialize the members of *WND-CLASS*. Here is a description of some of these members:

- *lpszClassName*. The *lpszClassName* member of *WNDCLASS* indicates the name of the window class. When you ask Windows to create a window of a certain class, it compares the class name of each registered class with the class name of the window you wish to create. If a matching registered class can be found, Windows creates the window and returns its window handle. If there is no registered class with the name you specified, Windows returns NULL.

- *hInstance*. The *hInstance* member of *WNDCLASS* identifies the owner or creator of the window class. For an application, this value is passed to the *WinMain* function. For DLLs, the information is passed to the *LibEntry* function. This value lets Windows automatically unregister the class when all instances of its creator terminate.

- *lpfnWndProc*. The *lpfnWndProc* member of *WNDCLASS* specifies the procedure that defines the behavior for all windows of the class. When something happens or is requested of the window, the window procedure is called and passed a message describing the event that occurred or the service that needs to be performed. The procedure then performs some operation to satisfy the request.

Windows supplies a default window procedure called *DefWindowProc*. The messages processed by this procedure mostly deal with the behavior of the window's system menu and non-client area. The complete list of recognized messages can be found in the *Microsoft Windows Programmer's Reference*. The table also describes, for each message, the operations *DefWindowProc* will perform. These operations are what Microsoft has defined as "standard" behavior for a window.

It's possible to set the *lpfnWndProc* member of *WNDCLASS* to *DefWindowProc* before registering the class. This will register a window class that has default, or standard, behavior. However, the window will not do anything interesting, so there's little point.

- *style*. The style member of the *WNDCLASS* structure specifies some of the behavioral aspects for windows of the class. WINDOWS.H defines the valid class styles that can be used to register a class. The list appears below:

Class style	WINDOWS.H identifier	ID value
Painting	CS_VREDRAW	0x0001
	CS_HREDRAW	0x0002
	CS_OWNDC	0x0020
	CS_CLASSDC	0x0040
	CS_PARENTDC	0x0080
	CS_SAVEBITS	0x0800
	CS_BYTEALIGNCLIENT	0x1000
	CS_BYTEALIGNWINDOW	0x2000
Input conversions	CS_KEYCVTWINDOW	0x0004
	CS_DBLCLKS	0x0008
	CS_NOKEYCVT	0x0100
	CS_NOCLOSE	0x0200
Class type	CS_GLOBALCLASS	0x4000

- *The Remaining Members.* The remaining members of the *WNDCLASS* structure are *cbClsExtra, cbWndExtra, hIcon, hCursor, hbrBackground,* and *lpszMenuName.* These members describe the default attributes and behavior that windows of the registered class should have.

How Windows Stores Window Classes Internally

When you call *RegisterClass*, Windows performs the following sequence of events:

1. The class name is checked to see if a class with the same name registered by the same module already exists. If so, *RegisterClass* returns NULL.
2. A block of memory is allocated to store information about the class. The block is large enough to hold all of the information in the *WNDCLASS* structure plus the number of bytes that were specified in the *cbClsExtra* member.
3. The contents of the *WNDCLASS* structure are copied into the memory block and the extra bytes are initialized to zero. These additional bytes are reserved for your application's use, and Windows does not use them at all. The information stored in the extra bytes is available to every window based on the registered class. The management of these extra bytes is left entirely up to the programmer.
4. Memory is allocated to store the name of the class' menu. The *lpszMenuName* field is changed to point to this memory block.
5. The handle of the module that is associated with the data instance handle specified in the *hInstance* member of the *WNDCLASS* structure is obtained. This module handle is then saved in the window class memory block. This is why the *GetClassWord* function uses a *GCW_HMODULE* identifier instead of a *GCW_HINSTANCE* identifier.
6. The class name is added to an atom table and the atom value is saved in the window class memory block. This value can later be retrieved by calling *GetClassWord* using the *GCW_ATOM* identifier.
7. Finally, the atom value obtained in the previous step is returned from the *RegisterClass* function. Once the atom value is known, it can be used in functions where the class name is a parameter. For example, to create an instance of a window that has just been registered, you could do the following:

```
atomClass = RegisterClass(&WndClass);
hWnd = CreateWindow(MAKEINTRESOURCE(atomClass), NULL, WS_CHILD, ...);
```

Figure 1-1 shows how a window class may be represented internally.

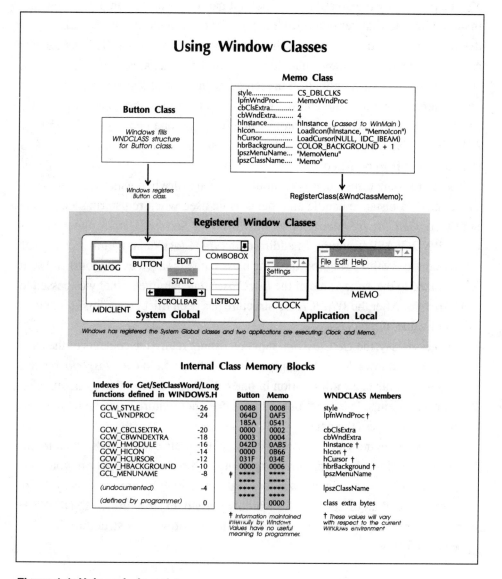

Figure 1-1. Using window classes

Windows contains functions that allow you to retrieve and modify the information in the class structure after the class has been registered. These functions are described in this section.

GetClassInfo can be used to fill a *WNDCLASS* structure with information about a previously registered class. The first parameter to the function is the data instance handle that registered the class. This value should be NULL if you desire the information for any of the Windows system classes. This parameter can also be a module instance handle instead of a data instance handle as demonstrated in the Voyeur application presented at the end of this chapter. The second parameter is either the address of a string containing the name of the class that you are interested in or the atom value for a class name passed by using the *MAKEINTRESOURCE* macro. The last parameter is the address of a *WNDCLASS* structure that is to be filled.

There are some things that you should be aware of when using *GetClassInfo*. Since the data instance handle and menu name used when registering a class are not saved, *GetClassInfo* does not set the *hInstance* and *lpszMenuName* members of the *WNDCLASS* structure. In addition, the *lpszClassName* member cannot be set to point to a valid string (because the class name is saved as an atom) and so it is initialized to the same value of the *lpszClassName* parameter that was passed to *GetClassInfo*. After the *WNDCLASS* structure has been filled, *GetClassInfo* returns the atom value of the class.

Needless to say, the *GetClassInfo* function cannot return the contents of the class extra bytes. Windows does not supply an inverse function to *GetClassInfo* that lets you change all the class information in one call. What differentiates this function from the remaining class functions is that it does not require a handle to an existing window to access the data.

GetClassLong and *GetClassWord* allow you to retrieve the individual members of the window class structure. To get any of the class information, you must supply a handle to an existing window that was created from the class you are interested in and an offset into the window class data structure. WINDOWS.H defines the offsets for all the elements in the window class structure. The list appears as follows:

Class element	WINDOWS.H identifier	Offset
Atom (After Windows 3.0)	GCW_ATOM	-32
Style	GCW_STYLE	-26
Window procedure	GCL_WNDPROC	-24
Class extra bytes	GCW_CBCLSEXTRA	-20
Window extra bytes	GCW_CBWNDEXTRA	-18
Owner's module instance	GCW_HMODULE	-16
Icon	GCW_HICON	-14
Cursor	GCW_HCURSOR	-12
Brush background	GCW_HBRBACKGROUND	-10
Menu name	GCL_MENUNAME	-8
Class name	(undefined)	-4
Start of class extra bytes	(programmer defined)	0

SetClassLong and *SetClassWord* allow you to change the individual members of the window class structure. To alter any of the class information, you must supply a handle to an existing window that was created from the class you are interested in, an offset into the window class data structure, and the desired new value. The WINDOWS.H identifiers listed above for *GetClassLong* and *GetClassWord* should be used for these functions as well.

Prior to Windows 3.1, these functions performed no parameter validation, meaning that you could pass in any index and change any of the class elements. However, in Windows 3.1, a great deal of parameter validation is performed. For example, Windows will now examine the value of the index parameter to guarantee that it refers to either a predefined index or is not a value that is greater than the number of class extra bytes that were specified when the class was registered. In addition, Windows will ignore any calls to *SetClassWord/Long* where the index is *GCL_MENUNAME*, *GCW_HMODULE*, or *GCW_ATOM* because changing any of these values would have disastrous effects on the system. Appendix C presents a method of accessing the class extra bytes that will ensure only valid indexes are used.

The most common reason for changing the window class structure is to change window attributes before creating a new window. The *SetClassLong* and *SetClass-Word* functions are inconvenient because they require a handle to a window of the desired class. Windows offers no satisfactory solution to this problem. To change an attribute of the window class structure, you must create a window of the desired class, call *SetClassLong* or *SetClassWord*, destroy the window, and create a new window of the same class.

Here is an example of how you could change all EDIT windows in all applications so that the mouse cursor will be an up-arrow instead of an I-beam:

```
// Create a window from the "EDIT" style.
hWndEdit = CreateWindow("EDIT", "", WS_OVERLAPPED, 0, 0, 0, 0,
    NULL, NULL, hInstance, 0l);
// Change the cursor handle to that of the up-arrow.
SetClassWord(hWndEdit, GCW_HCURSOR,
    LoadCursor(NULL, IDC_UPARROW));
// Destroy the edit window.
DestroyWindow(hWndEdit);
// From this point on, all edit windows will use an
// up-arrow instead of the I-beam mouse cursor.
```

Because Windows always refers to the window class structure when it's going to display a cursor, the up-arrow will appear for EDIT windows that have already been created as well as those that will be created in the future. Note that because EDIT is a system global class, this affects EDIT windows created by other applications as well as your own.

Creating and Destroying Window Instances

Windows are created by calling *CreateWindow* or *CreateWindowEx* with the name of the desired window class. This function sends several messages to the window procedure associated with the window class.

When *CreateWindow(Ex)* sends the *WM_NCCREATE* message to the window procedure, it's usually passed on to *DefWindowProc*. *DefWindowProc* allocates the block of memory used internally to describe this window instance, sets the window's caption, and initializes the scroll-bar values. The block of memory contains some information that is copied from the internal window class structure and some information from the parameters passed to *CreateWindow(Ex)*. If sufficient memory is not available for this memory block, *DefWindowProc* returns NULL.

When *CreateWindow(Ex)* sends the *WM_NCCREATE* message and NULL is returned, it stops sending messages to the window procedure and returns a NULL window handle to the caller.

During the creation of a window, *CreateWindow(Ex)* sends a *WM_CREATE* message (after the *WM_NCCREATE* message) so that any window-specific initialization may be performed. If you desire that the window not be created if initialization fails, return a value of -1 from your *WM_CREATE* processing. In addition to examining the return value from processing the *WM_NCCREATE* message, *CreateWindow(Ex)* examines the return value from the *WM_CREATE* message to see if the window should not be created. Note that the ability to halt window creation by returning -1 from *WM_CREATE* processing was undocumented before Windows 3.1; it does work correctly under Windows 3.0. The following code example demonstrates how to abort window creation if your initialization fails:

```
#define GCW_DATA            0
    .
    .
    .
case WM_CREATE:
    hGlobal = GlobalAlloc(GMEM_MOVEABLE, BUFFERSIZE);
    if (hGlobal == NULL)
        lResult = -1;      // Halt creation of window.
    else {
        SetClassWord(hWnd, GCW_DATA, hGlobal);
        // lResult was initialized to 0, Window creation OK.
    }
    break;

case WM_DESTROY:
    // Free block of memory created during WM_CREATE message.
    hGlobal = GetClassWord(hWnd, GCW_DATA);
    if (hGlobal != NULL)
        GlobalFree(hGlobal);
    break;
    .
    .
    .
return(lResult);
```

This code fragment also demonstrates how *WM_DESTROY* should be used to perform window cleanup. In this example, the global memory allocated by *WM_CRE-ATE* is freed. It is extremely important to note that Windows sends the *WM_DESTROY* message even if the return value from processing the *WM_CRE-ATE* message was -1. If the check to determine if *hGlobal* was NULL in the code fragment above was not done, we would be calling *GlobalFree* and passing it a handle of NULL. This is obviously something that must not be done.

Window Styles

CreateWindow's third parameter is the style of the window. As mentioned earlier, class style information affects all windows based on the class. Style information can also be specified for an individual instance of a class. The style parameter is a 32-bit value in which the high 16 bits specify style information that applies to all windows. WINDOWS.H defines styles that can be used for all windows. The list appears below:

Window style	WINDOWS.H identifier	ID value
Type	WS_OVERLAPPED	0x00000000L
	WS_POPUP	0x80000000L
	WS_CHILD	0x40000000L
States	WS_MINIMIZE	0x20000000L
	WS_VISIBLE	0x10000000L
	WS_DISABLED	0x08000000L
	WS_MAXIMIZE	0x01000000L
Clipping styles	WS_CLIPSIBLINGS	0x04000000L
	WS_CLIPCHILDREN	0x02000000L
Appearance	WS_CAPTION	0x00C00000L
	WS_BORDER	0x00800000L
	WS_DLGFRAME	0x00400000L
	WS_THICKFRAME	0x00040000L
	WS_HSCROLL	0x00100000L
	WS_VSCROLL	0x00200000L
	WS_SYSMENU	0x00080000L
Capabilities	WS_MINIMIZEBOX	0x00020000L
	WS_MAXIMIZEBOX	0x00010000L
Input focus sequence	WS_GROUP	0x00020000L
	WS_TABSTOP	0x00010000L

Note that the *WS_CAPTION* style is a combination of *WS_BORDER* and *WS_DLGFRAME*. Because a window cannot have both the *WS_BORDER* and *WS_DLGFRAME* styles, Windows interprets both bits being on as the *WS_CAP-TION* style.

Also note that the *WS_MINIMIZEBOX* and *WS_MAXIMIZEBOX* styles have identical values to the *WS_GROUP* and *WS_TABSTOP* identifiers. Windows treats these bits as *WS_GROUP* and *WS_TABSTOP* when the window is part of a dialog box to determine the input focus sequence. However, if the window is not part of a dialog box, Windows treats these bits as *WS_MINIMIZEBOX* and *WS_MAXIMIZEBOX*.

The low 16 bits of the window style parameter are specific to each class of window and have no predefined meaning to Windows itself. Microsoft has specified which styles apply to each of the system global classes. These can be combined with the window styles listed above to give greater control over the behavior of a window. WINDOWS.H defines the styles that can be used with each of the system global classes. Notice that each style for a class begins with a unique prefix.

System global class	Style prefix
DIALOG	*DS_*
BUTTON	*BS_*
COMBOBOX	*CBS_*
EDIT	*ES_*
LISTBOX	*LBS_*
MDICLIENT	*MDIS_*
SCROLLBAR	*SBS_*
STATIC	*SS_*

*DS_* styles are specified on the *STYLE* line in a dialog-box template. Windows knows to use these styles when the *DialogBox* or *CreateDialog* function implicitly creates the dialog-box window.

When examining the values for these identifiers in WINDOWS.H, you will notice that many of the values repeat. For example, *BS_DEFPUSHBUTTON* and *SS_CENTER* both have a value of 0x0001. This does not cause a problem because only the window procedure associated with the class will see these style bits. Each class will interpret the bits differently.

A window procedure can retrieve style information by using the *GetWindow-Long* function. Once the styles are retrieved, the procedure can *AND* the style with a particular identifier to see if the style is on or off. This information can be used to modify the behavior of the window.

Beginning with Windows 3.0, Microsoft added several new styles that can affect a window. To create a window using these new styles, you use *CreateWindowEx* instead of *CreateWindow*. The first parameter to *CreateWindowEx* represents the extended window styles. Like the window style value, the extended window style value is 32 bits long. WINDOWS.H defines the valid extended window styles. The list appears below:

Extended window style	WINDOWS.H identifier	ID value
Appearance	*WS_EX_DLGMODALFRAME*	0x80000000L
	WS_EX_TOPMOST	0x00000008L
	WS_EX_TRANSPARENT	0x00000020L
Communication	*WS_EX_NOPARENTNOTIFY*	0x40000000L
	WS_EX_ACCEPTFILES	0x00000010L

When you create a window using *CreateWindow*, the extended styles are considered to have a value of 0x00000000L.

How Windows Stores Window Instances Internally

The *CreateWindow* function can only create windows from a registered class. If Windows finds a class registered with the same name as the one requested, it allocates a block of memory to store information about the individual window. The block contains some of the information in the window class structure and some of the information that was passed to the *CreateWindow* function. Windows extends the size of the block by the number of bytes specified by the *cbWndExtra* value in the window class structure and initializes these bytes to zero.

Every window instance receives its own set of extra bytes. Like the class extra bytes, these are available solely for your application's use.

Figure 1-2 shows an example of how a window structure may be represented internally. Windows contains functions that allow you to retrieve and modify the information in the window structure after the window has been created. These functions are described in the following paragraphs.

The *GetClassName* function retrieves the class name that was used to create the window. The first parameter is the handle of the window, the second parameter is the address to a buffer that is to be filled with the class name, and the last parameter is the maximum length of this buffer. The return value indicates the atom value of the class.

The *GetWindowLong* and *GetWindowWord* functions allow you to retrieve the individual members of the window structure. To get any of the window information, you must supply a window handle and an offset into the window data structure. WINDOWS.H defines the offsets for all the elements in the window structure. The list appears below:

Window element	WINDOWS.H identifier	Offset
Extended style	*GWL_EXSTYLE*	-20
Style	*GWL_STYLE*	-16
ID	*GWW_ID*	-12
(undocumented)	(undocumented)	-10
Parent	*GWW_HWNDPARENT*	-8
Instance	*GWW_HINSTANCE*	-6
Window procedure	*GWL_WNDPROC*	-4
Start of window extra bytes	(programmer defined)	0

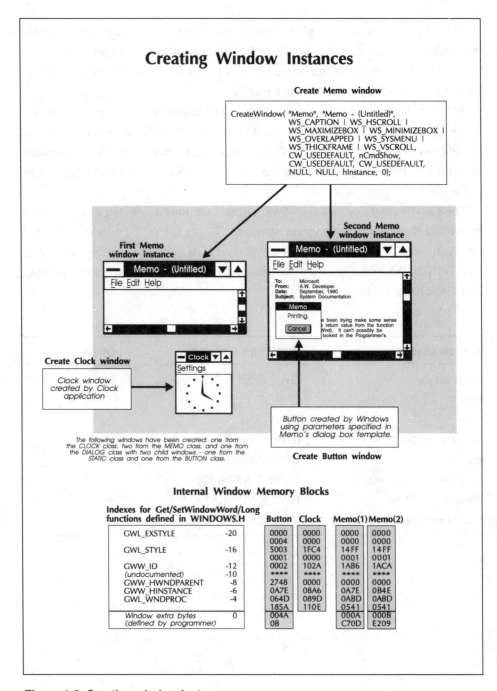

Figure 1-2. Creating window instances

The *SetWindowLong* and *SetWindowWord* functions let you change individual members of the window structure. To alter this information, you must supply a window handle, an offset into the window data structure, and the desired new value. The WINDOWS.H identifiers listed earlier for *GetWindowLong* and *GetWindow-Word* should be used for these functions as well.

The most common reason for changing the window structure is to store new values in the extra bytes. Here is an example of how you could keep track of how long an application has been running.

- *Step 1:* Define an ID to be used for referencing the window extra bytes:

```
#define GWL_STARTTIME    (0)
```

- *Step 2:* Register the class, making sure that four window extra bytes will be reserved for every window of this class:

```
WNDCLASS wc;
 .
 .
 .
wc.cbWndExtra = 4;
RegisterClass(&wc);
```

- *Step 3:* When the window is created, initialize the window extra bytes to the Windows system time:

```
case WM_CREATE:
    SetWindowLong(hWnd, GWL_STARTTIME, GetTickCount());
    break;
```

- *Step 4:* Determine the total time the application has been running:

```
DWORD dwSecondsRunning;
   .

   .

   .
dwSecondsRunning = (GetTickCount() -
    GetWindowLong(hWnd, GWL_STARTTIME)) / 1000;
```

Window Properties

Window properties give the programmer another way to associate data with windows. Properties are extremely useful if you want to associate data with a window instance for a class that you did not register yourself. If you didn't register the window class yourself, you don't know how many extra bytes were specified in the *WNDCLASS* structure. Although you can retrieve this information with *GetClassInfo*, you can be sure that if extra bytes were allocated they are being used by the window procedure that operates on this class. Using these extra bytes for your own purpose would surely interfere with the behavior of this window.

Properties allow you to associate data with a window by using a string name instead of modifying the information stored in the internal window structure. Only 16-bit values may be associated with a property. Because Windows must store property string names with a window, properties are slower to use and require more memory than window extra bytes.

Windows supplies four functions to manipulate properties of a window:

- The *SetProp* function associates a property with a window.
- The *RemoveProp* function removes a property associated with a window.
- The *GetProp* function retrieves the property associated with a window.
- The *EnumProps* function retrieves the list of all properties associated with a window.

The following is an example of how you could acquire some information in a modal dialog box and return that information to the caller.

• *Step 1:* The caller allocates memory for the information that will be retrieved by the modal dialog box:

```
#define MAX_USERS_NAME_LEN      (30)
    .

    .

    .

hLocal = LocalAlloc(LMEM_MOVEABLE | LMEM_ZEROINIT,
    MAX_USERS_NAME_LEN + 1);
DialogBoxParam(hInstance, "USERNAME", hWnd,
    UserNameDlgProc, (LONG) hLocal);
// The local memory block will contain the user's name.
    .

    .

    .
```

• *Step 2:* The dialog-box procedure associates the memory handle with the dialog-box window:

```
case WM_INITDIALOG:
    // The lParam contains the last parameter value passed to
    // DialogBoxParam. This is the handle to the local block of
    // memory.
    SetProp(hDlg, "Memory", (HLOCAL) lParam);
    // Perform any other initialization for the dialog box.
    .

    .

    .
```

- *Step 3:* The dialog box will fill the block of memory when the user clicks OK:

```
case IDOK:
    hLocal = GetProp(hDlg, "Memory");
    npszName = LocalLock(hLocal);
    GetDlgItemText(hDlg, ID_USERNAMEEDITBOX,
        (LONG) (LPSTR) npszName, MAX_USERS_NAME_LEN);
    LocalUnlock(hLocal);
    .
    .

    .
    EndDialog(hDlg, IDOK);
    break;
```

- *Step 4:* When the dialog box is destroyed, the property must be removed:

```
case WM_DESTROY:
    RemoveProp(hDlg, "Memory");
    break;
```

Window Messages

Windows are passive workers. When a manager (the user or Windows) requires that work be done, it sends a message to the window procedure instructing it to perform the work. The type of work to be done is specified by the message. When more information is needed to carry out the task, the *wParam* and *lParam* parameters relay the additional information. Window procedures have many alternatives for handling window messages:

1. Pass the message to *DefWindowProc*. This has the effect described in the *Microsoft Windows Programmer's Reference*. Any message not recognized by *DefWindowProc* is ignored and zero is returned.

2. Process the message. This is usually accomplished by including a case statement or a message cracker (from **WINDOWSX.H**) for the message

in your window procedure. Any operation may be performed. An appropriate value for the message should be returned.

3. Process the message and call *DefWindowProc* (in either order). This is usually accomplished by including a case statement for the message in your window procedure. However, the code for the case includes an explicit call to *DefWindowProc*. This executes the operations defined by *DefWindowProc* as well as any additional actions you may desire. An appropriate value for the message should be returned. This is usually the value returned by *DefWindowProc* but it does not have to be.

4. Ignore the message. No action is to be performed when the window procedure receives this message. An appropriate value for the message should be returned.

Kinds of Messages

Window messages are sent as unsigned integer values in the range of 0x0000 to 0xFFFF. Microsoft Windows divides this range into four sections:

Message range	Section description
0x0000 to *WM_USER - 1*	All standard window messages. This includes all messages that begin with the *WM_* prefix.
WM_USER to 0x7FFF	Class-defined integer messages.
0x8000 to 0xBFFF	Messages reserved by Microsoft for exclusive use by Windows.
0xC000 to 0xFFFF	System-global string messages. These are the message numbers returned by the *RegisterWindowMessage* function.

Note that *WM_USER* is defined in WINDOWS.H to be 0x0400.

Class-Defined Integer Messages

You can create messages that perform operations specific to a class of windows. Suppose you created an INFO window that maintained a block of memory and allowed other windows access to that block. You could create a class-specific message for the INFO window; when it received the message, it would return the handle of the block of memory. The list of class-specific messages should be placed in a header file, INFO.H. This file should be included by all modules that will send messages to INFO windows. INFO.H should look like this:

```
#define IM_GETMEMORY(WM_USER + 0)
```

In the file that contains the window procedure for an INFO window, INFO.C, the following code fragment should exist:

```
#include "INFO.H"
    .

    .

    .
case IM_GETMEMORY:
    lResult = GetWindowWord(hWnd, GWW_MEMORYHANDLE);
    break;
    .

    .

    .
    return(lResult);
```

Class-defined messages should only be sent to windows of the class that defines the messages. Sending a class-defined message to a window of another class will have an unpredictable effect.

WINDOWS.H defines class-specific messages that can be sent to most of the system global classes. Notice that each message begins with a unique prefix.

System global class	Message prefix
DIALOG	DM_
BUTTON	BM_
COMBOBOX	CB_
EDIT	EM_
LISTBOX	LB_
MDICLIENT	(none)
SCROLLBAR	(none)
STATIC	STM_ (After Windows 3.0)

System-Global String Messages

You create system-global string messages when you wish to send a message and are unsure of the receiving window's class. When you register a system-global message, you are telling the Windows environment that there is a new "standard" message that any window in any application can recognize.

We add a new system message by calling *RegisterWindowMessage*. This function accepts a character string and returns a numeric value in the range of 0xC000 to 0xFFFF. If another call to *RegisterWindowMessage* is placed from any application with the same character string, Windows returns the same value that was returned the first time. Because of this, different windows will be using the same integer value to represent the same type of message.

All applications that wish to use these new messages should call *RegisterWindowMessage* during initialization. Once a window message has been registered, it remains in existence during the entire Windows session. This is because Windows has no function to unregister a window message.

Sneaking a Peek at Windows

Voyeur, a sample application discussed here, is a tool that demonstrates most of the concepts explained in this chapter. Voyeur's client area shows all the information associated with a window on the screen. The user instructs Voyeur to begin peering into windows by selecting one of the two peer options on the system menu. At this point, the mouse cursor changes into a pair of eyes that can be positioned anywhere on the screen. When the cursor enters a window, a frame is drawn around the window and Voyeur updates its dialog box with information about the window.

Figure 1-3 shows Voyeur in action. In this example, Voyeur is displaying the information for the Main group window of Program Manager. To keep Voyeur from using too much screen real estate, Voyeur's menu options are part of the system menu instead of a separate menu bar. For convenience, Voyeur interprets the class styles, window styles, and extended window styles and fills list boxes with the appropriate style's text name. The actual hexadecimal value of the styles is given above the list box. Also, the class extra bytes and window extra bytes are shown in list boxes.

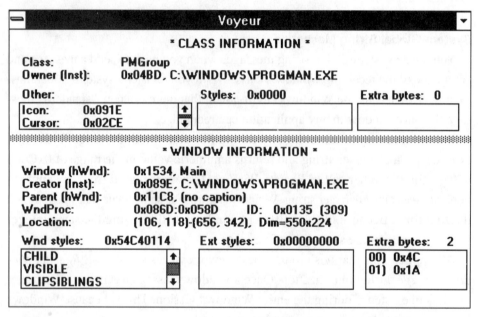

Figure 1-3. Voyeur displaying information for the Main group window of Program Manager

Voyeur adds two options to its system menu:

• *"Peer into window"* changes the mouse cursor into a pair of eyes and allows the user to examine different windows by positioning the cursor on them. As the cursor is moved, Voyeur determines which window is under the cursor and updates the information in Voyeur's dialog box.

- *"Drop back and peer"* is identical to "Peer into window" with one small exception. Due to Voyeur's size, it will often cover other windows on the screen. The "Drop back and peer" instruction puts Voyeur in the background; other windows rise to the top. After you have selected a window to examine by clicking the left mouse button, Voyeur will force itself to the top of the screen. This allows a clear view of Voyeur without having to move any windows out of the way.

Voyeur's Initialization

Voyeur first registers a window class for its main window and then tries to create the main window. The window procedure for the main window does all of its initialization during the *WM_CREATE* message processing as described in the "Creating and Destroying Window Instances" section earlier in this chapter. It's a good idea to halt Voyeur's main window creation if its dialog box cannot be created. In this case, *WinMain* would see NULL returned from the *CreateWindow* call and would terminate the program. The *WM_CREATE* message processing code can be found in the *VoyeurAppWndProc* function.

Voyeur now creates the modeless dialog box that will display information to the user. This is done using the VOYEUR template in the VOYEUR.RC file. Once the dialog box has been created, Voyeur's main window changes its size so that it fits snugly around the dialog box:

```
GetWindowRect(hWnd, &rc);
GetWindowRect(_hWndStats, &rcStatDlg);
MoveWindow(hWnd, rc.left, rc.top,
    rcStatDlg.right - rcStatDlg.left,
    rcStatDlg.bottom - rcStatDlg.top +
    GetSystemMetrics(SM_CYCAPTION), FALSE);
```

This gives the impression that the dialog box is the client area of Voyeur, when in fact it's a modeless dialog box covering the main window's client area. Since the *CreateWindow* call to create the Voyeur window uses *CW_USEDEFAULT* to specify the location of the window, Windows may place the window anywhere on the user's screen. Using the *MoveWindow* function with the values in *rc.left* and *rc.top* as the origin will not change Voyeur's screen position.

Note that we must take into consideration the height of a caption bar when chang-ing the height of Voyeur's main window. This is done by adding the height of a caption bar to the height of the modeless dialog box. The height of a caption bar can be obtained by using

```
GetSystemMetrics(SM_CYCAPTION)
```

Normally, dialog boxes are able to move independently of their parents. This is not desirable for Voyeur. If the user moves the Voyeur window, the modeless dia-log box should move with the window. This again gives the impression that Voyeur is one window and not made up of two independent windows. You can make the dialog box move with the main window by changing the *STYLE* line in the tem-plate for the dialog box.

If you refer to the VOYEUR.RC file, you will see the line

```
STYLE WS_VISIBLE | WS_CHILD
```

By default, Microsoft's dialog editor gives dialog boxes the *WS_POPUP* style. By manually changing *WS_POPUP* to *WS_CHILD*, we force Windows to move the dialog box with the main window.

While looking at the template for the dialog box, notice the line

```
FONT 8, "Helv"
```

This tells Windows that all the children in the dialog box should use the 8-point Helvetica font. This font is smaller than the system font, which Windows normally uses for dialog boxes. Because of the smaller font, Voyeur takes up less screen space.

The remainder of the initialization involves adding options to Voyeur's system menu. Options to be added to a system menu must have identifier values of less than 0xF000. This is because all of the pre-defined system menu IDs have values greater than or equal to 0xF000. Windows sends a *WM_SYSCOMMAND* message to the window procedure when an option from the system menu has been selected. The *wParam* variable contains the menu identifier of the selected option. Windows uses the bottom four bits of *wParam* internally. When you define option identifiers to be used in the system menu, select values that contain zeros in the last four bits.

Initializing the Statistics Dialog Box

When *VoyeurAppWndProc* calls the *CreateDialog* function, a *WM_INITDIA-LOG* message is sent to the dialog-box procedure, *VoyeurDlgProc*. This gives the dialog box a chance to do its initialization. The only initialization that needs to be performed is the setting of a tab stop in the "Other" list box that appears in the Class Information section of the dialog box.

Take a look at the "Other" list box in Figure 1-3. You will notice that all the data fields are flushed left within the box. If Windows used a fixed-pitch font, it would be easy to pad each heading with spaces so that the second column would be flushed left. However, Windows uses a proportionally spaced font, which makes flushing the column left much more difficult. We solve this problem by setting a tab stop within the list box and embedding tab characters in the strings. For a list box to process tabs, it must have the *LBS_USETABSTOPS* style specified in the dialog-box template.

To determine the correct location for the tab stop, we must first calculate the number of pixels required to display the widest heading. This is done by first getting a device context and selecting the font used by the dialog box into it:

```
hDC = GetDC(hDlg);
SelectObject(hDC, GetWindowFont(hDlg));
```

Next, each of the headings is passed as the second parameter into the *GetText-Extent* function. The *GetTextExtent* function examines this string and returns its dimensions in pixels—the width in the low word and the height in the high word. The first parameter to *GetTextExtent* is the handle to a device context (HDC) containing the font that the list box will use when it draws the text on the screen. The *GetTextExtent* function uses the font currently selected in the device context when determining the dimensions of the string. Naturally, a string will be wider using a 36-point font than the same text displayed in a 12-point font.

The *LB_SETTABSTOPS* message sets the position of a tab stop in a list box. The *wParam* value indicates the number of tab stops to be set. The *lParam* value is a far pointer to an array of integers. This array contains the list of tab-stop settings. Tab-stop settings are not in pixels, but in dialog units. The dialog units are based on the font that the list box is using. In this case, the list-box font is the same font being used by the whole dialog box. We'll now discuss how to convert the string width from screen to dialog-box units.

You may be familiar with the *MapDialogRect* function. This function converts the coordinates in a *RECT* structure from dialog-box units to screen units by performing the following code:

```
rc.left = (rc.left * nAveCharWidth) / 4;
rc.top = (rc.top  * nAveCharHeight) / 8;
rc.right = (rc.right * nAveCharWidth) / 4;
rc.bottom = (rc.bottom * nAveCharHeight) / 8;
```

In this code fragment, *nAveCharWidth* and *nAveCharHeight* represent the average width and height of characters in the font associated with the dialog box identified by the first parameter to *MapDialogRect*. Unfortunately, this is the opposite of what we need. We need to convert from screen coordinates to dialog-box units. So to do this, we must determine the number of pixels in a horizontal dialog-box unit and perform the calculation ourselves. To determine the number of pixels in a horizontal dialog-box unit, we first prepare a *RECT* structure and set the *left* member to four and the *top* member to eight. We then call *MapDialogRect*:

```
SetRect(&rc, 4, 8, 0, 0);
MapDialogRect(hDlg, &rc);
```

By passing in this rectangle, *MapDialogRect* will change the members in the rectangle so that the *RECT* structure contains the average character width and height (in screen coordinates) of the font associated with the dialog box. Once we have the number of pixels per average character width (in *rc.left*), we can calculate the tab-stop position in terms of dialog-box units as follows.

```
wTabStop = ((wMaxTextLen * 4) / rc.left) + 6;
```

In the line above, we multiply *wMaxTextLen* by four because four is the number of horizontal dialog-box units per average character width. We then divide by the number of pixels per four horizontal dialog-box units. Notice that the multiplication must be done before the division so that rounding errors do not occur giving us incorrect results. Finally, we add six dialog-box units so that some space (about a character and a half) appears between the columns in the list box. Finally, we can set the tab stops in the list box:

```
ListBox_SetTabStops(GetDlgItem(hDlg, ID_CLASSOTHERBOX), 1, &wTabStop);
```

Note that all of the calculations that we have done are based on the font that is selected into the dialog-box window instead of the list-box window. Ideally, we would have liked to use the font associated with the list-box window but the *MapDialogRect* function only works with a window that was created by calling one of the following functions: *DialogBox, DialogBoxParam, DialogBoxIndirect, DialogBoxIndirectParam, CreateDialog, CreateDialogParam, CreateDialogIndirect,* or *CreateDialogIndirectParam.* Since the font used by the list box is the same as that used by the dialog box, all of the calculations will be accurate. If the fonts were different, there would be no direct way to arrive at the information needed. You would first have to get the font for the list box, select it into the dialog box, perform all of the operations above, and restore the original dialog-box font:

```
hWndOtherBox = GetDlgItem(hDlg, ID_CLASSOTHERBOX);
hFont = GetWindowFont(hWndOtherBox);         // List-box font.
hFont = SetWindowFont(hDlg, hFont, FALSE);   // Returns dialog-box font.


// Perform calculations.
...
// Restore the original dialog-box font
SetWindowFont(hDlg, hFont, FALSE);           // Restore dialog-box font.
```

This may seem like an awful lot of trouble—and it is! The tab stop's position could have been determined by calculating its value ahead of time or even using trial-and-error methods. But the contents of the list box probably would not have lined up correctly on a monitor with a different resolution. This is because Windows selects fonts based on the screen resolution and often the average character widths and heights are different from one resolution to another. Also, if we changed a heading or added a field, we would have to recalculate the tab stop.

Device independence is one of Window's most powerful features, but it isn't automatic. Paying attention to this kind of detail makes a good application better.

Peering into Windows

Voyeur starts tracking the mouse and updating its dialog box after you have chosen "Peer into window." A *WM_SYSCOMMAND* message is sent to *VoyeurApp-WndProc*. The code looks like this:

```
case IDM_PEERINTOWINDOW:
    SetCapture(hWnd);
    SetCursor(LoadCursor(_hInstance, "Eyes"));
    hWndLastSubject = NULL;
    break;
```

First, we tell Windows that all mouse messages should be sent to *VoyeurApp-WndProc* no matter where the mouse is. Then we load the "Eyes" cursor from the resource section of the program file and make it the mouse cursor. This gives the user a visual indication that Voyeur is functioning. Finally a static variable, *hWnd-LastSubject* is initialized to NULL. This tells Voyeur that no window has been passed over by the mouse yet.

The *hWndLastSubject* variable contains the handle of the window that Voyeur was just looking at. This is because:

1. Voyeur can reduce flicker and increase program speed if the mouse moves within the same window. Since the window's information is already displayed in Voyeur's dialog box, there is no need to update it.

2. When the mouse cursor is positioned over a different window from *hWnd-LastSubject*, Voyeur must remove the frame it placed around the previous window.

The "Drop back and peer" option forces Voyeur to go behind all other windows on the screen. This allows any windows originally hidden by Voyeur to appear in front of it. This feature is useful because it allows access to windows that you might not otherwise be able to pass the mouse cursor over.

Windows maintains a list of all windows in the system. This is called the *window manager's list*. In addition to width and height, a window also has a position describing how close it is to the top of the screen. This front-to-back position is called the window's *z-order*, named for the z-axis of a three-dimensional coordinate system. The topmost window on the screen is the one at the top of the window manager's list. When painting the screen, Windows uses the z-order to clip display output. This guarantees that windows closer to the top of the window manager's list will not be overwritten by windows closer to the bottom of the list.

When the user clicks on an application's caption bar, Windows forces that window to the top of the window manager's list and activates the application. When this application's window is moved to the top of the window manager's list, all of its child windows and owned pop-up windows (including dialog boxes) are also moved to the top of the list. As you can see, windows can change their positions on this list very easily. Programs can use the *SetWindowPos* function to alter the z-order maintained by the window manager's list.

Starting with Windows 3.1, Microsoft has added a new extended window style, *WS_EX_TOPMOST*. Any window created with this style is always positioned in front of any windows that do not have this style. This style is most useful for things like keeping the clock always visible or for keeping the Windows Help system always visible—when the user switches back to the application, the window containing the help text will remain unobscured. Of course, Windows will guarantee that any children and owned–pop-ups of a window containing the *WS_EX_TOP-MOST* style are on top of the window even if they, themselves, do not have the *WS_EX_TOPMOST* style specified.

At a Windows 3.1 conference, one of the speakers stated that this new feature will probably be the most misused feature of 3.1—use this feature only when it adds value to your application. Another option is to let users decide how they wish to use your application—both the Clock and Windows Help have menu items that allow the user to determine whether or not to make the application window a topmost window.

The only way to change the topmost status of a window is by using the *SetWindowPos* function. This function can change a window's z-order position and will set or reset the *WS_EX_TOPMOST* flag in the window's extended styles. You cannot alter a window's topmost status by getting the window's current extended styles with *GetWindowLong*, toggling the *WS_EX_TOPMOST* bit, and then setting the new styles back with *SetWindowLong*. Windows will simply ignore your request if you attempt to do so.

The second parameter to *SetWindowPos* is used to change the z-order of the window. Normally, this parameter indicates the handle of the window behind which this window should be positioned. However, several new identifiers have been defined in WINDOWS.H that can be passed as the second parameter to *SetWindowPos* to alter a window's position in the z-order and the window's topmost status. The list appears below:

WINDOWS.H identifier	Value	Meaning
HWND_TOP	NULL	If the window is a topmost window, it is positioned above all topmost windows. If the window is a non-topmost window, it is positioned above all non-topmost windows.
HWND_BOTTOM	1	Positions the window at the bottom of the z-order. If the window was a topmost window, it loses its topmost status.
HWND_TOPMOST	-1	Changes the window's status, making it a topmost window.
HWND_NOTOPMOST	-2	Places the window above all non-topmost windows. If the window is a topmost window it is changed to a non-topmost window.

By using two of the identifiers above, we can position Voyeur's window at the top or bottom of the window manager's list. The line

```
SetWindowPos(hWnd, HWND_BOTTOM, 0, 0, 0, 0, SWP_NOMOVE | SWP_NOSIZE);
```

causes Voyeur's application window and modeless dialog-box window to be positioned at the bottom of the window manager's list. Any other application's windows originally hidden by Voyeur will be closer to the top of the screen and will automatically be sent *WM_NCPAINT* and *WM_PAINT* messages by Windows to be redrawn. The *SWP_NOMOVE* and *SWP_NOSIZE* flags cause the position and size parameters to be ignored.

The execution of the *SetWindowPos* function above is the only difference between the "Peer into window" and "Drop back and peer" menu options.

Any time an application processes the *WM_SYSCOMMAND* message, it must do all the processing for any menu items the application has appended to the system menu and not pass these messages to *DefWindowProc*. Also, for any "standard" system menu options, *WM_SYSCOMMAND* messages must be passed to *DefWindowProc*. The only exception to this rule is if we trap a "standard" menu item and perform some special processing before or instead of passing it to *DefWindowProc*.

Updating the Dialog Box

All windows normally receive *WM_MOUSEMOVE* messages only when the mouse cursor passes through the client area of the window. However, it's possible for a window to "steal" all the mouse messages from other windows and have Windows direct them to a particular window procedure. This is done with the *SetCapture* function. When Voyeur calls *SetCapture(hWnd)* during the *IDM_PEERIN-TOWINDOW* case of the *WM_SYSCOMMAND* message, it tells Windows that all mouse messages (*WM_LBUTTONDOWN, WM_LBUTTONUP, WM_LBUT-TONDBLCLK, WM_MOUSEMOVE*, and so on), regardless of the mouse-cursor position, should be directed to the window procedure for the window specified by the *hWnd* parameter to *SetCapture*.

The *GetCapture* function can determine the handle of the window that currently has capture. Normally no window has capture, and the *GetCapture* function returns

NULL. Because Voyeur should not update its dialog box if mouse capture has not been set to Voyeur's main window, we simply break out of the *switch* statement:

```
case WM_MOUSEMOVE:
    if (GetCapture() == NULL) break;
```

In fact, whenever *GetCapture* is called from within a mouse message (in this case, *WM_MOUSEMOVE*), the only return values possible are NULL and the window handle passed to the window procedure, *hWnd*. This is because the window procedure would never receive a mouse message if another window had captured the mouse.

If *GetCapture* doesn't return NULL, we must determine which window the mouse cursor is over. The value in the *lParam* parameter for a *WM_MOUSEMOVE* message is the location (in device units) of the mouse. These coordinates are relative to Voyeur's client area. The *ClientToScreen* function can be used to convert the value of *lParam* into coordinates relative to the entire screen:

```
ClientToScreen(hWnd, &MAKEPOINT(lParam));
```

Now, we can call the *WindowFromPoint* function to determine the handle of the window below the mouse cursor:

```
hWndSubject = WindowFromPoint(MAKEPOINT(lParam));
```

The *WindowFromPoint* function returns NULL if the mouse isn't over a window. Next, we check to see if the task that created the window is the same as Voyeur's task. This prevents the viewing of window and class information for any windows created by Voyeur.

If the mouse cursor is over a child window, the *WindowFromPoint* function returns the handle of the child's parent instead of the handle of the child window. To obtain the handle for the child window, we must use the *ChildWindowFrom-Point* function:

```
ScreenToClient(hWndSubject, &MAKEPOINT(lParam));
hWndChild = ChildWindowFromPoint(hWndSubject, MAKEPOINT(lParam));
```

Notice that the point in *lParam* must be converted again; this time so it is relative to the client area of the child's parent. If the point passed to *ChildWindowFromPoint* is outside the parent window's area, the return value is NULL. If the point is not over a child, the function will return the handle to the parent. If the function returns a valid window handle, this window is now our new subject.

If the window happens to be the same as our last subject, then the information in the dialog box will be the same as before and no further actions need to be taken. Otherwise, we remove the frame around the previous window and draw a frame around our new window. Both actions are done by calling *DrawWindowFrame*. *SetClassInfo* and *SetWindowInfo* are called to fill the dialog box with information relevant to our new window. Finally, we save our new window handle in the static variable *hWndLastSubject*.

Freezing the Dialog-Box Information

After choosing a window, the user can freeze the class and window information by clicking the left mouse button. When Voyeur gets a *WM_LBUTTONUP* message, it removes any frame around the most recently passed-over window and releases the mouse capture. The line

```
BringWindowToTop(hWnd);
```

tells Windows to bring Voyeur and its dialog box back to the top of the window manager's list. (Remember that if the user had selected "Drop back and peer" from the system menu, Voyeur would be placed behind all other windows.) This function causes Voyeur to return to the top so that the information can easily be seen by the user. If the "Peer into window" option was chosen, Voyeur was already the topmost window and bringing it to the top again doesn't do anything. We could have used

```
SetWindowPos(hWnd, HWND_TOP, 0, 0, 0, 0, SWP_NOMOVE | SWP_NOSIZE);
```

to accomplish the same operation. In fact, this is exactly how Microsoft has implemented the *BringWindowToTop* function.

Recall that Voyeur changed the mouse cursor to a pair of eyes after the user selected one of the "Peer" options from the system menu. If the mouse has not been captured, Windows sends a *WM_SETCURSOR* message to the window procedure associated with the window under the mouse cursor whenever the mouse moves within the window. The *DefWindowProc* function will automatically change the mouse cursor back to the cursor selected when the window's class was registered. For this reason, the mouse cursor will not maintain the shape of the eyes once we call the *ReleaseCapture* function. This is the desired behavior.

Drawing a Frame Around the Window

Voyeur's *DrawWindowFrame* function draws a frame around any window whose handle is passed to it. This function also removes the frame.

The main requirement for drawing a frame around a window is that the frame must be visible. This may sound obvious, but in a graphical environment where a window can be any color or combination of colors, what color do you choose? The best answer is whatever color the window is not. In other words, the frame should be drawn in the inverse color of the screen. This guarantees that the frame will be visible.

This has an added advantage for us. If we draw the frame again in the same location, the screen will be restored to its original colors. This has the effect of removing the frame. That way, only one function is needed to draw and remove the window's frame.

The code for *DrawWindowFrame* looks like this:

```
void NEAR DrawWindowFrame (HWND hWnd) {
    HDC hDC;
    RECT rc;
    HPEN hPen;

    GetWindowRect(hWnd, &rc);
    hDC = GetWindowDC(hWnd);
    SetROP2(hDC, R2_NOT);
    hPen = CreatePen(PS_INSIDEFRAME, 3 *
        GetSystemMetrics(SM_CXBORDER), RGB(0, 0, 0));
    SelectObject(hDC, hPen);
    SelectObject(hDC, GetStockObject(NULL_BRUSH));
    Rectangle(hDC, 0, 0, rc.right - rc.left, rc.bottom - rc.top);
```

```
ReleaseDC(hWnd, hDC);
DeleteObject(hPen);
}
```

This function first retrieves the rectangle (in screen coordinates) of the desired window. Next, we obtain a device context for the entire window using the *GetWindowDC* function. With the device context returned from this function, Windows gives us permission to write anywhere within the area occupied by the window. If we had used the *GetDC* function, Windows would only allow us to write in the client area of the window.

Before drawing a rectangle around the window, we must prepare the device context by specifying that drawing with the pen should yield the inverse of the screen color. This is done by setting the *ROP2* value to *R2_NOT*. Next, we create a thick pen so that our frame will be easily seen. We specify a pen style of *PS_INSIDE-FRAME* so Windows will draw the frame within the window's area. The width of the pen is specified as three times the width of a nonsizeable window border. This means it should look fine on any monitor with any resolution.

Let's say that you were running Windows with a screen resolution of 1 million pixels by 1 million pixels (don't we wish?!). Drawing a 1-pixel-high line across the screen will probably go completely unnoticed. However, Microsoft guarantees that the width of a nonsizeable window border will be visible, regardless of what resolution the user is running Windows. So, basing the width of the frame surrounding the window on the nonsizeable window border value guarantees that our frame will be visible.

The last parameter to the *CreatePen* function specifies the pen's color. Because the *ROP2* value is set to *R2_NOT*, the pen's color won't actually be used when the frame is drawn. For this reason the color may be any value. I arbitrarily selected black.

Because the *Rectangle* function fills the rectangle with the brush currently selected in the device context, we must select a *NULL_BRUSH*. This will let us draw a frame without obscuring the remaining contents of the window.

We draw the frame by calling *Rectangle*. Because the coordinates are relative to the device context, the top left corner of the rectangle is point (0, 0). The lower right corner is (width of window, height of window).

The remainder of the function releases the device context and deletes the pen. Note that the order of these lines is important. A device context must have handles to existing objects within it at all times. If we deleted the pen before releasing the device context, Windows would crash with a fatal exit. Once the device context has been released, the pen may be deleted.

Setting the Class and Window Information

SetClassInfo accepts a handle to the modeless dialog box and a handle to the window whose class information is displayed. *GetClassName* can be used to obtain the name of the class of the window. Once we have the class name, calling *GetClassInfo* fills a *WNDCLASS* structure with the rest of the information needed for the display. The *GetClassInfo* function requires the data or module instance handle of the application that registered the window class so that Windows can distinguish between two application local classes having the same name but created by different applications. The module handle of the application that registered the window class can be obtained from:

```
GetClassWord(hWnd, GCW_HMODULE)
```

After calling the *GetClassInfo* function, we execute the following line

```
WndClass.hInstance = GetClassWord(hWnd, GCW_HMODULE);
```

because the *GetClassInfo* function doesn't guarantee that the value in the *hInstance* member of the *WNDCLASS* structure will be the same one that was used when *RegisterClass* was called.

The *GetModuleFileName* function retrieves the name of the executable file that registered the class:

```
GetModuleFileName(WndClass.hInstance, szText, sizeof(szText));
```

This function will return the full path of a file associated with the module handle that is passed in.

The remainder of the *SetClassInfo* function formats the strings for display and sets them in the dialog box. Because each static box maintains the information most recently placed in it, the repainting of Voyeur's client area is the responsibility of the static windows. This way, our application never has to worry about processing *WM_PAINT* messages. Voyeur is also designed so that the location of text in the window is left entirely up to the dialog-box template. If we wish to move things around at a later time or add more information, this scheme is very flexible.

Filling the "Extra bytes:" list box is a small problem because Windows does not offer a *GetClassByte* function. We must call *GetClassWord* repeatedly, incrementing the offset by one each time and appending the value in the *LOBYTE* or *HIBYTE* of each returned word into the list box.

When Voyeur fills the contents of a list box, it sends a *WM_SETREDRAW* message to the list box with *wParam* set to FALSE. For example:

```
SetWindowRedraw(GetDlgItem(hDlg, ID_CLASSOTHERBOX), FALSE);
```

This tells the list box not to update its window while entries are being added or deleted. Normally, list boxes update their windows immediately as their contents are changed. By turning redraw off, we ensure that the list boxes don't flicker on the screen and make Voyeur's display of information significantly faster. After all the new entries have been added to the list box, Voyeur sends another *WM_SETRE-DRAW* message to the list box with *wParam* set to TRUE. This tells the list box that it's now OK for it to repaint the window. However, the list box does not automatically force a repaint when it receives this message. To force the contents of the list box to be updated, Voyeur must call *InvalidateRect*.

SetWindowInfo is similar to *SetClassInfo*. Most of its information is retrieved by the *GetWindowWord* and *GetWindowLong* functions. *GetWindowText* gets the captions of the window (and its parent, if it exists). Once again, *GetModuleFile-Name* gets the name of the executable file that created the window. The handle passed to *GetModuleFileName* is the data-instance handle of the task that created the window. This is obtained by calling *GetWindowWord* and passing it the *GWW_HINSTANCE* offset. The location and dimensions of the window are determined by calling *GetWindowRect*.

Filling the window "Extra bytes:" list box is the same as filling the class extra bytes list box. Since all windows of a class must have the same number of window extra bytes, this value is retrieved by calling *GetClassWord* and passing it the *GCW_CBWNDEXTRA* offset.

When the "Wnd styles:" list box is being filled, only the top 16 bits of the value returned by

```
GetWindowLong(hWnd, GWL_STYLE);
```

are examined. Remember, the bottom 16 bits are window-class specific. Voyeur cannot determine the meaning of these bits for the selected window.

Filling the Style List Boxes

Because Voyeur has three style list boxes—class styles, window styles, and extended window styles—its useful to have one function that is general enough to fill all three. *FillStyleBox* accepts a handle to the appropriate list box, a pointer to an array of *STYLELIST* structures, and a *DWORD* representing the style bits to be checked. Each *STYLELIST* structure contains a value for the style and a text string that should appear if that style bit is on. These style arrays are declared as follows:

```
typedef struct { DWORD dwID; char *szName; } STYLELIST;

STYLELIST _ClassStyle[] = {
    { CS_VREDRAW,              "VREDRAW"              },
    { CS_HREDRAW,              "HREDRAW"              },
        .
        .
        .
    { CS_GLOBALCLASS,          "GLOBALCLASS"          },
    { 0,                       NULL                   }
};

STYLELIST _WindowStyles[] = {
    { WS_POPUP,                "POPUP"                },
    { WS_CHILD,                "CHILD"                },
        .
        .
        .
```

```
    { WS_TABSTOP,                    "TABSTOP, MAXIMIZEBOX"      },
    { 0,                             NULL                        }
};


STYLELIST _ExtWindowStyles[] = {
    { WS_EX_DLGMODALFRAME,           "DLGMODALFRAME"             },
    { WS_EX_NOPARENTNOTIFY,          "NOPARENTNOTIFY"            },
        .

        .

        .

    { WS_EX_TRANSPARENT,             "TRANSPARENT"               },
    { 0,                             NULL                        }
};
```

This method is very general and easily expanded to accommodate styles that future versions of Windows might offer. Unfortunately, it does have some drawbacks. For example, an overlapped window is denoted by having no window style bits on. Voyeur will display an empty list box for this window instead of having *"OVERLAPPED"* in the list box. Styles represented by multiple bits are not displayed. For example, a window created with the *WS_CAPTION* style will be represented by *"BORDER"* and *"DLGFRAME"* in the list box instead of *"CAPTION."* Finally, Voyeur cannot determine if bit 17 of the window style's *DWORD* means *WS_TABSTOP* or *WS_MAX-IMIZEBOX*. This is also true for bit 18, *WS_GROUP* or *WS_MINIMIZEBOX*. For this reason, Voyeur displays both styles when applicable.

The Voyeur application, presented in Listings 1-1 through 1-7, illustrates the window attribute information.

Figure 1-4. VOYEUR.ICO

Figure 1-5. Voyeur eyes cursor for window peering

Listing 1-1. VOYEUR.C application source module

```
/*********************************************************************
Module name: VOYEUR.C
Programmer : Jeffrey M. Richter.
*********************************************************************/

#include <windows.h>
#include <windowsx.h>

#include "voyeur.h"

extern const HINSTANCE _cdecl _hInstance;

char _szAppName[] = "Voyeur";

HWND _hWndStats = NULL;

#define IDM_PEERINTOWINDOW        (0x0110)    // Must be < 0xF000
#define IDM_DROPBACKANDPEER       (0x0120)    // Must be < 0xF000


typedef struct { DWORD dwID; char *szName; } STYLELIST;
```

```
STYLELIST _ClassStyles[] = {
    { CS_VREDRAW,           "VREDRAW"               },
    { CS_HREDRAW,           "HREDRAW"               },
    { CS_KEYCVTWINDOW,      "KEYCVTWINDOW"          },
    { CS_DBLCLKS,           "DBLCLKS"               },
    { CS_OWNDC,             "OWNDC"                 },
    { CS_CLASSDC,           "CLASSDC"               },
    { CS_PARENTDC,          "PARENTDC"              },
    { CS_NOKEYCVT,          "NOKEYCVT"              },
    { CS_NOCLOSE,           "NOCLOSE"               },
    { CS_SAVEBITS,          "SAVEBITS"              },
    { CS_BYTEALIGNCLIENT,   "BYTEALIGNCLIENT"       },
    { CS_BYTEALIGNWINDOW,   "BYTEALIGNWINDOW"       },
    { CS_GLOBALCLASS,       "GLOBALCLASS"           },
    { 0,                    NULL                    }
};

STYLELIST _WindowStyles[] = {
    { WS_POPUP,             "POPUP"                 },
    { WS_CHILD,             "CHILD"                 },
    { WS_MINIMIZE,          "MINIMIZE"              },
    { WS_VISIBLE,           "VISIBLE"               },
    { WS_DISABLED,          "DISABLED"              },
    { WS_CLIPSIBLINGS,      "CLIPSIBLINGS"          },
    { WS_CLIPCHILDREN,      "CLIPCHILDREN"          },
    { WS_MAXIMIZE,          "MAXIMIZE"              },
    { WS_BORDER,            "BORDER"                },
    { WS_DLGFRAME,          "DLGFRAME"              },
    { WS_VSCROLL,           "VSCROLL"               },
    { WS_HSCROLL,           "HSCROLL"               },
    { WS_SYSMENU,           "SYSMENU"               },
    { WS_THICKFRAME,        "THICKFRAME"            },
    { WS_GROUP,             "GROUP, MINIMIZEBOX"    },
    { WS_TABSTOP,           "TABSTOP, MAXIMIZEBOX"  },
    { 0,                    NULL                    }
};

STYLELIST _ExtWindowStyles[] = {
    { WS_EX_DLGMODALFRAME,  "DLGMODALFRAME"         },
    { WS_EX_NOPARENTNOTIFY, "NOPARENTNOTIFY"        },
    { WS_EX_TOPMOST,        "TOPMOST"               },
    { WS_EX_ACCEPTFILES,    "ACCEPTFILES"           },
    { WS_EX_TRANSPARENT,    "TRANSPARENT"           },
    { 0,                    NULL                    }
};
```

```
typedef enum {
    CIH_ATOM, CIH_ICON, CIH_CURSOR, CIH_BACKGROUND,
    CIH_WNDPROC, CIH_MENU, CIH_END
} CLASSINFOHEAD;

char *szClassInfoHeading[] = {
    "Atom: ",
    "Icon: ",
    "Cursor: ",
    "Backgrnd: ",
    "WndProc: ",
    "Menu: ",
    NULL
};

ATOM NEAR RegisterAppWndClass (HINSTANCE hInstance);
LRESULT CALLBACK VoyeurAppWndProc
        (HWND hWnd, UINT uMsg, WPARAM wParam, LPARAM lParam);

// ****************************************************************
#pragma argsused
int WinMain (HINSTANCE hInstance, HINSTANCE hPrevInstance,
    LPSTR lpszCmdLine, int nCmdShow) {
    MSG msg;
    HWND hWnd;

    if (hPrevInstance == NULL)
        if (RegisterAppWndClass(hInstance) == NULL)
            return(0);

    hWnd = CreateWindow(_szAppName, _szAppName,
        WS_OVERLAPPED | WS_VISIBLE | WS_CLIPCHILDREN |
        WS_CAPTION | WS_SYSMENU | WS_MINIMIZEBOX,
        CW_USEDEFAULT, nCmdShow, CW_USEDEFAULT, CW_USEDEFAULT,
        NULL, NULL, hInstance, 0);

    if (hWnd == NULL) return(0);

    while (GetMessage(&msg, NULL, 0, 0)) {
        if (!IsDialogMessage(_hWndStats, &msg)) {
            TranslateMessage(&msg);
            DispatchMessage(&msg);
        }
    }

    return(0);
}
```

```
// ****************************************************************
// This function registers Voyeur's main window.

ATOM NEAR RegisterAppWndClass (HINSTANCE hInstance) {
    WNDCLASS WndClass;

    WndClass.style         = 0;
    WndClass.lpfnWndProc   = VoyeurAppWndProc;
    WndClass.cbClsExtra    = 0;
    WndClass.cbWndExtra    = 0;
    WndClass.hInstance     = hInstance;
    WndClass.hIcon         = LoadIcon(hInstance, _szAppName);
    WndClass.hCursor       = LoadCursor(NULL, IDC_ARROW);
    WndClass.hbrBackground = COLOR_WINDOW + 1;
    WndClass.lpszMenuName  = NULL;
    WndClass.lpszClassName = _szAppName;
    return(RegisterClass(&WndClass));
}


// ****************************************************************
// This function processes messages sent to the modeless dlg box.

#pragma argsused
BOOL CALLBACK VoyeurDlgProc
        (HWND hDlg, UINT uMsg, WPARAM wParam, LPARAM lParam) {
    BOOL fProcessed = TRUE;
    WORD wTextLen, wMaxTextLen = 0, wTabStop;
    NPSTR szHeading; HDC hDC;
    CLASSINFOHEAD ClassInfoHead;
        RECT rc;

    switch (uMsg) {
        case WM_INITDIALOG:
            // Determine where to place tab stops in list box.

            hDC = GetDC(hDlg);
            SelectObject(hDC, GetWindowFont(hDlg));

            ClassInfoHead = CIH_ATOM;
            while (ClassInfoHead != CIH_END) {
                szHeading = szClassInfoHeading[ClassInfoHead];

                // Get length (in pixels) of heading.
                wTextLen = LOWORD(GetTextExtent(hDC, szHeading,
                        lstrlen(szHeading)));
```

```
        // Find heading with maximum length.
        wMaxTextLen = max(wMaxTextLen, wTextLen);

        ClassInfoHead = (CLASSINFOHEAD) (ClassInfoHead + 1);
      }
      ReleaseDC(hDlg, hDC);

      // Convert pixels into dialog-box units.
      SetRect(&rc, 4, 8, 4, 8);
      MapDialogRect(hDlg, &rc);
      wTabStop = 6 + ((wMaxTextLen * 4) / rc.left);

      // Set tab-stop position in list box.  Note: list box must
      // have LBS_USETABSTOPS style in dialog-box template.
      (void) ListBox_SetTabStops(
          GetDlgItem(hDlg, ID_CLASSOTHERBOX), 1, &wTabStop);

      fProcessed = FALSE;
      break;
    default:
      fProcessed = FALSE;
      break;
  }

  return(fProcessed);
}


// ***************************************************************
// This function fills a list box with text names of the styles.
// It is used for the class styles, window styles, and extended
// window styles.

void NEAR FillStyleBox
      (HWND hWndListBox, STYLELIST Styles[], DWORD dwStyleFlags) {
  int x;

  // Turn off redraw so the list box will not flicker every time
  // an entry is added to it.  Also makes updating much faster.
  SetWindowRedraw(hWndListBox, FALSE);

  (void) ListBox_ResetContent(hWndListBox); // Empty list box.

  for (x = 0; Styles[x].szName != NULL; x++) {

    if (Styles[x].dwID & dwStyleFlags) {
        // If style bit is set, add style text to the list box.
        (void) ListBox_AddString(hWndListBox, Styles[x].szName);
```

```
      }
   }

   SetWindowRedraw(hWndListBox, TRUE);  // Turn redraw back on.

   // Force redraw of list box so that it shows proper information.
   InvalidateRect(hWndListBox, NULL, TRUE);
}

// ****************************************************************
// This function sets all of the static and list-box windows with
// the class information about the passed-in window (hWnd).

void NEAR SetClassInfo (HWND hDlg, HWND hWnd) {
   char szText[100], szBuf[100], y;
   WNDCLASS WndClass;
   WORD x;

   // Get the class name of the window.
   GetClassName(hWnd, szBuf, sizeof(szBuf));
   SetDlgItemText(hDlg, ID_CLASSNAME, szBuf);

   // Fill a WNDCLASS structure.  Note: We can pass a data
   // instance or a module instance handle.
   GetClassInfo(GetClassWord(hWnd, GCW_HMODULE), szBuf,
      &WndClass);
   WndClass.hInstance = GetClassWord(hWnd, GCW_HMODULE);

   // Get module name of application that registered this class.
   GetModuleFileName(WndClass.hInstance, szText, sizeof(szText));
   wsprintf(szBuf, "0x%04X, %s", WndClass.hInstance,
      (LPSTR) szText);
   SetDlgItemText(hDlg, ID_OWNER, szBuf);

   // Fill "Other" list box with information from WNDCLASS struct.

   SetWindowRedraw(GetDlgItem(hDlg, ID_CLASSOTHERBOX), FALSE);
   (void) ListBox_ResetContent(
      GetDlgItem(hDlg, ID_CLASSOTHERBOX));

   if (LOWORD(GetVersion()) > 0x0003) {
      wsprintf(szBuf, "%s\t0x%04X",
         (LPSTR) szClassInfoHeading[CIH_ATOM],
         GetClassWord(hWnd, GCW_ATOM));
   } else {
      wsprintf(szBuf, "%s\tWin3.1",
         (LPSTR) szClassInfoHeading[CIH_ATOM]);
```

```
}
(void) ListBox_AddString(
   GetDlgItem(hDlg, ID_CLASSOTHERBOX), szBuf);

wsprintf(szBuf, "%s\t0x%04X",
   (LPSTR) szClassInfoHeading[CIH_ICON], WndClass.hIcon);
(void) ListBox_AddString(
   GetDlgItem(hDlg, ID_CLASSOTHERBOX), szBuf);

wsprintf(szBuf, "%s\t0x%04X",
   (LPSTR) szClassInfoHeading[CIH_CURSOR], WndClass.hCursor);
(void) ListBox_AddString(
   GetDlgItem(hDlg, ID_CLASSOTHERBOX), szBuf);

wsprintf(szBuf, "%s\t0x%04X",
   (LPSTR) szClassInfoHeading[CIH_BACKGROUND],
   WndClass.hbrBackground);
(void) ListBox_AddString(
   GetDlgItem(hDlg, ID_CLASSOTHERBOX), szBuf);

wsprintf(szBuf, "%s\t0x%04X:0x%04X",
   (LPSTR) szClassInfoHeading[CIH_WNDPROC],
   HIWORD(WndClass.lpfnWndProc),
   LOWORD((LONG) WndClass.lpfnWndProc));
(void) ListBox_AddString(
   GetDlgItem(hDlg, ID_CLASSOTHERBOX), szBuf);

wsprintf(szBuf, "%s\t0x%04X:0x%04X",
   (LPSTR) szClassInfoHeading[CIH_MENU],
   HIWORD(WndClass.lpszMenuName),
   LOWORD((LONG) WndClass.lpszMenuName));
(void) ListBox_AddString(
   GetDlgItem(hDlg, ID_CLASSOTHERBOX), szBuf);

SetWindowRedraw(GetDlgItem(hDlg, ID_CLASSOTHERBOX), TRUE);
InvalidateRect(GetDlgItem(hDlg, ID_CLASSOTHERBOX), NULL, TRUE);

// Fill in all the "Class style" information.
wsprintf(szBuf, "0x%04X", WndClass.style);
SetDlgItemText(hDlg, ID_CLASSSTYLE, szBuf);

// Fill "Class style" list box with class style information.
FillStyleBox(GetDlgItem(hDlg, ID_CLASSSTYLEBOX),
   _ClassStyles, WndClass.style);

// Fill in all the "Class extra byte" information.
wsprintf(szBuf, "%u", WndClass.cbClsExtra);
```

```
    SetDlgItemText(hDlg, ID_CBCLSEXTRA, szBuf);

    // Fill the "Class extra bytes" list box.
    SetWindowRedraw(GetDlgItem(hDlg, ID_CBCLSEXTRABOX), FALSE);
    (void) ListBox_ResetContent(
        GetDlgItem(hDlg, ID_CBCLSEXTRABOX));

    for (x = 0; x < (WORD) WndClass.cbClsExtra; x++) {
        // These two lines are necessary so that we do not
        // step beyond the class' extra bytes.
        if (x == 0) y = LOBYTE(GetClassWord(hWnd, x));
        else y = HIBYTE(GetClassWord(hWnd, x - 1));
        wsprintf(szBuf, "%02u   0x%02X", x, y & 0x00ff);
        (void) ListBox_AddString(
            GetDlgItem(hDlg, ID_CBCLSEXTRABOX), szBuf);
    }

    SetWindowRedraw(GetDlgItem(hDlg, ID_CBCLSEXTRABOX), TRUE);

    // Force redraw of "Class extra bytes" list box.
    InvalidateRect(GetDlgItem(hDlg, ID_CBCLSEXTRABOX), NULL, TRUE);
}

// *****************************************************************
// This function sets all of the static and list-box windows with
// the window information about the passed-in window (hWnd).

void NEAR SetWindowInfo (HWND hDlg, HWND hWnd) {
    char szText[100], szBuf[100], y;
    HINSTANCE hInstance;
    WNDPROC lpfnWndProc;
    HWND hWndParent;
    RECT rc;
    WORD x, cbWndExtra;

    // Get caption of "peered" window.
    if (GetWindowText(hWnd, szText, sizeof(szText)) == 0)
        lstrcpy(szText, "(no caption)");
    wsprintf(szBuf, "0x%04X, %s", hWnd, (LPSTR) szText);
    SetDlgItemText(hDlg, ID_WINDOW, szBuf);

    // Get module name of application that created this window.
    hInstance = GetWindowWord(hWnd, GWW_HINSTANCE);
    if (GetModuleFileName(hInstance, szText, sizeof(szText)) == 0)
        lstrcpy(szText, "(no module name)");
    wsprintf(szBuf, "0x%04X, %s", hInstance, (LPSTR) szText);
    SetDlgItemText(hDlg, ID_CREATOR, szBuf);
```

```
// If window has a parent, get the parent's information.
hWndParent = GetParent(hWnd);
if (hWndParent == NULL)
   lstrcpy(szBuf, "(no parent window)");
else {
   if (GetWindowText(hWndParent, szText, sizeof(szText)) == 0)
      lstrcpy(szText, "(no caption)");
   wsprintf(szBuf, "0x%04X, %s", hWndParent, (LPSTR) szText);
}
SetDlgItemText(hDlg, ID_PARENT, szBuf);

// Get address of window's window procedure.
lpfnWndProc = (WNDPROC) GetWindowLong(hWnd, GWL_WNDPROC);
wsprintf(szBuf, "0x%04X:0x%04X",
   HIWORD(lpfnWndProc), LOWORD((LONG) lpfnWndProc));
SetDlgItemText(hDlg, ID_WNDPROC, szBuf);

// Get window's ID.
wsprintf(szBuf, "0x%04X  (%d)", GetWindowWord(hWnd, GWW_ID),
   GetWindowWord(hWnd, GWW_ID));
SetDlgItemText(hDlg, ID_ID, szBuf);

// Get screen coordinates of window.
// Show (left, top)-(right, bottom),  Dim=Width x Height.
GetWindowRect(hWnd, &rc);
wsprintf(szBuf, "(%d, %d)-(%d, %d),  Dim=%dx%d",
   rc.left, rc.top, rc.right, rc.bottom,
   rc.right - rc.left, rc.bottom - rc.top);
SetDlgItemText(hDlg, ID_LOCATION, szBuf);

// Fill in all the "Window style" information.
wsprintf(szBuf, "0x%08lX", GetWindowLong(hWnd, GWL_STYLE));
SetDlgItemText(hDlg, ID_WNDSTYLES, szBuf);

// Fill the "Window style" list box.
FillStyleBox(GetDlgItem(hDlg, ID_WNDSTYLESBOX),
   _WindowStyles, GetWindowLong(hWnd, GWL_STYLE));

// Fill in all the "Extended window style" information.
wsprintf(szBuf, "0x%08lX", GetWindowLong(hWnd, GWL_EXSTYLE));
SetDlgItemText(hDlg, ID_WNDEXTSTYLES, szBuf);

// Fill the "Extended window style" list box.
FillStyleBox(GetDlgItem(hDlg, ID_WNDEXTSTYLESBOX),
   _ExtWindowStyles, GetWindowLong(hWnd, GWL_EXSTYLE));
```

```
    // Fill in all the "Window extra byte" information.
    cbWndExtra = GetClassWord(hWnd, GCW_CBWNDEXTRA);
    wsprintf(szBuf, "%d", cbWndExtra);
    SetDlgItemText(hDlg, ID_CBWNDEXTRA, szBuf);

    // Fill the "Window extra bytes" list box.
    SetWindowRedraw(GetDlgItem(hDlg, ID_CBWNDEXTRABOX), FALSE);
    (void) ListBox_ResetContent(
        GetDlgItem(hDlg, ID_CBWNDEXTRABOX));

    for (x = 0; x < cbWndExtra; x++) {
        // These two lines are necessary so that we do not
        // step beyond the windows' extra bytes.
        if (x == 0) y = LOBYTE(GetWindowWord(hWnd, x));
        else y = HIBYTE(GetWindowWord(hWnd, x - 1));
        wsprintf(szBuf, "%02u  0x%02X", x, y & 0x00ff);
        (void) ListBox_AddString(
            GetDlgItem(hDlg, ID_CBWNDEXTRABOX), szBuf);
    }

    SetWindowRedraw(GetDlgItem(hDlg, ID_CBWNDEXTRABOX), TRUE);

    // Force redraw of "Window extra bytes" list box.
    InvalidateRect(GetDlgItem(hDlg, ID_CBWNDEXTRABOX), NULL, TRUE);
}


// ****************************************************************
// This functions draws a frame around a given window.  The frame
// is drawn in the inverse screen color.  This allows a second
// call to this function to restore the screen display to its
// original appearance.

void NEAR DrawWindowFrame (HWND hWnd) {
    HDC  hDC;
    RECT rc;
    HPEN hPen;

    // Retrieve location of window on screen.
    GetWindowRect(hWnd, &rc);

    // Get a Device context that allows us to write anywhere within
    // the window.  NOTE: GetDC would only allow us to write in the
    // window's client area.
    hDC = GetWindowDC(hWnd);

    // To guarantee that the frame will be visible, tell Windows to
    // draw the frame using the inverse screen color.
```

```
        SetROP2(hDC, R2_NOT);

        // Create a pen that is three times the width of a nonsizeable
        // border.  The color will not be used to draw the frame, so
        // its value could be anything.  PS_INSIDEFRAME tells windows
        // that the entire frame should be enclosed within the window.
        hPen = CreatePen(PS_INSIDEFRAME,
            3 * GetSystemMetrics(SM_CXBORDER), RGB(0, 0, 0));
        SelectObject(hDC, hPen);
        // We must select a NULL brush so that the contents of the
        // window will not be covered.
        SelectObject(hDC, GetStockObject(NULL_BRUSH));

        // Draw the frame.  Because the Device Context is relative to
        // the window, the left-top corner is (0, 0) and the
        // right-bottom corner is (width of window, height of window).
        Rectangle(hDC, 0, 0, rc.right - rc.left, rc.bottom - rc.top);

        ReleaseDC(hWnd, hDC);

        // We can only destroy the pen AFTER we have released the DC
        // because the DC must have valid "tools" in it at all times.
        DeleteObject(hPen);
}


// ******************************************************************
// This function processes all messages sent to the main window.

LRESULT CALLBACK VoyeurAppWndProc
        (HWND hWnd, UINT uMsg, WPARAM wParam, LPARAM lParam) {
    BOOL fCallDefProc = FALSE;
    LRESULT lResult = 0;
    HMENU hMenu;
    RECT rc, rcStatDlg;
    HWND hWndSubject, hWndChild;
    static HWND hWndLastSubject = NULL;

    switch (uMsg) {

        case WM_CREATE:
            // Try to create modeless dialog box.
            _hWndStats = CreateDialog(_hInstance, "VOYEUR", hWnd,
                (DLGPROC) VoyeurDlgProc);
            if (_hWndStats == NULL) {

                // If modeless dialog box couldn't be created, tell
                // Windows not to create the window and return.
```

```
        lResult = -1;
        break;
    }

    // Change Voyeur's window dimensions so that it exactly
    // surrounds the modeless dialog box.  Voyeur's position
    // on the screen should not be altered.
    GetWindowRect(hWnd, &rc);
    GetWindowRect(_hWndStats, &rcStatDlg);
    MoveWindow(hWnd, rc.left, rc.top,
        rcStatDlg.right - rcStatDlg.left,
        rcStatDlg.bottom - rcStatDlg.top +
        GetSystemMetrics(SM_CYCAPTION), FALSE)';

    // Get handle to Voyeur's System Menu.
    hMenu = GetSystemMenu(hWnd, 0);

    // Append separator bar & two options.
    AppendMenu(hMenu, MF_SEPARATOR, 0, 0);
    AppendMenu(hMenu, MF_STRING,
        IDM_PEERINTOWINDOW, "&Peer into window");
    AppendMenu(hMenu, MF_STRING,
        IDM_DROPBACKANDPEER, "&Drop back and peer");

    DrawMenuBar(hWnd);

    lResult = 0;    // Window has been created OK.
    break;

case WM_DESTROY:
    PostQuitMessage(0);
    break;

case WM_SYSCOMMAND:
    // Any menu option selected from Voyeur's System Menu.

    // Any options that we appended to System menu should be
    // processed by Voyeur and NOT passed to DefWindowProc.

    switch (wParam & 0xfff0) {

    case IDM_DROPBACKANDPEER:
        // Send Voyeur's window to back of Window Manager's
        // list.  This causes any windows that are overlapped
        // by Voyeur to become visible.  This allows these
        // windows to be "peered" into.
        SetWindowPos(hWnd, HWND_BOTTOM, 0, 0, 0, 0,
```

```
            SWP_NOMOVE | SWP_NOSIZE);

        // Fall through to IDM_PEERINTOWINDOW

    case IDM_PEERINTOWINDOW:
        // Force all mouse msgs to come here.
        SetCapture(hWnd);

        // Change the mouse cursor to eyes.  This provides a
        // visual indication to user that Voyeur is "peering."
        SetCursor(LoadCursor(_hInstance, "Eyes"));

        // Set Window handle of last viewed window to NULL.
        hWndLastSubject = NULL;
        break;

    default:
        // Any options that we do not process should be
        // passed to DefWindowProc.
        fCallDefProc = TRUE;
        break;
    }

    break;

case WM_MOUSEMOVE:
    // If we don't have capture, we shouldn't do anything.
    if (GetCapture() == NULL)
        break;

    // lParam contains the mouse location relative to
    // Voyeur's client area.

    // Convert the location to screen coordinates.
    ClientToScreen(hWnd, &MAKEPOINT(lParam));

    // Get the handle of the window under the mouse cursor.
    #pragma warn -stv
    hWndSubject = WindowFromPoint(MAKEPOINT(lParam));
    #pragma warn .stv

    // If mouse isn't over a window, return.
    if (hWndSubject == NULL) break;

    // If window as created by Voyeur, ignore it.
    if (GetWindowTask(hWndSubject) == GetCurrentTask())
        break;
```

```
    // Convert the mouse location into client coordinates
    // relative to the window that is under the mouse cursor.
    ScreenToClient(hWndSubject, &MAKEPOINT(lParam));
    // Get the handle of the child window under the cursor.
    #pragma warn -stv
    hWndChild = ChildWindowFromPoint(hWndSubject,
        MAKEPOINT(lParam));
    #pragma warn .stv

    // If point is over a child, our subject is the child.
    if (hWndChild != NULL)
        hWndSubject = hWndChild;

    // If our new subject is the same as our last subject,
    // there is no need to update our display.
    if (hWndLastSubject == hWndSubject)
        break;

    // If this is not our first window being viewed, remove
    // the frame surrounding the previously viewed window.
    if (hWndLastSubject != NULL)
        DrawWindowFrame(hWndLastSubject);

    UpdateWindow(hWndSubject);

    // Draw a frame around our new window.
    DrawWindowFrame(hWndSubject);

    // Fill status box with subject window's class info.
    SetClassInfo(_hWndStats, hWndSubject);

    // Fill status box with subject window's window info.
    SetWindowInfo(_hWndStats, hWndSubject);

    hWndLastSubject = hWndSubject;
    break;

case WM_LBUTTONUP:
    // If we don't have capture, we shouldn't do anything.
    if (GetCapture() != hWnd)
        break;

    // If we never "peered" into a window, we don't have to
    // remove its surrounding frame.
    if (hWndLastSubject != NULL)
        DrawWindowFrame(hWndLastSubject);
```

```
        // Allow other applications to receive mouse messages.
        ReleaseCapture();

        // Force Voyeur to appear on top of all other windows.
        BringWindowToTop(hWnd);

        break;

    default:
        fCallDefProc = TRUE;
        break;
    }

    if (fCallDefProc)
        lResult = DefWindowProc(hWnd, uMsg, wParam, lParam);

    return(lResult);
}
```

Listing 1-2. VOYEUR.H application header file

```
/******************************************************************
Module name: VOYEUR.H
Programmer : Jeffrey M. Richter.
******************************************************************/

#define ID_CBCLSEXTRA        105
#define ID_CBCLSEXTRABOX     106
#define ID_CBWNDEXTRA        118
#define ID_CBWNDEXTRABOX     119
#define ID_CLASSNAME         100
#define ID_CLASSOTHERBOX     102
#define ID_CLASSSTYLE        103
#define ID_CLASSSTYLEBOX     104
#define ID_CREATOR           108
#define ID_ID                112
#define ID_LOCATION          113
#define ID_NUMPROPS          140
#define ID_OWNER             101
#define ID_PARENT            110
#define ID_TASK              109
#define ID_WINDOW            107
#define ID_WINDOWHANDLE      121
#define ID_WNDEXTSTYLES      116
```

```
#define ID_WNDEXTSTYLESBOX    117
#define ID_WNDPROC            111
#define ID_WNDPROPBOX         141
#define ID_WNDSTYLES          114
#define ID_WNDSTYLESBOX       115
```

Listing 1-3. VOYEUR.RC application resource file

```
/*******************************************************************
Module name: VOYEUR.RC
Programmer : Jeffrey M. Richter.
*******************************************************************/

#include <windows.h>
#include "voyeur.h"

Voyeur    ICON      MOVEABLE DISCARDABLE Voyeur.Ico
Eyes      CURSOR    MOVEABLE DISCARDABLE Eyes.Cur

VOYEUR DIALOG 0, 0, 272, 160
FONT 8, "Helv"
STYLE WS_CHILD | WS_VISIBLE
BEGIN
   CONTROL "* CLASS INFORMATION *", -1, "static",
      SS_CENTER | WS_CHILD, 0, 4, 280, 8
   CONTROL "Class:", -1, "static",
      SS_LEFT | WS_CHILD, 2, 16, 28, 8
   CONTROL "", ID_CLASSNAME, "static",
      SS_LEFT | WS_CHILD, 60, 16, 172, 8
   CONTROL "Owner (Inst):", -1, "static",
      SS_LEFT | WS_CHILD, 2, 24, 48, 8
   CONTROL "", ID_OWNER, "static",
      SS_LEFT | WS_CHILD, 60, 24, 172, 8
   CONTROL "Other:", -1, "static",
      SS_LEFT | WS_CHILD, 2, 36, 32, 8
   CONTROL "", ID_CLASSOTHERBOX, "listbox", LBS_USETABSTOPS |
      WS_BORDER | WS_VSCROLL | WS_TABSTOP | WS_CHILD,
      2, 46, 104, 20
   CONTROL "Styles:", -1, "static",
      SS_LEFT | WS_CHILD, 110, 36, 28, 8
   CONTROL "", ID_CLASSSTYLE, "static",
      SS_LEFT | WS_CHILD, 134, 36, 32, 8
   CONTROL "", ID_CLASSSTYLEBOX, "listbox",
      WS_BORDER | WS_VSCROLL | WS_CHILD, 110, 46, 92, 20
   CONTROL "Extra bytes:", -1, "static",
```

```
      SS_LEFT | WS_CHILD, 208, 36, 48, 8
   CONTROL "", ID_CBCLSEXTRA, "static",
      SS_LEFT | WS_CHILD, 248, 36, 16, 8
   CONTROL "", ID_CBCLSEXTRABOX, "listbox",
      WS_BORDER | WS_VSCROLL | WS_CHILD, 208, 46, 60, 20
   CONTROL "", -1, "static",
      SS_GRAYRECT | WS_CHILD, 0, 66, 280, 4
   CONTROL "* WINDOW INFORMATION *", -1, "static",
      SS_CENTER | WS_CHILD, 0, 72, 280, 8
   CONTROL "Window (hWnd):", -1, "static",
      SS_LEFT | WS_CHILD, 2, 84, 68, 8
   CONTROL "", ID_WINDOW, "static",
      SS_LEFT | WS_CHILD, 60, 84, 184, 8
   CONTROL "Creator (Inst):", -1, "static",
      SS_LEFT | WS_CHILD, 2, 92, 68, 8
   CONTROL "", ID_CREATOR, "static",
      SS_LEFT | WS_CHILD, 60, 92, 184, 8
   CONTROL "Parent (hWnd):", -1, "static",
      SS_LEFT | WS_CHILD, 2, 100, 68, 8
   CONTROL "", ID_PARENT, "static",
      SS_LEFT | WS_CHILD, 60, 100, 184, 8
   CONTROL "WndProc:", -1, "static",
      SS_LEFT | WS_CHILD, 2, 108, 48, 8
   CONTROL "", ID_WNDPROC, "static",
      SS_LEFT | WS_CHILD, 60, 108, 64, 8
   CONTROL "ID:", -1, "static",
      SS_LEFT | WS_CHILD, 144, 108, 16, 8
   CONTROL "", ID_ID, "static",
      SS_LEFT | WS_CHILD, 160, 108, 84, 8
   CONTROL "Location:", -1, "static",
      SS_LEFT | WS_CHILD, 2, 116, 36, 8
   CONTROL "", ID_LOCATION, "static",
      SS_LEFT | WS_CHILD, 60, 116, 184, 8
   CONTROL "Wnd styles:", -1, "static",
      SS_LEFT | WS_CHILD, 2, 128, 48, 8
   CONTROL "", ID_WNDSTYLES, "static",
      SS_LEFT | WS_CHILD, 42, 128, 52, 8
   CONTROL "", ID_WNDSTYLESBOX, "listbox",
      WS_BORDER | WS_VSCROLL | WS_CHILD, 2, 138, 104, 20
   CONTROL "Ext styles:", -1, "static",
      SS_LEFT | WS_CHILD, 110, 128, 44, 8
   CONTROL "", ID_WNDEXTSTYLES, "static",
      SS_LEFT | WS_CHILD, 146, 128, 48, 8
   CONTROL "", ID_WNDEXTSTYLESBOX, "listbox",
      WS_BORDER | WS_VSCROLL | WS_CHILD, 110, 138, 92, 20
   CONTROL "Extra bytes:", -1, "static",
      SS_LEFT | WS_CHILD, 208, 128, 48, 8
```

```
   CONTROL "", ID_CBWNDEXTRA, "static",
      SS_LEFT | WS_CHILD, 250, 128, 12, 8
   CONTROL "", ID_CBWNDEXTRABOX, "listbox",
      WS_BORDER | WS_VSCROLL | WS_CHILD, 208, 138, 60, 20
END
```

Listing 1-4. VOYEUR.DEF application definitions file

```
; Module name: VOYEUR.DEF
; Programmer : Jeffrey M. Richter.

NAME          VOYEUR
DESCRIPTION   'Voyeur: Window Examination Application'
STUB          'WinStub.exe'
EXETYPE       WINDOWS
CODE          MOVEABLE DISCARDABLE PRELOAD
DATA          MOVEABLE MULTIPLE PRELOAD
HEAPSIZE      1024
STACKSIZE     5120
```

Listing 1-5. MAKEFILE for Voyeur application

```
#*******************************************************************
#Module name: MAKEFILE
#Programmer : Jeffrey M. Richter
#*******************************************************************

!include "..\builtins.jmr"

PROG = Voyeur

MODEL = s
CFLAGS = -P-c -c -f- -WS -p -v -w -m$(MODEL) -I$(INCLUDEDIR)
LFLAGS = /P/v/n/m/s/L$(LIBDIR)
LIBS = CW$(MODEL) Import

MODULES = $(PROG).obj

ICONS   = $(PROG).ico
BITMAPS =
CURSORS = Eyes.cur

$(PROG).Exe: $(MODULES) $(PROG).Def $(PROG).Res
```

```
    tlink $(LFLAGS) @&&!
COW$(MODEL) $(MODULES)
$(PROG), $(PROG), $(LIBS), $(PROG)
!
   rc -30 -T $(PROG).Res
   TDStrip -s $(PROG)

$(PROG).res: $(PROG).rc $(PROG).h $(RESOURCES)
```

CHAPTER 2

Subclassing and Superclassing Windows

The Microsoft Windows Software Development Kit (SDK) supplies a number of ready-to-use window classes, including LISTBOX, COMBOBOX, EDIT, and so on. These controls are intended to be general enough for use in any application. Sometimes, however, you may wish that one of the controls had slightly different behavior.

One solution to this problem is to design your own control from scratch. This is usually a significant task. It would be nice if Microsoft distributed the source code for controls so that we could modify their behavior. However, since Microsoft does not make the source code available, we cannot do this. Window subclassing and superclassing come to the rescue and save us from reinventing the wheel.

Subclassing and superclassing can also be used on your own window classes, including application windows and custom controls that you create. You can also modify the behavior of applications written by others through subclassing and superclassing.

How Window Subclassing Works

When registering a window class, you fill the members of the *WNDCLASS* structure and pass the structure to the *RegisterClass* function. The address of the window procedure is set using the *lpfnWndProc* member of the structure. This procedure processes messages pertaining to all instances of windows in this class.

Whenever a new window is created, Windows allocates a block of memory containing information specific to that window. The value of *lpfnWndProc* is copied from the block of memory for the window class into the block of memory allocated for the newly created window. When a message is dispatched to a window procedure, Windows examines the value of the window procedure in the window's memory block and calls the function whose address is stored there.

63

Windows does not examine the window class memory block when dispatching a message to a window.

To subclass a window, you change the window procedure address in the window's memory block to point to a new window procedure (Figure 2-1). Because the address is changed in one window's memory block, it does not affect any other windows created from the same class.

If Windows did not give each window instance its own copy of the window procedure address, then changing the class' address would alter the behavior of all windows in the class. If this were the case, subclassing a single EDIT control so that it would no longer accept letters would cause EDIT controls in all applications to stop accepting letters. This is certainly not desirable.

Once you have told Windows the address of your own window procedure, all messages destined for the window will be sent to your own window procedure. Your procedure must look exactly like a standard window procedure. In other words, it must have an identical prototype:

```
LRESULT CALLBACK WndSubClassProc (HWND hWnd, UINT uMsg,
    WPARAM wParam, LPARAM lParam);
```

Once the message destined for the original window procedure has been sent to your procedure, you may do one of the following:

1. Pass it to the original procedure. This is done for most messages. The reason for subclassing is usually to alter the behavior of a window only slightly. For this reason, most messages will be passed to the original procedure so that the default behavior for this class of window can be performed.

2. Stop the message from being passed to the original procedure. For example, if you wanted an EDIT control to stop accepting letters, you would examine *WM_CHAR* messages, check to see if the *wParam* value is between A and Z or a and z, and, if so, return from the *WndSubClassProc* function. If *wParam* is any other character, you would pass the message to the original window procedure for EDIT controls.

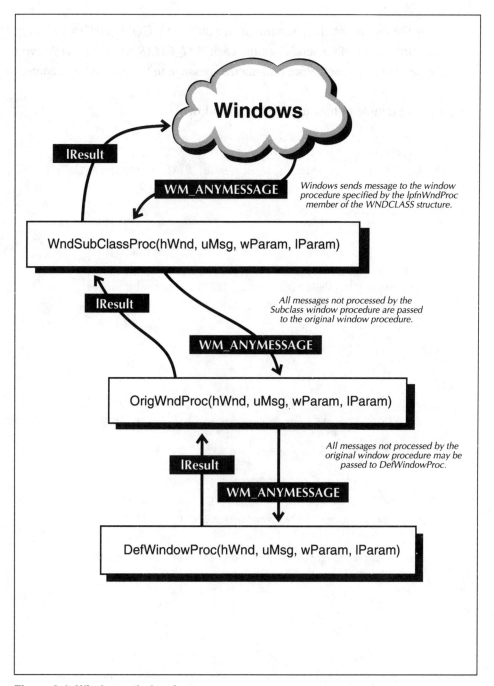

Figure 2-1. Window subclassing

3. Alter the message before sending it. If you want a COMBOBOX to accept only uppercase characters, examine each *WM_CHAR* message and convert the key to uppercase before passing the message to the original procedure.

Here is an example of how to subclass a window:

```
// Prototype for forward reference.
LRESULT CALLBACK EditSubClassProc (HWND, UINT, WPARAM, LPARAM);


WNDPROC _wpOrigWndProc;
     .

     .

     .

int WinMain (HINSTANCE hInstance, HINSTANCE hPrevInstance,
     LPSTR szCmdLine, int nCmdShow) {
   HWND hWndEdit;

     .

     .

     .

   hWndEdit = CreateWindow("EDIT", "", WS_CHILD,
      10, 20, 100, 16, hWndParent, NULL, hInstance, OL);


   // Set new address for window procedure and
   // save the address of the original window's window procedure.
   _wpOrigWndProc = SubclassWindow(hWndEdit, EditSubClassProc);

   // All messages destined for hWndEdit will be sent to
   // EditSubClassProc.
}
     .

     .

     .

LRESULT CALLBACK EditSubClassProc (HWND hWnd, UINT uMsg,
     WPARAM wParam, LPARAM lParam) {
```

```
    LRESULT lResult = 0;
    BOOL fCallOrigWndProc = TRUE;
    switch (uMsg) {
    .

    .

    .

    }
    if (fCallOrigWndProc)
        lResult = CallWindowProc(_wpOrigWndProc, hWnd, uMsg,
            wParam, lParam);

    return(lResult);
}
```

The only information required to subclass a window is its window handle. You'll notice that I have used the *SubclassWindow* macro above to perform the window subclassing. This macro is contained in the WINDOWSX.H file and is defined as follows:

```
#define SubclassWindow(hwnd, lpfn) \
        ((WNDPROC)SetWindowLong((hwnd), GWL_WNDPROC, \
        (LPARAM)(WNDPROC)(lpfn)))
```

You can see that, aside from some casting, it doesn't do anything more than simply calling *SetWindowLong* and changing the address of the window's window procedure. The return value from *SetWindowLong* is the address of the original window procedure and that is simply saved in the global variable *_wpOrigWndProc*. The function you write to intercept messages is identical in form to a window procedure. The only difference is that you pass the messages to the original window procedure instead of calling *DefWindowProc*. To have the original window perform its normal operations for a particular message, you must use the *CallWindowProc* function. This function is passed the address of the original window procedure, the window handle (*hWnd*), the message (*uMsg*), and the two data elements (*wParam* and *lParam*).

Limitations Imposed by Window Subclassing

Suppose we would like to further restrict our EDIT control subclass to accept only a certain range of numbers. We are not familiar with the way an EDIT control uses its extra class and window bytes, so we cannot use these bytes for storing information about the valid data range. Because subclassing requires that a window instance already exist before we can subclass it, increasing the number of class or window extra bytes is also impossible. The best way to associate data with a subclassed window is by using window properties, as explained in Chapter 1.

Of course, if you know how the window class uses its class and window extra bytes, it's OK to use them for yourself. You should, however, try to think ahead to how the subclassed class may change. Such changes may prevent your subclass window procedure from working correctly.

Finally, you can add your own user messages to a subclassed window if you approach the task carefully. An example: If we examine WINDOWS.H, we discover that the highest used BUTTON class-specific message is *BM_SETSTYLE*, defined as *WM_USER + 4*. We do not know if Microsoft has defined other, internal messages for the BUTTON class that do not appear in the WINDOWS.H file. If we added our own user message starting at *WM_USER + 5*, it could conflict with an undocumented message recognized by the BUTTON class. Actually, choosing any value—*WM_USER + 500*, for example—would be tempting fate. The only way to solve this problem is by using the *RegisterWindowMessage* function described in Chapter 1.

The Program Manager Restore Program

In my Windows environment, I have checked the "Minimize on Use" option that appears on the Options menu in Program Manager. This tells Program Manager to turn itself into an icon whenever I use it to launch an application. When the application terminates, Program Manager remains an icon.

Because the only action I can do now is open Program Manager, it would be convenient if Program Manager could detect that it is the only application running and restore itself automatically. The Program Manager Restore (PM Restore) program demonstrates how this function can be added to Program Manager via window subclassing.

PM Restore doesn't create any windows of its own; it subclasses Program Manager's window and just waits for messages. PM Restore also demonstrates how to add new menu items to an existing or already running application by appending "About PM Restore..." and "Remove PM Restore" to Program Manager's Options menu.

> **Note:** Subclassing a window for a class created by someone else can cause your application to fail when the company releases new versions of its application. Because PM Restore subclasses Microsoft's Program Manager application, it is possible that PM Restore will not function with future versions of Program Manager.
>
> PM Restore assumes that Program Manager is the shell application of Windows. This is specified by the *SHELL=PROGMAN.EXE* line in the SYSTEM.INI file. By default, all Windows installations set up Program Manager as the shell application. If your Windows setup has a different application from the Windows shell, the PM Restore application will not work.

How PM Restore Works

Windows sends notification messages to windows when something has happened. One of these is *WM_ACTIVATEAPP*, which is sent to the main window of the currently active application to notify it that it is being deactivated. The message is also sent to the main window of the application being activated. The *wParam* parameter associated with the *WM_ACTIVATEAPP* message can be examined to determine whether the application is being activated or deactivated.

When you terminate an application, Windows makes another application active. Since Program Manager is always running, Windows could make it the active application. If this happens, Program Manager receives a *WM_ACTIVATEAPP* message. PM Restore, which has subclassed Program Manager, intercepts the *WM_ACTIVATEAPP* message before Program Manager sees it.

PM Restore first determines whether Windows is activating or deactivating Program Manager. If Program Manager is being deactivated, PM Restore does not process the message; it's passed to Program Manager.

If Windows is activating Program Manager, PM Restore determines whether any other applications are running. If at least one other application is running, PM Restore does nothing and simply passes the *WM_ACTIVATEAPP* message to Program Manager's original window procedure.

If no other applications are running, PM Restore calls the *ShowWindow* function, which tells Program Manager to restore itself to its last "opened" size. The *WM_ACTIVATEAPP* message is then passed to Program Manager.

The *WinMain* Function

Because it doesn't make sense to run multiple instances of PM Restore, *hPrevInstance* is checked. If it's not NULL, PM Restore is not installed. The PM Restore application then stores its task-instance handle in a global variable:

```
HTASK _hTaskPMRestore;
    .
    .
    .
    _hTaskPMRestore = GetCurrentTask();
```

When Windows executes an instance of an application, each instance is assigned a unique task-instance handle. *GetCurrentTask* returns the task-instance handle of the currently executing task. When the PM Restore application calls *GetCurrentTask*, Windows returns the task-instance handle of the PM Restore application. This handle is used later so the user can remove PM Restore from memory. (The procedure for doing this is explained later in this section.) For a complete discussion of tasks and their instance handles, see Chapter 6.

To subclass Program Manager and add menu items to it, we must retrieve its window handle by calling *FindWindow:*

```
    _hWndPM = FindWindow(_szPMClass, NULL);
```

The first parameter is the class name of the window we are looking for (or NULL to find windows matching any class). The second parameter is the caption of that window (or NULL to match any caption). At first, you might think we should use the caption and specify NULL for the window class because we can see that the caption of Program Manager on the screen is "Program Manager" (Figure 2-2) and we don't know what Microsoft used as the class name for the window. However, we can easily change the caption of Program Manager by maximizing one of its child windows. If we maximize the Main group (Figure 2-3), the caption changes to "Program Manager - [Main]." If we had tried to locate Program Manager with

```
_hWndPM = FindWindow(NULL, "Program Manager");
```

_hWndPM would be NULL because a window would not exist with the specified caption.

So the best way to get Program Manager's window handle is to specify its class name. I discovered the class name by using the Voyeur application presented in Chapter 1. When I selected the "Peer into window" option under the system menu and positioned the mouse cursor over Program Manager's caption, Voyeur revealed the class name (PROGMAN) of Program Manager.

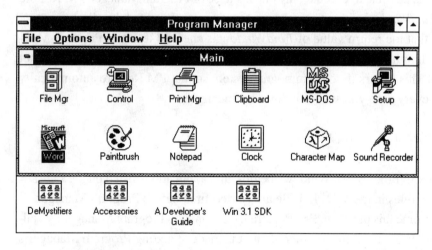

Figure 2-2. Program Manager window

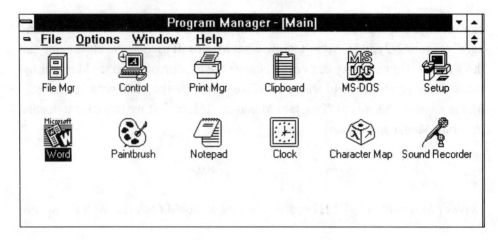

Figure 2-3. Program Manager - [Main] window

The *FindWindow* function can be extremely useful for locating windows to subclass. It has one drawback, however. If multiple windows of the same class exist and have the same caption, *FindWindow* will only locate the first one and its handle. Because it is possible to execute only one instance of Program Manager, PM Restore can use *FindWindow* without any chance of retrieving the wrong handle.

Notice that the return value of *FindWindow* is checked to see if Program Manager could, in fact, be found. If *_hWndPM* is NULL, Program Manager could not be found. This occurs if you set up your system so that PM Restore automatically executes every time you start Windows by specifying

```
LOAD=PMRest.EXE
```

in the WIN.INI file. When Windows begins, any applications listed on the *LOAD=* and *RUN=* lines in the WIN.INI file are started first, before Program Manager.

To overcome this problem, PM Restore tries to invoke Program Manager by calling the *WinExec* function. Another attempt is made at getting Program Manager's window handle. If we are unsuccessful this time, PM Restore cannot subclass Program Manager. It notifies the user and terminates.

After Windows has executed all the applications listed in the *LOAD=* and *RUN=* lines of the WIN.INI file, the shell application is executed. In our case, this would be Program Manager, except that it's already running. Fortunately, Microsoft designed Program Manager so that it only allows one instance of itself to execute. Otherwise, our Windows session would start with two Program Managers.

Changing Program Manager's Menus

Once we have the window handle of Program Manager, we can easily add new menu items to it. But first we must choose menu ID values that do not conflict with any of the values already selected by Microsoft for Program Manager menu options.

The commercial version of Voyeur, Microsoft's Spy, and Borland's WinSight can determine the ID values of all Program Manager menu options. Windows sends the *WM_SYSCOMMAND* message to a window procedure when the user has selected a menu option from a system menu (this includes the system menu of Multiple Document Interface, or MDI, children). Windows sends the *WM_COMMAND* message to a window procedure when the user has selected a menu option from a nonsystem menu. Because we will be adding our menu options to Program Manager's nonsystem menu, we must determine all the menu IDs assigned by Microsoft for use by that menu and select values that do not conflict.

I examined *WM_COMMAND* messages passed to Program Manager's window procedure. I selected each option in turn and recorded the *wParam* values, resulting in this table:

Menu item	Hex	Decimal
File menu		
New...	0x0065	101
Open	0x0066	102
Move...	0x0067	103
Copy...	0x0068	104
Delete	0x0069	105
Properties...	0x006A	106
Run...	0x006B	107
Exit Windows...	0x006C	108
Options menu		
Auto Arrange	0x00C9	201
Minimize on Use	0x00CA	202
Save Settings on Exit	0x00CC	204

(table continued on following page)

Menu item	Hex	Decimal
Window menu		
Cascade	0x012D	301
Tile	0x012E	302
Arrange Icons	0x012F	303
Group Window 1	0x01F4	500
.	.	.
.	.	.
.	.	.
Group Window 9	0x01FC	508
More Windows...	0x01FD	509
Help menu		
Contents	0x0191	401
Search for Help on...	0x0194	404
How to Use Help	0x0192	402
Windows Tutorial	0x0195	405
About Program Manager...	0x0193	403

Note that in an MDI application, Windows maintains the list of MDI child windows in the Window menu on behalf of the programmer. The programmer tells Windows the ID value of the first MDI child window. Windows will assign ID values in ascending order (incrementing each ID by one) to all MDI child windows created after the first. Each of the program group windows in Program Manager is an MDI child window. The first program group window will have an ID value of 0x01F4, the second, 0x01F5, and so on.

Now that we have this information, we just have to select menu IDs that do not conflict. I have selected a value of 4444 for *IDM_PMRESTOREABOUT* and a value of 4445 for *IDM_PMRESTOREREMOVE*. Since we want to append the new options to the menu that contains the "Auto Arrange" option, we must locate that menu and get its handle. At first, you might think that we could use

```
hMenu = GetSubMenu(GetMenu(_hWndPM), 1);
```

but this will not work if an MDI child window is maximized. The system menu for the MDI child becomes the first pop-up menu in the application's menu bar, pushing the index of all other pop-up menus up by one. Because of this, the line of code above will return to us the menu handle of the File menu. By setting the code up in a loop and checking the first menu option in each pop-up to see if its menu ID is *IDM_AUTO_ARRANGE* (0x00C9), we will be sure to add our option to the correct pop-up menu.

We now subclass Program Manager as follows:

```
// Set new window function for the Program Manager and
// save present window function for the Program Manager in global variable.
    _fpOrigPMProc = SubclassWindow(_hWndPM,
            MakeProcInstance((FARPROC) PMSubClass, hInstance));
```

This step passes the procedural instance address into SubclassWindow to cause the subclassing to take effect and saves the address of Program Manager's original window procedure in a global variable so it can be used in the call to the *Call-WindowProc* function that appears at the end of the *PMSubClass* function.

A Word About Procedural Instances

Back in the early days of Windows programming, the programmer struggled with issues such as Windows' task-switching, the segmented architecture of the Intel chips, and how to allow his or her application to cooperate with other running applications, including multiple instances of itself. One of the most misunderstood areas of Windows programming has always been the procedural instance and the use of the *MakeProcInstance* and *FreeProcInstance* functions as well as whether or not to list function names in the module's .DEF file.

In Windows, a task-switch means that Windows must save the current state of the CPU registers and set the registers back to what they were when the task that is about to become active is switched away.

For Windows (in protected mode), a task-switch is simply a matter of saving most of the CPU registers for the currently executing task and setting up the CPU registers for the task that is about to execute. When the Windows programming team was working on the task-switching code, they decided not to restore the *DS* register. Windows relegates this responsibility to the programmer. To help the programmer restore the *DS* register, Windows offers the *MakeProcInstance* and *FreeProcInstance* func-

WINDOWS 3.1: A DEVELOPER'S GUIDE

tions, a variety of compiler options, a set of compiler directives (such as _loadds, _export), and the module's .DEF file. You then use a combination of these to get your callback functions (window, dialog-box, and enumeration procedures) to restore the *DS* register to your application's data segment when they execute.

When I said *help* earlier, I used the term loosely because many programmers have found all of these settings/options to be more confusing than helpful. For example, whenever a window is sent a message, Windows performs a task-switch to the application that created the window. This means that Windows restores the registers for the task (except for *DS*). For the data segment, Windows looks at the value of the *hInstance* parameter that was passed to *CreateWindow(Ex)*. This value identifies the application's data segment. Windows then loads the *AX* register with the selector identifying the application's data segment. When the window procedure is called, the procedure PUSHes the current value of the *DS* register on the stack and loads the *DS* register with the value in the *AX* register. Now, any time that global or static variables are accessed from within the window procedure, the *DS* register will be set correctly. Of course, when the window procedure terminates, the original value of the *DS* register is POPed off the stack.

The window procedure knows to do this PUSHing and POPing because the function name was exported in the module's .DEF file. For functions that are not called by Windows directly, the *AX* register is not initialized to point to the application's data segment. If these functions loaded the *DS* register with the value of the *AX* register, the function would certainly crash Windows. You tell the function not to load the *DS* register by not exporting the function—this is the case for most functions in your application.

Let's examine a scenario. When your application creates an EDIT control or any other kind of system global window, your application passes into the *CreateWindow(Ex)* function the data instance handle for your application. When Windows sends a message to one of these windows, the *SS* register is set to your application's stack and the *AX* register will be set to your application's data segment. This means that the code in the system-global window class' window procedure will be using your application's stack. But it most certainly must not access data in your application's data segment pointed to by the *AX* register. After all, Microsoft doesn't know what the contents of your application's data segment are and any attempts to read or write to them are sure to cause confusion either in their control's window procedures or later in your own code. So, how does the system-global class' window procedure know to use its own data segment?

The address of the data segment is placed in the code itself. In fact, this is true for all exported functions in a dynamic-link library. So, when the EDIT control's window procedure receives a message, the value in the *AX* register is ignored and the *DS* register is set to the data segment for the library. While an application has a separate data segment for each running instance of the application, there can only ever be one data segment for a dynamic-link library; hence, the library's data segment address can be placed directly in the prologues for each function in the library.

This is all well and good for a window procedure, but what about dialog-box procedures? Well, Windows requires that you create a procedural instance address of the dialog-box procedure and pass the address of the procedural instance into the *DialogBox* function. Procedural instances are created by calling the *MakeProcInstance* function.

The *MakeProcInstance* function accepts two parameters. The first is the address of the procedure to be made into a procedural instance; the second is the data instance handle to your application's data segment. *MakeProcInstance* allocates a block of memory that contains some assembly language instructions to do the following:

1. Set the *AX* register to the value of the *hInstance* parameter.
2. Call the address specified by the first parameter to *MakeProcInstance*.

The address returned by *MakeProcInstance* is the address to this assembly code. Calling this address is just like calling the function directly except that the *AX* register is initialized to your data segment's address. When you no longer need the procedural instance, you can call *FreeProcInstance* to free the memory containing the assembly language instructions.

After developing Windows applications for a few years and having to put up with these annoyances, programmers discovered a trick. When a message is sent to a dialog box, Windows knows which application created the dialog box and performs a task-switch, setting the *SS* register to the application's data segment. Well, almost every Windows application has its stack contained in the application's data segment. Why couldn't each function simply load the *DS* register with the value of the *SS* register and ignore the *AX* register altogether? If the function prologues could be altered to do this, then there would be no need for calling *MakeProcInstance* or *FreeProcInstance* or even listing functions in the *EXPORT*s section of the application's .DEF file. Sounds great, right? Well, it is.

For those functions that were originally not exported, setting the *DS* register to the value in the *SS* register causes no harm whatsoever. So no distinction has to be made between exported and non-exported functions. And, instead of using the return value from calling *MakeProcInstance* in a call to *DialogBox*, the address of the function itself can be used.

Both the Borland C++ compiler (Version 2.0 and later) and the Microsoft C/C++ compiler (Version 7.0 and later) support a command-line option that instructs the compiler to generate function prologues that set *DS* to *SS*. This feature has been used in all of the programs in this book (except for PM Restore) as well as all of the commercial applications that I have been involved with.

You're probably asking yourself what all of this has to do with window subclassing. If your application creates a window and subclasses it, Windows is going to set the *SS* register to your application's data segment and the *AX* register to the address of your application's data segment identified by the *hInstance* parameter to *CreateWindow*. If your subclass window procedure is in your application, everything is OK. If your subclass window procedure is in a dynamic-link library, everything is still OK because the value in *AX* will be ignored and the *DS* register will be set up correctly.

When the message is passed on to the original window procedure, the *SS* register will be OK, but the *AX* register is bound to be incorrect after all of the processing that has just occurred in your own subclass window procedure. Somehow, the *AX* register must be set to identify PM Restore's data segment. This is what *CallWindowProc* does. *CallWindowProc* simply looks in the window's internal data structure for the *hInstance* member and loads the *AX* register with the address of the application's data segment. It then calls the function whose address you specify as the first parameter. By the way, the *CallWindowProc* function does not cause a task-switch to occur. This means that the value in the *SS* register does not change during this call and that the original window procedure will be using your application's stack.

Now, let's look at another scenario. The Program Manager application creates its main window and PM Restore (a different task) subclasses the Program Manager's window. When Windows sends a message to Program Manager's window, a task-switch occurs, making the Program Manager the active task. Both the *SS* and *AX* registers are set to the Program Manager's data segment. However, because PM Restore has subclassed the Program Manager's window, the subclass window procedure in PM Restore will be called. The active task is the Program Manager and, because *SS* contains the address of Program Manager's data segment, PM Restore will be using another application's stack. While this is OK, PM Restore's subclass window procedure needs to have access to its own data segment and has to determine what it is. To solve this problem, we *must* use *MakeProcInstance*.

Notice that when PM Restore subclasses the Program Manager's window, it first calls *MakeProcInstance* and passes it the address of the subclass window procedure and *_hInstance*. The procedural address is now passed to the *SubclassWindow* macro instead of the address itself. Now, when Windows sends a message to the Program Manager's window, the task-switch still occurs, setting the *SS* and *AX* registers to the Program Manager's data segment. But when the procedural instance address of the subclass window procedure is called, the *AX* register is changed to that of PM Restore's data segment. The subclass window procedure will use its own data segment.

Just before the subclass window procedure returns, it calls *CallWindowProc*. *CallWindowProc* sets the *AX* register to Program Manager's data segment and calls Program Manager's original window procedure.

The only reason that I went into this whole discussion is that PM Restore subclasses a window created by another task. This is extremely unusual for applications to do. Almost all applications will subclass windows that it created itself. In this case, you can forget about most of the problems associated with task-switching (*MakeProcInstance*, *FreeProcInstance*, and module .DEF files) and simply use the compiler's switches and directives (_export and _loadds).

It should be noted that I consider this implementation of PM Restore to be a little on the kludgy side; yet, I also believe that the concepts presented here are very important in Windows programming and are worth studying. I am sure that if you asked Microsoft, the company would not recommend that a task be able to subclass a window created by another task and in fact, this method will not work when running Windows in a government secure environment like Windows NT.

And now back to our story

If PM Restore is executed from Program Manager (rather than using the LOAD= method), Program Manager will be minimized as usual if "Minimize on Use" is checked in the Options menu. Since PM Restore does not create any windows, Windows will not make it the active application. Because of this, Windows will not send a *WM_ACTIVATEAPP* message to the Program Manager's window, allowing the subclass window procedure to restore the window to its original size. The following call:

```
FORWARD_WM_SYSCOMMAND(_hWndPM, SC_RESTORE, 0, 0, PostMessage);
```

forces Program Manager back to its restored state.

Finally, we want PM Restore to relinquish control to Windows without terminating. We do this by entering a message loop. If PM Restore did terminate without restoring the Program Manager's original window procedure, Windows would try to call a subclass function that is no longer in memory whenever a new message is sent to Program Manager. This would certainly crash Windows.

At this point, PM Restore has been initialized, Program Manager has been subclassed, and three new menu items have been added to Program Manager's menu. On the desktop, the only visual indication that everything has been performed successfully is the new menu items appearing under the Options menu of Program Manager.

The *PMSubClass* Function and Message Trapping

Since we wish to affect Program Manager in a very small way and not change the bulk of its behavior, our subclass function only intercepts two messages. *WM_ACTIVATEAPP* is intercepted so that PM Restore can perform the restore operation. *WM_COMMAND* is intercepted so that we can pop up our own About box and allow the user to remove PM Restore from memory.

This is the code associated with the *WM_ACTIVATEAPP* message:

```
case WM_ACTIVATEAPP:
    if (wParam == 0) break;
    if (!IsIconic(hWnd)) break;
```

```
fpProc = MakeProcInstance(AnyAppsRunning, _hInstance);
fAnyWindowsUp = (EnumWindows(fpProc, 0l) == 0);
FreeProcInstance(fpProc);
if (fAnyWindowsUp) break;
ShowWindow(hWnd, SW_RESTORE);
break;
```

If Program Manager is being deactivated or is not an icon, it will not need to be restored to its "open" size. That's why we perform the tests in the first two *if* conditions. Then we must discover whether any other applications are running. We ask Windows to enumerate all the parent windows on the screen by passing each window's handle to the specified callback function.

EnumWindows calls the specified procedural instance once for each parent window. The callback function has the option of continuing the enumeration or halting it. If the return value from *EnumWindows* is zero, our callback function saw a window from another running application and halted the enumeration. Program Manager will not be restored. If the enumeration continues to completion, no other applications are running and we call the *ShowWindow* function to pop Program Manager back to its open state. Notice that I had to call *MakeProcInstance* and *FreeProcInstance* above because the *PMSubClass* procedure is operating under the guise of another task. Also, because I am not able to use the smart-callback feature in the compiler for PM Restore, I had to export the *AnyAppsRunning* function. However, I did this by using the *_export* keyword in the program rather than listing the function in the EXPORTS section of the PMREST.DEF file.

As an aside, it is always better to use the *_export* keyword to export a function rather than listing the function in the .DEF file's EXPORTS section. First, if you change the name of the function, you only have to modify one file, the source code module. Second, if you are using C++, the compiler performs a process called name-mangling. This process causes the compiler to take the name of your function and change its internal representation. When the linker tries to export the function, it will not be able to find the functions listed in the EXPORTS section of the .DEF file and a linker error occurs.

Here's the code associated with the *WM_COMMAND* message:

```
case WM_COMMAND:
    switch (wParam) {
    case IDM_PMRESTOREABOUT:
        fpProc = MakeProcInstance(AboutProc, _hInstance);
        DialogBox(_hInstance, "About", hWnd, fpProc);
        FreeProcInstance(fpProc);
        fCallOrigProc = FALSE;
        break;

    case IDM_PMRESTOREREMOVE:
        // Stop window subclassing by putting back the address of
        // the original window procedure.
        SubclassWindow(hWnd, _fpOrigPMProc);

        // Get menu handle to Program Managers Options menu.
        hMenu = GetMenu(hWnd);

        // Remove the bottom two menu options.
        RemoveMenu(hMenu, IDM_PMRESTOREABOUT, MF_BYCOMMAND);
        RemoveMenu(hMenu, IDM_PMRESTOREREMOVE, MF_BYCOMMAND);

        // Get number of top-level menu items.
        nTopLevelMenuNum = GetMenuItemCount(hMenu) - 1;
        while (nTopLevelMenuNum) {
            // Get handle to pop-up menu.
            hMenuPopup = GetSubMenu(hMenu, nTopLevelMenuNum);
            // Is first option in pop-up menu IDM_AUTO_ARRANGE?
            if (IDM_AUTO_ARRANGE == GetMenuItemID(hMenuPopup, 0)) {
            // Remove separator bar.
                RemoveMenu(hMenuPopup, GetMenuItemCount(hMenuPopup) - 1,
                    MF_BYPOSITION);
                break;              // Stop checking menus.
```

```
        }
        nTopLevelMenuNum—;    // Try next menu.
    }
    DrawMenuBar(hWnd);         // Update new menu bar.
    // Post a WM_QUIT message to our application to remove it
    // from memory.
    PostAppMessage(_hTaskPMRestore, WM_QUIT, 0, 0);
    break;


default:
    break;
```

The subclass function will intercept *WM_COMMAND* messages each time a menu item is selected from within Program Manager. If the *wParam* is *IDM_PMRESTORE-ABOUT*, PM Restore will display the About dialog box. Notice that after the About box is closed, we set *fCallOrigProc* to FALSE. This will prevent us from calling the original window procedure for this *WM_COMMAND* message since Program Manager never expects a *wParam* value of 4444. If we allowed this message to be processed by the original window procedure, the results would be unpredictable.

When *wParam* is *IDM_PMRESTOREREMOVE*, the user has requested that the PM Restore application terminate and remove itself from memory. PM Restore does this by setting Program Manager's window bytes back to the original *WndProc* address. The three menu items that were appended to Program Manager are then removed. Finally, the *PostAppMessage* function is called, instructing PM Restore that it should terminate:

```
    PostAppMessage(_hTaskPMRestore, WM_QUIT, 0, 0);
```

PostAppMessage is similar to *PostMessage* except that its first parameter is a task-instance handle instead of a window handle. When this function is called, Windows places the specified message in the application queue identified by the first parameter. In this case, the *WM_QUIT* message is placed in PM Restore's application queue. The *GetMessage* function in PM Restore's *WinMain* function will retrieve the *WM_QUIT* message. Just before *GetMessage* returns, it checks to see if the message being returned is *WM_QUIT*. If it is, *GetMessage* returns zero, causing the *while* loop to terminate. Once the loop has terminated, PM Restore returns to Windows and is removed from memory.

When a message is dispatched to a window procedure, Windows sets the current task to the application that registered the window's class. If we were to call the *GetCurrentTask* function here, it would not return the task-instance handle of PM Restore, it would return Program Manager's task-instance handle instead. This is why PM Restore's task-instance handle had to be saved earlier in a global variable. For a complete discussion of tasks and queues, refer to Chapter 6.

For all other values of *wParam* associated with the *WM_COMMAND* message, the message is just passed to the original window procedure and handled normally. The other messages are not intercepted and are passed to the original window procedure.

The *AnyAppsRunning* Function

The Windows function *EnumWindows* calls *AnyAppsRunning* once for each parent window. If the window handle passed to this function is the handle for the desktop, a window associated with Program Manager, or an invisible window, we don't care about it and continue with the window enumeration. If it is not one of these, it must be a window for an application. At this point, we stop the enumeration and *EnumWindows* returns zero, telling *PMSubClass* that another application is running and not to restore Program Manager.

Running PM Restore

To run the program, start Windows and execute PMREST.EXE like any other Windows application. You could also place PMREST.EXE in the *LOAD=* line of your WIN.INI file to make it load automatically whenever you start Windows. Once invoked, PM Restore stays active during your entire Windows session. The only way to remove or disable PM Restore is by terminating Windows or selecting "Remove PM Restore" from Program Manager's Options menu.

Listings 2-1 through 2-7, the PM Restore application, illustrate window subclassing.

Listing 2-1. PMREST.C application source module

```
/********************************************************************
Module name: PMREST.C
Programmer : Jeffrey M. Richter.
********************************************************************/

#include <windows.h>
#include <windowsx.h>

extern const HINSTANCE _cdecl _hInstance;

   // Menu IDs from Program Manager's menu.
#define IDM_AUTO_ARRANGE          (0x00C9)
#define IDM_PMRESTOREABOUT        (4444)
#define IDM_PMRESTOREREMOVE       (4445)

char _szAppName[] = "Program Manager Restore";

   // Class name of the Program Manager window.
char _szPMClass[] = "PROGMAN";

   // Address for original window procedure.
WNDPROC _fpOrigPMProc = NULL;

   // Window handle of Program Manager.
HWND _hWndPM = NULL;

   // Our task handle.
HTASK _hTaskPMRestore = NULL;

   // Forward reference to subclass function.
LRESULT CALLBACK PMSubClass (HWND, UINT, WPARAM, LPARAM);

#pragma argsused
int WinMain (HINSTANCE hInstance, HINSTANCE hPrevInstance,
          LPSTR lpszCmdLine, int cmdShow) {
   MSG msg;
   HMENU hMenu, hMenuPopup;
   int nTopLevelMenuNum;

   // Don't allow second instance of "PMRest" to run.
   if (hPrevInstance != NULL) {
      MessageBox(GetFocus(), "Application already running.",
         _szAppName, MB_OK | MB_SYSTEMMODAL);
      return(FALSE);
```

```
    }

    // Get task-instance handle and store it in a global variable.
    _hTaskPMRestore = GetCurrentTask();

    // Find window handle of Program Manager.  Do not specify a
    // caption because the Program Manager's caption changes
    // depending whether a group is maximized or not.
    _hWndPM = FindWindow(_szPMClass, NULL);

    if (_hWndPM == NULL) {

        // If the Program Manager's window couldn't be found, try to
        // execute the Program Manager application.  This happens if
        // PMREST.EXE is in the LOAD= line of the WIN.INI file.
        WinExec("ProgMan", SW_SHOW);
        _hWndPM = FindWindow(_szPMClass, NULL);

        // If we still can't find PROGMAN, we must terminate.
        if (_hWndPM == NULL) {
            MessageBox(GetFocus(), "Cannot find Program Manager.",
                _szAppName, MB_OK);
            return(FALSE);
        }
    }

    // Get Menu handle to Program Manager's "Options" menu.
    hMenu = GetMenu(_hWndPM);

        // Get number of top-level menu items.
    nTopLevelMenuNum = GetMenuItemCount(hMenu) - 1;
    while (nTopLevelMenuNum) {

        // Get handle to pop-up menu.
        hMenuPopup = GetSubMenu(hMenu, nTopLevelMenuNum);

            // Is first option in the pop-up menu IDM_AUTO_ARRANGE?
        if (IDM_AUTO_ARRANGE == GetMenuItemID(hMenuPopup, 0)) {

            // Add a separator bar & menu item options to this menu.
            AppendMenu(hMenuPopup, MF_SEPARATOR, 0, 0);
            AppendMenu(hMenuPopup, MF_ENABLED | MF_STRING,
                IDM_PMRESTOREABOUT, "A&bout PM Restore...");
            AppendMenu(hMenuPopup, MF_ENABLED | MF_STRING,
                IDM_PMRESTOREREMOVE, "&Remove PM Restore");

            break;   // Stop check menus.
```

```
        }
        nTopLevelMenuNum--;          // Try next menu.
    }

    DrawMenuBar(_hWndPM);            // Update the new menu bar.

    // Set new window function for the Program Manager and save the
    // present window function in global variable.
    _fpOrigPMProc = SubclassWindow(_hWndPM,
        MakeProcInstance((FARPROC) PMSubClass, hInstance));

    // Running PMRest.EXE will minimize the Program Manager if
    // "Minimize on Use" is selected in the Options menu.  Since
    // there will not be a task-switch, our subclassing will not
    // restore the Program Manager automatically, so we must do it.
    FORWARD_WM_SYSCOMMAND(_hWndPM, SC_RESTORE, 0, 0, PostMessage);

    // Begin message loop.  This is so that our application doesn't
    // terminate.  If we terminated, our subclass function would be
    // removed from memory.  When Windows tried to call it, it
    // would jump to garbage and cause a General Protection Fault.
    while (GetMessage(&msg, NULL, 0, 0))
        DispatchMessage(&msg);

    return(0);
}


    // Function to process About Box.
BOOL CALLBACK _export AboutProc
        (HWND hDlg, UINT uMsg, WPARAM wParam, LPARAM lParam) {
    BOOL fProcessed = TRUE;

    switch (uMsg) {

        case WM_INITDIALOG:
            break;

        case WM_COMMAND:
            switch (wParam) {
                case IDOK: case IDCANCEL:
                    if (HIWORD(lParam) == BN_CLICKED)
                        EndDialog(hDlg, wParam);
                    break;
                default:
                    break;
            }
            break;
```

```
        default:
            fProcessed = FALSE; break;
    }
    return(fProcessed);
}


    // Forward reference to function called by EnumWindows.
BOOL CALLBACK _export AnyAppsRunning (HWND, LPARAM);

// Subclass function for the Program Manager. Any messages for the
// Program Manager window come here before reaching the original
// window function.
LRESULT CALLBACK _export PMSubClass
        (HWND hWnd, UINT uMsg, WPARAM wParam, LPARAM lParam) {
    FARPROC fpProc;
    BOOL fAnyWindowsUp, fCallOrigProc = TRUE;
    LRESULT lResult = 0L;
    HMENU hMenu, hMenuPopup;
    int nTopLevelMenuNum;

    switch (uMsg) {

    case WM_ACTIVATEAPP:
        // Program Manager is either being activated or deactivated.

        if (wParam == 0) break;        // PROGMAN being deactivated.
        if (!IsIconic(hWnd)) break;    // PROGMAN isn't an icon.

        // Program Manager is being made active and is an icon.
        // Check to see if any other applications are running.
        fpProc = MakeProcInstance((FARPROC) AnyAppsRunning,
            _hInstance);
        fAnyWindowsUp = (EnumWindows(fpProc, 0l) == 0);
        FreeProcInstance(fpProc);

        // If the enumeration was stopped prematurely, there must
        // be at least one other application running.
        if (fAnyWindowsUp) break;

        // No other apps running, restore PROGMAN to "open" state.
        ShowWindow(hWnd, SW_RESTORE);
        break;

    case WM_COMMAND:
        switch (wParam) {
```

```
case IDM_PMRESTOREABOUT:
    // Our added menu option to display
    // "About PM Restore..." was chosen.
    fpProc = MakeProcInstance((FARPROC) AboutProc,
        _hInstance);
    DialogBox(_hInstance, "About", hWnd, fpProc);
    FreeProcInstance(fpProc);

    // Don't pass this message to Original PROGMAN WndProc
    // because it wouldn't know what to do with it.
    fCallOrigProc = FALSE;
    break;

case IDM_PMRESTOREREMOVE:
    // Stop window subclassing by putting back the address
    // of the original window procedure.
    (void) SubclassWindow(hWnd, _fpOrigPMProc);
    // Get Menu handle to Program Manager's "Options" menu.
    hMenu = GetMenu(hWnd);
    RemoveMenu(hMenu, IDM_PMRESTOREABOUT, MF_BYCOMMAND);
    RemoveMenu(hMenu, IDM_PMRESTOREREMOVE, MF_BYCOMMAND);

        // Get number of top-level menu items.
    nTopLevelMenuNum = GetMenuItemCount(hMenu) - 1;
    while (nTopLevelMenuNum) {

        // Get handle to pop-up menu.
        hMenuPopup = GetSubMenu(hMenu, nTopLevelMenuNum);

            // Is first option in the pop-up IDM_AUTO_ARRANGE?
        if (IDM_AUTO_ARRANGE ==
            GetMenuItemID(hMenuPopup, 0)) {

            // Remove separator bar.
            RemoveMenu(hMenuPopup,
                GetMenuItemCount(hMenuPopup) - 1,
                MF_BYPOSITION);

            break;   // Stop check menus.
        }
        nTopLevelMenuNum--;  // Try next menu.
    }

    DrawMenuBar(hWnd);       // Update the new menu bar.

    // Post WM_QUIT to our task to remove it from memory.
    PostAppMessage(_hTaskPMRestore, WM_QUIT, 0, 0);
```

```
            break;

        default: // Pass other WM_COMMAND's to original procedure.
           break;
        }
        break;

    default: // Pass other messages to original procedure.
        break;

    }

    if (fCallOrigProc) {
        // Call original window procedure and return the result to
        // whoever sent this message to the Program Manager.
        lResult = CallWindowProc((FARPROC) _fpOrigPMProc, hWnd,
           uMsg, wParam, lParam);
    }

    return(lResult);
}

// Window's callback function to determine if any windows exist
// that should stop us from restoring the Program Manager.
#pragma argsused
BOOL CALLBACK _export AnyAppsRunning (HWND hWnd, LPARAM lParam) {

    // If window is the Window's desktop, continue enumeration.
    if (hWnd == GetDesktopWindow())
        return(1);

    // If the window is invisible (hidden), continue enumeration.
    if (!IsWindowVisible(hWnd))
        return(1);

    // If window was created by PROGMAN, continue enumeration.
    if (GetWindowTask(_hWndPM) == GetWindowTask(hWnd))
        return(1);
    // Any other type of window, stop enumeration.
    return(0);
}
```

Listing 2-2. PMREST.RC application resource file

```
/********************************************************************
Module name: PMREST.RC
Programmer : Jeffrey M. Richter.
********************************************************************/

#include <windows.h>

PM_Rest  ICON  MOVEABLE DISCARDABLE PMRest.Ico

ABOUT DIALOG 16, 20, 126, 59
CAPTION "About Program Manager Restore"
STYLE WS_BORDER | WS_CAPTION | WS_DLGFRAME | WS_SYSMENU |
      WS_VISIBLE | WS_POPUP
BEGIN
   CONTROL "PM_Rest", -1, "static",
      SS_ICON | WS_CHILD, 4, 16, 16, 16
   CONTROL "Program Manager Restore", -1, "static",
      SS_CENTER | WS_CHILD, 22, 8, 100, 12
   CONTROL "Written by:", -1, "static",
      SS_CENTER | WS_CHILD, 22, 20, 100, 12
   CONTROL "Jeffrey M. Richter", -1, "static",
      SS_CENTER | WS_CHILD, 22, 32, 100, 12
   CONTROL "&OK", IDOK, "button",
      BS_DEFPUSHBUTTON | WS_TABSTOP | WS_CHILD, 40, 44, 44, 12
END
```

Listing 2-3. PMREST.DEF definitions file

```
; Module name: PMREST.DEF
; Programmer : Jeffrey M. Richter.

NAME        PMREST
DESCRIPTION 'Program Manager Restore Application'
STUB        'WinStub.exe'
EXETYPE     WINDOWS
CODE        MOVEABLE NONDISCARDABLE PRELOAD
DATA        MOVEABLE MULTIPLE PRELOAD
HEAPSIZE    1024
STACKSIZE   5120
```

Listing 2-4. MAKEFILE for PMRest application

```
#******************************************************************
#Module name: MAKEFILE
#Programmer : Jeffrey M. Richter
#******************************************************************

!include "..\builtins.jmr"

PROG = PMRest

MODEL = s
CFLAGS = -P-c -c -f- -W -p -v -w -m$(MODEL) -I$(INCLUDEDIR)
LFLAGS = /P/v/n/m/s/L$(LIBDIR)
LIBS = CW$(MODEL) Import

MODULES = $(PROG).obj

ICONS   = $(PROG).ico
BITMAPS =
CURSORS =

$(PROG).Exe: $(MODULES) $(PROG).Def $(PROG).Res
     tlink $(LFLAGS) @&&!
COW$(MODEL) $(MODULES)
$(PROG), $(PROG), $(LIBS), $(PROG)
!
   rc -30 -T $(PROG).Res
   TDStrip -s $(PROG)

$(PROG).res:   $(PROG).rc $(RESOURCES)
```

Figure 2-4. PMREST.ICO

92

How Window Superclassing Works

Window superclassing is similar to window subclassing. The idea is that messages intended for the window procedure of the original class are routed to a different procedure that you supply. At the bottom of this procedure, the message is passed to the original window procedure instead of *DefWindowProc*. This is done by calling the *CallWindowProc* function.

Superclassing alters the behavior of an existing window class. This window class is called the *base class*. The base is usually a system global class like BUTTON or COMBOBOX, but it may be any window class.

When you superclass a window class, you must register a new window class with Windows. The *lpfnWndProc* member of the *WNDCLASS* structure points to your superclass window procedure. When a message is dispatched to the superclassed window (Figure 2-5), Windows examines the memory block for the window and calls the superclass window procedure. After the superclass window procedure processes the message, it passes the message to the window procedure associated with the base class.

Many more steps are necessary to create a superclass than to subclass a window. The process of superclassing a window begins with a call to the *GetClassInfo* function passing it the name of the desired base class. This fills a *WNDCLASS* structure with most of the statistics regarding the base class.

This *WNDCLASS* structure serves as a starting point for the new window class. The next step is to give the new class a name. This is done by setting the *lpszClassName* member to the new name for the class. The value of the *hInstance* member should be set to the value of *hInstance* that was passed to *WinMain* when the application that is registering the superclass was invoked, since this new class is being registered by your application.

It is important to save the value of the original *lpfnWndProc* member (usually in a global variable). This value is the address of the base class window procedure. This variable will be used later in the superclass window procedure as the first parameter to the *CallWindowProc* function. The *lpfnWndProc* member of the *WNDCLASS* structure is then set to the address of the superclass window procedure. This procedure must be prototyped like any window procedure. That is, it must be a FAR function, and use the PASCAL calling convention.

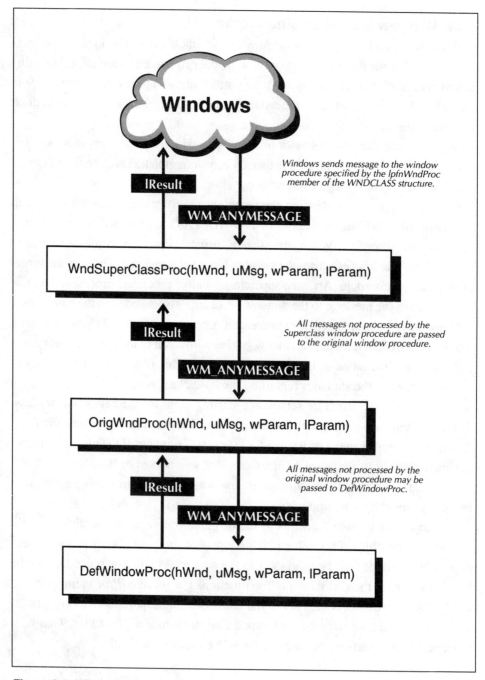

Figure 2-5. Window superclassing

Because a new window class is going to be registered, you can increase the values of the *cbClsExtra* and *cbWndExtra* members of the *WNDCLASS* structure. These additional bytes may be used by your superclass function. This is a big advantage of superclassing over subclassing. But be careful when using the class or window extra bytes for a superclassed window class. The base class window procedure was written with the assumption that the class extra bytes from zero to *cbClsExtra*-1 and the window extra bytes from zero to *cbWndExtra*-1 are for its own use. The superclass window procedure must not access the class and window extra bytes within these ranges unless it knows exactly how they are used by the base class.

If the superclass window procedure is going to add class and window extra bytes, it must save the original values of the *cbClsExtra* and *cbWndExtra* members of the *WNDCLASS* structure, usually in global variables, before changing the values of those members. When the superclass window procedure wants to access any of the window extra bytes, it must add the original value of *cbWndExtra* to the index so that it does not reference the window extra bytes used by the base class. Here is an example of how to prepare and access additional window bytes added to the superclass:

```
// Global variables to save the number of class extra bytes,
// window extra bytes, and the window procedure address of the
// LISTBOX base class.
int _cbClsExtraOrig;
int _cbWndExtraOrig;
WNDPROC _lpfnWndProcOrig;

// Index into window extra bytes where our LISTBOX data can be
// found.
// This data follows the data required by the base class.
#define GWW_LISTBOXDATA (_cbWndExtraOrig + 0)
    .
    .
    .
ATOM RegisterSuperClass (void) {
    WNDCLASS WndClass;
```

```
// Fill WNDCLASS structure with information about
// LISTBOX class.
GetClassInfo(NULL, "LISTBOX", &WndClass);

// Save the information we need later in global variables.
_cbClsExtraOrig = WndClass.cbClsExtra;
_cbWndExtraOrig = WndClass.cbWndExtra;
_lpfnWndProcOrig = WndClass.lpfnWndProc;
    .
    .
    .

// Add two window extra bytes to account for our LISTBOX data.
WndClass.cbWndExtra += 2;

// Register the new window class
return(RegisterClass(&WndClass));
}
    .
    .
    .


LRESULT CALLBACK LBSuperClsWndProc (HWND hWnd, UINT uMsg,
    WPARAM wParam, LPARAM lParam) {
  int wListBoxData;
    .
    .
    .

  // Retrieve our LISTBOX data from the added window extra bytes.
  wListBoxData = GetWindowWord(hWnd, GWW_LISTBOXDATA);
    .
    .
    .

  // Call base class window procedure for remainder of processing.
  return(CallWindowProc(_lpfnWndProcOrig, hWnd, uMsg,
    wParam, lParam));
}
```

Of course, it is possible to associate data with a superclassed window via window properties as explained in Chapter 1. However, it is always better to store information in window extra bytes because properties require more data space and take more time to access.

The *lpszMenuName* member of *WNDCLASS* may also be changed to give the new class a new menu. If a new menu is used, the IDs for the menu options should correspond to the IDs in the "standard" menu for the base class. This is not necessary if the superclass window procedure processes the *WM_COMMAND* message in its entirety and does not pass this message to the base class window procedure.

The remaining members of the *WNDCLASS* structure—*style*, *hIcon*, *hCursor*, and *hbrBackground*—may be changed in any way you desire. For example, if you want your new window class to use a different mouse cursor or a different icon, change the *hCursor* and *hIcon* members of the *WNDCLASS* structure accordingly.

Finally, call the *RegisterClass* function to notify Windows of the new class. This will let you create new windows of this class.

The main difference between subclassing and superclassing is that subclassing alters the behavior of an existing window, while superclassing alters the behavior of all windows instances created from an existing window class. It is better to use superclassing when you wish to change the operation of many windows. This is because it is easier to register a new class, give it a new name, and create windows of this new class than it is to create all the desired windows and use the *SetWindowLong* function or *SubclassWindow* macro to change the address of each of their window procedures.

The most common use for superclassing is for a dialog box containing several of the superclassed controls. When a dialog box is created, the dialog-box manager goes through the dialog-box template and creates windows based on each *CONTROL* line in the template. If the template contains several LISTBOX windows that require altered behavior, it is much easier to specify NEWLISTBOX in each *CONTROL* line of the template. With window subclassing, the dialog-box manager would have to create all the LISTBOX windows before you could subclass these windows, one at a time, during the processing of the *WM_INITDIALOG* message. This is an unduly tedious process.

Another advantage of superclassing is that the superclass window procedure gets to perform its own initialization for the window. This is because Windows knows about the superclass window procedure from the class memory block before a window is created. When the window is created, the superclass window procedure receives the *WM_NCCREATE* and *WM_CREATE* messages. During the processing of these messages, the superclass window procedure may initialize its class or window extra bytes or do any other processing it desires.

Both of these messages should be passed to the base class window procedure, whether the superclass window procedure processes them or not. Windows must perform initialization for each window in response to *WM_NCCREATE*. If this message wasn't passed to the original window procedure, *DefWindowProc* would never be called and the window would not be initialized properly. By passing the *WM_NCCREATE* message to the base class procedure, we ensure that *DefWindowProc* will eventually be called. Similarly, the *WM_CREATE* message should also be passed to the base class window procedure.

You can add your own user messages for a superclassed window class using *RegisterWindowMessage*. Here, the same rules apply to superclassed window classes as to subclassed windows.

The following table summarizes the differences between window subclassing and superclassing.

Subclassing	Superclassing
Recommended if few windows need to have altered behavior.	Recommended if many windows need to have the same type of altered behavior.
No new window class is registered.	A new window class must be registered.
Subclass function may not use any class or window extra bytes.	Superclass function may use additional class and window extra bytes.
Window must have been created before it can be subclassed.	Superclassing does not require that a window be created first.
Subclassed windows cannot intercept the window's initialization messages (*WM_NCCREATE* and *WM_CREATE*).	Superclassed windows can intercept the window's initialization messages (*WM_NCCREATE* and *WM_CREATE*).

An Example of Window Superclassing

The sample program that demonstrates window superclassing, NOALPHA.EXE, creates a window that contains nothing but a menu bar. The one option on this menu bar evokes a dialog box that contains several windows. Two of these windows are of the NoAlpha class, a superclass based on the system global EDIT class. The NoAlpha class behaves just like an EDIT window except that it does not accept lowercase or uppercase letters. In fact, when the user tries to type a letter into a NoAlpha window, the computer beeps, notifying the user that letters are not allowed.

A window created using the NoAlpha superclass can restrict input to a programmer-specified range of values. A new window message is registered that allows an application using a NoAlpha window to change the legal range of values. Another new message is registered that allows an application using a NoAlpha window to check to see if the value in the window is within the legal range.

The source code for this example is split between two source files: NOALPHA.C and SUPERCLS.C.

The Window Superclassing Package: SUPERCLS.C

SUPERCLS.C contains source code that could easily be incorporated into your own applications. The functions in this module help you register new window superclasses and aid in the manipulation of any class and window extra bytes that you may add when superclassing a window class.

Some of the information obtained from the base class must be used when processing superclassed windows, including the number of class and window extra bytes and the address of the base class window procedure. Instead of storing this information in global variables, the *RegisterSuperClass* function in SUPERCLS.C adds eight bytes to the class extra bytes and stores the information there. This is a much cleaner method for working with superclasses.

The prototype for the *RegisterSuperClass* function is:

```
ATOM WINAPI RegisterSuperClass (LPWNDCLASS WndClass,
WNDPROC lpfnSCWndProc,
        int cbClsAdditional, int cbWndAdditional);
```

To register a new superclass, your application should first prepare a *WNDCLASS* structure by calling *GetClassInfo*. It should then change any of the *WNDCLASS* members necessary with the exception of the *cbClsExtra*, *cbWndExtra*, and *lpfn-WndProc* members. These values will be altered by the *RegisterSuperClass* function. When *RegisterSuperClass* is called, the first parameter is the address of the *WNDLCASS* structure followed by the address of the superclass window procedure as well as the number of additional class and window extra bytes that you desire for the superclass.

After *RegisterSuperClass* is called, it saves the address of the superclass window procedure and the base class values of the *cbClsExtra*, *cbWndExtra*, and *lpfn-WndProc* members in a *SUPERCLSINIT* structure variable:

```
SuperClsInit.lpfnSuperClsWndProc = lpfnSCWndProc;
SuperClsInit.lpfnBCWndProc = WndClass->lpfnWndProc;
SuperClsInit.cbBCClsExtra    = WndClass->cbClsExtra;
SuperClsInit.cbBCWndExtra    = WndClass->cbWndExtra;
```

Then we increment the *cbClsExtra* member by the value in the *cbClsAdditional* parameter plus eight. The eight bytes at the end will hold the base class' *cbClsExtra*, *cbWndExtra*, and *lpfnWndProc* data. We then increment *cbWndExtra* by the value of the *cbWndAdditional* parameter. Finally, we set *lpfnWndProc* to the address of a special window procedure in this SUPERCLS.C module, *SuperClsInitWndProc*:

```
#define MINCBCLSADDITIONAL \
    (sizeof(WNDPROC) + sizeof(int) + sizeof(int))
    .
    .
    .
WndClass->cbClsExtra += cbClsAdditional + MINCBCLSADDITIONAL;
WndClass->cbWndExtra += cbWndAdditional;
WndClass->lpfnWndProc = SuperClsInitWndProc;
```

Now that the *WNDCLASS* structure has been prepared, we register the window class using *RegisterClass*. If the class is registered successfully, we must now set the last eight class extra bytes to the values that were saved in the *SUPERCLSINIT* structure variable. Unfortunately, Windows doesn't offer a way to alter a class' extra bytes without first having a handle to a window of the desired class. Following is the solution to this problem.

RegisterSuperClass saves the base class values of the *cbClsExtra*, *cbWndExtra*, and *lpfnWndProc* members of *WNDCLASS* as well as the new superclass window procedure in the *SUPERCLSINIT* structure variable. The *cbClsExtra*, *cbWndExtra*, and *lpfnWndProc* members are initialized as described above, and the new class is registered by calling *RegisterClass*.

Setting the last eight class extra bytes requires a window of the new class to be created first so that its handle can be passed to the *SetClassWord* and *SetClassLong* functions. So, *RegisterSuperClass* now creates a window of this class. The creation of the window causes the class extra bytes to be initialized, which we will look at in a moment. After the initialization, *RegisterSuperClass* immediately destroys the window that it created.

While the window is being created, Windows sends *WM_GETMINMAXINFO*, *WM_NCCREATE*, *WM_NCCALCSIZE*, and *WM_CREATE* messages (in that order) to the special window procedure, *SuperClsInitWndProc*, because its address was loaded into the *lpfnWndProc* member of the *WNDCLASS* structure when the window class was registered. When *RegisterSuperClass* calls the *CreateWindow* function, it passes the address of the *SuperClsInit* structure variable as the last parameter. When the *SuperClsInitWndProc* function receives a *WM_CREATE* message, the *lParam* parameter contains the address of a *CREATESTRUCT* structure whose *lpCreateParams* member contains the address of the *SuperClsInit* structure variable passed to *CreateWindow*. This address is saved temporarily in the class extra bytes so that it can be retrieved and used when *SuperClsInitWndProc* receives a *WM_NCDESTROY* message.

When the *WM_NCDESTROY* message is received, the following code is executed:

```
cbClsTotal = GetClassWord(hWnd, GCW_CBCLSEXTRA);

// Retrieve the address of the LPSUPERCLSINIT struct.
lpSuperClsInit = (LPSUPERCLSINIT)
   GetClassLong(hWnd, cbClsTotal - BCWNDPROCINDEX);
```

```
SetClassLong(hWnd, cbClsTotal - BCWNDPROCINDEX,
    (LONG) lpSuperClsInit->lpfnBCWndProc);

SetClassWord(hWnd, cbClsTotal - CBBCCLSEXTRAINDEX,
    lpSuperClsInit->cbBCClsExtra);

SetClassWord(hWnd, cbClsTotal - CBBCWNDEXTRAINDEX,
    lpSuperClsInit->cbBCWndExtra);

SetClassLong(hWnd, GCL_WNDPROC,
    (LONG) lpSuperClsInit->lpfnSuperClsWndProc);
```

This code first retrieves the number of class extra bytes set aside for the class. It then saves the original window procedure as well as the original number of class and window extra bytes in the last eight bytes of the class extra bytes. Finally, the address of the class' window procedure needs to be changed to the address of the superclass procedure that the user originally passed as the *lpfnSCWndProc* parameter to the *RegisterSuperClass* function.

You may be wondering why we change this address during the *WM_NCDESTROY* message rather than during the *WM_DESTROY*, *WM_CREATE*, or *WM_NCCREATE* message. The reason is that after the address is changed any future messages destined for this window will be sent to the new superclass window procedure. This could have disastrous effects. The *WM_NCDESTROY* message is the last message ever received by a window.

Let's assume that the new superclass window procedure is written so that it allocates memory during the processing of its *WM_CREATE* message and frees that memory when it receives a *WM_DESTROY* message. If we change the window procedure address when the *SuperClsInitWndProc* function receives the *WM_CREATE* message, the *WM_DESTROY* message would be sent to the new superclass window procedure. This procedure would then try to free memory that never was allocated, causing all kinds of potential problems.

The following table shows the contents of the class extra bytes after *Register-SuperClass* has been called. The Example column shows the index into the class extra bytes if the base class required two extra class bytes and the superclass required four additional class bytes.

Offset	Example	Contents
The *GCW_* and *GCL_* defines in WINDOWS.H (all have negative offset)	*GCW_STYLE* (-32) to -1	All the class information contained in the *WNDCLASS* structure.
0 to *cbClsExtra* - 1 (retrieved from the *GetClassInfo* call)	0 to 1	All the class extra bytes needed by the base class.
cbClsExtra to (*cbClsExtra* + *cbClsAdditional* - 1)	2 to 5	All the class extra bytes needed by the superclass.
(*cbClsExtra* + *cbClsAdditional*) to (*cbClsExtra* + *cbClsAdditional* + 1)	6 to 7	The number of window extra bytes needed by base class. Used by functions in SUPERCLS.C.
(*cbClsExtra* + *cbClsAdditional* + 2) to (*cbClsExtra* + *cbClsAdditional* + 3)	8 to 9	The number of class extra bytes needed by base class. Used by functions in SUPERCLS.C.
(*cbClsExtra* + *cbClsAdditional* + 4) to (*cbClsExtra* + *cbClsAdditional* + 7)	10 to 13	The address of the base window procedure. Used by *GetBCWndProc* function in SUPERCLS.C.

Now that everything has been initialized properly, the new superclass window procedure will receive all messages for any future windows created by this class. When that window procedure needs to pass a message onto the base class window procedure, it simply makes the following call.

```
lResult =
    CallWindowProc(GetBCWndProc(hWnd), hWnd, uMsg, wParam, lParam);
```

The call to *GetBCWndProc* (in SUPERCLS.C) causes the base class' window procedure to be retrieved from the superclass' class extra bytes and returned.

The *CalcClassByteIndex* function is only used by other functions in this module. It's declared as

```
static int NEAR CalcClassByteIndex (HWND hWnd, int nIndex);
```

This function accepts a window handle to a superclassed window and an index into the class extra bytes. This index is zero-based and allows us to ignore any class extra bytes needed by the base class. If the specified index is negative, it refers to information that is part of the *WNDCLASS* structure. If the number is greater than or equal to zero, it refers to class bytes that are needed by the superclass window procedure. The index into the class extra bytes for the superclassed extra bytes is calculated by retrieving the number of class extra bytes required by the base class and adding it to the *nIndex* parameter. The new value of *nIndex* is the index that should be used with the *Get/SetClassWord/Long* functions for class extra bytes associated with the superclassed window.

CalcWindowByteIndex is identical to *CalcClassByteIndex* except that it calculates the index into the window extra bytes. The new value of *nIndex* is the index that should be used with the *Get/SetWindowWord/Long* functions for window extra bytes associated with the superclassed window.

The remaining functions (*SetSCClassWord*, *GetSCClassWord*, *SetSCClassLong*, *GetSCClassLong*, *SetSCWindowWord*, *GetSCWindowWord*, *SetSCWindowLong*, and *GetSCWindowLong*) are used by the application whenever any class or window extra bytes must be referenced. These functions prevent the calling application from altering the class and window extra bytes of the base class window procedure.

The Application Program: NOALPHA.C

Initializing the Application

NoAlpha's initialization code registers its application window class (NoAlphaApp) and the superclass window class (NoAlpha). The *RegisterNoAlphaWndClass* function simply fills a *WNDCLASS* structure by calling the *GetClassInfo* function, using EDIT as the base class. The *lpszClassName* and *hInstance* members of the *WND-CLASS* structure are modified to point to NoAlpha and the value of the *hInstance* parameter, respectively. The NoAlpha class does not change any of the other members of the *WNDCLASS* structure. However, when you create other superclasses you may change these values.

Because *RegisterNoAlphaWndClass* uses functions from SUPERCLS.C, the *cbClsExtra*, *cbWndExtra*, and *lpfnWndProc* members are not changed here. The desired values are passed to *RegisterSuperClass*, which fixes the *WNDCLASS* structure and calls *RegisterClass* on behalf of the application.

When the call to *RegisterSuperClass* returns, the *WNDCLASS* structure contains all the appropriate values for the superclassed window class. The return value from *RegisterSuperClass* is returned to the caller of the *RegisterNo-AlphaWndClass* function.

The new superclass (NoAlpha) requires no additional class extra bytes. However, it does use four additional window extra bytes. These two words contain the low and high values representing the valid range for numbers in the NoAlpha window. We want to let applications send messages to the NoAlpha window to set the valid range and to return a Boolean, indicating whether the value in the window is within the valid range. Because NoAlpha is a superclass, it would not be prudent to create messages based on the *WM_USER* method. The only way we can guarantee that message values do not conflict with any other message values is by using *RegisterWindowMessage*.

After the NoAlpha superclass is registered, the NoAlpha class-specific messages "ValidRange" and "SetRange" are defined and their values saved in global variables:

```
_ValidRangeMsg = RegisterWindowMessage("ValidRange");
_SetRangeMsg = RegisterWindowMessage("SetRange");
```

If another instance of this application is running, neither the application window class nor the NoAlpha superclass should be registered. However, this new instance of the application needs to be aware of the values for the "ValidRange" and "SetRange" messages. These values are simply determined by passing the *RegisterWindowMessage* function the same message string used for the first instance of the application. Windows remembers the value that was returned when the message was first registered and returns the same value. (Once a window message has been registered, Windows remembers its value for the entire session, even if all instances of the application terminate.)

The Superclass Window Procedure

NoAlphaWndProc is the superclass window procedure. All messages destined for a window of the NoAlpha class are directed to this function. The first thing this function does is determine if the message is one of the two NoAlpha class-specific messages ("SetRange" or "ValidRange"). Because the values of these messages must be obtained from variables, *case* statements cannot be used. Checking for these messages must be done with *if* statements. If the message is "SetRange," the lowest value in the range is in the low word of the *lParam* parameter and the highest value is in the high word.

The *SetSCWindowWord* function in SUPERCLS.C changes the window extra bytes to reflect the new valid range:

```
#define NOALPHA_CBWNDEXTRA    (4)
#define GSCWW_LOVALUE         (0)
#define GSCWW_HIVALUE         (2)

.

.

.

SetSCWindowWord(hWnd, GSCWW_LOVALUE, LOWORD(lParam));
SetSCWindowWord(hWnd, GSCWW_HIVALUE, HIWORD(lParam));
```

Because this message is our own, it should not be passed to the base window procedure. If this message were passed to the base window procedure, that procedure should ignore the message anyway.

If the message is "ValidRange," the text of the NoAlpha window is copied to a buffer and converted to an integer:

```
GetWindowText(hWnd, szValue, sizeof(szValue));
nValue = atoi(szValue);
```

The low and high values are retrieved from the window extra bytes

```
nLoValue = GetSCWindowWord(hWnd, GSCWW_LOVALUE);
nHiValue = GetSCWindowWord(hWnd, GSCWW_HIVALUE);
```

and the result of the message processing is the result of *nLoValue <= nValue <= nHiValue*:

```
lResult = (nLoValue <= nValue) && (nValue <= nHiValue);
```

The remaining messages can be processed using the familiar *switch-case* construct.

The *WM_CREATE* message initializes the two window extra words so that the default low range of legal values is -32,767 and the default high range is +32,767. If this were not done, the default range would be from zero to zero.

The *WM_CHAR* message checks the value of the *wParam* parameter to determine if a letter was pressed. If a letter were pressed, the base window procedure should not be called. This prohibits the message from ever being seen by the EDIT class' window procedure and guarantees that no letters will ever appear in a NoAlpha window. The *MessageBeep* function notifies the user that an illegal key has been pressed.

Any other messages destined for the NoAlpha window are passed directly to the base class window procedure for default or standard EDIT window processing:

```
CallWindowProc(GetBCWndProc(hWnd), hWnd, uMsg,
    wParam, lParam);
```

The call to the *GetBCWndProc* function (found in the SUPERCLS.C module) looks into the class extra bytes and retrieves the address of the base class window procedure.

The Dialog-Box Function

DlgProc processes all messages for the dialog box shown in Figure 2-6. During the *WM_INITDIALOG* message, the valid range for the two NoAlpha windows is set:

```
SendDlgItemMessage(hDlg, ID_NOALPHA1, _SetRangeMsg,
    0, MAKELONG(100, 200));
SendDlgItemMessage(hDlg, ID_NOALPHA2, _SetRangeMsg,
    0, MAKELONG(-300, 100));
```

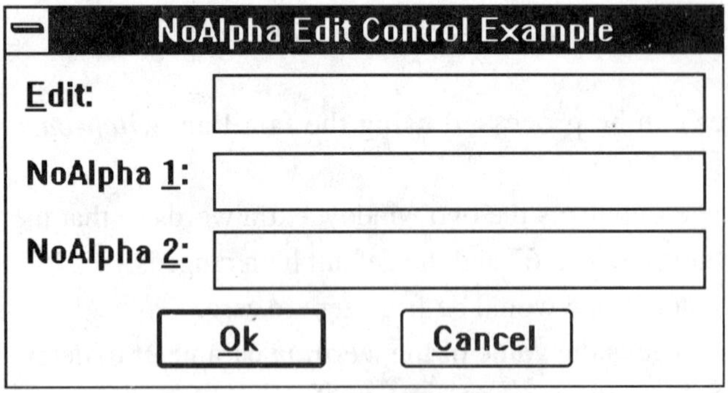

Figure 2-6. Dialog box containing EDIT control and two NoAlpha controls

When a *BN_CLICKED* message is received from the "OK" button, a message is sent to the first NoAlpha window to assess whether the entered value is within the legal range:

```
fOk = SendDlgItemMessage(hWnd, ID_NOALPHA1, _ValidRangeMsg, 0, 0);
```

If the value is not in the legal range, the *MessageBox* function displays a notice to that effect. The *SetFocus* function changes the input focus to the first NoAlpha window so that the user can correct the value.

If the window contains a valid value, the second NoAlpha window is checked in the same fashion. Only when the user has entered legal values in both NoAlpha windows is the *EndDialog* function called, closing the dialog box.

The NoAlpha edit control demo application, shown in Listings 2-8 through 2-16, demonstrates window superclassing.

Figure 2-7. NOALPHA.ICO

Listing 2-5. NOALPHA.C application source module

```
/******************************************************************
Module name: NOALPHA.C
Programmer : Jeffrey M. Richter.
******************************************************************/

#include <windows.h>
#include <stdlib.h>

#include "supercls.h"
#include "noalpha.h"
extern const HINSTANCE _cdecl _hInstance;

char _szAppName[] = "NoAlphaApp";

//*****************************************************************
// Registered msg integers to be prcessed by superclass procedure.
WORD _SetRangeMsg = WM_NULL, _ValidRangeMsg = WM_NULL;
```

```
   // Forward reference to various functions.
ATOM NEAR RegisterAppWndClass (HINSTANCE hInstance);
ATOM NEAR RegisterNoAlphaWndClass (HINSTANCE hInstance);
BOOL CALLBACK DlgProc (HWND, UINT, WPARAM, LPARAM);
LRESULT CALLBACK NoAlphaAppWndProc (HWND, UINT, WPARAM, LPARAM);

// ****************************************************************
#pragma argsused
int WinMain (HINSTANCE hInstance, HINSTANCE hPrevInstance,
   LPSTR lpszCmdLine, int cmdShow) {
   MSG msg;
   HWND hWnd;

   if (hPrevInstance == NULL) {  // First instance running.

      // Register NoAlpha's main window's class.
      if (RegisterAppWndClass(hInstance) == NULL)
         return(0);

      // Register the NoAlpha class.  This is a superclass based
      // on the standard Window's "EDIT" control.
      if (RegisterNoAlphaWndClass(hInstance) == NULL)
         return(0);
   }

   // Register two new window messages called, "ValidRange" &
   // "SetRange".  If these messages have been registered before,
   // Windows returns the same values that were returned the
   // first time these messages were registered.
   _ValidRangeMsg = RegisterWindowMessage("ValidRange");
   _SetRangeMsg   = RegisterWindowMessage("SetRange");

   // Create NoAlpha's application window.
   hWnd = CreateWindow(_szAppName, _szAppName,
      WS_OVERLAPPEDWINDOW, CW_USEDEFAULT, SW_SHOW, CW_USEDEFAULT,
      CW_USEDEFAULT, NULL, NULL, hInstance, 0);

   if (hWnd == NULL) return(0);
   ShowWindow(hWnd, cmdShow);
   UpdateWindow(hWnd);

   while (GetMessage(&msg, NULL, 0, 0)) {
      TranslateMessage(&msg);
      DispatchMessage(&msg);
   }
   return(0);
```

```
}

// ****************************************************************
// This function registers NoAlpha's application window.
ATOM NEAR RegisterAppWndClass (HINSTANCE hInstance) {
   WNDCLASS WndClass;

   WndClass.style        = 0;
   WndClass.lpfnWndProc  = NoAlphaAppWndProc;
   WndClass.cbClsExtra   = 0;
   WndClass.cbWndExtra   = 0;
   WndClass.hInstance    = hInstance;
   WndClass.hIcon        = LoadIcon(hInstance, _szAppName);
   WndClass.hCursor      = LoadCursor(NULL, IDC_ARROW);
   WndClass.hbrBackground = COLOR_WINDOW + 1;
   WndClass.lpszMenuName = _szAppName;
   WndClass.lpszClassName = _szAppName;
   return(RegisterClass(&WndClass));
}

// ****************************************************************
// This function processes messages sent to application window.

LRESULT CALLBACK NoAlphaAppWndProc (HWND hWnd, UINT uMsg,
   WPARAM wParam, LPARAM lParam) {
   BOOL fCallDefProc = FALSE;
   LRESULT lResult = 0;

   switch (uMsg) {
      case WM_DESTROY:
         PostQuitMessage(0);
         break;

      case WM_COMMAND:
         switch (wParam) {
         case IDM_DIALOGBOX:
            DialogBox(_hInstance, "DlgBox", hWnd,
               (DLGPROC) DlgProc);
            break;

         default:
            break;
         }
         break;

      default:
         fCallDefProc = TRUE; break;
```

```
        }

    if (fCallDefProc)
        lResult = DefWindowProc(hWnd, uMsg, wParam, lParam);

    return(lResult);
}

// *****************************************************************
// This function processes messages sent to NoAlpha's dialog box.

BOOL CALLBACK DlgProc (HWND hDlg, UINT uMsg, WPARAM wParam,
    LPARAM lParam) {
    BOOL fProcessed = TRUE, fInRange;

    switch (uMsg) {
        case WM_INITDIALOG:
            // Set valid range in both NoAlpha controls.
            SendDlgItemMessage(hDlg, ID_NOALPHA1, _SetRangeMsg, 0,
                MAKELONG(100, 200));

            SendDlgItemMessage(hDlg, ID_NOALPHA2, _SetRangeMsg, 0,
                MAKELONG(-300, 100));
            break;

        case WM_COMMAND:
            switch (wParam) {
                case IDOK:
                    if (HIWORD(lParam) != BN_CLICKED) break;

                    // Send message to first NoAlpha control to see if
                    // its value is in range.
                    fInRange = (BOOL) SendDlgItemMessage(hDlg,
                        ID_NOALPHA1, _ValidRangeMsg, 0, 0l);
                    if (!fInRange) {
                        // Display error message to user.
                        MessageBox(hDlg, "Value is out of range.",
                            _szAppName, MB_OK);

                        // Set focus to "NoAlpha" control so user can
                        // change its value.
                        SetFocus(GetDlgItem(hDlg, ID_NOALPHA1));
                        break;
                    }

                    // Send message to second NoAlpha control to see
                    // if its value is in range.
```

```
                    fInRange = (BOOL) SendDlgItemMessage(hDlg,
                       ID_NOALPHA2, _ValidRangeMsg, 0, 0l);

                    if (!fInRange) {
                       // Display error message to user.
                       MessageBox(hDlg, "Value is out of range.",
                          _szAppName, MB_OK);

                       // Set focus to "NoAlpha" control so user can
                       // change its value.
                       SetFocus(GetDlgItem(hDlg, ID_NOALPHA2));
                       break;
                    }

                    EndDialog(hDlg, wParam);
                    break;

                 case IDCANCEL:
                    EndDialog(hDlg, wParam);
                    break;
              }
          default:
              fProcessed = FALSE; break;
       }
       return(fProcessed);
}

//*****************************************************************
// Window words for the NoAlpha Super Class.
#define NOALPHA_CBCLSEXTRA      (0)

#define NOALPHA_CBWNDEXTRA      (4)
#define GSCWW_LOVALUE           (0)
#define GSCWW_HIVALUE           (2)

LRESULT CALLBACK NoAlphaWndProc (HWND hWnd, UINT uMsg,
   WPARAM wParam, LPARAM lParam);

// *****************************************************************
// This function registers the NoAlpha class.  This is a
// superclassed class based on the standard "EDIT" control.
ATOM NEAR RegisterNoAlphaWndClass (HINSTANCE hInstance) {
   WNDCLASS WndClass;

   // Retrieve class information for "EDIT" system global class.
   GetClassInfo(NULL, "EDIT", &WndClass);
```

```
        // Our new class should have a new name.
        WndClass.lpszClassName = "NoAlpha";
        WndClass.hInstance     = hInstance;

        // The following WNDCLASS members are not changed for NoAlpha:
        //      style, hIcon, hCursor, hbrBackground, lpszMenuName.

        // Register the new window class.
        return(RegisterSuperClass(
            &WndClass,             // Address of WNDCLASS structure.
            NoAlphaWndProc,        // Addr of superclass window procedure.
            NOALPHA_CBCLSEXTRA,    // # of additional class extra bytes.
            NOALPHA_CBWNDEXTRA     // # of additional window extra bytes.
            ));
}


// **************************************************************
// This function processes all messages sent to "NoAlpha" windows.

LRESULT CALLBACK NoAlphaWndProc (HWND hWnd, UINT uMsg,
    WPARAM wParam, LPARAM lParam) {
    LRESULT lResult = 0L;
    BOOL fCallBaseClassWndProc = TRUE;
    char szValue[10];
    int nValue, nLoValue, nHiValue;

    // Check if message is the registered message: "SetRange".
    if (uMsg == _SetRangeMsg) {

        // Change window extra bytes to reflect new valid range.
        SetSCWindowWord(hWnd, GSCWW_LOVALUE, LOWORD(lParam));
        SetSCWindowWord(hWnd, GSCWW_HIVALUE, HIWORD(lParam));

        // Message should not be passed to base class procedure.
        fCallBaseClassWndProc = FALSE;
    }

    // Check if message is the registered message: "ValidRange".
    if (uMsg == _ValidRangeMsg) {

        // Get value in NoAlpha window.
        GetWindowText(hWnd, szValue, sizeof(szValue));
        // Convert number to integer.
        nValue = atoi(szValue);
        // Retrieve valid range from window extra bytes.
        nLoValue = GetSCWindowWord(hWnd, GSCWW_LOVALUE);
        nHiValue = GetSCWindowWord(hWnd, GSCWW_HIVALUE);
```

```
    // Determine if user's values is within legal range.
    lResult = (nLoValue <= nValue) && (nValue <= nHiValue);

    // Message should not be passed to base class procedure.
    fCallBaseClassWndProc = FALSE;
}

switch (uMsg) {
    case WM_CREATE:
        // By default, set valid range to -32767 to + 32767
        SetSCWindowWord(hWnd, GSCWW_LOVALUE, -32767);
        SetSCWindowWord(hWnd, GSCWW_HIVALUE, +32767);
        break;

    case WM_CHAR:
        // Prohibit message from being sent to base class
        // procedure if wParam is a letter.
        if (wParam >= 'A' && wParam <= 'Z')
            fCallBaseClassWndProc = FALSE;

        if (wParam >= 'a' && wParam <= 'z')
            fCallBaseClassWndProc = FALSE;

        // If message is a letter, notify user that key is
        // illegal for a NoAlpha window by beeping.
        if (fCallBaseClassWndProc == FALSE) MessageBeep(0);
        break;
    default: // Pass other messages to base class procedure.
        break;

}

if (fCallBaseClassWndProc) {
    // Call the base class window procedure and return its
    // result to the caller.
    lResult =
        CallWindowProc((FARPROC) GetBCWndProc(hWnd), hWnd,
            uMsg, wParam, lParam);
}

return(lResult);
}
```

Listing 2-6. NOALPHA.H application header module

```
/********************************************************************
Module name: NOALPHA.H
Programmer : Jeffrey M. Richter.
********************************************************************/


#define IDM_DIALOGBOX    (100)

#define ID_EDIT          (100)
#define ID_NOALPHA1      (101)
#define ID_NOALPHA2      (102)
```

Listing 2-7. NOALPHA.RC application resource file

```
/********************************************************************
Module name: NOALPHA.RC
Programmer : Jeffrey M. Richter.
********************************************************************/


#include <windows.h>
#include "noalpha.h"


NoAlphaApp  ICON  MOVEABLE DISCARDABLE NoAlpha.Ico


NoAlphaApp MENU
BEGIN
    MENUITEM "See &NoAlpha class...", IDM_DIALOGBOX
END


DLGBOX DIALOG LOADONCALL MOVEABLE DISCARDABLE 8, 26, 152, 68
CAPTION "NoAlpha Edit Control Example"
STYLE WS_BORDER | WS_CAPTION | WS_DLGFRAME | WS_SYSMENU |
     WS_VISIBLE | WS_POPUP
BEGIN
    CONTROL "&Edit:", -1, "static",
        SS_LEFT | WS_CHILD, 4, 4, 32, 12
    CONTROL "", ID_EDIT, "edit",
        ES_LEFT | WS_BORDER | WS_TABSTOP | WS_CHILD, 44, 4, 104, 12
    CONTROL "NoAlpha &1:", -1, "static",
        SS_LEFT | WS_CHILD, 4, 20, 40, 12
    CONTROL "", ID_NOALPHA1, "noalpha",
        0 | WS_BORDER | WS_TABSTOP | WS_CHILD, 44, 20, 104, 12
    CONTROL "NoAlpha &2:", -1, "static",
```

```
            SS_LEFT | WS_CHILD, 4, 36, 40, 12
        CONTROL "", ID_NOALPHA2, "noalpha",
            0 | WS_BORDER | WS_TABSTOP | WS_CHILD, 44, 36, 104, 12
        CONTROL "&Ok", IDOK, "button",
            BS_DEFPUSHBUTTON | WS_TABSTOP | WS_CHILD, 32, 52, 36, 12
        CONTROL "&Cancel", IDCANCEL, "button",
            BS_PUSHBUTTON | WS_TABSTOP | WS_CHILD, 84, 52, 36, 12
END
```

Listing 2-8. NOALPHA.DEF definitions file

```
; Module name: NOALPHA.DEF
; Programmer : Jeffrey M. Richter.

NAME          NOALPHA
DESCRIPTION   'NoAlpha: EDIT Superclass Application'
STUB          'WinStub.exe'
EXETYPE       WINDOWS
CODE          MOVEABLE DISCARDABLE PRELOAD
DATA          MOVEABLE MULTIPLE PRELOAD
HEAPSIZE      1024
STACKSIZE     5120
```

Listing 2-9. MAKEFILE for NoAlpha application

```
#*******************************************************************
#Module name: MAKEFILE
#Programmer : Jeffrey M. Richter
#*******************************************************************

!include "..\builtins.jmr"

PROG = NoAlpha
MODEL = s
CFLAGS = -P-c -c -f- -WS -p -v -w -m$(MODEL) -I$(INCLUDEDIR)
LFLAGS = /P/v/n/m/s/L$(LIBDIR)
LIBS = CW$(MODEL) Import

MODULES = $(PROG).obj SuperCls.obj

ICONS   = $(PROG).ico
BITMAPS =
CURSORS =
```

```
$(PROG).Exe: $(MODULES) $(PROG).Def $(PROG).Res
     tlink $(LFLAGS) @&&!$(PROG).lnk
COW$(MODEL) $(MODULES)
$(PROG), $(PROG), $(LIBS), $(PROG)
!
   rc -30 -T $(PROG).Res
   TDStrip -s $(PROG)

$(PROG).res:   $(PROG).rc $(PROG).h $(RESOURCES)
```

Listing 2-10. SUPERCLS.C window superclassing source module

```c
/********************************************************************
Module name: SUPERCLS.C
Programmer : Jeffrey M. Richter.
********************************************************************/

#include <windows.h>
#include "supercls.h"

// Offsets of base class values from the high-end of superclass
// class extra bytes.
#define BCWNDPROCINDEX      (sizeof(WNDPROC))
#define CBBCCLSEXTRAINDEX   (sizeof(WNDPROC) + sizeof(int))
#define CBBCWNDEXTRAINDEX   \
   (sizeof(WNDPROC) + sizeof(int) + sizeof(int))

#define MINCBCLSADDTIONAL   \
       (sizeof(WNDPROC) + sizeof(int) + sizeof(int))

typedef struct {
   WNDPROC lpfnSuperClsWndProc;
   WNDPROC lpfnBCWndProc;
   int cbBCClsExtra;
   int cbBCWndExtra;
} SUPERCLSINIT, FAR *LPSUPERCLSINIT;


LRESULT CALLBACK SuperClsInitWndProc (HWND hWnd, UINT uMsg,
   WPARAM wParam, LPARAM lParam) {
   LPSUPERCLSINIT lpSuperClsInit;
   WORD cbClsTotal;

   switch (uMsg) {
      case WM_CREATE:
```

```
            // Save the address of the LPSUPERCLSINIT struct passed
            // in the class extra bytes temporarily so that it can
            // be retrieved during the WM_NCDESTROY processing.
            cbClsTotal = GetClassWord(hWnd, GCW_CBCLSEXTRA);

            SetClassLong(hWnd, cbClsTotal - BCWNDPROCINDEX,
                (LONG) (((LPCREATESTRUCT) lParam)->lpCreateParams));
            break;

        case WM_NCDESTROY:
            cbClsTotal = GetClassWord(hWnd, GCW_CBCLSEXTRA);
            // Retrieve the address of the LPSUPERCLSINIT struct.
            lpSuperClsInit = (LPSUPERCLSINIT)
                GetClassLong(hWnd, cbClsTotal - BCWNDPROCINDEX);

            SetClassLong(hWnd, cbClsTotal - BCWNDPROCINDEX,
                (LONG) lpSuperClsInit->lpfnBCWndProc);

            SetClassWord(hWnd, cbClsTotal - CBBCCLSEXTRAINDEX,
                lpSuperClsInit->cbBCClsExtra);

            SetClassWord(hWnd, cbClsTotal - CBBCWNDEXTRAINDEX,
                lpSuperClsInit->cbBCWndExtra);

            SetClassLong(hWnd, GCL_WNDPROC,
                (LONG) lpSuperClsInit->lpfnSuperClsWndProc);

        break;
    }
    return(DefWindowProc(hWnd, uMsg, wParam, lParam));
}

ATOM WINAPI RegisterSuperClass (LPWNDCLASS WndClass,
    WNDPROC lpfnSCWndProc, int cbClsAdditional,
    int cbWndAdditional) {
    HWND hWnd;
    SUPERCLSINIT SuperClsInit;

    SuperClsInit.lpfnSuperClsWndProc = lpfnSCWndProc;
    SuperClsInit.lpfnBCWndProc = WndClass->lpfnWndProc;
    SuperClsInit.cbBCClsExtra  = WndClass->cbClsExtra;
    SuperClsInit.cbBCWndExtra  = WndClass->cbWndExtra;

    WndClass->cbClsExtra += cbClsAdditional + MINCBCLSADDTIONAL;
    WndClass->cbWndExtra += cbWndAdditional;
    WndClass->lpfnWndProc = SuperClsInitWndProc;
```

```
    if (RegisterClass(WndClass) == NULL) return(NULL);
    hWnd = CreateWindow(WndClass->lpszClassName, "", 0, 0, 0, 0, 0,
        NULL, NULL, WndClass->hInstance, (LPSTR) &SuperClsInit);

    if (hWnd == NULL) {
        UnregisterClass(WndClass->lpszClassName,
            WndClass->hInstance);
        return(FALSE);
    }

    DestroyWindow(hWnd);
    return(TRUE);
}

WNDPROC WINAPI GetBCWndProc (HWND hWnd) {
    return((WNDPROC) GetClassLong(hWnd,
        GetClassWord(hWnd, GCW_CBCLSEXTRA) - BCWNDPROCINDEX));
}

//*****************************************************************
// Function used internally by Get/SetClassWord/Long functions.
static int NEAR CalcClassByteIndex (HWND hWnd, int nIndex) {
    int cbBCClsExtraIndex, cbBCClsExtra;

    // If nIndex is negative, nIndex points to internal window
    // memory block, same index should be returned.
    if (nIndex < 0) return(nIndex);

    // Retrieve index into class extra bytes for the number of
    // class extra bytes used by the base class.
    cbBCClsExtraIndex =
        GetClassWord(hWnd, GCW_CBCLSEXTRA) - CBBCCLSEXTRAINDEX;

    // Retrieve number of class extra bytes used by the base class.
    cbBCClsExtra = GetClassWord(hWnd, cbBCClsExtraIndex);

    // Return desired (index + number) of class extra bytes
    // used by base class.
    return(nIndex + cbBCClsExtra);
}

// Function used internally by Get/SetWindowWord/Long functions.
static int NEAR CalcWindowByteIndex (HWND hWnd, int nIndex) {
    int cbBCWndExtraIndex, cbBCWndExtra;

    // If nIndex is negative, nIndex points to internal window
    // memory block, same index should be returned.
```

```
    if (nIndex < 0) return(nIndex);

    // Retrieve index into class extra bytes for the number of
    // window extra bytes used by the base class.
    cbBCWndExtraIndex =
        GetClassWord(hWnd, GCW_CBCLSEXTRA) - CBBCWNDEXTRAINDEX;

    // Retrieve number of window extra bytes used by base class.
    cbBCWndExtra = GetClassWord(hWnd, cbBCWndExtraIndex);

    // Return desired (index + number) of window extra bytes
    // used by base class.
    return(nIndex + cbBCWndExtra);
}

//*******************************************************************
// The four Get/SetClassWord/Long functions.

WORD WINAPI SetSCClassWord (HWND hWnd, int nIndex,
    WORD wNewWord) {
    nIndex = CalcClassByteIndex(hWnd, nIndex);
    return(SetClassWord(hWnd, nIndex, wNewWord));
}

WORD WINAPI GetSCClassWord (HWND hWnd, int nIndex) {
    nIndex = CalcClassByteIndex(hWnd, nIndex);
    return(GetClassWord(hWnd, nIndex));
}

DWORD WINAPI SetSCClassLong (HWND hWnd, int nIndex,
    DWORD dwNewLong) {
    nIndex = CalcClassByteIndex(hWnd, nIndex);
    return(SetClassLong(hWnd, nIndex, dwNewLong));
}

DWORD WINAPI GetSCClassLong (HWND hWnd, int nIndex) {
    nIndex = CalcClassByteIndex(hWnd, nIndex);
    return(GetClassLong(hWnd, nIndex));
}

//*******************************************************************
// The four Get/SetWindowWord/Long functions.

WORD WINAPI SetSCWindowWord (HWND hWnd, int nIndex,
    WORD wNewWord) {
    nIndex = CalcWindowByteIndex(hWnd, nIndex);
    return(SetWindowWord(hWnd, nIndex, wNewWord));
```

```
}

WORD WINAPI GetSCWindowWord (HWND hWnd, int nIndex) {
   nIndex = CalcWindowByteIndex(hWnd, nIndex);
   return(GetWindowWord(hWnd, nIndex));
}

DWORD WINAPI SetSCWindowLong (HWND hWnd, int nIndex,
   DWORD dwNewLong) {
   nIndex = CalcWindowByteIndex(hWnd, nIndex);
   return(SetWindowLong(hWnd, nIndex, dwNewLong));
}

DWORD WINAPI GetSCWindowLong (HWND hWnd, int nIndex) {
   nIndex = CalcWindowByteIndex(hWnd, nIndex);
   return(GetWindowLong(hWnd, nIndex));
}
```

Listing 2-11. SUPERCLS.H window superclassing header module

```
/******************************************************************
Module name: SUPERCLS.H
Programmer : Jeffrey M. Richter.
******************************************************************/

ATOM WINAPI RegisterSuperClass (LPWNDCLASS WndClass,
   WNDPROC lpfpSCWndProc, int cbClsAdditional,
   int cbWndAdditional);

WNDPROC WINAPI GetBCWndProc (HWND hWnd);

WORD  WINAPI SetSCClassWord (HWND hWnd, int nIndex,
   WORD wNewWord);

WORD  WINAPI GetSCClassWord (HWND hWnd, int nIndex);

DWORD WINAPI SetSCClassLong (HWND hWnd, int nIndex,
   DWORD dwNewLong);

DWORD WINAPI GetSCClassLong (HWND hWnd, int nIndex);

WORD  WINAPI SetSCWindowWord (HWND hWnd, int nIndex,
   WORD wNewWord);

WORD  WINAPI GetSCWindowWord (HWND hWnd, int nIndex);
```

```
DWORD WINAPI GetSCWindowLong (HWND hWnd, int nIndex);

DWORD WINAPI SetSCWindowLong (HWND hWnd, int nIndex,
    DWORD dwNewLong);
```

CHAPTER 3

Dialog-Box Techniques

Dialog boxes are a consistent, convenient way for applications to request information from the user. The dialog editor that comes with the Windows SDK makes it easy to design dialog boxes. It relieves the programmer of responsibility for many tedious details, such as calculating window locations for controls. The dialog editor can also be used by non-programmers, allowing much of the application's interface to be designed by other members of a design team.

The Voyeur application in Chapter 1 uses a dialog box to display information to the user. Much of the work was done by the dialog-box mechanism, and less by the application. Since the information fields were handled by the dialog mechanism, we can move them around to improve the application's appearance without rewriting any of the program code.

This chapter discusses various techniques for working with dialog boxes. Here's a brief preview of the dialog-box techniques we'll discuss:

- The *SetWindowPos* dialog box lets the programmer create new controls and add them to a dialog box after it has been displayed. The programmer can also use this technique to alter the tab-stop order of the controls.

- The *Options* >> dialog box seems to be appearing more and more often in commercial applications. It presents a dialog box to the user, but some of the controls are not shown. When the "Options >>" button is selected, the dialog box expands and the user gains access to the remaining controls. For an example of this type of dialog box, open the Windows Control Panel application and select Printers. In the Printers dialog box is a button marked "Add >>." If this button is pressed, the dialog box expands to include the controls necessary to add more printers to the Windows environment.

- The *modalless* dialog box is a cross between a modal dialog box and a modeless dialog box. It allows the programmer to display what appears to be a modal dialog box to the user. However, when the user closes the dialog box, the box is not destroyed . . . and neither are the settings the user selected. This lets the programmer retrieve the settings via standard Windows Applications Programming Interface (API) functions.

- The *dynamic* dialog box allows the programmer to create a dialog-box template at run time. This is useful for database applications and applications similar to the SDK's Dialog Editor.

- The *mode selection* dialog box allows the programmer to replace a whole subset of child controls, depending on the mode selected by the user. For an example of this type of dialog box, execute Word for Windows (Version 2.0) and select "Options ..." from the "Tools" menu. In the Options dialog box is a list box on the left with bitmaps representing the possible modes selectable by the user. Whenever the user selects a different mode, all of the other controls in this dialog box are replaced by a new set of controls.

All the techniques discussed in this chapter are demonstrated by the dialog-techniques application, DLGTECH.EXE. This application consists of five C modules. The first, DLGTECH.C, contains the *WinMain* function, initialization code for the application, and the window procedure for the main window. The dialog-box function demonstrating the *SetWindowPos* technique is also contained in DLGTECH.C.

The remaining source files contain dialog-box functions as well as functions necessary for supporting the demonstrated technique. A header file also exists for each file. The header file contains all the prototypes for the support functions. The following are the techniques and the files in which they're implemented:

The Options >> technique:	DLG-OPTS.C and DLG-OPTS.H
The modalless dialog-box technique:	DLG-MDLS.C and DLG-MDLS.H
The dynamic dialog-box technique:	DLG-DYNA.C and DLG-DYNA.H
The mode selection dialog-box technique:	DLG-MODE.C and DLG-MODE.H

The *SetWindowPos* Dialog Box

The window manager maintains an internal list of every existing window. When the dialog-box manager creates child controls, they are inserted one by one into the list. For operations that affect the windows of a dialog box, Windows consults the list. If the dialog box is hidden, for example, all of its children are likewise hidden. The same is true if the dialog box is destroyed.

When the user presses the Tab key within a dialog box, Windows searches through the window manager's list for children of the dialog box, locates the child that has focus, and searches forward for the next child window that has the *WS_TABSTOP* style set. Change the order of the windows in the window manager's list and you've changed the tab-stop order.

Figure 3-1 shows the dialog box for the *SetWindowPos* example.

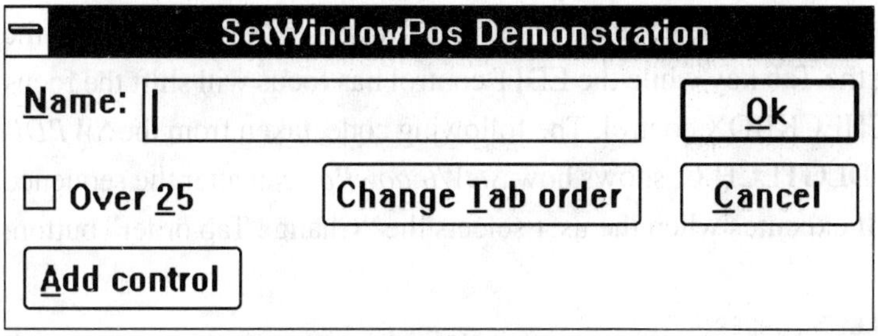

Figure 3-1. The SetWindowPos dialog box

This dialog box is created from the following template, which is from the file DLGTECH.RC.

```
SETWINDOWPOS DIALOG LOADONCALL MOVEABLE DISCARDABLE 8, 29, 176, 52
CAPTION "SetWindowPos Demonstration"
STYLE WS_BORDER | WS_CAPTION | WS_DLGFRAME | WS_SYSMENU | WS_POPUP
BEGIN
    CONTROL "&Name:", ID_NAMETEXT, "static", SS_LEFT | WS_CHILD,
        4, 4, 24, 8
    CONTROL "", ID_NAME, "edit", ES_LEFT | WS_BORDER | WS_GROUP |
        WS_TABSTOP | WS_CHILD, 28, 4, 100, 12
```

```
CONTROL "Over &25", ID_OVER25, "button", BS_AUTOCHECKBOX |
    WS_GROUP | WS_TABSTOP | WS_CHILD, 4, 20, 40, 12
CONTROL "Change &Tab order", ID_CHANGETABORDER, "button",
    BS_PUSHBUTTON | WS_GROUP | WS_TABSTOP | WS_CHILD, 64,
    20, 64, 12
CONTROL "&Add control", ID_ADDCONTROL, "button", BS_PUSHBUTTON
    | WS_GROUP | WS_TABSTOP | WS_CHILD, 4, 36, 44, 12
CONTROL "&OK", IDOK, "button", BS_DEFPUSHBUTTON | WS_GROUP |
    WS_TABSTOP | WS_CHILD, 136, 4, 36, 12
CONTROL "&Cancel", IDCANCEL, "button", BS_PUSHBUTTON | WS_GROUP
    | WS_TABSTOP | WS_CHILD, 136, 20, 36, 12
END
```

Because Windows creates the controls in the order in which they are listed in the template, pressing the Tab key while the EDIT control has focus will shift the focus to the "Over 25" CHECKBOX control. The following code, taken from the *SWPDlgProc* function in DLGTECH.C, shows how *SetWindowPos* can alter the sequence of these controls. It executes when the user selects the "Change Tab order" button.

```
case ID_CHANGETABORDER:
    if (HIWORD(lParam) != BN_CLICKED)
        break;

    SetWindowPos(GetDlgItem(hDlg, ID_OVER25),
        GetDlgItem(hDlg, ID_NAMETEXT),
        0, 0, 0, 0, SWP_NOMOVE | SWP_NOSIZE);

    SetWindowPos(GetDlgItem(hDlg, ID_NAMETEXT),
        GetDlgItem(hDlg, ID_OVER25),
        0, 0, 0, 0, SWP_NOMOVE | SWP_NOSIZE);

    SetFocus(GetNextDlgTabItem(hDlg, LOWORD(lParam), 0));
    EnableWindow(LOWORD(lParam), FALSE);
    break;
```

In the window manager's list, the controls are initially in order by ID: *ID_NAMETEXT*, *ID_NAME*, *ID_OVER25*. The first call to *SetWindowPos* changes this order so that the control identified by *ID_OVER25* is placed after the control identified by *ID_NAMETEXT,* resulting in a new tab order: *ID_NAMETEXT*, *ID_OVER25*, *ID_NAME*. The second call to *SetWindowPos* places the control identified by *ID_NAMETEXT* after the control identified by *ID_OVER25*. The final order is *ID_OVER25*, *ID_NAMETEXT*, *ID_NAME*. Pressing the Tab key while the "Over 25" check box has focus will shift the focus to the EDIT control.

The "Change Tab order" button was the last control to have focus. We should set the focus to some other control in the dialog box by calling the *SetFocus* function. The call to *GetNextDlgTabItem* tells Windows to search through the window manager's list and find the next (or previous) control that has the *WS_TABSTOP* style.

The *Windows Programmer's Reference* (for Version 3.0) states that *GetNextDlgTabItem* searches for the previous control if the third parameter is zero and the next control if this parameter is nonzero. This is incorrect; the description of the third parameter is backward. To search for the next control with the *WS_TABSTOP* style, the third parameter must be zero.

Finally, the code disables the "Change Tab order" button so that the user cannot select this option again.

You might be thinking that this is a cute thing to know but really isn't useful. I agree. But by building on this concept, we can dynamically add controls to a dialog box after it has been created. When the "Add control" button is pressed, the following code in the *SWPDlgProc* function executes:

```
case ID_ADDCONTROL:
   if (HIWORD(lParam) != BN_CLICKED)
      break;

   // Position control at (64, 36), width = 64, height = 12.
   SetRect(&rc, 64, 36, 64 + 64, 36 + 12);
   // Convert from dialog-box units to screen units.
   MapDialogRect(hDlg, &rc);
```

```
hWndControl = CreateWindow("scrollbar", "",
    SBS_HORZ | WS_CHILD | WS_TABSTOP | WS_GROUP,
    rc.left, rc.top, rc.right - rc.left, rc.bottom - rc.top,
    hDlg, ID_SCROLLBAR, _hInstance, 0);

SetWindowPos(hWndControl, LOWORD(lParam),
    0, 0, 0, 0, SWP_NOMOVE | SWP_NOSIZE | SWP_SHOWWINDOW);

// Set the focus to the control after this button.
SetFocus(GetNextDlgTabItem(hDlg, LOWORD(lParam), 0));

EnableWindow(LOWORD(lParam), FALSE);
break;
```

Here's how it works:

First, we prepare a rectangle with the (left, top) and (right, bottom) coordinates desired for the control in dialog-box units. The *MapDialogRect* function is then called to convert the rectangle from dialog-box coordinates to screen (pixel) coordinates.

Next, we create a new control with *CreateWindow*. The style parameter should have the same values that the dialog editor would have used. For example, the *WS_CHILD* style must be specified. If the control is to be a tab stop, specify the *WS_TABSTOP* style.

The control's parent window is the handle to the dialog box. When you create a child control with the *CreateWindow* function, the parameter after the parent window is the ID value that the child should have. After the child control has been created, the window is inserted into the window manager's list using the *SetWindowPos* function. Remember that the placement of the control affects how the Tab key changes the order in which controls gain focus.

Because the "Add control" button received focus when the user selected it, we must change the focus to another control. This button is also disabled in this demonstration so that the user cannot select it again.

The Options Dialog Box

Any new application involves a learning curve for the user. To help a user learn, the application can initially "hide" some of its functionality. Then, as the user becomes more adept, the program can reveal its advanced features. Many modern applications offer this kind of hand-holding.

For example, Microsoft Word for Windows (Version 1.x) and Microsoft Excel (Version 3.0) offer "Short Menus" and "Full Menus" options. The "Short Menus" option hides some of the advanced features from the user. When the user is more confident and familiar with the program, the "Full Menus" option is ready to allow full access to the programs features.

This feature tiering can also be applied to dialog boxes. When the user selects the "Style..." option from the Format menu in Word for Windows (Version 2.0), the dialog box in Figure 3-2 appears. Figure 3-3 shows the Style dialog box after the "Define >>" button is pressed.

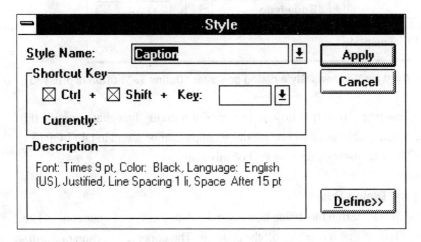

Figure 3-2. Word for Windows Style dialog box before "Define >>" button is pressed

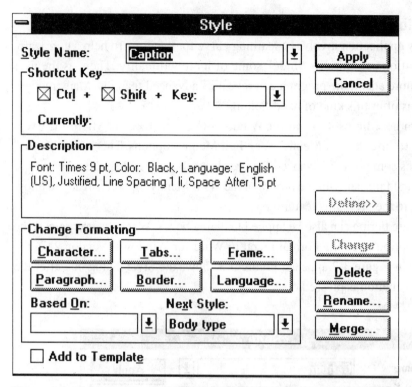

Figure 3-3. Word for Windows Style dialog box after "Define >>" button is pressed

The next few pages describe how to implement a dialog box that contains this type of functionality. The source code for this example can be found in DLG-OPTS.C and DLG-OPTS.H (presented at the end of this chapter).

Designing the Dialog Box

The first step is to design the dialog box using the dialog editor of your choice. Create the dialog box so that it contains all the controls. The upper left portion of the dialog box should contain the controls that will always be displayed. This is called the *default area* because it is the part of the dialog box that is always visible.

Once the entire dialog box has been laid out, add a STATIC control called the *default area control*. Change the style of this control so that it is a black rectangle. This will allow you to identify it easily while you work with the dialog box. The identifier assigned to this control will be used by the functions contained in the DLG-OPTS.C file and, therefore, must be unique.

Position the default area control so that its lower right corner is where you want the lower right corner of the default area to be. Figure 3-4 shows the final dialog box.

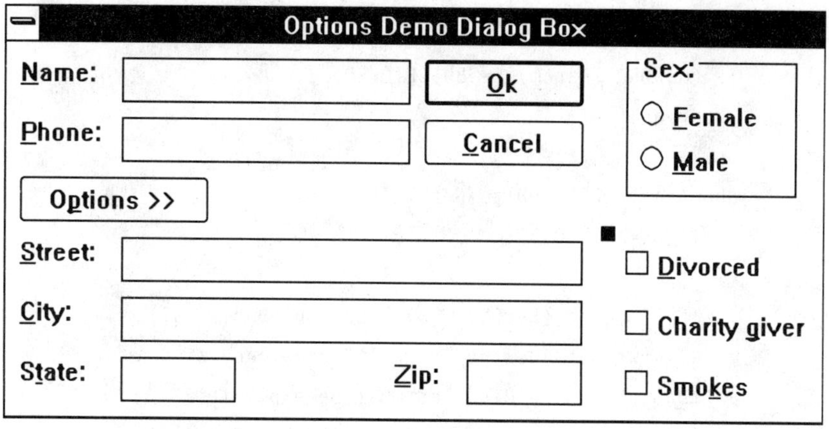

Figure 3-4. Options Demo dialog box

The Dialog-Box Function

The function that processes this dialog box is called *OptionsDlgProc*. It can be found in DLG-OPTS.C. The code is shown as follows:

```
BOOL CALLBACK OptionsDlgProc (HWND hDlg, UINT uMsg, WPARAM wParam,
     LPARAM lParam) {
  BOOL fProcessed = TRUE;

  switch (uMsg) {
    case WM_INITDIALOG:
       ShowArea(TRUE, hDlg, GetDlgItem(hDlg, ID_DEFAULTBOX));
       break;

    case WM_COMMAND:

       switch (wParam) {
         case IDOK:
         case IDCANCEL:
```

```
            EndDialog(hDlg, wParam);
            break;

        case ID_OPTIONS:
            if (HIWORD(lParam) != BN_CLICKED)
                break;

            ShowArea(FALSE, hDlg, GetDlgItem(hDlg,
                ID_DEFAULTBOX));

            // The ShowArea(FALSE, ...) function enables all
            // windows outside the "default" area. Any windows
            // that should be disabled must be explicitly
            // disabled here. Note that the status of the win-
            // dows within the default area is NOT changed.

            SetFocus(GetNextDlgTabItem(hDlg,
                LOWORD(lParam), 0));
            EnableWindow(LOWORD(lParam), FALSE);
            break;
        default:
            fProcessed = FALSE;
            break;
        }
        break;

    default:
        fProcessed = FALSE;
        break;
    }
    return(fProcessed);
}
```

When *OptionsDlgProc* receives the *WM_INITDIALOG* message, all the child controls have been created but the dialog box has not yet been displayed. Here's the prototype for the *ShowArea* function:

```
void WINAPI ShowArea (BOOL fShowDefAreaOnly, HWND hDlg,
    HWND hWndDefArea);
```

When we call *ShowArea* and pass TRUE as the first parameter, the dialog box is shrunk so that its lower right corner is the same as the lower right corner of the default area control. *ShowArea* disables all the controls that appear to the right of or below the default area control. This function also hides the default area control so the black rectangle is not visible to the user.

When the user presses the Tab key, Windows sets the window focus to the next enabled control that has the *WS_TABSTOP* style. Although shrinking the dialog box clips the controls beyond the default area, they are still enabled. A clipped control could get focus, but the user would not be able to see it. By disabling these controls, *ShowArea* ensures that the Tab key will allow the user to traverse only the controls in the default area.

This time, *ShowArea* is called when the user selects the "Options >>" button with the first parameter set to FALSE. The function restores the dialog box to its original size and enables the controls outside the default area, allowing the user to access them by pressing the Tab key. Of course, the user may also select these controls with the mouse.

Sometimes you will want some of the controls to remain disabled. *ShowArea* cannot determine which specific controls you may want to enable or disable. For this reason, you must explicitly disable individual controls in the options area after the call to *ShowArea*.

Once the additional controls are available to the user, focus is set to the next control after the "Options >>" button; the button is then disabled so it cannot be selected again.

The *ShowArea* Function

The main purpose of *ShowArea* (found in DLG-OPTS.C) is to expand or shrink the dialog box. If the *fShowDefAreaOnly* parameter is TRUE, the dialog box is shrunk. If *fShowDefAreaOnly* is FALSE, the dialog box is expanded to show all of its controls.

When the dialog box is shrunk, all the controls outside the default area control must be disabled. This is done by cycling through all of the dialog box's child windows with the following loop:

```
// Retrieve coordinates for default area window.
GetWindowRect(hWndDefArea, &rcDefArea);

hWndChild = GetFirstChild(hDlg);

for (; hWndChild != NULL; hWndChild = GetNextSibling(hWndChild)) {

    // Calculate rectangle occupied by child window in screen coordi-
    // nates.
    GetWindowRect(hWndChild, &rc);

    // Enable/Disable child if its:
    // right  edge is >= the right  edge of hWndDefArea.
    // bottom edge is >= the bottom edge of hWndDefArea.
    if ((rc.right  >= rcDefArea.right) ||
        (rc.bottom >= rcDefArea.bottom))
        EnableWindow(hWndChild, !fShowDefAreaOnly);
}
```

For each child window in the dialog box, it is determined if its bottom right corner is above and to the left of the location of the default area window. If it is, the window is either enabled or disabled, depending on the value of the *fShowDefAreaOnly* parameter.

When *ShowArea* is called via the *WM_INITDIALOG* message, the dialog box has been created full size (although not displayed yet). The original width and height of the dialog box must be saved so that it can be restored to this size later. It would be convenient if we could use the window extra bytes associated with the dialog box, but because we do not know how these bytes are used they should not be altered. However, we can convert the width and height values to a string and then save the contents of the string in the default area control. Here's the code that does the job:

```
// Turns a style ON for a window.
#define SetStyleOn(hWnd, Style) \
    SetWindowLong(hWnd, GWL_STYLE, Style | \
    GetWindowLong(hWnd, GWL_STYLE));
// Turns a style OFF for a window.
#define SetStyleOff(hWnd, Style) \
    SetWindowLong(hWnd, GWL_STYLE, ~Style & \
    GetWindowLong(hWnd, GWL_STYLE));

  .

  .

  .

wsprintf(szDlgDims, "%05u %05u",
    rcDlg.right - rcDlg.left, rcDlg.bottom - rcDlg.top);


SetStyleOff(hWndDefArea, SS_BLACKRECT);
SetStyleOn(hWndDefArea, SS_LEFT);
SetWindowText(hWndDefArea, szDlgDims);
```

Since the default area control is not visible, it will not display the information it contains. The *SetStyleOff* and *SetStyleOn* macros turn off the *SS_BLACKRECT* style and turn on the *SS_LEFT* style of this control. If this were not done, the default window control would ignore the *SetWindowText* call.

After the width and height are saved, the dialog box is resized:

```
SetWindowPos(hDlg, NULL, 0, 0,
    rcDefArea.right - rcDlg.left, rcDefArea.bottom - rcDlg.top,
    SWP_NOZORDER | SWP_NOMOVE);
```

and the default area control is hidden:

```
ShowWindow(hWndDefArea, SW_HIDE);
```

When *ShowArea* is called upon receipt of a *BN_CLICKED* notification from the "Options >>" button, the controls outside the dialog box must be enabled and the dialog box restored to its full size. The controls are enabled using the code explained above. Here's how the dialog box is restored to its full size:

```
GetWindowText(hWndDefArea, szDlgDims, sizeof(szDlgDims));


SetWindowPos(hDlg, NULL, 0, 0,
    atoi(szDlgDims), atoi(szDlgDims + 6),
    SWP_NOZORDER | SWP_NOMOVE);
```

First, the text associated with the default area control is retrieved. Remember, this string was set during processing of the *WM_INITDIALOG* message. It contains the width and height of the full-size dialog box. The numbers in the string must first be converted to integers using *atoi* and then passed to *SetWindowPos* so that the dialog box is restored to its original size.

Modalless Dialog Boxes

Modal dialog boxes are used to request additional information from a user before continuing with an action. When the dialog box is displayed, the user fills in the required information. The user selects the "OK" button, the dialog box is destroyed and the user's settings are lost. Most Windows programs save the user's settings in global variables when the "OK" button is selected.

Windows offers the *DialogBoxParam* and *DialogBoxIndirectParam* functions that can be used to pass the address of a memory block to the dialog-box procedure. The dialog procedure can use this memory block to save the user's settings when the "OK" button is selected. Since this address is sent to the dialog-box procedure only during the processing of the *WM_INITDIALOG* message, the procedure must somehow save this value.

This section describes a type of dialog box called a *modalless* dialog box. To Windows, this is a modeless dialog box. To the user, it operates like a modal dialog box. To the programmer, it is created and destroyed like a modeless dialog but is displayed and hidden like a modal dialog box.

Because the dialog box is modeless, it exists even when it is not displayed. This allows the application to use Windows API functions to set and retrieve data from the controls in the dialog box.

Working with Modalless Dialog Boxes

Modalless dialog boxes are created by calling the *CreateModalLessDlgBox* function in the DLG-MDLS.C file. During processing of the *WM_CREATE* message in the *AppWndProc* function (found in DLGTECH.C), the modalless dialog box is created:

```
_hDlgModalLess = CreateModalLessDlgBox(_hInstance, "Modalless",
    hWnd, ModalLessDemoProc, 0);
if (_hDlgModalLess == NULL) {
    MessageBox(hWnd, "Cant create modalless dialog box.",
        _szAppName, MB_OK);
    EnableMenuItem(GetMenu(hWnd), IDM_MODALLESSDEMO, MF_BYCOMMAND |
        MF_GRAYED);
}
break;
```

If the modalless dialog box cannot be created, the application displays a notice to the user and disables the menu item that activates the modalless dialog-box demonstration.

The modalless dialog box is destroyed when the *AppWndProc* function processes the *WM_CLOSE* message:

```
if (_hDlgModalLess)
    DestroyModalLessDlgBox(_hDlgModalLess);
fCallDefProc = TRUE;
break;
```

Notice that the *fCallDefProc* variable must be set to TRUE so that the standard processing for *WM_CLOSE* is performed.

Once a modalless dialog box is created, the functions that access it are similar to those for modal dialog boxes. Below is a table showing the modal dialog-box functions and their equivalent modalless dialog-box functions.

Action	Modal Dialog- Box Function	Modalless Dialog- Box Function
Display dialog box	*DialogBox* *DialogBoxParam*	*ModalLessDlgBox* *ModalLessDlgBox*
Terminate dialog-box usage	*EndDialog*	*EndModalLessDlgBox*

When the application wants the modalless dialog box to be displayed, the *Modal-LessDlgBox* function is called:

```
nResult = ModalLessDlgBox(_hDlgModalLess, hWnd, 0);
```

This function requires the window handle to the modalless dialog box, the window handle to the window that is to be disabled, and a long data value. The long value may contain any value the application would like to pass to the modalless dialog box just before the box is displayed. This function will not return to the caller until the modalless dialog-box function has called the *EndModalLessDlgBox* function.

Here's the dialog-box procedure that demonstrates the use of modalless dialog boxes:

```
BOOL CALLBACK ModalLessDlgProc (HWND hDlg, UINT uMsg,
    WPARAM wParam, LPARAM lParam) {
  BOOL fProcessed = TRUE;

  if (uMsg == RegisterWindowMessage(SZMODALLESSSHOWMSG)) {
    // lParam is the data value passed to ModalLessDlgBox
    // function. Initialize the EDIT control with some text
    // whenever the dialog box is about to be shown.
    SetDlgItemText(hDlg, ID_NAME, "Default text");
    SetFocus(GetDlgItem(hDlg, ID_NAME));
  }

  switch (uMsg) {
    case WM_INITDIALOG:
      break;
```

```
case WM_COMMAND:
    switch (wParam) {
        case IDOK:
        case IDCANCEL:
            if (HIWORD(lParam) == BN_CLICKED)
                EndModalLessDlgBox(hDlg, wParam);
            break;

        default:
            break;
    }
    break;

default:
    fProcessed = FALSE;
    break;
}
return(fProcessed);
}
```

When the dialog box is created with *CreateModalLessDlgBox*, a *WM_INITDI-ALOG* message is sent to the dialog-box procedure. This is when any one-time initialization should be performed on the dialog box. Just before the dialog box is displayed (called by the *ModalLessDlgBox* function) it receives a message. This message is represented by the ASCII string defined in the DLG-MDLS.H file *SZMODALLESSSHOWMSG*. This is defined as "*ModalLessShowMsg*."

When the modalless dialog-box procedure receives a message, it first checks to see if the message is *SZMODALLESSSHOWMSG*. If it is, the necessary actions are performed to prepare the dialog box for display. In our example, default text is placed in the EDIT control, and this control receives the input focus.

EndModalLessDlgBox removes the dialog box from the screen and returns control to the calling application. The first parameter is the handle of the dialog box; the second is the value to be returned to the caller of the *ModalLessDlgBox* function. This function is similar to the *EndDialog* function for modal dialog boxes.

How Modalless Dialog Boxes Work

The DLG-MDLS.H file contains prototypes for all the functions defined in DLG-MDLS.C that may be called from your application. The macro *SZMODAL-LESSSHOWMSG* is also defined. This message notifies the dialog-box procedure when the dialog box is about to be shown. The functions in DLG-MDLS.C are described below:

- *CreateModalLessDlgBox* creates a modeless dialog box and returns its window handle. It is simply a call to *CreateDialogParam*.

- *DestroyModalLessDlgBox* destroys the modeless dialog box created by *CreateModalLessDlgBox*. It is simply a call to *DestroyWindow*.

- *ModalLessDlgBox* displays a modalless dialog box to the user. Like the *DialogBox* and *DialogBoxParam* functions for modal dialog boxes, this function will not return until the modalless dialog box has been closed by a call to *EndModalLessDlgBox* (described later).

The *ModalLessDlgBox* function requires the handle to the modalless dialog box (created via a call to the *CreateModalLessDlgBox* function), the handle of the window to be disabled when this dialog box appears, and a long value that is passed during the *SZMODALLESSSHOWMSG* message loop.

After *ModalLessDlgBox* disables the window defined in the second parameter, the *SZMODALLESSSHOWMSG* message is sent to *ModalLessDlgProc* and the dialog box is made visible:

```
uModalLessShowMsg = RegisterWindowMessage(SZMODALLESSSHOWMSG);
SendMessage(hDlg, uModalLessShowMsg, 0, lParam);
ShowWindow(hDlg, SW_SHOW);
```

A message loop must be initiated so control does not immediately return to the calling application:

```
while (!fPropFound) {
    GetMessage(&msg, NULL, 0, 0);
        if (!IsDialogMessage(hDlg, &msg)) {
            TranslateMessage(&msg);
            DispatchMessage(&msg);
        }
    nResult = GetProp(hDlg, _szModalLessResult);
    fPropFound = RemoveProp(hDlg, _szModalLessResult) != NULL;
}
```

A modalless dialog box returns a result by calling *EndModalLessDlgBox*. This function associates a window property with the dialog box. During the message loop, the *GetProp* function is called to see if *EndModalLessDlgBox* has been called. If the value returned by *GetProp* is zero, it means that the property has not yet been associated with the window or that the *nResult* parameter to the *End-ModalLessDlgBox* function was zero. We can determine which of these cases it was by calling the *RemoveProp* function. If this function is unable to remove a property with the specified name, NULL is returned. This means that the message loop should not terminate.

If the property was removed, the message loop terminates, the disabled parent window is enabled, the modalless dialog box is hidden, and the result from the *Get-Prop* function is returned to the application:

```
EnableWindow(hWndParent, TRUE);
ShowWindow(hDlg, SW_HIDE);
return(nResult);
```

The final function, *EndModalLessDlgBox*, is called from the modalless dialog-box function when the dialog box is to be removed from the screen. The parameters are identical to the parameters for *EndDialog*. Associating the window property with the dialog box notifies the message loop in *ModalLessDlgBox* that *EndModalLessDlgBox* has been called:

```
return(SetProp(hDlg, _szModalLessResult, nResult));
```

However, an attempt to set a property can fail. The return value is zero if the property could not be associated. This means that the dialog cannot be terminated.

Dynamic Dialog Boxes

Sometimes it is necessary to design dialog boxes while the application is running. For example, a database application may allow the user to design the entry form and then create a dialog box based on this form for adding records to the database.

Windows offers four functions for creating dialog boxes at run time. *Dialog-BoxIndirect* and *DialogBoxIndirectParam* create modal dialog boxes, while *CreateDialogIndirect* and *CreateDialogIndirectParam* create modeless dialog boxes. Dynamic dialog boxes are created by building a dialog template in a global memory block and passing this memory block to one of these functions.

The *Windows Programmer's Reference* describes the three data structures necessary for building dialog-box templates in memory: *DLGTEMPLATE*, *FONTINFO*, and *DLGITEMTEMPLATE*. If you search through the WINDOWS.H file, you won't find any of these structures defined; you must define them yourself. All these structures consist of a fixed portion at the beginning and a variable-length portion at the end. While this method conserves memory, it makes dialog-box templates much more difficult to create and use.

The first data structure, *DLGTEMPLATE*, holds information that applies to the entire dialog box. This structure must appear at the beginning of the memory block in the following format:

```
typedef struct {
    long dtStyle;
    BYTE dtItemCount;
    int dtX;
    int dtY;
    int dtCX;
    int dtCY;
    // char dtMenuName[];          // Variable-length string.
    // char dtClassName[];         // Variable-length string.
    // char dtCaptionText[];       // Variable-length string.
} DLGTEMPLATE, FAR *LPDLGTEMPLATE;
```

The fixed elements of this data structure describe the dialog box's style, number of controls, position, and dimensions. The variable-length portion of the data structure describes the dialog box's menu name, class name, and caption text. Each of these fields is a zero-terminated string.

The second data structure is *FONTINFO,* which specifies the font Windows should use when drawing text in the dialog box. If the *DS_SETFONT* style is specified in the *DLGTEMPLATE* structure, then the *FONTINFO* structure must appear immediately after *DLGTEMPLATE* in memory. If *DS_SETFONT* is not specified, *FONTINFO* should not appear in the memory block at all. This structure has the following format:

```
typedef struct {
    short int PointSize;
    // char szTypeFace[];        // Variable-length string.
} FONTINFO, FAR *LPFONTINFO;
```

The fixed element of this data structure is the point size of the font specified in the variable-length part. The typeface name must specify a font that was previously loaded via WIN.INI or the *LoadFont* function.

The third data structure is *DLGITEMTEMPLATE.* This structure must appear once for every control that will appear in the dialog-box template. This is the value of the *dtItemCount* member of the *DLGTEMPLATE* structure. The first of these structures appears immediately after the *FONTINFO* structure (or after the *DLGTEM-PLATE* structure if the *DS_SETFONT* style is not specified). The *DLGITEMTEM-PLATE* structure has the following format:

```
typedef struct {
    int dtilX;
    int dtilY;
    int dtilCX;
    int dtilCY;
    int dtilID;
    long dtilStyle;
    // char dtilClass[];          // Variable-length string.
```

```
    // char dtilText[];              // Variable-length string.
    // BYTE dtilInfo;                // # of bytes in following memory
                                     // block.
    // PTR dtilData;                 // Variable-length memory block.
} DLGITEMTEMPLATE, FAR *LPDLGITEMTEMPLATE;
```

The fixed elements of this structure contain each control's position, dimensions, ID value, and styles. The variable-length elements are zero-terminated strings that hold the control's class name and window text.

The next byte, *dtilInfo*, specifies the number of bytes in the remaining field, *dtilData*. The *dtilData* field is a variable-length block of bytes. When Windows creates the control specified by this *DLGITEMTEMPLATE* structure, it calls the *CreateWindow* function and passes the address to the *dtilData* memory block in the last parameter. The window procedure for this control can examine the *dtilData* bytes while processing the *WM_NCCREATE* and *WM_CREATE* messages. When Windows sends a *WM_NCCREATE* or *WM_CREATE* message to a window procedure, the *lParam* parameter is a pointer to a *CREATESTRUCT* data structure. The address of the *dtilData* bytes is located in the *lpCreateParams* member of this structure.

The *dtilInfo* member is necessary so that when Windows creates the dialog boxes, it knows how many bytes to skip to get to the beginning of the next *DLGITEMTEMPLATE* structure.

Once the memory block has been initialized (Figure 3-5), one of the dialog-box functions may be called. The functions that create modal dialog boxes accept the handle to this block of memory as their second parameter:

```
int DialogBoxIndirect(HINSTANCE hInstance, HGLOBAL hGlblDialogTem-
    plate, HWND hWndParent, DLGPROC lpDialogFunc);

int DialogBoxIndirectParam(HINSTANCE hInstance, HGLOBAL
    hGlblDialogTemplate, HWND hWndParent, DLGPROC lpDialogFunc, LPARAM
    lParam);
```

When the modal dialog box has been removed, the block of memory may be freed using the *GlobalFree* function.

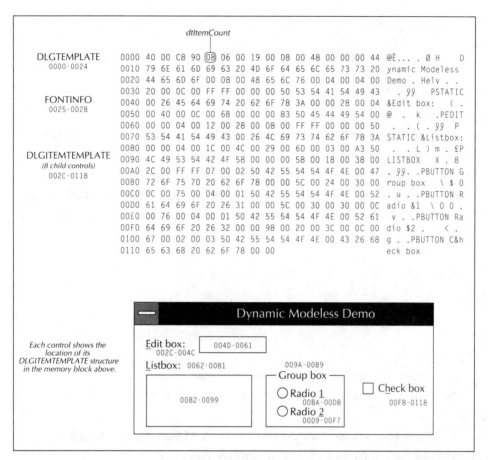

Figure 3-5. Memory block used with *CreateDialogIndirect* to make dynamic modeless demo dialog box

The dialog techniques application demonstrates how to create modal and modeless dialog boxes (the source code for DlgTech appears at the end of this chapter). When the "Dynamic modal demo..." option is chosen, the following code fragment executes:

```
case IDM_DYNAMICMODALDEMO:
    hGlbl = BuildDynamicDlgBox(FALSE);
    if (hGlbl == NULL) {
        MessageBox(hWnd, "Insufficient memory.", _szAppName, MB_OK);
        break;
```

```
    }
    DialogBoxIndirect(_hInstance, hGlbl, hWnd, (DLGPROC) DynamicDlgProc);
    GlobalFree(hGlbl);
    break;
```

The *BuildDynamicDlgBox* function in the DLG-DYNA.C file performs all the work to create the dialog-box template in memory. If there is insufficient memory, NULL is returned; otherwise, the global memory handle to the template is returned.

The functions that create modeless dialog boxes require that the block of memory be locked by the *GlobalLock* function and that the address be passed as the second parameter:

```
    int CreateDialogIndirect(HINSTANCE hInstance,
        const void FAR *lpDialogTemplate, HWND hWndParent,
        DLGPROC lpDialogFunc);

    int CreateDialogIndirectParam(HINSTANCE hInstance,
        const void FAR * lpDialogTemplate, HWND hWndParent,
        DLGPROC lpDialogFunc, LPARAM lParam);
```

Once the dialog box has been created, the block of memory may be unlocked and freed using the *GlobalUnlock* and *GlobalFree* functions.

When the "Dynamic modeless demo..." option is chosen in the dialog techniques application, the following code fragment executes:

```
    case IDM_DYNAMICMODELESSDEMO:
        if (_hDlgDynamic != NULL) {
            DestroyWindow(_hDlgDynamic);
            _hDlgDynamic = NULL;
            CheckMenuItem(GetMenu(hWnd), wParam,
                MF_BYCOMMAND | MF_UNCHECKED);
            break;
        }
        hGlbl = BuildDynamicDlgBox(TRUE);
```

```
if (hGlbl == NULL) {
   MessageBox(hWnd, "Insufficient memory.", _szAppName, MB_OK);
   break;
}

_hDlgDynamic = CreateDialogIndirect(_hInstance,
   GlobalLock(hGlbl), hWnd, (DLGPROC) DynamicDlgProc);
GlobalUnlock(hGlbl);
GlobalFree(hGlbl);
CheckMenuItem(GetMenu(hWnd), wParam, MF_BYCOMMAND |
   MF_CHECKED);
break;
```

The _hDlgDynamic_ global variable contains the handle of the modeless dynamic dialog box. If the dialog box does not exist, it is NULL. If the dialog box exists, choosing the "Dynamic modeless demo..." option destroys the dialog box. If the dialog box doesn't exist, this menu option creates it.

The first test in the code above ascertains whether the dialog box already exists. If it does, it is destroyed and _hDlgDynamic_ is set to NULL to indicate that the dialog box may be created again. The menu item "Dynamic modeless demo..." is unchecked to show the user that the dialog box does not exist.

If the dialog box does not exist, the template for it is created in memory. If the global handle returned is NULL, the user is notified that there is insufficient memory. If the dialog-box template is created successfully, the memory block is locked and _CreateDialogIndirect_ is called with the template's address. Immediately after the dialog box has been created, the memory is unlocked and freed. Finally, the "Dynamic modeless demo..." option is checked to indicate to the user that the dialog box is active.

Building the Dialog-Box Template

BuildDynamicDlgBox calls various functions in the DLG-DYNA.C file to create the dialog-box template. The only parameter to this function is a Boolean value, _fModeless_, which specifies whether a modal or modeless dialog box is to be created.

The call to *CreateDlgTemplate* performs the initial memory allocation and fills in the *DLGTEMPLATE* structure at the beginning of the memory block:

```
HGLOBAL WINAPI  CreateDlgTemplate(
    LONG dtStyle,
    int dtX, int dtY,              // In dialog-box units.
    int dtCX, int dtCY,           // In dialog-box units.
    LPSTR dtMenuName,             // "" if no menu.
    LPSTR dtClassName,            // "" if standard dialog-box class.
    LPSTR dtCaptionText,
    short int PointSize,          // Only used if DS_SETFONT style
                                  // specified.

    LPSTR szTypeFace);            // Only used if DS_SETFONT style
                                  // specified.
        .
        .
        .
if(fModeless)
    hGlbl = CreateDlgTemplate(
        WS_BORDER | WS_CAPTION | WS_DLGFRAME |
        WS_SYSMENU | WS_VISIBLE | WS_POPUP | DS_SETFONT,
        6, 25, 216, 72, "", "","Dynamic Modeless Demo", 8, "Helv");
else
    hGlbl = CreateDlgTemplate(
        WS_BORDER | WS_CAPTION | WS_DLGFRAME |
        WS_SYSMENU | WS_VISIBLE | WS_POPUP,
        6, 25, 216, 72, "", "","Dynamic Modal Demo", 0,"");
```

Because the *DS_SETFONT* flag is specified when the modeless dialog box is created, the last two parameters (*8* and *"Helv"*) indicate the font that should be used when the dialog box is created. The *DS_SETFONT* flag is not specified for the modal dialog box, so *CreateDlgTemplate* will ignore the last two parameters. The number of controls that will appear in the dialog-box template is not specified to *CreateDlgTemplate*; it is set to zero initially and is incremented with each call to the *AddDlgControl* function.

Once the *DLGTEMPLATE* structure has been placed in the memory block, the individual controls are appended. *BuildDynamicDlgBox* uses the following data structure to create those controls.

```
#define MAXDLGITEMDATA    (10)

struct {
    int x, y, cx, cy, id;
    long Style;
    LPSTR szClass, szText;
    BYTE Info;
    BYTE Data[MAXDLGITEMDATA];
} DynamicDlgBoxData[] = {
    { 4, 4, 32, 12, -1, SS_LEFT, "STATIC", "&Edit box:", 0,
      { 0 } },
    { 40, 4, 64, 12, ID_EDITBOX, ES_LEFT | WS_BORDER | WS_TABSTOP |
      WS_GROUP, "EDIT", "", 0, { 0 } },
    { 4, 18, 40, 8, -1, SS_LEFT, "STATIC", "&Listbox:", 0, { 0 } },
    .

    .

    .

    { 0, 0, 0, 0, 0, 0, NULL, NULL, 0, { 0 } }
};
```

AddDlgControl is called for each item in this data structure, and a new *DLGITEMTEMPLATE* structure is appended to the end of the memory block:

```
// LOWORD = Success(TRUE)/Failure(FALSE), HIWORD=New hGlbl.
DWORD WINAPI AddDlgControl (
    HGLOBAL hGlbl,              // Handle from CreateDlgTemplate or
                               // AddDlgControl.
    int dtilX, int dtilY,      // In dialog-box units.
    int dtilCX, int dtilCY,    // In dialog-box units.
    int dtilID,
```

```
        long dtilStyle,             // WS_CHILD is automatically added;
        LPSTR dtilClass,            // may be: "BUTTON", "EDIT", "STATIC"
                                    // "LISTBOX", "SCROLLBAR", "COMBOBOX".
        LPSTR dtilText,
        BYTE dtilInfo,              // Number of additional data bytes.
        LPBYTE dtilData);           // Address of additional bytes.
    .
    .
    .
for (x = 0; DynamicDlgBoxData[x].szClass != NULL; x++) {
    // Do not add the "OK" and "Cancel" buttons if a modeless
    // dialog box is being created.
    if (fModeless) {
      if (DynamicDlgBoxData[x].id == IDOK ||
        DynamicDlgBoxData[x].id == IDCANCEL)
        continue;
    }

    dwAddDlgControlResult = AddDlgControl(hGlbl,
      DynamicDlgBoxData[x].x,  DynamicDlgBoxData[x].y,
      DynamicDlgBoxData[x].cx, DynamicDlgBoxData[x].cy,
      DynamicDlgBoxData[x].id, DynamicDlgBoxData[x].Style | WS_VISIBLE,
      DynamicDlgBoxData[x].szClass,  DynamicDlgBoxData[x].szText,
      DynamicDlgBoxData[x].Info,     DynamicDlgBoxData[x].Data);

    // LOWORD is FALSE if insufficient memory exists.
    if (LOWORD(dwAddDlgControlResult) == FALSE) break;

    // HIWORD is handle to new block of memory.
    hGlbl = HIWORD(dwAddDlgControlResult);
}
```

The "OK" and "Cancel" buttons are not included in the modeless version of this dialog-box template (they are not usually included in modeless dialog boxes).

After the template has been created successfully, *DoneAddingControls* performs some internal cleanup in the memory block and the memory handle is returned to the application.

Managing the Dialog Templates Memory Block

The functions that manage the block of memory are *CreateDlgTemplate*, *AddDlgControl*, and *DoneAddingControls*.

CreateDlgTemplate performs the initial global memory allocation. This allocation must be large enough to contain a *DLGTEMPLATE* structure and its three variable-length fields: *dtMenuName*, *dtClassName*, and *dtCaptionText*. If the dialog template includes the *DS_SETFONT* style, the memory block must be large enough to include the *FONTINFO* structure, including its variable-length field, *szTypeFace*.

An additional two bytes are included in the size of the memory block. This word contains the number of bytes used in the block so far, letting the *AddDlgControl* function know where to begin appending its *DLGITEMTEMPLATE* structures. After the memory block is allocated, *CreateDlgTemplate* fills the memory block with the values passed in the parameters to the function and the *dtilItemCount* member is initialized to zero. The handle to the memory block is then returned to the caller.

AddDlgControl appends new controls to the end of a memory block that was created by *CreateDlgTemplate*. This function first calculates the number of bytes required to contain a *DLGITEMTEMPLATE* structure and its three variable-length fields: *dtilClass*, *dtilText*, and *dtilData*. Before the memory block can be enlarged, this function must determine the number of bytes already used. The Windows *GlobalSize* function cannot be used because Windows sometimes allocates more bytes than requested when satisfying a memory allocation. To solve this problem, the first word in the memory block contains the number of bytes used in the block. This was updated by *CreateDlgTemplate* or a previous call to *AddDlgControl*. Now, *AddDlgControl* can add the value in the first word of the block to the number of bytes required by the new control and call *GlobalReAlloc*:

```
wBlockLen += * (WORD FAR *) GlobalLock(hGlbl);
GlobalUnlock(hGlbl);
hGlblNew = GlobalReAlloc(hGlbl, wBlockLen, GMEM_MOVEABLE |
    GMEM_ZEROINIT);
```

Because *GlobalReAlloc* does not necessarily return the same memory handle that was passed to it, *AddDlgControl* must notify the calling application of the new handle by returning it.

With the memory block now large enough to hold the additional control, the new *DLGITEMTEMPLATE* structure is appended after the number of bytes used in the block. When a new control is added, the *dtItemCount* member in *DLGTEMPLATE* is incremented. Before the memory block is unlocked, the first word in the block is updated to reflect the total number of bytes now used in the block.

Once the application is done adding controls to the dialog-box template, the *DoneAddingControls* function must be called. This function simply locks the memory block and does a memory move to shift all the information in the block toward the beginning by two bytes. This removes the number-of-bytes-used information. Once this is done, the *AddDlgControl* function may no longer be called for this memory block. The memory block is now in the correct format to be used by the *DialogBoxIndirect(Param)* and *CreateDialogIndirect(Param)* functions.

Mode-Select Dialog Boxes

Dialog boxes let the user select from a set of options. Today's applications offer so many options that the user could end up spending all day configuring the application by going from one dialog box to the next. An excellent example of an option-filled application is Word for Windows 2.0. Word offers 11 different categories of configurable settings. After the user chooses a category, the set of options that apply to that category is displayed. Word's Options dialog box appears in Figure 3-6.

In this figure, the "View" category has been selected on the left and the options pertaining to "View" are displayed on the right. Figure 3-7 shows what the dialog box looks like after the "General" category has been selected. You can see that all of the options on the right have been changed. This method of replacing controls in a dialog box not only conserves screen real estate, it also makes selecting options much easier for the end user. Options pertaining to a specific subject are displayed together. Options having nothing to do with the displayed category are not shown to the user. The advantage of this scheme is that the user can go to one place for setting the options that affect the application.

When you consider that the alternatives to this method are either flooding the dialog box with all possible controls or having the user first select a category and then click a button to bring up another dialog box, I'm sure you will agree that the method employed by Word for Windows is much better.

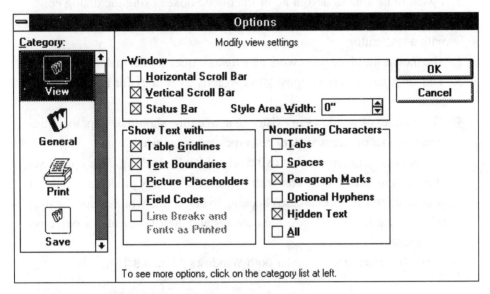

Figure 3-6. Word's Option dialog box

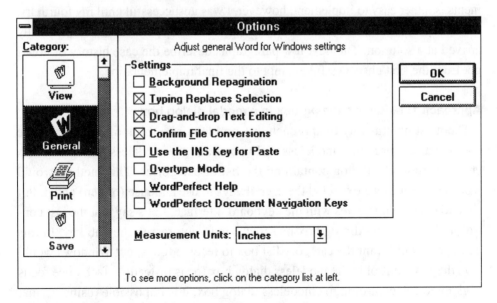

Figure 3-7. Dialog box after selection of "General" category

There are a number of features I consider extremely important for this technique:

1. I want to be able to design all of the dialog boxes using the dialog editor and not by having to create CONTROL statements in an .RC or .DLG file with a text editor.
2. The mouse interface must work exactly as it does for normal dialog boxes.
3. The keyboard interface must work exactly as it does for normal dialog boxes.
4. The number of windows in existence at one time should be kept to a minimum so that precious system resources are not wasted.
5. I want code implementation extremely clean by making each option set appear as its own dialog box with its own dialog-box procedure. (I don't want to code any special-case checking to determine which mode the user selected and how to process the controls and their notifications based on that mode.)
6. I want the code to work under both Windows 3.0 and 3.1.

On the surface, you might think that a method conforming to the above requirements is rather easy to implement; however, I was unsuccessful until my fourth try. Some of you might be interested in how I approached the problem and how I finally arrived at a solution. The next few paragraphs describe the case history of how I got from the first unsuccessful attempt to the final implementation.

Approach 1: Modeless dialog box in a modal dialog box

The most natural way to approach this problem is to think of the replaceable controls as children of a modeless dialog box and the modeless dialog box as a child to the modal dialog containing the list of categories. This method would work very well if we expected the user always to use a mouse (or pen) and didn't have to concern ourselves with the keyboard interface. Let's say that the last control in the modeless dialog box had focus and you pressed the Tab key. In this case, you would want the category list box to receive focus, but Windows would give the first control in the modeless dialog box focus instead. In fact, once focus is given to any control in the modeless dialog box, it is impossible (using normal Windows methods or dialog-box processing) to give the focus to any control that is a direct child of the modal dialog box by using the keyboard. Of course, you could try subclassing some of the controls and doing all of the Tabbing, Shift-Tabbing, arrow keys, and Alt-Mnemonic processing yourself, but this would be a lot of code and you can bet that some situation would be forgotten by the time you thought you were done.

Actually, I didn't even attempt to implement this solution. After thinking about it for a while and what it would require to process all of the keyboard possibilities, my head began to spin. Once my dizziness started to fade, I felt that the only way to get the keyboard processing to work correctly (and easily) was to make the new controls direct children of the modal dialog box itself, period. So, on to the next approach.

Approach 2: Using the *SetParent* function

This approach begins by devising a scheme for setting up all of the dialog-box templates. This scheme is also used in the third and final approaches. Figures 3-8 through 3-11 show what the four dialog-box templates look like in the example application. All of the dialog boxes must meet the following requirements:

1. The first dialog-box template is the frame dialog and sets the stage for the remaining templates. The location, size, caption text, font, and styles that you assign here are the settings used for the lifetime of the dialog box as it appears on the screen. When the controls from any of the other templates are merged into this dialog box, their dialog-boxes' settings are ignored. To aid you in the creation of the remaining templates, I recommend that you begin each template using the same settings as the frame-dialog template.

2. In the frame dialog, create all of the controls that should always be visible no matter which mode the user selects. The other templates do not have this information repeated.

3. Create a STATIC control in the frame dialog that encompasses the area where controls will be replaced when a new mode is selected by the user. I call this STATIC control the *ChangeableArea* window. This STATIC control must appear in all of the dialog-box templates and is used as a reference to help you know where controls can and cannot be placed. Make sure that the ID of this STATIC control is the same in every template as well.

4. Order the controls in the frame dialog to achieve the Tab order that you desire. When controls from other templates are merged into the frame, they are merged immediately following the STATIC control.

5. Create all other templates. When you are assigning IDs to the controls, you may not use an ID value that conflicts with a control's ID in the frame dialog. However, you may use an ID that conflicts with a control in another template.

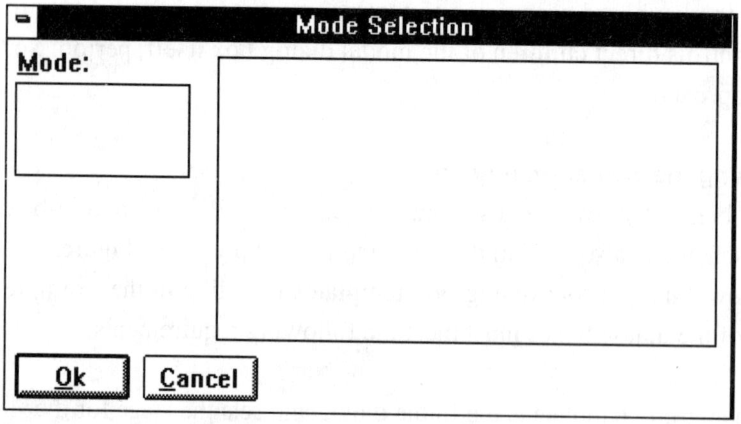

Figure 3-8. The frame dialog template

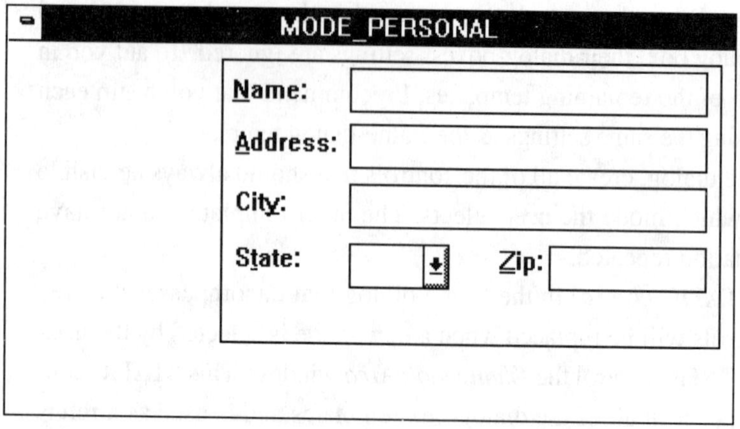

Figure 3-9. Dialog template for the first mode

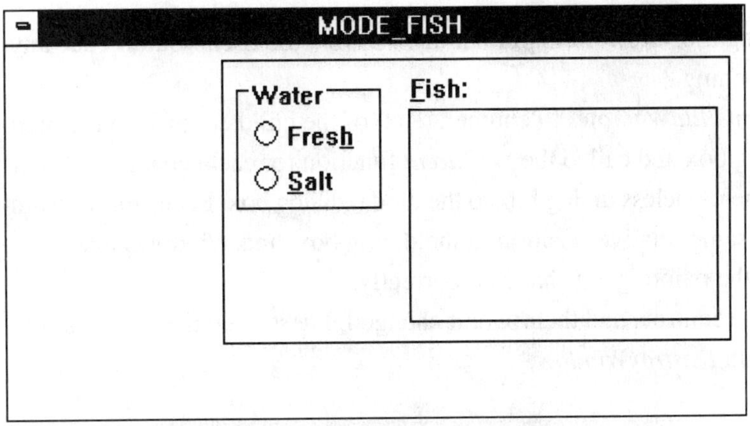

Figure 3-10. Dialog template for the second mode

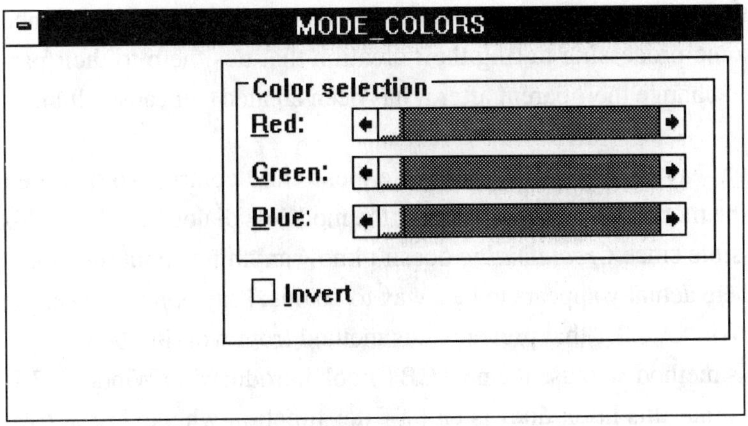

Figure 3-11. Dialog template for the third mode

Having laid out a couple of templates to work from and experiment with, I began implementing my ideas. They went something like this:

First, I called *DialogBox* to create the modal dialog box containing the controls that always appear, regardless of the mode a user might select (such as the Category list box and the "OK" and "Cancel" buttons). Then, for cases when a user selects a new Category, I performed the following steps.

1. Destroyed all of the category-specific controls in the modal dialog box.
2. Called *CreateDialog* to load the new template from the executable into mem-

ory, keeping the whole dialog box hidden so that the user wouldn't see anything happening.

3. Used *EnumChildWindows* to enumerate all of the child controls in the modeless dialog box and called the *SetParent* function for each, changing its parent from the modeless dialog box to the modal dialog box. Each control maintained the same relative position in the dialog box, and Windows made sure that all of the painting was handled correctly.

4. After all the controls had their parent changed, I destroyed the modeless dialog box with *DestroyWindow*.

This method actually appeared to work until I added EDIT controls to any of the dialog-box templates. After I did this, the call to *SetParent* caused a General Protection Violation to occur. It turns out that EDIT controls, list boxes, and combo boxes perform some processing during their creation that ties them to their parent. Attempting to change their parent after it has been created can cause all kinds of problems.

Now, I needed a way to have Windows create these child controls so that their parent is always the modal dialog box and never the modeless dialog box. Well, this may seem impossible since *CreateDialog* doesn't know anything about the modal dialog box, but there actually appears to be a way to do this. I say *appears*, because there is a bug in Windows 3.1 that prevents this method from working.

The idea for this method is to use the new CBT hook introduced in Windows 3.1. One of the things that this hook does is call a filter function whenever the *CreateWindow* function is about to create a window. When this happens, the hook filter function, *CBTProc*, is sent a hook code of *HCBT_CREATEWND*. The value in the *lParam* parameter to the hook function receives an address to a *CBT_CREATEWND* structure, which contains a *CREATESTRUCT* structure. You may recall that the *CREATESTRUCT* structure contains all information about the window that is about to be created.

The documentation for the hook states:

> *At the time of the* HCBT_CREATEWND *notification, the window has been created, but its final size and position may not have been determined, nor has its parent window been established.*

I took my cue from this line and attempted to change the *hwndParent* member of the *CREATESTRUCT* structure from the modeless dialog box to that of the modal dialog box. The problem here was that although the documentation states that you can change a window's parent, you can't—this is a bug in Windows 3.1. The other thing that I don't like about this method is that it violates Requirement 6—the solution should work with both Windows 3.0 and 3.1.

The more time I spent playing with this problem, the more it just seemed like I would have to read the dialog-box template from the executable and parse each control's information out of it myself, which leads us to the Final Approach.

Final Approach: The brute force method

In this approach, we pretty much do everything ourselves without much help from Windows. The most important function that this method performs is the task of merging all the controls in a dialog-box template into an existing dialog box. This function, *MergeControlsIntoDlg* (found in the module DLG-MODE.C), accepts four parameters. The first, *hDlg*, is the handle of the dialog box that the controls are to be merged into. The second parameter, *uIDChangeableArea*, identifies the control that immediately precedes the first control to be merged. This is important so that a logical sequence is maintained when the user presses the Tab key to give different controls focus.

The parameter, *hInstance*, is required so that Windows knows which module to access when trying to find the dialog-box template. The last parameter, *szDlgTemplate*, identifies the name of the resource in the executable or dynamic-link library.

The function begins by locating the resource representing the dialog-box template, loading it into memory and getting the address to the beginning of the dialog-box template:

```
HRSRC hrsrcDialog;
HGLOBAL hGlblDlgTemplate;
LPDLGTEMPLATE lpDlgTemplate;
    .

    .

    .
hrsrcDialog = FindResource(hInstance, szDlgTemplate, RT_DIALOG);
```

```
if (hrsrcDialog == NULL) return(FALSE);
hGlblDlgTemplate = LoadResource(hInstance, hrsrcDialog);
lpDlgTemplate = (LPDLGTEMPLATE) LockResource(hGlblDlgTemplate);
if (lpDlgTemplate == NULL) return(FALSE);
```

The call to *FindResource* instructs Windows to look into the executable or DLL identified by the *hInstance* parameter and to find the resource whose name is specified in the second parameter. This parameter is usually a zero-terminated string or a number converted to a string with the *MAKEINTRESOURCE* macro. The third parameter identifies the type of resource that Windows should look for. In the line above, *FindResource* will locate a dialog box because *RT_DIALOG* is specified. The table below shows the list of possible resource types and their identifiers that may be passed to *FindResource*:

Resource type	Identifier (from WINDOWS.H)
Accelerator table	RT_ACCELERATOR
Bitmap	RT_BITMAP
Cursor	RT_CURSOR
Dialog-box template	RT_DIALOG
Font	RT_FONT
Font directory	RT_FONTDIR
Icon	RT_ICON
Menu	RT_MENU
User-defined data	RT_RCDATA
String table	RT_STRING

This function is a little strange because Microsoft states that *FindResource* must not be used to load icons, cursors, or strings. You must use the *LoadIcon, LoadCursor,* and *LoadString* functions instead. In addition, Microsoft recommends that the *LoadAccelerators, LoadBitmap*, and *LoadMenu* functions be used to load their associated resources instead of using *FindResource* followed by *LoadResource*. This pretty much just leaves us with calling *FindResource* only for dialog-box templates, fonts, font directories, and user-defined resources.

After we locate the dialog-box template and have its resource handle in the *hrsrcDialog* variable, we tell Windows to load the resource into memory by calling *LoadResource*. The first parameter again identifies the executable or DLL containing the resource, and the second parameter is the resource handle returned from *FindResource*. *LoadResource* doesn't actually load the resource into memory. Instead, it allocates a handle to a discarded global block of memory. When a call is later placed to *LockResource*, Windows sees that the block has been discarded, reallocates it so that it is large enough to hold the requested resource, loads the resource into the block, locks the block, and returns a pointer to the first byte. It is possible that insufficient memory will exist to reallocate the block to a larger size and; therefore, *LockResource* may fail and return NULL—check for this in your own applications.

After we have called *LockResource* in the *MergeControlsIntoDlg* function, the pointer returned is to the dialog-box template containing the controls that are to be merged. Of course, the memory block consists of the *DLGTEMPLATE*, *FONTINFO*, and multiple *DLGITEMTEMPLATE* structures that were presented in the preceding section, "Dynamic Dialog Boxes."

We must now get the number of controls that are in the template via:

```
bNumControls = lpDlgTemplate->dtItemCount;
```

and create each of the child controls by cycling through each *DLGITEMTEM-PLATE* structure.

For each control, we must first determine the class of the control. The control's class name is found starting at the first byte after the *dtilStyle* member of the *DLGITEMTEMPLATE* structure. Most of the controls in a dialog box are one of the system global window classes (EDIT, LISTBOX, BUTTON, and so on). To make dialog-box templates smaller in size, Microsoft devised a scheme where if the first byte of the class name in the template is greater than or equal to 0x80, the class is one of the system global classes. The next byte following the 0x8? is the first byte of the control's caption. This scheme saves space because all of the system global classes are represented by one byte rather than a zero-terminated string. The following table shows the values that were assigned to each system global class.

Class name	Value
BUTTON	0x80
EDIT	0x81
STATIC	0x82
LISTBOX	0x83
SCROLLBAR	0x84
COMBOBOX	0x85

When creating a child control from the template, we must first check to see if the first byte of the class name is one of the values listed above and if it is, determine the string name for the class and use that when calling *CreateWindowEx*.

Remember that the *dtilX*, *dtilY*, *dtilCX*, and *dtilCY* members in the *DLGITEMTEM-PLATE* structure contain the position of the child control in dialog-box units. These units must be converted to screen units before *CreateWindowEx* can be called:

```
SetRect(&rc, lpDlgItemTemplate->dtilX, lpDlgItemTemplate->dtilY,
    lpDlgItemTemplate->dtilX + lpDlgItemTemplate->dtilCX,
    lpDlgItemTemplate->dtilY + lpDlgItemTemplate->dtilCY);
MapDialogRect(hDlg, &rc);
```

After all of this preparation is complete, the control can be created:

```
hWndChild = CreateWindowEx(WS_EX_NOPARENTNOTIFY, (LPCSTR) lpszClass,
    (LPCSTR) lpszText, lpDlgItemTemplate->dtilStyle, rc.left, rc.top,
    rc.right - rc.left, rc.bottom - rc.top,
    hDlg, (HMENU) lpDlgItemTemplate->dtilID, hInstance,
    lpCreateParams + 1);
```

Notice that we have passed in the handle to the modal dialog box to be the parent of this child control.

If the control was created successfully, we must set its font to be the same as that of the modal dialog box, and we must position the control properly in the window z-order:

```
SetWindowFont(hWndChild, hFont, FALSE);

// Fix the z-order of the controls.
SetWindowPos(hWndChild, hWndPrevChild, 0, 0, 0, 0,
        SWP_NOMOVE | SWP_NOSIZE);
hWndPrevChild = hWndChild;
```

The *hFont* variable above was first obtained by calling *GetWindowFont* and passing in the handle to the modal dialog box. The z-order is corrected by calling *SetWindowPos* and passing in the handle to the previously created child window, *hWndPrevChild*. When *MergeControlIntoDlg* is first called, *hWndPrevChild* is initialized to be the handle of the *ChangeableArea* window. After the first child is positioned immediately after this window, *hWndPrevChild* is set to the handle of the window just repositioned so that future controls will be inserted in succession.

After all of the controls have been merged, the global block of memory containing the template is unlocked and freed:

```
UnlockResource(hGlblDlgTemplate);
FreeResource(hGlblDlgTemplate);
```

The *MergeControlsIntoDlg* function adds controls into the modal dialog box. However, we also need a function that removes the controls that are already in there. This is the job of the *DestroyControlsInChangeableArea* function:

```
void WINAPI DestroyControlsInChangeableArea (HWND hDlg,
    UINT uIChangeableArea) {
    // Destroy all controls inside the control identified
    // by the "uIDChangeableArea" parameter.
    EnumChildWindows(hDlg, (WNDENUMPROC) EnumChildProc,
            GetDlgItem(hDlg, uIDChangeableArea));
}
```

This function doesn't do much at all but call *EnumChildWindows* and pass it the window handle of the STATIC control identified by the *uIDChangeableArea* ID.

165

When it does this, the *EnumChildProc* function checks to see if each child window passed to it is within the area occupied by the STATIC control and destroys that window if it is:

```
static BOOL CALLBACK EnumChildProc (HWND hWnd, LPARAM lParam) {
    RECT rcChild, rcChangeable;

    if (hWnd == (HWND) lParam)
        return(TRUE);  // Don't destroy the ID_CHANGEABLE window.

    GetWindowRect(hWnd, &rcChild);
    GetWindowRect((HWND) lParam, &rcChangeable);

    if (IntersectRect(&rcChild, &rcChangeable, &rcChild) != 0) {
        // Rectangles intersect—destroy the window.
        DestroyWindow(hWnd);
    }
    return(TRUE);  // Continue the enumeration.}
```

The remainder of the DLG-MODE.C module demonstrates how to use the functions explained above. At the root of the implementation are the following data structures and an array, *_ModeInfo*, initialized to have three elements:

```
typedef BOOL (CALLBACK* xDLGPROC)(HWND, UINT, WPARAM, LPARAM);

struct {
    char *szModeName, *szDlgTemplate;
    xDLGPROC fpDlgProc;
    UINT uChangeAwayMsg;
} _ModeInfo[] = {
    { "Personal",      "MODE_PERSONAL", PersonalDlgProc, MS_CHANGEAWAY},
```

```
    { "Fish report",   "MODE_FISH",      FishDlgProc,      MS_CHANGEAWAY},
    { "Color options", "MODE_COLORS",    ColorDlgProc,     MS_CHANGEAWAY}
};
```

Each entry in the array identifies a mode that the user may select. For each mode, the data structure defines four members. The first member, *szModeName*, is the zero-terminated string that appears to the user in the Mode list box. The *szDlgTemplate* member identifies the name of the dialog template containing the controls that must be merged with the modal dialog box when the user selects the mode.

The *fpDlgProc* member contains the address of the pseudo–dialog-box procedure that processes messages when this mode is selected. Once the controls have been merged with the modal dialog box, any messages or notifications from them will enter the dialog-box procedure. This procedure is responsible for dispatching the message to the proper function to handle the message. I call the function a pseudo–dialog-box procedure because it looks exactly like a dialog-box procedure but it is not called directly by Windows. You'll also notice that I have defined my own data type, *xDLGPROC*. The reason for this is that the prototype for the *DLGPROC* type defined in WINDOWS.H does not include the parameters in the *typedef* unless you use the *STRICT* option when compiling. Because these parameters are important in the remainder of the code's implementation, I used my own type.

The final member, *uChangeAwayMsg*, is the unsigned integer representing the message that is passed to the pseudo–dialog-box procedure when the user is changing the mode away from the selected mode. This integer may be different for each of the pseudo–dialog-box procedures, but I have made them the same in this example. This message and its usage will be described later. For now, let's turn our attention to the procedure for the modal dialog box.

The dialog-box procedure for the modal dialog box is called *ModeSelDlgProc*. This procedure is responsible for managing the selection of modes by the user and dispatching messages to the proper pseudo–dialog-box procedure. When *ModeSelDlgProc* receives the *WM_INITDIALOG* message, it performs the following tasks:

1. It associates a window property with the dialog box. For reasons that we will see later, it is important that the dialog box know which mode is currently selected by the user. Initially, there is no mode selected and so the value of

the associated property is set to negative one:

```
SetProp(hDlg, szPreviousMode, (HANDLE) -1);    // No mode was previ-
                                               // ously selected.
```

When the dialog-box procedure receives the *WM_DESTROY* message, it removes the property:

```
case WM_DESTROY:
    RemoveProp(hDlg, szPreviousMode);
    break;
```

2. The template for the dialog box contains a STATIC window that defines the area where controls are to be destroyed and replaced by controls in other dialog-box templates. This is the *ChangeableArea* window. Since this window should not be visible to the user, it is hidden when the dialog box is created; it must not be destroyed because it is used elsewhere in the dialog-box procedure.
3. The "Mode" list box is filled with the zero-terminated strings from the *_Mode-Info* data structure described above.
4. The first mode in the *_ModeInfo* structure is set as the default mode by selecting it in the list box and forcing an *LBN_SELCHANGE* notification code to be sent to the dialog-box procedure:

```
ListBox_SetCurSel(hWndT, 0);    // Select first entry in _ModeInfo.
FORWARD_WM_COMMAND(hDlg, ID_MODE_LIST, hWndT, LBN_SELCHANGE,
    SendMessage);
```

It is the *LBN_SELCHANGE* notification that causes the dialog procedure to change away from one mode and switch to another mode. When this notification is received, the dialog-box procedure performs the following tasks:

1. It notifies the currently selected mode that the user is switching away from it. It does this by retrieving the previously selected mode (remember that the *LBN_SELCHANGE* notification entered the dialog-box procedure *after* the

user has selected a new mode), and calling the pseudo–dialog-box procedure for that mode, passing it the *MSG_CHANGEAWAY* message:

```
x = (UINT) GetProp(hDlg, szPreviousMode);
if (x != (UINT) -1) {
   // A mode was previously selected.
   (_ModeInfo[x].fpDlgProc)(hDlg, _ModeInfo[x].uChangeAwayMsg, 0, 0);
}
```

2. All of the controls that were merged from the previously selected mode must be destroyed. This is done by calling the *DestroyControlsInChangeableArea* function and passing it the handle to the modal dialog box and the ID of the STATIC control:

```
DestroyControlsInChangeableArea(hDlg, ID_MODE_CHANGEABLEAREA);
```

3. The newly selected mode is determined, the controls from that mode's dialog-box template are merged into the modal dialog box, and the new mode number is saved in the window's property:

```
x = ListBox_GetCurSel(LOWORD(lParam));
MergeControlsIntoDlg(hDlg, ID_MODE_CHANGEABLEAREA, _hInstance,
   _ModeInfo[x].szDlgTemplate);
SetProp(hDlg, szPreviousMode, (HANDLE) x);
```

4. Now that all of the controls for the mode have been merged, we force a *WM_INITDIALOG* message into the pseudo–dialog-box procedure so that it can do whatever initialization of controls needed:

```
(_ModeInfo[x].fpDlgProc)(hDlg, WM_INITDIALOG, 0, 0);
```

At the bottom of the *ModeSelDlgProc* function, we must pass on any message that was not processed to the pseudo–dialog-box function for the currently active mode. The following code fragment does this:

```
      .
      .
      .
if (!fProcessed) {
        x = (UINT) GetProp(hDlg, szPreviousMode);
        if (x != (UINT) -1)
                fProcessed = (_ModeInfo[x].fpDlgProc)(hDlg, uMsg,
                        wParam, lParam);
}
return(fProcessed);
}
```

That's it for the processing of the modal dialog box. The pseudo–dialog-box functions look almost exactly like a regular dialog-box procedure. The only differences are the following.

1. Pseudo–dialog-box procedures receive a *WM_INITDIALOG* message whenever the mode that they are associated with is selected by the user. During this message, the procedure should initialize any of the merged controls.
2. When the user selects a different mode, the pseudo–dialog-box procedure receives a *MS_CHANGEAWAY* message. During this message, the procedure should do any cleanup or saving of data in the controls so that they can be initialized with this data later if the user re-selects the mode.

Due to the way that this implementation has been laid out, it should be very easy to take code for existing dialog boxes in your own applications and convert them in an extremely short time to use the Mode-Selection method described here.

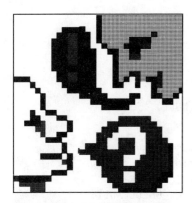

Figure 3-12. DLGTECH.ICO

Listing 3-1. DLGTECH.C application source module

```
/*******************************************************************
Module name: DLGTECH.C
Programmer : Jeffrey M. Richter.
*******************************************************************/

#include <windows.h>
#include "dlg-opts.h"
#include "dlg-mdls.h"
#include "dlg-dyna.h"

#include "dlgtech.h"

extern const HINSTANCE _cdecl _hInstance;

char _szAppName[] = "DlgTech";
static HWND _hDlgDynamic = NULL;
static HWND _hDlgModalLess = NULL;

ATOM NEAR RegisterAppWndClass (HINSTANCE hInstance);

LRESULT CALLBACK AppWndProc
      (HWND hWnd, UINT uMsg, WPARAM wParam, LPARAM lParam);
BOOL CALLBACK SWPDlgProc
      (HWND hDlg, UINT uMsg, WPARAM wParam, LPARAM lParam);
BOOL CALLBACK ModeSelDlgProc
      (HWND hDlg, UINT Msg, WPARAM wParam, LPARAM lParam);

#pragma argsused
```

```
int WinMain (HINSTANCE hInstance, HINSTANCE hPrevInstance,
                    LPSTR lpszCmdLine, int cmdShow) {
    MSG msg;
    HWND hWnd;

    if (hPrevInstance == NULL)
        if (RegisterAppWndClass(hInstance) == NULL)
            return(0);

    hWnd = CreateWindow(_szAppName, _szAppName, WS_OVERLAPPED |
        WS_VISIBLE | WS_CLIPCHILDREN | WS_CAPTION | WS_SYSMENU |
        WS_MINIMIZEBOX | WS_MAXIMIZEBOX | WS_THICKFRAME,
        CW_USEDEFAULT, SW_SHOW, CW_USEDEFAULT, CW_USEDEFAULT,
        NULL, NULL, hInstance, 0);

    if (hWnd == NULL) return(0);
    ShowWindow(hWnd, cmdShow);
    UpdateWindow(hWnd);

    while (GetMessage(&msg, NULL, 0, 0)) {
        if (!IsWindow(_hDlgDynamic) ||
            !IsDialogMessage(_hDlgDynamic, &msg)) {
            TranslateMessage(&msg);
            DispatchMessage(&msg);
        }
    }

    return(0);
}

ATOM NEAR RegisterAppWndClass (HINSTANCE hInstance) {
    WNDCLASS WndClass;

    WndClass.style          = 0;
    WndClass.lpfnWndProc    = AppWndProc;
    WndClass.cbClsExtra     = 0;
    WndClass.cbWndExtra     = 0;
    WndClass.hInstance      = hInstance;
    WndClass.hIcon          = LoadIcon(hInstance, _szAppName);
    WndClass.hCursor        = LoadCursor(NULL, IDC_ARROW);
    WndClass.hbrBackground  = COLOR_WINDOW + 1;
    WndClass.lpszMenuName   = _szAppName;
    WndClass.lpszClassName  = _szAppName;
    return(RegisterClass(&WndClass));
}
```

```
// ******************************************************************
// This function processes all messages sent to the main window.

LRESULT CALLBACK AppWndProc (HWND hWnd, UINT uMsg, WPARAM wParam,
      LPARAM lParam) {
   BOOL fCallDefProc = FALSE;
   LRESULT lResult = 0;
   HGLOBAL hGlbl;
   int nResult;
   char szBuf[100], szName[50];

   switch (uMsg) {
      case WM_CREATE:
         _hDlgModalLess =
            CreateModalLessDlgBox(_hInstance, "ModalLess", hWnd,
               (DLGPROC) ModalLessDlgProc, 0);
         if (_hDlgModalLess == NULL) {
            MessageBox(hWnd, "Can't create modalless dialog box.",
               _szAppName, MB_OK);
            EnableMenuItem(GetMenu(hWnd), IDM_MODALLESSDEMO,
               MF_BYCOMMAND | MF_GRAYED);
         }
         break;

      case WM_CLOSE:
         if (_hDlgModalLess)
            DestroyModalLessDlgBox(_hDlgModalLess);
         fCallDefProc = TRUE;
         break;

      case WM_DESTROY:
         PostQuitMessage(0);
         break;

      case WM_COMMAND:
         switch (wParam) {

         case IDM_OPTIONSDEMO:
            DialogBox(_hInstance, "Options", hWnd,
               (DLGPROC) OptionsDlgProc);
            break;

         case IDM_DYNAMICMODALDEMO:
            hGlbl = BuildDynamicDlgBox(FALSE);
            if (hGlbl == NULL) {
               MessageBox(hWnd, "Insufficient memory.",
                  _szAppName, MB_OK);
```

```
            break;
        }
        DialogBoxIndirect(_hInstance, hGlbl, hWnd,
            (DLGPROC) DynamicDlgProc);
        GlobalFree(hGlbl);
        break;

    case IDM_DYNAMICMODELESSDEMO:
        if (_hDlgDynamic != NULL) {
            DestroyWindow(_hDlgDynamic);
            _hDlgDynamic = NULL;
            CheckMenuItem(GetMenu(hWnd), wParam,
                MF_BYCOMMAND | MF_UNCHECKED);
            break;
        }

        hGlbl = BuildDynamicDlgBox(TRUE);
        if (hGlbl == NULL) {
            MessageBox(hWnd, "Insufficient memory.",
                _szAppName, MB_OK);
            break;
        }

        _hDlgDynamic = CreateDialogIndirect(_hInstance,
            GlobalLock(hGlbl), hWnd, (DLGPROC) DynamicDlgProc);

        GlobalUnlock(hGlbl);
        GlobalFree(hGlbl);
        CheckMenuItem(GetMenu(hWnd), wParam,
            MF_BYCOMMAND | MF_CHECKED);
        break;

    case IDM_MODALLESSDEMO:
        nResult = ModalLessDlgBox(_hDlgModalLess, hWnd, 0);
        GetDlgItemText(_hDlgModalLess, ID_NAME, szName,
            sizeof(szName));
        wsprintf(szBuf, "Button: %s, Name: %s",
            (nResult == IDOK) ? (LPSTR) "Ok"
            : (LPSTR) "Cancel", (LPSTR) szName);
        MessageBox(hWnd, szBuf, _szAppName, MB_OK);
        break;

    case IDM_SETWINDOWPOSDEMO:
        DialogBox(_hInstance, "SetWindowPos", hWnd,
            (DLGPROC) SWPDlgProc);
        break;
    case IDM_MODESELECTDEMO:
```

```
      DialogBox(_hInstance, "MODE_SELECT", hWnd,
         (DLGPROC) ModeSelDlgProc);
      break;

   default:
      // Any options that we do not process should be
      // passed to DefWindowProc.
      fCallDefProc = TRUE;
      break;
   }

   break;

default:
   fCallDefProc = TRUE; break;
}

if (fCallDefProc)
   lResult = DefWindowProc(hWnd, uMsg, wParam, lParam);

return(lResult);
}


//*****************************************************************
// Functions for the SetWindowPos Dialog-Box Demonstration.

BOOL CALLBACK SWPDlgProc (HWND hDlg, UINT uMsg, WPARAM wParam,
      LPARAM lParam) {
   BOOL fProcessed = TRUE;
   HWND hWndControl;
   RECT rc;

   switch (uMsg) {
      case WM_INITDIALOG:
         break;

      case WM_COMMAND:
         switch (wParam) {
            case IDOK:
            case IDCANCEL:
               if (HIWORD(lParam) == BN_CLICKED)
                  EndDialog(hDlg, wParam);
               break;

            case ID_CHANGETABORDER:
               if (HIWORD(lParam) != BN_CLICKED)
                  break;
```

```
// Order is "&Name:", "EDIT", "Over &25".
// Move "Over &25" after "&Name:" field.
SetWindowPos(GetDlgItem(hDlg, ID_OVER25),
    GetDlgItem(hDlg, ID_NAMETEXT),
    0, 0, 0, 0, SWP_NOMOVE | SWP_NOSIZE);

// Order is "&Name:", "Over &25", "EDIT".
// Move "&Name:" after "Over &25" field.
SetWindowPos(GetDlgItem(hDlg, ID_NAMETEXT),
    GetDlgItem(hDlg, ID_OVER25),
    0, 0, 0, 0, SWP_NOMOVE | SWP_NOSIZE);

// Order is "Over &25", "&Name:", EDIT.

// Set the focus to the control after this button.
SetFocus(
    GetNextDlgTabItem(hDlg, LOWORD(lParam), 0));

EnableWindow(LOWORD(lParam), FALSE);
break;

case ID_ADDCONTROL:
    if (HIWORD(lParam) != BN_CLICKED)
        break;

    // Position control at (64, 36), w = 64, h = 12.
    SetRect(&rc, 64, 36, 64 + 64, 36 + 12);

    // Convert from dialog-box units to screen units.
    MapDialogRect(hDlg, &rc);

    hWndControl = CreateWindow("scrollbar", "",
        SBS_HORZ | WS_CHILD | WS_TABSTOP | WS_GROUP,
        rc.left, rc.top,
        rc.right - rc.left, rc.bottom - rc.top,
        hDlg, ID_SCROLLBAR, _hInstance, 0);

    SetWindowPos(hWndControl, LOWORD(lParam), 0, 0,
        0, 0, SWP_NOMOVE | SWP_NOSIZE | SWP_SHOWWINDOW);

    // Set the focus to the control after this button.
    SetFocus(
        GetNextDlgTabItem(hDlg, LOWORD(lParam), 0));
    EnableWindow(LOWORD(lParam), FALSE);
    break;
```

```
            default:
                break;
        }
        break;

    default:
        fProcessed = FALSE; break;
    }
  return(fProcessed);
}
```

Listing 3-2. DLGTECH.H application header module

```c
/********************************************************************
Module name: DLGTECH.H
Programmer : Jeffrey M. Richter.
********************************************************************/

#define IDM_SETWINDOWPOSDEMO          (100)
#define IDM_OPTIONSDEMO               (101)
#define IDM_MODALLESSDEMO             (102)
#define IDM_DYNAMICMODALDEMO          (103)
#define IDM_DYNAMICMODELESSDEMO       (104)
#define IDM_MODESELECTDEMO            (105)

#ifdef _DEMO
#define ID_ADDCONTROL        100
#define ID_CARITY            101
#define ID_CHANGETABORDER    102
#define ID_CHECKBOX          103
#define ID_CITY              104
#define ID_DEFAULTBOX        105
#define ID_DIVORCED          106
#define ID_EDITBOX           107
#define ID_FEMALE            108
#define ID_LISTBOX           109
#define ID_MALE              110
#define ID_NAME              111
#define ID_NAMFTEXT          112
#define ID_OPTIONS           113
#define ID_OVER25            114
#define ID_PHONE             115
#define ID_QUEST             116
#define ID_RADIO1            117
#define ID_RADIO2            118
```

```
#define ID_SCROLLBAR          119
#define ID_SMOKES             120
#define ID_STATE              121
#define ID_STREET             122
#define ID_XBUTTON            123
#define ID_ZIP                124

// IDs for the Mode-Select Technique.
#define ID_MODE_LIST                  200
#define ID_MODE_CHANGEABLEAREA        201
#define ID_MODE_PERSONAL_NAME         202
#define ID_MODE_PERSONAL_ADDR         203
#define ID_MODE_PERSONAL_CITY         204
#define ID_MODE_PERSONAL_STATE        205
#define ID_MODE_PERSONAL_ZIP          206
#define ID_MODE_FISH_FRESH            207
#define ID_MODE_FISH_SALT             208
#define ID_MODE_FISH_LIST             209
#define ID_MODE_COLORS_RED            210
#define ID_MODE_COLORS_GREEN          211
#define ID_MODE_COLORS_BLUE           212
#define ID_MODE_COLORS_INVERT         213
#endif
```

Listing 3-3. DLG-OPTS.C Options dialog-box source module

```
/******************************************************************
Module name: DLG-OPTS.C
Programmer : Jeffrey M. Richter.
******************************************************************/

#include <windows.h>
#include <windowsx.h>
#include <stdlib.h>
#include "dlgtech.h"
#include "dlg-opts.h"

extern const HINSTANCE _cdecl _hInstance;

// Turns a style ON for a window.
#define SetStyleOn(hWnd, Style) \
   SetWindowLong(hWnd, GWL_STYLE, \
      Style | GetWindowLong(hWnd, GWL_STYLE));

// Turns a style OFF for a window.
```

```
#define SetStyleOff(hWnd, Style) \
    SetWindowLong(hWnd, GWL_STYLE, \
        ~Style & GetWindowLong(hWnd, GWL_STYLE));

void WINAPI ShowArea (BOOL fShowDefAreaOnly, HWND hDlg,
        HWND hWndDefArea) {
    RECT rcDlg, rcDefArea;
    char szDlgDims[25];
    HWND hWndChild;
    RECT rc;

    // Save original width and height of dialog box.
    GetWindowRect(hDlg, &rcDlg);

    // Retrieve coordinates for default area window.
    GetWindowRect(hWndDefArea, &rcDefArea);

    hWndChild = GetFirstChild(hDlg);

    for (; hWndChild != NULL;
        hWndChild = GetNextSibling(hWndChild)) {

        // Calculate rectangle occupied by child window in
        // screen coordinates.
        GetWindowRect(hWndChild, &rc);

        // Enable/Disable child if its:
        // right  edge is >= the right  edge of hWndDefArea.
        // bottom edge is >= the bottom edge of hWndDefArea.
        if ((rc.right  >= rcDefArea.right) ||
            (rc.bottom >= rcDefArea.bottom))
            EnableWindow(hWndChild, !fShowDefAreaOnly);
    }

    if (fShowDefAreaOnly) {
        wsprintf(szDlgDims, "%05u %05u",
            rcDlg.right - rcDlg.left, rcDlg.bottom - rcDlg.top);

        SetStyleOff(hWndDefArea, SS_BLACKRECT);
        SetStyleOn(hWndDefArea, SS_LEFT);
        SetWindowText(hWndDefArea, szDlgDims);
        // Resize dialog box to fit only default area.
        SetWindowPos(hDlg, NULL, 0, 0,
            rcDefArea.right - rcDlg.left,
            rcDefArea.bottom - rcDlg.top,
            SWP_NOZORDER | SWP_NOMOVE);
```

```
        // Make sure that the Default area box is hidden.
        ShowWindow(hWndDefArea, SW_HIDE);

    } else {
        GetWindowText(hWndDefArea, szDlgDims, sizeof(szDlgDims));

        // Restore dialog box to its original size.
        SetWindowPos(hDlg, NULL, 0, 0,
            atoi(szDlgDims), atoi(szDlgDims + 6),
            SWP_NOZORDER | SWP_NOMOVE);
    }
}

#ifdef _DEMO

//******************************************************************
// Functions for the ModalLess Dialog-Box Demonstration.

BOOL CALLBACK OptionsDlgProc (HWND hDlg, UINT uMsg,
    WPARAM wParam, LPARAM lParam) {
    BOOL fProcessed = TRUE;

    switch (uMsg) {

        case WM_INITDIALOG:
            // During initialization, before any windows are shown,
            // resize the dialog box so that only the "default"
            // portion is shown.
            ShowArea(TRUE, hDlg, GetDlgItem(hDlg, ID_DEFAULTBOX));
            break;

        case WM_COMMAND:
            switch (wParam) {

                case IDOK:
                case IDCANCEL:
                    // Terminate dialog box if user selects the "OK" or
                    // "Cancel" button.
                    EndDialog(hDlg, wParam);
                    break;

                case ID_OPTIONS:
                    if (HIWORD(lParam) != BN_CLICKED)
                        break;

                    // User selected "Options >>" button, show entire
                    // dialog box.
```

```
            ShowArea(FALSE, hDlg,
                GetDlgItem(hDlg, ID_DEFAULTBOX));

            // The ShowArea(FALSE, ...) function enables all
            // windows outside the "default" area.  Any windows
            // that should be disabled, must be made explicitly
            // disabled here.  Note, the status of the windows
            // within the "default" area is NOT changed.

            // Set the focus to the desired control.
            SetFocus(
                GetNextDlgTabItem(hDlg, LOWORD(lParam), 0));

            // Disable "Options>>" button.
            EnableWindow(LOWORD(lParam), FALSE);
            break;
         default:
            fProcessed = FALSE;
            break;
      }
      break;

   default:
      fProcessed = FALSE;
      break;
   }
   return(fProcessed);
}
#endif
```

Listing 3-4. DLG-OPTS.H Options dialog-box header module

```
/*****************************************************************
Module name: DLG-OPTS.H
Programmer : Jeffrey M. Richter.
*****************************************************************/

void WINAPI ShowArea (BOOL fShowDefAreaOnly, HWND hDlg,
     HWND hWndDefArea);

#ifdef _DEMO
//***************************************************************
// Functions for the "Options >>" Dialog-Box Demonstration.
```

```
BOOL CALLBACK OptionsDlgProc (HWND hDlg, UINT uMsg, WPARAM wParam,
     LPARAM lParam);
#endif
```

Listing 3-5. DLG-MDLS.C modalless dialog-box source module

```
/********************************************************************
Module name: DLG-MDLS.C
Programmer : Jeffrey M. Richter.
********************************************************************/

#include <windows.h>
#include "dlgtech.h"
#include "dlg-mdls.h"

extern const HINSTANCE _cdecl _hInstance;

static char _szModalLessResult[] = "ModalLessResult";


HWND WINAPI CreateModalLessDlgBox (HINSTANCE hInstance,
   LPCSTR szTemplateName, HWND hWndParent, DLGPROC DialogFunc,
   LPARAM lParamInit) {

   return(CreateDialogParam(hInstance, szTemplateName,
      hWndParent, DialogFunc, lParamInit));
}

BOOL WINAPI DestroyModalLessDlgBox (HWND hDlg) {
   return(DestroyWindow(hDlg));
}

int WINAPI ModalLessDlgBox (HWND hDlg, HWND hWndParent,
     LPARAM lParam) {
   BOOL fPropFound = FALSE;
   int nResult = NULL;
   UINT uModalLessShowMsg;
   MSG msg;
   EnableWindow(hWndParent, FALSE);

   // Register and send the "ModalLessShowMsg" msg to the
   // modalLess dialog box.
   uModalLessShowMsg = RegisterWindowMessage(SZMODALLESSSHOWMSG);
   SendMessage(hDlg, uModalLessShowMsg, 0, lParam);
```

```
// Display the modalless dialog box.
ShowWindow(hDlg, SW_SHOW);

// Continue the message loop until the "ModalLessResult"
// property has been associated with the modalless dialog box.
// This happens when the dialog-box function calls the
// EndModalLessDlgBox function.

while (!fPropFound) {
    GetMessage(&msg, NULL, 0, 0);
    if (!IsDialogMessage(hDlg, &msg)) {
        TranslateMessage(&msg);
        DispatchMessage(&msg);
    }

    // Get value of "ModalLessResult" property.  If property
    // does not exist, GetProp returns zero.
    nResult = GetProp(hDlg, _szModalLessResult);

    // Try to remove the property.  If RemoveProp returns NULL,
    // the property was never associated with the window and the
    // message loop must continue.
    fPropFound = RemoveProp(hDlg, _szModalLessResult) != NULL;
}

EnableWindow(hWndParent, TRUE);
// Hide the modalless dialog box and return the result to the
// application.
ShowWindow(hDlg, SW_HIDE);
return(nResult);
}

BOOL WINAPI EndModalLessDlgBox (HWND hDlg, int nResult) {
    return(SetProp(hDlg, _szModalLessResult, nResult));
}

#ifdef _DEMO
//*****************************************************************
// Functions for the ModalLess Dialog-Box Demonstration.

BOOL CALLBACK ModalLessDlgProc (HWND hDlg, UINT uMsg,
        WPARAM wParam, LPARAM lParam) {
    BOOL fProcessed = TRUE;

    if (uMsg == RegisterWindowMessage(SZMODALLESSSHOWMSG)) {
        // lParam is the data value passed to ModalLessDlgBox
```

```
        // function.  Initialize the EDIT control with some text
        // whenever the dialog box is about to be shown.
        SetDlgItemText(hDlg, ID_NAME, "Default text");

        // Make the EDIT window have the focus.
        SetFocus(GetDlgItem(hDlg, ID_NAME));
    }

    switch (uMsg) {
        case WM_INITDIALOG:
            break;
        case WM_COMMAND:
            switch (wParam) {
                case IDOK:
                case IDCANCEL:
                    if (HIWORD(lParam) == BN_CLICKED)
                        EndModalLessDlgBox(hDlg, wParam);
                    break;

                default:
                    break;
            }
            break;

        default:
            fProcessed = FALSE;
            break;
    }
    return(fProcessed);
}
#endif
```

Listing 3-6. DLG-MDLS.H modalless dialog-box header module

```
/******************************************************************
Module name: DLG-MDLS.H
Programmer : Jeffrey M. Richter.
******************************************************************/

#define SZMODALLESSSHOWMSG     "ModalLessShowMsg"

HWND WINAPI CreateModalLessDlgBox (HINSTANCE hInstance,
     LPCSTR szTemplateName, HWND hWndParent, DLGPROC DialogFunc,
     LPARAM lParamInit);
```

```
BOOL WINAPI DestroyModalLessDlgBox (HWND hDlg);

int  WINAPI ModalLessDlgBox (HWND hDlg, HWND hWndParent,
      LPARAM lParam);

BOOL WINAPI EndModalLessDlgBox (HWND hDlg, int nResult);

#ifdef _DEMO
//****************************************************************
// Functions for the ModalLess Dialog-Box Demonstration.

BOOL CALLBACK ModalLessDlgProc (HWND hDlg, UINT uMsg,
      WPARAM wParam, LPARAM lParam);
#endif
```

Listing 3-7. DLG-DYNA.C dynamic dialog-box source module

```
/****************************************************************
Module name: DLG-DYNA.C
Programmer : Jeffrey M. Richter.
****************************************************************/

#include <windows.h>
#include <memory.h>

#include "dlgtech.h"
#include "dlg-dyna.h"

extern const HINSTANCE _cdecl _hInstance;

typedef struct {
   long dtStyle;
   BYTE dtItemCount;
   int  dtX;
   int  dtY;
   int  dtCX;
   int  dtCY;
// char dtMenuName[];      // Variable-length string.
// char dtClassName[];     // Variable-length string.
// char dtCaptionText[];   // Variable-length string.
} DLGTEMPLATE, FAR *LPDLGTEMPLATE;

typedef struct {
   short int PointSize;
// char  szTypeFace[];     // Variable-length string.
```

```
} FONTINFO, FAR *LPFONTINFO;

typedef struct {
    int  dtilX;
    int  dtilY;
    int  dtilCX;
    int  dtilCY;
    int  dtilID;
    long dtilStyle;
// char dtilClass[];        // Variable-length string.
// char dtilText[];         // Variable-length string.
// BYTE dtilInfo;           // # bytes in following memory block.
// BYTE dtilData;           // Variable-length memory block.
} DLGITEMTEMPLATE, FAR *LPDLGITEMTEMPLATE;

HGLOBAL WINAPI CreateDlgTemplate(
    LONG dtStyle,
    int dtX, int dtY,        // In dialog-box units.
    int dtCX, int dtCY,      // In dialog-box units.
    LPSTR dtMenuName,        // "" if no menu.
    LPSTR dtClassName,       // "" if standard dialog-box class.
    LPSTR dtCaptionText,
    short int PointSize,     // Only used if DS_SETFONT specified.
    LPSTR szTypeFace) {      // Only used if DS_SETFONT specified.
    HGLOBAL hGlbl;
    WORD wBlockLen, FAR *wNumBytes;
    WORD wMenuNameLen, wClassNameLen,
        wCaptionTextLen, wTypeFaceLen;
    LPSTR szDlgTemplate, szDlgTypeFace;
    LPDLGTEMPLATE lpDlgTemplate;
    LPFONTINFO lpFontInfo;

    // Calculate number of bytes required by following fields:
    wMenuNameLen    = 1 + lstrlen(dtMenuName);
    wClassNameLen   = 1 + lstrlen(dtClassName);
    wCaptionTextLen = 1 + lstrlen(dtCaptionText);

    // Block must be large enough to contain the following:
    wBlockLen =
        sizeof(WORD) +          // Stores # of bytes used in block.
        sizeof(DLGTEMPLATE) +   // # bytes: fixed part DLGTEMPLATE.
        wMenuNameLen +          // # bytes: menu name.
        wClassNameLen +         // # bytes: dialog-class name.
        wCaptionTextLen;        // # bytes: dialog-box caption.

    if (dtStyle & DS_SETFONT) {
        // Dialog box uses font other than System font.
```

```
    // Calculate # of bytes required for typeface name.
    wTypeFaceLen = 1 + lstrlen(szTypeFace);

    // Block must be large enough to include font information.
    wBlockLen +=
        sizeof(short int) +  // # bytes for font's point size.
        wTypeFaceLen;         // # bytes for font typeface name.

} else {
    // Dialog box uses the System font.
    wTypeFaceLen = 0;

    // Block length does not change.
}

// Allocate global block of memory for Dialog template.
hGlbl = GlobalAlloc(GMEM_MOVEABLE | GMEM_ZEROINIT, wBlockLen);
if (hGlbl == NULL) return(hGlbl);

// wNumBytes points to beginning of memory block.
wNumBytes = (WORD FAR *) GlobalLock(hGlbl);

// Store in first two bytes the # of bytes used in the block.
*wNumBytes = (WORD) wBlockLen;

// lpDlgTemplate points to start of DLGTEMPLATE in block.
lpDlgTemplate = (LPDLGTEMPLATE) (wNumBytes + 1);

// Set the members of the DLGTEMPLATE structure.
lpDlgTemplate->dtStyle = dtStyle;
lpDlgTemplate->dtItemCount = 0;  // Incremented with calls
                                 // to AddDlgControl.
lpDlgTemplate->dtX = dtX;
lpDlgTemplate->dtY = dtY;
lpDlgTemplate->dtCX = dtCX;
lpDlgTemplate->dtCY = dtCY;

// szDlgTemplate points to start of variable
// part of DLGTEMPLATE.
szDlgTemplate = (LPSTR) (lpDlgTemplate + 1);

// Append the menu name, class name, and caption text to block.
_fmemcpy(szDlgTemplate, dtMenuName, wMenuNameLen);
szDlgTemplate += wMenuNameLen;
_fmemcpy(szDlgTemplate, dtClassName, wClassNameLen);
szDlgTemplate += wClassNameLen;
_fmemcpy(szDlgTemplate, dtCaptionText, wCaptionTextLen);
```

```
    szDlgTemplate += wCaptionTextLen;

    if (dtStyle & DS_SETFONT) {
        // Dialog box uses font other that System font.

        // lpFontInfo points to start of FONTINFO structure.
        lpFontInfo = (LPFONTINFO) szDlgTemplate;

        // Set the members of the FONTINFO structure.
        lpFontInfo->PointSize = PointSize;

        // szTypeFace points to start of variable part of FONTINFO.
        szDlgTypeFace = (LPSTR) (lpFontInfo + 1);

        // Append the typeface name to the block.
        _fmemcpy(szDlgTypeFace, szTypeFace, wTypeFaceLen);
    }

    GlobalUnlock(hGlbl);
    return(hGlbl);
}

// LOWORD = Success(TRUE)/Failure(FALSE), HIWORD=New hGlbl.
DWORD WINAPI AddDlgControl (
    HGLOBAL hGlbl,          // Handle from CreateDlgTemplate
                            // or AddDlgControl.
    int dtilX, int dtilY,   // In dialog-box units.
    int dtilCX, int dtilCY, // In dialog-box units.
    int dtilID,
    long dtilStyle,         // WS_CHILD is automatically added.
    LPSTR dtilClass,        // May be: "BUTTON", "EDIT", "STATIC",
                            // "LISTBOX", "SCROLLBAR",
                            // "COMBOBOX".
    LPSTR dtilText,
    BYTE dtilInfo,          // Number of additional data bytes.
    LPBYTE dtilData) {      // Value passed through lpCreateParams
                            // of CREATESTRUCT.

    HGLOBAL hGlblNew;
    WORD wBlockLen, wClassLen, wTextLen, FAR *wNumBytes;
    LPDLGTEMPLATE lpDlgTemplate;
    LPDLGITEMTEMPLATE lpDlgItemTemplate;
    LPSTR szDlgItemTemplate;

    // Calculate number of bytes required by following fields:
    wClassLen = 1 + lstrlen(dtilClass);
    wTextLen  = 1 + lstrlen(dtilText);
```

```
// Block must be increased by to contain the following:
wBlockLen =
    sizeof(DLGITEMTEMPLATE) +  // # bytes for fixed part
                               // of DLGITEMTEMPLATE.
    wClassLen +                // # bytes for control class.
    wTextLen +                 // # bytes for control text.
    sizeof(BYTE) +             // One byte  for # of dtilInfo
                               // bytes (below).
    dtilInfo;                  // # bytes for extra data.

// Guarantee that all controls have WS_CHILD style.
dtilStyle |= WS_CHILD;

// Get number of bytes currently in the memory block.
wBlockLen += * (WORD FAR *) GlobalLock(hGlbl);
GlobalUnlock(hGlbl);

// Increase size of memory block to include new dialog item.
hGlblNew = GlobalReAlloc(hGlbl, wBlockLen,
                GMEM_MOVEABLE | GMEM_ZEROINIT);
if (hGlblNew == NULL)
    return(MAKELONG(FALSE, hGlbl));

// wNumBytes points to beginning of memory block.
wNumBytes = (WORD FAR *) GlobalLock(hGlblNew);

// lpDlgTemplate points to start of DLGTEMPLATE in block.
lpDlgTemplate = (LPDLGTEMPLATE) (wNumBytes + 1);

// Increment the number of controls in the template.
lpDlgTemplate->dtItemCount++;

// lpDlgItemTemplate points to start of new DLGITEMTEMPLATE.
// This is at the end of the memory block.
lpDlgItemTemplate = (LPDLGITEMTEMPLATE)
                    (((LPSTR) wNumBytes) + *wNumBytes);

// Set the members of the DLGITEMTEMPLATE structure.
lpDlgItemTemplate->dtilX = dtilX;
lpDlgItemTemplate->dtilY = dtilY;
lpDlgItemTemplate->dtilCX = dtilCX;
lpDlgItemTemplate->dtilCY = dtilCY;
lpDlgItemTemplate->dtilID = dtilID;
lpDlgItemTemplate->dtilStyle = dtilStyle;
// szDlgTemplate points to start of variable part
// of DLGITEMTEMPLATE.
szDlgItemTemplate = (LPSTR) (lpDlgItemTemplate + 1);
```

```
    // Append the control's class name, text to the block.
    _fmemcpy(szDlgItemTemplate, dtilClass, wClassLen);
    szDlgItemTemplate += wClassLen;
    _fmemcpy(szDlgItemTemplate, dtilText, wTextLen);
    szDlgItemTemplate += wTextLen;

    // Append the control's dtilInfo member.
    *szDlgItemTemplate = dtilInfo;
    szDlgItemTemplate += sizeof(BYTE);

    // Append the control's dtilData member.
    _fmemcpy(szDlgItemTemplate, dtilData, dtilInfo);
    szDlgItemTemplate += dtilInfo;

    // Store in the first two bytes the # of bytes used in block.
    *wNumBytes = (WORD) (szDlgItemTemplate - (LPSTR) wNumBytes);

    GlobalUnlock(hGlblNew);
    return(MAKELONG(TRUE, hGlblNew));
}

void WINAPI DoneAddingControls (HGLOBAL hGlbl) {
    WORD FAR *wNumBytes;

    // wNumBytes points to beginning of memory block.
    wNumBytes = (WORD FAR *) GlobalLock(hGlbl);

    // Move all of the bytes in the block down two bytes.
    _fmemcpy(wNumBytes, wNumBytes + 1, *wNumBytes - 2);
    GlobalUnlock(hGlbl);
    // Once this function is executed, no more items can be
    // added to the dialog-box template.
}

#ifdef _DEMO

//********************************************************************
// Functions for the Dynamic Modal and Modeless Dialog-Box demos.
#define MAXDLGITEMDATA  (10)

struct {
    int x, y, cx, cy, id;
    long Style;
    LPSTR szClass, szText;
    BYTE Info;
    BYTE Data[MAXDLGITEMDATA];
```

```
} DynamicDlgBoxData[] = {

    { 4, 4, 32, 12, -1, SS_LEFT, "STATIC", "&Edit box:",
      0, { 0 } },

    { 40,  4, 64, 12, ID_EDITBOX,
      ES_LEFT | WS_BORDER | WS_TABSTOP | WS_GROUP, "EDIT", "",
      0, { 0 } },

    { 4, 18, 40,  8, -1, SS_LEFT, "STATIC", "&Listbox:",
      0, { 0 } },

    { 4, 28, 76, 41, ID_LISTBOX, LBS_NOTIFY | LBS_SORT |
      LBS_STANDARD | WS_BORDER | WS_VSCROLL | WS_TABSTOP |
      WS_GROUP, "LISTBOX", "", 0, { 0 } },

    { 132,  4, 36, 12, IDOK, BS_DEFPUSHBUTTON | WS_TABSTOP |
      WS_GROUP, "BUTTON", "&Ok", 0, { 0 } },

    { 176,  4, 36, 12, IDCANCEL, BS_PUSHBUTTON | WS_TABSTOP |
      WS_GROUP, "BUTTON", "&Cancel", 0, { 0 } },

    { 88, 24, 56, 44, -1, BS_GROUPBOX | WS_GROUP, "BUTTON",
      "Group box", 0, { 0 } },

    { 92, 36, 48, 12, ID_RADIO1, BS_RADIOBUTTON | WS_TABSTOP,
      "BUTTON", "Radio &1", 0, { 0 } },

    { 92, 48, 48, 12, ID_RADIO2, BS_RADIOBUTTON | WS_TABSTOP,
      "BUTTON", "Radio &2", 0, { 0 } },

    { 152, 32, 60, 12, ID_CHECKBOX, BS_CHECKBOX | WS_TABSTOP |
      WS_GROUP, "BUTTON", "C&heck box", 0, { 0 } },

    { 0, 0, 0, 0, 0, 0, NULL, NULL, 0, { 0 } }
};

BOOL CALLBACK DynamicDlgProc (HWND hDlg, UINT uMsg,
      WPARAM wParam, LPARAM lParam) {
    BOOL fProcessed = TRUE;
    switch (uMsg) {

        case WM_INITDIALOG:
            break;
        case WM_COMMAND:
            switch (wParam) {
                case IDOK:
```

```
            case IDCANCEL:
                // Although the two push buttons for IDOK and
                // IDCANCEL are not included in the modeless
                // version of this dialog box, these options can
                // still come through to here if the user
                // presses the "Enter" or "Esc" keys respectively.

                // In the case of a modeless dialog box, we cannot
                // call the EndDialog() function.  We can determine
                // if this window is the modeless one because it
                // does not have the IDOK button within it.  In
                // this case, GetDlgItem() below returns NULL.
                if (GetDlgItem(hDlg, IDOK) == NULL)
                    break;

                if (HIWORD(lParam) == BN_CLICKED)
                    EndDialog(hDlg, wParam);
                break;

            default:
                break;
        }
        break;

    default:
        fProcessed = FALSE; break;
    }
    return(fProcessed);
}

HGLOBAL WINAPI BuildDynamicDlgBox (BOOL fModeless) {
    HGLOBAL hGlbl;
    WORD x;
    DWORD dwAddDlgControlResult;

    // Create the dynamic dialog-box header information.
    if (fModeless)
        hGlbl = CreateDlgTemplate(
            WS_BORDER | WS_CAPTION | WS_DLGFRAME | WS_SYSMENU |
            WS_VISIBLE | WS_POPUP | DS_SETFONT, 6, 25, 216, 72,
            "", "", "Dynamic Modeless Demo", 8, "Helv");
    else
        hGlbl = CreateDlgTemplate(
            WS_BORDER | WS_CAPTION | WS_DLGFRAME |
            WS_SYSMENU | WS_VISIBLE | WS_POPUP,
            6, 25, 216, 72, "", "", "Dynamic Modal Demo", 0, "");
```

```
    if (hGlbl == NULL)
        return(hGlbl);

    // Add each of the controls in the DynamicDlgBoxData array.
    for (x = 0; DynamicDlgBoxData[x].szClass != NULL; x++) {

        // Do not add the "OK" and "Cancel" buttons if a modeless
        // dialog box is being created.
        if (fModeless) {
            if (DynamicDlgBoxData[x].id == IDOK ||
                DynamicDlgBoxData[x].id == IDCANCEL)
                continue;
        }

        dwAddDlgControlResult = AddDlgControl(hGlbl,
            DynamicDlgBoxData[x].x,        DynamicDlgBoxData[x].y,
            DynamicDlgBoxData[x].cx,       DynamicDlgBoxData[x].cy,
            DynamicDlgBoxData[x].id,
            DynamicDlgBoxData[x].Style | WS_VISIBLE,
            DynamicDlgBoxData[x].szClass,
            DynamicDlgBoxData[x].szText,
            DynamicDlgBoxData[x].Info,
            DynamicDlgBoxData[x].Data);

        // LOWORD is FALSE if insufficient memory exists.
        if (LOWORD(dwAddDlgControlResult) == FALSE) break;

        // HIWORD is handle to new block of memory.
        hGlbl = HIWORD(dwAddDlgControlResult);
    }

    // LOWORD is FALSE if insufficient memory exists; free what
    // we have and return NULL to caller.
    if (LOWORD(dwAddDlgControlResult) == FALSE) {
        GlobalFree(hGlbl);
        hGlbl = NULL;
    } else {
        // Cleanup the dialog-box information.
        DoneAddingControls(hGlbl);
    }

    // Return the handle to the dynamic dialog-box information.
    return(hGlbl);
}
#endif
```

Listing 3-8. DLG-DYNA.H dynamic dialog-box header module

```
/********************************************************************
Module name: DLG-DYNA.H
Programmer : Jeffrey M. Richter.
********************************************************************/

HGLOBAL WINAPI CreateDlgTemplate(
    LONG dtStyle,
    int dtX, int dtY,         // In dialog-box units.
    int dtCX, int dtCY,       // In dialog-box units.
    LPSTR dtMenuName,         // "" if no menu.
    LPSTR dtClassName,        // "" if standard dialog-box class.
    LPSTR dtCaptionText,
    short int PointSize,      // Only used if DS_SETFONT specified.
    LPSTR szTypeFace);        // Only used if DS_SETFONT specified.

// LOWORD = Success(TRUE)/Failure(FALSE), HIWORD=New hGlbl.
DWORD WINAPI AddDlgControl (
    HGLOBAL hGlbl,            // Handle from CreateDlgTemplate
                             // or AddDlgControl.
    int dtilX, int dtilY,    // In dialog-box units.
    int dtilCX, int dtilCY,  // In dialog-box units.
    int dtilID,
    long dtilStyle,          // WS_CHILD is automatically added.
    LPSTR dtilClass,         // May be: "BUTTON", "EDIT",
                             // "STATIC", "LISTBOX",
                             // "SCROLLBAR", "COMBOBOX".
    LPSTR dtilText,
    BYTE dtilInfo,           // Number of additional data bytes.
    LPBYTE dtilData);        // Value passed through lpCreateParams
                             // of CREATESTRUCT.

void WINAPI DoneAddingControls (
    HGLOBAL hGlbl);          // Handle from CreateDlgTemplate
                             // or AddDlgControl.

#ifdef _DEMO
//******************************************************************
// Functions for the Dynamic Dialog-Box Demonstrations.

BOOL CALLBACK DynamicDlgProc (HWND hDlg, UINT uMsg, WPARAM wParam,
        LPARAM lParam);
HGLOBAL WINAPI BuildDynamicDlgBox (BOOL fModeless);
#endif
```

Listing 3-9. DLG-MODE.C source module

```
/*******************************************************************
Module name: DLG-MODE.C
Programmer : Jeffrey M. Richter.
*******************************************************************/

#include <windows.h>
#include <windowsx.h>
#include <stdlib.h>
#include "dlgtech.h"
#include "dlg-mode.h"

extern const HINSTANCE _cdecl _hInstance;

typedef struct {
    long dtStyle;
    BYTE dtItemCount;
    int  dtX;
    int  dtY;
    int  dtCX;
    int  dtCY;
// char dtMenuName[];       // Variable-length string.
// char dtClassName[];      // Variable-length string.
// char dtCaptionText[];    // Variable-length string.
} DLGTEMPLATE, FAR *LPDLGTEMPLATE;

typedef struct {
    short int PointSize;
// char  szTypeFace[];      // Variable-length string.
} FONTINFO, FAR *LPFONTINFO;

typedef struct {
    int   dtilX;
    int   dtilY;
    int   dtilCX;
    int   dtilCY;
    int   dtilID;
    long  dtilStyle;
// char dtilClass[];        // Variable-length string.
// char dtilText[];         // Variable-length string.
// BYTE dtilInfo;           // Number of bytes in following memory block.
// BYTE dtilData;           // Variable-length memory block.
} DLGITEMTEMPLATE, FAR *LPDLGITEMTEMPLATE;

static BOOL CALLBACK EnumChildProc (HWND hWnd, LPARAM lParam) {
```

```
      RECT rcChild, rcChangeable;

      if (hWnd == (HWND) lParam)
         return(TRUE);  // Don't destroy the ID_CHANGEABLE window.

      GetWindowRect(hWnd, &rcChild);
      GetWindowRect((HWND) lParam, &rcChangeable);

      if (IntersectRect(&rcChild, &rcChangeable, &rcChild) != 0) {
         // Rectangles intersect-destroy the window.
         DestroyWindow(hWnd);
      }

      return(TRUE);  // Continue the enumeration.
}

void WINAPI DestroyControlsInChangeableArea
      (HWND hDlg, UINT uIDChangeableArea) {

      // Destroy all controls inside the control identified
      // by the "uIDChangeableArea" parameter.
      EnumChildWindows(hDlg, (WNDENUMPROC) EnumChildProc,
         GetDlgItem(hDlg, uIDChangeableArea));
}


//****************************************************************

#define PREDEFINEDCNTRLBIT        0x80
#define BUTTONCNTRLCODE           0x80
#define EDITCNTRLCODE             0x81
#define STATICCNTRLCODE           0x82
#define LISTBOXCNTRLCODE          0x83
#define SCROLLBARCNTRLCODE        0x84
#define COMBOBOXCNTRLCODE         0x85

static char *szPredefinedClassNames[] =
   { "BUTTON", "EDIT", "STATIC",
   "LISTBOX", "SCROLLBAR", "COMBOBOX" };

BOOL WINAPI MergeControlsIntoDlg
      (HWND hDlg, UINT uIDChangeableArea,
      HINSTANCE hInstance, LPCSTR szDlgTemplate) {

   HWND hWndPrevChild = GetDlgItem(hDlg, uIDChangeableArea);
   HFONT hFont;
   LPBYTE p, lpszClass, lpszText, lpCreateParams;
   LPDLGTEMPLATE lpDlgTemplate;
```

```
LPDLGITEMTEMPLATE lpDlgItemTemplate;
LPFONTINFO lpFontInfo;
HWND hWndChild;
BYTE bNumControls;
HRSRC hrsrcDialog;
HGLOBAL hGlblDlgTemplate;
RECT rc;

hrsrcDialog =
    FindResource(hInstance, szDlgTemplate, RT_DIALOG);
if (hrsrcDialog == NULL) return(FALSE);
hGlblDlgTemplate = LoadResource(hInstance, hrsrcDialog);
lpDlgTemplate = (LPDLGTEMPLATE) LockResource(hGlblDlgTemplate);
if (lpDlgTemplate == NULL) return(FALSE);

hFont = GetWindowFont(hDlg);

// Ignore everything in dialog template except for the number
// of controls.
bNumControls = lpDlgTemplate->dtItemCount;

p = (LPBYTE) (&lpDlgTemplate->dtCY + 1);  // Start of menu name.
while (*p++ != 0) ;            // Skip the menu name string.
while (*p++ != 0) ;            // Skip the class name string.
while (*p++ != 0) ;            // Skip the caption string.
lpFontInfo = (LPFONTINFO) p;  // Start of FONTINFO (if exists)

// Find address of first DLGITEMTEMPLATE structure
if (lpDlgTemplate->dtStyle & DS_SETFONT) {
    p = (LPBYTE) (&lpFontInfo->PointSize + 1);
    while (*p++ != 0) ;  // Skip the type face name string.
    lpDlgItemTemplate = (LPDLGITEMTEMPLATE) p;
} else lpDlgItemTemplate = (LPDLGITEMTEMPLATE) lpFontInfo;

// Create all of the child controls.
while (bNumControls- != 0) {

    lpszClass = (LPBYTE) (&lpDlgItemTemplate->dtilStyle + 1);
    if (*lpszClass & PREDEFINEDCNTRLBIT) {
        lpszText = lpszClass + 1;
        lpszClass = (LPBYTE) szPredefinedClassNames
            [(WORD)(*lpszClass) - PREDEFINEDCNTRLBIT];
    } else for (lpszText = lpszClass; *lpszText++ != 0; ) ;

    // Find address of number-of-bytes-in-additional-data.
    for (lpCreateParams = lpszText; *lpCreateParams++ != 0; ) ;
    // Do not create any windows with an ID of uIDChangeableArea.
```

```
      // This control was used for reference when the template was
      // created and should not be created.
      if (lpDlgItemTemplate->dtilID == uIDChangeableArea)
         goto NextControl;

      SetRect(&rc, lpDlgItemTemplate->dtilX,
         lpDlgItemTemplate->dtilY,
         lpDlgItemTemplate->dtilX + lpDlgItemTemplate->dtilCX,
         lpDlgItemTemplate->dtilY + lpDlgItemTemplate->dtilCY);
      MapDialogRect(hDlg, &rc);

      hWndChild = CreateWindowEx(WS_EX_NOPARENTNOTIFY,
         (LPCSTR) lpszClass, (LPCSTR) lpszText,
         lpDlgItemTemplate->dtilStyle,
         rc.left, rc.top,
         rc.right - rc.left, rc.bottom - rc.top,
         hDlg, (HMENU) lpDlgItemTemplate->dtilID, hInstance,
         lpCreateParams + 1); // +1 to point to first byte of data.

      if (hWndChild == NULL) {
         // The child couldn't be create.
         UnlockResource(hGlblDlgTemplate);
         FreeResource(hGlblDlgTemplate);
         return(FALSE);
      }

      // Tell the new control to use the same font as dialog box.
      SetWindowFont(hWndChild, hFont, FALSE);

      // Fix the z-order of the controls.
      SetWindowPos(hWndChild, hWndPrevChild, 0, 0, 0, 0,
         SWP_NOMOVE | SWP_NOSIZE);
      hWndPrevChild = hWndChild;

      NextControl:
      // Point to the next DlgItemTemplate.
      lpDlgItemTemplate = (LPDLGITEMTEMPLATE)
         (lpCreateParams + 1 + *lpCreateParams);
   }

   UnlockResource(hGlblDlgTemplate);
   FreeResource(hGlblDlgTemplate);
   return(TRUE);
}

#ifdef _DEMO
//**************************************************************
// Functions for the mode-select dialog-box demonstration.
```

```
#define ARRAY_LEN(Array)        (sizeof(Array) / sizeof(Array[0]))

// You really should use RegisterWindowMessage but this makes
// the demonstration more understandable.
#define MS_CHANGEAWAY        (WM_USER + 200)

BOOL CALLBACK PersonalDlgProc
     (HWND hDlg, UINT uMsg, WPARAM wParam, LPARAM lParam);
BOOL CALLBACK FishDlgProc
     (HWND hDlg, UINT uMsg, WPARAM wParam, LPARAM lParam);
BOOL CALLBACK ColorDlgProc
     (HWND hDlg, UINT uMsg, WPARAM wParam, LPARAM lParam);

typedef BOOL (CALLBACK* xDLGPROC)(HWND, UINT, WPARAM, LPARAM);

struct {
   char *szModeName, *szDlgTemplate;
   xDLGPROC fpDlgProc;
   UINT uChangeAwayMsg;
} _ModeInfo[] = {
   { "Personal",       "MODE_PERSONAL", PersonalDlgProc,
     MS_CHANGEAWAY },
   { "Fish report",    "MODE_FISH",     FishDlgProc,
     MS_CHANGEAWAY },
   { "Color options", "MODE_COLORS",   ColorDlgProc,
     MS_CHANGEAWAY }
};

BOOL CALLBACK ModeSelDlgProc
     (HWND hDlg, UINT uMsg, WPARAM wParam, LPARAM lParam) {
   BOOL fProcessed = TRUE;
   char szPreviousMode[] = "PrevMode";
   HWND hWndT;
   UINT x;

   switch (uMsg) {

      case WM_INITDIALOG:
         // No mode was previously selected.
         SetProp(hDlg, szPreviousMode, (HANDLE) -1);
         // Hide the "ChangeableArea" window.
         ShowWindow(GetDlgItem(hDlg, ID_MODE_CHANGEABLEAREA),
            SW_HIDE);

         // Initialize the dialog box by loading the list box with
         // the set of selectable modes.
         hWndT = GetDlgItem(hDlg, ID_MODE_LIST);
```

```
        (void) ListBox_ResetContent(hWndT);
        for (x = 0; x < ARRAY_LEN(_ModeInfo); x++)
           (void) ListBox_AddString(hWndT,
               _ModeInfo[x].szModeName);

        // Select the default mode.

        (void) ListBox_SetCurSel(hWndT, 0); // Select "Personal"

        // Make dialog think that the user selected the mode.
        FORWARD_WM_COMMAND(hDlg, ID_MODE_LIST, hWndT,
           LBN_SELCHANGE, SendMessage);
        break;

   case WM_DESTROY:
        RemoveProp(hDlg, szPreviousMode);
        break;

   case WM_COMMAND:
        switch (wParam) {

            case IDOK:
                // Notify current mode-select dialog procedure that
                // the user is switching away FROM it.

                EndDialog(hDlg, wParam);
                break;

            case IDCANCEL:
                EndDialog(hDlg, wParam);
                break;

            case ID_MODE_LIST:
                if (HIWORD(lParam) != LBN_SELCHANGE)
                   break;

                // Notify current mode-select dialog procedure
                // that the user is switching away FROM it.
                x = (UINT) GetProp(hDlg, szPreviousMode);
                if (x != (UINT) -1) {
                   // A mode was previously selected
                   (_ModeInfo[x].fpDlgProc)
                       (hDlg, _ModeInfo[x].uChangeAwayMsg, 0, 0);
                }
                // Destroy the controls from the previous mode.
                DestroyControlsInChangeableArea(hDlg,
                   ID_MODE_CHANGEABLEAREA);
```

```
                // Determine which NEW mode was selected.
                x = ListBox_GetCurSel(LOWORD(lParam));

                // Replace the controls in the "Changeable Area".
                MergeControlsIntoDlg(hDlg, ID_MODE_CHANGEABLEAREA,
                    _hInstance, _ModeInfo[x].szDlgTemplate);

                // Set this before sending WM_INITDIALOG so that
                // any messages sent from dialog function and
                // passed through here are sent to the proper
                // procedure in the code below this "switch".
                SetProp(hDlg, szPreviousMode, (HANDLE) x);

                // Notify the new mode-select dialog procedure that
                // the user is switching TO it.
                (_ModeInfo[x].fpDlgProc)
                    (hDlg, WM_INITDIALOG, 0, 0);
                break;

            default:
                fProcessed = FALSE;
                break;
        }
        break;

    default:
        fProcessed = FALSE;
        break;
    }

    if (!fProcessed) {
        x = (UINT) GetProp(hDlg, szPreviousMode);
        if (x != (UINT) -1) {
            // If the message was not processed by this
            // dialog-box procedure, pass it to the selected
            // mode's dialog-box procedure.
            fProcessed =
                (_ModeInfo[x].fpDlgProc)(hDlg, uMsg, wParam, lParam);
        }
    }
    return(fProcessed);
}

//**************************************************************
#pragma argsused
BOOL CALLBACK PersonalDlgProc
        (HWND hDlg, UINT uMsg, WPARAM wParam, LPARAM lParam) {
    static char *szStates[] = {
```

```
                "AK", "AL", "AR", "AZ", "CA", "CO", "CT", "DC", "DE",
                "FL", "GA", "HI", "IA", "ID", "IL", "IN", "KS", "KY",
                "LA", "MA", "MD", "ME", "MI", "MN", "MO", "MS", "MT",
                "NC", "ND", "NE", "NH", "NJ", "NM", "NV", "NY", "OH",
                "OK", "OR", "PA", "RI", "SC", "SD", "TN", "TX", "UT",
                "VA", "VT", "WA", "WI", "WV", "WY"
        };

        static struct {
            char szName[25], szAddr[25], szCity[25], szZip[15];
            UINT uState;
        } Personal;

        BOOL fProcessed = TRUE;
        UINT x;

        switch (uMsg) {
            case WM_INITDIALOG:
                // Initialize the new controls.
                Edit_LimitText(GetDlgItem(hDlg, ID_MODE_PERSONAL_NAME),
                    sizeof(Personal.szName));
                Edit_LimitText(GetDlgItem(hDlg, ID_MODE_PERSONAL_ADDR),
                    sizeof(Personal.szAddr));
                Edit_LimitText(GetDlgItem(hDlg, ID_MODE_PERSONAL_CITY),
                    sizeof(Personal.szCity));
                Edit_LimitText(GetDlgItem(hDlg, ID_MODE_PERSONAL_ZIP),
                    sizeof(Personal.szZip));

                SetDlgItemText(hDlg, ID_MODE_PERSONAL_NAME,
                    Personal.szName);
                SetDlgItemText(hDlg, ID_MODE_PERSONAL_ADDR,
                    Personal.szAddr);
                SetDlgItemText(hDlg, ID_MODE_PERSONAL_CITY,
                    Personal.szCity);
                SetDlgItemText(hDlg, ID_MODE_PERSONAL_ZIP,
                    Personal.szZip);

                for (x = 0; x < ARRAY_LEN(szStates); x++)
                    (void) ComboBox_AddString(
                        GetDlgItem(hDlg, ID_MODE_PERSONAL_STATE),
                        szStates[x]);

                (void) ComboBox_SetCurSel(GetDlgItem(hDlg,
                    ID_MODE_PERSONAL_STATE), Personal.uState);
                break;

            case MS_CHANGEAWAY:
                GetDlgItemText(hDlg, ID_MODE_PERSONAL_NAME,
```

```
            Personal.szName, sizeof(Personal.szName));
         GetDlgItemText(hDlg, ID_MODE_PERSONAL_ADDR,
            Personal.szAddr, sizeof(Personal.szAddr));
         GetDlgItemText(hDlg, ID_MODE_PERSONAL_CITY,
            Personal.szCity, sizeof(Personal.szCity));
         GetDlgItemText(hDlg, ID_MODE_PERSONAL_ZIP,
            Personal.szZip, sizeof(Personal.szZip));
         Personal.uState = ComboBox_GetCurSel(
            GetDlgItem(hDlg, ID_MODE_PERSONAL_STATE));
         break;

      case WM_COMMAND:
         switch (wParam) {
            case ID_MODE_PERSONAL_NAME:
            case ID_MODE_PERSONAL_ADDR:
            case ID_MODE_PERSONAL_CITY:
            case ID_MODE_PERSONAL_STATE:
            case ID_MODE_PERSONAL_ZIP:
               break;
         }
         break;

      default:
         fProcessed = FALSE;
         break;
   }
   return(fProcessed);
}


//****************************************************************

#pragma argsused
BOOL CALLBACK FishDlgProc
        (HWND hDlg, UINT uMsg, WPARAM wParam, LPARAM lParam) {

   static BOOL fFreshWater;

   static char *szFishFresh[] = {
      "Cichlid",
      "Clown loach",
      "Cory Catfish",
      "Danio",
      "Gourami",
      "Oscar",
      "Pleco",
      "Rope Fish"
   };
```

```
static char *szFishSalt[] = {
    "Barracuda",
    "Hammer-head shark",
    "Dog face puffer",
    "Star fish",
    "Sting ray"
};

BOOL fProcessed = TRUE;
HWND hWndT;
UINT x, y;

switch (uMsg) {
    case WM_INITDIALOG:
        // Initialize the new controls
        x = fFreshWater ? ID_MODE_FISH_FRESH : ID_MODE_FISH_SALT;
        CheckRadioButton(hDlg, ID_MODE_FISH_FRESH,
            ID_MODE_FISH_SALT, fFreshWater ? ID_MODE_FISH_FRESH :
            ID_MODE_FISH_SALT);
        FORWARD_WM_COMMAND(hDlg, x, GetDlgItem(hDlg, x),
            BN_CLICKED, SendMessage);
        break;

    case MS_CHANGEAWAY:
        fFreshWater = Button_GetCheck(
            GetDlgItem(hDlg, ID_MODE_FISH_FRESH));
        break;

    case WM_COMMAND:
        switch (wParam) {
            case ID_MODE_FISH_FRESH:
            case ID_MODE_FISH_SALT:
                hWndT = GetDlgItem(hDlg, ID_MODE_FISH_LIST);
                (void) ListBox_ResetContent(hWndT);
                y = (wParam == ID_MODE_FISH_FRESH)
                    ? ARRAY_LEN(szFishFresh)
                        : ARRAY_LEN(szFishSalt);
                for (x = 0; x < y; x++)
                    (void) ListBox_AddString(hWndT,
                        (wParam == ID_MODE_FISH_FRESH)
                        ? szFishFresh[x] : szFishSalt[x]);
                (void) ListBox_SetCurSel(hWndT, 0);
                break;

            case ID_MODE_FISH_LIST:
                break;
        }
        break;
```

```
        default:
            fProcessed = FALSE;
            break;
    }
    return(fProcessed);
}

//*****************************************************************
#pragma argsused
BOOL CALLBACK ColorDlgProc
        (HWND hDlg, UINT uMsg, WPARAM wParam, LPARAM lParam) {
    static UINT uRed, uGreen, uBlue;
    static BOOL fInvert;

    BOOL fProcessed = TRUE;

    switch (uMsg) {
        case WM_INITDIALOG:
            // Initialize the new controls.
            ScrollBar_SetRange(
                GetDlgItem(hDlg, ID_MODE_COLORS_RED),
                0, 255, FALSE);
            ScrollBar_SetRange(
                GetDlgItem(hDlg, ID_MODE_COLORS_GREEN),
                0, 255, FALSE);
            ScrollBar_SetRange(
                GetDlgItem(hDlg, ID_MODE_COLORS_BLUE),
                0, 255, FALSE);

            ScrollBar_SetPos(
                GetDlgItem(hDlg, ID_MODE_COLORS_RED),   uRed,   TRUE);
            ScrollBar_SetPos(
                GetDlgItem(hDlg, ID_MODE_COLORS_GREEN), uGreen, TRUE);
            ScrollBar_SetPos(
                GetDlgItem(hDlg, ID_MODE_COLORS_BLUE),  uBlue,  TRUE);

            Button_SetCheck(
                GetDlgItem(hDlg, ID_MODE_COLORS_INVERT), fInvert);
            break;

        case MS_CHANGFAWAY:
            uRed   = ScrollBar_GetPos(
                GetDlgItem(hDlg, ID_MODE_COLORS_RED));
            uGreen = ScrollBar_GetPos(
                GetDlgItem(hDlg, ID_MODE_COLORS_GREEN));
            uBlue  = ScrollBar_GetPos(
                GetDlgItem(hDlg, ID_MODE_COLORS_BLUE));
```

```
            fInvert = Button_GetCheck(
                GetDlgItem(hDlg, ID_MODE_COLORS_INVERT));
            break;

        case WM_COMMAND:
            switch (wParam) {
                case ID_MODE_COLORS_RED:
                case ID_MODE_COLORS_GREEN:
                case ID_MODE_COLORS_BLUE:
                case ID_MODE_COLORS_INVERT:
                    break;
            }
            break;

        default:
            fProcessed = FALSE;
            break;
    }
    return(fProcessed);
}

#endif   // _DEMO
```

Listing 3-10. DLGMODE.H header module

```
/********************************************************************
Module name: DLG-MODE.H
Programmer : Jeffrey M. Richter.
********************************************************************/

void WINAPI ChangeControls (HWND hDlg, WORD wIDChangeable,
    WORD wIDDlgNew);

BOOL WINAPI MergeDialogs(HINSTANCE hInstance, LPCSTR lpszDlgName,
    HWND hDlg, HWND hWndPrevChild, UINT NotifyMsg,
    LPARAM lParam);
#ifdef _DEMO
//*****************************************************************
// Functions for the "Select Mode" dialog-box demonstration.

BOOL CALLBACK OptionsDlgProc (HWND hDlg, UINT uMsg, WPARAM wParam,
    LPARAM lParam);
#endif
```

Listing 3-11. DLGTECH.RC application resource file

```
/********************************************************************
Module name: DLGTECH.RC
Programmer : Jeffrey M. Richter.
********************************************************************/

#include <windows.h>
#define _DEMO
#include "dlgtech.h"


DlgTech  ICON     MOVEABLE DISCARDABLE DlgTech.Ico

DlgTech MENU
BEGIN
    POPUP     "&Examples"
      BEGIN
      MENUITEM "&SetWindowPos demo...",      IDM_SETWINDOWPOSDEMO
      MENUITEM "&Options demo...",           IDM_OPTIONSDEMO
      MENUITEM "&ModalLess demo...",         IDM_MODALLESSDEMO
      MENUITEM "&Dynamic modal demo...",     IDM_DYNAMICMODALDEMO
      MENUITEM "D&ynamic modeless demo...",  IDM_DYNAMICMODELESSDEMO
      MENUITEM "Mode-se&lect demo...",       IDM_MODESELECTDEMO
      END
END

OPTIONS DIALOG LOADONCALL MOVEABLE DISCARDABLE 9, 24, 228, 100
CAPTION "Options Demo Dialog Box"
STYLE WS_BORDER | WS_CAPTION | WS_DLGFRAME | WS_SYSMENU |
      WS_VISIBLE | WS_POPUP
BEGIN
    CONTROL "&Name:", -1, "static", SS_LEFT | WS_CHILD,
        4, 4, 24, 12
    CONTROL "", ID_NAME, "edit",
        ES_LEFT | WS_BORDER | WS_GROUP | WS_TABSTOP | WS_CHILD,
        32, 4, 80, 12
    CONTROL "&Phone:", -1, "static", SS_LEFT | WS_CHILD,
        4, 20, 24, 12
    CONTROL "", ID_PHONE, "edit",
        ES_LEFT | WS_BORDER | WS_GROUP | WS_TABSTOP | WS_CHILD,
        32, 20, 80, 12
    CONTROL "&Ok", IDOK, "button",
        BS_DEFPUSHBUTTON | WS_GROUP | WS_TABSTOP | WS_CHILD,
        116, 4, 44, 12
    CONTROL "&Cancel", IDCANCEL, "button",
        BS_PUSHBUTTON | WS_GROUP | WS_TABSTOP | WS_CHILD,
```

```
      116, 20, 44, 12
   CONTROL "O&ptions >>", ID_OPTIONS, "button",
      BS_PUSHBUTTON | WS_GROUP | WS_TABSTOP | WS_CHILD,
      4, 36, 52, 12
   CONTROL "", ID_DEFAULTBOX, "static", SS_BLACKRECT | WS_CHILD,
      165, 48, 4, 4
   CONTROL "&Street:", -1, "static", SS_LEFT | WS_CHILD,
      4, 52, 24, 12
   CONTROL "", ID_STREET, "edit",
      ES_LEFT | WS_BORDER | WS_GROUP | WS_TABSTOP | WS_CHILD,
      32, 52, 128, 12
   CONTROL "&City:", -1, "static", SS_LEFT | WS_CHILD,
      4, 68, 20, 12
   CONTROL "", ID_CITY, "edit",
      ES_LEFT | WS_BORDER | WS_GROUP | WS_TABSTOP | WS_CHILD,
      32, 68, 128, 12
   CONTROL "S&tate:", -1, "static", SS_LEFT | WS_CHILD,
      4, 84, 24, 12
   CONTROL "", ID_STATE, "edit",
      ES_LEFT | WS_BORDER | WS_GROUP | WS_TABSTOP | WS_CHILD,
      32, 84, 32, 12
   CONTROL "&Zip:", -1, "static", SS_LEFT | WS_CHILD,
      108, 84, 16, 12
   CONTROL "", ID_ZIP, "edit",
      ES_LEFT | WS_BORDER | WS_GROUP | WS_TABSTOP | WS_CHILD,
      128, 84, 32, 12
   CONTROL "Sex:", -1, "button", BS_GROUPBOX | WS_CHILD,
      172, 0, 48, 40
   CONTROL "&Female", ID_FEMALE, "button",
      BS_AUTORADIOBUTTON | WS_TABSTOP | WS_CHILD, 176, 12, 36, 12
   CONTROL "&Male", ID_MALE, "button",
      BS_AUTORADIOBUTTON | WS_TABSTOP | WS_CHILD, 176, 24, 28, 12
   CONTROL "&Divorced", ID_DIVORCED, "button",
      BS_AUTOCHECKBOX | WS_GROUP | WS_TABSTOP | WS_CHILD,
      172, 52, 44, 12
   CONTROL "Charity &giver", ID_CARITY, "button",
      BS_AUTOCHECKBOX | WS_GROUP | WS_TABSTOP | WS_CHILD,
      172, 68, 52, 12
   CONTROL "Smo&kes", ID_SMOKES, "button",
      BS_AUTOCHECKBOX | WS_GROUP | WS_TABSTOP | WS_CHILD,
      172, 84, 52, 12
END

SETWINDOWPOS DIALOG LOADONCALL MOVEABLE DISCARDABLE 8, 29, 176, 52
CAPTION "SetWindowPos Demonstration"
STYLE WS_BORDER | WS_CAPTION | WS_DLGFRAME | WS_SYSMENU | WS_POPUP
BEGIN
```

```
    CONTROL "&Name:", ID_NAMETEXT, "static", SS_LEFT | WS_CHILD,
        4, 4, 24, 8
    CONTROL "", ID_NAME, "edit",
        ES_LEFT | WS_BORDER | WS_GROUP | WS_TABSTOP | WS_CHILD,
        28, 4, 100, 12
    CONTROL "Over &25", ID_OVER25, "button",
        BS_AUTOCHECKBOX | WS_GROUP | WS_TABSTOP | WS_CHILD,
        4, 20, 40, 12
    CONTROL "Change &Tab order", ID_CHANGETABORDER, "button",
        BS_PUSHBUTTON | WS_GROUP | WS_TABSTOP | WS_CHILD,
        64, 20, 64, 12
    CONTROL "&Add control", ID_ADDCONTROL, "button",
        BS_PUSHBUTTON | WS_GROUP | WS_TABSTOP | WS_CHILD,
        4, 36, 44, 12
    CONTROL "&Ok", IDOK, "button",
        BS_DEFPUSHBUTTON | WS_GROUP | WS_TABSTOP | WS_CHILD,
        136, 4, 36, 12
    CONTROL "&Cancel", IDCANCEL, "button",
        BS_PUSHBUTTON | WS_GROUP | WS_TABSTOP | WS_CHILD,
        136, 20, 36, 12
END

MODALLESS DIALOG LOADONCALL MOVEABLE DISCARDABLE 9, 27, 132, 36
CAPTION "ModalLess Dialog Box Demo"
STYLE WS_BORDER | WS_CAPTION | WS_DLGFRAME | WS_SYSMENU | WS_POPUP
BEGIN
    CONTROL "&Name:", -1, "static", SS_LEFT | WS_CHILD,
        4, 4, 24, 12
    CONTROL "", ID_NAME, "edit",
        ES_LEFT | WS_BORDER | WS_TABSTOP | WS_CHILD, 28, 4, 100, 12
    CONTROL "&Ok", IDOK, "button",
        BS_DEFPUSHBUTTON | WS_TABSTOP | WS_CHILD, 24, 20, 36, 12
    CONTROL "&Cancel", IDCANCEL, "button",
        BS_PUSHBUTTON | WS_TABSTOP | WS_CHILD, 72, 20, 36, 12
END

// All of the dialog-box templates for demonstrating
// the mode-select dialog-box technique.

MODE_SELECT DIALOG 18, 18, 204, 100
CAPTION "Mode Selection"
STYLE DS_MODALFRAME | WS_POPUP | WS_CAPTION | WS_SYSMENU
BEGIN
    CONTROL "&Mode:", -1, "STATIC",
        SS_LEFT | WS_CHILD | WS_VISIBLE | WS_GROUP, 4, 2, 24, 8
    CONTROL "", ID_MODE_LIST, "LISTBOX",
        LBS_NOTIFY | WS_CHILD | WS_VISIBLE | WS_BORDER |
```

```
        WS_VSCROLL | WS_GROUP | WS_TABSTOP, 4, 12, 48, 24
    CONTROL "", ID_MODE_CHANGEABLEAREA, "static",
        SS_BLACKFRAME | WS_CHILD | WS_VISIBLE, 60, 4, 140, 76
    CONTROL "&Ok", IDOK, "BUTTON", BS_DEFPUSHBUTTON |
        WS_CHILD | WS_VISIBLE | WS_GROUP | WS_TABSTOP,
        4, 84, 32, 12
    CONTROL "&Cancel", IDCANCEL, "BUTTON",
        BS_PUSHBUTTON | WS_CHILD | WS_VISIBLE | WS_TABSTOP,
        40, 84, 32, 12
END

MODE_PERSONAL DIALOG 18, 32, 204, 100
CAPTION "MODE_PERSONAL"
STYLE DS_MODALFRAME | WS_POPUP | WS_CAPTION | WS_SYSMENU
BEGIN
    CONTROL "", ID_MODE_CHANGEABLEAREA, "static",
        SS_BLACKFRAME | WS_CHILD | WS_VISIBLE, 60, 4, 140, 76
    CONTROL "&Name:", -1, "STATIC",
        SS_LEFT | WS_CHILD | WS_VISIBLE | WS_GROUP, 63, 8, 24, 8
    CONTROL "", ID_MODE_PERSONAL_NAME, "EDIT",
        ES_LEFT | WS_CHILD | WS_VISIBLE | WS_BORDER | WS_TABSTOP,
        96, 6, 100, 12
    CONTROL "&Address:", -1, "STATIC",
        SS_LEFT | WS_CHILD | WS_VISIBLE | WS_GROUP, 64, 22, 32, 8
    CONTROL "", ID_MODE_PERSONAL_ADDR, "EDIT",
        ES_LEFT | WS_CHILD | WS_VISIBLE | WS_BORDER | WS_TABSTOP,
        96, 21, 100, 12
    CONTROL "Cit&y:", -1, "STATIC",
        SS_LEFT | WS_CHILD | WS_VISIBLE | WS_GROUP, 64, 38, 28, 8
    CONTROL "", ID_MODE_PERSONAL_CITY, "EDIT",
        ES_LEFT | WS_CHILD | WS_VISIBLE | WS_BORDER | WS_TABSTOP,
        96, 37, 100, 12
    CONTROL "S&tate:", -1, "STATIC",
        SS_LEFT | WS_CHILD | WS_VISIBLE | WS_GROUP, 64, 53, 28, 8
    CONTROL "", ID_MODE_PERSONAL_STATE, "COMBOBOX",
        CBS_DROPDOWNLIST | CBS_SORT | WS_CHILD | WS_VISIBLE |
        WS_VSCROLL | WS_GROUP | WS_TABSTOP, 96, 53, 28, 48
    CONTROL "&Zip:", -1, "STATIC",
        SS_LEFT | WS_CHILD | WS_VISIBLE | WS_GROUP, 138, 53, 16, 8
    CONTROL "", ID_MODE_PERSONAL_ZIP, "EDIT",
        ES_LEFT | WS_CHILD | WS_VISIBLE | WS_BORDER | WS_TABSTOP,
        152, 53, 44, 12
END

MODE_FISH DIALOG 18, 18, 204, 100
CAPTION "MODE_FISH"
STYLE DS_MODALFRAME | WS_POPUP | WS_CAPTION | WS_SYSMENU
```

```
BEGIN
    CONTROL "", ID_MODE_CHANGEABLEAREA, "static",
        SS_BLACKFRAME | WS_CHILD | WS_VISIBLE, 60, 4, 140, 76
    CONTROL "Water", -1, "button",
        BS_GROUPBOX | WS_CHILD | WS_VISIBLE, 64, 8, 40, 36
    CONTROL "Fres&h", ID_MODE_FISH_FRESH, "BUTTON",
        BS_AUTORADIOBUTTON | WS_CHILD | WS_VISIBLE | WS_TABSTOP,
        69, 18, 32, 12
    CONTROL "&Salt", ID_MODE_FISH_SALT, "BUTTON",
        BS_AUTORADIOBUTTON | WS_CHILD | WS_VISIBLE | WS_TABSTOP,
        69, 30, 28, 12
    CONTROL "&Fish:", -1, "STATIC",
        SS_LEFT | WS_CHILD | WS_VISIBLE | WS_GROUP, 112, 8, 24, 8
    CONTROL "", ID_MODE_FISH_LIST, "LISTBOX",
        LBS_NOTIFY | WS_CHILD | WS_VISIBLE | WS_BORDER |
        WS_VSCROLL | WS_GROUP | WS_TABSTOP, 112, 18, 84, 60
END
MODE_COLORS DIALOG 18, 18, 204, 100
CAPTION "MODE_COLORS"
STYLE DS_MODALFRAME | WS_POPUP | WS_CAPTION | WS_SYSMENU
BEGIN
    CONTROL "", ID_MODE_CHANGEABLEAREA, "static",
        SS_BLACKFRAME | WS_CHILD | WS_VISIBLE, 60, 4, 140, 76
    CONTROL "Color selection", -1, "button",
        BS_GROUPBOX | WS_CHILD | WS_VISIBLE, 64, 6, 132, 52
    CONTROL "&Red:", -1, "STATIC",
        SS_LEFT | WS_CHILD | WS_VISIBLE | WS_GROUP, 68, 17, 16, 8
    CONTROL "", ID_MODE_COLORS_RED, "SCROLLBAR",
        SBS_HORZ | WS_CHILD | WS_VISIBLE | WS_GROUP | WS_TABSTOP,
        96, 17, 92, 9
    CONTROL "&Green:", -1, "STATIC",
        SS_LEFT | WS_CHILD | WS_VISIBLE | WS_GROUP, 68, 30, 24, 8
    CONTROL "", ID_MODE_COLORS_GREEN, "SCROLLBAR",
        SBS_HORZ | WS_CHILD | WS_VISIBLE | WS_GROUP | WS_TABSTOP,
        96, 30, 92, 9
    CONTROL "&Blue:", -1, "STATIC",
        SS_LEFT | WS_CHILD | WS_VISIBLE | WS_GROUP, 68, 42, 16, 8
    CONTROL "", ID_MODE_COLORS_BLUE, "SCROLLBAR",
        SBS_HORZ | WS_CHILD | WS_VISIBLE | WS_GROUP | WS_TABSTOP,
        96, 43, 92, 9
    CONTROL "&Invert colors", ID_MODE_COLORS_INVERT, "BUTTON",
        BS_AUTOCHECKBOX | WS_CHILD | WS_VISIBLE | WS_TABSTOP,
        68, 60, 28, 12
END
```

Listing 3-12. DLGTECH.DEF application definitions file

```
; Module name: DLGTECH.DEF
; Programmer : Jeffrey M. Richter.

NAME          DLGTECH
DESCRIPTION   'DlgTech: Dialog techniques Application'
STUB          'WinStub.exe'
EXETYPE       WINDOWS
CODE          MOVEABLE DISCARDABLE PRELOAD
DATA          MOVEABLE MULTIPLE PRELOAD
HEAPSIZE      1024
STACKSIZE     5120
```

Listing 3-13. MAKEFILE for dialog techniques application

```
#********************************************************************
#Module name: MAKEFILE
#Programmer : Jeffrey M. Richter.
#********************************************************************

!include "..\builtins.jmr"

PROG = DlgTech

MODEL = s
CFLAGS = -P-c -c -f- -D_DEMO -WS -p -v -w -m$(MODEL) -I$(INCLUDEDIR)
LFLAGS = /P/v/n/m/s/L$(LIBDIR)
LIBS = CW$(MODEL) Import

MODULES = $(PROG).obj dlg-dyna.obj dlg-opts.obj
MODULES = $(MODULES) dlg-mdls.obj dlg-mode.obj
ICONS   = $(PROG).ico
BITMAPS =
CURSORS =

$(PROG).Exe: $(MODULES) $(PROG).Def $(PROG).Res
     tlink $(LFLAGS) @&&!
COW$(MODEL) $(MODULES)
$(PROG), $(PROG), $(LIBS), $(PROG)
!
   rc -30 -T $(PROG).Res
   TDStrip -s $(PROG)

$(PROG).res: $(PROG).rc $(PROG).h $(RESOURCES)
```

CHAPTER 4

Designing Custom Child Controls

The System Global child control classes supplied by Windows provide standard elements of the user interface. Microsoft endowed these controls with many features so they would be suitable for use in almost any application. However, there may be occasions when one of the supplied child controls just doesn't have the features your application requires. The solution is to design and implement your own child controls. These custom controls may be used in dialog boxes or as stand-alone windows.

In this chapter, we'll create two custom child controls. The first one, Meter, lets a user know how much of a job has been completed. This type of control is frequently used by installation software to indicate the percentage of the files that have been copied from the floppy disk to the hard drive. In fact, the setup program used to install Microsoft Windows uses this type of control (see Figure 4-1).

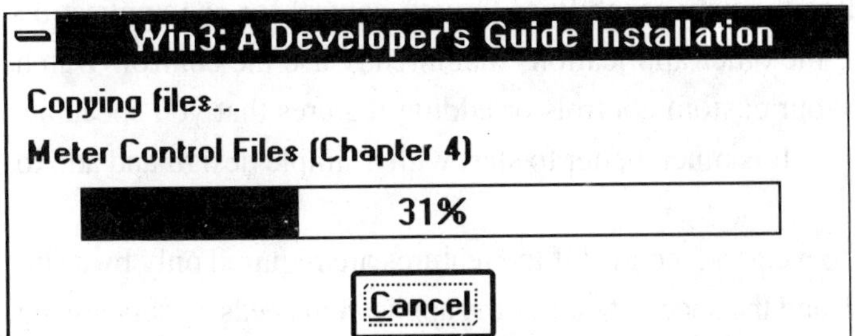

Figure 4-1. Meter custom child control

The second control is called a *spin button*. The spin button lets mouse users scroll through a list of values. It is a small window that usually appears just to the right of an edit control. The Microsoft Windows Control Panel application uses several.

Spin buttons appear to the right of the date and time fields in Control Panel, as shown in Figure 4-2.

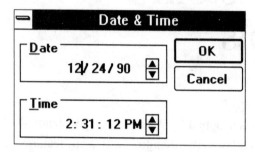

Figure 4-2. Spin button controls

Rules for Designing Custom Child Controls

Designing custom child controls and designing normal window classes are very similar. It is slightly more difficult to design custom child controls than to design an application's main window because most child controls are designed so that several instances of them may exist at one time.

A child control should be designed with the knowledge that its capabilities can be enhanced in the future. As you write applications, you will hear yourself saying, "I could use that custom child control if it only had (fill in the desired feature)." You will find that adding the new capabilities to your control for one application will generally enhance the other applications that already use the control. Watch out for overdesigning your custom controls or adding features that you speculate might be useful *someday*. It is much better to start with a simple design and add to it as necessary.

Do not add features to a custom control if the features are required only by a single application. Instead, add the special features the application needs by subclassing or superclassing the custom child control.

You can implement your custom control as part of an application or as a DLL. There are two advantages to using a DLL. The first is that all of your applications may use the same control, and the window procedure for the control is only loaded into memory once. The second advantage is that the control can be accessed by dialog editor applications like Borland's Resource Workshop or Microsoft's

Dialog Editor. This allows you to design dialog boxes using your own child control as though it were one of the system global child controls, like LISTBOX and EDIT. Later in this chapter, I'll demonstrate how to use custom child controls in Microsoft's Dialog Editor.

One of the most important design issues to keep in mind when implementing a custom control is that it should not use any global or static variables. Unlike application windows, child controls are usually created in bunches. For application windows, if several instances of the same application are running, each has its own data segment containing a separate copy of its global and static variables. This is not true for child controls since there is only one copy of the global and static variables shared among all instances of the custom control. Changes made to global and static variables will affect all child controls of a single class, and this is usually not desired. For example, if windows created from the EDIT class stored their text in a global variable, all EDIT windows on the screen would always contain and display the same text.

A custom child control requires a cleanly designed programmatic interface that explains, in detail, all the capabilities of the custom child control and how the programmer can manage the control's actions. Designing the programmer's interface involves creating a list of #*defined* values that should be placed in a header file for the control. Any application that is going to use the custom child control must include this header file.

Each custom child control class may have specific window styles associated with it. These styles allow the programmer to fine-tune the control's behavior and appearance. A window's style is specified by the *dwStyle* parameter passed to the *CreateWindow* and *CreateWindowEx* functions.

The top 16 bits are used for window styles that are specific to all created windows. These include the *WS_BORDER*, *WS_VISIBLE*, and *WS_POPUP* styles, to name just a few.

The low 16 bits are specific to each class. For example, all the styles specific to the BUTTON class begin with *BS_*, and all the styles specific to the LISTBOX class begin with *LBS_*. When you design a custom child control, you also define the styles that can be used in these low 16 bits to modify the control's behavior.

Each custom child control may have messages specific to its window class. The first class-specific message should be defined as (*WM_USER* + 0). The next should be (*WM_USER* + 1), and so on. Like the styles, these messages should be listed in the control's header file.

Comments should completely explain what the message does, what the return value means (if anything), and the values of the *wParam* and *lParam* parameters. For example, the *LB_DELETESTRING* message for the LISTBOX class requires that the *wParam* parameter contain the index of the string to be deleted. The *lParam* parameter is not used. The return from this message is the number of strings remaining or *LB_ERR* if an error occurs. If this information is documented as a comment in the custom child control's header file, it will be very easy for the programmer to use this control.

The last part of the programmer's interface is the notification codes sent by the control to its parent when some action takes place. Each code, which may be any value, should be defined in the header file. The control notifies the parent of the action by sending a *WM_COMMAND* message: the *wParam* parameter contains the ID for the child control. The *lParam* parameter contains the notification code in the high word and the child control's window handle in the low word.

To help send notification codes to the parent, the following function may be used:

```
LRESULT NEAR NotifyParent (HWND hWndControl,
       WORD wNotifyCode) {
   LRESULT lResult;
   lResult = SendMessage(GetParent(hWndControl), WM_COMMAND,
           GetWindowWord(hWndControl, GWW_ID),
               MAKELONG(hWndControl, wNotifyCode));
   return(lResult);
}
```

Or, alternatively, the *FORWARD_WM_COMMAND* macro from the WINDOWSX.H file may be used. This offers a slightly more convenient syntax:

```
LRESULT NEAR NotifyParent (HWND hWndControl,
       WORD wNotifyCode) {
   LRESULT lResult;
   lResult = FORWARD_WM_COMMAND(GetParent(hWndControl),
```

```
        GetWindowWord(hWndControl, GWW_ID), hWndControl,
        wNotifyCode, SendMessage);
    return(lResult);
}
```

Both of these functions create a *WM_COMMAND* message with the proper parameters and send it to the control's parent window. If the notification message requires
a return value from the parent, this value is returned to the control. In most Windows applications, controls are usually created as children of a dialog box. When
a control sends a *WM_COMMAND* message to the dialog box, the dialog box
receives the notification and can do any processing that it wishes. However, your
dialog-box function may not return a value back to the control sending the notification. This is because the Windows dialog-box window procedure always returns
zero in response to a *WM_COMMAND* message. In fact, Windows' dialog-box
window procedure always returns zero in response to any message except for the
following: *WM_CTLCOLOR*, *WM_COMPAREITEM*, *VM_VKEYTOITEM*,
WM_CHARTOITEM, *WM_QUERYDRAGICON*, or *WM_INITDIALOG*. Starting
with Windows 3.1, Microsoft has documented a method so that your dialog-box
function may return a value other than zero in response to any message. Your dialog-box function must use the *SetDlgMsgResult* macro defined in the WIN-
DOWSX.H file included in the SDK:

```
#define     SetDlgMsgResult(hwnd, msg, result) \
    (((msg) == WM_CTLCOLOR || (msg) == WM_COMPAREITEM || \
    (msg) == WM_VKEYTOITEM || \
    (msg) == WM_CHARTOITEM || (msg) == WM_QUERYDRAGICON || \
    (msg) == WM_INITDIALOG) \
    ? (BOOL)LOWORD(result) : \
    (SetWindowLong((hwnd), DWL_MSGRESULT, \
(LPARAM)(lRESULT)(result)), TRUE))
```

As you can see, if your dialog-box function is processing any of the special six
messages, this macro simply returns the LOWORD (result) after casting it to a
BOOL. However, if any other message is being processed, this macro saves the

value that you wish to return in the dialog box's window extra bytes and returns TRUE to the Windows dialog-box window procedure. This procedure sees that you have returned TRUE, retrieves the return value from the window extra bytes, and returns this value to the function that originally called *SendMessage*. By the way, this macro works for both Windows 3.0 and 3.1.

To use this macro, you simply change the last line of your dialog-box procedure from:

```
return(fProcessed)
```

to:

```
return(SetDlgMsgResult(hDlg, uMsg, fProcessed));
```

Once the programmer's interface has been designed and the control's header file created, you need to determine what information, if any, the custom child control will need internally. For example, each LISTBOX control must remember the number of items in the list, which item is selected, which item is at the top of the box, and other information.

If a small amount of information is common to all instances of the particular custom child control, the class' extra bytes can be used. To store a larger amount of information, a block of memory should be allocated and its handle stored in the class extra bytes.

For information that pertains to each instance of the custom child control, use the window extra bytes. Again, if the amount of information required is large, a block of memory should be allocated and its handle stored in the window extra bytes. Although it is possible to use window properties to store information, storing the data in the window extra bytes is preferred due to the memory and performance overhead associated with window properties.

Implementing a Meter Control

The Meter control is used when an application is about to begin a lengthy process and wants to notify the user of its progress. The programmer first tells the control how many parts make up the entire job. Then, as the job is processing, the programmer notifies the Meter control after each part has completed. This causes Meter to update its display, which graphically depicts the percentage of the job that is complete.

Designing the Meter Programmer's Interface

The programmer's interface for the Meter control should be designed first. This control has no class-specific styles. However, Meter does define four class-specific window messages:

Message	Description	Returns	wParam	lParam
MM_SETPARTSINJOB	Tells the control how many parts are in the job.	N/A	Number of parts in job.	Not used
MM_GETPARTSINJOB	Returns the number of parts in the job.	Number of parts in job.	Not used	Not used
MM_SETPARTSCOMPLETE	Tells the control how many parts of the job have been completed.	N/A	Number of completed parts.	Not used
MM_GETPARTSCOMPLETE	Returns the number of parts that have been completed.	Number of completed parts.	Not used	Not used

An application must initialize a Meter control after creating it by telling it how many parts make up the completed job. For example, if an installation program has 10 files to copy, the program would send the following message to the Meter control to tell it that the job is divided into 10 parts:

```
SendDlgItemMessage(hDlg, ID_METER, MM_SETPARTSINJOB, 10, 0);
```

After each part of the job has been performed, the application sends a message to the Meter control telling it how many have been completed. So after each file has been copied from the floppy disk to the hard drive, the application must notify the Meter control:

```
for (nFileNum = 0; nFileNum < 10; nFileNum++) {
    // Code to copy file from floppy disk to hard drive.
        .
        .
        .
    SendDlgItemMessage(hDlg, ID_METER, MM_SETPARTSCOMPLETE,
        nFileNum + 1, 0);
}
```

After the Meter control receives the *MM_SETPARTSCOMPLETE* message, it computes the percentage of work done and updates its window. After the program has copied the fourth file, for example, Meter determines that four files out of 10 is 40 percent and redraws its window so that the left-most 40 percent of the window is one color and the right-most 60 percent is another color. The string "40%" is displayed in the center of Meter's window.

Should an application need to know how many parts the job is divided into, the application can send an *MM_GETPARTSINJOB* message:

```
wMaxValue = (WORD) SendDlgItemMessage(hDlg, ID_METER,
    MM_GETPARTSINJOB, 0, 0);
```

Likewise, an application may determine the number of parts of the job that have been completed by using the *MM_GETPARTSCOMPLETE* message:

```
wPartsDone = (WORD) SendDlgItemMessage(hDlg, ID_METER,
    MM_GETPARTSCOMPLETE, 0, 0);
```

Although all the preceding examples have demonstrated how messages would be sent to the Meter control if it were part of a dialog box, any custom child control may be created outside of a dialog box using the *CreateWindow* or *CreateWindowEx* functions. The Meter control would then be manipulated with the *SendMessage* function instead of *SendDlgItemMessage*. The first parameter of the *SendMessage* function must be the window handle of the control.

The Meter control's header file, METER.H, contains all the *#defines* discussed earlier.

Implementing the Meter Control Code

When a custom child control is implemented using a DLL, the window class for the control should register upon initialization of the library. The following is the code for the *LibMain* function:

```
HINSTANCE _hInstance = NULL;
    .
    .
    .
BOOL WINAPI LibMain (HINSTANCE hInstance, WORD wDataSeg,
      WORD wHeapSize, LPSTR lpszCmdLine) {
   BOOL fOk;
   _hInstance = hInstance;
   if (wHeapSize != 0)
      UnlockData(0);        // Let data segment move.

   fOk = (RegisterControlClass(hInstance) != NULL);
   return(fOk);            // TRUE if initialization is successful.
}
```

Once the control's window class has been registered, any application can create windows of the class. The *RegisterControlClass* function fills the *WNDCLASS* structure and returns the following result of the call to *RegisterClass*:

```
static ATOM LOCAL RegisterControlClass (HINSTANCE hInstance) {
   WNDCLASS wc;
   wc.style          = CS_GLOBALCLASS | CS_HREDRAW | CS_VREDRAW;
   wc.lpfnWndProc    = MeterWndFn;
   wc.cbClsExtra     = 0;
   wc.cbWndExtra     = CBWNDEXTRA;
   wc.hInstance      = hInstance;
   wc.hIcon          = NULL;
```

```
wc.hCursor          = LoadCursor(NULL, IDC_ARROW);
wc.hbrBackground    = NULL;
wc.lpszMenuName     = NULL;
wc.lpszClassName    = _szControlName;
return(RegisterClass(&wc));
}
```

Although the DLL registers the Meter control class, windows of this class are created by applications. Therefore, the Meter control must be registered as an application global class. This is done by *OR*ing the *CS_GLOBALCLASS* style with any other desired class styles. Failing to use this style will cause the Meter class to be registered as an application local class (local to the DLL), and Windows would not allow any applications to create windows of this class.

Specifying the *CS_HREDRAW* and *CS_VREDRAW* styles causes Windows to invalidate the entire window whenever its size changes. If these styles are not included, Windows does not invalidate any part of the window when the window is made smaller and invalidates only the uncovered area of a window when the window is made larger. Because Meters should be completely redrawn whenever the size of the window is changed, these two styles must be specified. It should be noted, however, that the size of a Meter control, like most controls in a dialog box, usually does not change after it is created.

Since most custom child controls maintain some internal information, the *cbWnd-Extra* member of the *WNDCLASS* structure is usually not zero. The Meter control must maintain a value representing the number of parts in the whole job and the number of parts that have been completed. In addition, almost all controls that paint text allow the application to tell a control which font it should use. The handle to this font is also saved in window extra bytes. Because each of these values requires a word, six extra bytes are necessary for Meter windows. The *#defines* to access this information are found at the top of the METER.C file:

```
#define CBWNDEXTRA          (6)
#define GWW_PARTSINJOB      (0)
#define GWW_PARTSCOMPLETE   (2)
#define GWW_FONT            (4)
```

The last member of note in the *WNDCLASS* structure is *hbrBackground*. When *BeginPaint* is called, Windows sends a *WM_ERASEBKGND* message to the window procedure. Normally, window procedures pass this message directly to the *DefWindowProc* function for processing. If the *hbrBackground* member's value is NULL, *DefWindowProc* doesn't paint the windows' background and returns zero, indicating that the background has not been erased. Because the *WM_PAINT* message in the Meter control's window procedure draws the window, including its background, painting the window is faster if *DefWindowProc* doesn't also have to paint the background. Also, Meter's background varies, depending on the number of parts that have been completed. If *DefWindowProc* were allowed to erase the background, Meter's window would flash because it would first be painted with the background color specified when the class was registered; that color would change when the *WM_PAINT* message redrew the background.

When the DLL that registered the custom child control's window class terminates, the window exit procedure (*WEP*) is called. This procedure removes the custom child control's window class by calling the *UnregisterClass* function. The *WEP* procedure for the Meter control is as follows:

```
int WINAPI WEP (int nSystemExit) {
   switch (nSystemExit) {
      case WEP_SYSTEM_EXIT:    // System is shutting down.
         break;
      case WEP_FREE_DLL:       // Usage count is zero.
         break;
   }
   UnregisterClass(_szControlName, _hInstance);
   return(1);                  // Termination successful.
}
```

Before the class is unregistered, all windows created from the class must be destroyed. This is the responsibility of the application that created the windows. At the end of the chapter, we will discuss how an application loads the DLL and how it tells Windows when the DLL is no longer needed.

Special Messages for Child Controls

Meter's window procedure, *MeterWndFn*, is almost identical to any other window procedure except it processes a few additional messages, *WM_GETDLGCODE, WM_SETFONT, WM_GETFONT*, and *WM_ENABLE*.

The dialog-box manager periodically sends *WM_GETDLGCODE* messages to windows that are in a dialog box. If the user presses a key while a dialog box is active, the dialog-box manager receives the key. It then sends the *WM_GETDLG-CODE* message to the window that currently has the input focus, asking it what type of keys it is interested in receiving. The control must respond by using a combination of the following identifiers defined in WINDOWS.H ORed together.

Identifier	Value	Meaning
DLGC_BUTTON	0x2000	Control can be checked.
DLGC_DEFPUSHBUTTON	0x0010	Control is a default push button.
DLGC_HASSETSEL	0x0008	Control processes *EM_SETSEL* messages.
DLGC_RADIOBUTTON	0x0040	Control is a radio button.
DLGC_STATIC	0x0100	Control doesn't process any keys.
DLGC_UNDEFPUSHBUTTON	0x0020	Control is not a default push button.
DLGC_WANTALLKEYS	0x0004	Control processes all keys. Same as *DLGC_WANTMESSAGE*.
DLGC_WANTARROWS	0x0001	Control processes arrow keys.
DLGC_WANTCHARS	0x0080	Control wants *WM_CHAR* messages.
DLGC_WANTMESSAGE	0x0004	Control processes all keys. Same as *DLGC_WANTALLKEYS*.
DLGC_WANTTAB	0x0002	Control processes the Tab key.

This message allows a control to let the dialog-box manager know which keys it would like to receive. For example, if the EDIT control's window procedure responded to the *WM_GETDLGCODE* message by returning *DLG_WANT-ALLKEYS*, the Tab key would be sent to the control and the dialog-box manager would not change the input focus to the next control, as would ordinarily be expected.

Because Meter does not process any keystrokes, it simply returns the *DLGC_STA-TIC* value:

```
LRESULT CALLBACK MeterWndProc (HWND hDlg, UINT uMsg, WPARAM
wParam,
      LPARAM lParam) {
   LRESULT lResult = 0;

   switch (uMsg) {
      case WM_GETDLGCODE:
         lResult = DLGC_STATIC;
         break;
         .

         .

         .

      }
         .

         .

         .

      return(lResult);
   }
```

The next two special messages are the *WM_SETFONT* and *WM_GETFONT* messages. These messages allow an application to tell the control which font it should use when displaying text. When an application tells a control which font to use to display text by sending it a *WM_SETFONT* message, the *wParam* parameter must contain the handle of a valid font. This font must remain valid for the lifetime of the control. The *lParam* parameter should be TRUE if the application wants the control to be repainted and FALSE if the control should not be repainted. The code for processing the *WM_SETFONT* message in the Meter control is shown below.

```
   case WM_SETFONT:
      SetWindowWord(hWnd, GWW_FONT, (HFONT) wParam);
      if (lParam) // Redraw the control immediately.
         InvalidateRect(hWnd, NULL, FALSE);

      break;   // lResult is zero, indicating that we processed the
               // message.
```

An application can also ask a control which font it is using by sending it a *WM_GETFONT* message. Meter processes this message as follows.

```
case WM_GETFONT:
    lResult = GetWindowWord(hWnd, GWW_FONT);
break;
```

The last special message processed by many controls is the *WM_ENABLE* message. Windows sends this message to a window when that window is being activated or deactivated. When a window is deactivated, Windows no longer sends hardware messages to that window (for example, keystroke and mouse messages). Usually, when a window is deactivated, it paints its contents on the screen in a grayed state.

To make a control's appearance consistent with its state, the control calls the *InvalidateRect* function upon receiving a *WM_ENABLE* message so the contents of the control will be repainted. When the control later receives the *WM_PAINT* message, it checks the enabled status of the control by calling *IsWindowEnabled(hWnd)* and paints itself accordingly. By the way, when the control originally receives the *WM_ENABLE* message, the *wParam* parameter indicates whether the the control is being enabled (TRUE) or disabled (FALSE). The window procedure usually ignores this parameter.

Since the Meter control is a static-like control that never receives any kind of input, it is unnecessary for *MeterWndFn* to trap the *WM_ENABLE* message at all. However, it is added for demonstration purposes.

Painting the Meter Control

Most of the work done by the Meter control is in the *WM_PAINT* message. First, the values used by Meter must be retrieved by sending the *MM_GETPARTSINJOB* and *MM_GETPARTSCOMPLETE* messages:

```
wPartsInJob = (WORD) SendMessage(hWnd, MM_GETPARTSINJOB, 0, 0l);
wPartsComplete = (WORD) SendMessage(hWnd, MM_GETPARTSCOMPLETE,
    0, 0l);
```

These values are retrieved by sending a message to the control instead of accessing the window's extra bytes directly with *GetWindowWord*. If Meter's implementation is someday changed so that these values are stored in a local block of memory, our code to retrieve the values would not have to change; only the processing for the *MM_GETPARTSINJOB* and *MM_GETPARTSCOMPLETE* messages would need to be modified. This is good programming practice because it places fewer dependencies in the code.

Now that we have these values, we create a string reflecting the percentage of the job completed:

```
wsprintf(szPercentage, "%d%%", (100 * wPartsComplete) /
    wPartsInJob);
```

The *BeginPaint* function gets a device context for the window. We then check to see if the application wishes the control to paint the percentage value using a font other than the default system font. This is done by retrieving the control's font and selecting it into the device context if it is not NULL. Next, the window's background and text colors are set to what the user has chosen in the colors section of Control Panel by default:

```
BeginPaint(hWnd, &ps);

hFont = GetWindowFont(hWnd);
if (hFont != NULL)
    SelectObject(ps.hdc, hFont);
SetBkColor(ps.hdc, GetSysColor(COLOR_WINDOW));
SetTextColor(ps.hdc, GetSysColor(COLOR_WINDOWTEXT));
```

Most child controls allow the parent to alter their colors. For example, an application may let the user select a color by presenting three scroll bars: one for the amount of red, one for the amount of green, and one for the amount of blue. Just before each scroll bar is about to paint itself, it allows the parent to alter the colors it will use. This way, the parent can make the scroll bars appear as red, green, and blue.

Child controls let parents alter their colors by sending a *WM_CTLCOLOR* message before the child paints its window. When the parent receives this message, *wParam* contains the handle to the device context the child will use when painting; *lParam* contains the child control's window handle in the low word and an identifier for the control type in the high word. The following identifiers are used to notify the parent of the type of control that is about to begin painting:

WINDOWS.H identifier	WINDOWS.H value	Type of control
CTLCOLOR_BTN	3	BUTTON control
CTLCOLOR_DLG	4	Dialog box
CTLCOLOR_EDIT	1	EDIT control
CTLCOLOR_LISTBOX	2	LISTBOX or COMBOBOX control
CTLCOLOR_SCROLLBAR	5	SCROLLBAR control
CTLCOLOR_STATIC	6	STATIC control

You may define an identifier for your own custom child controls via a *CTLCOLOR_** identifier in the header file for your control. Make sure you select a value that does not conflict with any of the previous values. METER.H defines the following identifier for use with the *WM_CTLCOLOR* message:

```
#define CTLCOLOR_METER          (100)
```

By passing the handle to the device context in *wParam*, the parent can use *SetBkColor* and *SetTextColor* to change the color the control will use for painting. The parent also has the option of changing any of the other attributes associated with a device context. When the parent receives a *WM_CTLCOLOR* message, it must return the handle of a valid brush. If the parent does not trap the *WM_CTLCOLOR* message, *DefWindowProc* does not alter anything in the device context; it just returns a valid brush handle on behalf of the parent. The code that processes the *WM_PAINT* message in the control's window procedure must select this brush into the device context before painting:

```
HBRUSH hBrush;
    .
    .
    .
```

```
hBrush = FORWARD_WM_CTLCOLOR(GetParent(hWnd), ps.hdc, hWnd,
CTLCOLOR_METER, SendMessage)
SelectObject(ps.hdc, hBrush);
    .

    .

    .
// Paint the window using the DC modified by parent and
// the brush returned by parent.
    .

    .

    .
EndPaint(hWnd, &ps);
```

The control's parent is responsible for destroying the brush. Brushes are usually created by the dialog box during *WM_INITDIALOG* message processing and destroyed during *WM_DESTROY* message processing.

Meter takes the window's background and text colors and displays their inverse to represent the part of the task that has been completed:

```
dwColor = GetBkColor(ps.hdc);
SetBkColor(ps.hdc, SetTextColor(ps.hdc, dwColor));
```

The left part of the window indicates the percentage of the job completed, while the right indicates the remaining percentage of the job. In the middle of the window is the percentage completed shown as a number. The rectangle that bounds the area to be drawn in the percent-completed color is calculated as follows:

```
GetClientRect(hWnd, &rcClient);
SetRect(&rcPrcnt, 0, 0, (rcClient.right * wPartsComplete) /
    wPartsInJob, rcClient.bottom);
```

The *ExtTextOut* function draws the left side of the window:

```
SetTextAlign(ps.hdc, TA_CENTER | TA_TOP);
ExtTextOut(ps.hdc, rcClient.right / 2,
```

```
(rcClient.bottom - HIWORD(GetTextExtent(ps.hdc, "X", 1))) / 2,
ETO_OPAQUE | ETO_CLIPPED, &rcPrcnt,
szPercentage, lstrlen(szPercentage), NULL);
```

The first parameter to *ExtTextOut* is the same for all functions that perform output, the handle to the device context. The second and third parameters specify the x- and y-coordinates where the string is to be placed. Because the text alignment is set to *TA_CENTER*, the text string will always be displayed centered in the middle of the window (*rcClient.right / 2*). To center the text vertically, the height of a capital letter X is subtracted from the height of the window and the result divided by two. The fourth parameter specifies that the background color should be used to fill the rectangle (*ETO_OPAQUE*) and that no text should be drawn outside the clipping rectangle (*ETO_CLIPPED*). The next parameter is the address of the clipping rectangle to be used. The address of the string containing the text and the length of the string are specified next. The final parameter is NULL, indicating that you want Windows to use normal spacing for displaying the text.

The coordinates of the rectangle are now changed to fill the right part of the window. First, the colors are inverted again:

```
rcPrcnt.left = rcPrcnt.right;
rcPrcnt.right = rcClient.right;

dwColor = GetBkColor(ps.hdc);
SetBkColor(ps.hdc, SetTextColor(ps.hdc, dwColor));
```

ExtTextOut is called again with the same parameters as before. This paints the right part of Meter's window.

Let's look at an example. If the job is 50 percent complete, Meter should display the string "50%" in the center of the window. The left half of the window should be in one color and the right half in a different color. If the background were drawn first and the string placed on top of it, some of the string would be unreadable because the text color would be the same as the background color. The solution: Write the string to the screen twice, first with the clipping rectangle on the left half of the window and then with the clipping rectangle on the right. *ExtTextOut* will not allow any text to be written outside the clipping rectangle because of the *ETO_CLIPPED* option. In the case of our string, the first call to *ExtTextOut* draws the five and the left half of the zero. The second call draws the right half of the zero and the percent symbol.

The remaining messages processed by Meter's window procedure are class specific. *MM_GETPARTSINJOB* and *MM_GETPARTSCOMPLETE* simply place calls to *GetWindowWord* and return the result to the caller. *MM_SETPARTSINJOB* and *MM_SETPARTSCOMPLETE* call *SetWindowWord,* passing it the value in *wParam.* Because a value has changed, making the contents of Meter's window inaccurate, we call *InvalidateRect* so a *WM_PAINT* message for the Meter control will be placed in the application's message queue.

Windows will not examine any window's message queue until the executing application yields control. This happens when the application calls Windows' function *PeekMessage*, *GetMessage,* or *WaitMessage.* When copying files from the floppy drive to the hard disk, for instance, the application may not yield control to Windows until all the files have been copied. This means the *WM_PAINT* message might not be sent to Meter until all files have been copied. Meter would report "0%" complete until the job was done, then suddenly jump to "100%" complete. The user would never see any intermediate progress.

To force Meter to reflect the true percentage complete when the application sends a *MM_SETPARTSINJOB* or *MM_SETPARTSCOMPLETE* message, you must call *UpdateWindow.* This forces Windows to send the *WM_PAINT* message to the window immediately.

The last section in this chapter, "Integrating Custom Child Controls with Microsoft's Dialog Editor," demonstrates how the Meter control can be added to dialog boxes with the Dialog Editor and how to manipulate Meter controls from your application. Because additional functions are necessary to integrate Meter with the Dialog Editor, the module-definitions file (METER.DEF) and the MAKE-FILE appear later in this chapter. The Meter source and header modules appear in Listings 4-1 and 4-2.

Listing 4-1. METER.H DLL header module

```
/*******************************************************************
Module name: METER.H
Programmer : Jeffrey M. Richter.
*******************************************************************/

// Meter control sends WM_CTLCOLOR message to parent window
// with the following identifier with in the HIWORD of the lParam.
#define CTLCOLOR_METER      (100)

// Meter control doesn't have any class-specific window styles.

// Meter control's class-specific window messages.
#define MM_SETPARTSINJOB        (WM_USER + 0)
#define MM_GETPARTSINJOB        (WM_USER + 1)
#define MM_SETPARTSCOMPLETE     (WM_USER + 2)
#define MM_GETPARTSCOMPLETE     (WM_USER + 3)

// Meter control has no notification codes to send to parent.

#define DLG_STYLEDLG    1000
#define ID_VALUE        100
```

Listing 4-2. METER.C DLL source module

```
/*******************************************************************
Module name: METER.C
Programmer : Jeffrey M. Richter.
*******************************************************************/

#include <windows.h>
#include <windowsx.h>

#include "meter.h"

extern const HINSTANCE _cdecl _hInstance;

char _szControlName[] = "Meter";

#define CBWNDEXTRA          (6)
#define GWW_PARTSINJOB      (0)
#define GWW_PARTSCOMPLETE   (2)
#define GWW_FONT            (4)
```

```
ATOM NEAR RegisterControlClass (HINSTANCE hInstance);
LRESULT CALLBACK MeterWndFn
        (HWND hWnd, UINT uMsg, WPARAM wParam, LPARAM lParam);

/******** Dynamic-Link Library Initialization Routines **********/

#pragma argsused
BOOL WINAPI LibMain (HINSTANCE hInstance, WORD wDataSeg,
   WORD wHeapSize, LPSTR lpszCmdLine) {
   BOOL fOk;
   if (wHeapSize != 0) UnlockData(0);  // Let data segment move.
   fOk = (RegisterControlClass(hInstance) != NULL);
   return(fOk);   // Return TRUE if initialization is successful.
}

int WINAPI WEP (int nSystemExit) {
   switch (nSystemExit) {
      case WEP_SYSTEM_EXIT:   // System is shutting down.
         break;

      case WEP_FREE_DLL:      // Usage count is zero (0).
         break;
   }
   UnregisterClass(_szControlName, _hInstance);
   return(1);                 // WEP function successful.
}

ATOM NEAR RegisterControlClass (HINSTANCE hInstance) {
   WNDCLASS wc;
   wc.style         = CS_GLOBALCLASS | CS_HREDRAW | CS_VREDRAW;
   wc.lpfnWndProc   = MeterWndFn;
   wc.cbClsExtra    = 0;
   wc.cbWndExtra    = CBWNDEXTRA;
   wc.hInstance     = hInstance;
   wc.hIcon         = (HICON) NULL;
   wc.hCursor       = LoadCursor((HCURSOR) NULL, IDC_ARROW);
   wc.hbrBackground = (HBRUSH) NULL;
   wc.lpszMenuName  = NULL;
   wc.lpszClassName = _szControlName;
   return(RegisterClass(&wc));
}

LRESULT CALLBACK MeterWndFn
      (HWND hWnd, UINT uMsg, WPARAM wParam, LPARAM lParam) {
   LRESULT lResult = 0;
```

```
char szPercentage[10];
RECT rcClient, rcPrcnt;
PAINTSTRUCT ps;
WORD wPartsInJob, wPartsComplete;
HBRUSH hBrush;
DWORD dwColor;
HFONT hFont;

switch (uMsg) {
   case WM_GETDLGCODE:
      lResult = DLGC_STATIC;
      break;

   case WM_SETFONT:
      SetWindowWord(hWnd, GWW_FONT, (HFONT) wParam);
      if (lParam) // Redraw the control immediately.
         InvalidateRect(hWnd, NULL, FALSE);

      break;

   case WM_GETFONT:
      lResult = GetWindowWord(hWnd, GWW_FONT);
      break;

   case WM_ENABLE:
      InvalidateRect(hWnd, NULL, FALSE);
      break;

   case WM_CREATE:   // lParam == &CreateStruct.
      SendMessage(hWnd, MM_SETPARTSINJOB, 100, 0l);
      SendMessage(hWnd, MM_SETPARTSCOMPLETE, 50, 0);
      break;

   case WM_PAINT:
      wPartsInJob = (WORD)
         SendMessage(hWnd, MM_GETPARTSINJOB,  0, 0l);
      wPartsComplete = (WORD)
         SendMessage(hWnd, MM_GETPARTSCOMPLETE, 0, 0l);
      if (wPartsInJob == 0) {
         wPartsInJob = 1;
         wPartsComplete = 0;
      }

      wsprintf(szPercentage, "%d%%",
         (100 * wPartsComplete) / wPartsInJob);
```

```
BeginPaint(hWnd, &ps);
hFont = GetWindowFont(hWnd);
if (hFont != NULL)
   SelectObject(ps.hdc, hFont);

// Setup default foreground and background text colors.
SetBkColor(ps.hdc, GetSysColor(COLOR_WINDOW));
SetTextColor(ps.hdc, GetSysColor(COLOR_WINDOWTEXT));

// Send WM_CTLCOLOR message to parent in case parent
// wants to use a different color in the Meter control.
hBrush = FORWARD_WM_CTLCOLOR(GetParent(hWnd),
   ps.hdc, hWnd, CTLCOLOR_METER, SendMessage);

// Always use brush returned by parent.
SelectObject(ps.hdc, hBrush);

// Invert the foreground and background colors.
dwColor = GetBkColor(ps.hdc);
SetBkColor(ps.hdc, SetTextColor(ps.hdc, dwColor));

// Set rectangle coordinates to include only left
// percentage of the window.
GetClientRect(hWnd, &rcClient);
SetRect(&rcPrcnt, 0, 0,
   (rcClient.right * wPartsComplete) / wPartsInJob,
   rcClient.bottom);

// Output the percentage value in the window.
// Function also paints left part of window.
SetTextAlign(ps.hdc, TA_CENTER | TA_TOP);
ExtTextOut(ps.hdc, rcClient.right / 2,
   (rcClient.bottom -
   HIWORD(GetTextExtent(ps.hdc, "X", 1))) / 2,
   ETO_OPAQUE | ETO_CLIPPED, &rcPrcnt,
   szPercentage, lstrlen(szPercentage), NULL);

// Adjust rectangle so that it includes the remaining
// percentage of the window.
rcPrcnt.left = rcPrcnt.right;
rcPrcnt.right = rcClient.right;

// Invert the foreground and background colors.
dwColor = GetBkColor(ps.hdc);
SetBkColor(ps.hdc, SetTextColor(ps.hdc, dwColor));
```

```
        // Output the percentage value a second time.
        // Function also paints right part of window.
        ExtTextOut(ps.hdc, rcClient.right / 2,
            (rcClient.bottom -
            HIWORD(GetTextExtent(ps.hdc, "X", 1))) / 2,
            ETO_OPAQUE | ETO_CLIPPED, &rcPrcnt,
            szPercentage, lstrlen(szPercentage), NULL);

        EndPaint(hWnd, &ps);
        break;

    case MM_SETPARTSINJOB:
        SetWindowWord(hWnd, GWW_PARTSINJOB, wParam);
        InvalidateRect(hWnd, NULL, FALSE);
        UpdateWindow(hWnd);
        break;

    case MM_GETPARTSINJOB:
        lResult = (LONG) GetWindowWord(hWnd, GWW_PARTSINJOB);
        break;

    case MM_SETPARTSCOMPLETE:
        SetWindowWord(hWnd, GWW_PARTSCOMPLETE, wParam);
        InvalidateRect(hWnd, NULL, FALSE);
        UpdateWindow(hWnd);
        break;

    case MM_GETPARTSCOMPLETE:
        lResult = (LONG) GetWindowWord(hWnd, GWW_PARTSCOMPLETE);
        break;

    default:
        lResult = DefWindowProc(hWnd, uMsg, wParam, lParam);
        break;
    }
  return(lResult);
}
```

A Homespun Spin Button

Although many of the applications that come with Windows use spin buttons, Microsoft has not designed one as a system global class that can be used by our applications.

A spin button allows the user to cycle through a list of values. It should only be used when the choices are in consecutive order and the user can anticipate the next value.

There should always be a default value in the edit field. A spin button is a convenience for mouse users only and never receives the keyboard input focus. Therefore, the EDIT control associated with the spin button should let the user type directly into the field and allow the use of the up and down arrow keys to cycle through the choices.

The programmer must tell the Spin Button control the range of possible values. For example, an application may associate a spin button with a month field. In this case, the application would tell the spin button that the valid range is one to 12. The spin button also maintains a value, within the valid range, that indicates the current value. If the month displayed in the edit field is July, the current value associated with the spin button is seven.

Designing the Spin Button Programmer's Interface

The first step in designing the programmer's interface for the spin button is deciding what styles, if any, can be specified to modify the behavior of the custom child control. Our spin button supports only one style, *SPNS_WRAP*. It is defined in SPIN.H as

```
#define SPNS_WRAP 0x0001L
```

By examining the Windows Control Panel application, you see spin buttons behaving in two ways. In the "Date/Time" option, the spin button wraps around when the value reaches a maximum or minimum. For example, if the month is 12 and the spin button is used to increment the month, the value wraps around to the value one. Similarly, decrementing the month when it is at one changes the value to 12.

If you choose the "Desktop" option in the Control Panel, you'll notice that the range associated with the Granularity field is zero to 49 and the value will not wrap. That is, using the spin button to increment the Granularity field when it is at 49 has no effect on the value.

By default, our spin button will not allow wrapping. If the application wishes to create a spin button that does allow wrapping, you must *OR* the *SPNS_WRAP* style with the other window styles when creating the custom child control. The header file, SPIN.H, includes all the styles that can be used when creating a Spin Button control and must be included by applications that use this control. If spin buttons are created in dialog boxes that have been defined in the resource file, this header file must also be included there so that the resource compiler knows the values of any control-specific styles.

The next part of the programmer's interface is the messages that are to be recognized by the control. The Spin Button control recognizes five messages (four for use by applications using the Spin control, which are defined in SPIN.H, and one for the Spin control's private use.) The messages and their descriptions are as follows:

Message	Description	Returns	wParam	lParam
SPNM_SETRANGE	Sets the valid range.	N/A	Not used	Bottom of range in the low word. Top of range in the high word.
SPNM_GETRANGE	Gets the valid range.	Bottom of range in low word. Top of range in high word.	Not used	Not used
SPNM_SETCRNTVALUE	Sets the current value.	N/A	New value	Not used
SPNM_GETCRNTVALUE	Gets the current value.	Current value	Not used	Not used
SPNM_SCROLLVALUE	Increments or decrements the current value. The message is sent from the spin button itself. It is not sent from other windows.			

It is sometimes necessary for a control to recognize messages that can only be sent from the control itself. For example, the spin button's window procedure sends a *SPNM_SCROLLVALUE* message to itself while the user holds down the mouse button. This message should never be sent from any other window. The message should not be placed in the control's header file but in the file containing the window procedure. It should be defined so that its value will not interfere with the values assigned to messages that may be sent from other windows. For example, defining the *SPNM_SCROLLVALUE* message as

```
#define SPNM_SCROLLVALUE        (WM_USER + 500)
```

leaves room for 500 public class-specific messages, (*WM_USER* + 0) to (*WM_USER* + 499). This should be more than enough. Remember that the values of class-specific messages must be within the range of (*WM_USER* + 0) to 0x7FFF. In WINDOWS.H, *WM_USER* is defined as 0x0400.

The last part of the programmer's interface defines the notification codes that can be sent from the custom child control. Notification codes are always sent via *WM_COMMAND* messages to the control's parent. The notification code *SPNN_VALUECHANGE* sent from a spin button notifies the parent whenever the spin button's value has changed.

Implementing the Spin Button Code

The *LibMain* and *WEP* functions in the spin button's source code are identical to those in Meter. *RegisterControlClass* is also identical, except that the *hbrBackground* member of the *WNDCLASS* structure is set to *COLOR_BTNFACE* + 1. Because of this, the spin button's background will have the same color as a push button.

The Spin Button control must maintain a value representing the valid range as well as the current value. Because the range consists of a low number and a high number, a *DWORD* is required. The current value requires a *WORD*. The spin button also needs to maintain an additional *WORD* value that is used internally. This value is explained later. The *#define*s to access this information are found at the top of the SPIN.C file:

```
#define CBWNDEXTRA              (8)
#define GWL_RANGE               (0)
#define GWW_CRNTVALUE           (4)
#define GWW_TRIANGLEPRESSED     (6)
```

Painting the Spin Button Control

The push buttons in Windows are complicated to draw because of their three-dimensional effect. To maintain this effect, the *WM_PAINT* message in the window procedure for a push button control ignores any changes made to the device context when the control's parent processes the *WM_CTLCOLOR* message. Instead, colors are retrieved by calling *GetSysColor* using the *COLOR_BTNFACE*, *COLOR_BTNSHADOW*, and *COLOR_BTNTEXT* identifiers. Because spin buttons use the same colors as push buttons, the spin button does not send a *WM_CTL-COLOR* message to its parent when processing a *WM_PAINT* message.

The code that processes the spin buttons *WM_PAINT* message is shown below:

```
hDC = BeginPaint(hWnd, &ps);
GetClientRect(hWnd, &rc);
x = rc.right / 2;
y = rc.bottom / 2;

// Draw middle separator bar.
MoveTo(hDC, 0, y);
LineTo(hDC, rc.right, y);

// Whenever a DC is retrieved, it is created with a WHITE_BRUSH
// by default. We must change this to a BLACK_BRUSH so that we
// can fill the triangles.
SelectObject(hDC, GetStockObject(BLACK_BRUSH));

// Draw top triangle and fill it in.
MoveTo(hDC, x, 2);
LineTo(hDC, rc.right - 2, y - 2);
LineTo(hDC, 2, y - 2);
LineTo(hDC, x, 2);
FloodFill(hDC, x, y - 3, RGB(0, 0, 0));

// Draw bottom triangle and fill it in.
MoveTo(hDC, 2, y + 2);
LineTo(hDC, rc.right - 2, y + 2);
LineTo(hDC, x, rc.bottom - 2);
LineTo(hDC, 2, y + 2);
FloodFill(hDC, x, y + 3, RGB(0, 0, 0));

EndPaint(hWnd, &ps);
break;
```

When *BeginPaint* is called, Windows repaints the background of the window using the color selected in the *hbrBackground* member of *WNDCLASS* when the class is registered. In this case, this is the color used for button faces, *COLOR_BTN-FACE*. The x and y values are calculated to be the middle of the window. The spin button must draw a horizontal bar across the middle of the window and draw the two triangles.

Because the triangles are always drawn in black, *BLACK_BRUSH* is selected into the device context. Once the outline of each triangle has been drawn, a point is selected that is known to be within each triangle, and *FloodFill* fills the triangle with black.

Figure 4-3 shows how the interior of the spin button is drawn.

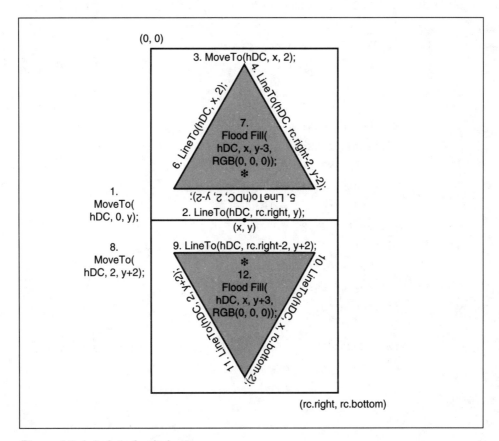

Figure 4-3. Interior of spin button

Changing a Value with the Spin Button

A *WM_LBUTTONDOWN* message is sent to the spin button's window procedure when the user clicks the mouse. During this procedure, the spin button must determine whether the mouse is over the up-triangle or the down-triangle. This can easily be computed because the *lParam* for a *WM_LBUTTONDOWN* message contains the x- and y-coordinates of the mouse cursor relative to the window's client area:

```
typedef enum { TP_NONE, TP_UP, TP_DOWN } TRIANGLEPRESSED;

    .
    .
    .

LRESULT CALLBACK SpinWndFn (HWND hWnd, UINT uMsg, WPARAM wParam,
    LPARAM lParam) {
  TRIANGLEPRESSED TrianglePressed;

    .
    .
    .

  case WM_LBUTTONDOWN:
    GetClientRect(hWnd, &rc);
    if ((int) HIWORD(lParam) < rc.bottom / 2) {
      // Mouse over up-triangle.
      TrianglePressed = TP_UP;
      rc.bottom /= 2;
    } else {
      // Mouse over down-triangle.
      TrianglePressed = TP_DOWN;
      rc.top = rc.bottom / 2;
    }
    SetWindowWord(hWnd, GWW_TRIANGLEPRESSED, TrianglePressed);

    .
    .
    .

  }
```

TrianglePressed is an enumerated type that represents the triangle the mouse was last over. This value is stored in the window extra bytes for the spin button so that it can be used later by the *SPNM_SCROLLVALUE* message.

Using the updated value in the *RECT* variable, *rc*, you invert the half of the spin button over which the mouse is clicked to indicate to the user that the spin button has been activated:

```
hDC = GetDC(hWnd);
InvertRect(hDC, &rc);
ReleaseDC(hWnd, hDC);
```

Let's tackle a common problem faced by many child controls and applications: How to continue scrolling when no messages are entering the window procedure.

Suppose you are marking text in a Notepad-like application by clicking the mouse on the start of the desired text and dragging the mouse below the window. Once the mouse moves below the window, the window no longer receives mouse messages. One way to continue scrolling is by setting a timer when the *WM_LBUT-TONDOWN* message is received. This will cause *WM_TIMER* messages to come to your window procedure periodically. With each timer message, the window could be scrolled.

This method has some disadvantages:

1. Other applications are allowed to run while your application is scrolling and your window procedure is waiting for *WM_TIMER* messages. While this may seem like an advantage, the effect to the user is uneven, jerky scrolling. In fact, this may even give the appearance that your application has stopped working completely if another application does not relinquish control for you to receive another *WM_TIMER* message.

2. It requires a timer. Windows allows only a small number of timers to be active at any one time. While this is usually sufficient, users do not expect to see an "Out of timers!" message when they want to begin scrolling through their text.

The spin button window procedure for scrolling avoids the problems associated with using timers. This method starts a loop that compares the current Windows system time with the time the next event should occur. The system time is retrieved by using the *GetTickCount* function. If the system time is earlier than the event start time, the loop repeats. When the Windows system time is later than the event start time, the event is executed and the new event start time is set to the current Windows system time plus a programmer-defined delay period. The cycle then repeats.

It is important to decide on a time delay between scrolling events. The spin button uses an identifier at the top of its source code:

```
// Delay between scrolling events in milliseconds.
#define TIME_DELAY          (150)
```

We then calculate the time of the first event by retrieving the current Windows system time and subtracting the time delay from it. This ensures that the scrolling event occurs at least once:

```
dwEventTime = GetTickCount() - TIME_DELAY;
```

The *do...while* loop below continues to send *SPNM_SCROLLVALUE* messages to the spin button's window procedure, telling it to scroll the button's value until the user has released the left mouse button:

```
do {
    if (dwEventTime > GetTickCount()) continue;
    SendMessage(hWnd, SPNM_SCROLLVALUE, 0, 0l);
    dwEventTime = GetTickCount() + TIME_DELAY;
} while (GetAsyncKeyState(VK_LBUTTON) & 0x8000);
```

The *GetAsyncKeyState* function tests the status of virtual keys. In this case, you test the status of the left mouse button (*VK_LBUTTON*). If the most significant bit of the return value is one, the virtual key is still held down and the loop continues.

At the top of the loop, check to see if the current Windows system time is later than the event time. If it isn't, no actions are performed and the loop condition is tested again. If the event time has passed, the *SPNM_SCROLLVALUE* message is sent, causing the spin button to update its value. After the value has been scrolled, *dwEventTime* is set to the time the next event should occur and the loop continues.

Once the user has released the left mouse button, the Spin Button window must be redrawn to remove the half that is currently inverted:

```
InvalidateRect(hWnd, NULL, TRUE);
```

The *InvalidateRect* function instructs Windows to send a *WM_PAINT* message to the window procedure, redrawing the window in its "normal" state.

Scrolling the Spin Button

The value in the spin button is scrolled while the *SPNM_SCROLLVALUE* message is being processed. This is an internal message that is only sent by the spin button to itself. For this reason, the message is not in the header file, SPIN.H, but is defined at the top of the SPIN.C source file (presented at the end of this section):

```
#define SPNM_SCROLLVALUE     (WM_USER + 500)
```

This message is generated at 150-millisecond intervals for as long as the user holds down the left mouse button.

You may notice by experimenting with the spin buttons in the "Date/Time" section of the Control Panel application that the user is able to change the scrolling direction while the mouse button is held down. That is, if the user activates the spin button by clicking on its down-triangle, the month value will begin to decrease. If the user now moves the mouse over the up-triangle without releasing the mouse button, the month values begin to increase and the spin button is inverted to indicate the directional change. Also notice that when the mouse cursor is not over the spin button at all, no scrolling occurs, even if the mouse button is held down.

The processing for the *SPNM_SCROLLVALUE* message is responsible for making our spin button behave the same way. First, if the mouse cursor is outside the spin button's window, nothing should happen. The following code accomplishes this:

```
GetCursorPos(&pt);
ScreenToClient(hWnd, &pt);
GetClientRect(hWnd, &rc);
if (!PtInRect(&rc, pt)) break;
```

The *GetCursorPos* function retrieves the current mouse position in screen coordinates. This value must be converted to client coordinates before the *PtIn-Rect* function can determine whether the mouse cursor is within the spin button's client area.

Next, the current value and the valid range of the spin button are retrieved from the window extra bytes:

```
nNewVal = (int) SendMessage(hWnd, SPNM_GETCRNTVALUE, 0, 0l);
nCrntVal = nNewVal;
dwRange = SendMessage(hWnd, SPNM_GETRANGE, 0, 0l);
```

The function also determines whether this particular spin button was created with the *SPNS_WRAP* flag. This data will be used later.

```
fWrap = (BOOL) (GetWindowLong(hWnd, GWL_STYLE) & SPNS_WRAP);
```

To see if the user has changed direction by moving the mouse cursor over a different triangle, we must determine which triangle the mouse was over last and which half it is over now:

```
OldTrianglePressed = (TRIANGLEPRESSED)
   GetWindowWord(hWnd, GWW_TRIANGLEPRESSED);
TrianglePressed = (pt.y < rc.bottom / 2) ? TP_UP : TP_DOWN;
```

If the user has changed directions, the window must be inverted to give visual feedback to the user that the spin button has recognized this. Remember that the initial processing in the *WM_LBUTTONDOWN* message has already inverted half of the window. Inverting the entire window has the effect of restoring the half that was already inverted and inverting the new half:

```
if (OldTrianglePressed != TrianglePressed) {
   hDC = GetDC(hWnd);
   InvertRect(hDC, &rc);
   ReleaseDC(hWnd, hDC);
}
```

Finally, you can scroll the value:

```
if (TrianglePressed == TP_UP) {
   // If value is not at top of range, increment it.
   if ((int) HIWORD(dwRange) > nCrntVal) nNewVal++;
   else {
      // If value is at top of range and the "wrap" flag is
      // set, set the value to the bottom of the range.
      if (fWrap) nNewVal = (int) LOWORD(dwRange);
   }
} else {
   // If value is not at bottom of range, decrement it.
   if ((int) LOWORD(dwRange) < nCrntVal) nNewVal-;
   else {
      // If value is at bottom of range and the "wrap" flag is
      // set, set the value to the top of the range.
      if (fWrap) nNewVal = (int) HIWORD(dwRange);
   }
}
```

After the new value has been determined, if it differs from the previous value the *SPNM_SETCRNTVALUE* message is sent to the spin button telling it the new value:

```
if (nNewVal != nCrntVal)
   SendMessage(hWnd, SPNM_SETCRNTVALUE, nNewVal, 0l);
```

This also notifies the parent window that the spin button's value has changed because the code that processes the *WM_SETCRNTVALUE* message sends a

WM_COMMAND message with the *SPNN_VALUECHANGE* notification code to the parent.

Just before the processing of the *SPNM_SCROLLVALUE* message terminates, the new triangle that is down must be stored so you will know how to update the window when the next scroll event occurs:

```
SetWindowWord(hWnd, GWW_TRIANGLEPRESSED, TrianglePressed);
```

The spin button must also maintain the current value. Since this is a relatively small amount of information, it's best to use the window extra bytes.

The "Integrating Custom Child Controls with Microsoft's Dialog Editor" section, which appears later in this chapter, demonstrates how the Spin Button control can be added to dialog boxes with the Dialog Editor and how to manipulate Spin Button controls from your application. Because additional functions are necessary to integrate the Spin Button control with the Dialog Editor, the module definitions file (SPIN.DEF) and the MAKEFILE appear later in this chapter.

Listing 4-3. SPIN.H DLL header module

```
/****************************************************************
Module name: SPIN.H
Programmer : Jeffrey M. Richter.
****************************************************************/

// Spin button doesn't send WM_CTLCOLOR message to parent window.


// Spin button's class-specific window styles.
#define SPNS_WRAP          0x0001L


// Spin button's class-specific window messages.
#define SPNM_SETRANGE       (WM_USER + 0)
#define SPNM_GETRANGE       (WM_USER + 1)
#define SPNM_SETCRNTVALUE   (WM_USER + 2)
#define SPNM_GETCRNTVALUE   (WM_USER + 3)

// Spin button's notification codes sent in HIWORD of lParam
// during a WM_COMMAND message.
```

```
#define SPNN_VALUECHANGE    (1)

#define ID_VALUE     100
#define ID_WRAP      101
```

Listing 4-4. SPIN.C DLL source module

```
/*******************************************************************
Module name: SPIN.C
Programmer : Jeffrey M. Richter.
*******************************************************************/

#include <windows.h>

#include "spin.h"

extern const HINSTANCE _cdecl _hInstance;

#define CBWNDEXTRA              (8)
#define GWL_RANGE               (0)
#define GWW_CRNTVALUE           (4)
#define GWW_TRIANGLEPRESSED     (6)

#define SPNM_SCROLLVALUE        (WM_USER + 500)

    // Time delay between scrolling events in milliseconds.
#define TIME_DELAY              (150)

typedef enum { TP_NONE, TP_UP, TP_DOWN } TRIANGLEPRESSED;

char _szControlName[] = "Spin";

ATOM NEAR RegisterControlClass (HINSTANCE hInstance);
LRESULT CALLBACK SpinWndFn
    (HWND hWnd, UINT uMsg, WPARAM wParam, LPARAM lParam);

/*** Window's Dynamic-Link Library Initialization Routines ******/

#pragma argsused
BOOL WINAPI LibMain (HINSTANCE hInstance, WORD wDataSeg,
    WORD wHeapSize, LPSTR lpszCmdLine) {
    BOOL fOk;
    if (wHeapSize != 0) UnlockData(0);  // Let data segment move
    fOk = (RegisterControlClass(hInstance) != NULL);
    return(fOk);    // Return TRUE if initialization is successful.
}
```

```
int WINAPI WEP (int nSystemExit) {

   switch (nSystemExit) {
      case WEP_SYSTEM_EXIT:   // System is shutting down.
         break;
      case WEP_FREE_DLL:      // Usage count is zero (0).
         break;
   }
   UnregisterClass(_szControlName, _hInstance);
   return(1);                  // WEP function successful.
}

ATOM NEAR RegisterControlClass (HINSTANCE hInstance) {
   WNDCLASS wc;
   wc.style          = CS_GLOBALCLASS | CS_HREDRAW | CS_VREDRAW;
   wc.lpfnWndProc    = SpinWndFn;
   wc.cbClsExtra     = 0;
   wc.cbWndExtra     = CBWNDEXTRA;
   wc.hInstance      = hInstance;
   wc.hIcon          = (HICON) NULL;
   wc.hCursor        = LoadCursor((HCURSOR) NULL, IDC_ARROW);
   wc.hbrBackground  = COLOR_BTNFACE + 1;
   wc.lpszMenuName   = NULL;
   wc.lpszClassName  = _szControlName;
   return(RegisterClass(&wc));
}


static LRESULT NEAR NotifyParent
         (HWND hWndControl, WORD wNotifyCode) {
   LRESULT lResult;
   lResult = SendMessage(GetParent(hWndControl), WM_COMMAND,
            GetWindowWord(hWndControl, GWW_ID),
            MAKELPARAM(hWndControl, wNotifyCode));
   return(lResult);
}

LRESULT CALLBACK SpinWndFn
         (HWND hWnd, UINT uMsg, WPARAM wParam, LPARAM lParam) {
   LRESULT lResult = 0;
   HDC hDC;
   POINT pt;
   RECT rc;
   PAINTSTRUCT ps;
   int nCrntVal, nNewVal, x, y;
   TRIANGLEPRESSED TrianglePressed, OldTrianglePressed;
   DWORD dwEventTime, dwRange;
```

```
BOOL fWrap;

switch (uMsg) {
    case WM_GETDLGCODE:
        lResult = DLGC_STATIC;
        break;
    case WM_ENABLE:
        InvalidateRect(hWnd, NULL, FALSE);
        break;

    case WM_CREATE:    // lParam == &CreateStruct.
        SendMessage(hWnd, SPNM_SETRANGE, 0, MAKELPARAM(0, 0));
        SendMessage(hWnd, SPNM_SETCRNTVALUE, 0, 0);
        break;

    case WM_PAINT:
        // Calling BeginPaint sends a WM_ERASEBKGND message.
        // Because that message is not trapped, DefWindowProc
        // uses the system color COLOR_BTNFACE because it was
        // specified in the hbrBackground member of the
        // WNDCLASS structure when this class was registered.
        hDC = BeginPaint(hWnd, &ps);

        GetClientRect(hWnd, &rc);
        x = rc.right / 2;
        y = rc.bottom / 2;

            // Draw middle separator bar.
        MoveTo(hDC, 0, y);
        LineTo(hDC, rc.right, y);

        // Whenever a DC is retrieved, it contains a WHITE_BRUSH
        // by default; change this to a BLACK_BRUSH so that you
        // can fill the triangles.
        SelectObject(hDC, GetStockObject(BLACK_BRUSH));

            // Draw top triangle and fill it in.
        MoveTo(hDC, x, 2);
        LineTo(hDC, rc.right - 2, y - 2);
        LineTo(hDC, 2, y - 2);
        LineTo(hDC, x, 2);
        FloodFill(hDC, x, y - 3, RGB(0, 0, 0));

            // Draw bottom triangle and fill it in.
        MoveTo(hDC, 2, y + 2);
        LineTo(hDC, rc.right - 2, y + 2);
```

```
        LineTo(hDC, x, rc.bottom - 2);
        LineTo(hDC, 2, y + 2);
        FloodFill(hDC, x, y + 3, RGB(0, 0, 0));
        EndPaint(hWnd, &ps);
        break;

case WM_LBUTTONDOWN:
    // Get coordinates for the Spin Button's window.
    GetClientRect(hWnd, &rc);

    if ((int) HIWORD(lParam) < rc.bottom / 2) {  // Up arrow
        TrianglePressed = TP_UP;
        // Change coordinates so rectangle includes
        // only the top-half of the window.
        rc.bottom /= 2;
    } else {
        TrianglePressed = TP_DOWN;

        // Change coordinates so rectangle includes
        // only the bottom-half of the window.
        rc.top = rc.bottom / 2;
    }

    // Save the triangle the mouse was clicked over.
    SetWindowWord(hWnd,
        GWW_TRIANGLEPRESSED, TrianglePressed);

    // Invert the top or bottom half of the window where the
    // mouse was clicked.
    hDC = GetDC(hWnd);
    InvertRect(hDC, &rc);
    ReleaseDC(hWnd, hDC);

    SetCapture(hWnd);

    // Subtract TIME_DELAY so action is done at least once.
    dwEventTime = GetTickCount() - TIME_DELAY;

    do {
        // Is it time to execute the event?
        if (dwEventTime > GetTickCount())
            continue;

        // Execute the event; scroll value in spin button.
        SendMessage(hWnd, SPNM_SCROLLVALUE, 0, 0l);
```

```
        // Get time of next scroll event.
        dwEventTime = GetTickCount() + TIME_DELAY;

        // Check if left mouse button is still down.
    } while (GetAsyncKeyState(VK_LBUTTON) & 0x8000);

    ReleaseCapture();

    // Invalidate the entire window. This will force Windows
    // to send a WM_PAINT message restoring the window to its
    // original colors.
    InvalidateRect(hWnd, NULL, TRUE);
    break;

case SPNM_SCROLLVALUE:
    // Get the location of the mouse.
    GetCursorPos(&pt);

    // Convert the point from screen coordinates
    // to client coordinates.
    ScreenToClient(hWnd, &pt);

    // If the point is NOT is spin's client area, nothing to do.
    GetClientRect(hWnd, &rc);
    #pragma warn -stv
    if (!PtInRect(&rc, pt)) break;
    #pragma warn .stv

    // Get the spin button's current value and range.
    nNewVal = (int)
        SendMessage(hWnd, SPNM_GETCRNTVALUE, 0, 0l);
    nCrntVal = nNewVal;
    dwRange = SendMessage(hWnd, SPNM_GETRANGE, 0, 0l);

    // Get spin button's styles and test if the
    // "wrap" flag is set.
    fWrap = (BOOL)
        (GetWindowLong(hWnd, GWL_STYLE) & SPNS_WRAP);

    // Determine which triangle was selected.
    OldTrianglePressed = (TRIANGLEPRESSED)
        GetWindowWord(hWnd, GWW_TRIANGLEPRESSED);

    // Determine which triangle the mouse is now over.
    TrianglePressed = (pt.y < rc.bottom / 2)
        ? TP_UP : TP_DOWN;
```

253

```
    // If the user has switched triangles, invert the entire
    // rectangle. This restores the half that was inverted in
    // the WM_LBUTTONDOWN message and inverts the new half.
    if (OldTrianglePressed != TrianglePressed) {
        hDC = GetDC(hWnd);
        InvertRect(hDC, &rc);
        ReleaseDC(hWnd, hDC);
    }

    if (TrianglePressed == TP_UP) {
        // If value is not at top of range, increment it.
        if ((int) HIWORD(dwRange) > nCrntVal) nNewVal++;
        else {
            // If value at top of range and the "wrap" flag
            // is set, set value to the bottom of the range.
            if (fWrap) nNewVal = (int) LOWORD(dwRange);
        }

    } else {
        // If value is not at bottom of range, decrement it.
        if ((int) LOWORD(dwRange) < nCrntVal) nNewVal-;
        else {
            // If value at bottom of range and the "wrap" flag
            // is set, set the value to the top of the range.
            if (fWrap) nNewVal = (int) HIWORD(dwRange);
        }
    }

    // If the value has been changed, set the new value.
    if (nNewVal != nCrntVal)
        SendMessage(hWnd, SPNM_SETCRNTVALUE, nNewVal, 0l);

    // Set the new triangle pressed for the next call to here.
    SetWindowWord(hWnd,
        GWW_TRIANGLEPRESSED, TrianglePressed);
    break;

case SPNM_SETRANGE:
    SetWindowLong(hWnd, GWL_RANGE, lParam);
    break;

case SPNM_GETRANGE:
    lResult = GetWindowLong(hWnd, GWL_RANGE);
    break;

case SPNM_SETCRNTVALUE:
    SetWindowWord(hWnd, GWW_CRNTVALUE, wParam);
```

```
        NotifyParent(hWnd, SPNN_VALUECHANGE);
        break;

    case SPNM_GETCRNTVALUE:
        lResult = (LRESULT) GetWindowWord(hWnd, GWW_CRNTVALUE);
        break;

    default:
        lResult = DefWindowProc(hWnd, uMsg, wParam, lParam);
        break;
    }
    return(lResult);
}
```

Integrating Custom Child Controls with Microsoft's Dialog Editor

This section demonstrates how to add functions to custom child controls so you may use them with Microsoft's Dialog Editor application. The method described in this section also allows you to use your custom controls in Borland's Resource Workshop. In addition, Borland has extended the interface of its Resource Workshop to allow several custom controls to be contained in one DLL. The changes that you would have to make to the DLL to support this added capability are not difficult.

The Dialog Editor that comes with the Windows' SDK lets you design dialog boxes with custom child controls. The custom child control's source code cannot be part of a Windows application; it must be within a DLL. In addition to the custom control's window procedure, a number of other functions must also be contained in this DLL. The source module CNTL-DE.C and its associated header file, CNTL-DE.H, contain functions that make adding Dialog Editor support for custom child controls much easier. These files may be compiled and linked with your own custom child controls. For example, the Meter and Spin controls are both linked with the CNTL-DE.OBJ to produce DLLs that can be used with the Dialog Editor.

Preparing the Dialog Editor

To inform the Dialog Editor of a new custom child control, select the "Open Custom..." option from the File menu. The dialog box shown in Figure 4-4 will appear.

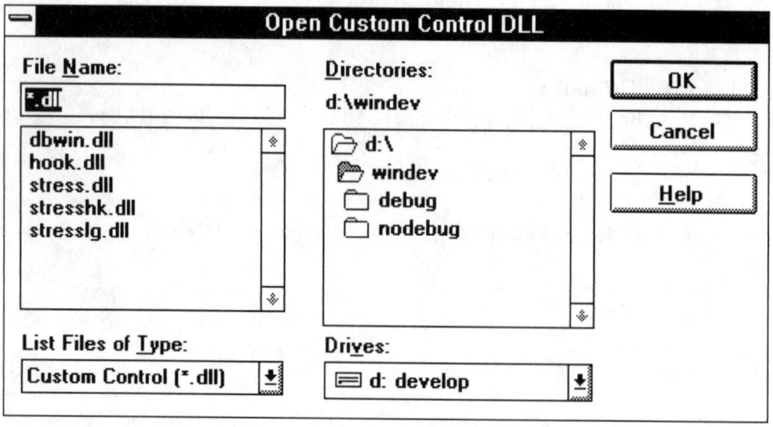

Open Custom Control DLL

File Name:
`*.dll`

dbwin.dll
hook.dll
stress.dll
stresshk.dll
stresslg.dll

Directories:
d:\windev

d:\
windev
debug
nodebug

OK

Cancel

Help

List Files of Type:
Custom Control (*.dll)

Drives:
d: develop

Figure 4-4. Dialog box used to integrate a custom child control with the Dialog Editor

Custom child controls may be removed from the Dialog Editor by choosing the "Remove Custom..." option from the File menu.

The Dialog Editor maintains a list of all the controls that have been added to a dialog-box template. Controls are added by selecting the desired control from the toolbox. To add a custom child control to the dialog template, choose the "..." option from the toolbox. After selecting this tool, a dialog box (shown in Figure 4-5) containing a list of the custom child controls will appear.

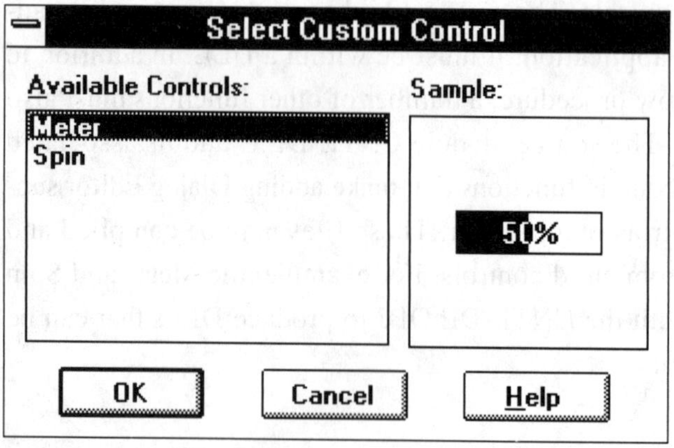

Select Custom Control

Available Controls:

Meter
Spin

Sample:

50%

OK   Cancel   Help

Figure 4-5. Selecting a custom child control to add to a dialog-box template

256

In the "Sample" window, the Dialog Editor creates a window of the selected class and displays it so you can see what the control looks like before placing it in the dialog-box template. Once the control is in the template, you may drag and resize it with the mouse as if it were one of the predefined Windows controls.

The ID, text, or style of a custom child control is changed by selecting the "Styles..." option from the Edit menu or double-clicking on the desired control. Because the content of the Styles dialog box for each custom child control differs, the DLL for the control is responsible for the dialog-box's display and operation. When the Dialog Editor saves your dialog template in the .DLG file, the information about each control is in the following format:

```
CONTROL "ControlText", ControlID, "ControlClassName",
    ControlStyles, X, Y, CX, CY
```

The Dialog Editor knows the *ControlClassName* because that's how you selected a control to add to the template. The *X*, *Y*, *CX*, and *CY* values are determined by the position and size of the control in the dialog box. The remaining fields—*ControlText*, *ControlID*, and *ControlStyles*—are changed in the Styles dialog box and are maintained by the Dialog Editor.

Adding the Dialog Editor Support Functions to Custom Controls

The DLL for custom controls must contain seven functions that the Dialog Editor can call to retrieve information about the custom child control. The functions are shown in the following table.

Function name	Description
LibMain	This function is called by Windows when the DLL is first loaded into memory. This function should already be a part of your DLL; it does not need to change.
WEP	This function is called by Windows when the DLL is removed from memory. This function should already be a part of your DLL; it does not need to change.

Function name	Description
Class*WndFn*	This is the window procedure for the custom child control. It should already be a part of your DLL; it does not need to change.
Class*Info*	This function is called by the Dialog Editor to inform it of the controls supported by this DLL.
Class*Flags*	This function is called by the Dialog Editor when the user saves the dialog template. It interprets the control's styles value and creates a string expanding the class-specific style IDs.
Class*Style*	This function is called by the Dialog Editor when the user wishes to change the ID, text, or styles of the custom control by displaying the Styles dialog box.
Class*DlgFn*	This is the dialog-box function used for the Styles dialog box.

In this table, *Class* is a placeholder for the class name of the control. All the functions except *LibMain* must be listed in the *EXPORTS* section of the DLL's .DEF file. In fact, all six functions must be exported by the following ordinal values:

Function name	Ordinal value
WEP	1
Class*WndFn*	5
Class*Info*	2
Class*Flags*	4
Class*Style*	3
Class*DlgFn*	6

The CUSTCNTL.H file that comes with the Windows' SDK must be *#included* in the source files containing the functions that support the Dialog Editor. This file defines a number of data structures and constants that are used when the Dialog Editor interacts with the control's DLL. In addition, CNTL-DE.C and CNTL-DE.H (given later) provide helper functions that may be used to simplify the process of adding Dialog Editor support for your own custom child controls. The following examples describe how each *Class* function is implemented for the spin button.

The Class*Info* Function

The Dialog Editor calls Class*Info* upon initialization. The DLL must allocate a block of memory that is to contain a *CTLINFO* structure and initialize this structure. The *CTLINFO* structure is defined in the CUSTCNTL.H file supplied with the Windows' SDK.

```
#define CTLTYPES            12
#define CTLCLASS            20
#define CTLTITLE            94
      .
      .
      .


typedef struct tagCTLINFO
{
    UINT    wVersion;             /* control version */
    UINT    wCtlTypes;            /* control types */
    char    szClass[CTLCLASS];    /* control class name */
    char    szTitle[CTLTITLE];    /* control title */
    char    szReserved[10];       /* reserved for future use */
    CTLTYPE Type[CTLTYPES];       /* control type list */
} CTLINFO;
```

The source code for the *SpinInfo* function is shown below:

```
HGLOBAL WINAPI SpinInfo (void) {
    HGLOBAL hGlblCtlInfo = NULL;
    hGlblCtlInfo = ControlInfo(0x0100, _szControlName,
        _szControlName);
    if (hGlblCtlInfo == NULL) return(hGlblCtlInfo);
    AddControlType(hGlblCtlInfo, 0, 7, 12, WS_BORDER | WS_CHILD,
        _szControlName);
    return(hGlblCtlInfo);
}
```

259

This function first calls *ControlInfo,* in CNTL-DE.C, which allocates a global block of memory to hold a *CTLINFO* structure. The parameters passed to the function describe the control's version, class name, and title. These values are stored in *CTLINFO. ControlInfo* returns the handle to the memory block or NULL if the block could not be allocated.

```
HGLOBAL WINAPI ControlInfo
      (WORD wVersion, LPSTR szClass, LPSTR szTitle) {
   HGLOBAL hGlbl = NULL;
   LPCTLINFO lpCtlInfo;

   hGlbl = GlobalAlloc(GMEM_MOVEABLE | GMEM_ZEROINIT,
      (DWORD) sizeof(CTLINFO));
   if (hGlbl == NULL) return(hGlbl);
   lpCtlInfo = (LPCTLINFO) GlobalLock(hGlbl);
   lpCtlInfo->wVersion = wVersion;
   lpCtlInfo->wCtlTypes = 0;
   lstrcpy(lpCtlInfo->szClass, szClass);
   lstrcpy(lpCtlInfo->szTitle, szTitle);
   GlobalUnlock(hGlbl);
   return(hGlbl);
}
```

CTLINFO also has a member called *wCtlTypes.* This is the number of control types that are supported by the window class. This value must be less than the *CTL-TYPES* identifier *#defin*ed in CUSTCNTL.H. In both Windows 3.0 and 3.1, this value is 12. The *ControlInfo* function initializes this value to zero. Every time the *ClassInfo* function calls the *AddControlType* function (described below), the *wCtl-Types* value is incremented.

Once the initial memory block has been prepared, each control type may be added to the block with *AddControlType.* Since only one type of control is supported by the spin button, *AddControlType* is called only once. This function determines the number of individual controls that have already been inserted into the array of *CTL-TYPE* structures and adds the new control to the end of the array. A *CTLTYPE* structure has the following members:

```
#define CTLDESCR 22

    .

    .

    .

typedef struct tagCTLTYPE
{
    UINT    wType;                  /* type style */
    UINT    wWidth;                 /* suggested width */
    UINT    wHeight;                /* suggested height */
    DWORD   dwStyle;                /* default style */
    char    szDescr[CTLDESCR];      /* description */
} CTLTYPE;
```

AddControlType accepts the handle to the *CTLINFO* structure returned from *ControlInfo* and a number of parameters that describe the control to be added. *CTLINFO* is checked to see if the maximum number of control types supported by the Dialog Editor have already been added. If so, the new control is not added and FALSE is returned to the caller. Otherwise, the information describing the new control is copied into the array of *CTLTYPE* structures.

The *wType* parameter is not currently used by the Dialog Editor and should always be set to 0. The *wWidth* and *wHeight* parameters describe the default dimensions for the control. If the high bits of the *wWidth* and *wHeight* parameters are one, the lower 15 bits specify the dimensions in pixels. If the high bit is zero, the lower 15 bits specify the dimensions in dialog-box units.

The *dwStyle* parameter specifies the default styles the control should have. The *szDescr* parameter is not used by the current Dialog Editor but may be used by future development tools.

```
BOOL WINAPI AddControlType (HGLOBAL hGlbl, WORD wType,
    WORD wWidth, WORD wHeight, DWORD dwStyle, LPSTR szDescr) {
  LPCTLINFO lpCtlInfo; WORD wNumTypes;
  lpCtlInfo = (LPCTLINFO) GlobalLock(hGlbl);
  wNumTypes = lpCtlInfo->wCtlTypes;
  if (wNumTypes == CTLTYPES) {
```

```
      GlobalUnlock(hGlbl);
      return(FALSE);
   }
   lpCtlInfo->Type[wNumTypes].wType = wType;
   lpCtlInfo->Type[wNumTypes].wWidth = wWidth;
   lpCtlInfo->Type[wNumTypes].wHeight = wHeight;
   lpCtlInfo->Type[wNumTypes].dwStyle = dwStyle;
   lstrcpy(lpCtlInfo->Type[wNumTypes].szDescr, szDescr);
   lpCtlInfo->wCtlTypes++;
   GlobalUnlock(hGlbl);
   return(TRUE);
}
```

Once all the control types have been added, the handle to the global memory block is returned by the Class*Info* function to the Dialog Editor. If the memory block could not be created, Class*Info* returns NULL.

The Class*Style* and Class*DlgFn* Functions

The Class*Style* function is called by the Dialog Editor whenever the user wants to change any of the style information for a custom control. The user indicates this by double-clicking on the custom control's window. (The user may also change style information by selecting the "Styles..." option from the Edit menu.) The function that processes the dialog box must be called Class*DlgFn*.

The source code for the *SpinStyle* function is shown below:

```
BOOL WINAPI SpinStyle (HWND hWnd, HGLOBAL hGlblCtlStyle,
   LPFNSTRTOID lpfnStrToId, LPFNIDTOSTR lpfnIdToStr) {

   return(ShowStyleDlg(_hInstance, "StyleDlg", hWnd,
      (DLGPROC) SpinDlgFn, 0, hGlblCtlStyle, lpfnStrToId,
      lpfnIdToStr));
}
```

The *ShowStyleDlg* function supplied in CNTL-DE.C does most of the work necessary before presenting the dialog box to the user on behalf of the custom child control. The *hWnd* parameter is the handle to the Dialog Editor's main window. This is the window that will own the control's Styles dialog box. The *hGlblCtlStyle* parameter is a handle to a global block of memory. It contains information about the individual custom control the user wishes to change. The memory is in the form of a *CTLSTYLE* structure:

```
#define CTLCLASS 20
#define CTLTITLE 94
    .
    .
    .
typedef struct tagCTLSTYLE
{
    UINT    wX;                /* x origin of control */
    UINT    wY;                /* y origin of control */
    UINT    wCx;               /* width of control */
    UINT    wCy;               /* height of control */
    UINT    wId;               /* control child id */
    DWORD   dwStyle;           /* control style */
    char    szClass[CTLCLASS]; /* name of control class */
    char    szTitle[CTLTITLE]; /* control text */
} CTLSTYLE;
```

The control's upper left corner and dimensions are specified by *wX*, *wY*, *wCx*, and *wCy*. The *wId* member of the structure indicates the ID assigned to this control. The *dwStyle* member specifies the window and class-specific styles assigned to the control. The *szClass* member is the class name of the control. The *szTitle* member stores text for controls that have text associated with them. The spin button has no text associated with it and does not alter this member.

Every control is assigned an ID value. This value is usually a text string defined as an integer in a header file. The *CTLSTYLE* structure passes the numeric value of the ID in its *wId* member. However, when the Styles dialog box is displayed, the string equivalent of the ID value should be displayed to the user.

The last two parameters passed to the Class*Style* function, *lpfnStrToId* and *lpfnId-ToStr*, are addresses of two functions in the Dialog Editor and are called by the control's Styles dialog box. The first function, *lpfnStrToId*, has the following prototype:

```
typedef DWORD   (CALLBACK* LPFNSTRTOID)(LPCSTR);
```

This function converts the string used for a control's ID to the value for the string. This is possible because the Dialog Editor maintains the header file in memory. The return value indicates whether the ID string is in the header file. If the low-order word is nonzero, the high-order word contains the numeric value of the identifier. If the low-order word is zero, the ID string cannot be found.

The second function, *lpfnIdToStr*, performs the opposite operation and has the following prototype:

```
typedef UINT   (CALLBACK* LPFNIDTOSTR)(UINT, LPSTR, UINT);
```

This function converts a numeric ID to its string equivalent. The first parameter specifies the numeric ID value of the control. The last two parameters specify the address of the string buffer to receive the string and the maximum size of the string. The return value indicates the number of characters copied into the string buffer. It is zero if the function fails.

The last three values passed to the Class*Style* function (*hGlblCtlStyle*, *lpfnStr-ToId*, and *lpfnIdToStr*) are really not used directly by this function at all. They're accessed by the dialog-box procedure for the Styles dialog box. The *ShowStyleDlg* function (in CNTL-DE.C) packages these parameters in a *CTLSTYLEDLG* structure that can be accessed from within the dialog-box procedure. The *CTLSTYLEDLG* structure and the *ShowStyleDlg* function are shown below:

```
typedef struct {
    HGLOBAL hGlblCtlStyle;      // Memory handle holds CTLSTYLE
                                // for control.
    LPFNSTRTOID lpfnStrToId;  // DIALOG function to convert
                                // string ID to number.
    LPFNIDTOSTR lpfnIdToStr;  // DIALOG function to convert
                                // numeric ID to string.
```

```
} CTLSTYLEDLG, FAR *LPCTLSTYLEDLG, NEAR *NPCTLSTYLEDLG;
.

.

.


int WINAPI ShowStyleDlg (HINSTANCE hInstance, LPSTR szTemplate,
    HWND hWndParent, DLGPROC fpDlgProc, LPARAM lParam,
    HGLOBAL hGlblCtlStyle, LPFNSTRTOID lpfnStrToId,
    LPFNIDTOSTR lpfnIdToStr) {

  HLOCAL hLclCtlStyleDlg;
  NPCTLSTYLEDLG npCtlStyleDlg;
  int x;
  hLclCtlStyleDlg = LocalAlloc(LMEM_MOVEABLE | LMEM_ZEROINIT,
      sizeof(CTLSTYLEDLG));
  if (hLclCtlStyleDlg == NULL) return(FALSE);

  npCtlStyleDlg = (NPCTLSTYLEDLG) LocalLock(hLclCtlStyleDlg);
  npCtlStyleDlg->hGlblCtlStyle = hGlblCtlStyle;
  npCtlStyleDlg->lpfnStrToId = lpfnStrToId;
  npCtlStyleDlg->lpfnIdToStr = lpfnIdToStr;
  LocalUnlock(hLclCtlStyleDlg);

  SetProp(hWndParent, _szCtlProp, hLclCtlStyleDlg);

  x = DialogBoxParam(hInstance, szTemplate, hWndParent,
      fpDlgProc, lParam);
  RemoveProp(hWndParent, _szCtlProp);
  LocalFree(hLclCtlStyleDlg);
  return(x == IDOK);
}
```

ShowStyleDlg allocates a local block of memory large enough to contain a *CTL-STYLEDLG* structure. This structure is declared in CNTL-DE.C and is not part of the standard Dialog Editor interface and the CUSTCNTL.H file. The structure is then filled with three values, the handle to the *CTLSTYLE* memory block, the address of *lpfnStrToId*, and the address of *lpfnIdToStr*. The handle to this local block of memory is then associated with the Dialog Editor's window as a window property.

The dialog box is displayed using the *DialogBoxParam* function. This allows the Class*Style* function to pass some value in the *lParam* parameter to the dialog-box procedure if it wants to. When the user closes the dialog box (by selecting the "OK" or "Cancel" button), the property is removed from the Dialog Editor's window and the local block of memory is freed. The Class*Style* function must return TRUE or FALSE to the Dialog Editor, indicating whether the *CTLSTYLE* structure has been changed.

The function that processes messages for the spin button's Styles dialog box is called *SpinDlgFn*. During *SpinDlgFn*'s *WM_INITDIALOG* message, the *GetIDString* help function is called. The spin button's Style dialog box appears in Figure 4-6.

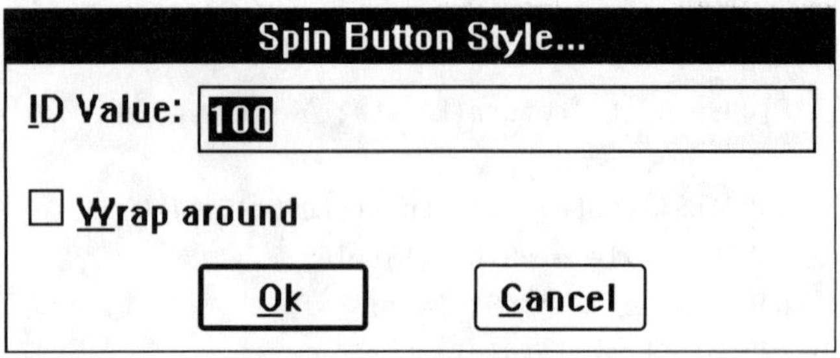

Figure 4-6. Spin Button Style dialog box

```
WORD WINAPI GetIdString (HWND hDlg, LPSTR szId,
    WORD wIdMaxLen) {
HLOCAL hLclCtlStyleDlg;
NPCTLSTYLEDLG npCtlStyleDlg;
LPCTLSTYLE lpCtlStyle;
WORD wIdLen;

hLclCtlStyleDlg = (HLOCAL) GetProp(GetParent(hDlg), _szCtlProp);
if (hLclCtlStyleDlg == NULL) return(0);

npCtlStyleDlg = (NPCTLSTYLEDLG) LocalLock(hLclCtlStyleDlg);
lpCtlStyle = (LPCTLSTYLE)
    GlobalLock(npCtlStyleDlg->hGlblCtlStyle);
```

```
wIdLen = (*npCtlStyleDlg->lpfnIdToStr)
         (lpCtlStyle->wId, szId, wIdMaxLen);
GlobalUnlock(npCtlStyleDlg->hGlblCtlStyle);
LocalUnlock(hLclCtlStyleDlg);
return(wIdLen);
}
```

GetStringId is called with the window handle of the styles dialog box, the address of a buffer where the string equivalent of the control's ID is to go, and the maximum size of this buffer. The function then calls the *GetProp* function to locate the handle of the *CTLSTYLEDLG* memory block. Remember that the window property was associated with the Dialog Editor, not the dialog box itself. This requires that the *GetParent* function be called to get the window handle of the Dialog Editor before calling the *GetProp* function.

Once the handle to the *CTLSTYLEDLG* structure has been obtained, *GetIdString* calls the *lpfnIdToStr* function. This function fills the *szId* parameter with the name of the ID from the header file corresponding to the ID value of the control. The function returns the length of the ID's string or zero if an error occurred. The dialog-box function can then call the *SetDlgItemText* function to place the ID's text value in the EDIT field associated with the "ID Value:" STATIC window.

CNTL-DE.C contains two functions that allow the dialog-box function to retrieve information about the custom control being processed. These functions, *CtlStyleLock* and *CtlStyleUnlock*, both require the window handle of the styles dialog box. From this window handle, the *GetParent* and *GetProp* functions are used as in *GetIdStr* to retrieve the memory handle of *CTLSTYLEDLG*. With this memory handle, *CtlStyleLock* calls *GlobalLock* to lock the memory block containing *CTLSTYLE*. The address of this block is then returned to the caller. When the caller no longer wishes to access the *CTLSTYLE* structure, the *CtlStyleUnlock* function is called to unlock the block.

In the processing of the *WM_INITDIALOG* message, *CtlStyleLock* is called to retrieve the value of the custom control's *dwStyle* member. This value can now be used to activate check boxes or set radio buttons to reflect the current styles of the custom control. The spin button has only one valid style, *SPNS_WRAP*. The complete processing for the *WM_INITDIALOG* message appears as follows:

```
case WM_INITDIALOG:
    GetIdString(hDlg, szId, sizeof(szId));
    SetDlgItemText(hDlg, ID_VALUE, szId);
    lpCtlStyle = CtlStyleLock(hDlg);
    SendDlgItemMessage(hDlg, ID_WRAP, BM_SETCHECK,
        (BOOL) (lpCtlStyle->dwStyle & SPNS_WRAP), 01);
    CtlStyleUnlock(hDlg);
    break;
```

The only other processing in the dialog-box function that is specific to integrating custom controls with the Dialog Editor is for the *WM_COMMAND* message. The code for this processing appears as follows:

```
case IDOK:
    GetDlgItemText(hDlg, ID_VALUE, szId, sizeof(szId));
    dwResult = SetIdValue(hDlg, szId);
    if (LOWORD(dwResult) == 0) break;
    lpCtlStyle = CtlStyleLock(hDlg);
    lpCtlStyle->dwStyle &= 0xffff0000; // Clear control-specific
                                       // styles.
    if (SendDlgItemMessage(hDlg, ID_WRAP, BM_GETCHECK, 0, 01))
        lpCtlStyle->dwStyle |= SPNS_WRAP;
    CtlStyleUnlock(hDlg);
    // Fall through to IDCANCEL case.

case IDCANCEL:
    EndDialog(hDlg, wParam);
    break;
```

When the user selects the "OK" button, the ID value in the EDIT control must be checked to see if the string exists in the header file being used by the Dialog Editor. This is done by calling the *SetIdValue* function in the CNTL-DE.C module:

```
DWORD WINAPI SetIdValue (HWND hDlg, LPSTR szId) {
    HLOCAL hLclCtlStyleDlg;
    NPCTLSTYLEDLG npCtlStyleDlg;
    LPCTLSTYLE lpCtlStyle;
    DWORD dwResult = 0;

    hLclCtlStyleDlg = (HLOCAL) GetProp(GetParent(hDlg), _szCtlProp);
    if (hLclCtlStyleDlg == NULL) return(dwResult);

    npCtlStyleDlg = (NPCTLSTYLEDLG) LocalLock(hLclCtlStyleDlg);
    dwResult = (*npCtlStyleDlg->lpfnStrToId)(szId);
    LocalUnlock(hLclCtlStyleDlg);
    if (LOWORD(dwResult) == 0)
        return(dwResult);
    lpCtlStyle = CtlStyleLock(hDlg);
    lpCtlStyle->wId = HIWORD(dwResult);
    CtlStyleUnlock(hDlg);
    return(dwResult);
}
```

This function calls *lpfnIdToStr* to see whether the ID value string passed in the *szId* parameter is in the header file being used by the Dialog Editor. If the string is not in the header file, the Dialog Editor automatically asks the user if the string should be added. If the user adds the string, *lpfnStrToId* returns nonzero in the high-order word and updates the value in the *CTLSTYLE* structure. If the user does not add the ID to the header file, *lpfnStrToId* returns zero in the low-order word, does not update the *CTLSTYLE* structure, and returns to the caller.

If the dialog-box function sees that the *SetIdValue* function returned zero in the low-order word, the Styles dialog box is not terminated and the user can either cancel the dialog box or enter a different ID value string.

Now, the style information for the control must be determined. First, the *dwStyle* member of the *CTLSTYLE* structure is ANDed with 0xffff0000. This clears all the bits that represent class-specific styles. Remember that the other bits are for the general window styles, all beginning with *WS_*. Because the spin button does not allow the user to change its window styles, these should not be reset.

Next, we check all radio buttons and check boxes to determine which class-specific styles should be turned on. Because the spin button has only one style, only one check box has to be examined. If the call to *SendDlgItemMessage* using the *BM_GETCHECK* message returned TRUE, the *SPNS_WRAP* flag is set in the *dwStyle* member. Otherwise, no class-specific style bits are set.

Finally, the *CTLSTYLE* structure is updated to reflect the changes. At this point, the *IDOK* case falls through to *IDCANCEL*. This case calls the *EndDialog* function, returning the value of the *wParam* parameter (*IDOK* or *IDCANCEL*).

The Class*Flags* Function

The last function in SPINDLG.C is *SpinFlags*. This function is called by the Dialog Editor when the user saves the dialog box. The Dialog Editor creates a .DLG file that contains *CONTROL* statements for every control the user added to the dialog-box template. In each line there is a list of identifiers representing the styles chosen for the particular control. For custom child controls, the Dialog Editor doesn't know the names associated with the class-specific styles. *SpinFlags* retrieves the names so they can be included in the .DLG file:

```
WORD WINAPI SpinFlags (DWORD dwFlags, LPSTR szString,
    WORD wMaxString) {
WORD x;
*szString = 0;
if (dwFlags & SPNS_WRAP) lstrcat(szString, "SPNS_WRAP | ");
x = lstrlen(szString);
if (x > 0) { x -= sizeof(" | ") - 1; *(szString + x) = 0; }
return(x);
}
```

This function is passed the *dwFlags* parameter, which contains the window and class-specific style bits for the control. It is also passed the address of a buffer, *szString*, where the expanded string identifiers are to be placed. The last parameter, *wMaxString*, specifies the maximum number of characters that may be placed in the buffer.

The function places a zero in the first byte of the string buffer. It then appends the text (and symbol representing C's Boolean *OR* operation) for each style that has a style bit set in the *dwFlags* parameter to the buffer. When the string buffer has been filled, the trailing *OR* symbol is removed and the number of characters in the string is returned to the Dialog Editor. The Dialog Editor then appends the text for the generic window styles to this buffer and outputs the completed line to the .DLG file.

The source code for SPINDLG.C contains all the functions necessary to interface the spin button with the Dialog Editor. Although we have not discussed the functions to access the Meter control with the Dialog Editor, the functions appear in METERDLG.C. This completes the interface required for the Dialog Editor to access custom child controls.

Listing 4-5. SPINDLG.C Spin interface for Dialog Editor source module

```
/****************************************************************
Module name: SPINDLG.C
Programmer : Jeffrey M. Richter.
****************************************************************/

#include <windows.h>
#include <custcntl.h>

#include "cntl-de.h"

#include "spin.h"

extern const HINSTANCE _cdecl _hInstance;

extern char _szControlName[];

BOOL CALLBACK SpinDlgFn
   (HWND hDlg, UINT uMessage, WPARAM wParam, LPARAM lParam);

HGLOBAL WINAPI SpinInfo (void) {
   HGLOBAL hGlblCtlInfo = (HGLOBAL) NULL;

   hGlblCtlInfo =
      ControlInfo(0x0100, _szControlName, _szControlName);
   if (hGlblCtlInfo == NULL) return(hGlblCtlInfo);
   AddControlType(hGlblCtlInfo, 0, 7, 12,
      WS_BORDER | WS_CHILD, _szControlName);
```

```
    return(hGlblCtlInfo);
}

BOOL WINAPI SpinStyle (HWND hWnd, HGLOBAL hGlblCtlStyle,
         LPFNSTRTOID lpfnStrToId, LPFNIDTOSTR lpfnIdToStr) {
    return(ShowStyleDlg(_hInstance, "StyleDlg", hWnd,
       (DLGPROC) SpinDlgFn, 0, hGlblCtlStyle,
       lpfnStrToId, lpfnIdToStr));
}

BOOL CALLBACK SpinDlgFn
        (HWND hDlg, UINT uMsg, WPARAM wParam, LPARAM lParam) {
    BOOL fProcessed = TRUE;
    char szId[20];
    DWORD dwResult;
    LPCTLSTYLE lpCtlStyle;

    switch (uMsg) {
       case WM_INITDIALOG:
          // Fill the EDIT control with name of this control's ID.
          GetIdString(hDlg, szId, sizeof(szId));
          SetDlgItemText(hDlg, ID_VALUE, szId);

          // Initialize check box reflecting spin control's styles.
          lpCtlStyle = CtlStyleLock(hDlg);
          SendDlgItemMessage(hDlg, ID_WRAP, BM_SETCHECK,
             (BOOL) (lpCtlStyle->dwStyle & SPNS_WRAP), 0l);
          CtlStyleUnlock(hDlg);
          break;

       case WM_COMMAND:
          switch(wParam) {
             case IDOK:

                // Convert the string ID value to its
                // numeric equivalent.
                GetDlgItemText(hDlg, ID_VALUE, szId, sizeof(szId));
                dwResult = SetIdValue(hDlg, szId);

                // If string ID not found or added,
                // do NOT end dialog box.
                if (LOWORD(dwResult) == 0) break;

                // Calculate the new control's styles.
                lpCtlStyle = CtlStyleLock(hDlg);
```

```
            // Clear control-specific flags
            lpCtlStyle->dwStyle &= 0xffff0000L;

            if (SendDlgItemMessage(hDlg, ID_WRAP,
                BM_GETCHECK, 0, 0l))
                lpCtlStyle->dwStyle |= SPNS_WRAP;

            CtlStyleUnlock(hDlg);

            // Fall through to IDCANCEL case.

        case IDCANCEL:
            // Terminate dialog box returning IDOK or IDCANCEL.
            EndDialog(hDlg, wParam);
            break;

        case ID_VALUE:
            // Disable IDOK button if no text in ID_VALUE box.
            if (HIWORD(lParam) == EN_CHANGE)
                EnableWindow(GetDlgItem(hDlg, IDOK),
                    SendMessage(LOWORD(lParam),
                        WM_GETTEXTLENGTH, 0, 0L) ? TRUE : FALSE);
            break;

        default: fProcessed = FALSE; break;
        }
        break;

    default: fProcessed = FALSE; break;
    }
    return(fProcessed);
}


#pragma argsused
WORD WINAPI SpinFlags
        (DWORD dwFlags, LPSTR szString, WORD wMaxString) {
    WORD x;
    *szString = 0;
    if (dwFlags & SPNS_WRAP) lstrcat(szString, "SPNS_WRAP | ");
    x = lstrlen(szString);
    if (x > 0) { x -= sizeof(" | ") - 1; *(szString + x) = 0; }
    return(x);
}
```

Listing 4-6. SPIN.RC DLL resource file

```
/*********************************************************************
Module name: SPIN.RC
Programmer : Jeffrey M. Richter.
*********************************************************************/

#include <windows.h>
#include "spin.h"

STYLEDLG DIALOG LOADONCALL MOVEABLE DISCARDABLE 83, 73, 156, 52
CAPTION "Spin Button Style..."
STYLE WS_BORDER | WS_CAPTION | WS_DLGFRAME | WS_POPUP
BEGIN
    CONTROL "&ID Value:", -1, "static",
        SS_LEFT | WS_CHILD, 4, 4, 32, 12
    CONTROL "", ID_VALUE, "edit",
        ES_LEFT | WS_BORDER | WS_TABSTOP | WS_CHILD,
        36, 4, 116, 12
    CONTROL "&Wrap around", ID_WRAP, "button",
        BS_AUTOCHECKBOX | WS_TABSTOP | WS_CHILD, 4, 20, 56, 12
    CONTROL "&Ok", IDOK, "button",
        BS_DEFPUSHBUTTON | WS_TABSTOP | WS_CHILD, 36, 36, 32, 12
    CONTROL "&Cancel", IDCANCEL, "button",
        BS_PUSHBUTTON | WS_TABSTOP | WS_CHILD, 88, 36, 32, 12
END
```

Listing 4-7. SPIN.DEF module definitions file

```
; Module name: SPIN.DEF
; Programmer : Jeffrey M. Richter.

LIBRARY       SPIN
DESCRIPTION 'Spin Button Custom Control Library'
EXETYPE       WINDOWS
STUB          'WinStub.Exe'
CODE          MOVEABLE PRELOAD DISCARDABLE
DATA          MOVEABLE PRELOAD SINGLE
HEAPSIZE      1024
EXPORTS
    WEP           @1      RESIDENTNAME
    SpinInfo      @2
    SpinStyle     @3
    SpinFlags     @4
    SpinWndFn     @5
    SpinDlgFn     @6
```

Listing 4-8. MAKEFILE for Spin custom control DLL

```
#**********************************************************************
#Module name: MAKEFILE
#Programmer : Jeffrey M. Richter.
#**********************************************************************

!include "..\builtins.jmr"

PROG  = Spin

MODEL = s
CFLAGS = -O2 -d -c -f- -WD -P-c -p -v -w -w-bbf -m$(MODEL)! -
I$(INCLUDEDIR)
LFLAGS = /P/v/n/m/s/L$(LIBDIR)
!if $(MODEL) == m
LIBS = CWL
!else
LIBS = CWS
!endif


LIBS = $(LIBS) Import


MODULES = $(PROG).obj $(PROG)Dlg.obj Cntl-DE.obj

ICONS   =
BITMAPS =
CURSORS =

$(PROG).DLL: $(MODULES) $(PROG).Def $(PROG).Res
     tlink $(LFLAGS) @&&!
COD$(MODEL) $(MODULES)
$(PROG), $(PROG), $(LIBS), $(PROG)
!
     rc -30 -T -Fe$(PROG).DLL $(PROG).Res
     TDStrip -s $(PROG).DLL
     copy $(PROG).dll ..\custcntl.04
     copy $(PROG).tds ..\custcntl.04

$(PROG).res: $(PROG).rc $(PROG).h $(RESOURCES)
```

Listing 4-9. METERDLG.C Meter interface for Dialog Editor source module

```
/*********************************************************************
Module name: METERDLG.C
Programmer : Jeffrey M. Richter.
*********************************************************************/

#include <windows.h>
#include <custcntl.h>

#include "cntl-de.h"

#include "meter.h"

extern const HINSTANCE _cdecl _hInstance;

extern char _szControlName[];

BOOL CALLBACK MeterDlgFn
        (HWND hDlg, UINT uMsg, WPARAM wParam, LPARAM lParam);
HGLOBAL WINAPI MeterInfo (void) {
   HGLOBAL hGlblCtlInfo = (HGLOBAL) NULL;

   hGlblCtlInfo =
      ControlInfo(0x0100, _szControlName, _szControlName);
   if (hGlblCtlInfo == NULL) return(hGlblCtlInfo);
   AddControlType(hGlblCtlInfo, 0, 40, 12,
      WS_BORDER | WS_CHILD, _szControlName);
   return(hGlblCtlInfo);

}

BOOL WINAPI MeterStyle (HWND hWnd, HGLOBAL hGlblCtlStyle,
        LPFNSTRTOID lpfnStrToId, LPFNIDTOSTR lpfnIdToStr) {
   return(ShowStyleDlg(_hInstance, MAKEINTRESOURCE(DLG_STYLEDLG),
      hWnd, (DLGPROC) MeterDlgFn, 0, hGlblCtlStyle,
      lpfnStrToId, lpfnIdToStr));
}

BOOL CALLBACK MeterDlgFn
        (HWND hDlg, UINT uMsg, WPARAM wParam, LPARAM lParam) {
   BOOL fResult = TRUE;
   char szId[20];
   DWORD dwResult;

   switch (uMsg) {
```

```
        case WM_INITDIALOG:
            GetIdString(hDlg, szId, sizeof(szId));
            SetDlgItemText(hDlg, ID_VALUE, szId);
            break;

        case WM_COMMAND:
            switch (wParam) {
                case IDOK:
                    GetDlgItemText(hDlg, ID_VALUE, szId, sizeof(szId));
                    dwResult = SetIdValue(hDlg, szId);
                    if (LOWORD(dwResult) == 0) break;
                    // Fall through to IDCANCEL case.

                case IDCANCEL:
                    EndDialog(hDlg, wParam);
                    break;

                case ID_VALUE:
                    if (HIWORD(lParam) == EN_CHANGE)
                        EnableWindow(GetDlgItem(hDlg, IDOK),
                            SendMessage(LOWORD(lParam),
                                WM_GETTEXTLENGTH, 0, 0L) ? TRUE : FALSE);
                    break;

                default: fResult = FALSE; break;
            }
            break;

        default: fResult = FALSE; break;
    }
    return(fResult);
}


#pragma argsused
WORD WINAPI MeterFlags
        (DWORD dwFlags, LPSTR szString, WORD wMaxString) {
    WORD x;
    *szString = 0;
    x = lstrlen(szString);
    if (x > 0) { x -= sizeof(" | ") - 1; *(szString + x) = 0; }
    return(x);
}
```

Listing 4-10. METER.DEF DLL definitions file

```
; Module name: METER.DEF
; Programmer : Jeffrey M. Richter.

LIBRARY      METER
DESCRIPTION 'Meter Custom Control Library'
EXETYPE      WINDOWS
STUB         'WinStub.Exe'

; The code segment is marked as PRELOAD FIXED NONDISCARDABLE
; because this module is used by the setup application
; presented in Chapter 10. In a DLL, Windows allows code
; segments to be discarded if FIXED is not specified. This is
; why FIXED appears below.
CODE         PRELOAD FIXED NONDISCARDABLE
DATA         MOVEABLE PRELOAD SINGLE
HEAPSIZE     1024
EXPORTS
    WEP            @1      RESIDENTNAME
    MeterInfo      @2
    MeterStyle     @3
    MeterFlags     @4
    MeterWndFn     @5
    MeterDlgFn     @6
```

Listing 4-11. METER.RC DLL resource file

```
/******************************************************************
Module name: METER.RC
Programmer : Jeffrey M. Richter.
******************************************************************/

#include <windows.h>
#include "meter.h"

DLG_STYLEDLG DIALOG LOADONCALL MOVEABLE DISCARDABLE
    83, 73, 156, 36
CAPTION "Meter Style..."
STYLE WS_BORDER | WS_CAPTION | WS_DLGFRAME | WS_POPUP
BEGIN
    CONTROL "&ID Value:", -1, "static",
        SS_LEFT | WS_CHILD, 4, 4, 32, 12
    CONTROL "", ID_VALUE, "edit",
        ES_LEFT | WS_BORDER | WS_TABSTOP | WS_CHILD, 36, 4, 116, 12
```

```
    CONTROL "&Ok", IDOK, "button",
        BS_DEFPUSHBUTTON | WS_TABSTOP | WS_CHILD, 36, 20, 32, 12
    CONTROL "&Cancel", IDCANCEL, "button",
        BS_PUSHBUTTON | WS_TABSTOP | WS_CHILD, 88, 20, 32, 12
END
```

Listing 4-12. MAKEFILE for Meter custom control DLL

```
#**********************************************************************
#Module name: MAKEFILE
#Programmer : Jeffrey M. Richter.
#**********************************************************************

!include "..\builtins.jmr"

PROG  = Meter

MODEL = s
CFLAGS = -O2 -d -c -f- -WD -P-c -p -v -w -w-bbf -m$(MODEL)! -
I$(INCLUDEDIR)
LFLAGS = /P/v/n/m/s/L$(LIBDIR)
!if $(MODEL) == m
LIBS = CWL
!else
LIBS = CWS
!endif

LIBS = $(LIBS) Import


MODULES = $(PROG).obj $(PROG)Dlg.obj Cntl-DE.obj

ICONS   =
BITMAPS =
CURSORS =

$(PROG).DLL: $(MODULES) $(PROG).Def $(PROG).Res
     tlink $(LFLAGS) @&&!
COD$(MODEL) $(MODULES)
$(PROG), $(PROG), $(LIBS), $(PROG)
!
     rc -30 -T -Fe$(PROG).DLL $(PROG).Res
     TDStrip -s $(PROG).DLL
     copy $(PROG).dll ..\custcntl.04
     copy $(PROG).tds ..\custcntl.04

$(PROG).res: $(PROG).rc $(PROG).h $(RESOURCES)
```

Listing 4-13. CNTL-DE.C Custom Control helper functions for Dialog Editor interface source module

```
/*******************************************************************
Module name: CNTL-DE.C
Programmer : Jeffrey M. Richter.
*******************************************************************/

#include <windows.h>
#include <custcntl.h>

#include "cntl-de.h"

// Property string used internally to store local handle of
// CTLSTYLEDLG data structure.
static char _szCtlProp[] = "CtlDlgStyleData";
// Data structure used internally to get information into the
// style dialog-box function.
typedef struct {
    HGLOBAL       hGlblCtlStyle;// Handle holds control's CTLSTYLE.
    LPFNSTRTOID   lpfnStrToId;  // Func to cnvrt string ID to number.
    LPFNIDTOSTR   lpfnIdToStr;  // Func to cnvrt number ID to string.
} CTLSTYLEDLG, FAR *LPCTLSTYLEDLG, NEAR *NPCTLSTYLEDLG;

// This function should be called first in the ClassInfo
// function to initialize the new control.
HGLOBAL WINAPI ControlInfo
        (WORD wVersion, LPSTR szClass, LPSTR szTitle) {

    HGLOBAL hGlbl = (HGLOBAL) NULL;
    LPCTLINFO lpCtlInfo;

    hGlbl = GlobalAlloc(GMEM_MOVEABLE | GMEM_ZEROINIT,
                        (DWORD) sizeof(CTLINFO));
    if (hGlbl == NULL) return(hGlbl);
    lpCtlInfo = (LPCTLINFO) GlobalLock(hGlbl);
    lpCtlInfo->wVersion = wVersion;

    // Initialize wCtlTypes to zero, incremented by
    // AddControlType function.
    lpCtlInfo->wCtlTypes = 0;
    lstrcpy(lpCtlInfo->szClass, szClass);
    lstrcpy(lpCtlInfo->szTitle, szTitle);
    GlobalUnlock(hGlbl);
    return(hGlbl);
}
```

```
// This function should be called repeatedly to add new control
// types to the structure returned by the ControlInfo function.
// This function should be called in the ClassInfo function.
BOOL WINAPI AddControlType (HGLOBAL hGlbl, WORD wType,
        WORD wWidth, WORD wHeight, DWORD dwStyle, LPSTR szDescr) {

    LPCTLINFO lpCtlInfo; WORD wNumTypes;
    lpCtlInfo = (LPCTLINFO) GlobalLock(hGlbl);
    wNumTypes = lpCtlInfo->wCtlTypes;
    if (wNumTypes == CTLTYPES) {
        GlobalUnlock(hGlbl);
        return(FALSE);
    }
    lpCtlInfo->Type[wNumTypes].wType   = wType;
    lpCtlInfo->Type[wNumTypes].wWidth  = wWidth;
    lpCtlInfo->Type[wNumTypes].wHeight = wHeight;
    lpCtlInfo->Type[wNumTypes].dwStyle = dwStyle;
    lstrcpy(lpCtlInfo->Type[wNumTypes].szDescr, szDescr);
    lpCtlInfo->wCtlTypes++;
    GlobalUnlock(hGlbl);
    return(TRUE);
}


// This function displays the control's style dialog box and
// should be called from the ClassStyle function.
int WINAPI ShowStyleDlg (HINSTANCE hInstance, LPCSTR szTemplate,
        HWND hWndParent, DLGPROC fpDlgProc, LPARAM lParam,
        HGLOBAL hGlblCtlStyle, LPFNSTRTOID lpfnStrToId,
        LPFNIDTOSTR lpfnIdToStr) {

    HLOCAL hLclCtlStyleDlg;
    NPCTLSTYLEDLG npCtlStyleDlg;
    int x;

    hLclCtlStyleDlg = LocalAlloc(LMEM_MOVEABLE | LMEM_ZEROINIT,
        sizeof(CTLSTYLEDLG));
    if (hLclCtlStyleDlg == NULL) return(FALSE);

    npCtlStyleDlg = (NPCTLSTYLEDLG) LocalLock(hLclCtlStyleDlg);
    npCtlStyleDlg->hGlblCtlStyle = hGlblCtlStyle;
    npCtlStyleDlg->lpfnStrToId = lpfnStrToId;
    npCtlStyleDlg->lpfnIdToStr = lpfnIdToStr;
    LocalUnlock(hLclCtlStyleDlg);

    // Associate property with dialog editor's window.
    SetProp(hWndParent, _szCtlProp, hLclCtlStyleDlg);
```

```
    // Display control's styles dialog box.
    x = DialogBoxParam(hInstance, szTemplate, hWndParent,
        fpDlgProc, lParam);

    // Remove property associated with dialog editor's window.
    RemoveProp(hWndParent, _szCtlProp);

    LocalFree(hLclCtlStyleDlg);
    return(x == IDOK);    // Return whether CTLSTYLE has changed.
}

// This function should only be called from the ClassDlgFn
// function. It locks the memory block containing the CTLSTYLE
// structure for the selected control and returns the FAR address
// to that structure.
LPCTLSTYLE WINAPI CtlStyleLock (HWND hDlg) {
    HLOCAL hLclCtlStyleDlg;
    NPCTLSTYLEDLG npCtlStyleDlg;
    LPCTLSTYLE lpCtlStyle = NULL;

    // Property is associated with dialog editor's window.
    // Parent of the dialog box is the dialog editor.
    hLclCtlStyleDlg = GetProp(GetParent(hDlg), _szCtlProp);

    if (hLclCtlStyleDlg == NULL) return(lpCtlStyle);
    npCtlStyleDlg = (NPCTLSTYLEDLG) LocalLock(hLclCtlStyleDlg);
    lpCtlStyle = (LPCTLSTYLE)
        GlobalLock(npCtlStyleDlg->hGlblCtlStyle);
    LocalUnlock(hLclCtlStyleDlg);
    return(lpCtlStyle);
}

// This function should only be called from the ClassDlgFn
// function. It unlocks the memory block containing the CTLSTYLE
// structure for the selected control and returns whether the
// block was successfully unlocked.
BOOL WINAPI CtlStyleUnlock (HWND hDlg) {
    HLOCAL hLclCtlStyleDlg;
    NPCTLSTYLEDLG npCtlStyleDlg;
    BOOL fOk = FALSE;

    // Property is associated with dialog editor's window.
    // Parent of the dialog box is the dialog editor.
    hLclCtlStyleDlg = GetProp(GetParent(hDlg), _szCtlProp);

    if (hLclCtlStyleDlg == NULL) return(fOk);
```

```
    npCtlStyleDlg = (NPCTLSTYLEDLG) LocalLock(hLclCtlStyleDlg);
    fOk = GlobalUnlock(npCtlStyleDlg->hGlblCtlStyle);
    LocalUnlock(hLclCtlStyleDlg);
    return(fOk);
}


// This function should only be called from the ClassDlgFn
// function. It converts the ID value for the control into a
// identifier string and stores the string in the address passed
// in. The number of characters in the string is returned.
WORD WINAPI GetIdString (HWND hDlg, LPSTR szId, WORD wIdMaxLen) {
    HLOCAL hLclCtlStyleDlg;
    NPCTLSTYLEDLG npCtlStyleDlg;
    LPCTLSTYLE lpCtlStyle;
    WORD wIdLen;

    // Property is associated with dialog editor's window.
    // Parent of the dialog box is the dialog editor.
    hLclCtlStyleDlg = GetProp(GetParent(hDlg), _szCtlProp);
    if (hLclCtlStyleDlg == NULL) return(0);

    npCtlStyleDlg = (NPCTLSTYLEDLG) LocalLock(hLclCtlStyleDlg);
    lpCtlStyle = (LPCTLSTYLE)
        GlobalLock(npCtlStyleDlg->hGlblCtlStyle);

    // Call the lpfnIdToStr function to convert the numeric ID
    // to its string equivalent.
    wIdLen = (*npCtlStyleDlg->lpfnIdToStr)
        (lpCtlStyle->wId, szId, wIdMaxLen);

    GlobalUnlock(npCtlStyleDlg->hGlblCtlStyle);
    LocalUnlock(hLclCtlStyleDlg);
    return(wIdLen);
}


// This function should only be called from the ClassDlgFn
// function. It converts an ID string value into its numeric
// equivalent and stores the numeric value in the CTLSTYLE
// structure for the control. If the low word of the result is zero,
// the ID is invalid; otherwise, the high word contains the numeric
// value of the ID.
DWORD WINAPI SetIdValue (HWND hDlg, LPSTR szId) {
    HLOCAL hLclCtlStyleDlg;
    NPCTLSTYLEDLG npCtlStyleDlg;
    LPCTLSTYLE lpCtlStyle;
    DWORD dwResult = 0;
```

```
hLclCtlStyleDlg = GetProp(GetParent(hDlg), _szCtlProp);
if (hLclCtlStyleDlg == NULL) return(dwResult);

npCtlStyleDlg = (NPCTLSTYLEDLG) LocalLock(hLclCtlStyleDlg);

// Call the lpfnStrToId function to convert the string ID
// to its numeric equivalent.
dwResult = (*npCtlStyleDlg->lpfnStrToId)(szId);

LocalUnlock(hLclCtlStyleDlg);
// If LOWORD is zero, string NOT found.
if (LOWORD(dwResult) == 0)
    return(dwResult);

// LOWORD is not zero, numeric ID is in the HIWORD.
lpCtlStyle = CtlStyleLock(hDlg);
lpCtlStyle->wId = HIWORD(dwResult);
CtlStyleUnlock(hDlg);
return(dwResult);
}
```

Listing 4-14. CNTL-DE.H Custom Control helper functions for Dialog Editor interface header module

```
/******************************************************************
Module name: CNTL-DE.H
Programmer : Jeffrey M. Richter.
******************************************************************/

// This function should be called first in the ClassInfo
// function to initialize the new control.
HGLOBAL WINAPI ControlInfo (WORD wVersion, LPSTR szClass,
    LPSTR szTitle);

// This function should be called repeatedly to add new control
// types to the structure returned by the ControlInfo function.
// This function should be called in the ClassInfo function.
BOOL WINAPI AddControlType (HGLOBAL hGlbl, WORD wType,
    WORD wWidth, WORD wHeight, DWORD dwStyle, LPSTR szDescr);

// This function displays the control's style dialog box and
// should be called from the ClassStyle function.
int WINAPI ShowStyleDlg (HINSTANCE hInstance, LPCSTR szTemplate,
    HWND hWndParent, DLGPROC fpDlgProc, LPARAM lParam,
    HGLOBAL hGlblCtlStyle, LPFNSTRTOID lpfnStrToId,
    LPFNIDTOSTR lpfnIdToStr);
```

```
// This function should only be called from the ClassDlgFn
// function. It locks the memory block containing the CTLSTYLE
// structure for the selected control and returns the FAR
// address to that structure.
LPCTLSTYLE WINAPI CtlStyleLock (HWND hDlg);

// This function should only be called from the ClassDlgFn
// function. It unlocks the memory block containing the CTLSTYLE
// structure for the selected control and returns whether the
// block was successfully unlocked.
BOOL WINAPI CtlStyleUnlock (HWND hDlg);

// This function should only be called from the ClassDlgFn
// function. It converts the ID value for the control into an
// identifier string and stores the string in the address passed
// in. The number of characters in the string is returned.
WORD WINAPI GetIdString (HWND hDlg, LPSTR szId, WORD wIdMaxLen);

// This function should only be called from the ClassDlgFn
// function. It converts an ID string value into its numeric
// equivalent and stores the numeric value in the CTLSTYLE
// structure for the control. If the low word of the result is zero,
// the ID is invalid; otherwise, the high word contains the numeric
// value of the ID.
DWORD WINAPI SetIdValue (HWND hDlg, LPSTR szId);
```

Using Custom Controls in an Application

This section describes the steps necessary to use custom child controls in your own applications. Keep in mind that all the DLLs for your custom child controls must be distributed with your application's executable file. The sample application, CUSTCNTL.EXE, demonstrates the use of the Meter and Spin Button controls in a dialog box. The Meter control is also used in Chapter 10, "Installing Commercial Applications."

When your application is executed, each custom control's class must be registered. This is done by calling the *LoadLibrary* function to load each custom control's DLL. The *LoadLibrary* function locates the .DLL file and its *LibEntry* function. *LibEntry* is a small assembly language function in the LIBENTRY.ASM file included with the Windows SDK. The object file is also included.

LibEntry calls the *LibMain* function you wrote for the DLL. This function registers the window class for the custom child control. Once the class has been registered, the application may create dialog boxes containing these controls or individual windows of the class. The following is an example of how an application that uses the Meter and Spin Button controls might perform its initialization:

```
int WinMain (HINSTANCE hInstance, HINSTANCE hPrevInstance,
    LPSTR lpszCmdLine, int nCmdShow) {
  HINSTANCE hInstMeter, hInstSpin;
  hInstMeter = LoadLibrary("METER.DLL");
  if (hInstMeter < HINSTANCE_ERROR)
    return(0);
  hInstSpin = LoadLibrary("SPIN.DLL");
  if (hInstSpin < HINSTANCE_ERROR) {
    FreeLibrary(hInstMeter);
    return(0);
  }
  .
  .
  .

  // Perform any other initialization and start message loop.
  .

  .

  .


  FreeLibrary(hInstSpin);
  FreeLibrary(hInstMeter);
  return(0);
}
```

Before the application terminates, it must call *FreeLibrary* to subtract 1 from the reference count of the library. When the reference count reaches zero, the *WEP* function is called. This function calls the *UnregisterClass* function to remove the custom child control class from Windows.

Once the custom child control's library has been loaded, the control class can be used like any other window class. This means windows may be created directly by calling *CreateWindow* or *CreateWindowEx*, or indirectly by creating dialog boxes containing the custom control if its class name is referenced in the dialog box's template.

Figure 4-7. CUSTCNTL.ICO

Listing 4-15. CUSTCNTL.C application source module

```
/****************************************************************
Module name: CUSTCNTL.C
Programmer : Jeffrey M. Richter.
****************************************************************/

#include <windows.h>

#include "custcntl.h"

extern const HINSTANCE _cdecl _hInstance;

char _szAppName[] = "CustCntl";

#define IDM_DEMO    (0x0110)    // Must be < 0xF000 (GetSystemMenu).

ATOM NEAR RegisterAppWndClass (HINSTANCE hInstance);
BOOL CALLBACK CustCntlDlgProc
    (HWND hDlg, UINT uMsg, WPARAM wParam, LPARAM lParam);
LRESULT CALLBACK AppWndProc
```

```
    (HWND hWnd, UINT uMsg, WPARAM wParam, LPARAM lParam);

//**************************************************************
#pragma argsused
int WinMain (HINSTANCE hInstance, HINSTANCE hPrevInstance,
          LPSTR lpszCmdLine, int nCmdShow) {
   MSG msg;
   HWND hWnd;
   HMENU hMenu;
   HINSTANCE hLibMeter, hLibSpin;
   if (hPrevInstance == NULL)
      if (RegisterAppWndClass(hInstance) == NULL)
         return(0);

   hWnd = CreateWindow(_szAppName, _szAppName,
      WS_OVERLAPPEDWINDOW | WS_VISIBLE,
      CW_USEDEFAULT, nCmdShow, CW_USEDEFAULT, CW_USEDEFAULT,
      NULL, NULL, hInstance, 0);
   if (hWnd == NULL) return(0);

   // Get handle to application's system menu.
   hMenu = GetSystemMenu(hWnd, 0);

   // Append separator bar and two options.
   AppendMenu(hMenu, MF_SEPARATOR, 0, 0);
   AppendMenu(hMenu, MF_STRING,
      IDM_DEMO, "&Custom control demo...");
   DrawMenuBar(hWnd);

   hLibMeter = LoadLibrary("METER.DLL");
   if (hLibMeter < HINSTANCE_ERROR) return(0);

   hLibSpin  = LoadLibrary("SPIN.DLL");
   if (hLibSpin < HINSTANCE_ERROR) {
      FreeLibrary(hLibMeter);
      return(0);
   }

   while (GetMessage(&msg, NULL, 0, 0)) {
      TranslateMessage(&msg);
      DispatchMessage(&msg);
   }

   FreeLibrary(hLibMeter);
   FreeLibrary(hLibSpin);
   return(0);
}
```

```
// *****************************************************************
// This function registers the application's main window.

ATOM NEAR RegisterAppWndClass (HINSTANCE hInstance) {
   WNDCLASS WndClass;

   WndClass.style         = 0;
   WndClass.lpfnWndProc   = AppWndProc;
   WndClass.cbClsExtra    = 0;
   WndClass.cbWndExtra    = 0;
   WndClass.hInstance     = hInstance;
   WndClass.hIcon         = LoadIcon(hInstance, _szAppName);
   WndClass.hCursor       = LoadCursor(NULL, IDC_ARROW);
   WndClass.hbrBackground = COLOR_WINDOW + 1;
   WndClass.lpszMenuName  = NULL;
   WndClass.lpszClassName = _szAppName;
   return(RegisterClass(&WndClass));
}


// *****************************************************************
// This function processes messages sent to a modeless dialog box.

BOOL CALLBACK CustCntlDlgProc
         (HWND hDlg, UINT uMsg, WPARAM wParam, LPARAM lParam) {
   BOOL fProcessed = TRUE;
   int x;

   switch (uMsg) {
      case WM_INITDIALOG:
         // Tell Meter control that the job consists of 25 parts.
         SendDlgItemMessage(hDlg, ID_METER,
            MM_SETPARTSINJOB, 25, 0);

         // Tell Meter control that the zero parts are complete.
         SendDlgItemMessage(hDlg, ID_METER,
            MM_SETPARTSCOMPLETE, 0, 0);

         // Tell spin button that the valid range is 0 to 25.
         SendDlgItemMessage(hDlg, ID_SPIN, SPNM_SETRANGE, 0,
            MAKELPARAM(0, 25));

         // Tell spin button that the current value is 0.
         SendDlgItemMessage(hDlg, ID_SPIN,
            SPNM_SETCRNTVALUE, 0, 0);
         break;
```

```
        case WM_COMMAND:
          switch (wParam) {
            case ID_SPIN:
              switch (HIWORD(lParam)) {
                case SPNN_VALUECHANGE:
                  // User has changed the current value
                  // of the spin button.

                  // Request the current value
                  // from the spin button.
                  x = (int) SendMessage(LOWORD(lParam),
                      SPNM_GETCRNTVALUE, 0, 0);

                  // Tells the Meter control the new number of
                  // parts that are complete.
                  SendDlgItemMessage(hDlg, ID_METER,
                      MM_SETPARTSCOMPLETE, x, 0);

                  // Update the static window to reflect the
                  // current value in the spin button.
                  SetDlgItemInt(hDlg, ID_SPINVALUE, x, FALSE);
                  break;
              }
              break;

            case IDOK:
            case IDCANCEL:
              EndDialog(hDlg, wParam);
              break;

            default: break;
          }
          break;

        default:
          fProcessed = FALSE;
          break;
      }

    return(fProcessed);
}

// *************************************************************
// This function processes messages sent to the app's main window.

LRESULT CALLBACK AppWndProc
        (HWND hWnd, UINT uMsg, WPARAM wParam, LPARAM lParam) {
```

```
BOOL fCallDefProc = FALSE;
LRESULT lResult = 0;

switch (uMsg) {
   case WM_DESTROY:
      PostQuitMessage(0);
      break;
   case WM_SYSCOMMAND:
      // Any menu option selected from CustCntl's System Menu.

      // Any options that you appended to System menu should be
      // processed by CustCntl and NOT passed to DefWindowProc.

      switch (wParam & 0xfff0) {

      case IDM_DEMO:
         // Display about box.
         DialogBox(_hInstance, "CustCntl",
            hWnd, (DLGPROC) CustCntlDlgProc);
         break;

      default:
         // Any options that you do not process should be
         // passed to DefWindowProc.
         fCallDefProc = TRUE;
         break;
      }

      break;

   default:
      fCallDefProc = TRUE; break;
}

if (fCallDefProc)
   lResult = DefWindowProc(hWnd, uMsg, wParam, lParam);

return(lResult);
}
```

Listing 4-16. CUSTCNTL.H application header module

```
/********************************************************************
Module name: CUSTCNTL.H
Programmer : Jeffrey M. Richter.
********************************************************************/

#include "..\spin.04\spin.h"
#include "..\meter.04\meter.h"

#define ID_SPINVALUE     100
#define ID_SPIN          101
#define ID_METER         102
```

Listing 4-17. CUSTCNTL.DEF Custom Control application definitions file

```
; Module name: CUSTCNTL.DEF
; Programmer : Jeffrey M. Richter.

NAME          CUSTCNTL
DESCRIPTION   'CustCntl: Custom Child Control Application'
STUB          'WinStub.exe'
EXETYPE       WINDOWS
CODE          MOVEABLE DISCARDABLE PRELOAD
DATA          MOVEABLE MULTIPLE PRELOAD
HEAPSIZE      1024
STACKSIZE     5120
```

Listing 4-18. CUSTCNTL.RC application resource file

```
/********************************************************************
Module name: CUSTCNTL.RC
Programmer : Jeffrey M. Richter.
********************************************************************/

#include <windows.h>
#include "custcntl.h"

CustCntl ICON     MOVEABLE DISCARDABLE CustCntl.Ico

CUSTCNTL DIALOG LOADONCALL MOVEABLE DISCARDABLE 11, 22, 144, 36
CAPTION "Custom control demonstration"
STYLE WS_BORDER | WS_CAPTION | WS_DLGFRAME | WS_SYSMENU |
    WS_VISIBLE | WS_POPUP
```

```
BEGIN
    CONTROL "&Spin value:", -1, "static",
        SS_LEFT | WS_CHILD, 4, 4, 40, 12
    CONTROL "", ID_SPINVALUE, "static",
        SS_LEFT | WS_BORDER | WS_CHILD, 44, 4, 32, 12
    CONTROL "Text", ID_SPIN, "spin",
        WS_BORDER | WS_CHILD, 76, 4, 8, 12
    CONTROL "Text", ID_METER, "meter",
        WS_BORDER | WS_CHILD, 4, 20, 96, 12
    CONTROL "&Cancel", IDCANCEL, "button",
        BS_DEFPUSHBUTTON | WS_TABSTOP | WS_CHILD, 104, 4, 36, 12
END
```

Listing 4-19. MAKEFILE for Custom Control application

```
#*******************************************************************
#Module name: MAKEFILE
#Programmer : Jeffrey M. Richter.
#*******************************************************************

!include "..\builtins.jmr"

PROG = CustCntl

MODEL = s
CFLAGS = -P-c -c -f- -WS -p -v -w -m$(MODEL) -I$(INCLUDEDIR)
LFLAGS = /P/v/n/m/s/L$(LIBDIR)
LIBS = CW$(MODEL) Import

MODULES = $(PROG).obj

ICONS   = $(PROG).ico
BITMAPS =
CURSORS =

$(PROG).Exe: $(MODULES) $(PROG).Def $(PROG).Res
    tlink $(LFLAGS) @&&!
COW$(MODEL) $(MODULES)
$(PROG), $(PROG), $(LIBS), $(PROG)
!
    rc -30 -T $(PROG).Res
    TDStrip -s $(PROG)

$(PROG).res:    $(PROG).rc $(PROG).h $(RESOURCES)
```

CHAPTER 5

Setting Up Printers

Since Windows 3.0, Windows gives your applications much greater control over printer settings than previously. In earlier versions, printer settings were system-wide. When the user changed the settings, the new settings affected all the applications running under Windows. For example, if the user changed the printer's settings so that it would print in landscape mode for a spreadsheet application, the printer would remain in landscape mode when printing from a word-processing application.

Beginning with Version 3.0 of Windows, each application can maintain its own print settings. In fact, an application may maintain several different print settings at once. This allows a word-processing application to remember the settings for a particular document. For example, the user may desire that interoffice memos always print from the laser printer's paper Bin 1 and that corporate correspondence always print from Bin 2.

This chapter explains how Windows manages printers and how applications can access various printer settings. It continues with a discussion of the Print Setup common dialog box supplied by Microsoft in COMMDLG.DLL. The chapter concludes with a sample application that uses the Print Setup common dialog box to request various printer settings from the user and prints a sample page using the selected settings.

How Windows Manages Printers

Users install, configure, set up, and remove printers from the Windows environment using the Printers dialog box in the Control Panel (Figure 5-1).

```
┌──────────────────────────────────────────────────────────────┐
│ ▬                         Printers                             │
├────────────────────────────────────────┬───────────────────── │
│ ┌Default Printer──────────────────────┐ │   ┌─────────────┐    │
│ │ TI microLaser PS35 on LPT1:          │ │   │   Cancel    │    │
│ └──────────────────────────────────────┘ │   └─────────────┘    │
│ ┌Installed Printers:──────────────────┐ │   ┌─────────────┐    │
│ │ IBM Graphics on COM2:            ▲  │ │   │  Connect... │    │
│ │ NEC Pinwriter P6 on FILE:           │ │   └─────────────┘    │
│ │ TI microLaser PS35 on LPT1:         │ │   ┌─────────────┐    │
│ │ TI microLaser PS35 on LPT2:         │ │   │  Setup...   │    │
│ │ WINFAX on CAS                    ▼  │ │   └─────────────┘    │
│ │                                     │ │   ┌─────────────┐    │
│ │      ┌──────────────────────────┐   │ │   │  Remove     │    │
│ │      │ Set As Default Printer   │   │ │   └─────────────┘    │
│ │      └──────────────────────────┘   │ │   ┌─────────────┐    │
│ └──────────────────────────────────────┘ │   │  Add >>     │    │
│ ☒ Use Print Manager                      │   └─────────────┘    │
│                                          │   ┌─────────────┐    │
│ List of Printers:                        │   │   Help      │    │
│ ┌──────────────────────────────────────┐ │   └─────────────┘    │
│ │ Install Unlisted or Updated Printer ▲│ │                     │
│ │ Generic / Text Only                  │ │                     │
│ │ Agfa 9000 Series PS                  │ │   ┌─────────────┐    │
│ │ Agfa Compugraphic 400PS              │ │   │  Install... │    │
│ │ Agfa Compugraphic Genics             │ │   └─────────────┘    │
│ │ Apple LaserWriter                    │ │                     │
│ │ Apple LaserWriter II NT              │ │                     │
│ │ Apple LaserWriter II NTX          ▼ │ │                     │
│ └──────────────────────────────────────┘ │                     │
└──────────────────────────────────────────┴──────────────────── ┘
```

Figure 5-1. Printers dialog box

When the user selects the "Add >>" push button, the list of available printers appears in the "List of Printers:" list box. This list is obtained from the *[io.device]* section of the CONTROL.INF file distributed with Windows. Each line in this section contains the information necessary to install a single printer. The entire *[io.device]* section is far too long to be reproduced here, so only the beginning of it is shown:

```
[io.device]
; (printers, plotters, etc.)
; The filename is followed by
;
; - the descriptive string which will appear in Control Panel and
;   which will appear in WIN.INI
; - 1 or 2 strings indicating the scaling for this device.
;
; There may be more than one line for a driver, corresponding to
;   different printers.
```

```
6:TTY.DRV,"Generic / Text Only","DEVICESPECIFIC"
6:pscript.DRV,"Agfa 9000 Series PS","DEVICESPECIFIC"
6:pscript.DRV,"Agfa Compugraphic 400PS","DEVICESPECIFIC"
6:HPPCL.DRV,6:unidrv.dll,"Agfa Compugraphic Genics","DEVICESPECIFIC"
6:pscript.DRV,"Apple LaserWriter","DEVICESPECIFIC"
6:pscript.DRV,"Apple LaserWriter II NT","DEVICESPECIFIC"
6:pscript.DRV,"Apple LaserWriter II NTX","DEVICESPECIFIC"
6:pscript.DRV,"Apple LaserWriter Plus","DEVICESPECIFIC"
6:HPPCL.DRV,6:unidrv.dll,"Apricot Laser","DEVICESPECIFIC"
6:pscript.DRV,"AST TurboLaser/PS","DEVICESPECIFIC"
6:HPPLOT.DRV,"AT&T 435","CONTINUOUSSCALING"
6:CITOH.DRV,6:unidrv.dll,"AT&T 470/475","DEVICESPECIFIC"
6:oki9ibm.DRV,6:unidrv.dll,"AT&T 473/478","DEVICESPECIFIC"
6:CITOH.DRV,6:unidrv.dll,"C-Itoh 8510","DEVICESPECIFIC"
6:CANON10e.DRV,6:unidrv.dll,"Canon Bubble-Jet BJ-10e","DEVICESPECIFIC"
6:CANON130.DRV,6:unidrv.dll,"Canon Bubble-Jet BJ-130e","DEVICESPECIFIC"
6:CANON330.DRV,6:unidrv.dll,"Canon Bubble-Jet BJ-300","DEVICESPECIFIC"
6:CANON330.DRV,6:unidrv.dll,"Canon Bubble-Jet BJ-330","DEVICESPECIFIC"
6:lbpiii.DRV,6:gendrv.dll,"Canon LBP-4","DEVICESPECIFIC"
6:LBPII.DRV,6:gendrv.dll,"Canon LBP-8 II","DEVICESPECIFIC"
6:lbpiii.DRV,6:gendrv.dll,"Canon LBP-8 III","DEVICESPECIFIC"
6:CIT9US.DRV,6:unidrv.dll,"Citizen 120D","DEVICESPECIFIC"
6:CIT9US.DRV,6:unidrv.dll,"Citizen 180D","DEVICESPECIFIC"
6:CIT9US.DRV,6:unidrv.dll,6:dmcolor.dll,"Citizen 200GX","DEVICESPECIFIC"
6:CIT9US.DRV,6:unidrv.dll,6:dmcolor.dll,"Citizen 200GX/15","DEVICESPECIFIC"
6:CIT24US.DRV,6:unidrv.dll,6:dmcolor.dll,"Citizen GSX-130","DEVICESPECIFIC"
6:CIT24US.DRV,6:unidrv.dll,6:dmcolor.dll,"Citizen GSX-140","DEVICESPECIFIC"
6:CIT24US.DRV,6:unidrv.dll,6:dmcolor.dll,"Citizen GSX-140+","DEVICESPECIFIC"
6:CIT24US.DRV,6:unidrv.dll,6:dmcolor.dll,"Citizen GSX-145","DEVICESPECIFIC"
6:CIT9US.DRV,6:unidrv.dll,6:dmcolor.dll,"Citizen HSP-500","DEVICESPECIFIC"
6:CIT9US.DRV,6:unidrv.dll,6:dmcolor.dll,"Citizen HSP-550","DEVICESPECIFIC"
6:CIT24US.DRV,6:unidrv.dll,"Citizen PN48","DEVICESPECIFIC"
6:pscript.DRV,"Dataproducts LZR-2665","DEVICESPECIFIC"
6:diconix.DRV,6:unidrv.dll,"Diconix 150 Plus","DEVICESPECIFIC"
```

```
6:pscript.DRV,6:DECCOLOR.WPD,"Digital Colormate PS","DEVICESPECIFIC"
6:pscript.DRV,6:DEC1150.WPD,"Digital DEClaser 1150","DEVICESPECIFIC"
6:pscript.DRV,6:DEC2150.WPD,"Digital DEClaser 2150","DEVICESPECIFIC"
6:pscript.DRV,6:DEC2250.WPD,"Digital DEClaser 2250","DEVICESPECIFIC"
6:pscript.DRV,6:DEC3250.WPD,"Digital DEClaser 3250","DEVICESPECIFIC"
6:pscript.DRV,"Digital LN03R ScriptPrinter","DEVICESPECIFIC"
      .
      .
      .
```

Each line contains the list of files needed to drive the printer. The first file listed is the main device driver. Each driver filename starts with a diskette number that indicates on which of the Windows retail distribution diskettes the file exists. After the list of driver files is the text indicating the specific printer's model and one or two strings specifying device scaling information. The scaling information tells Windows if some special screen fonts should be loaded to make it easier to design documents on the screen that are destined for the printer.

When the user wishes to install a new printer, the Control Panel first determines if the specified device driver is already installed. If it is, the Control Panel asks the user if it should use the current printer driver or replace it with a new one.

The third field is the line of text the Control Panel places in the "List of Printers:" list box. Some lines contain the printer's type, which is enclosed in square brackets.

PSCRIPT.DRV is used for many different printers. If you examine the complete CONTROL.INF file on your computer, you will notice that several other drivers are used for a variety of printers. For example, the EPSON9.DRV file is used for all nine-pin Epson printers and the NEC24PIN.DRV file is used for all 24-pin NEC printers. Although the features and capabilities of PostScript printers vary, the actual translation of data for the particular printer remains the same.

After the user has installed a new printer, the installed printer's information is inserted in the "Installed Printers:" list box of the dialog box.

Each printer must be assigned a port. The *[ports]* section of the WIN.INI file defines the ports Windows should recognize. By default, the following ports exist:

```
[ports]
LPT1:=
LPT2:=
LPT3:=
COM1:=9600,n,8,1
COM2:=9600,n,8,1
COM3:=9600,n,8,1
COM4:=9600,n,8,1
EPT:=
FILE:=
LPT1.DOS=
LPT2.DOS=
```

The table below briefly explains the default ports. When new printers are installed, the Control Panel assigns them to the LPT1: port by default.

Printer	Description
LPT1:, LPT2:, LPT3:	The printer is connected to one of the line-printer ports and may be used for printing.
COM1:, COM2:, COM3:, COM4:	The printer is connected to one of the communications ports and may be used for printing.
EPT:	The printer is connected to the EPT port and may be used for printing. The EPT port is part of a hardware card that gets inserted into the computer to drive an IBM Personal Pageprinter.
FILE:	Printing to this printer will cause all output to be sent to a file. When printing begins, the user will be prompted for a filename.
LPT1.DOS, LPT2.DOS	Printing to this printer will cause all output to be sent to the path name specified. These ports are used when Windows is running in a DOS compatibility box under OS/2.

The Control Panel lets more than one printer be assigned to the same port. Windows makes it the sole responsibility of the user to know which printer is physically connected and choose the correct one from within the application before printing.

Every time the user exits the Printers dialog box, the Control Panel saves the printer information in the *[PrinterPorts]* section of the WIN.INI file:

```
[PrinterPorts]
Generic / Text Only=TTY,LPT2:,15,45
HP LaserJet Series II=HPPCL,LPT1:,15,45
IBM Graphics=oki9ibm,COM2:,15,45
NEC Pinwriter P6=NEC24pin,FILE:,15,45
TI microLaser PS35=pscript,LPT1:,15,90,LPT2:,15,90
WINFAX=WINFAX,CAS,15,45
```

On the left of the equal sign is the text describing the printer that has been installed. Following the equal sign is the name of the main device driver, not including its extension, used to access that printer. The remainder of the line specifies the port the printer is connected to, the "Device Not Selected:" timeout, and the "Transmission Retry:" timeout. If more than one printer of this type has been installed, these last three fields are repeated for each printer installed. For example, the *[PrinterPorts]* section shows that two TI microLaser PS35 printers have been installed:

Port	Device not selected	Transmission retry
LPT1:	15	90
LPT2:	15	90

Although an application may refer to the information in *[PrinterPorts]* to determine which printers are available, this section is usually used only by the Control Panel. Applications should reference the *[devices]* section (also updated by the Control Panel) of the WIN.INI file to determine which printers are available:

```
[devices]
Generic / Text Only=TTY,LPT2:
HP LaserJet Series II=HPPCL,LPT1:
IBM Graphics=oki9ibm,COM2:
NEC Pinwriter P6=NEC24pin,FILE:
TI microLaser PS35=pscript,LPT1:,LPT2:
WINFAX=WINFAX,CAS
```

As in the *[PrinterPorts]* section of the WIN.INI file, the item to the left of the equal sign is the device name of the installed printer. Immediately following the equal sign is the name of the main printer device driver. The remainder of the line specifies which port or ports the printer is connected to. This section does not contain the "Device Not Selected" and "Transmission Retry" fields.

In addition to assigning printers to various ports, Windows lets the user select a default printer. The "Default Printer" box in the Control Panel shows the default printer. Applications use this printer if the user has not explicitly chosen a different printer. The default printer is set by selecting the desired default printer in the "Installed Printers" list box and by clicking the "Set As Default Printer" button.

The Control Panel saves this information in the *[windows]* section of the WIN.INI file:

```
[windows]
 .

 .

 .

device=TI microLaser PS35,pscript,LPT1:
 .

 .

 .
```

Following the equal sign is the text describing the device name of the printer, the printer's main device driver file, and the port to which the printer is connected. When no default printer is selected, the line has the following appearance:

```
device=
```

When an application finds that no default printer has been selected, any options that would allow the user to print should be disabled. In addition, if an application requires some knowledge of a printer's capabilities before it can perform some actions, these actions should also be disabled. For example, a word-processing program might not be able to calculate the number of pages in a document if it cannot calculate the paper size for any printer.

Printer Device Drivers

Because there are so many different kinds of printers, it would be impossible for Microsoft to support all of them in Windows itself. For this reason, a special device driver must be developed for each type of printer. Even though Microsoft distributes most of the drivers with Windows, the device drivers are often available directly from the printer manufacturer.

Although the printer device driver file has a .DRV instead of a .DLL extension, it *is* a DLL. The most important responsibility of a printer device driver is to translate device-independent GDI function calls into a series of commands and data that can be sent to the printer. Printer drivers are also responsible for providing device-dependent characteristics such as printer technology (raster, vector, plotter) and horizontal and vertical resolution to an application. Finally, printer drivers let the user and applications change printer settings, such as paper orientation.

When the user selects the "Setup..." button from the Printers dialog box in the Control Panel, another dialog box appears. It contains settings applicable to the selected printer. Because each printer supports different settings, the template for the settings dialog box and the code to process it are contained in the printer's device driver file. The settings dialog box for a TI microLaser PS35 printer is shown in Figure 5-2.

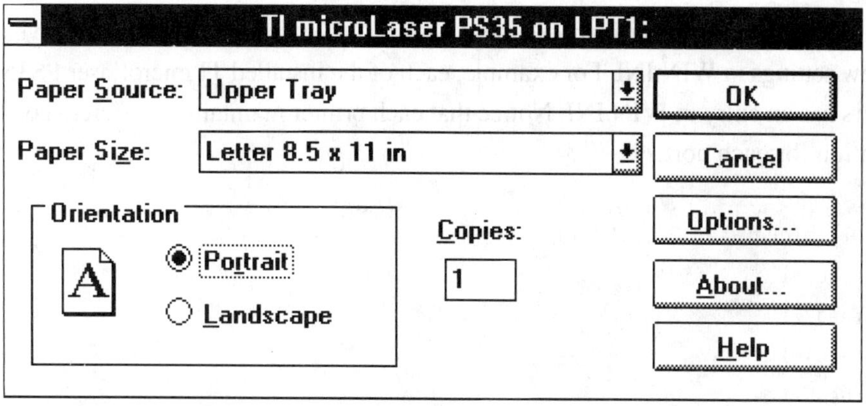

```
 ┌──────────────────────────────────────────────────────────────┐
 │ ▭        TI microLaser PS35 on LPT1:                           │
 ├──────────────────────────────────────────────────────────────┤
 │                                                                │
 │  Paper Source:  ┌─────────────────────────┬─┐  ┌───────────┐   │
 │                 │ Upper Tray              │▼│  │    OK     │   │
 │                 └─────────────────────────┴─┘  └───────────┘   │
 │  Paper Size:    ┌─────────────────────────┬─┐  ┌───────────┐   │
 │                 │ Letter 8.5 x 11 in      │▼│  │  Cancel   │   │
 │                 └─────────────────────────┴─┘  └───────────┘   │
 │  ┌─ Orientation ──────────────┐                ┌───────────┐   │
 │  │                   Copies:   │  Options...│   │
 │  │  ┌───┐  ◉ Portrait          │  ┌───┐         └───────────┘   │
 │  │  │ A │                      │  │ 1 │         ┌───────────┐   │
 │  │  └───┘  ○ Landscape         │  └───┘         │  About... │   │
 │  │                             │                └───────────┘   │
 │  └─────────────────────────────┘                ┌───────────┐   │
 │                                                  │   Help    │   │
 │                                                  └───────────┘   │
 └──────────────────────────────────────────────────────────────┘
```

Figure 5-2. Settings dialog box for TI microLaser PS35

The settings dialog box for an NEC Pinwriter P6 is shown in Figure 5-3.

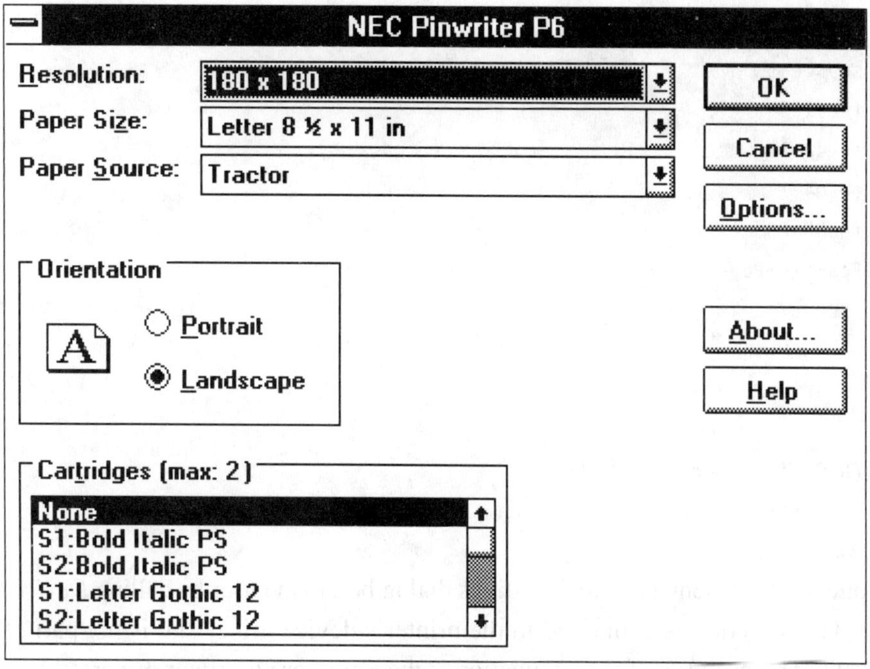

```
 ┌──────────────────────────────────────────────────────────────┐
 │ ▭              NEC Pinwriter P6                                │
 ├──────────────────────────────────────────────────────────────┤
 │  Resolution:   ┌─────────────────────────┬─┐  ┌───────────┐   │
 │                │ 180 x 180               │▼│  │    OK     │   │
 │                └─────────────────────────┴─┘  └───────────┘   │
 │  Paper Size:   ┌─────────────────────────┬─┐  ┌───────────┐   │
 │                │ Letter 8 ½ x 11 in      │▼│  │  Cancel   │   │
 │                └─────────────────────────┴─┘  └───────────┘   │
 │  Paper Source: ┌─────────────────────────┬─┐  ┌───────────┐   │
 │                │ Tractor                 │▼│  │ Options...│   │
 │                └─────────────────────────┴─┘  └───────────┘   │
 │  ┌─ Orientation ──────────────┐                                │
 │  │                             │                ┌───────────┐   │
 │  │  ┌───┐  ○ Portrait          │                │  About... │   │
 │  │  │ A │                      │                └───────────┘   │
 │  │  └───┘  ◉ Landscape         │                ┌───────────┐   │
 │  │                             │                │   Help    │   │
 │  └─────────────────────────────┘                └───────────┘   │
 │  ┌─ Cartridges (max: 2) ──────────────────┐                    │
 │  │ None                              ▲│                    │
 │  │ S1:Bold Italic PS                 ░│                    │
 │  │ S2:Bold Italic PS                 ░│                    │
 │  │ S1:Letter Gothic 12               ░│                    │
 │  │ S2:Letter Gothic 12               ▼│                    │
 │  └─────────────────────────────────────┘                    │
 └──────────────────────────────────────────────────────────────┘
```

Figure 5-3. Settings dialog box for NEC Pinwriter P6

When the Control Panel changes these settings, the printer device driver saves the new settings in WIN.INI. For example, each of the installed TI microLaser PS35 printers has an entry in WIN.INI. Notice that each printer maintains a different configuration for each port.

```
[TI microLaser PS35,LPT1]
feed1=1
feed2=1
feed4=1
feed5=1
EpsFile=
orient=1

[TI microLaser PS35,LPT2]
orient=2
source=5
feed1=5
feed2=1
feed4=1
feed5=20
EpsFile=Paper
Size=37



[NEC Pinwriter P6,FILE]
Orientation=2
```

Applications present a printer's settings dialog box to the user by calling *Device-Mode*. This function is contained in the printer's device driver and is not part of Windows. The prototype for this function is the same for all printer drivers:

```
void WINAPI DeviceMode(HWND hWnd, HMODULE hModLibrary,
    LPSTR szDeviceName, LPSTR szPort);
```

Because this function is in a DLL, the library must be loaded before the function can be called. The following code fragment demonstrates how to call *DeviceMode*:

```
typedef void WINAPI FNDEVICEMODE(HWND, HMODULE, LPSTR, LPSTR);
typedef FNDEVICEMODE FAR *LPFNDEVICEMODE;
.
.
.
BOOL WINAPI CallDeviceModeFunc (HWND hWnd, LPSTR szDriver,
      LPSTR szDeviceName, LPSTR szPort) {
   HMODULE hModLibrary;
   LPFNDEVICEMODE lpfnDeviceMode;
   BOOL fOk = FALSE;

   hModLibrary = (HMODULE) LoadLibrary(szDriver);
   if (hModLibrary < HINSTANCE_ERROR) {
      // Library could not be loaded.
      return(fOk);
   }
   lpfnDeviceMode = (LPFNDEVICEMODE)
      GetProcAddress(hModLibrary, "DeviceMode");
   if (lpfnDeviceMode != NULL) {
      lpfnDeviceMode(hWnd, hModLibrary, szDeviceName, szPort);
      fOk = TRUE;
   } else {
      // DeviceMode function not in library.
   }
   FreeLibrary(hModLibrary);
   return(fOk);
}
```

Because this function displays a dialog box to the user, a window handle that will own the dialog box must be passed as the first parameter. The second parameter to *CallDeviceModeFunc* is the name of the printer device driver file to be loaded. The third parameter is the device name of the printer driver. This is the same text that appears in the *[PrinterPorts]* and *[devices]* sections of the WIN.INI file. The last parameter is the null-terminated string representing the output port (for instance, LPT1: or FILE:).

CallDeviceModeFunc attempts to load the DLL using the *LoadLibrary* function. If the library cannot be loaded, *LoadLibrary* returns a value of less than *HIN-STANCE_ERROR* identifying the reason why. Once the handle to the library has been obtained, *GetProcAddress* can locate the address of *DeviceMode* in the DLL. The following line could appear also:

```
lpfnDeviceMode = GetProcAddress(hModLibrary, PROC_OLDDEVICEMODE);
```

The *PROC_OLDDEVICEMODE* identifier can be found in the PRINT.H file included with the Windows SDK.

If *GetProcAddress* returns NULL, the library does not contain a *DeviceMode* function. Otherwise, this function is called with all the parameters passed to *CallDeviceModeFunc* (except that it gets the handle to the library instead of the library's name). This causes the printer device driver library to present the settings dialog box to the user.

When the *DeviceMode* function returns, the *FreeLibrary* function releases the memory used by the library. *CallDeviceModeFunc* returns TRUE or FALSE, indicating whether the call to the *DeviceMode* function was successful.

Although *DeviceMode* is declared as returning no value (*void*), most printer drivers have implemented their *DeviceMode* functions so that they return TRUE or FALSE. However, this is not a rule that developers of device drivers must follow; so, don't rely on it unless you're sure that the printer drivers your applications access implement this feature.

The *DEVMODE* Structure and Printer Environments

When the user selects the "OK" button from the printer settings dialog box, the device driver gathers all the settings and places them in a *DEVMODE* structure.

This structure is defined in the PRINT.H file included with the Windows SDK:

```
#define CCHDEVICENAME           32
.
.
.
typedef struct tagDEVMODE
{
    char   dmDeviceName[CCHDEVICENAME];
    UINT   dmSpecVersion;
    UINT   dmDriverVersion;
    UINT   dmSize;
    UINT   dmDriverExtra;
    DWORD  dmFields;
    int    dmOrientation;
    int    dmPaperSize;
    int    dmPaperLength;
    int    dmPaperWidth;
    int    dmScale;
    int    dmCopies;
    int    dmDefaultSource;
    int    dmPrintQuality;
    int    dmColor;
    int    dmDuplex;
    int    dmYResolution;
    int    dmTTOption;
} DEVMODE;
```

The *DEVMODE* structure consists of three distinct parts:

Part	Description	Members in DEVMODE structure
Header	Specifies information about the device driver that initialized the *DEVMODE* structure.	*dmDeviceName, dmSpecVersion, dmDriverVersion, dmSize, dmDriverExtra*
Device-independent	These members specify information that may apply to any printer.	*dmFields, dmOrientation, dmPaperSize, dmPaperLength, dmPaperWidth, dmScale, dmCopies, dmDefaultSource, dmPrintQuality, dmColor, dmDuplex, dmYResolution, dmTTOption*
Device-dependent	These members specify information specific to this printer driver.	These members begin after the data structure; their length is specified by the *dmDriverExtra* member.

The table below describes each of the *DEVMODE* structure's members:

Member	Description
dmDeviceName	Null-terminated string specifying the printer that the remainder of the structure describes. May be up to 32 characters, including the zero byte.
dmSpecVersion	Specifies the version of the *DEVMODE* specification. This value is the same as the version of Windows and, therefore, is currently 0x030A.
dmDriverSpec	Specifies the version of the printer driver. This value is assigned by the printer driver.
dmSize	Specifies the number of bytes in the header and device-independent parts of the *DEVMODE* structure. This value may change with future versions of Windows (it has changed between Windows 3.0 and 3.1). It is safer for applications to use this field rather than s*izeof(DEVMODE)*.
dmDriverExtra	Specifies the number of bytes in the device-dependent part of the *DEVMODE* structure.

Member	Description
dmFields	Specifies which of the structure members are recognized by the printer's device driver. The following identifiers may be *ANDed* with this member to determine which of the remaining members contain useful information:

DM_ORIENTATION	DM_PAPERSIZE
DM_PAPERLENGTH	DM_PAPERWIDTH
DM_SCALE	DM_COPIES
DM_DEFAULTSOURCE	DM_PRINTQUALITY
DM_COLOR	DM_DUPLEX
DM_YRESOLUTION	DM_TTOPTION

Member	Description
dmOrientation	Specifies the orientation of the paper. It is one of the following identifiers:

DMORIENT_PORTRAIT	DMORIENT_LANDSCAPE

Member	Description
dmPaperSize	Specifies the size of the paper. It is one of the following identifiers:

DMPAPER_LETTER	(8½ x 11 in)
DMPAPER_LETTERSMALL	(8½ x 11 in)
DMPAPER_TABLOID	(11 x 17 in)
DMPAPER_LEDGER	(17 x 11 in)
DMPAPER_LEGAL	(8½ x 14 in)
DMPAPER_STATEMENT	(5½ x 8½ in)
DMPAPER_EXECUTIVE	(7½ x 10 in)
DMPAPER_A3	(297 x 420 mm)
DMPAPER_A4	(210 x 297 mm)
DMPAPER_A4SMALL	(210 x 297 mm)
DMPAPER_A5	(148 x 210 mm)
DMPAPER_B4	(250 x 354 mm)
DMPAPER_B5	(182 x 257 mm)
DMPAPER_FOLIO	(8½ x 13 in)
DMPAPER_QUARTO	(215 x 275 mm)
DMPAPER_10X14	(10 x 14 in)
DMPAPER_11X17	(11 x 17 in)
DMPAPER_NOTE	(8½ x 11 in)
DMPAPER_ENV_9	(3⅞ x 8⅞ in)
DMPAPER_ENV_10	(4⅛ x 9 in)

Member	Description	
	DMPAPER_ENV_11	(4½ x 10⅜ in)
	DMPAPER_ENV_12	(4¾ x 11 in)
	DMPAPER_ENV_14	(5 x 11½ in)
	DMPAPER_CSHEET	(C size sheet)
	DMPAPER_DSHEET	(D size sheet)
	DMPAPER_ESHEET	(E size sheet)
	DMPAPER_ENV_DL	(110 x 220 mm)
	DMPAPER_ENV_C5	(162 x 229 mm)
	DMPAPER_ENV_C3	(324 x 458 mm)
	DMPAPER_ENV_C4	(229 x 324 mm)
	DMPAPER_ENV_C6	(114 x 162 mm)
	DMPAPER_ENV_C65	(114 x 229 mm)
	DMPAPER_ENV_B4	(250 x 353 mm)
	DMPAPER_ENV_B5	(176 x 250 mm)
	DMPAPER_ENV_B6	(176 x 125 mm)
	DMPAPER_ENV_ITALY	(110 x 230 mm)
	DMPAPER_ENV_MONARCH	(3.875 x 7.5 in)
	DMPAPER_ENV_PERSONAL	(3⅝ x 6½ in)
	DMPAPER_FANFOLD_US	(14⅞ x 11 in)
	DMPAPER_FANFOLD_STD_GERMAN	(8½ x 12 in)
	DMPAPER_FANFOLD_LGL_GERMAN	(8½ x 13 in)
dmPaperLength	Overrides the paper length specified in dmPaperSize member. Length of paper is specified in tenths of millimeters. If dmPaperLength and dmPaperWidth are both specified, dmPaperSize may be zero.	
dmPaperWidth	Overrides the paper width specified in dmPaperSize member. Width of paper is specified in tenths of millimeters. If dmPaperLength and dmPaperWidth are both specified, dmPaperSize may be zero.	
dmScale	Specifies the percentage by which the page is scaled. A value of 50 will cause printed output to be half its width and height.	
dmCopies	Specifies the number of copies to be printed for each page.	
dmDefaultSource	Specifies the paper bin to use when printing. It is one of the following identifiers:	
	DMBIN_ONLYONE DMBIN_UPPER	

Member	Description
	DMBIN_LOWER DMBIN_MIDDLE DMBIN_MANUAL DMBIN_ENVELOPE DMBIN_ENVMANUAL DMBIN_AUTO DMBIN_TRACTOR DMBIN_SMALLFMT DMBIN_LARGEFMT DMBIN_LARGECAPACITY DMBIN_CASSETTE
dmPrintQuality	Specifies the resolution to be used when printing. If it is a positive value, it specifies the number of dots per inch, making this member device-dependent. If dmYResolution is initialized, this value represented the x-resolution. Otherwise, this value represents both the x- and y-resolutions. This member may also be one of the following negative identifiers: DMRES_HIGH DMRES_MEDIUM DMRES_LOW DMRES_DRAFT
dmColor	Specifies whether the printer should print in color or monochrome. It is one of the following identifiers: DMCOLOR_COLOR DMCOLOR_MONOCHROME
dmDuplex	Specifies duplex printing. It is one of the following identifiers: DMDUP_SIMPLEX DMDUP_HORIZONTAL DMDUP_VERTICAL
dmYResolution	Specifies the y-resolution of the printer in dots per inch. If the printer initializes this member, the dmPrintQuality member specifies the x-resolution of the printer in dots per inch.
dmTTOption	Specifies how TrueType fonts should be printed. It can be one of the following identifiers: DMTT_BITMAP DMTT_DOWNLOAD DMTT_SUBDEV

Printer Environments

Once the printer driver has filled in the *DEVMODE* structure, it uses the values in the structure to write settings to the user's WIN.INI file (like the *[TI microLaser PS35,LPT2]* entry shown earlier). This *DEVMODE* structure is also saved in a printer environment, a block of memory maintained by Windows that retains the most recent settings for a particular printer port.

When Windows is first invoked, no printer environments are in memory. As the user changes settings for various printers, each printer's device driver saves its printer environment. There can only be one printer environment for each printer port.

When the user selects the "OK" button in *DeviceMode*'s dialog box, the device driver calls *SetEnvironment* to store the current printer settings in memory. Prior to Windows 3.1, *SetEnviroment* was documented in the Windows SDK documentation. Now, it is documented in the Windows DDK documentation. The prototype for this function is:

```
int SetEnvironment(LPCSTR lpszPort, const void FAR *lpvEnviron,
    UINT cbMaxCopy);
```

The first parameter is the name of the port. If an environment already exists for this port, it is deleted. The second parameter is the address of the *DEVMODE* structure that contains the user's printer settings. The last parameter specifies the number of bytes in the complete *DEVMODE* structure. After the environment is set, *SetEnvironment* returns the number of bytes copied into the environment or zero if an error occurred.

You can delete a printer environment by specifying the *cbMaxCopy* parameter to *SetEnvironment* as zero. In this case, *SetEnvironment* returns -1 if the printer environment has been successfully deleted.

Once the new environment is set, the printer driver's *DeviceMode* function calls the *SendMessage* function as follows:

```
SendMessage(HWND_BROADCAST, WM_DEVMODECHANGE, 0,
    (LONG) (LPSTR) DevMode->dmDeviceName);
```

This causes the *WM_DEVMODECHANGE* message to be sent to all overlapped and pop-up windows in the Windows system. The message notifies them that the printer environment has changed for the device whose name is specified by the *lParam* parameter. This allows applications that are using the default settings for a particular printer to retrieve the new settings by calling *GetEnvironment*. Just like the *SetEnvironment* function, this function is now documented in the Windows DDK instead of the SDK. The prototype for this function is:

```
int GetEnvironment(LPCSTR lpszPort, void FAR *lpvEnviron,
    UINT cbMaxCopy);
```

The first parameter specifies the port for which an environment should be retrieved. The second parameter is the address of a *DEVMODE* structure where the environment information is to be copied. The last parameter specifies the maximum number of bytes to copy into the *DEVMODE* structure pointed to by the *lpvEnviron* parameter. The *GetEnvironment* function returns the number of bytes copied to the memory block pointed to by *lpvEnviron*. If the printer environment cannot be located for the specified port, the return value is zero.

An application can determine the number of bytes required to contain the complete *DEVMODE* structure by calling *GetEnvironment* and passing NULL as the *lpvEnviron* parameter. An application can call this function once to retrieve the size of the *DEVMODE* structure, allocate a block of memory that size, then call *GetEnvironment* again to fill the memory block.

The following outline describes the actions performed by *DeviceMode*:

A. *DeviceMode* fills a *DEVMODE* structure.
   1. The *GetEnvironment* function is called to retrieve the most recent printer settings.
   2. If the printer environment cannot be found (*GetEnvironment* returned zero), the driver tries to fill a *DEVMODE* structure from entries in the WIN.INI file.
   3. If no entry exists in the WIN.INI file, the driver fills the *DEVMODE* structure with default values.

B. The printer settings dialog box is displayed to the user, and the controls within it are set to reflect the values in the *DEVMODE* structure.

C. User changes settings in the dialog box until the "OK" or "Cancel" button is selected.
   1. If the "Cancel" button is selected:
      a. The dialog box is removed.
      b. Control is returned to the application.
   2. If the "OK" button is selected:
      a. The *DEVMODE* structure is updated with the new settings in the dialog box.
      b. The new settings are written to the WIN.INI file (like the *[TI micro-Laser PS35,LPT2]* entry shown earlier).
      c. The *SetEnvironment* function is called to save the new settings in memory.
      d. The *SendMessage* function is called to send the *WM_DEVMODE-CHANGE* message to all top-level windows.
      e. The dialog box is removed.
      f. Control is returned to the application.

The *ExtDeviceMode* Function

Starting with version 3.0 of Windows, a new function is defined that should be included in printer device drivers. This function, *ExtDeviceMode*, allows an application to have greater control over the processing of printer settings. As with *Device-Mode*, an application gains access to *ExtDeviceMode* by loading the printer driver's DLL and retrieving the address of the function with *GetProcAddress*:

```
lpfnExtDeviceMode =
   (LPFNDEVMODE) GetProcAddress(hModLibrary, "ExtDeviceMode");
```

or

```
lpfnExtDeviceMode =
   (LPFNDEVMODE) GetProcAddress(hModLibrary, PROC_EXTDEVICEMODE);
```

314

The PRINT.H file contains the following definitions to help you work with the *ExtDeviceMode* function:

```
#define PROC_EXTDEVICEMODE        MAKEINTRESOURCE(90)
        .

        .

        .
typedef UINT (CALLBACK* LPFNDEVMODE)(HWND, HMODULE, DEVMODE FAR*,
    LPSTR, LPSTR, DEVMODE FAR*, LPSTR, UINT);
```

Although all printer device drivers must include *DeviceMode*, it is not guaranteed that any printer driver will include *ExtDeviceMode*. In fact, in Windows 3.0 most of the printer drivers did not contain *ExtDeviceMode*. In Windows 3.1, however, this situation has been improved and all the printer drivers except for one (HPPLOT.DRV) include this function. The prototype for *ExtDeviceMode* is:

```
int ExtDeviceMode(HWND hWnd, HMODULE hDriver,
    LPDEVMODE lpdmOutput, LPSTR lpszDevice, LPSTR lpszPort,
    LPDEVMODE lpdmInput, LPSTR lpszProfile, WORD fwMode);
```

The meanings of the *hWnd*, *hDriver*, *lpszDevice*, and *lpszPort* parameters are identical to those used by *DeviceMode*. The *fwMode* parameter specifies the action or actions *ExtDeviceMode* is to take. The table below lists the possible actions:

Values in *fwMode* (may be *OR*ed together)	Action
DM_MODIFY	Modifies the current printer settings to reflect the changes specified by the *DEVMODE* structure pointed to by the *lpdmInput* parameter.
DM_PROMPT	Allows the user to change any of the printer's settings by presenting the printer settings dialog box to the user.

Values in *fwMode* (may be *OR*ed together)	Action
DM_COPY	Causes the printer settings to be copied to the *DEVMODE* structure pointed to by the *lpdmOutput* parameter.
DM_UPDATE	Writes the new printer settings to the environment and file specified by the *lpszProfile* parameter.

If the *fwMode* parameter is zero, the *ExtDeviceMode* function returns the number of bytes required to contain a complete *DEVMODE* structure. Otherwise, if the *DM_PROMPT* identifier is specified, the return value is either *IDOK* or *IDCANCEL*, depending on which button the user selected. If *DM_PROMPT* is not specified, the return value is *IDOK* if the function is successful or a negative value if the function fails.

An application may modify a printer's settings by specifying *DM_MODIFY*. This identifier instructs *ExtDeviceMode* to take the *DEVMODE* structure representing the current printer's settings and change some of its members. The *DEVMODE* structure pointed to by *lpdmInput* must have its five header members initialized and should contain in its *dmFields* member the list of fields to be changed.

The *dmFields* member of *DEVMODE* identifies the fields supported by the particular printer. However, *dmFields* has a slightly different meaning when used in the *DEVMODE* structure pointed to by the *lpdmInput* parameter. In this case, *dmFields* specifies which fields of the current printer settings you wish to change. For example, if an application wants to change the *dmOrientation* and *dmCopies* values of the current printers settings, it should initialize the following members before calling *ExtDeviceMode*:

```
// Initialize DEVMODE header fields.
lstrcpy(DevMode->dmDeviceName, szDeviceName);
DevMode->dmSpecVersion = DM_SPECVERSION;
DevMode->dmDriverVersion = 0;
DevMode->dmSize = sizeof(DEVMODE);
DevMode->dmDriverExtra = 0;
```

```
// Specify which fields we wish to change.
DevMode->dmFields = DM_ORIENTATION | DM_COPIES

// Set the new, desired values.
DevMode->dmOrientation = DM_LANDSCAPE;
DevMode->dmCopies = 2;

// Call the ExtDeviceMode function using DM_MODIFY and
// any other desired DM_ flags.
```

Because the code won't modify any of the driver's device-dependent information, the *dmDriverVersion* member and the *dmDriverExtra* member may be set to zero.

Initializing the *dmOrientation* and *dmCopies* members tells *ExtDeviceMode* to use the current *DEVMODE* structure for the printer, changing its orientation to landscape and the number of copies to two. No other fields will be altered. Because some of the device-independent information does not apply to all printers, Windows printer drivers ignore any settings in this structure that do not apply. For example, the driver for a printer that does not support color will ignore any values set in the *dmColor* member, even if the *DM_COLOR* identifier is *OR*ed in the *dmFields* member.

Specifying the *DM_PROMPT* identifier forces the *ExtDeviceMode* function to display the printer settings dialog box to the user. If the *DM_MODIFY* identifier was also specified, the *DEVMODE* structure is modified before the dialog box appears. The user may now change any of the settings in the dialog box. When the user selects the "OK" button, the *DEVMODE* structure maintained by *ExtDevice-Mode* contains the new information.

Unless the *DM_COPY* or *DM_UPDATE* identifier is included with the *fwMode* parameter, this updated *DEVMODE* structure will be destroyed, having no effect when the *ExtDeviceMode* function terminates. *DM_COPY* makes *ExtDeviceMode* copy the updated *DEVMODE* structure to the *DEVMODE* structure pointed to by the *lpdmOutput* parameter.

The *DM_UPDATE* identifier causes the *ExtDeviceMode* function to perform the same actions as the *DeviceMode* function:

1. Call *SetEnvironment,* passing it the updated *DEVMODE* structure.
2. Call *SendMessage* using the *WM_DEVMODECHANGE* message to notify all top-level windows of the printer environment change.
3. Save the updated settings in the file specified by the *lpszProfile* parameter. If *lpszProfile* is NULL, the updated settings are saved in the WIN.INI file.

Calling the *ExtDeviceMode* function with

```
ExtDeviceMode(hWnd, hModLibrary, NULL, szDeviceName, lpPort,
     NULL, NULL, DM_PROMPT | DM_UPDATE);
```

has the same effect as calling the *DeviceMode* function. In fact, many printer drivers implement their *DeviceMode* functions using this exact syntax. This line causes the *ExtDeviceMode* function to perform the following actions:

1. It retrieves the printer's current settings by calling *GetEnvironment.* If the environment is not found, the initialization file specified by the *lpszProfile* parameter is used. This is WIN.INI because *lpszProfile* is NULL. Finally, if the settings cannot be found, the driver uses built-in default settings.
2. Because *DM_MODIFY* is not specified, *lpdmInput* may be NULL and the current printer settings are not changed.
3. The printer settings dialog box is displayed because the *DM_PROMPT* identifier is specified.
4. Since the *DM_COPY* identifier is not specified, the updated settings are not copied to the *DEVMODE* structure pointed to by the *lpdmOutput* parameter. Therefore, the *lpdmOutput* parameter may be NULL.
5. The *DM_UPDATE* identifier causes the updated settings to be saved in a printer environment and changed in WIN.INI. Again, the WIN.INI file is used because *lpszProfile* is NULL.

Sending Output to a Printer

Before sending information to a printer, a Windows application must create a device context for the printer. This is done with the *CreateDC* function. The prototype for this function is:

```
HDC CreateDC(LPCSTR lpszDriver, LPCSTR lpszDevice, LPCSTR lpszPort,
    LPDEVMODE lpDevMode);
```

The *lpszDriver* parameter is the name of the printer device driver file and must not include the extension. The *lpszDevice* parameter specifies the device name of the printer driver. The *lpszPort* parameter is the name of the port to which the printer is connected. The port name uses standard DOS conventions and should be suffixed with a colon (though this is not mandatory). If *lpszPort* is FILE:, the user will be requested to enter a filename when printing begins. This *lpszPort* parameter may also specify the full path name of a file where the information is to be sent. If you specify a path name directly, do not terminate it with a colon.

The *lpDevMode* parameter is a pointer to a *DEVMODE* structure. If this parameter is NULL, *CreateDC* will call *GetEnvironment* to retrieve the default printer settings for the specified port. If, on the other hand, *lpDevMode* points to a *DEVMODE* structure, the structure must be complete, including both device-independent and device-dependent information. Although you can create a complete *DEVMODE* structure manually, the structure should be filled by a call to *GetEnvironment* or *ExtDeviceMode*. This guarantees that all members are filled with the appropriate values for the driver you are using. Once the device context has been created, standard GDI functions may be used to send information to the printer.

Now, let's say that the user is working on a document in his or her word processor. The user desires that all pages be printed in portrait orientation except page 7, which is to be printed in landscape orientation. Prior to Windows 3.1, there was no way to do this except by terminating the job after page 6, starting and stopping a new one-page job for page 7, and then sending the remaining pages as a third job. However, in Windows 3.1, Microsoft has added a new function that allows an application to change the printer settings during a single print job. This function is called *ResetDC* and has the following prototype:

```
HDC ResetDC(HDC hDC, DEVMODE FAR *lpDevMode);
```

The first parameter to *ResetDC* is the handle of the device context originally retrieved by a call to *CreateDC* or a previous call to *ResetDC*. The second parameter is the address of a *DEVMODE* structure containing the new print settings. If the function is successful at changing the settings, a new DC is returned. This DC will be the same as the *hDC* parameter passed to the function. *ResetDC* returns NULL if it was unsuccessful. Be aware that you cannot use this function to change the driver name, device name, or output port. To do this, you must call *DeleteDC* to terminate the current print job and begin another print job by calling *CreateDC* with the new driver name, device name, or output port.

Getting Printer-Specific Information

Applications often need to query a printer device driver for device-dependent information. For example, a program may call *EnumFonts* or *EnumFontFamilies* to retrieve a list of fonts and sizes supported by the printer. The *GetDeviceCaps* function can be used to determine device-specific information about the printer.

Printer device drivers that support *ExtDeviceMode* also support *DeviceCapabilities*. This function is contained in the printers device driver file, just like *DeviceMode* and *ExtDeviceMode*. An application that wishes to use *DeviceCapabilities* must retrieve its address from the DLL the same way the *DeviceMode* and *ExtDevice-Mode* functions are retrieved:

```
lpfnDevCaps = (LPFNDEVCAPS)
    GetProcAddress(hModLibrary, "DeviceCapabilities");
```

or

```
lpfnDevCaps = (LPFNDEVCAPS)
    GetProcAddress(hModLibrary, PROC_DEVICECAPABILITIES);
```

The PRINT.H file contains the following definitions to help you work with *Device-Capabilities*:

```
#define PROC_DEVICECAPABILTIES MAKEINTRESOURCE(91)
    .
    .
    .
typedef DWORD  (CALLBACK* LPFNDEVCAPS)(LPSTR, LPSTR, UINT, LPSTR,
    DEVMODE FAR*);
```

The prototype for *DeviceCapabilities* is:

```
DWORD DeviceCapabilities(LPCSTR lpszDevice, LPCSTR lpszPort,
    WORD fwCapability, LPSTR lpOutput, LPDEVMODE lpdm);
```

The *lpszDevice* parameter specifies the device name of the printer driver for which information is requested. The *lpszPort* parameter is the name of the port to which the device is connected. The *fwCapability* parameter specifies the type of information that is requested. The possible values are listed in the SDK's PRINT.H file and are shown below:

BC_BINNAMES	DC_BINS	DC_COPIES
DC_DRIVER	DC_DUPLEX	DC_ENUMRESOLUTIONS
DC_EXTRA	DC_FIELDS	DC_FILEDEPENDENCIES
DC_MAXEXTENT	DC_MINEXTENT	DC_ORIENTATION
DC_PAPERNAMES	DC_PAPERS	DC_PAPERSIZE
DC_SIZE	DC_TRUETYPE	DC_VERSION

The *lpOutput* parameter is a pointer to a buffer that is to receive data corresponding to the type of information requested. For example, the *DC_PAPERS* index causes *DeviceCapabilities* to treat the *lpOutput* parameter as a far pointer to an array of *WORD*s. It then fills the array with the paper sizes supported by this driver. The return value indicates the number of entries copied into the array.

The *lpDevMode* parameter specifies where *DeviceCapabilities* should look for values. If *lpDevMode* is NULL, the device driver examines the current default settings for the printer. If *lpDevMode* points to a *DEVMODE* structure, *Device-Capabilities* returns information about the *DEVMODE* structure. For example, calling *DeviceCapabilities* with the *fwCapability* parameter set to *DC_EXTRA* will return the number of extra bytes used for the current default settings if *lpDe-vMode* is NULL. If *lpDevMode* is not NULL, *DeviceCapabilities* returns the value in the *dmDriverExtra* member of the *DEVMODE* structure pointed to by the *lpDev-Mode* parameter.

Printer Driver Caveats

Earlier versions of Windows offered insufficient support for controlling printers from applications. Microsoft noticed this need and has begun addressing improved printer support by standardizing a data structure to hold printer settings (*DEVMODE*) and defining functions that can be called from our own applications to alter these settings.

Printer drivers that do not support the *ExtDeviceMode* function may also not support the *DEVMODE* structure. *DEVMODE* was defined for version 3.0 of Windows and did not exist prior to it. Because of this, Windows 2.x printer device drivers used a proprietary data structure for saving the printer's settings. This structure was then saved and retrieved using the *SetEnvironment* and *GetEnvironment* functions. Both functions ignore the actual data structure passed in their *lpvEnviron* parameters and just store the data in memory. The only requirement of this data structure was that the first member had to have the name of the device that created the structure. This way, a driver could tell if the data retrieved by a call to *GetEnvironment* was created by the same driver.

When an application calls *CreateDC*, a function is called in the printer driver. If the *lpInitData* parameter to *CreateDC* is NULL, the device driver calls the *GetEn-vironment* function to retrieve the most current settings for the printer and creates the device context using these settings. If the *lpInitData* parameter is not NULL, it must point to a data structure that was retrieved by a call to *GetEnvironment*. This means the printer device driver was the only program that processed the data structure used to store the particular printers settings.

Until updated printer drivers are available, programmers will have to be very cautious when it comes to manipulating printer environments and *DEVMODE* structures.

The Print and Print Setup Common Dialog Boxes

There are several situations in a Windows application where dialog boxes are presented to the user when the application requires more information before it can continue. Some of these situations are opening a file, saving a file, printing a file, or selecting a font. Since these kinds of operations are generic to most applications, Microsoft created the Common Dialog-Box Library. This dynamic-link library contains dialog-box templates and dialog-box procedures for the most common types of dialog boxes presented to users. The purpose is to give Windows a more consistent look and feel across applications as well as to cut the coding time required for developers. Microsoft has done an excellent job of attaining this goal. The common dialogs take almost everything into account, are simple to use, and can be extended for any special needs required by an application.

Of course, the common dialog boxes that I will be discussing here are the Print and Print Setup dialogs shown in Figures 5-4 and 5-5. Most of the information presented in this chapter explains how the Print Setup Common dialog box operates. If your application uses this dialog box you may be able to avoid having to know how Windows manages the various printer settings. On the other hand, if your application is greatly concerned with the quality of printed output, knowing how Windows manages the printer settings is extremely important.

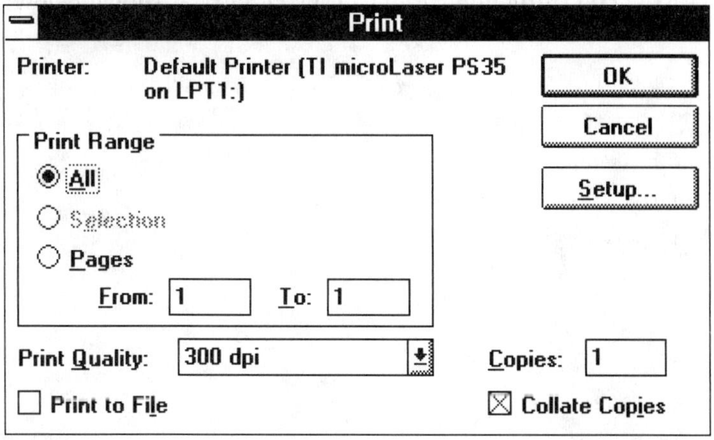

Figure 5-4. The Print Dialog Box

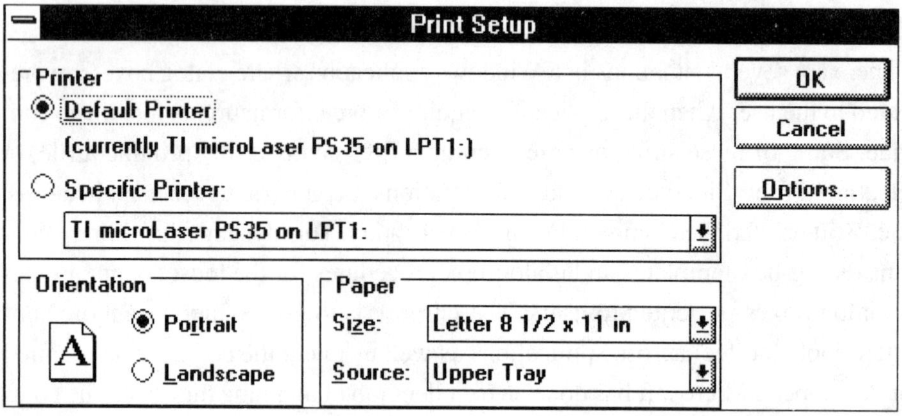

Figure 5-5. The Print Setup Dialog Box

Typically, the Print dialog is presented to the user immediately after the user has instructed the application to print a document, and the Print Setup dialog is presented when the user wishes to use a different printer or wishes to change the selected printer's settings. This is usually done by selecting the "Print setup..." option from the application's File menu or by pushing the "Setup..." button in the Print dialog box.

To use any of the common dialog boxes, you must first allocate the proper structure for the dialog box, and then call the Windows API function that presents that dialog box to the user. For the Print and Print Setup dialog boxes, we use the *PRINT-DLG* structure. The *PRINTDLG* structure (from COMMDLG.H) is shown below:

```
typedef struct tagPD {
    DWORD       lStructSize;
    HWND        hwndOwner;
    HGLOBAL     hDevMode;
    HGLOBAL     hDevNames;
    HDC         hDC;
    DWORD       Flags;
    UINT        nFromPage;
    UINT        nToPage;
    UINT        nMinPage;
    UINT        nMaxPage;
    UINT        nCopies;
```

```
HINSTANCE  hInstance;
LPARAM     CustData;
UINT       (CALLBACK* lpfnPrintHook)(HWND, UINT, WPARAM, LPARAM);
UINT       (CALLBACK* lpfnSetupHook)(HWND, UINT, WPARAM, LPARAM);
LPCSTR     lpPrintTemplateName;
LPCSTR     lpSetupTemplateName;
HGLOBAL    hPrintTemplate;
HGLOBAL    hSetupTemplate;
} PRINTDLG;
```

To call the Print or Print Setup dialog boxes, you must initialize this *PRINTDLG* structure and pass the address of this structure to the *PrintDlg* function. The function examines the data structure on input to initialize the dialog box and presents the dialog box to the user. When the user dismisses the dialog box, the function replaces some of the members in the data structure, reflecting the results of the user's selections. Below is a table that explains the meaning of each member in the *PRINTDLG* structure. For a complete description of the members, see the *Microsoft Windows Programmer Reference, Volume 3: Messages, Structures, and Macros.*

Member	When filled	Meaning
lStructSize	Input	As with all of the structures used with the common dialogs, the first member, *lStructSize*, must be initialized with the size of the structure in bytes. If Microsoft needs to add more members to the structure in a future version of Windows, its code can determine which version of the common dialog your application was using by checking this value.
hwndOwner	Input	Identifies the owner of the dialog box.
hDevMode	Input	The handle to a global block of memory containing a *DEVMODE* structure. When the dialog box is displayed, the controls in the box

Member	When filled	Meaning
		are updated to reflect these settings. The block of memory passed in is freed by the *PrintDlg* function.
hDevMode	Output	The handle to a global block of memory containing a *DEVMODE* structure with the user's new settings. This handle will probably be different from the one passed on input to the function even if the user presses the "Cancel" button to terminate the function.
hDevNames	Input	The handle to a global block of memory containing a *DEVNAMES* structure. When the dialog box is displayed, the controls in the box are updated to reflect these settings. The block of memory passed in is freed by the *PrintDlg* function.
hDevNames	Output	The handle to a global block of memory containing a *DEVNAMES* structure with the user's newly selected printer and port. This handle will probably be different from the one passed on input to the function even if the user presses the "Cancel" button to terminate the function.
hDC	Output	The handle to a device context or an information context created by the *PrintDlg* function if either the *PD_RETURNDC* or *PD_RETURNIC* flag is specified in the *Flags* member. Otherwise, this member is undefined.
Flags	Input	Allows the application to fine-tune the behavior of the Print and Print Setup common dialog boxes. The flags are discussed later.
Flags	Output	Informs the application about selections made by the user. The flags are discussed later.

Member	When filled	Meaning
nFromPage	Input	The default starting page displayed to the user in the Print dialog.
nFromPage	Output	The starting page number selected by the user.
nToPage	Input	The default stopping page displayed to the user in the Print dialog.
nToPage	Output	The stopping page number selected by the user.
nMinPage	Input	The minimum page number that may be selected by the user.
nMaxPage	Input	The maximum page number that may be selected by the user.
nCopies	Input	The default number of copies displayed to the user in the Print dialog.
nCopies	Output	The number of copies selected by the user.
hInstance	Input	Identifies the application containing a dialog-box template that should be used in place of the Print and/or Print Setup dialogs.
lCustData	Input	A data value that can be passed to a common dialog hook function.
lpfnPrintHook	Input	Address to a Print dialog hook function.
lpfnSetupHook	Input	Address to a Print Setup hook function.
lpPrintTemplateName	Input	Identifies an application-supplied Print dialog-box template.
lpSetupTemplateName	Input	Identifies an application-supplied Print Setup dialog-box template.
hPrintTemplate	Input	Identifies an application-supplied Print dialog-box template contained in a global memory block.

Member	When filled	Meaning
hSetupTemplate	Input	Identifies an application-supplied Print Setup dialog-box template contained in a global memory block.

Below are a list of the possible settings for the *Flags* member above. For a complete description of the flags, see the *Microsoft Windows Programmer Reference, Volume 3: Messages, Structures, and Macros*. Several identifiers are specified by ORing them together:

Identifier	When set	Meaning
PD_ALLPAGES	Input	Causes the ALL radio button in the Print Range group box to be selected by default.
PD_ALLPAGES	Output	Indicates if the user selected this option.
PD_COLLATE	Input	Causes the Collate Copies check box to be selected by default.
PD_COLLATECOPIES	Output	Indicates if the user selected this option.
PD_DISABLEPRINTTOFILE	Input	Disables the Print to File check box.
PD_ENABLEPRINTHOOK	Input	Enables the hook function specified in the *lpfnPrintHook* member.
PD_ENABLEPRINT-TEMPLATE	Input	Causes *PrintDlg* to use the dialog-box template specified in the *hInstance* and *lpPrintTemplateName* members.
PD_ENABLEPRINT-TEMPLATEHANDLE	Input	Causes *PrintDlg* to use the dialog-box template specified in the *hPrintTemplate* member.
PD_ENABLESETUPHOOK	Input	Enables the hook function specified in the *lpfnSetupHook* member.

Identifier	When set	Meaning
PD_ENABLESETUP-TEMPLATE	Input	Causes *PrintDlg* to use the dialog-box template specified in the *hInstance* and *lpSetupTemplateName* members.
PD_ENABLESETUP-TEMPLATEHANDLE	Input	Causes *PrintDlg* to use the dialog-box template specified in the *hSetupTemplate* member.
PD_HIDEPRINTTOFILE	Input	Causes the Print to file check box to be hidden.
PD_NOPAGENUMS	Input	Disables the Pages radio button.
PD_NOSELECTION	Input	Disables the Selection radio button.
PD_NOWARNING	Input	Prevents a warning message from being displayed if no default printer has been set.
PD_PAGENUMS	Input	Causes the Pages radio button to be set by default.
PD_PAGENUMS	Output	Indicates if the user selected this option.
PD_PRINTSETUP	Input	Causes *PrintDlg* to display the Print Setup dialog instead of the Print dialog.
PD_PRINTTOFILE	Input	Causes the Print to File check box to be selected by default.
PD_RETURNDC	Input	Causes *PrintDlg* to call the *CreateDC* function for the selected printer and return the handle to the device context that was created.
PD_RETURNDEFAULT	Input	Causes *PrintDlg* to allocate block for the *DEVMODE* and *DEVNAMES* structure that represented the system default printer. The global memory handles are returned in the *hDevMode* and *hDevNames* members.

Identifier	When set	Meaning
PD_RETURNIC	Input	Causes *PrintDlg* to call the *CreateIC* function for the selected printer and return the handle to the information context that was created.
PD_SELECTION	Input	Causes the Selection radio button to be set by default.
PD_SELECTION	Output	Indicates if the user selected this option.
PD_SHOWHELP	Input	Causes a Help push button to appear in the Print and Print Setup dialog-boxes.
PD_USEDEVMODECOPIES	Input	Use this flag to instruct *PrintDlg* that you want the selected printer driver to be responsible for handling multiple copies of a document instead of your application.

By preparing this data structure and calling the *PrintDlg* function, you avoid all of the problems of parsing the WIN.INI file, determining if drivers contain the *ExtDeviceMode* function, and determining which capabilities are supported by any particular driver. In addition, your Print and Print Setup dialog boxes will look very similar to those presented in other Windows applications. This spells ease-of-use for the end user.

There is one feature that I would like Microsoft to add in future versions of the Print and Print Setup dialog boxes. This is the ability to call *PrintDlg*, passing it the handles to *DEVMODE* and *DEVNAMES* structures in the *hDevMode* and *hDev-Names* members respectively and having it create a device context without displaying any dialog boxes at all. Without this capability, you must parse the contents of the *DEVNAMES* structure yourself and call *CreateDC*. The function below, *CreatePrinterDC*, demonstrates how to do this:

```
HDC WINAPI CreatePrinterDC (HGLOBAL hGlblDevNames,
    HGLOBAL hGlblDevMode) {
```

```
HDC hDC;
LPDEVNAMES lpDevNames;
LPDEVMODE  lpDevMode = NULL;

if (hGlblDevNames == NULL)
   return(NULL);

lpDevNames = (LPDEVNAMES) GlobalLock(hGlblDevNames);

if (hGlblDevMode != NULL)
   lpDevMode = (LPDEVMODE) GlobalLock(hGlblDevMode);

hDC = CreateDC(
   ((LPCSTR) lpDevNames) + lpDevNames->wDriverOffset,
   ((LPCSTR) lpDevNames) + lpDevNames->wDeviceOffset,
   ((LPCSTR) lpDevNames) + lpDevNames->wOutputOffset,
   lpDevMode);

if (hGlblDevMode != NULL)
   GlobalUnlock(hGlblDevMode);

GlobalUnlock(hGlblDevNames);
return(hDC);
}
```

Printer Setup Demonstration Application

The sample application, PRNTDEMO.C, demonstrates how to maintain two different sets of printer settings for printing a document. The application also demonstrates how to use the *PRINTDLG* structure and *PrintDlg* functions to allow the user to change printers and settings.

With this application, you can prepare two printers and configure their settings. For example, you can prepare the first printer to be the TI microLaser PS 35 connected to LPT1: and the second printer to be the NEC Pinwriter P6 connected to FILE:. You may also set the TI microLaser PS 35 so it prints in portrait mode and the NEC Pinwriter P6 so it prints in landscape mode. The sample application remembers these settings and allows you to print a page using these printers and their settings.

This application defines two sets of printer settings. Each set consists of two global memory handles. The first, _hGlblDevNames1, is a handle to a DEVNAMES structure containing the selected device, driver, and output port. The second handle, _hDevMode1, is a handle to a DEVMODE structure containing the settings most recently selected by the user. The handles for the second printer's settings are _hGlblDevNames2 and _hDevMode2.

During the processing of the WM_CREATE message, the device name information and DEVMODE information for the system default printer are saved. This is done by preparing a PRINTDLG structure and passing it to PrintDlg:

```
PRINTDLG PD;

.

.

.

_fmemset(&PD, 0, sizeof(PD));    // Set all members to zero
PD.lStructSize = sizeof(PD);
PD.Flags = PD_RETURNDEFAULT;
PrintDlg(&PD);
_hGlblDevNames1 = PD.hDevNames;
_hGlblDevMode1 = PD.hDevMode;
```

This is repeated for the second set of printer settings, _hGlblDevNames2 and _hGlblDevMode2. Once these have been initialized, the user may select the "Print setup 1..." or the "Print setup 2..." option to alter the printer settings for either of these two printers. When either menu option is selected, the WM_COMMAND message is sent and the following code executes:

```
case IDM_PRINTSETUP1:
case IDM_PRINTSETUP2:
    _fmemset(&PD, 0, sizeof(PD));
    PD.lStructSize = sizeof(PD);
    PD.hwndOwner = hWnd;
```

```
PD.Flags = PD_PRINTSETUP;

if (wParam == IDM_PS1) {
   PD.hDevMode = _hGlblDevMode1;
   PD.hDevNames = _hGlblDevNames1;
} else {
   PD.hDevMode = _hGlblDevMode2;
   PD.hDevNames = _hGlblDevNames2;
}
PrintDlg(&PD);
if (wParam == IDM_PS1) {
   _hGlblDevMode1  = PD.hDevMode;
   _hGlblDevNames1 = PD.hDevNames;
} else {
   _hGlblDevMode2  = PD.hDevMode;
   _hGlblDevNames2 = PD.hDevNames;
}
```

To print a single page using print settings for printer 1 or printer 2 is simply a matter of selecting either the "Print 1" or "Print 2" menu option. This causes the following code to execute:

```
case IDM_PRINT1:
case IDM_PRINT2:
   if (wParam == IDM_PRINT1) {
      hDC = CreatePrinterDC(_hGlblDevNames1, _hGlblDevMode1);
   } else {
      hDC = CreatePrinterDC(_hGlblDevNames2, _hGlblDevMode2);
   }

   if (hDC == NULL) {
      MessageBox(hWnd, "Cannot print.", _szAppName,
         MB_OK | MB_ICONEXCLAMATION);
      break;
```

```
}
Escape(hDC, STARTDOC, lstrlen(_szAppName), _szAppName, 0);
TextOut(hDC, 10, 10, _szText, lstrlen(_szText));
Escape(hDC, NEWFRAME, 0, 0, 0);
Escape(hDC, ENDDOC, 0, 0, 0);
DeleteDC(hDC);
```

The code above simply calls the *CreatePrinterDC* function described earlier in this chapter and passes it the handles to the printer's *DEVNAMES* and *DEVMODE* structures. This function parses the contents of the *DEVNAMES* structure and creates a device context with the settings specified in the *DEVMODE* structure. The *hDC* that is returned from *CreatePrinterDC* is then used in calls to the normal GDI functions to print a single page on the selected printer.

Figure 5-6. PRINT.ICO.

Listing 5-1. PRNTDEMO.C application source module

```
/******************************************************************
Module name: PRNTDEMO.C
Programmer : Jeffrey M. Richter.
******************************************************************/

#include <windows.h>
#include <print.h>
#include <commdlg.h>
#include <string.h>
```

```
#include "PrntDemo.h"

extern const HINSTANCE _cdecl _hInstance;

char _szAppName[] = "PrntDemo";
char _szText[] = "This is a text line!";

LRESULT CALLBACK WndProc (HWND hWnd, UINT uMsg, WPARAM wParam,
      LPARAM lParam);
HDC WINAPI CreatePrinterDC (HGLOBAL hGlblDevNames,
      HGLOBAL hGlblDevMode);

#pragma argsused
int WinMain (HINSTANCE hInstance, HINSTANCE hPrevInstance,
                  LPSTR lpszCmdLine, int nCmdShow) {
   HWND hWnd;
   MSG msg;
   WNDCLASS wc;

   if (!hPrevInstance) {
      wc.style          = 0;
      wc.lpfnWndProc    = WndProc;
      wc.cbClsExtra     = 0;
      wc.cbWndExtra     = 0;
      wc.hInstance      = hInstance;
      wc.hIcon          = LoadIcon(hInstance, _szAppName);
      wc.hCursor        = LoadCursor(NULL, IDC_ARROW);
      wc.hbrBackground  = COLOR_WINDOW + 1;
      wc.lpszMenuName   = _szAppName;
      wc.lpszClassName  = _szAppName;
      if (RegisterClass(&wc) == NULL)
         return(0);
   }

   hWnd = CreateWindow(_szAppName, "Printer Setup Demonstration",
      WS_OVERLAPPED | WS_VISIBLE | WS_CAPTION |
      WS_SYSMENU | WS_MINIMIZEBOX | WS_MAXIMIZEBOX |
      WS_THICKFRAME, CW_USEDEFAULT, nCmdShow, CW_USEDEFAULT,
      CW_USEDEFAULT, NULL, NULL, hInstance, 0);
   if (hWnd == NULL) return(0);

   while (GetMessage(&msg, NULL, 0, 0)) {
      TranslateMessage(&msg);
      DispatchMessage(&msg);
   }

   return(0);
}
```

```
HGLOBAL _hGlblDevNames1 = NULL, _hGlblDevMode1 = NULL;
HGLOBAL _hGlblDevNames2 = NULL, _hGlblDevMode2 = NULL;

LRESULT CALLBACK WndProc (HWND hWnd, UINT uMsg, WPARAM wParam,
      LPARAM lParam) {
   BOOL fCallDefProc = FALSE;
   LRESULT lResult = 0;
   HDC hDC;
   PRINTDLG PD;

   switch (uMsg) {
      case WM_CREATE:
         // Prepare the PrintDlg structure.
         _fmemset(&PD, 0, sizeof(PD));
         PD.lStructSize = sizeof(PD);
         PD.hwndOwner = hWnd;
         PD.hDevMode = NULL;
         PD.hDevNames = NULL;
         PD.hDC = NULL;
         PD.Flags = PD_RETURNDEFAULT;
         PrintDlg(&PD);

         // Save the DEVNAMES and DEVMODE structure handles.
         _hGlblDevNames1 = PD.hDevNames;
         _hGlblDevMode1 = PD.hDevMode;
         if (_hGlblDevNames1 == NULL)
            EnableMenuItem(GetMenu(hWnd), IDM_PRINT1,
               MF_GRAYED | MF_BYCOMMAND);

         // Do it again for the second printer.
         _fmemset(&PD, 0, sizeof(PD));
         PD.lStructSize = sizeof(PD);
         PD.hwndOwner = hWnd;
         PD.hDevMode = NULL;
         PD.hDevNames = NULL;
         PD.hDC = NULL;
         PD.Flags = PD_RETURNDEFAULT;
         PrintDlg(&PD);
         _hGlblDevNames2 = PD.hDevNames;
         _hGlblDevMode2 = PD.hDevMode;
         if (_hGlblDevNames2 == NULL)
            EnableMenuItem(GetMenu(hWnd), IDM_PRINT2,
               MF_GRAYED | MF_BYCOMMAND);
         break;

      case WM_DESTROY:
         if (_hGlblDevNames1 != NULL)
            GlobalFree(_hGlblDevNames1);
```

```
          if (_hGlblDevMode1 != NULL)
             GlobalFree(_hGlblDevMode1);

          if (_hGlblDevNames2 != NULL)
             GlobalFree(_hGlblDevNames2);
          if (_hGlblDevMode2 != NULL)
             GlobalFree(_hGlblDevMode2);

          PostQuitMessage(0);
          break;

     case WM_COMMAND:
          switch (wParam) {

               case IDM_PRINTSETUP1:
               case IDM_PRINTSETUP2:
                    // Prepare the PrintDlg structure
                    _fmemset(&PD, 0, sizeof(PD));
                    PD.lStructSize = sizeof(PD);
                    PD.hwndOwner = hWnd;
                    PD.hDC = NULL;
                    PD.Flags = PD_PRINTSETUP;

                    // Use the appropriate printer settings.
                    if (wParam == IDM_PRINTSETUP1) {
                       PD.hDevMode = _hGlblDevMode1;
                       PD.hDevNames = _hGlblDevNames1;
                    } else {
                       PD.hDevMode = _hGlblDevMode2;
                       PD.hDevNames = _hGlblDevNames2;
                    }
                    PrintDlg(&PD);

                    // Save the user's new settings.
                    if (wParam == IDM_PRINTSETUP1) {
                       _hGlblDevMode1  = PD.hDevMode;
                       _hGlblDevNames1 = PD.hDevNames;
                    } else {
                       _hGlblDevMode2  = PD.hDevMode;
                       _hGlblDevNames2 = PD.hDevNames;
                    }
                    break;

               case IDM_PRINT1:
               case IDM_PRINT2:
                    // Create a DC for the selected printer.
                    if (wParam == IDM_PRINT1) {
                       hDC = CreatePrinterDC(_hGlblDevNames1,
```

```
                          _hGlblDevMode1);
                } else {
                  hDC = CreatePrinterDC(_hGlblDevNames2,
                    _hGlblDevMode2);
                }

                if (hDC == NULL) {
                  MessageBox(hWnd, "Cannot print.", _szAppName,
                    MB_OK | MB_ICONEXCLAMATION);
                  break;
                }

                // Print a dummy page of information.
                Escape(hDC, STARTDOC, lstrlen(_szAppName),
                  _szAppName, 0);
                TextOut(hDC, 10, 10, _szText, lstrlen(_szText));
                Escape(hDC, NEWFRAME, 0, 0, 0);
                Escape(hDC, ENDDOC, 0, 0, 0);
                DeleteDC(hDC);
                break;
            }
          break;

      default:
          fCallDefProc = TRUE;
          break;
    }
    if (fCallDefProc)
      lResult = DefWindowProc(hWnd, uMsg, wParam, lParam);
    return(lResult);
}


// This function accepts a DEVNAMES structure and creates a
// device context for the printer described in it.
HDC WINAPI CreatePrinterDC (HGLOBAL hGlblDevNames,
    HGLOBAL hGlblDevMode) {
  HDC hDC;
  LPDEVNAMES lpDevNames;
  LPDEVMODE  lpDevMode;

  if (hGlblDevNames == NULL)
      return(NULL);

  lpDevNames = (LPDEVNAMES) GlobalLock(hGlblDevNames);

  if (hGlblDevMode != NULL)
     lpDevMode = (LPDEVMODE) GlobalLock(hGlblDevMode);
  hDC = CreateDC(
```

```
    ((LPCSTR) lpDevNames) + lpDevNames->wDriverOffset,
    ((LPCSTR) lpDevNames) + lpDevNames->wDeviceOffset,
    ((LPCSTR) lpDevNames) + lpDevNames->wOutputOffset,
    lpDevMode);

  if (hGlblDevMode != NULL)
    GlobalUnlock(hGlblDevMode);

  GlobalUnlock(hGlblDevNames);
  return(hDC);
}
```

Listing 5-2. PRNTDEMO.H application header module

```
/******************************************************************
Module name: PRNTDEMO.H
Programmer : Jeffrey M. Richter.
******************************************************************/

#define IDM_PRINTSETUP1    (100)
#define IDM_PRINTSETUP2    (101)
#define IDM_PRINT1         (102)
#define IDM_PRINT2         (103)
```

Listing 5-3. MAKEFILE for printer setup application

```
#******************************************************************
#Module name: MAKEFILE
#Programmer : Jeffrey M. Richter
#******************************************************************

!include "..\builtins.jmr"

PROG = PrntDemo

MODEL = s
CFLAGS = -c -f- -WS -p -v -w -m$(MODEL) -I$(INCLUDEDIR)
LFLAGS = /P/v/n/m/s/L$(LIBDIR)
LIBS = CW$(MODEL) Import

MODULES = $(PROG).obj

ICONS   = $(PROG).ico
BITMAPS =
CURSORS =
```

```
$(PROG).Exe: $(MODULES) $(PROG).Def $(PROG).Res
     tlink $(LFLAGS) @&&!
COW$(MODEL) $(MODULES)
$(PROG), $(PROG), $(LIBS), $(PROG)
!
   rc -30 -T $(PROG).Res
   TDStrip -s $(PROG)

$(PROG).res:    $(PROG).rc $(PROG).h $(RESOURCES)
```

Listing 5-4. PRNTDEMO.DEF Print definitions file

```
; Module name: PRNTDEMO.DEF
; Programmer : Jeffrey M. Richter.

NAME        PRNTDEMO
DESCRIPTION 'PRNTDEMO: Demonstration Application'
STUB        'WinStub.exe'
EXETYPE     WINDOWS
CODE        MOVEABLE DISCARDABLE PRELOAD
DATA        MOVEABLE MULTIPLE PRELOAD
HEAPSIZE    1024
STACKSIZE   5120
```

Listing 5-5. PRNTDEMO.RC application resource file

```
/*******************************************************************
Module name: PRNTDEMO.RC
Programmer : Jeffrey M. Richter.
*******************************************************************/

#include <windows.h>

#include "PrntDemo.h"

PrntDemo ICON     MOVEABLE DISCARDABLE PrntDemo.Ico

PrntDemo MENU
BEGIN
   POPUP    "&Examples"
      BEGIN
      MENUITEM "Printer setup &1...",      IDM_PRINTSETUP1
      MENUITEM "Printer setup &2...",      IDM_PRINTSETUP2
      MENUITEM "&Print using PS1",         IDM_PRINT1
      MENUITEM "P&rint using PS2",         IDM_PRINT2
      END
END
```

340

CHAPTER 6

Tasks and Queues

By now, you are familiar with many of the different types of handles used to manipulate data in Microsoft Windows. Handles are used to keep track of windows, local memory blocks, global memory blocks, brushes, pens, and much more. In this chapter, we discuss three more types of handles and how Windows uses them to manage the most important of system resources: your applications. We also discuss how Windows uses system and application queues to synchronize applications.

Tasks and Their Handles

Windows maintains three handles for each running application: the data-instance handle, the module-instance handle, and the task-instance handle. There has always been confusion in Windows as to which handle means what and under which circumstances you use each handle. To add to the confusion, the WINDOWS.H file supplied with the SDK only ever had one data type to describe all of these handles, *HANDLE*. However, starting with Windows 3.1, WINDOWS.H defines separate data types for each of these handles (*HINSTANCE* for data-instance handles, *HMODULE* for module-instance handles, and *HTASK* for task-instance handles). Having separate data types for each handle helps your understanding of how Windows operates. In addition, when you need to use a Windows API function, you'll have a much better idea of which handle type the function expects. Programmers frequently pass the wrong handle type to an SDK function. Let's begin our discussion with a description of the three handle types.

The data-instance handle is the most familiar. This is the handle that is passed as the first parameter to your applications *WinMain* function. Windows uses this handle to identify the data segment for the current instance of the application.

When an application is executed, Windows creates a data segment for the new instance of the application and assigns it a data-instance handle. Windows then calls the application's *WinMain* function and passes the data-instance handle as the *hInstance* parameter. The second parameter, *hPrevInstance*, contains the data-instance handle for another instance of the application if one is running. Otherwise, *hPrevInstance* contains NULL.

Applications use *hPrevInstance* in the following ways:

1. To allow only one instance of your application to run at a time, check the value of the *hPrevInstance* parameter. If the value is not NULL, the application can immediately return to Windows, terminating the new instance of the executing application:

```
int WinMain (HINSTANCE hInstance, HINSTANCE hPrevInstance,
    LPSTR lpszCmdLine, int nCmdShow) {
    .
    .
    .
    if (hPrevInstance != NULL) return(0);
    .
    .
    .
```

2. Because applications should only register window classes when the first instance of the application is started, the code for registering window classes should only be executed if *hPrevInstance* is NULL:

```
int WinMain (HINSTANCE hInstance, HINSTANCE hPrevInstance,
    LPSTR lpszCmdLine, int nCmdShow) {
    .
    .
    if (hPrevInstance == NULL) {
        // Register window classes used by this application.
    }
    .
    .
```

Although a new data segment is created for each instance of a running application, Windows allows all the instances to share the same code segments. Also, when a new application is invoked, it must register any window classes used by the application. If additional instances of the same application are executed, the new instances should not attempt to register the window classes again, but should assume that the classes have already been registered.

Windows maintains a single module-instance handle for all occurrences (data-instances) of a particular application. When an application registers a window class, it must initialize a *WNDCLASS* structure and call the *RegisterClass* function. The *hInstance* member of the *WNDCLASS* structure must be initialized to the data-instance handle that was passed as the *hInstance* parameter to *WinMain*. *Register-Class* examines the *hInstance* member of *WNDCLASS* and determines the module-instance handle associated with it. *RegisterClass* then registers the new window class using the module-instance handle. You may have noticed that you can call the *GetClassWord* function and pass it an identifier of *GCW_HMODULE*. This instructs Windows to return the module-instance handle for which the window class was registered. Also, notice that there is no *GCW_HINSTANCE* identifier for use with this function. This is because *RegisterClass* does not save the data-instance handle passed in *WNDCLASS*'s *hInstance* member but instead saves the module-instance handle of the application registering the class.

The Voyeur application presented in Chapter 1 is a useful tool for studying this scheme. Try executing an instance of the Calc application supplied with Windows, then use Voyeur to peer into Calc's window by choosing "Peer into window" from Voyeur's system menu and positioning the mouse cursor over Calc's caption bar. Voyeur's window is shown in Figure 6-1.

The *Owner* field in the *Class Information* section identifies the module-instance handle associated with the registered window class (0x262F). This isn't the same as the value associated with the *Creator* field in the *Window Information* section (0x25DE). The *Creator* field identifies the data-instance handle (*hInstance* parameter) passed to *CreateWindow* or *CreateWindowEx* when the window was created.

When a window is being created, Windows first determines the module-instance handle associated with the *hInstance* parameter passed to *CreateWindow* or *CreateWindowEx*. It then scans all the registered window classes that have the same module-instance handle and class name. This explains why window classes do not have to be registered for each instance of an application.

```
┌─────────────────────────────────────────────────────────────────┐
│ ━                          Voyeur                            ▼   │
├───────────────────────────────────────────────────────────────────┤
│                    * CLASS INFORMATION *                          │
│ Class:          SciCalc                                           │
│ Owner (Inst):   0x262F, C:\WINDOWS\CALC.EXE                       │
│ Other:                       Styles: 0x0000        Extra bytes: 0 │
│ ┌───────────────────────┐ ┌─────────────────────┐ ┌─────────────┐ │
│ │Atom:     0xC7CA     ▲ │ │                     │ │             │ │
│ │Icon:     0x25AE     ▼ │ │                     │ │             │ │
│ └───────────────────────┘ └─────────────────────┘ └─────────────┘ │
│                                                                   │
│                   * WINDOW INFORMATION *                          │
│ Window (hWnd):  0x2584, Calculator                                │
│ Creator (Inst): 0x25DE, C:\WINDOWS\CALC.EXE                       │
│ Parent (hWnd):  (no parent window)                                │
│ WndProc:        0x25FF:0x051C          ID:  0x11A8  (4520)         │
│ Location:       (400, 360)-(661, 629), Dim=261x269                │
│ Wnd styles: 0x14CA0000      Ext styles: 0x00000000  Extra bytes: 30│
│ ┌───────────────────────┐ ┌─────────────────────┐ ┌─────────────┐ │
│ │VISIBLE              ▲ │ │                     │ │00)  0x00  ▲ │ │
│ │CLIPSIBLINGS         ▼ │ │                     │ │01)  0x00  ▼ │ │
│ └───────────────────────┘ └─────────────────────┘ └─────────────┘ │
└───────────────────────────────────────────────────────────────────┘
```

Figure 6-1. Voyeur peering into Calc

To reinforce this concept, perform the following experiment. Without terminating the Calc application, start another instance of Calc. Use Voyeur again to peer into the new Calc's window. You will see that the *Owner* field in Voyeur's *Class Information* section is identical to the *Owner* field in the first instance of Calc.

In Voyeur, the pathname of the owner (module that registered the window class) and the creator (module that created the window instance) is retrieved by calling the *GetModuleFileName* function. Although this function is prototyped as expecting a data-instance handle (*HINSTANCE*) as its first parameter, this function will actually accept either a data-instance handle or a module-instance handle (*HMODULE*). For Voyeur to display the pathname of the module that registered the class, it passes in the value returned from calling *GetClassWord* with the *GCW_HMODULE* identifier to *GetModuleFileName*. It displays the pathname of the module that created the selected window instance by passing the result of calling *GetWindowWord* with the *GWW_HINSTANCE* identifier to *GetModuleFileName*.

When you are using Voyeur to look at the first instance of Calc's window, the same module was used both to register the class and to create the window instance. If you use Voyeur again and peer into the number field area in Calc, you will find that the window is a STATIC control. In this case, Voyeur will report that the window was registered by USER.EXE but was created by CALC.EXE.

In addition to module- and data-instance handles, applications have task-instance handles. Windows creates a task-instance handle for every instance of an executing application. The Windows scheduler uses the task-instance handles when scheduling events to be processed by the executing tasks. Any modules that do not require scheduling do not receive a task-instance handle. Modules that do not require scheduling are dynamic-link libraries. When a DLL is loaded into Windows, it receives a module-instance handle and a data-instance handle but does not receive a task-instance handle.

To help put all these handles into perspective, let's assume Program Manager, Paintbrush, and two instances of Calc are running. This means that Windows is maintaining four module instances (one for each different application and Paintbrush's dynamic-link library, PBRUSH.DLL), five data instances (one for each running application and PBRUSH.DLL), and four task instances (one for each running application).

	PROGMAN .EXE	PBRUSH.EXE	PBRUSH.DLL	CALC.EXE (First instance)	CALC.EXE (Second instance)
Module instance	I	II	III	IV	
Data instance	A	B	C	D	E
Task instance	i	ii		iii	iv

There is always exactly one active task in Windows. The active task is the application that created the window that is processing a message. For example, when an application retrieves a message from its application queue, Windows makes that application the active task. When an application sends a message to a window that is registered by another application, Windows performs a task switch during the *SendMessage* function before calling the other window's window procedure. When the window procedure returns, Windows performs another task switch back to the application that sent the message.

As mentioned earlier, Windows does not consider DLLs tasks. That's why DLLs are only assigned module- and data-instance handles, not task-instance handles. In addition, only one instance of any DLL can ever be loaded into Windows at one

time, so exactly one module- and one data-instance handle is assigned to a DLL.
So, if you send a message to a system global class, a task switch does not occur
because USER.EXE (a dynamic-link library in spite of its extension) registered all
system global classes.

Although Windows no longer supports real mode with expanded memory (EMS),
it is useful to examine how Windows managed tasks in this mode. Both Windows
3.0 and 3.1 are really stepping stones to the next versions of Windows, Windows-
32 running on top of Windows-NT. In many ways, future versions of Windows will
operate more like real-mode Windows with EMS.

In real-mode Windows with EMS, only the active task's code and data are banked
into the real-mode addressing space. All the code and data belonging to inactive
tasks are banked out of the real-mode addressing space.

This has some important ramifications for the programmer. Let's say Application
A has a memory block that is to be filled by sending a message to a window whose
window procedure is in Application B. Application A calls the *SendMessage* function and passes the address of the memory block as the *lParam* parameter. Windows performs a task switch and banks out the code and data associated with Application A. When the window procedure in Application B writes to the address pointed
to by the *lParam* parameter, it will actually write over data belonging to Application B...*not* Application A.

The correct way to pass large amounts of information between applications is by
using dynamic data exchange. After a DDE conversation is initiated, Application
B should allocate a memory block using the *GlobalAlloc* function with the
GMEM_DDESHARE flag. When a memory block is allocated this way, Windows
creates the block above the EMS bank line. Then Application B sends a DDE message identifying the memory block's handle to Application A. When Application
A calls the *GlobalLock* function, Windows notices that the block has the
GMEM_DDESHARE flag set and allocates a new block of memory above the EMS
bank line, where Application A is now located. Windows then copies the data from
the first memory block to the new memory block. When Application A calls the
GlobalUnlock function, Windows frees the newly allocated block, leaving the original with Application B.

Global memory blocks allocated by functions within DLLs are owned by the current task, not the library. This means that if a DLL function allocated a block of mem-

ory on behalf of an application, that memory block would be freed when the application terminates, not when the DLL terminates. Another example will help explain this.

Application A and Application B use the same DLL. Application A calls a function in the DLL, which in turn calls *GlobalAlloc*. If Application A now terminates, the memory block is freed. However, the DLL continues to exist in memory because Application B is still using it.

There is one exception to this rule. Memory blocks allocated with the *GMEM_DDESHARE* or *GMEM_SHARE* flag are owned by the module (not task) that called *GlobalAlloc*. Lets look at how this affects the lifetime of the data in the memory block.

When an instance of an application terminates, any global memory allocated explicitly by the application is freed. However, if any of those blocks have the *GMEM_DDESHARE* or *GMEM_SHARE* flag, Windows does not free the block until all the instances of the application have been freed. If the block was allocated by a DLL, Windows does not free the block until the DLL is no longer needed and is removed from memory.

Windows supplies the following functions for working with tasks:

- *GetNumTasks* retrieves the number of tasks that are currently running under Windows.
- *GetCurrentTask* retrieves the task-instance handle of the currently executing task.
- *GetWindowTask* retrieves the task-instance handle of the task associated with the specified window handle.
- *IsTask* determines if the task-instance handle passed into it is valid.

In addition to these functions, the new TOOLHELP.DLL supplied with Windows 3.1, offers several additional functions for working with tasks.

You may recall that the Voyeur application presented in Chapter 1 will not allow the user to peer into any of the windows that were created by Voyeur. The program determines the task-instance handle of the task that created the window under the mouse cursor by calling *GetWindowTask* and passing it the handle of a window. If the task-instance handle matches that returned by *GetCurrentTask*, the window was created by Voyeur. Voyeur can now ignore this window. Because *GetCurrentTask* is called from within the processing of the *WM_MOUSEMOVE* message, the current task will always be Voyeur.

Looking Toward the Future

Anyone who has written a Windows application is familiar with the Global Protection Violation error. This error occurs when your application tries to access a memory address that contains no data. However, if your application creates a pointer that references memory in another application's data segment, a Global Protection Violation will *not* occur.

While neither Windows 3.0 (without EMS) nor 3.1 offer support to protect one application from accessing the data of another application, future versions of Windows will. In this environment, when a task-switch occurs, Windows tells the processor to "hide" all of the data and code from all non-active tasks so that the active task has no access to it. This level of protection would not allow an application to inadvertently retrieve or modify data belonging to another application. Windows will, of course, make code and data segments of DLLs unprotected so they may be accessed by any application at any time.

Application Queues

Windows creates a message queue for each task when it is started. By default, the queue is large enough to hold eight messages. This may seem like a small number, but the queue is actually used infrequently. This is because Windows does not allow events from the system queue to accumulate in the application's queue and because most Windows functions, like *SetFocus*, send *WM_SETFOCUS* and *WM_KILLFOCUS* messages directly to the window procedure instead of posting them to the application's queue. However, if an application requires a queue that is capable of holding more than eight messages, it can simply call *SetMessageQueue*:

```
BOOL SetMessageQueue (int cMsg);
```

This function deletes the current queue for the application and attempts to allocate a new one. The size of the queue is set by the *cMsg* parameter, which specifies the maximum number of messages the queue should hold.

Attempting to allocate a queue could result in insufficient memory. If this happens, *SetMessageQueue* returns zero; the application can try to create a queue of a smaller size. The application must decide whether it can execute with the finally allocated queue size and, if not, immediately return to Windows. The *SetMessageQueue* function should be called before any windows are created because all the messages in the queue are destroyed when the function is called.

Three functions can append messages to the end of the application queue: *PostMessage*, *PostQuitMessage*, and *PostAppMessage*.

PostMessage has the following prototype:

```
BOOL PostMessage (HWND hWnd, UINT uMsg, WPARAM wParam, LPARAM lParam);
```

This function determines which application queue to post the message to by determining which task created the window identified by the *hWnd* parameter. The message is then appended to the queue. If the queue is full, *PostMessage* returns a zero, indicating that the message could not be posted. Note that the *PostMessage* function does not wait for the message to be processed; it returns immediately after the message has been appended to the application's queue.

PostQuitMessage has the following prototype:

```
void PostQuitMessage (nExitCode);
```

This function adds a *WM_QUIT* message to the end of the queue used by the currently executing task. The *nExitCode* parameter may be used by the application to determine what steps to take upon termination. Most applications ignore this value. When this message is retrieved from the application's queue, the *hWnd* and *lParam* members of the *MSG* structure contain zeros. The *wParam* member contains the value that was passed to *PostQuitMessage*.

The last function, *PostAppMessage*, has the following prototype:

```
BOOL PostAppMessage (HTASK hTask, UINT uMsg, WPARAM wParam,
    LPARAM lParam);
```

This function can be used to post a message to an application that did not create any windows. It's identical to *PostMessage* except that the first parameter specifies a task-instance handle instead of a window handle. The return value is nonzero if the message was successfully posted to the application's queue. When a message placed in the queue by a call to *PostAppMessage* is retrieved, the *hWnd* member of the *MSG* structure is zero. Since the *hWnd* member is zero, an application can determine the actions it wants to take by examining the *message* member. This test should be performed in the application's message loop immediately after *GetMessage* returns. The Program Manager Restore application presented in the window subclassing section of Chapter 2 demonstrates the use of *PostAppMessage*.

Some other Windows API functions, like *TranslateMessage*, can alter the application's queue. *TranslateMessage* examines the message being passed to it and, if the message is *WM_KEYDOWN* or *WM_SYSKEYDOWN*, posts a *WM_CHAR* or *WM_SYSCHAR* message to the application's queue. However, this message is not appended; it is inserted at the front of the queue, where it will be retrieved by the next call to *GetMessage* or *PeekMessage*.

Whenever an application calls *InvalidateRect* or *InvalidateRgn*, Windows places a *WM_PAINT* message in the queue. But Windows treats *WM_PAINT* messages differently from most other messages. When an application calls *GetMessage*, Windows will only return the *WM_PAINT* message if no other messages are pending in the queue. Because repainting the screen is one of the slowest operations under Windows, holding *WM_PAINT* messages until all other messages are processed makes Windows run much faster than if it updated the screen after every change. To force a *WM_PAINT* message to be sent to a window, use *UpdateWindow*. This function looks directly into the application's queue and checks for a *WM_PAINT* message. If one exists, Windows sends the *WM_PAINT* message to the window's window procedure. If a *WM_PAINT* message is not in the queue, *UpdateWindow* does nothing and returns.

The *WM_PAINT* message has another unusual attribute. When a *WM_PAINT* message is received by a window procedure, Windows does not remove the message from the application's queue. The only way a *WM_PAINT* message can be removed from the queue is by calling *ValidateRect* or *ValidateRgn*. These functions tell Windows that all or part of the window's client area is up to date. If Windows sees that all of the window's client area is up to date, the *WM_PAINT* message is removed from the queue. Because the *BeginPaint* function calls the *ValidateRect* function, Windows will remove the *WM_PAINT* message from your application's queue.

If you do not use *BeginPaint* and *EndPaint* or *ValidateRect* and *ValidateRgn* during the *WM_PAINT* message processing in your window procedure, Windows will start an infinite loop. Imagine that your window needs to be painted and is sent the *WM_PAINT* message. This message is processed as follows:

```
case WM_PAINT
    hDC = GetDC(hWnd);
    TextOut(hDC,0,0,"Some text",9);
    ReleaseDC(hWnd,hDC);
    break;
```

In this example, the invalid client area has never been validated. This means that the *WM_PAINT* message will still exist in the application's queue and Windows will again send the *WM_PAINT* message to the window's procedure. Windows will continue to loop in this fashion until your application is terminated.

The *WM_TIMER* message is also handled distinctively. Windows places a *WM_TIMER* message in your application's queue whenever the time specified in the call to *SetTimer* has expired. However, like *WM_PAINT*, *GetMessage* returns a *WM_TIMER* message only when the application's queue contains no other messages (except *WM_PAINT*). In addition, Windows will not put more than one *WM_TIMER* message for a given window in an application's queue.

Suppose your application creates a timer that goes off every 100 milliseconds. If another application starts a printing process that requires 15 seconds, Windows does not put 150 *WM_TIMER* messages in your application's queue. Instead, when control is returned to your application, only one *WM_TIMER* message will be retrieved from the queue. You can imagine how quickly your application's queue would fill up if every *WM_TIMER* message were placed in it.

The System and Application Queues

Although each instance of an application has its own application queue, Windows maintains a single system queue. The system queue stores all keyboard and mouse events.

Each event in the system queue is in the form of an *EVENTMSG* structure (defined in WINDOWS.H):

```
typedef struct tagEVENTMSG
{
    UINT    message;
    UINT    paramL;
    UINT    paramH;
    DWORD   time;
} EVENTMSG;
```

The message member contains one of the following keyboard or mouse messages:

```
WM_MOUSEMOVE

WM_LBUTTONDOWN      WM_MBUTTONDOWN      WM_RBUTTONDOWN

WM_LBUTTONUP        WM_MBUTTONUP        WM_RBUTTONUP

WM_KEYDOWN          WM_SYSKEYDOWN

WM_KEYUP            WM_SYSKEYUP
```

The *paramL* and *paramH* members contain additional information about the message. The last member, *time*, contains the time the event occurred. This time is measured in milliseconds since the Windows session began. The current system time can be retrieved by calling *GetTickCount* or *GetCurrentTime*.

The *WM_MOUSEMOVE* event is treated differently from other events stored in the system queue. Windows only stores the most recent *WM_MOUSEMOVE* message in the system queue. An example will illustrate why Windows behaves this way.

Let's assume your application is covering most of the screen and the user is just moving the mouse back and forth over your application's window area. If another application is processing a lengthy job, Windows does not have a chance to send the *WM_MOUSEMOVE* messages to your application. It's not until your application regains control that Windows sends the last *WM_MOUSEMOVE* message identifying the most recent position of the mouse.

When Windows initializes, it creates a system queue of a fixed size that is not changed during the Windows session. If Windows placed every mouse-movement event in the system queue, the queue would fill up very quickly. The queue can still become saturated with events if the user presses keys or mouse buttons while an application is in the middle of a lengthy process. When this happens, Windows indicates to the user that the system queue is full by beeping.

To retrieve a message from either the system or application queue, an application calls either the *GetMessage* or *PeekMessage* function. These functions can only examine and retrieve messages destined for the application that is calling *GetMessage* or *PeekMessage*. Messages destined for other applications cannot be retrieved. The prototypes for both of these functions appear below:

```
BOOL GetMessage (MSG FAR *lpMsg, HWND hWnd, UINT uMsgFilterFirst,
    UINT uMsgFilterLast);
BOOL PeekMessage (MSG FAR *lpMsg, HWND hWNd, UINT uMsgFilterFirst,
    UINT uMsgFilterLast, UINT fuRemove);
```

When determining which queue to retrieve a message from, both of these functions first look into the application's queue for a message to be processed. If a message cannot be found in that queue or the only messages are *WM_TIMER* and *WM_PAINT*, the system queue is checked for messages.

Now, here are the meanings of the parameters to these functions. The first parameter, *lpMsg*, is an address to an *MSG* structure that will be filled with information about the message to be processed. The structure has the following appearance:

```
typedef struct tagMSG
{
    HWND            hwnd;
    UINT            message;
    WPARAM          wParam;
    LPARAM          lParam;
    DWORD           time;
    POINT           pt;
} MSG;
```

If *GetMessage* or *PeekMessage* wind up returning a value from the system queue instead of the application's queue, the message is converted from the *EVENTMSG* structure described above to the *MSG* structure.

The second parameter, *hWnd*, tells *GetMessage* and *PeekMessage* that you are only interested in messages destined for the window identified by this parameter. Usually, this parameter is NULL, which means that you are interested in any messages destined for any window in your application.

The third and fourth parameters, *uMsgFilterFirst* and *uMsgFilterLast*, indicate the message range that you are interested in. For example, if you only wanted to process any mouse messages that were pending in the queue, you would set *uMsgFilterFirst* and *uMsgFilterLast* to WM_MOUSEFIRST and WM_MOUSELAST respectively. Usually both of these parameters are set to NULL so that any message in the queue will be returned.

Now, let's discuss the difference between *GetMessage* and *PeekMessage*.

GetMessage causes your application to go to sleep if no messages are waiting for it. For example, when your application calls *GetMessage* and no messages are pending for your application, Windows checks the application queues for other applications running in the system. If another application has messages pending, Windows causes a task-switch to that application and allows its messages to be processed. After that application has processed its messages, Windows checks the queue of another application and starts the whole thing over again.

Eventually, another message will be destined for a window in your application. When this happens, Windows fills the *MSG* structure that you had passed to it when you called *GetMessage* and return to your application.

When your application calls *PeekMessage*, *PeekMessage* simply looks into the queue to see if any messages are pending and returns. If a message is not pending, *PeekMessage* checks to see if another application has pending messages and if so, allows that application to run. This is just like *GetMessage*. However, when no more messages are pending for any applications, *PeekMessage* returns to your application. This is the main difference between *GetMessage* and *PeekMessage*. *GetMessage* would not return until a message was in a queue destined for your application.

With this in mind, we can now discuss the last parameter to *PeekMessage*. This parameter is one or more flags *OR*ed together that allow you to fine-tune how *PeekMessage* should work. The flags are listed as follows:

Identifier	Description
PM_NOREMOVE	If *PeekMessage* finds a message, it fills the *MSG* structure and returns. However, the message will not be removed from the queue. A future call to *GetMessage* or *PeekMessage* (with the *PM_REMOVE* flag) is required to remove the message from the queue.
PM_REMOVE	If *PeekMessage* finds a message, it fills the *MSG* structure and returns. The message will be removed from the queue.
PM_NOYIELD	Tells *PeekMessage* not to check other applications' queues for messages if no messages exist in the current application's queue.

The last thing to discuss about these two functions are their return values. The *GetMessage* function returns TRUE if the message retrieved is not a *WM_QUIT* message. If the message is *WM_QUIT*, FALSE is returned. This is useful because most applications use a *GetMessage* loop in their application that looks something like this:

```
int WinMain (...) {
  MSG msg;
    .
    .
    .

  while (GetMessage(&msg, (HWND) NULL, 0, 0)) {
    TranslateMessage(&msg);
    DispatchMessage(&msg);
  }
    .
    .
    .

  return(msg.wParam);
}
```

When the application's main window is closed, it usually calls *PostQuitMessage* so that a *WM_QUIT* message will eventually be retrieved by *GetMessage*. When

GetMessage does retrieve the *WM_QUIT* message, it knows that the application wanted to terminate and returns FALSE so that the *while* loop terminates, allowing the rest of *WinMain* to execute. When the remainder of the code in *WinMain* is finished executing and *WinMain* returns, the application is officially terminated and taken out of memory.

For the *PeekMessage* function, the return value indicates whether a message was found or not. A message was not found if the function returns FALSE. It is possible to design your application's main loop around the *PeekMessage* function instead of the *GetMessage* function. It would look something like this:

```
int WinMain (...) {
   MSG msg;
   .
   .
   .
   while (TRUE) {
      if (!PeekMessage(&msg, (HWND) NULL, 0, 0, PM_REMOVE))
         continue;
      if (msg.message == WM_QUIT)
         break;
      TranslateMessage(&msg);
      DispatchMessage(&msg);
   }
   .
   .
   .
   return(msg.wParam);
}
```

Even though the code shown above will work, you don't want to do this! The main difference here (as compared to the *GetMessage* method) is that *PeekMessage* always returns, even if no messages are in your application's queue. In the case when no messages are in the queue, *PeekMessage* returns FALSE, and the loop starts over again by calling *PeekMessage*. The problem is that the application doesn't give up control to Windows when there is nothing to do. This is a problem for battery-operated computers.

The batteries available for laptops and notebook computers average about three or four hours of continuous use before dying. This is simply not enough time—especially if you use your computer on cross-country plane rides. However, Windows 3.1 offers some power management features. If Windows sees that no application has received a message in a long time (usually about a minute or two), Windows can shut off power to some of the computer's peripherals to help conserve battery power. When it sees that a message does need to be processed, power is restored to the necessary peripherals. However, if you design your application around a *PeekMessage* loop as shown above, you trick Windows into believing that your application is busy doing something all the time and that power is needed for all the peripherals.

Believe me, customers will soon discover which applications are using *PeekMessage* loops and which are using *GetMessage* loops by how long their batteries last. And with the growing numbers of laptops, notebooks, and even pen computers, this is becoming more and more of an issue. For those of you who are more interested in this topic, Microsoft offers an *Advanced Power Management Specification Guide* and you can also explore Windows 3.1's new *WM_POWER* message.

Now seems like a good time to mention another function, *WaitMessage*. This function causes Windows to look in your application's queue for a message and not to return until a message exists. By using this function in conjunction with the *PeekMessage* function you could write your message loop as follows:

```
int WinMain (...) {
MSG msg;

   .

   .

   .

   while (TRUE) {
      WaitMessage();
      PeekMessage(&msg, (HWND) NULL, 0, 0, PM_REMOVE);
      if (msg.message == WM_QUIT)
         break;
      TranslateMessage(&msg);
```

```
        DispatchMessage(&msg);
    }
    .
    .
    .
    return(msg.wParam);
    }
```

In the loop above, *WaitMessage* is called first to check if any messages are in the applications' queue. If no messages are in the queue, Windows will allow other applications to run until a message exists for this application. After *Wait-Message* returns, *PeekMessage* is called to retrieve the message. Note that in this case, you don't have to check the return value from *PeekMessage* because you know that there is a message in the queue. The remainder of the code is identical to the preceding example.

In Windows 3.1, a new function was introduced that allows an application to see what kinds of messages are in the queue. This function executes extremely quickly and doesn't have the overhead of copying messages into *MSG* structures or checking to see if a message exists for an individual window. The prototype for this function appears below:

```
    DWORD GetQueueStatus(UINT fuFlags);
```

The *fuFlags* parameter can be any of the following flags *OR*ed together:

Identifier	Description
QS_KEY	Is there a *WM_CHAR* message in the queue?
QS_MOUSE	Is there a WM_MOUSEMOVE, WM_?BUTTONDOWN, or a WM_?BUTTONUP message in the queue?
QS_MOUSEMOVE	Is there a WM_MOUSEMOVE message in the queue?
QS_MOUSEBUTTON	Is there a WM_?BUTTONDOWN or a WM_?BUTTONUP message in the queue?

Identifier	Description
QS_PAINT	Is there a WM_PAINT message in the queue?
QS_POSTMESSAGE	Is there a posted message other than those listed above in the queue?
QS_SENDMESSAGE	Is there a sent message in the queue?
QS_TIMER	Is there a WM_TIMER message in the queue?

After being called, *GetQueueStatus* checks the queue to see if any of the message types are in the application's queue and if any have been added since the last call to *GetQueueStatus*, *GetMessage*, or *PeekMessage*. The HIWORD of the return value indicates which message types are in the queue. The *QS_** values can be ANDed with this value to determine which message types are in the queue. For example, to see if a *WM_PAINT* message is in the queue an application could do the following:

```
BOOL fPaintMsgInQueue = HIWORD(GetQueueStatus(QS_PAINT)) & QS_PAINT;
```

The LOWORD of the *GetQueueStatus'* return value indicates which messages have been added to the queue since the last call to *GetQueueStatus*, *GetMessage*, or *PeekMessage*.

Now that you have retrieved a message from the queue, you must have that message processed by the appropriate window. This is the job of the *DispatchMessage* function. This function accepts the *MSG* structure containing the message, determines the address of the window procedure used for the window specified by the *hwnd* member, and calls the function, passing it the values in the *message*, *wParam*, and *lParam* members. The window procedure does not receive the *time* and *pt* members of the *MSG* structure. These members contain the system time when the message was posted to the application's queue and the position of the mouse cursor in screen coordinates when the message was posted. If the window procedure needs this information, the *GetMessageTime* and *GetMessagePos* functions may be used.

Our discussion wouldn't be complete if we didn't discuss *SendMessage*. If the sender and receiver of the message belong to the same application, Windows does not insert the message into the application's queue but simply calls the window procedure associated with *SendMessage*'s *hWnd* parameter.

If, on the other hand, the sender and receiver are from different applications, Windows first inserts the sent message at the front of the receiver's queue. It then allows Windows to perform a task-switch so that the receiver application can process the message. After the message has been processed, Windows makes the sending task the active task and returns. Windows actually does a lot of work here—this is a simplified version. For instance, Windows must also copy the *uMsg*, *wParam*, and *lParam* parameters to the receiver's stack before allowing the receiver to process the message.

Because Windows operates this way, some interesting scenarios can occur causing Windows to hang. For example, let's say that Application A calls *SendMessage* to have a message processed by a window in Application B. Application A must put itself in waiting while the window in Application B processes the message. Now, let's say that Application B's window procedure displays a dialog box causing Application B to check the contents of the system queue. If a message for Application A is at the head of the queue, Windows puts Application B in waiting until Application A has had a chance to process the system queue event. When Application A receives the event, it cannot process it because it is still waiting for Application B to return from the original call to *SendMessage* —the system is hung.

You can solve this problem by using the *ReplyMessage* function:

```
void ReplyMessage(LRESULT lResult);
```

This function causes Windows to reply to a sent message immediately. After the window that sent the message receives the result, it continues processing. When that application gives up control to Windows, Windows switches tasks back to the task that was sent the original message and allows it to continue processing after the call to *ReplyMessage*. Here's an example:

Application A sends a message to a window in Application B.

```
uSomeVal = SendMessage(hWndInAppB, UM_SOMETHING, 0, 0);
if (uSomeVal == 0) {
    .

    .

    .

}
    .

    .

    .
```

The window procedure in Application B processes the message as follows:

```
case UM_SOMETHING:
    ReplyMessage(_uSomeValue);

    MessageBox(hWnd, "Some text", "Some title", MB_OK);
    lResult = _uSomeValue;
    break;
    .

    .

    .
```

When this code executes, the call to *ReplyMessage* causes *SendMessage* (in Application A) to return the value of Application B's global variable *_uSomeValue* immediately. The line following *ReplyMessage*, *MessageBox*, does not execute. After Application A has finished its processing, Windows activates Application B again and starts executing the code following the call to *ReplyMessage*. That's right, Windows jumps right back to where it left off—you have to see this with a debugger to believe it!

The story is a little different if the sender and receiver are the same application. When *ReplyMessage* is called, it checks to see if it is processing a message sent by a different task. If the message is from the same task, *ReplyMessage* does nothing and simply returns, allowing the call to *MessageBox* to execute. By the way, an application can determine if it is processing a message sent to it by the same application by calling the *InSendMessage* function:

```
BOOL InSendMessage (void);
```

This function returns nonzero if the application is processing a message sent to it from another task. If the application is processing a message that it sent to itself, this function returns FALSE.

CHAPTER 7

Hooks

I consider hooks to be one of Windows most powerful features. They give an application a way to trap various events that are about to occur with respect to the application or the entire Windows system. In fact, not only can an application be notified when a particular event is about to happen but for most hooks, the application can tell Windows to stop the event from occurring at all. In spite of the powerful capabilities that hooks offer, many applications have been written that never take advantage of them. There are several reasons for this.

1. Microsoft's documentation has always been less than adequate.

Many of the structures and data types referred to in the documentation are not even defined in WINDOWS.H. However, in Windows 3.1, Microsoft has greatly improved the documentation and has also added many new data structures and types to WINDOWS.H.

Even though the documentation has been improved there are still many incorrect statements made within it. The reason for this is that Windows 3.1 offers a completely new method for installing and using hooks. But for backward compatibility, the old hook method will still work. You are strongly encouraged to use the new hook method over the old. In fact, I will not even discuss the old hook method in this chapter. Unfortunately, Microsoft did not make as strong a commitment to the new hook method as it should have when writing the documentation. As a result, the descriptions presented in the *Microsoft Windows' SDK Programmer's Reference* mix information about the old and the new methods but do not state which method it is referring to. For example, the description in many of the hook procedures (for example *KeyboardProc*) explains that if the *wParam* parameter is negative, the *CallNextHookEx* function must be called and that the filter function should perform no further processing. This is true for the old hook method but is not true for the new one. Actually, for the old hook method, the function is *DefHookProc* and not *CallNextHookEx*. Misleading information like this is certain to put the novice hook implementor in quite a tizzy.

I have taken special care to make sure that everything in this chapter is correct and accurate. Of course, it is possible that you may interpret something slightly differently than I intended. The main idea that I want to get across is to read the SDK documentation carefully, read my information carefully, and trust your instincts above all else.

2. Most hooks affect system performance.

Every time an event is about to occur in the system, Windows notifies a hook. If many hooks are installed, Windows has to notify all of them. This can noticeably downgrade Windows' performance. Windows 3.1 goes a big step in improving performance by allowing the application installing a hook to be notified only of events that are relevant to the application rather than the whole system.

3. Prior to Windows 3.1, Microsoft made the individual applications responsible for maintaining the list of hook procedures to be called.

If an application installed a hook and terminated without removing the hook, Windows would still attempt to call the hook, causing Windows to crash. Starting in Version 3.1, Windows maintains the installed hooks and when an application terminates, Windows automatically unhooks any hooks that were installed by that application.

4. The application's code to process almost every hook has to be in a dynamic-link library.

There is a lot of overhead in creating a dynamic-link library just for one small hook function. For hooks that are called only within the context of a single application, this is not necessary; the hook function can be part of the application's executable file.

5. Windows previously offered seven different types of hooks.

In many cases, if an application wanted to be notified of something, it had to install a hook that gave much more information than needed. The application would then filter out anything that it really wasn't interested in. In Windows 3.1, there are now 12 different hook types.

Hook Basics

Although Windows now offers 12 hooks, the methods used for installing and removing them are identical. Later in this chapter, we will discuss the details of each hook and when to use each one.

An application installs a hook by calling *SetWindowsHookEx*. The prototype for this function appears below:

```
HHOOK SetWindowsHookEx (int idHook, HOOKPROC hkPrc, HINSTANCE hInst,
    HTASK hTask);
```

When this function is called, Windows allocates a block of memory containing an internal data structure describing the newly-installed hook. All of these data structures are linked together to form a linked list with each new node (data structure) being placed at the front. After the node has been inserted into the list, *SetWindowsHookEx* returns a handle to the node. This value must be saved by the application and is used whenever the application needs to refer to the hook. We will see examples of this later.

The first parameter, *idHook*, specifies the type of hook the application wishes to install. This is one of the values listed in the following table:

Hook identifier	Description
WH_CALLWNDPROC	When this hook is installed, Windows calls the associated hook function every time a message is sent to a window using the *SendMessage* function.
WH_GETMESSAGE	When this hook is installed, Windows calls the associated hook function every time a message is retrieved by a call to the *GetMessage* or *PeekMessage* function.
WH_KEYBOARD	When this hook is installed, Windows calls the associated hook function every time an application calls the *GetMessage* or *PeekMessage* function and a *WM_KEYDOWN* or *WM_KEYUP* message is retrieved.
WH_MOUSE	When this hook is installed, Windows calls the associated hook function every time an application calls the *GetMessage* or *PeekMessage* function and a mouse message is retrieved.

Hook identifier	Description
WH_HARDWARE	When this hook is installed, Windows calls the associated hook function every time a hardware message is retrieved by a call to the *GetMessage* or *PeekMessage* function returns and that message is not related to the keyboard or the mouse.
WH_SYSMSGFILTER	When this hook is installed, Windows calls the associated hook function every time a dialog box, menu, or scroll bar is about to process a message.
WH_MSGFILTER	When this hook is installed, Windows calls the associated hook function every time a dialog box, menu, or scroll bar belonging to the application that installed the hook is about to process a message.
WH_JOURNALRECORD	When this hook is installed, Windows calls the associated hook function every time a message is retrieved from the Windows system queue.
WH_JOURNALPLAYBACK	When this hook is installed, Windows calls the associated hook function every time an event is requested from the Windows system queue.
WH_CBT	When this hook is installed, Windows calls the associated hook function before activating, creating, destroying, minimizing, maximizing, moving, or sizing a window; before completing a system command; before removing a mouse or keyboard event from the system message queue; before setting the input focus; or before synchronizing with the system message queue.
WH_SHELL	When this hook is installed, Windows calls the associated hook function whenever a top-level, unowned window is created or destroyed or when the shell application should activate its main window.
WH_DEBUG	When this hook is installed, Windows calls the associated hook function before calling any other hook.

The second parameter, *hkPrc*, is a procedural-instance address of the filter function that should process messages for the identified hook. The following rules apply to this second parameter:

1. If the filter function is in a DLL and *SetWindowsHookEx* is called from within the same DLL, the *hkPrc* parameter should simply be the name of the filter function. Because DLLs have only one instance, there is no need to create a procedural-instance for the filter function by calling *MakeProcInstance*.

2. If the call to *SetWindowsHookEx* is in an application (as opposed to a DLL) and the filter function is in a DLL, the *hkPrc* parameter can simply be the name of the filter function. In this case, the function is usually prototyped in a header file for the DLL and the application must be linked with the .LIB file associated with the DLL containing the filter function. Alternatively, an application can call *GetProcAddress* to retrieve the address of the filter function from the DLL and pass this value to the *SetWindowsHookEx* function.

3. If the call to *SetWindowsHookEx* is in an application and the filter function is in the same application, the *hkPrc* parameter must be the procedural-instance address of the filter function. This address is obtained by calling *MakeProcInstance* and passing it the name of the filter function. If your compiler supports a switch that loads the *DS* register with the *SS* register upon function entry, you do not have to call *MakeProcInstance*. Both the Borland C++ Version 2.0 or later and the Microsoft C/C++ Version 7.0 or later compilers support this feature.

The third parameter, *hInst*, is a data-instance handle identifying the instance of the module containing the hook function. If the hook function is in an application, this value is the same as that which was passed to your application's *WinMain* function in the *hinstCurrent* parameter. If the hook function is in a DLL, this value is the same that was passed to the DLL's *LibMain* function in the *hInst* parameter.

The last parameter, *hTask*, is a task-instance handle identifying the instance of the task that is installing the hook function. This parameter tells Windows whether the hook function should be called for an event occurring anywhere in the system or only for a specific task. If an application wants to install a task-specific hook, it can call *GetCurrentTask* to get the task-instance handle for itself (assuming that it is the active task when it calls this function) or, the application may call *GetWindowTask* to determine the task-instance handle of an application that created a specific window. Either of these task-instance handles may be passed as the *hTask* parameter. If an application wants to install a system-wide hook, the value of the *hTask* parameter should be NULL. If you install a hook function having system scope, the code for that function must be in a DLL. A hook function that has task scope may have its code in an executable or a DLL.

It is always a better idea to use task-specific hooks instead of system hooks whenever possible for the following reasons:

1. Windows calls system hook functions when an event occurs that affects any task. This can really affect Windows' performance. Task-specific hooks are called only when an event occurs that effects the individual task.

2. Task-specific hooks can be placed in the application's executable whereas the code for a system-wide hook must be placed in a DLL. If you wish, an application's hook function may be placed in a DLL, but this is not required.

3. Windows NT is a government secure operating system that will not allow an application to install system-wide hooks. Using only task-specific hooks now will cut down on the time required to port your application to this new environment.

Most of the different hook types may be installed having either system or task scope. However, the *WH_JOURNALRECORD, WH_JOURNALPLAYBACK*, and *WH_SYSMSGFILTER* hooks can only be installed having system scope. In addition, the *WH_SYSMSGFILTER* hooks are called before any *WH_MSGFILTER* hooks are called.

When Windows calls a hook function, it calls the hook functions that have task scope before calling hook functions that have requested system scope. For example, let's say that Application A installs a *WH_KEYBOARD* hook and requests that it have task scope. Application B is now executed and also installs a *WH_KEY-BOARD* hook but requests that it have system scope. If Application A is active and the user presses a key, Application A's hook function will be notified of the event first followed by Application B's hook function.

Now, let's say that Application B is active and the user presses a key. In this case, Application B's hook function will be notified of the event but Application A's hook function will not be notified at all. This is because the event did not occur while Application A was active.

Also, because Application A's hook function has task scope, the code for the function may be in Application A's executable code. However, Application B's hook function must be in a DLL because it has system scope.

Whenever an event occurs that is associated with the type of hook you have installed, Windows calls the filter function specified during the call to *SetWindows-HookEx*. The filter function must have the following prototype, regardless of the type of hook that has been installed:

```
LRESULT CALLBACK FilterFunc (int nCode, WPARAM wParam, LPARAM lParam);
```

The name of the function, *FilterFunc*, is a place holder for your own function's name. The first parameter, *nCode*, specifies the hook code. The domain of values for this parameter depends on the type of hook being installed. The values of the *wParam* and *lParam* parameters depend on the type of value passed in the *nCode* parameter.

A hook filter function's structure is similar to that of a window procedure. That is, the *nCode* parameter identifies the type of action (or message) that is to be performed by the filter function. The meanings of the *wParam* and *lParam* parameters depend on the type of action specified in *nCode*. We will examine the specific values of *nCode* and its associated values for *wParam* and *lParam* later in this chapter.

The code fragment below shows a possible function skeleton for a *WH_KEY-BOARD* hook:

```
// The "_hHook" global variable will be set to
// the return value from the call to the SetWindowsHookEx function.
static HHOOK _hHook = NULL;
 .

 .

 .

LRESULT CALLBACK KybdHook (int nCode, WPARAM wParam, LPARAM lParam) {
    BOOL fCallNextProc = FALSE;
    LRESULT lResult = 0;

    switch (nCode) {

        case HC_ACTION:
            // Do HC_ACTION processing.
            break;

        case HC_NOREMOVE:
            // Do HC_NOREMOVE processing.
            break;

        default:
            fCallNextProc = TRUE;
            break;
    }
    if (fCallNextProc)
        lResult = CallNextHookEx(_hHook, nCode, wParam, lParam);
    return(lResult);
}
```

A filter-function chain is formed when many applications install hooks of a particular type. When a particular event occurs, Windows calls the most recently-installed filter function for that hook. For example, if Application A installs a system-wide *WH_KEYBOARD* hook, Windows will call this filter function whenever a keyboard message is retrieved. If Application B also installs a system-wide *WH_KEYBOARD* hook, Windows will no longer call the filter function installed by Application A and will only call the one installed by Application B. It is the responsibility of each filter function to make sure that any previously installed filter functions are called.

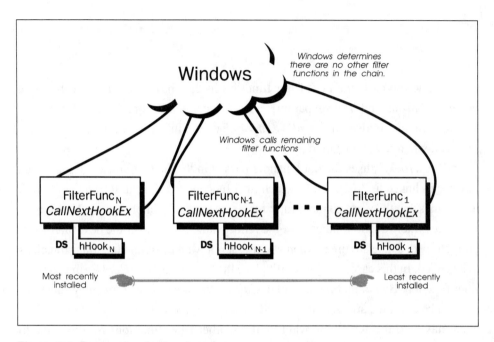

Figure 7-1. Processing for hook codes

The *SetWindowsHookEx* function returns the handle of a newly-installed filter function. The function that is installing the new filter function must save this address in a global variable:

```
static HHOOK _hHook = NULL;
   .
   .
   .
_hHook = SetWindowsHookEx(WH_KEYBOARD, KybdHook, hInst, NULL);
   .
   .
   .
```

If an error occurs, *SetWindowsHookEx* returns NULL.

If you want the previously-installed filter functions to be called after your filter function executes, you must place a call to *CallNextHookEx:*

```
LRESULT CallNextHookEx(HHOOK hhook, int nCode, WPARAM wParam,
    LPARAM lParam);
```

This function calls the next filter function in the chain and passes it the same *nCode*, *wParam*, and *lParam* parameters as it received. Before the next filter function terminates, it also calls *CallNextHookEx,* passing it the hook handle that it received when it was installed.

CallNextHookEx uses the hook handle passed in the first parameter so that it can traverse its linked list to determine which filter function to call next. If *CallNextHookEx* determines that there are no more filter functions to call, it simply returns NULL back to the last filter function; otherwise, the return value is whatever the next filter function returned. There are times when you might not want the remaining filter functions to be called. In this case, you just don't place the call to *CallNextHookEx* in your own filter function. By not putting the call to *CallNextHookEx* in, the remaining functions will not be executed and you may specify your own return value for this hook. There even may be times when you want to allow other filter functions for this hook to process first and when they have completed, do your own processing. This is done by placing the call to *CallNextHookEx* at the top of your filter function instead of at the bottom as shown above. Then, just before your filter function returns, you may return your own value or the value that was returned by the call to *CallNextHookEx.* The return value expected from a filter function depends on the type of hook installed and the value of the *nCode* parameter.

Here is an example of when you might not want to call the remaining filter functions in the chain. Let's say an application copies the window contents under the mouse cursor to the clipboard whenever the F9 key is pressed. The application must install a system-wide *WH_KEYBOARD* hook that examines each keystroke for an F9 key. For each keystroke that is not an F9, the next filter function in the chain should be called. However, once the filter function detects the F9 key, it performs the operations necessary to copy the window contents to the clipboard and immediately returns—without calling the next filter function in the chain. In fact, the *WH_KEYBOARD* filter function should return one to Windows, telling it to discard the keystroke event and not pass it to the application. This prohibits any applications from ever receiving the F9 key.

Removing a Filter Function from the Chain

When an application no longer needs its hooks, they are removed by calling *UnhookWindowsHookEx*:

```
BOOL UnhookWindowsHookEx (HHOOK hHook);
```

The *hHook* parameter specifies the handle of the hook that you wish to remove. This handle was originally returned from the call to *SetWindowsHookEx* when the hook was first installed. The return value from *UnhookWindowsHookEx* indicates whether the filter function has been successfully removed from the chain. If so, a nonzero value is returned.

Windows does not require that hook filter functions be removed in the reverse of the order in which they were installed. Whenever a hook is removed, Windows destroys the block of memory identifying the node and updates the links in the list.

The *WH_CALLWNDPROC* and *WH_GETMESSAGE* Hooks

One of the most useful utilities for debugging Windows programs is the Spy application supplied with the SDK. This application allows you to monitor the messages sent to a particular window (or to all windows). By using the *WH_CALLWNDPROC* and *WH_GETMESSAGE* hooks, Spy intercepts all messages sent to a window and displays that information in its own client area.

When an application calls *SendMessage*, Windows checks to see whether a *WH_CALLWNDPROC* hook filter function has been installed. If it has, Windows calls the first *WH_CALLWNDPROC* filter function in the chain. The table below summarizes the value expected by the filter function and the return value expected by Windows:

nCode	wParam	lParam	lResult
HC_ACTION	The message is being sent by the current task if wParam is nonzero.	Points to a CALLWNDPROC structure.	Not used, return zero.

The *HC_ACTION* hook code notifies the filter function that a message has been sent to a window. The *lParam* parameter points to a *CALLWNDPROC* structure that has the following prototype:

```
typedef struct {
    WORD hlParam;  // High-order word of lParam.
    WORD llParam;  // Low-order word of lParam.
    WPARAM wParam;
    UINT uMsg;
    HWND hWnd;
} CALLWNDPROC;
```

For some unknown reason, Microsoft did not include this structure definition in the WINDOWS.H file so you will have to define it yourself if your want to use this hook. If you compare this structure with the one given in the description of the *Call-WndProc* function in the *SDK Programmer's Reference*, Volume 2, you'll see that they don't match. The one in the *Programmer's Reference* is incorrect. If you examine the structure above, you might find that it looks very familiar to you. This structure is the same as an upside-down *MSG* structure except that it does not include the *pt* and *time* members.

Normally, when Windows is about to send a message, it pushes the *hWnd*, *uMsg*, *wParam*, and *lParam* parameters on the stack and then calls the appropriate window procedure. When a *WH_CALLWNDPROC* hook is installed, Windows still pushes all of these values onto the stack, but first it calls the filter function. The filter function is actually passed the address on the stack to where the parameters were pushed. But because the stack builds down, parameters are in reverse order. This has two important consequences. First, the *lParam* value cannot be used directly. Instead, you must use the two members *hlParam* and *llParam* to form a full long value:

```
MAKELONG(lpCallWndProc->llParam, lpCallWndProc->hlParam)
```

Second, since the parameters are on the stack all ready to be passed to the window procedure, the filter function can examine the contents of this structure and modify any or all of its members. At the end of the filter function, *CallNextHookEx* may be called so that any other functions in the chain have a chance to monitor or modify the structure. When all the filter functions have had a chance to process the message, Windows sends the modified message to the proper window.

Because messages to carry out operations are sent so frequently in Windows, installing a *WH_CALLWNDPROC* hook filter function will hurt Windows' performance dramatically. For this reason, the *WH_CALLWNDPROC* hook function is usually only used for debugging purposes. Do not be confused; this hook may be used with the retail version of Windows as well as the debugging version.

The *WH_CALLWNDPROC* hook intercepts messages sent to a window procedure during a call to *SendMessage*. To intercept messages retrieved from the application's queue (by calls to the *GetMessage* and *PeekMessage* functions), you must install a *WH_GETMESSAGE* hook filter function. The table below summarizes the value expected by the filter function and the return value expected by Windows:

nCode	wParam	lParam	lResult
HC_ACTION	NULL	Points to an MSG structure.	Not used, return zero.

The *WH_KEYBOARD* Hook

The *WH_KEYBOARD* hook is used by an application when it wants to examine keystrokes, even when it does not have the input focus. For example, the Recorder application supplied with Windows uses this hook. The Recorder allows the user to define a specific keystroke that activates a prerecorded sequence of events. While the Recorder is running, it uses the keyboard to watch the keyboard messages to see if the user presses a key that initiates a macro. The Recorder watches all keystrokes, even when it is not the active application.

When the user presses or releases a key, this event is placed in the Windows' system queue. This event is retrieved when an application makes a call to *GetMessage* or *PeekMessage*. Just before Windows returns the keystroke event, it calls the first *WH_KEYBOARD* filter function in the chain. The table below summarizes the values expected by the filter function and the return value expected by Windows:

nCode	wParam	lParam	lResult
HC_ACTION	Specifies the virtual key code of the key.	Specifies the same information as sent in the *lParam* parameter to a window procedure when it receives a *WM_KEYDOWN* message (see below).	Zero if message should be processed; one if the message should be discarded.
HC_NOREMOVE	Specifies the virtual key code of the key.	Specifies the same information as sent in the *lParam* parameter to a window procedure when it receives a *WM_KEYDOWN* message (see below).	Zero if message should be processed; one if the message should be discarded.

If the keystroke event is being retrieved from the system queue because the application called the *PeekMessage* function with the *PM_NOREMOVE* flag, the filter function will receive a hook code of *HC_NOREMOVE*. Any other time a keystroke event occurs, the *HC_ACTION* hook code is received.

When the hook code is *HC_ACTION* or *HC_NOREMOVE*, the *wParam* parameter identifies the virtual key code representing the pressed or released key. The list of virtual key codes supported by Windows is in Appendix B of the *Microsoft Windows' SDK Programmer's Reference (Messages, Structure, and Macros)*, Volume 3.

The *lParam* parameter contains additional information about the keystroke event:

Bits in *lParam*	Description
0 through 15	Repeat count (number of times the keystroke is repeated as a result of the user holding down the key).
16 through 23	Scan code of key.
24	This bit is on if the key is extended. Extended keys are function keys or keys on the numeric keypad.

Bits in *lParam*	Description
25 through 26	Not used.
27 through 28	Used internally by Windows.
29	This bit is on if the Alt key was held down while the key was pressed.
30	This bit is on if the key is down before the message is sent.
31	This bit is on if the key is being released, off if it is being pressed.

Windows does not allow a *WH_KEYBOARD* filter function to change the values in the *wParam* or *lParam* parameter before sending messages to an application. If you want to write a hook filter function that converts all occurrences of one keystroke to another, you have to use *WH_CALLWNDPROC* and *WH_GETMESSAGE* because these hooks allow their filter functions to modify messages.

The *WH_MOUSE* Hook

The *WH_MOUSE* hook is used by an application when it wants to examine mouse movements and button clicks, even when it does not have mouse capture. For example, let's say that some company is producing a product to help end users learn how to work with Windows. When the user loads the application, it installs a mouse hook and pops up a little help window on the screen. Now, whenever the mouse is moved over a screen element (such as a system menu, minimize box, scroll bar, caption, or desktop window), the mouse hook function can determine which screen element the cursor is over and display some help text in its little window. When this application does this, it does not interfere in any way with the normal processing of the mouse and any other application being used.

Whenever the user presses or releases a button on the mouse or moves the mouse, this event is placed in the Windows' system queue. This event is retrieved when an application makes a call to *GetMessage* or *PeekMessage*. Just before Windows returns the mouse event, it calls the first *WH_MOUSE* filter function in the chain. The following table summarizes the values expected by the filter function and the return values expected by Windows:

nCode	wParam	lParam	lResult
HC_ACTION	Specifies the mouse message.	Points to a MOUSEHOOKSTRUCT structure.	Zero if message should be processed; one if the message should be discarded.
HC_NOREMOVE	Specifies the mouse message.	Points to a MOUSEHOOKSTRUCT structure.	Zero if message should be processed; one if the message should be discarded.

If the mouse event is being retrieved from the system queue because the application called the *PeekMessage* function with the *PM_NOREMOVE* flag, the filter function will receive a hook code of *HC_NOREMOVE*. Any other time a mouse event occurs, the *HC_ACTION* hook code is received.

When the hook code is *HC_ACTION* or *HC_NOREMOVE*, the *wParam* parameter identifies the mouse message (WM_MOUSEMOVE, WM_LBUTTON-DOWN, WM_RBUTTONUP and so on).

The *lParam* parameter is a pointer to a *MOUSEHOOKSTRUCT* that looks like:

```
typedef struct tagMOUSEHOOKSTRUCT {
    POINT    pt;
    HWND     hwnd;
    UINT     wHitTestCode;
    DWORD    dwExtraInfo;
} MOUSEHOOKSTRUCT;
```

When the address of this structure is passed to the filter function, the *pt* member contains the coordinates of the mouse cursor in screen coordinates; the *hwnd* member identifies the handle of the window that is about to receive the mouse message; the *wHitTestCode* member contains a hit test code identifying which screen element the mouse is over. For a full list of hit test codes, see the *WM_NCHITTEST* message in the *SDK Programmer's Reference (Messages, Structures, and Macros)*, Volume 3.

The last member in this structure, *dwExtraInfo*, specifies extra information associated with the mouse event. This information can be set by using the *hardware_event* function and is normally retrieved in a window procedure by calling the *GetMessageExtraInfo* function.

The *WH_HARDWARE* Hook

The *WH_HARDWARE* hook is used by an application when it wants to examine hardware events other than keyboard and mouse events. This hook exists mostly for applications that run under Windows with the pen extensions.

Whenever a hardware event occurs, this event is placed in the Windows system queue. The event is retrieved when an application makes a call to *GetMessage* or *PeekMessage*. Just before Windows returns the hardware event (and it is not a keyboard or mouse event), it calls the first *WH_HARDWARE* filter function in the chain. The table below summarizes the values expected by the filter function and the return values expected by Windows:

nCode	wParam	lParam	lResult
HC_ACTION	NULL	Points to a *HARDWAREHOOKSTRUCT* structure.	Zero if message should be processed; one if the message should be discarded.
HC_NOREMOVE	NULL	Points to a *HARDWAREHOOKSTRUCT* structure.	Zero if message should be processed; one if the message should be discarded.

If the hardware event is being retrieved from the system queue because the application called the *PeekMessage* function with the *PM_NOREMOVE* flag, the filter function will receive a hook code of *HC_NOREMOVE*. Any other time a hardware event occurs, the *HC_ACTION* hook code is received.

When the hook code is *HC_ACTION* or *HC_NOREMOVE*, the *lParam* parameter is a pointer to a *HARDWAREHOOKSTRUCT* that looks like:

```
typedef struct tagHARDWAREHOOKSTRUCT {
    HWND    hWnd;
```

```
    UINT    wMessage;
    WPARAM  wParam;
    LPARAM  lParam;
} HARDWAREHOOKSTRUCT;
```

If you can't guess by now what all the members of this structure represent, you should put down this book and retire as a Windows programmer.

The *WH_SYSMSGFILTER* and *WH_MSGFILTER* Hooks

Windows calls the *WH_SYSMSGFILTER* and *WH_MSGFILTER* hook filter-function chains whenever a message is about to be processed by a dialog box, menu, or scroll bar. While the *WH_SYSMSGFILTER* hook can be used to monitor messages sent to any application, the *WH_MSGFILTER* hook can only be used to monitor messages sent to dialog boxes, messages boxes, menus, and scroll bars that were created by the application that installed the hook. A *WH_SYSMSGFILTER* hook can only be given system-wide scope and, therefore, must exist in a DLL.

Whenever a dialog box, menu, or scroll bar is about to process a message, Windows calls the first *WH_MSGFILTER* filter function in the chain for the active application. If none of the filter functions in that chain tells Windows to discard the message, Windows calls the first *WH_SYSMSGFILTER* filter function. The table below summarizes the values expected by both the *WH_MSGFILTER* and the *WH_SYSMSGFILTER* filter functions and the return value expected by Windows:

nCode	wParam	lParam	lResult
MSGF_DIALOGBOX	NULL	Points to an MSG structure.	Zero if message should be processed; one if the message should be discarded.
MSGF_MENU	NULL	Points to an MSG structure.	Zero if message should be processed; one if the message should be discarded.

nCode	wParam	lParam	lResult
MSGF_SCROLLBAR	NULL	Points to an MSG structure.	Zero if message should be processed; one if the message should be discarded.
MSGF_NEXTMENU	NULL	Points to an MSG structure.	Zero if message should be processed; one if the message should be discarded.

The *lParam* parameter for *WH_SYSMSGFILTER* and *WH_MSGFILTER* points to an *MSG* structure identifying the message to be processed. A filter function may alter any of the values in this structure before returning.

These hooks can also be used to process messages sent to a message box. In this case, the *nCode* parameter to the filter function will be *MSGF_DIALOGBOX*.

The *MSGF_NEXTWINDOW* hook code arrives at a *WM_SYSMSGFILTER* hook's filter function whenever the user presses the Alt-Tab or Alt-Esc keys to make another application active. The *MSGF_NEXTWINDOW* hook code is received by a *WH_MSGFILTER* hook function having task scope only if the user presses the Alt-Tab or Alt-Esc key combination when the application that installed the hook is the active task.

You can also tap into the *WH_SYSMSGFILTER* and *WH_MSGFILTER* hooks if you want. Let's say that you have designed a custom child control and you would like Windows to call these hooks at the top of your child control's window procedure to determine if the message should be processed or to allow the hook filter functions to alter some of the members of the *MSG* structure for the message. To do this, you can place a call to the *CallMsgFilter* function in your control's window procedure just before the switch statement:

```
#define MSGF_CUSTOMCONTROL    (MSGF_USER + 2763)
    .
    .
    .
```

```
LRESULT CALLBACK WndProc (HWND hWnd, UINT uMsg, WPARAM wParam,
    LPARAM lParam) {
    MSG Msg;
    LRESULT lResult = 0;

    // Load the message information into an MSG structure.
    Msg.hwnd = hWnd;
    Msg.message = uMsg;
    Msg.wParam = wParam;
    Msg.lParam = lParam;
    Msg.time = GetMessageTime();
    Msg.pt = GetMessagePos();

    // Send the Msg information to the WH_SYSMSGFILTER and WH_MSGFILTER
    // hooks.
    if (CallMsgFilter(&Msg, MSGF_CUSTOMCONTROL))
        return(0);

    // Filter functions want us to continue; so, load the altered
    // values back into the normal parameters.
    hWnd = Msg.hwnd;
    uMsg = Msg.message;
    wParam = Msg.wParam;
    lParam = Msg.lParam;

    // Do the normal window processing.
    switch (uMsg) {
    .

    .

    .

    }
    return(lResult);
}
```

The first parameter to *CallMsgFilter* is the address to an *MSG* structure containing the information about the message about to be processed. This address will be passed to the filter functions as the *lParam* parameter.

The second parameter is a value that will be passed into the *nCode* parameter to the filter functions. Care must be taken with this parameter. For example, let's say that two different applications each create a custom child control using this *CallMsgFilter* method and both install for itself a *WH_SYSMSGFILTER* hook. Since *WH_SYSMSGFILTER* hooks are system-wide, whenever a message is about to be processed by the first application's child control, the second application's *WH_SYSMSGFILTER* hook function is called. If both applications used the same value for *nCode*, the filter function has no way of knowing what type of control is receiving the message.

This problem can be alleviated somewhat by having your application install a *WH_MSGFILTER* hook instead of a *WH_SYSMSGFILTER* hook. In this case, you would know that when your filter function is called, it must be processing a message for a control in your application. However, any other application that has installed a *WH_SYSMSGFILTER* hook will also be notified that your control is about to process a message.

Ideally, we would like to select a value for the *nCode* parameter that is guaranteed not to conflict with a value chosen by another application. It would be nice if Windows offered a function like *RegisterWindowMessage*, called something like *RegisterMsgFilterCode*, that allowed an application to create unique message filter codes. But because Windows does not offer this, it is impossible to create unique code values. Windows does offer an *MSGF_USER* identifier in WINDOWS.H defined as 4096. Because it is not documented, I assume that this identifier exists to tell us that Windows wants to reserve the first 4096 values for its own use and that we may use any value as long as it is greater than 4095. But by having this identifier defined by Microsoft, it is much more likely that programmers will choose conflicting values. The natural tendency for every programmer is to define a new *MSG_* value as (MSGF_USER + 0). If all application developers do this, the number will, of course, conflict. That is why I added 2763 to *MSGF_USER* in the code fragment above; I figure it is unlikely that another programmer will select this value.

Now that we have discussed the *nCode* value, it's time to discuss what happens in the previous code fragment. When *CallMsgFilter* is called, Windows calls the first filter function installed for the *WH_SYSMSGFILTER* hook. If the last filter function executed for this hook returns nonzero, *CallMsgFilter* returns nonzero. This informs your window procedure that the filter functions want you to ignore this message and simply return. However, if the *WH_SYSMSGFILTER* hook functions return zero, *CallMsgFilter* calls the filter functions installed for the *WH_MSGFILTER* hook. Whatever the last filter function executed for this hook returns, *CallMsgFilter* returns to your window procedure. Again, if the value is nonzero, you should not process the message. If the return value is zero, you should process the message using the values that you passed to the hook in the *MSG* structure. Remember that some or all of the filter functions could have changed members in this MSG structure.

The *WH_JOURNALRECORD* and *WH_JOURNALPLAYBACK* Hooks

Perhaps the most commonly used hooks are *WH_JOURNALRECORD* and *WH_JOURNALPLAYBACK*, which add macro recording facility to applications such as the Windows Recorder.

When a *WH_JOURNALRECORD* hook is installed, Windows calls the *WH_JOURNALRECORD* hook filter-function chain whenever a message is retrieved from the Windows' system queue. Recall that the Windows' system queue is used to store all the user's input (mouse, keyboard, and other hardware events). The table below summarizes the values expected by the filter function and the return values expected by Windows:

nCode	wParam	lParam	lResult
HC_ACTION	NULL	Points to an EVENTMSG structure.	Not used, return zero.
HC_SYSMODALON	NULL	NULL	Not used, return zero.
HC_SYSMODALOFF	NULL	NULL	Not used, return zero.

When the hook code to a *WH_JOURNALRECORD* hook filter function is *HC_ACTION*, the *lParam* parameter points to an *EVENTMSG* structure. If you examine the documentation for the *JournalRecordProc* in the *SDK Programmer's Reference*, Volume 2, the documentation states that the *lParam* parameter points to an *MSG* structure—this is incorrect. The *lParam* points to an *EVENTMSG* structure:

```
typedef struct tagEVENTMSG {
    UINT    message;
    UINT    paramL;
    UINT    paramH;
    DWORD   time;
} EVENTMSG;
```

For macro recording to be implemented in an application, a *WH_JOURNALRECORD* filter function should append each *EVENTMSG* structure received to a block of memory. This technique is demonstrated by the Echo application discussed later.

The *HC_SYSMODALON* and *HC_SYSMODALOFF* hook codes are used to notify a *WH_JOURNALRECORD* filter function when a system modal dialog box appears or is removed, respectively. The filter function should watch for the *HC_SYSMODALON* hook code and temporarily stop appending *EVENTMSG* structures to the memory block. Depending on the application, it might be even better to turn the recording off completely and notify the user that a system modal dialog box has appeared. The user should not be notified until after that dialog box has been removed. The Echo application shows how to implement this logic. You may also want to experiment with the Recorder application supplied with Windows to see how it operates.

After the *WH_JOURNALRECORD* hook has been removed, *WH_JOURNAL-PLAYBACK* is used to play back the sequence of events. When a *WH_JOURNAL-PLAYBACK* hook is installed, Windows ignores all mouse and keyboard input from the user and retrieves system events by calling the *WH_JOURNALPLAY-BACK* filter function. While a *WH_JOURNALPLAYBACK* hook is installed, the mouse will not effect the position of the mouse cursor on the screen. The table below summarizes the values expected by the filter function and the return values expected by Windows:

nCode	wParam	lParam	lResult
HC_GETNEXT	NULL	Points to an EVENTMSG structure.	Number of clock ticks. Windows should wait before processing the message.
HC_SKIP	NULL	NULL	Not used, return zero.
HC_SYSMODALON	NULL	NULL	Not used, return zero.
HC_SYSMODALOFF	NULL	NULL	Not used, return zero.

HC_SYSMODALON and HC_SYSMODALOFF notify the WH_JOURNAL-PLAYBACK filter function that a system modal dialog box has appeared or been removed. Windows stops calling the filter function while the dialog box is on the screen. Because a system modal dialog box usually means that some serious action must be taken, a WH_JOURNALPLAYBACK hook can watch for the HC_SYS-MODALON hook code and unhook itself. It would not be wise to continue playing the events after the dialog box is removed. Once the dialog box has been removed, Windows resumes calling the WH_JOURNALPLAYBACK filter function.

When the filter function receives the HC_GETNEXT hook code, the next EVENTMSG structure in the memory block should be copied to the EVENTMSG structure pointed to by the lParam parameter.

The HC_SKIP hook code notifies the WH_JOURNALPLAYBACK filter function that Windows is done processing the current event and to prepare the next one. This means that the filter function should continue to return the first event in the sequence every time Windows sends the HC_GETNEXT hook code. When Windows sends the HC_SKIP hook code, the filter function should prepare to return the next event in the sequence in response to the next HC_GETNEXT hook code sent from Windows. When the filter function receives the HC_SKIP hook code and determines that all the saved events have been played, the filter function can call the Unhook-WindowsHookEx function to remove itself from the chain. A WH_JOURNAL-PLAYBACK filter function should not unhook itself during the processing of a HC_GETNEXT hook code.

When the filter function returns from processing HC_GETNEXT, the time member of the EVENTMSG structure (pointed to by the lParam parameter) must contain the system time when the message should occur. To accomplish this, I recommend updating the *time* member of all the saved events immediately after the *WH_JOURNALRECORD* hook's filter function is removed. The result should have the *time* member in each *EVENTMSG* structure, reflecting the number of clock ticks that have elapsed since recording started. The following code fragment shows how to calculate this:

```
LPEVENTMSG lpEventMsg;
WORD wNumEvents;
  .
  .
  .

while (wNumEvents--)
    lpEventMsg[wNumEvents].time -= lpEventMsg[0].time;
  .
  .
  .
```

The *lpEventMsg* variable points to an array of saved *EVENTMSG* structures, and the *wNumEvents* variable contains the number of events that have been recorded.

When the *WH_JOURNALPLAYBACK* hook is installed, the application should save the current system time:

```
HHOOK _hHook;
DWORD _dwStartPlaybackTime;
  .
  .
  .

_hHook = SetWindowsHookEx(WH_JOURNALPLAYBACK,
    (HOOKPROC) JrnlPlayBackHook, hInst, NULL);
_dwStartPlaybackTime = GetTickCount();
  .
  .
  .
```

Then, when the *HC_GETNEXT* hook code is passed to the filter function, the function can copy the current *EVENTMSG* to the location pointed to by the *lParam* parameter and change that copy's *time* member to the proper playback time:

```
((LPEVENTMSG) lParam)->time += _dwStartPlaybackTime;
```

The return value from the filter function indicates the number of milliseconds Windows should wait before playing back the event. If the playback time has passed, the function should return zero. The code fragment below shows how to calculate this value:

```
LRESULT lResult;
    .
    .
    .
switch (nCode) {
    case HC_GETNEXT:
        // Copy current event to EVENTMSG structure pointed to
        // by lParam.
        *((LPEVENTMSG) lParam) = lpEventMsg[wCurrentEvent];

        // Update time member in copy to system playback time.
        ((LPEVENTMSG) lParam)->time += _dwStartPlaybackTime;

        // Return # of milliseconds Windows should wait before
        // processing event.
        lResult = ((LPEVENTMSG) lParam)->time - GetTickCount();
        if ((signed long) lResult < 0) lResult = 0;
        break;
    .
    .
    .
}
```

```
    .
    .
    .
    return(lResult);
```

If you would like to have the recorded macros played back at full speed instead of recorded speed, the filter function should change the *time* member in the copied structure to the current system time and return zero:

```
LRESULT lResult;
    .
    .
    .
switch (nCode) {
    case HC_GETNEXT:
        // Copy current event to EVENTMSG structure pointed to
        // by lParam.
        *((LPEVENTMSG) lParam) = lpEventMsg[wCurrentEvent];

        // Update time member in copy to system playback time.
        ((LPEVENTMSG) lParam)->time = GetTickCount();

        // Return # of milliseconds Windows should wait before
        // processing event.
        lResult = 0;
        break;
        .
        .
        .
    }
    .
    .
    .
    return(lResult);
```

There are some issues to keep in mind when recording and playing back macros. Use of the mouse should be kept to a minimum. The *EVENTMSG* structures that *WH_JOURNALRECORD* receives contain the position of the mouse in screen coordinates. When a macro is played back, the windows on the screen may be in different locations or different sizes than when the macro was recorded. This may cause the mouse events to be sent to a window other than the original one. In addition, macros could be played back on a monitor having a different screen resolution from that of the monitor used when the events were recorded. Finally, incompatibilities could result when a macro recorded on one keyboard is played back on a machine connected to a keyboard with a different country setting.

The *WH_SHELL* Hook

The *WH_SHELL* hook is used by a shell application when it wants to know when application windows are being created and destroyed in the system. For example, you might want to write a program that keeps track of which applications a user was using and how long the user ran those applications. A program to do this would first install a *WH_SHELL* hook. Then every time it was notified that a top-level, unowned window was created, it would record the window's caption and the system time. When the shell application was notified that a top-level, unowned window was being destroyed, it would update its record, determining which application was being closed, and would note the system time again.

The following table summarizes the values expected by the *WH_SHELL* filter function and the return values expected by Windows:

nCode	wParam	lParam	lResult
HSHELL_WINDOWCREATED	Handle of window being created.	NULL	Not used, return zero.
HSHELL_WINDOWDESTROYED	Handle of window being destroyed.	NULL	Not used, return zero.
HSHELL_ACTIVATESHELLWINDOW	NULL	NULL	Not used, return zero.

Whenever a top-level, unowned window is being created or destroyed, Windows calls the first *WH_SHELL* filter function and passes it a value of *HSHELL_WINDOWCREATED* or *HSHELL_WINDOWDESTROYED* respectively. If the *nCode* parameter is *HSHELL_WINDOWCREATED*, the window has been created and you may send messages to it at this point. If the *nCode* parameter is *HSHELL_WINDOWDESTROYED*, the window has not yet been destroyed and you may again send messages to it.

When an active window is destroyed, Windows calls the first *WH_SHELL* filter function and passes it a value of *WSHELL_ACTIVATESHELLWINDOW*. This value tells the shell application that it should make itself the active application by calling the *PostMessage* function.

The *WH_CBT* Hook

The *WH_CBT* hook is used by an application that wishes to offer computer-based training (CBT) facilities to its users. When this hook is installed, Windows calls the associated hook function before activating, creating, destroying, minimizing, maximizing, moving, or sizing a window; before completing a system command; before removing a mouse or keyboard event from the system message queue; before setting the input focus; or before synchronizing with the system message queue. The application's hook function can monitor a user's progress with the application and can aid the user by performing certain tasks automatically.

For example, an application can give the user instructions on how to complete a certain process at the beginning of the session. Then later, the application can tell the user to execute that process. The CBT hook can be used to see if the user has executed the process successfully. In addition, many applications that offer CBT often present main concepts to the new user but force the program to move quickly through more mundane tasks. For instance, a user might be learning how to format a document in a word processing application. There is no need for the application to force the user to enter a paragraph of text before demonstrating the formatting functions. In this case, a *WH_CBT* hook might install a *WH_JOURNALPLAYBACK* hook that will force keystrokes into the application creating the paragraph of text for the user. After all of the keystrokes have been played, the *WH_JOURNALPLAYBACK* hook would be removed.

The following table summarizes the values expected by the *WH_CBT* filter function and the return values expected by Windows:

nCode	wParam	lParam	lResult
HCBT_ACTIVATE	Handle of window being activated.	Points to a *CBT_ACTIVATESTRUCT* structure.	Zero if window should be activated; one to prevent it.
HCBT_CREATEWND	Handle of window being created.	Points to a *CBT_CREATEWND* structure.	Zero if window should be created; one to prevent it.
HCBT_DESTROYWND	Handle of window being destroyed.	NULL	Zero if window should be destroyed; one to prevent it.
HCBT_MINMAX	Handle of window being minimized or maximized.	LOWORD specifies a show value (*SW_*).	Zero if window should be minimized or maximized; one to prevent it.
HCBT_MOVESIZE	Handle of window being moved or sized.	Points to a *RECT* structure.	Zero if window should be moved or sized; one to prevent it.
HCBT_SETFOCUS	Handle of window gaining input focus.	LOWORD specifies handle of window losing input focus.	Zero if input focus should be changed; one to prevent it.
HCBT_SYSCOMMAND	Specifies the system command selected by the user.	If *wParam* is *SC_HOTKEY*, LOWORD is handle of window that will be made active. If *wParam* is not *SC_HOTKEY* and the system command was chosen with the mouse, LOWORD and HIWORD represent the x- and y-coordinates of the mouse cursor. For any other condition, *lParam* is undefined.	Zero if system command should be executed; one to prevent it.

nCode	wParam	lParam	lResult
HCBT_CLICKSKIPPED	Identifies the mouse message removed from the queue.	Points to a MOUSEHOOKSTRUCT structure.	Not used, return zero.
HCBT_KEYSKIPPED	Identifies the keyboard message removed from the queue.	Specifies the same information as sent in lParam to a window procedure when it receives a WM_KEYDOWN message.	Not used, return zero.
HCBT_QS	NULL	NULL	Not used, return zero.

Whenever a new window is about to be activated, Windows calls the first *WH_CBT* filter function and passes it a value of *HCBT_ACTIVATE*. The *wParam* contains the handle of the window being activated and the *lParam* parameter points to a *CBTACTIVATESTRUCT* structure:

```
typedef struct tagCBTACTIVATESTRUCT {
    BOOL    fMouse;
    HWND    hWndActive;
} CBTACTIVATESTRUCT;
```

The *fMouse* member is TRUE if the window is being activated as the result of a mouse click. The *hWndActive* member indicates the handle of the window that is currently active.

Whenever a new window is about to be created, Windows calls the first *WH_CBT* filter function and passes it a value of *HCBT_CREATEWND*. The *wParam* contains the handle of the window created. At this point, Windows has actually created the window's data structure in memory but has not sent any messages to the window (such as *WM_NCCREATE* or *WM_CREATE*). If the filter function returns one in response to this code, the window will be destroyed and *CreateWindow(Ex)* will return NULL to the application attempting to create the window. If the filter function returns zero, the window is created and the *WM_NCCREATE* and *WM_CREATE* messages are sent to it.

Although the window has not been sent the *WM_NCCREATE* and *WM_CRE-ATE* messages by the time the filter function receives the *HCBT_CREATEWND* code, the filter function may send messages to the window. But beware that the window has not been fully initialized and that sending some messages may cause Global Protection Violations or will return incorrect values. Avoid doing this if you can.

When the *HCBT_CREATEWND* code is received by the filter function, the *lParam* parameter points to a *CBT_CREATEWND* structure:

```
typedef struct tagCBT_CREATEWND {
    CREATESTRUCT FAR* lpcs;
    HWND      hwndInsertAfter;
} CBT_CREATEWND;
```

The *lpcs* member is a pointer to a *CREATESTRUCT* structure containing all of the parameters that were passed to *CreateWindow(Ex)* when the application attempted to create the window. The *hwndInsertAfter* member in the *HCBT_CRE-ATEWND* structure indicates the handle of the window that this new window will be inserted after in the z-order. When the filter function receives the *HCBT_CRE-ATEWND* notification, it can examine these values and modify any of them. However, there is a bug in Windows 3.1 that will not allow you to change the parent of the window. If the filter function changes the *hwndParent* member of the *CRE-ATESTRUCT* structure, Windows ignores the change when completing the creation of the window. The parent will always be the same as the *hwndParent* parameter passed to the *CreateWindow(Ex)* function.

The *HCBT_CLICKSKIPPED* code is used by an application when it wants to know when the user has clicked the mouse over a window so that the application can install a *WH_JOURNALPLAYBACK* hook to force hardware events into the system queue, causing a process to execute automatically. Windows calls the first *WH_CBT* filter function and passes it a value of *HCBT_CLICKEDSKIPPED* when a mouse-click message is removed from the queue, sent to a *WH_MOUSE* hook, and the last filter function executed for the *WH_MOUSE* hook told Windows to ignore the message. At this point, the *WH_CBT* filter function receiving the *HCBT_CLICKSKIPPED* code would install the *WH_JOURNALPLAYBACK* hook.

For example, a spreadsheet application might want to check if the user has clicked over a particular cell. It would do this by checking in its *HW_MOUSE* filter function if the mouse was over the desired cell. If it were, the filter function would return one, informing Windows that the message should not be processed by the application. At this point, Windows calls the *WH_CBT* filter function and passes it the *HCBT_CLICKSKIPPED* code so that the application can install a *WH_JOURNALPLAYBACK* hook to repeat a sequence of events like summing a row or column.

The *wParam* parameter for the *HCBT_CLICKSKIPPED* code identifies the mouse message that occurred, and the *lParam* parameter points to the same *MOUSE-HOOKSTRUCT* structure that was sent to the *WH_MOUSE* hook filter functions. See the discussion of the *WH_MOUSE* hook earlier in this chapter for a description of this structure.

The *HCBT_KEYSKIPPED* code is used by an application when it wants to know when the user has pressed a key on the keyboard so that the application can install a *WH_JOURNALPLAYBACK* hook to force hardware events into the system queue, causing a process to execute automatically. Windows calls the first *WH_CBT* filter function and passes it a value of *HCBT_KEYSKIPPED* when a keystroke message is removed from the queue, sent to a *WH_KEYBOARD* hook and the last filter function executed for the *WH_KEYBOARD* hook told Windows to ignore the message. At this point, the *WH_CBT* filter function receiving the *HCBT_KEYSKIPPED* code would install the *WH_JOURNALPLAYBACK* hook.

For example, a word-processing application might want the user to enter a line of text and perform some action after a period is entered. It would do this by checking in its *WH_KEYBOARD* filter function when the period was typed. When it is, the filter function would return one, informing Windows that the message should not be processed by the application. At this point, Windows calls the *WH_CBT* filter function and passes it the *HCBT_KEYSKIPPED* code so that the application can install a *WH_JOURNALPLAYBACK* hook to play back a sequence of events such as spell checking the sentence.

The *wParam* parameter for the *HCBT_KEYSKIPPED* code identifies the keyboard message that occurred and the *lParam* parameter identifies the same value that was sent to the *WH_KEYBOARD* hook filter functions. See the discussion of the *WH_KEYBOARD* hook earlier in this chapter for a description of this parameter.

Whenever a *WM_QUEUESYNC* message is retrieved from the system message queue, Windows calls the first *WH_CBT* filter function and passes it a value of *HCBT_QS*. In a CBT application, *WH_JOURNALPLAYBACK* hooks are frequently installed and removed so that tasks may be performed automatically by the application while the user watches. Just before an application installs the *WH_JOUR-NALPLAYBACK* hook, it should place a *WM_QUEUESYNC* message in the queue. The first *WH_CBT* hook filter function receives a *HCBT_QS* notification and knows that it should stop monitoring events while the journal of hardware events is being played back. When the *WH_JOURNALPLAYBACK* hook is removed, the application should again place a *WM_QUEUESYNC* message in the queue, so that the *WH_CBT* hook filter function knows that new events it receives are due to the user's actions.

The *WH_DEBUG* Hook

The *WH_DEBUG* hook is used by an application when it wants to monitor all hooks that are being processed by the system. This allows an application to see what hooks are being called and which module is processing the hook.

Remember, when a new hook is installed, Windows calls that hook filter function first. That hook filter function can decide to call the next filter function in the chain or to stop the processing. If you install a hook and determine that your filter function is not being called, it may be that another hook was installed after yours. The *WH_DEBUG* hook can be used to determine which application has installed hooks.

Whenever Windows is about to call any hook filter functions, it calls the first *WH_DEBUG* filter function in the chain. The following table summarizes the values expected by the filter function and the return values expected by Windows:

nCode	wParam	lParam	lResult
HC_ACTION	Task-instance handle of the task that installed the hook about to be called.	Points to a DEBUGHOOKINFO structure.	Zero if the hook about to be called should be executed; one to prevent it.

Whenever a hook filter function (other than *WH_DEBUG*) is about to be called, Windows calls the first *WH_DEBUG* filter function and passes it a value of *HC_ACTION*. The *wParam* parameter identifies the task-instance handle of the application that installed the filter function that is about to be called. From this parameter, you can determine which application installed the hook by using the *TaskFindHandle* function included in the new TOOLHELP.DLL. The *lParam* parameter points to a *DEBUGHOOKINFO* structure:

```
typedef struct tagDEBUGHOOKINFO {
    HMODULE     hModuleHook;
    LPARAM      reserved;
    LPARAM      lParam;
    WPARAM      wParam;
    int         code;
} DEBUGHOOKINFO;
```

The *hModuleHook* member is the module-instance handle of the module that contains the filter function about to be called. From this handle, you can determine the executable or dynamic-link library that contains the function by calling the *ModuleFindHandle* function, also supplied in TOOLHELP.DLL or by using *GetModuleFileName*. The next member, *reserved*, is for Windows' own use. You should not attempt to use this member for anything.

The remaining members in the structure, *lParam*, *wParam*, and *code*, are the parameters that are to be passed to the filter about to be called. You may inspect these values and modify them if you wish.

To allow the next *WH_DEBUG* hook filter function in the chain to be called, *Call-NextHookEx,* as with all of the hooks, must be called from the *WH_DEBUG* filter function passing it the same parameters that were passed to the first filter function. Do not call *CallNextHookEx* and pass it the members in the *DEBUGHOOKINFO* structure.

The Screen-Blanker Utility

Ever since Windows was introduced, company after company has written some type of screen-blanking program. You know the kind I mean: The computer sits idle for a while, the screen turns black, and some animated design moves across it. The sample application SCRNBLNK.EXE demonstrates how to implement one of these screen blankers. It uses the *WH_JOURNALRECORD* hook to monitor input from the user. When no user input has been detected after five minutes, the application blanks the user's screen and draws some multicolored circles. To continue working with Windows, the user can press any key or a mouse button.

Screen blankers have become so popular, that Microsoft has published a formal specification on how to implement a screen blanker so that the user may select the screen blanker from the Windows' Control Panel. When a screen blanker is written this way, Windows manages all the nitty-gritty details of when to blank the screen. All you have to concentrate on is the animation that the screen blanker performs. For more information on how to implement a screen blanker this way, refer to Chapter 14 (*Screen-Saver Library*) in the *SDK Programmer's Reference*, Volume 1. The screen blanker application presented in this chapter does not follow this specification.

The screen blanker initializes by registering two window classes, SCRNBLNK and SCRNBLNKPOPUP. The SCRNBLNK class is the application's main window. This window is created as an icon and refuses to be opened by the user. (This is done by intercepting *WM_QUERYOPEN* and returning zero.) The main window serves as an indicator to the user that the screen blanker is loaded and allows the user to select options from the application's system menu. During *WM_CREATE* message processing, a new menu item is added to the system menu, "Preferences." The "Preferences" menu presents a dialog box that allows the user to change the number of minutes that the user must be idle before blanking the screen (the default is five minutes). After the menu item has been appended, the *InstallJrnlHook* function is called, passing TRUE as its parameter. This function is in the SBDLL.C file:

```
static HHOOK _hHook = NULL;
static DWORD _dwLastEventTime = 0;
.

.

.

void WINAPI InstallJrnlHook (BOOL fInstall) {
   if (fInstall) {
      _hHook = SetWindowsHookEx(WH_JOURNALRECORD,
         (HOOKPROC) JrnlRcrdHookFunc, _hInstance, NULL);
      _dwLastEventTime = GetTickCount();
   } else {
      UnhookWindowsHookEx(_hHook);
      _hHook = NULL;
      _dwLastEventTime = 0;
   }
}
```

Because the hook is being installed (*fInstall* is TRUE), this function sets the
WH_JOURNALRECORD hook into the chain and initializes the *_dwLastEventTime*
variable equal to the current system time. This global variable is updated every time
a system event is passed to the *WH_JOURNALRECORD* filter function. This function is shown below:

```
LRESULT CALLBACK JrnlRcrdHookFunc (int nCode, WPARAM wParam,
   LPARAM lParam) {
   switch (nCode) {

      case HC_ACTION:
         _dwLastEventTime = ((LPEVENTMSG) lParam)->time;
         break;

      case HC_SYSMODALON:
      case HC_SYSMODALOFF:
         break;
```

```
        default:
            break;
    }


    return(CallNextHookEx(_hHook, nCode, wParam, lParam));
}
```

After the hook has been installed, the screen blanker creates a SCRNBLNKPOPUP window with the following call:

```
_hWndBlnk = CreateWindowEx(WS_EX_TOPMOST, _szBlnkClass, NULL,
    WS_POPUP, 0, 0, GetSystemMetrics(SM_CXSCREEN),
    GetSystemMetrics(SM_CYSCREEN), NULL, NULL, hInstance, 0);
```

As you can see, the window is created using the *WS_EX_TOPMOST* extended style and has the dimension of the entire screen. It is important the window contain the *WS_EX_TOPMOST* style so that it covers any other windows already on the screen containing this style. You will also notice that the *WS_POPUP* style is used when creating the window and that no parent window is specified (this is called an unowned pop-up window). The following discussion explains why the screen blanker needs an unowned pop-up.

The logic that controls when the screen blanker should clear the screen is in the processing of the *WM_TIMER* messages in the *BlnkWndProc* window procedure:

```
switch (uMsg) {
    case WM_TIMER:
        if (!IsWindowVisible(hWnd)) {
            if (GetTickCount() - GetLastEventTime())
                    > _wMinutes * 60000ul) {
                ShowWindow(hWnd, SW_SHOW);
                ShowCursor(FALSE);
            }
            break;
        }
```

```
// Draw in the blank window.
    .
    .
    .
```

   We can determine whether the SCRNBLNKPOPUP window is already visible by calling *IsWindowVisible*. If this function returns TRUE, draw some circles in the blank window. But if *IsWindowVisible* returns FALSE, you must see if the user has been idle for at least the number of minutes specified in the *_wMinutes* variable. Examine the last time an event occurred by calling the *GetLastEventTime* function in SBDLL.C. This function simply returns the value of the *_dwLastEventTime* variable contained in the data segment of the DLL.

   If the user has been idle for the requested period, the SCRNBLNKPOPUP window is made visible via a call to *ShowWindow* and the mouse cursor is hidden. When the window appears, Windows sends a *WM_ERASEBKGND* message to its window procedure. Because this message is not intercepted, it is passed to *DefWindowProc*, which examines the value of the *hbrBackground* member for the registered class and paints the window's background in that color. SCRNBLNKPOPUP sets the *hbrBackground* member of the *WNDCLASS* structure as follows:

```
WndClass.hbrBackground = GetStockObject(BLACK_BRUSH);
```

Windows will make the entire screen black when the window is visible.

   Now, we can discuss why the SCRNBLNKPOPUP window had to be an unowned pop-up. When a window is a child or an owned pop-up, Windows prohibits that window from being visible when its parent or owner is an icon. Since the application's main window is always an icon, Windows would never allow the SCRN-BLNKPOPUP window to be seen if it weren't an unowned pop-up.

   The user can continue to work with Windows by pressing a key or mouse button. When one of these events occurs, the following code fragment executes:

```
case WM_LBUTTONDOWN:
case WM_MBUTTONDOWN:
case WM_RBUTTONDOWN:
```

```
case WM_KEYDOWN:
case WM_SYSKEYDOWN:
    ShowCursor(TRUE);
    ShowWindow(hWnd, SW_HIDE);
    break;
```

This causes the mouse cursor to be shown again and hides the SCRN-BLNKPOPUP window. When this window is hidden, the windows beneath it are no longer obscured and Windows automatically sends *WM_PAINT* messages to all the visible windows.

You may have noticed that the *PeekMessage* function is called twice during the processing of the *WM_TIMER* message. If the user presses a mouse button while the drawing algorithm is still drawing, the pop-up window won't be hidden until the drawing cycle is complete. To solve this problem, the *PeekMessage* function is called in the drawing loop:

```
fForceStop =
    PeekMessage(&msg, hWnd, WM_KEYFIRST, WM_KEYLAST,
        PM_NOYIELD | PM_NOREMOVE) ||
    PeekMessage(&msg, hWnd, WM_LBUTTONDOWN, WM_MOUSELAST,
        PM_NOYIELD | PM_NOREMOVE);
if (fForceStop) break;
```

If a keyboard or mouse event is found, *fForceStop* is set to TRUE and the drawing algorithm is prematurely terminated.

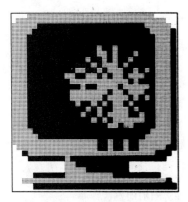

Figure 7-2. SCRNBLNK.ICO

Listing 7-1. SCRNBLNK.C application source module

```
/**************************************************************************
Module name: SCRNBLNK.C
Programmer : Jeffrey M. Richter.
**************************************************************************/

#include <windows.h>
#include <stdlib.h>
#include <math.h>

#include "ScrnBlnk.h"

char _szAppName[] = "ScrnBlnk";
char _szBlnkClass[] = "ScrnBlnkPopup";

extern const HINSTANCE _cdecl _hInstance;

#define IDM_PREFERENCES     (0x0110)    // Must be < 0xF000.

static WORD _wMinutes = 5;              // Default to five minutes idle time.
static HWND _hWnd, _hWndBlnk;

ATOM NEAR RegisterWndClasses (HINSTANCE hInstance);
LRESULT CALLBACK AppWndProc (HWND hWnd, UINT uMsg, WPARAM wParam,
    LPARAM lParam);
LRESULT CALLBACK BlnkWndProc (HWND hWnd, UINT uMsg, WPARAM wParam,
    LPARAM lParam);
BOOL CALLBACK PrefProc (HWND hDlg, UINT uMsg, WPARAM wParam,
    LPARAM lParam);
```

```
// **************************************************************************
#pragma argsused
int WinMain (HINSTANCE hInstance, HINSTANCE hPrevInstance,
        LPSTR lpszCmdLine, int nCmdShow) {
    MSG msg;

    if (hPrevInstance != NULL) return(0);

    if (RegisterWndClasses(hInstance) == 0) return(0);

    // Create application's main window. Show only as iconic (WS_MINIMIZE).
    _hWnd = CreateWindow(_szAppName, _szAppName,
        WS_OVERLAPPED | WS_CAPTION | WS_SYSMENU | WS_MINIMIZE,
        0, 0, 0, 0, NULL, NULL, hInstance, 0);

    if (_hWnd == NULL) return(0);

    ShowWindow(_hWnd, SW_MINIMIZE);
    UpdateWindow(_hWnd);

    // Create hidden unowned pop-up window that covers user's entire screen.
    _hWndBlnk = CreateWindowEx(WS_EX_TOPMOST, _szBlnkClass, NULL,
        WS_POPUP, 0, 0, GetSystemMetrics(SM_CXSCREEN),
        GetSystemMetrics(SM_CYSCREEN), NULL, NULL, hInstance, 0);

    if (_hWndBlnk == NULL) return(0);

    // Send WM_TIMER messages to unowned pop-up window every second.
    if (0 == SetTimer(_hWndBlnk, 1, 1000, NULL)) {
        MessageBox(_hWnd, "Not enough timers!", _szAppName, MB_OK);
        return(0);
    }

    while (GetMessage(&msg, NULL, 0, 0)) {
        TranslateMessage(&msg);
        DispatchMessage(&msg);
    }

    KillTimer(_hWndBlnk, 1);
    DestroyWindow(_hWndBlnk);

    return(0);
}

// **************************************************************************
ATOM NEAR RegisterWndClasses (HINSTANCE hInstance) {
    WNDCLASS WndClass;
```

```
WndClass.style          = 0;
WndClass.lpfnWndProc    = AppWndProc;
WndClass.cbClsExtra     = 0;
WndClass.cbWndExtra     = 0;
WndClass.hInstance      = hInstance;
WndClass.hIcon          = LoadIcon(hInstance, _szAppName);
WndClass.hCursor        = NULL;
WndClass.hbrBackground  = NULL;
WndClass.lpszMenuName   = NULL;
WndClass.lpszClassName  = _szAppName;
if (0 == RegisterClass(&WndClass)) return(0);

WndClass.style          = 0;
WndClass.lpfnWndProc    = BlnkWndProc;
WndClass.cbClsExtra     = 0;
WndClass.cbWndExtra     = 0;
WndClass.hInstance      = hInstance;
WndClass.hIcon          = LoadIcon(hInstance, _szAppName);
WndClass.hCursor        = NULL;

// Unowned pop-up window's background is always BLACK so that
// contents of screen are removed.
WndClass.hbrBackground = GetStockObject(BLACK_BRUSH);

WndClass.lpszMenuName   = NULL;
WndClass.lpszClassName  = _szBlnkClass;
return(RegisterClass(&WndClass));


// ************************************************************************
// This function processes all messages sent to ScrnBlnk's main window.

LRESULT CALLBACK AppWndProc (HWND hWnd, UINT uMsg, WPARAM wParam,
   LPARAM lParam) {
   BOOL fCallDefProc = FALSE;
   LRESULT lResult = 0;
   HMENU hMenu;
   WORD wIdleTime;

   switch (uMsg) {
      case WM_CREATE:
         // Append the "Preferences" option to the system menu.
         hMenu = GetSystemMenu(hWnd, 0);
         AppendMenu(hMenu, MF_SEPARATOR, 0, 0);
         AppendMenu(hMenu, MF_STRING, IDM_PREFERENCES, "&Preferences...");
         DrawMenuBar(hWnd);
```

```
            // Install the WH_JOURNALRECORD hook filter function.
            InstallJrnlHook(TRUE);
            break;

        case WM_DESTROY:
            // Remove the WH_JOURNALRECORD hook filter function.
            InstallJrnlHook(FALSE);

            PostQuitMessage(0);
            break;

        case WM_QUERYOPEN:
            // Do not allow the application to open; show only as icon.
            lResult = 0;
            break;

        case WM_SYSCOMMAND:
            switch (wParam & 0xfff0) {
                case IDM_PREFERENCES:
                    // Prompt user for idle time in minutes.
                    // The last parameter is the current settings of _wMinutes.
                    wIdleTime = DialogBoxParam(_hInstance, "Preferences",
                        hWnd, PrefProc, _wMinutes);

                    // If wIdleTime == -1, the user pressed "Cancel",
                    // else wIdleTime is the idle time.
                    if ((int) wIdleTime != -1) _wMinutes = wIdleTime;
                    break;

                default:
                    fCallDefProc = TRUE; break;
            }
            break;

    default:
        fCallDefProc = TRUE;
        break;
}
if (fCallDefProc)
    lResult = DefWindowProc(hWnd, uMsg, wParam, lParam);

return(lResult);
}
```

```
// ************************************************************************
#define GETRANDOM(Min, Max) ((rand() % (int)(((Max)+1) - (Min))) + (Min))

#define DEGTORAD(Deg) ((Deg * 3.14159) / 180)

LRESULT CALLBACK BlnkWndProc (HWND hWnd, UINT uMsg, WPARAM wParam,
   LPARAM lParam) {
   BOOL fCallDefProc = FALSE, fForceStop = FALSE;
   LRESULT lResult = 0;
   WORD wXCenter, wYCenter, wCircle, wRadius, wTheta, wInc;
   WORD wRed, wGreen, wBlue;
   RECT rc;
   HPEN hPen, hOldPen;
   HDC hDC;
   MSG msg;

   switch (uMsg) {
      case WM_TIMER:

         // If window is already visible, animate drawing.
         if (!IsWindowVisible(hWnd)) {

            // Every second, check if the idle time has elapsed.
            // Is system time minus the time of the last user event
            // greater than the number of minutes the user specified?
            if (GetTickCount() - GetLastEventTime() > _wMinutes * 60000ul) {
               ShowWindow(hWnd, SW_SHOW);
               ShowCursor(FALSE);
            }
            break;
         }

         // Animate the circle drawing in the blank window.
         GetWindowRect(hWnd, &rc);

         // Select random center point for circle.
         wXCenter = GETRANDOM(0, rc.right - 1);
         wYCenter = GETRANDOM(0, rc.bottom - 1);

         // Select random radius length for circle.
         wRadius = GETRANDOM(rc.right / 20, rc.right - 1);

         // Select random theta angle.
         wInc = GETRANDOM(1, 5);

         hDC = GetDC(hWnd);
         SetBkMode(hDC, TRANSPARENT);
```

407

```
// Draw circle twice:
//   First time: Circle is drawn in multicolors.
//   Second time: Circle is drawn in all black, effectively
//   removing it.
for (wCircle = 0; !fForceStop && wCircle < 2; wCircle++) {

    for (wTheta = 0; wTheta < 360; wTheta += wInc) {
        // Drawing takes a long time, so check if user becomes
        // active again by pressing a mouse button or key on the
        // keyboard.
        fForceStop =
            PeekMessage(&msg, hWnd, WM_KEYFIRST, WM_KEYLAST,
                PM_NOYIELD | PM_NOREMOVE) ||
            PeekMessage(&msg, hWnd, WM_LBUTTONDOWN, WM_MOUSELAST,
                PM_NOYIELD | PM_NOREMOVE);

        // If either type of event (mouse or keyboard) in queue,
        // stop drawing the circle prematurely.
        if (fForceStop) break;

        // Select a random color for the spoke of the circle.
        // Do not allow a spoke to be BLACK (RGB(0, 0, 0)).
        do {
            wRed   = GETRANDOM(0, 32);
            wGreen = GETRANDOM(0, 32);
            wBlue  = GETRANDOM(0, 32);
        } while (wRed == 0 && wGreen == 0 && wBlue == 0);

        // Create a pen using a cycling style and the random color.
        hPen = CreatePen((wTheta % 3), 1,
            RGB(wRed * 7, wGreen * 7, wBlue * 7));
        hOldPen = SelectObject(hDC, hPen);

        // Start at the center of the circle and draw the spoke.
        MoveTo(hDC, wXCenter, wYCenter);
        LineTo(hDC,
            (int) (wRadius * cos(DEGTORAD(wTheta))) + wXCenter,
            (int) (wRadius * sin(DEGTORAD(wTheta))) + wYCenter);

        // Restore original pen in hDC and delete the created pen.
        SelectObject(hDC, hOldPen);
        DeleteObject(hPen);
    }

    // For the second time the circle is drawn, set the ROP2 code
    // R2_BLACK. This causes all of the spokes to be painted black,
```

```
         // no matter what colors were used to create the pen.
         SetROP2(hDC, R2_BLACK);
      }
      ReleaseDC(hWnd, hDC);
      break;

   case WM_LBUTTONDOWN:
   case WM_MBUTTONDOWN:
   case WM_RBUTTONDOWN:
   case WM_KEYDOWN:
   case WM_SYSKEYDOWN:
      // If any of the above events occur, the user is active and you
      // must show the mouse cursor and hide yourself.
      ShowCursor(TRUE);
      ShowWindow(hWnd, SW_HIDE);
      break;

   default:
      fCallDefProc = TRUE; break;
   }

   if (fCallDefProc)
      lResult = DefWindowProc(hWnd, uMsg, wParam, lParam);

   return(lResult);
}

// ************************************************************************
// This function processes all messages sent to the Preferences dialog box.

BOOL CALLBACK PrefProc (HWND hDlg, UINT uMsg, WPARAM wParam, LPARAM lParam) {
   BOOL fProcessed = TRUE, fTranslated;
   WORD wMinutes;

   switch (uMsg) {

      case WM_INITDIALOG:
         // The lParam parameter contains the current settings of the
         // _wMinutes variable. This should be shown as the default value.
         SetDlgItemInt(hDlg, ID_MINUTES, (WORD) lParam, FALSE);
         break;

      case WM_COMMAND:
         switch (wParam) {
            case IDOK:
               if (HIWORD(lParam) != BN_CLICKED) break;
               wMinutes =
```

409

```
                    GetDlgItemInt(hDlg, ID_MINUTES, &fTranslated, FALSE);
                if (!fTranslated || wMinutes == 0) {
                  MessageBox(hDlg, "Invalid value for minutes.",
                     _szAppName, MB_OK); break;
                }
                // Return the new value that the user entered.
                EndDialog(hDlg, wMinutes);
                break;

            case IDCANCEL:
                if (HIWORD(lParam) != BN_CLICKED) break;
                // Return -1, indicating that the user pressed "Cancel".
                EndDialog(hDlg, -1);
                break;
            default:
                break;
          }
          break;

      default:
          fProcessed = FALSE; break;
    }
    return(fProcessed);
}
```

Listing 7-2. SCRNBLNK.H application header module

```
/***************************************************************************
Module name: SCRNBLNK.H
Programmer : Jeffrey M. Richter.
***************************************************************************/

#define ID_MINUTES    100

// Functions imported from SBDLL.DLL.
void CALLBACK InstallJrnlHook (BOOL fInstall);
DWORD WINAPI GetLastEventTime (void);
```

Listing 7-3. SCRNBLNK.DEF ScrnBlnk application definitions file

```
; Module name: SCRNBLNK.DEF
; Programmer : Jeffrey M. Richter.

NAME        SCRNBLNK
DESCRIPTION 'ScrnBlnk: Windows Screen Blanking Application'
STUB        'WinStub.exe'
EXETYPE     WINDOWS
CODE        MOVEABLE DISCARDABLE PRELOAD
DATA        MOVEABLE MULTIPLE PRELOAD
HEAPSIZE    1024
STACKSIZE   5120
```

Listing 7-4. SCRNBLNK.RC application resource file

```
/*****************************************************************************
Module name: SCRNBLNK.RC
Programmer : Jeffrey M. Richter.
*****************************************************************************/

#include <windows.h>
#include "ScrnBlnk.h"

ScrnBlnk ICON MOVEABLE DISCARDABLE ScrnBlnk.Ico

PREFERENCES DIALOG LOADONCALL MOVEABLE DISCARDABLE 7, 20, 88, 36
CAPTION "Preferences"
STYLE WS_BORDER | WS_CAPTION | WS_DLGFRAME | WS_SYSMENU | WS_VISIBLE |
WS_POPUP
BEGIN
    CONTROL "&Minutes til blank:", -1, "static", SS_LEFT | WS_CHILD, 4, 4,
60, 12
    CONTROL "", ID_MINUTES, "edit", ES_LEFT | WS_BORDER | WS_TABSTOP |
WS_CHILD, 64, 4, 20, 12
    CONTROL "&Ok", IDOK, "button", BS_DEFPUSHBUTTON | WS_TABSTOP |
WS_CHILD, 8, 20, 32, 12
    CONTROL "&Cancel", IDCANCEL, "button", BS_PUSHBUTTON | WS_TABSTOP |
WS_CHILD, 48, 20, 32, 12
END
```

411

Listing 7-5. MAKEFILE for screen-blanking application

```
#*******************************************************************
#Module name: MAKEFILE
#Programmer : Jeffrey M. Richter.
#*******************************************************************

!include "..\builtins.jmr"

PROG = ScrnBlnk

MODEL = s
CFLAGS = -P-c -c -f -WS -p -v -w -m$(MODEL) -I$(INCLUDEDIR)
LFLAGS = /P/v/n/m/s/L$(LIBDIR)
LIBS = CW$(MODEL) MathW$(MODEL) Import SBDLL

MODULES = $(PROG).obj

ICONS   = $(PROG).ico
BITMAPS =
CURSORS =

$(PROG).Exe: $(MODULES) $(PROG).Def $(PROG).Res
    tlink $(LFLAGS) @&&!
COW$(MODEL) $(MODULES)
$(PROG), $(PROG), $(LIBS), $(PROG)
!
   rc -31 -T $(PROG).Res
   TDStrip -s $(PROG)

$(PROG).res:   $(PROG).rc $(PROG).h $(RESOURCES)
```

Listing 7-6. SBDLL.C DLL source module

```
/*******************************************************************
Module name: SBDLL.C
Programmer : Jeffrey M. Richter.
*******************************************************************/

#include <windows.h>

extern const HINSTANCE _cdecl _hInstance;

static HHOOK _hHook = NULL;
```

```
static DWORD _dwLastEventTime = 0;

LRESULT CALLBACK JrnlRcrdHookFunc (int nCode, WPARAM wParam,
   LPARAM lParam);

#pragma argsused
BOOL WINAPI LibMain (HINSTANCE hInstance, WORD wDataSeg, WORD cbHeapSize,
   LPSTR lpCmdLine) {
   if (cbHeapSize != 0) UnlockData(0); // Let data segment move.
   return(TRUE);  // Return TRUE if initialization is successful.
}

int WINAPI WEP (int nSystemExit) {
   switch (nSystemExit) {
      case WEP_SYSTEM_EXIT:   // System is shutting down.
         break;
      case WEP_FREE_DLL:      // Usage count is zero (0).
         break;
   }
   return(1);                 // WEP function successful.
}

void WINAPI InstallJrnlHook (BOOL fInstall) {
   if (fInstall) {
      _hHook = SetWindowsHookEx(WH_JOURNALRECORD,
         (HOOKPROC) JrnlRcrdHookFunc, _hInstance, NULL);
      _dwLastEventTime = GetTickCount();
   } else {
      UnhookWindowsHookEx(_hHook);
      _hHook = NULL;
      _dwLastEventTime = 0;
   }
}

DWORD WINAPI GetLastEventTime (void) {
   return(_dwLastEventTime);
}

LRESULT CALLBACK JrnlRcrdHookFunc (int nCode, WPARAM wParam, LPARAM lParam)
{
   switch (nCode) {

      case HC_ACTION:
         _dwLastEventTime = ((LPEVENTMSG) lParam)->time;
         break;

      case HC_SYSMODALON:
```

```
        case HC_SYSMODALOFF:
           break;

        default:
           break;
    }

    return(CallNextHookEx(_hHook, nCode, wParam, lParam));
}
```

Listing 7-7. SBDLL.DEF DLL definitions file

```
; Module name: SBDLL.DEF
; Programmer : Jeffrey M. Richter.

LIBRARY      SBDLL
DESCRIPTION  'Screen Blanker Dynamic-link library'
EXETYPE      WINDOWS
STUB         'WinStub.Exe'
CODE         NONDISCARDABLE FIXED PRELOAD
DATA         MOVEABLE PRELOAD SINGLE
HEAPSIZE     1024
EXPORTS
    WEP                 @1      RESIDENTNAME
    JrnlRcrdHookFunc
    InstallJrnlHook
    GetLastEventTime
```

Listing 7-8. SBDLL.RC DLL resource file

```
// No resources.
```

Listing 7-9. SBDLL.MKF (MAKEFILE for screen-blanking DLL)

```
#******************************************************************
#Module name: SBDLL.MKF
#Programmer : Jeffrey M. Richter.
#******************************************************************

!include "..\builtins.jmr"

PROG = SBDLL

MODEL = s
CFLAGS = -P-c -c -f- -WD -p -v -w -m$(MODEL)! -I$(INCLUDEDIR)
LFLAGS = /P/v/n/m/s/L$(LIBDIR)
!if $(MODEL) == m
LIBS = CWL
```

```
!else
LIBS = CWS
!endif

LIBS = $(LIBS) Import

MODULES = $(PROG).obj

ICONS   =
BITMAPS =
CURSORS =

$(PROG).DLL: $(MODULES) $(PROG).Def $(PROG).Res
    tlink $(LFLAGS) @&&!
COD$(MODEL) $(MODULES)
$(PROG).DLL, $(PROG), $(LIBS), $(PROG)
!
   rc -31 -T -Fe$(PROG).DLL $(PROG).Res
   TDStrip -s $(PROG).DLL
   implib $(PROG).LIB $(PROG).DEF

$(PROG).res: $(PROG).rc $(RESOURCES)
```

The Echo Application (a Macro Recorder)

The Echo sample application discussed here shows how to implement an input event recorder using the *WH_JOURNALRECORD* and *WH_JOURNALPLAYBACK* hooks. The user starts recording events by choosing the "Record" option from the application's Macro menu. At this point, every mouse movement and keystroke is recorded until the user selects the "Stop" option. When the user has stopped the recorder, the "Playback" option will repeat the recorded events.

This application also shows how the F1 key can be intercepted so that help information can be displayed using a *WH_KEYBOARD* hook. When the user presses the F1 key while Echo is the active application, Echo calls the Windows' help engine.

Recording and Playing Events

All the procedures for recording and playing back events can be found in the RECORD.C file. This module consists of three functions: *Recorder*, *JrnlRecHookFunc*, and *JrnlPlybkHookFunc*. The Recorder function is the controlling function for all the recorder's operations. The following table shows the values that may be passed to the Recorder:

Record mode	wParam	lParam	Return value
RM_STARTRECORD	Not used.	The low-order word contains the window handle that will be notified when the recording stops. The high-order word contains the message sent to this window.	REC_ACTIVE if the recorder is currently recording or playing. REC_NOMEMORY if insufficient memory exists to begin recording. REC_OK if recording started successfully.
RM_STOPRECORD	Not used.	Not used.	REC_INACTIVE if the recorder was not recording. REC_OK if recording stopped successfully.
RM_STARTPLAY	Global memory handle containing recorded events.	The low-order word contains the window handle that will be notified when the playback stops. The high-order word contains the message sent to this window.	REC_ACTIVE if recorder is currently recording or playing. REC_NOEVENTS if there are no events in the memory block. REC_OK if playback started successfully.
RM_STOPPLAY	Not used.	Not used.	REC_INACTIVE if recording is not currently playing. REC_OK if playback stopped successfully.

Notice that the *RM_STARTRECORD* and *RM_STARTPLAY* modes expect a window handle and a message number passed in as the *lParam* parameter. The Recorder saves this information in static variables. When the Recorder stops saving or playing events, it sends the specified message to the specified window to notify it that it has stopped. The *wParam* parameter of the message will then contain the global memory handle containing the recorded events. The *lParam* parameter contains either *REC_OK*, *REC_TOOMANY* or *REC_SYSMODALON*.

The table below shows the four ways journal recording can be stopped and the value that will be sent to the specified window in the *lParam* parameter:

Method of stopping the Recorder while recording	Value in *lParam* parameter
When the user chooses the "Stop" option from the Macro menu in the application.	REC_OK
When the *HC_ACTION* hook code is sent to the *JrnlRecHookFunc* function, the *GlobalReAlloc* function is called to increase the size of the memory block. If there is insufficient memory, the Recorder is stopped.	REC_NOMEMORY
When the *HC_ACTION* hook code is sent to the *JrnlRecHookFunc* function, a check is made to see if more than 65,535 events have been placed in the memory block. If so, the Recorder is stopped.	REC_TOOMANY
When the *HC_SYSMODALOFF* hook code is sent to the *JrnlRecHookFunc* function, the Recorder is stopped.	REC_SYSMODALON

If the *JrnlRecHookFunc* function receives the *HC_SYSMODALON* hook code, it sets a static variable, *fPause,* to TRUE. When this variable is TRUE, the *JrnlRecHookFunc* function ignores all *HC_ACTION* hook codes. Once the system modal dialog box is removed, an *HC_SYSMODALOFF* hook code is sent to the filter function. This stops the Recorder and sends the *REC_SYSMODALON* identifier to the window handle specified when recording started.

To notify the user that Echo has stopped recording events, a message box is displayed. However, the appearance of a system modal dialog box usually means that something critical has happened to the Windows system. Echo should not display its message box until the user has dealt with the system modal dialog box. This is why the Recorder notifies the application that it has stopped recording after the system modal dialog box has been destroyed. This same approach is used when a system modal dialog box appears during playback.

When the Recorder stops playing, it sends the specified message to the specified window to notify the window that the recorder has stopped. If the Recorder has stopped playing, the *wParam* parameter of the message will contain zero. The *lParam* parameter contains either *REC_OK* or *REC_SYSMODALON*. The table below shows the two methods used to stop playing back the events and the value that will be sent to the specified window in the *lParam* parameter:

Method of stopping the Recorder during playback	Value in *lParam* parameter
When the *HC_SKIP* hook code is sent to the *JrnlPlybkHookFunc* function and all the events in the memory block have been played, the player is stopped.	REC_OK
When the *HC_SYSMODALOFF* hook code is sent to the *JrnlPlybkHookFunc* function, the player is stopped.	REC_SYSMODALON

The user-defined message that Echo passes to the Recorder function is *USER_RECORDER*. Echo monitors this message so it can set the static *fRecording* and *fPlaying* flags that are used to determine which menu items should be disabled in the Macro menu. The processing for this message is also used to display message boxes telling the user why recording or playing has been halted.

Requesting Help

Aside from recording and playing back input events, the Echo application also shows how to detect when the user has pressed a key, regardless of where the user is in the application. After this specific key has been detected, the Windows *WinHelp* function can be called to display help information to the user.

In the Echo application, keystrokes are intercepted by installing a *WH_KEYBOARD* hook just before Echo's message loop is started:

```
_hHookKybd = SetWindowsHookEx(WH_KEYBOARD,
    (HOOKPROC) KybdHookFunc, hInstance, GetCurrentTask());
while (GetMessage(&msg, NULL, 0, 0)) {
    TranslateMessage(&msg);
    DispatchMessage(&msg);
}
UnhookWindowsHookEx(_hHookKybd);
```

This code installs the *WH_KEYBOARD* hook as a task-specific hook by passing the return value from *GetCurrentTask* as the last parameter to *SetWindowsHookEx* above. Because the hook is task-specific, the code to process it (in the *KybdHookFunc* function) is contained in the application code itself rather than in a dynamic-link library. The hook handle that *SetWindowsHookEx* returns is saved in a global variable, *_hHookKybd*, so that it can be accessed from the *KybdHookFunc* function. When the application is terminated the *WH_KEYBOARD* hook is removed by calling *UnhookWindowsHookEx* and passing the handle of the hook to be removed.

The code that processes any and all keystrokes for the application is shown as follows.

```
LRESULT CALLBACK KybdHookFunc (int nCode, WPARAM wParam,
   LPARAM lParam) {
   BOOL fCallNextHookProc = TRUE;
   LRESULT lResult = 0;

   switch (nCode) {

      case HC_ACTION:
         if ((wParam != VK_F1) || (lParam & 0x80000000L))
            break;

         WinHelp(_hWndApp, NULL, HELP_HELPONHELP, NULL);
         fCallNextHookProc = FALSE;  // Don't call remaining filter
                                     // functions.
         lResult = 1;                // Don't send the keystroke onto
                                     // the focus window.
         break;

      case HC_NOREMOVE:
         break;

      default:
         break;
   }

   if (fCallNextHookProc)
      lResult = CallNextHookEx(_hHookKybd, nCode, wParam, lParam);

   return(lResult);
}
```

When a keystroke is removed from the queue, Windows calls *KybdHookFunc* and passes it a value of *HC_ACTION* in the *nCode* parameter. First check to see if the key pressed is not the F1 key (*wParam != VK_F1*) or if the user is releasing a key rather than pressing one (*lParam & 0x80000000L*). Remember that Windows sends the virtual key code of the key pressed in *wParam* and a set of flags about the keystroke event in the *lParam*. Bit 31 in the *lParam* indicates whether the key was depressed or released. If the bit is on, the key was released.

In the case where the user has pressed the F1 key, the call to *WinHelp* causes Windows to invoke the Windows help engine. We then set *fCallNextHookProc* to FALSE. This is our flag to tell us not to call *CallNextHookEx*, allowing other *WH_KEYBOARD* filter functions to process the event. We also tell *KybdHook-Func* to return one. When Windows sees that the filter function has returned one, it will not pass the *WM_KEYDOWN* message onto the window that currently has focus.

Because this is only a simulation no useful help is displayed, only the help information on how to use help is displayed. The Windows' help engine identifies the application requesting help by the window handle that is passed to the *WinHelp* function as the first parameter. The first parameter to *WinHelp* is, therefore, the handle to the application's main window. When the Echo application terminates, the processing for the *WM_DESTROY* message calls the *WinHelp* function again:

```
case WM_DESTROY:
    WinHelp(hWnd, NULL, HELP_QUIT, NULL);
```

The first parameter to this call to *WinHelp* is the window handle that was used in the filter function. All applications that use the Windows help engine should call *WinHelp* when they terminate and pass it the *HELP_QUIT* identifier. This informs the help engine that the application will no longer require help and instructs it to terminate itself, along with the application.

Figure 7-3. ECHO.ICO

Listing 7-10. ECHO.C application source module

```
/***************************************************************************
Module name: ECHO.C
Programmer : Jeffrey M. Richter.
***************************************************************************/

#include <windows.h>

#include "Echo.h"
#include "Record.h"


//*************************************************************************
char _szAppName[] = "Echo";

extern const HINSTANCE _cdecl _hInstance;
static HWND  _hWndApp = NULL;       // Main application's window handle.
static HHOOK _hHookKybd = NULL;

LRESULT CALLBACK AppWndProc (HWND hWnd, UINT uMsg, WPARAM wParam,
   LPARAM lParam);
LRESULT CALLBACK KybdHookFunc (int nCode, WPARAM wParam, LPARAM lParam);

#pragma argsused
int WinMain (HINSTANCE hInstance, HINSTANCE hPrevInstance,
   LPSTR lpszCmdLine, int nCmdShow) {
   WNDCLASS WndClass;
   MSG msg;
```

```
    WndClass.style          = 0;
    WndClass.lpfnWndProc    = AppWndProc;
    WndClass.cbClsExtra     = 0;
    WndClass.cbWndExtra     = 0;
    WndClass.hInstance      = hInstance;
    WndClass.hIcon          = LoadIcon(hInstance, _szAppName);
    WndClass.hCursor        = LoadCursor(NULL, IDC_ARROW);
    WndClass.hbrBackground  = COLOR_WINDOW + 1;
    WndClass.lpszMenuName   = _szAppName;
    WndClass.lpszClassName  = _szAppName;
    RegisterClass(&WndClass);

    // Create application window; store in global variable.
    _hWndApp = CreateWindow(_szAppName, _szAppName, WS_OVERLAPPEDWINDOW,
        CW_USEDEFAULT, SW_SHOW, CW_USEDEFAULT, CW_USEDEFAULT,
        NULL, NULL, hInstance, 0);

    if (_hWndApp == NULL) return(0);
    ShowWindow(_hWndApp, nCmdShow);
    UpdateWindow(_hWndApp);

    _hHookKybd = SetWindowsHookEx(WH_KEYBOARD,
        (HOOKPROC) KybdHookFunc, hInstance, GetCurrentTask());
    while (GetMessage(&msg, NULL, 0, 0)) {
        TranslateMessage(&msg);
        DispatchMessage(&msg);
    }
    UnhookWindowsHookEx(_hHookKybd);
    return(0);
}

// Window defined message sent by the Recorder function in the RECORD.C
// DLL when recording or playing of events is stopped.
#define USER_RECORDER    (WM_USER + 0)

LRESULT CALLBACK AppWndProc (HWND hWnd, UINT uMsg, WPARAM wParam,
    LPARAM lParam) {
    static BOOL fRecording = FALSE, fPlaying = FALSE;
    static HGLOBAL hGlblMacro;  // Global handle containing recorded events.
    BOOL fCallDefProc = FALSE;
    LRESULT lResult = 0;
    RECRESULT RecResult = REC_OK;
    char *szRecMsg = NULL;

    switch (uMsg) {
```

```
case WM_DESTROY:
    // Close the Windows' help engine.
    WinHelp(hWnd, NULL, HELP_QUIT, NULL);
    PostQuitMessage(0);
    break;

case USER_RECORDER:
    // Message sent when recording or playing is stopped.
    if (wParam == 0) {    // Playing stopped.
        fPlaying = FALSE;
        if ((RECRESULT) lParam == REC_SYSMODALON)
            MessageBox(hWnd, "System Modal Dialog Box - Playing Halted",
                _szAppName, MB_SYSTEMMODAL | MB_ICONHAND | MB_OK);
        break;
    }

    // Recording stopped.
    // wParam = HGLOBAL of block, lParam = RECRESULT.
    fRecording = FALSE;
    hGlblMacro = wParam;

    if ((RECRESULT) lParam == REC_TOOMANY)
        MessageBox(NULL, "Out of memory", _szAppName,
            MB_SYSTEMMODAL | MB_ICONHAND | MB_OK);

    if ((RECRESULT) lParam == REC_SYSMODALON)
        MessageBox(hWnd, "System Modal Dialog Box - Recording Halted",
            _szAppName, MB_SYSTEMMODAL | MB_ICONHAND | MB_OK);
    break;

case WM_INITMENU:
    // User is working with the menu, enable/disable options.
    EnableMenuItem(GetMenu(hWnd), IDM_STARTRECORD,
        MF_BYCOMMAND |
        ((fRecording || fPlaying) ? MF_GRAYED : MF_ENABLED));
    EnableMenuItem(GetMenu(hWnd), IDM_STOPRECORD,
        MF_BYCOMMAND | (fRecording ? MF_ENABLED : MF_GRAYED));
    EnableMenuItem(GetMenu(hWnd), IDM_STARTPLAYBACK,
        MF_BYCOMMAND |
        ((fRecording || fPlaying || hGlblMacro == NULL)
        ? MF_GRAYED : MF_ENABLED));
    break;

case WM_COMMAND:
    switch (wParam) {
```

```
case IDM_EXIT:
   SendMessage(hWnd, WM_CLOSE, 0, 0);
   break;

case IDM_STARTRECORD:
   // If a macro was already recorded, free it.
   if (hGlblMacro != NULL) GlobalFree(hGlblMacro);

   fRecording = TRUE;

   // Last parameter is handle to this window and message that
   // should be sent when recording is stopped.
   RecResult = Recorder(RM_STARTRECORD, 0,
      MAKELONG(hWnd, USER_RECORDER));
   break;

case IDM_STOPRECORD:
   RecResult = Recorder(RM_STOPRECORD, 0, 0);
   break;

case IDM_STARTPLAYBACK:
   fPlaying = TRUE;

   // Last parameter is handle to this window and message that
   // should be sent when playing is stopped.
   RecResult = Recorder(RM_STARTPLAY, hGlblMacro,
      MAKELONG(hWnd, USER_RECORDER));
   break;

default:
   break;
}

// Inform user if an error occurred with the recorder.
switch (RecResult) {
   case REC_ACTIVE:
      szRecMsg = "Recorder already recording/playing.";
      break;

   case REC_INACTIVE:
      szRecMsg = "Recorder already stopped.";
      break;

   case REC_NOMEMORY:
      szRecMsg = "Insufficient memory to start recording.";
      break;
```

```
            case REC_NOEVENTS:
                szRecMsg = "No events to playback.";
                break;
        }

        if (szRecMsg != NULL)
            MessageBox(hWnd, szRecMsg, _szAppName,
                MB_OK | MB_ICONINFORMATION);

        break;

    default:
        fCallDefProc = TRUE; break;
    }

    if (fCallDefProc)
        lResult = DefWindowProc(hWnd, uMsg, wParam, lParam);

    return(lResult);
}

// **************************************************************************
LRESULT CALLBACK KybdHookFunc (int nCode, WPARAM wParam, LPARAM lParam) {
    BOOL fCallNextHookProc = TRUE;
    LRESULT lResult = 0;

    switch (nCode) {

        case HC_ACTION:
            if ((wParam != VK_F1) || (lParam & 0x80000000L))
                break;

            WinHelp(_hWndApp, NULL, HELP_HELPONHELP, NULL);
            fCallNextHookProc = FALSE;
            lResult = 1;  // Don't send the keystroke on.
            break;

        case HC_NOREMOVE:
            break;

        default:
            break;
    }

    if (fCallNextHookProc)
        lResult = CallNextHookEx(_hHookKybd, nCode, wParam, lParam);
```

```
    return(lResult);
}
```

Listing 7-11. ECHO.H application header module

```
/*************************************************************************
Module name: ECHO.H
Programmer : Jeffrey M. Richter.
*************************************************************************/

#define IDM_EXIT          100
#define IDM_STARTRECORD   101
#define IDM_STOPRECORD    102
#define IDM_STARTPLAYBACK 103
```

Listing 7-12. ECHO.DEF application definitions file

```
; Module name: ECHO.DEF
; Programmer : Jeffrey M. Richter.

NAME        ECHO
DESCRIPTION 'Echo: Windows Recorder Application'
STUB        'WinStub.exe'
EXETYPE     WINDOWS
CODE        MOVEABLE DISCARDABLE PRELOAD
DATA        MOVEABLE MULTIPLE PRELOAD
HEAPSIZE    1024
STACKSIZE   5120
```

Listing 7-13. ECHO.RC application resource file

```
/*************************************************************************
Module name: ECHO.RC
Programmer : Jeffrey M. Richter.
*************************************************************************/

#include <windows.h>
#include "echo.h"

Echo ICON MOVEABLE DISCARDABLE Echo.Ico

Echo MENU
BEGIN
   POPUP "&File"
```

```
   BEGIN
      MENUITEM "E&xit",        IDM_EXIT
   END

   POPUP "&Macro"
   BEGIN
      MENUITEM "&Record",     IDM_STARTRECORD
      MENUITEM "&Stop",       IDM_STOPRECORD
      MENUITEM "&Playback",   IDM_STARTPLAYBACK
   END
END
```

Listing 7-14. MAKEFILE for Echo application

```
#*****************************************************************************
#Module name   : MAKEFILE
#Programmer    : Jeffrey M. Richter.
#*****************************************************************************

!include "..\builtins.jmr"

PROG = Echo

MODEL = s
CFLAGS = -P-c -c -f- -WS -p -v -w -m$(MODEL) -I$(INCLUDEDIR)
LFLAGS = /P/v/n/m/s/L$(LIBDIR)
LIBS = CW$(MODEL) Import Record

MODULES = $(PROG).obj

ICONS   = $(PROG).ico
BITMAPS =
CURSORS =

$(PROG).Exe: $(MODULES) $(PROG).Def $(PROG).Res
     tlink $(LFLAGS) @&&!
COW$(MODEL) $(MODULES)
$(PROG), $(PROG), $(LIBS), $(PROG)
!
     rc -31 -T $(PROG).Res
     TDStrip -s $(PROG)

$(PROG).res: $(PROG).rc $(PROG).h $(RESOURCES)
```

Listing 7-15. RECORD.C DLL source module

```c
/*********************************************************************
Module name: RECORD.C
Programmer : Jeffrey M. Richter.
*********************************************************************/

#include <windows.h>
#include "Record.h"

extern const HINSTANCE _cdecl _hInstance;

//*******************************************************************
static HHOOK      _hHookJrnl = NULL;
static HGLOBAL    _hGlblEvents = NULL;
static RECRESULT _PrematureHalt = REC_OK;

LRESULT CALLBACK JrnlRecHookFunc (int nCode, WPARAM wParam,
   LPARAM lParam);
LRESULT CALLBACK JrnlPlybkHookFunc (int nCode, WPARAM wParam,
   LPARAM lParam);

// Statistical information that appears at start of memory block.
typedef struct {
   WORD wNumEvents, wNumEventsPlayed; DWORD dwStartTime;
} RECORDSTAT, FAR *LPRECORDSTAT;

#pragma argsused
BOOL WINAPI LibMain (HINSTANCE hInstance, WORD wDataSeg,
   WORD cbHeapSize, LPSTR lpCmdLine) {
   if (cbHeapSize != 0) UnlockData(0); // Let data segment move.
   return(TRUE);  // Return TRUE if initialization is successful.
}

int WINAPI WEP (int nSystemExit) {
   switch (nSystemExit) {
      case WEP_SYSTEM_EXIT:   // System is shutting down.
         break;
      case WEP_FREE_DLL:      // Usage count is zero (0).
         break;
   }
   return(1);                 // WEP function successful.
}

RECRESULT WINAPI Recorder (RECORDMODE RecordMode, WPARAM wParam,
   LPARAM lParam) {
```

```
static HWND hWndNotify = NULL;
static UINT uMsgNotify = WM_NULL;
static RECORDMODE LastRecordMode = -1;
RECRESULT RecResult = REC_OK;
WORD wNumEvents;
LPRECORDSTAT lpRecordStat;
LPEVENTMSG lpEvent;

switch (RecordMode) {

    case RM_STARTRECORD:
        // wParam: Not used.
        // LOWORD(lParam): hWnd to end stop msg to.
        // HIWORD(lParam): Message to send to hWnd.
        // Returns: REC_ACTIVE, REC_NOMEMORY, REC_OK.

        if (_hGlblEvents) { RecResult = REC_ACTIVE; break; }

        // Save information so it can be used by RM_STOPRECORD.
        hWndNotify = (HWND) LOWORD(lParam);
        uMsgNotify = (UINT) HIWORD(lParam);

        // Assume the recording will be stopped by the user.
        _PrematureHalt = REC_OK;

        // Allocate memory block to hold the statistical data.
        _hGlblEvents =
            GlobalAlloc(GMEM_MOVEABLE, sizeof(RECORDSTAT));
        if (_hGlblEvents == NULL) {
            RecResult = REC_NOMEMORY;
            break;
        }

        // Initialize the statistical data.
        lpRecordStat = (LPRECORDSTAT) GlobalLock(_hGlblEvents);
        lpRecordStat->wNumEvents =
            lpRecordStat->wNumEventsPlayed = 0;
        GlobalUnlock(_hGlblEvents);

        // Turn on the event recording.
         hHookJrnl = SetWindowsHookEx(WH_JOURNALRECORD,
            (HOOKPROC) JrnlRecHookFunc, _hInstance, NULL);

        RecResult = REC_OK;
        break;

    case RM_STOPRECORD:
```

```
                // wParam: Not used.
                // lParam: Not used.
                // Returns: REC_INACTIVE, REC_OK.

                if (_hGlblEvents == NULL) {
                   RecResult = REC_INACTIVE;
                   break;
                }

                if (LastRecordMode == RM_STARTPLAY) { break; }

                // Stop the recording of events.
                UnhookWindowsHookEx(_hHookJrnl);
                _hHookJrnl = NULL;

                // Modify all the 'time' members in the EVENTMSG structs.
                lpRecordStat = (LPRECORDSTAT) GlobalLock(_hGlblEvents);
                lpEvent = (LPEVENTMSG) &lpRecordStat[1];
                wNumEvents = lpRecordStat->wNumEvents;
                while (wNumEvents > 1)
                   lpEvent[-wNumEvents].time -= lpEvent[0].time;

                lpEvent[0].time = 0;
                GlobalUnlock(_hGlblEvents);
                RecResult = REC_OK;

                // Send message to specified window to notify it
                // that recording has stopped.
                SendMessage(hWndNotify, uMsgNotify, _hGlblEvents,
                   _PrematureHalt);

                _hGlblEvents = NULL;
                break;

         case RM_STARTPLAY:
                // wParam: HGLOBAL to macro.
                // lParam: LOWORD(lParam) = hWnd to end stop msg to.
                // lParam: HIWORD(lParam) = Message to send to hWnd.
                // Returns: REC_ACTIVE, REC_OK, REC_NOEVENTS.

                if (_hGlblEvents != NULL) {
                   RecResult = REC_ACTIVE;
                   break;
                }

                // Save information so it can be used by RM_STOPRECORD.
                hWndNotify = (HWND) LOWORD(lParam);
```

```
            uMsgNotify = (UINT) HIWORD(lParam);

            // Assume the playing will be stopped after all
            // events have been played.
            _PrematureHalt = REC_OK;

            _hGlblEvents = (HGLOBAL) wParam;

            // Initialize statistical data.
            lpRecordStat = (LPRECORDSTAT) GlobalLock(_hGlblEvents);
            wNumEvents = lpRecordStat->wNumEvents;
            lpRecordStat->wNumEventsPlayed = 0;

            // Save the time when playback is started.
            lpRecordStat->dwStartTime = GetTickCount();

            GlobalUnlock(_hGlblEvents);
            if (wNumEvents == 0) {
                RecResult = REC_NOEVENTS;
                break;
            }

            _hHookJrnl = SetWindowsHookEx(WH_JOURNALPLAYBACK,
                (HOOKPROC) JrnlPlybkHookFunc, _hInstance, NULL);

            break;

        case RM_STOPPLAY:
            // Stop playing the recorded events.
            UnhookWindowsHookEx(_hHookJrnl);
            _hHookJrnl = NULL;
            _hGlblEvents = NULL;
            RecResult = REC_OK;

            // Send message to specified window to notify it
            // that playing has stopped.
            SendMessage(hWndNotify, uMsgNotify, 0, _PrematureHalt);
            break;
    }

    LastRecordMode = RecordMode;
    return(RecResult);
}

LRESULT CALLBACK JrnlRecHookFunc (int nCode, WPARAM wParam,
    LPARAM lParam) {
    static BOOL fPause = FALSE;
```

431

```
LPRECORDSTAT lpRecordStat;
LPEVENTMSG lpEvent;
BOOL fCallNextHookProc = FALSE;
LRESULT lResult = 0;
WORD wNumEvents;
HGLOBAL hMemTemp;

switch (nCode) {

   case HC_ACTION:
      fCallNextHookProc = TRUE;

      // If system modal dialog box is up, don't record event.
      if (fPause) break;

      // Determine number of events in the memory block now.
      lpRecordStat = (LPRECORDSTAT) GlobalLock(_hGlblEvents);
      wNumEvents = lpRecordStat->wNumEvents + 1;
      GlobalUnlock(_hGlblEvents);
      if (wNumEvents == 0xffff) {
         // Too many events recorded, stop recording.
         _PrematureHalt = REC_TOOMANY;
         Recorder(RM_STOPRECORD, 0, 0);
         break;
      }

      // Increase size of the memory block to hold new event.
      hMemTemp = GlobalReAlloc(_hGlblEvents,
         sizeof(RECORDSTAT) + wNumEvents * sizeof(EVENTMSG),
         GMEM_MOVEABLE);
      if (hMemTemp == NULL) {
         // Insufficient memory, stop recording.
         _PrematureHalt = REC_NOMEMORY;
         Recorder(RM_STOPRECORD, 0, 0);
         break;
      }

      _hGlblEvents = hMemTemp;

      // Append the new event to the end of the memory block.
      lpRecordStat = (LPRECORDSTAT) GlobalLock(_hGlblEvents);
      lpEvent = (LPEVENTMSG) &lpRecordStat[1];
      lpEvent[lpRecordStat->wNumEvents] =
         *((LPEVENTMSG) lParam);
      lpRecordStat->wNumEvents++;
      GlobalUnlock(_hGlblEvents);
      break;
```

```
    case HC_SYSMODALON:
        // Stop recording while system modal dialog box is up.
        fPause = TRUE;
        fCallNextHookProc = TRUE;
        break;

    case HC_SYSMODALOFF:
        // The system modal dialog box is gone; stop recording
        // and notify the user that recording has stopped.
        fPause = FALSE;
        _PrematureHalt = REC_SYSMODALON;
        Recorder(RM_STOPRECORD, 0, 0);
        break;

    default:
        fCallNextHookProc = TRUE;
        break;
    }

    if (fCallNextHookProc)
        lResult = CallNextHookEx(_hHookJrnl, nCode, wParam, lParam);

    return(lResult);
}

LRESULT CALLBACK JrnlPlybkHookFunc (int nCode, WPARAM wParam,
    LPARAM lParam) {
    BOOL fCallNextHookProc = FALSE;
    LRESULT lResult = 0;
    LPRECORDSTAT lpRecordStat;
    LPEVENTMSG lpEvent;

    lpRecordStat = (LPRECORDSTAT) GlobalLock(_hGlblEvents);
    switch (nCode) {

        case HC_SKIP:
            // Prepare to return the next event the next time the
            // hook code is HC_GETNEXT. If all events have been
            // played, stop playing.
            if (++lpRecordStat->wNumEventsPlayed ==
                lpRecordStat->wNumEvents)
                Recorder(RM_STOPPLAY, 0, 0);
            break;
```

```
      case HC_GETNEXT:
          // Copy the current event to the EVENTMSG
          // structure pointed to by lParam.
          lpEvent = (LPEVENTMSG) &lpRecordStat[1];
          *((LPEVENTMSG) lParam) =
              lpEvent[lpRecordStat->wNumEventsPlayed];

          // Adjust 'time' by adding time that playback started.
          ((LPEVENTMSG) lParam)->time += lpRecordStat->dwStartTime;

          // Return the number of milliseconds Windows should wait
          // before processing the event.
          lResult = ((LPEVENTMSG) lParam)->time - GetTickCount();

          // If the event occurred in the past, have Windows
          // process it now.
          if (lResult < 0) lResult = 0;
          break;

      case HC_SYSMODALOFF:
          // When the system modal dialog box is removed, stop
          // playing the events and notify the application.
          _PrematureHalt = REC_SYSMODALON;
          Recorder(RM_STOPPLAY, 0, 0);
          fCallNextHookProc = TRUE;
          break;

      case HC_SYSMODALON:
      default:
          fCallNextHookProc = TRUE;
          break;

  }
  GlobalUnlock(_hGlblEvents);

  if (fCallNextHookProc)
      lResult = CallNextHookEx(_hHookJrnl, nCode, wParam, lParam);

  return(lResult);
}
```

Listing 7-16. RECORD.RC DLL resource file

```
// No resources
```

Listing 7-17. RECORD.H DLL header module

```
/*****************************************************************************
Module name: RECORD.H
Programmer : Jeffrey M. Richter.
*****************************************************************************/

typedef enum {
    REC_OK,          // Operation was successful.
    REC_ACTIVE,      // Attempt to start recording while already recording.
                     // Attempt to start play while already playing.
    REC_INACTIVE,    // Attempt to stop recording while NOT recording.
    REC_NOMEMORY,    // When attempting to start recording or during recording,
    REC_NOEVENTS,    // attempt playback with no events in memory block.
    REC_TOOMANY,     // Attempt to record more than 65535 events.
    REC_SYSMODALON,  // Recording/playing halted because a system modal
                     // dialog box appeared.
} RECRESULT;

typedef enum {
    RM_STARTRECORD, RM_STOPRECORD, RM_STARTPLAY, RM_STOPPLAY
} RECORDMODE;

RECRESULT WINAPI Recorder (RECORDMODE RecordMode, WPARAM wParam,
    LPARAM lParam);
```

Listing 7-18. RECORD.DEF DLL definitions file

```
; Module name: RECORD.DEF
; Programmer : Jeffrey M. Richter.

LIBRARY      RECORD
DESCRIPTION 'Record: Journal hook routines for Echo'
STUB        'WinStub.exe'
EXETYPE     WINDOWS
CODE        FIXED PRELOAD
DATA        MOVEABLE SINGLE PRELOAD
HEAPSIZE    1024
EXPORTS
    WEP                @1    RESIDENTNAME
    Recorder           @2
    JrnlRecHookFunc    @3
    JrnlPlybkHookFunc  @4
```

Listing 7-19. RECORD.MKF (MAKEFILE for Record DLL)

```
#*************************************************************************
#Module name: RECORD.MKF
#Programmer : Jeffrey M. Richter.
#*************************************************************************

!include "..\builtins.jmr"

PROG = Record

MODEL = s
CFLAGS = -P-c -c -f- -WD -p -v -w -m$(MODEL)! -I$(INCLUDEDIR)
LFLAGS = /P/v/n/m/s/L$(LIBDIR)
!if $(MODEL) == m
LIBS = CWL
!else
LIBS = CWS
!endif

LIBS = $(LIBS) Import

MODULES = $(PROG).obj

ICONS   =
BITMAPS =
CURSORS =

$(PROG).DLL: $(MODULES) $(PROG).Def $(PROG).Res
     tlink $(LFLAGS) @&&!
COD$(MODEL) $(MODULES)
$(PROG).DLL, $(PROG), $(LIBS), $(PROG)
!
     rc -31 -T -Fe$(PROG).DLL $(PROG).Res
     TDStrip -s $(PROG).DLL
     implib $(PROG).LIB $(PROG).DEF

$(PROG).res: $(PROG).rc $(RESOURCES)
```

CHAPTER 8

MDI Application Techniques

The Multiple Document Interface standard is not new to Windows, but its implementation in Windows 3.x makes developing MDI applications much simpler. This chapter explains how to design and implement extensions to MDI applications.

MDI Application Basics

Every MDI application consists of a Frame window, an MDICLIENT window, and multiple MDI Child windows. The application registers the Frame window's class and MDI Child window classes. If the application allows the user to work on three types of documents (spreadsheets, charts, and macros, for instance), three MDI Child window classes will be registered. Instances of these windows are created as children of the MDICLIENT window, which was created as a child of the Frame window. The MDICLIENT window class is a System Global class that is registered by Windows when the session begins.

The Frame window is like the main overlapped window used by non-MDI applications. All windows created by the MDI application are descendants of this Frame window. One of the first duties of the Frame window is to create an instance of an MDICLIENT window class during the processing of the *WM_CRE-ATE* message. The MDICLIENT window is responsible for maintaining all of the MDI Child windows.

MDI applications behave differently because the Frame window calls *Def-FrameProc* instead of *DefWindowProc* when default processing for a message is desired. The parameters that would normally be passed to *DefWindowProc* are passed to *DefFrameProc*. The following pseudo-C code shows the messages processed by *DefFrameProc* and their default actions:

```
LRESULT WINAPI DefFrameProc (HWND hWndFrame, HWND hWndMDIClient,
    UINT uMsg, WPARAM wParam, LPARAM lParam) {
  LRESULT lResult = 0;
  BOOL fCallDefProc = FALSE;

  if ((hWndMDIClient == NULL) || !IsWindow(hWndMDIClient))
    return(DefWindowProc(hWndFrame, uMsg, wParam, lParam));

  switch (uMsg) {

    case WM_COMMAND:
      if ("More Windows..." Option from "Window" Menu selected) {
        hWndChildSelected = DialogBoxParam("More Windows..." Dialog
          Box);
        if (!IsWindow(hWndChildSelected))    // User pressed "Cancel".
          break;
      } else {
        if (MDI Child selected from "Window" menu)
          hWndChildSelected = GetMDIChildhWndFromMenuID(wParam);
      }

      if (IsWindow(hWndChildSelected)) {
        SendMessage(hWndMDIClient, WM_MDIACTIVATE,
          hWndChildSelected, 0);
        if (IsMinimized(hWndChildSelected))
          ShowWindow(hWndChildSelected, SW_SHOWNORMAL);
        break;
      }

      // The SC_* IDs come from the system menu of a maximized
      // MDI child.
      switch (wParam & 0xFFF0) {
        case SC_CLOSE:
        case SC_MAXIMIZE:
```

```
        case SC_MINIMIZE:
        case SC_MOVE:
        case SC_NEXTWINDOW:
        case SC_PREVWINDOW:
        case SC_RESTORE:
        case SC_SIZE:
            if (IsMaximized(hWndActiveChild)) {
                lResult = SendMessage(hWndActiveChild,
                    WM_SYSCOMMAND, wParam, lParam);
                break;
            }
        }
        fCallDefProc = TRUE;
        break;

    case WM_MENUCHAR:
        if (!IsMinimized(hWndFrame) && (wParam == '-')) {
            if (IsMaximized(hWndActiveChild))
                lResult = MAKELRESULT(0, 2);
            else
                if (IsWindow(hWndActiveChild)) {
                    PostMessage(hWndActiveChild, WM_SYSCOMMAND,
                        SC_KEYMENU, MAKELPARAM(-, 0));
                    lResult = MAKELRESULT(0, 1);
                }
        }
        fCallDefProc = TRUE;
        break;

    case WM_NCACTIVATE:
        SendMessage(hWndMDIClient, WM_NCACTIVATE, wParam, lParam);
        fCallDefProc = TRUE;
        break;
```

```
case WM_NEXTMENU:
   if (!IsMinimized(hWndFrame) && IsWindow(hWndActiveChild) &&
      !IsMaximized(hWndActiveChild)) {
      if (((wParam == VK_LEFT) && (LOWORD(lParam) ==
         GetMenu(hWndFrame))) ||
           ((wParam == VK_RIGHT) && (LOWORD(lParam) ==
              GetSystemMenu(hWndFrame, FALSE))) {
         lResult = MAKELRESULT(GetSystemMenu(hWndActiveChild,
            FALSE), hWndActiveChild);
         break;
      }
   }
   break;

case WM_SETFOCUS:
   SetFocus(hWndMDIClient);
   break;

case WM_SETTEXT:
   if (IsMaximized(hWndActiveChild))
      Add child's caption text to Frame's caption
   break;

case WM_SIZE:
   if ((WORD) wParam != SIZE_MINIMIZED)
      MoveWindow(hWndMDIClient, 0, 0, LOWORD(lParam),
         HIWORD(lParam), TRUE);
   else {
      GetClientRectOfNonMinimizedWindow(hWndFrame, &rc);
      MoveWindow(hWndMDIClient, 0, 0, rc.right, rc.bottom,
         TRUE);
   }
   fCallDefProc = TRUE;
   break;
```

```
    default:
        fCallDefProc = TRUE;
        break;
    }
    if (fCallDefProc)
        lResult = DefWindowProc(hWndFrame, uMsg, wParam, lParam);
    return(lResult);
}
```

Actions that occur within MDI Child windows are communicated to the MDI-CLIENT window by calling *DefMDIChildProc* in each MDI Child's window procedure. The parameters expected by *DefMDIChildProc* are identical to those expected by *DefWindowProc*. The following pseudo-C code shows the messages processed by the *DefMDIChildProc* function and their default actions:

```
LRESULT WINAPI DefMDIChildProc (HWND hWndMDIChild, UINT uMsg,
    WPARAM wParam, LPARAM lParam) {
    LRESULT lResult = 0;
    BOOL fCallDefProc = FALSE;

    if ((GetParent(hWndMDIChild) == NULL)  ||
        (GetClassWord(GetParent(hWndMDIChild), GCW_ATOM) !=
            AtomForMDICLIENTClass)) {
        return(DefWindowProc(hWndMDIChild, uMsg, wParam, lParam));
    }

    switch (uMsg) {

        case WM_CHILDACTIVATE:
            Activate the MDI Child;
            break;

        case WM_CLOSE:
            SendMessage(GetParent(hWndMDIChild), WM_MDIDESTROY,
```

```
       hWndMDIChild, 0);
   break;

case WM_GETMINMAXINFO:
   Do Normal Processing For Children;
   break;

case WM_MENUCHAR:
   PostMessage(GetParent(GetParent(hWndMDIChild)),
      WM_SYSCOMMAND, SC_KEYMENU, wParam);
   lResult = MAKELRESULT(0, 1);
   break;

case WM_MOVE:
   if (!IsMaximized(hWndMDIChild) {
      Calculate New Scroll Bar Ranges For hWndMDIClient;
   fCallDefProc = TRUE;
   break;

case WM_NEXTMENU:
   if (wParam == VK_LEFT)
      lResult = MAKELRESULT(GetSystemMenu(
         GetParent(GetParent(hWndMDIChild)), FALSE),
         GetParent(GetParent(hWndMDIChild)));
   else
      lResult = MAKELRESULT(GetMenu(GetParent(GetParent
         (hWndMDIChild))),
         GetParent(GetParent(hWndMDIChild)));
   break;

case WM_SETFOCUS:
   if (hWndMDIChild != hWndActiveMDIChild)
      // Attempt to activate the child.
      // Note that an MDI Child can abort the activation.
```

```
    // The frame's caption may need updating.
    // The Window menu needs to have the checkmark moved
    // if (activation successful).
        SendMessage(hWndNewActiveMDIChild, WM_MDIACTIVATE, TRUE,
            MAKELPARAM(hWndNewActiveMDIChild,
                hWndOldActiveMDIChild));
    }
    fCallDefProc = TRUE;
    break;


case WM_SETTEXT:
    DefWindowProc(hWndMDIChild, uMsg, wParam, lParam);
    Modify Menu Item In Frames "Window" Menu;
    if (IsMaximized(hWndMDIChild))
        Redraw Frames Non-Client Area;
    break;


case WM_SIZE:
    Do Normal Processing For MDI Child;
    // This includes determining if scroll bars are necessary
    // in MDI Client's window.
    fCallDefProc = TRUE;
    break;


case WM_SYSCOMMAND:
    switch (wParam & 0xFFF0) {
        case SC_NEXTWINDOW:
            SendMessage(GetParent(hWndMDIChild), WM_MDINEXT,
                hWndMDIChild, 0);
            break;

        case SC_PREVWINDOW:
            SendMessage(GetParent(hWndMDIChild), WM_MDINEXT,
                hWndMDIChild, MAKELPARAM(1, 0));
```

```
                    break;

              case SC_MOVE:
              case SC_SIZE:
                  if (IsMaxmized(hWndMDIChild)) break;
                  else fCallDefProc = TRUE;
                  break;

              case SC_MAXIMIZE:
                  if (IsMaxmized(hWndMDIChild))
                     lResult = SendMessage(GetParent(GetParent
                        (hWndMDIChild)), WM_SYSCOMMAND,
                        SC_MAXIMIZE, lParam);
                  else fCallDefProc = TRUE;
                  break;

              default:
                  fCallDefProc = TRUE;
          }
          break;
      }

  if (fCallDefProc)
      lResult = DefWindowProc(hWndMDIChild, uMsg, wParam, lParam);

  return(lResult);
  }
```

The MDI Sample Application

The MDI sample application shows how to implement various features in your own MDI programs. The initialization code for the MDI application can be found in the MDI.C module. This module creates the Frame window and the ribbon that may appear under the Frame's menu bar.

FRAME.C contains the function that registers the Frame window class and the window procedure that processes messages for this window. The application registers two MDI Child classes, Sheet and Chart. The functions that register the MDI Child classes and the window procedures required to process messages for these classes can be found in SHEET.C and CHART.C, presented later in this chapter.

MDI.H contains a number of values that are used for menu resources and string tables throughout the application. The *#define:*

```
#define GETFRAME(hWnd)   GetParent(GetParent(hWnd))
```

is frequently used in the window procedures for the two MDI Child classes. It returns the handle of the application's Frame window.

Several user-defined messages are also established in MDI.H. The MDI application is written entirely by using the message crackers supplied by Microsoft in the SDK's WINDOWSX.H file. Because of this, message crackers have also been created for the user-defined messages as well. The prefix used for each message identifies the window class that processes the message. The following table shows each message prefix and its meaning:

Message prefix	Window class that processes the message
FW	Processed by the Frame window.
AC	Processed by all the MDI Child windows.
AW	Processed by the Frame window and the MDI Child windows.

At the bottom of MDI.H are macro definitions that access class and window extra bytes. These macros are explained in Appendix B.

The remainder of this chapter discusses the various features that have been implemented in the MDI sample application.

Closing MDI Child Windows

Like applications, MDI Child windows can be closed by selecting the "Close" option from the Child's system menu. As a convenience to the user, Windows allows applications to be closed by double-clicking on the system menu. In fact, the bitmap used to represent the application's system menu is sometimes called the *Close Box*. Windows allows MDI Child windows to be closed when the user double-clicks on the MDI Child's Close Box. However, a bug in the Windows 3.0 implementation of MDI prevents a maximized MDI Child from being closed this way. In Windows 3.1, this bug has been corrected but the code below can be used to allow MDI Child windows to be closed under both Windows 3.0 and 3.1 and also demonstrates a useful method for determining how to conclude which screen element (for example, menu, maximize box, or border) was selected by the user with the mouse.

The following function, *Frame_OnNCLButtonDown*, is called in response to a *WM_NCLBUTTONDBLCLK* message sent to the MDI's Frame window. It can be used to correct the close bug in Windows 3.0:

```
void Frame_OnNCLButtonDown (HWND hwnd, BOOL fDoubleClick,
   int x, int y, UINT codeHitTest) {
   RECT rc; HBITMAP hBitmap; BITMAP Bitmap; POINT pt;
   BOOL fIsMDIChildMaximized;
   HWND hWndActiveMDIChild;
   if (!fDoubleClick) goto DWP;

   // Code to allow double-clicking the MDI Child's system menu
   // to close the MDI Child window.

   // If mouse wasn't clicked in the application's menu, nothing to do.
   if (codeHitTest != HTMENU) goto DWP;

   // If the active child is not maximized, nothing to do.
   hWndActiveMDIChild = GetActiveMDIChild(&fIsMDIChildMaximized);
   if (!fIsMDIChildMaximized) goto DWP;

   // The following code gets the position and dimensions of the MDI
   // Child's system menu in the Frame's menu bar.

   // Get position and dimensions of the Frame window.
   GetWindowRect(hwnd, &rc);
```

```
      // Get handle to the CLOSE BOX bitmaps.
      hBitmap = LoadBitmap(NULL, MAKEINTRESOURCE(OBM_CLOSE));

      // Get dimensions of the bitmaps.
      GetObject(hBitmap, sizeof(BITMAP), (LPSTR) (LPBITMAP) &Bitmap);
      DeleteBitmap(hBitmap);

      // Adjust the rectangle.
      rc.top += GetSystemMetrics(SM_CYCAPTION) +
         GetSystemMetrics(SM_CYFRAME);
      rc.bottom = rc.top + Bitmap.bmHeight;
      rc.left += GetSystemMetrics(SM_CXFRAME);

      // The close bitmap includes the Application and MDI Child CLOSE
      // boxes. So, we only want half of the bitmap's width.
      rc.right = rc.left + Bitmap.bmWidth / 2;
      // If the mouse cursor is within this rectangle, tell the
      // MDI Child window to close.
      pt.x = x;
      pt.y = y;
      if (!PtInRect(&rc, pt)) goto DWP;

      FORWARD_WM_SYSCOMMAND(hWndActiveMDIChild, SC_CLOSE, 0, 0, SendMessage);
      return;

DWP:
      FORWARD_WM_NCLBUTTONDOWN(hwnd, fDoubleClick, x, y, codeHitTest,
         Frame_DefProc);
}
```

When an MDI Child window is maximized, *DefMDIChildProc* alters the Frame window's menu bar by placing the MDI Child's system menu at the beginning and its "Restore" button at the end. Figure 8-1 shows how the menu bar is changed.

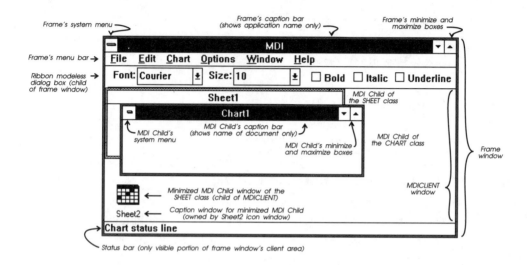

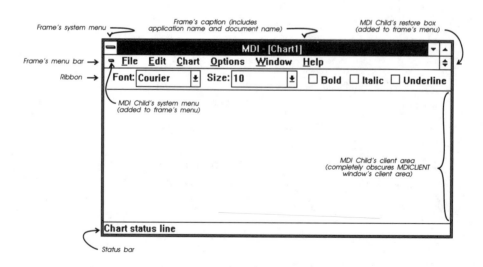

Figure 8-1. MDI applications before and after an MDI Child is maximized

When the user double-clicks on a window outside the client area, the Frame's window procedure calls *Frame_OnNCLButtonClick*. The first thing this function does is determine if it should even process the message. The message processes if the mouse was not double-clicked or if the mouse was not over the application's menu. Checking if the mouse was double-clicked is simply a matter of checking the *fDoubleClick* parameter and calling *DefFrameProc* if it is FALSE.

The *codeHitTest* parameter indicates which screen element of the window's non-client area the mouse was over. (For a complete list of hit codes, see the *WM_NCHITTEST* message in the *Windows' Programmer's Reference*.) If the value of *codeHitTest* is not *HTMENU*, the mouse was not over the application's menu and *DefFrameProc* is called for normal processing.

Once you know that the mouse was double-clicked in the Frame window's menu bar and there is a maximized MDI Child window, you must determine if the mouse is over the rectangular area occupied by the MDI Child's Close Box.

GetWindowRect returns the screen coordinates of the Frame window. This includes the window's caption bar and resizing borders. By adding the height of a caption bar and the height of the thick frame to *rc.top*, you get the y-coordinate (in screen units) of the top of the menu bar. You can store this value in *rc.top*. Then add the width of the thick frame to *rc.left* to get the x-coordinate where the left of the menu bar starts. Store this value in *rc.left*.

Now, calculate the width and height of the bitmap used to represent an MDI Child's Close Box. The *LoadBitmap* function is used to retrieve a handle to this bitmap. Windows has several bitmaps that any application can access. The *LoadBitmap* function uses the data-instance handle to determine which .EXE file (or .DLL file) to retrieve bitmaps from. If this value is NULL, *LoadBitmap* retrieves one of the predefined bitmaps as described in the *Windows' SDK Programmer's Reference* for the *LoadBitmap* function.

Use *OBM_CLOSE* to retrieve the handle of the Close Box bitmap. To finish defining the rectangular area, we must calculate the bottom coordinate:

```
rc.bottom = rc.top + Bitmap.bmHeight;
```

The right edge is equal to the left edge's coordinate plus half the width of the bitmap:

```
rc.right = rc.left + Bitmap.bmWidth / 2;
```

You need to divide the width of the Close Box bitmap by two because it contains the images for application Close Boxes (on the left) and MDI Child Close Boxes (on the right).

With the *rc* variable set to the screen coordinates of the MDI Child's Close Box, the *PtInRect* function can now be used to determine if the mouse cursor is within the rectangle. If it is, a *WM_SYSCOMMAND* message is forwarded via *SendMessage* to the active MDI Child window with the *wParam* parameter set to *SC_CLOSE*, telling the window that the user has tried to close it.

Eating Mouse Messages

When the user clicks the left button of the mouse over a window that is currently inactive, Windows activates the window and sends the *WM_LBUTTONDOWN* message to its window procedure. However, some applications may prefer that Windows activate the window without sending the *WM_LBUTTONDOWN* message. Let's perform an experiment using Microsoft's Word for Windows.

In Word for Windows, open two document windows. Only one window is active; select a region of text in that window. Make the other document window active by clicking the left mouse button within its client area. If you now click the mouse button over the client area of the first document's window, Word for Windows simply activates the document window. The text in the window remains selected. It isn't until you press the mouse button again that Word deselects the text and positions the caret at the mouse cursor's location.

The developers of Word for Windows had to make a deliberate effort for Word to behave this way. Normally, when an MDI Child window is activated by the mouse, a *WM_MOUSEACTIVATE* message is sent to the MDI Child, followed by a *WM_LBUTTONDOWN* message. Word ignores the *WM_LBUTTONDOWN* message when it is associated with the activation of an MDI Child window.

Whenever a click of the mouse activates a window, Windows sends a *WM_MOUSEACTIVATE* message to the window procedure. The *wParam* parameter contains the handle to the topmost parent window of the window being activated. The *lParam* parameter contains the hit test code in the low-order word and the mouse message (*WM_?BUTTONDOWN* or *WM_NC?BUTTONDOWN*) in the high-order word. The value returned while a *WM_MOUSEACTIVATE* message is being processed tells Windows how it should handle the *WM_?BUTTONDOWN* or *WM_NC?BUTTONDOWN* message. The possible return values are:

Identifier	Meaning
MA_ACTIVATE	Activate the window and send the mouse message.
MA_NOACTIVATE	Do not activate the window.
MA_ACTIVATEANDEAT	Activate the window but do not send the mouse message.
MA_NOACTIVATEANDEAT	Don't activate the window and don't send the mouse message.

You might expect that your MDI Child's window procedure could simply intercept the *WM_MOUSEACTIVATE* message and return *MA_ACTIVATEANDEAT* to cause the mouse event to be thrown away. However, there is a catch. Windows never considers a window with the *WS_CHILD* style active. That is, the *GetActiveWindow* function will never return a handle to a child window. Instead, Windows goes up the window hierarchy until it finds a window that does not have the *WS_CHILD* style and makes it the active window. In an MDI application, this is always the application's Frame window. When an MDI Child window is active, it just means that the window has the input focus and that its caption bar should be painted using the *COLOR_ACTIVECAPTION* color.

All of this means that a *WM_MOUSEACTIVATE* message is sent every time a mouse button is clicked over an MDI Child window. If the return value from this message were always *MA_ACTIVATEANDEAT*, the MDI Child's window procedure would never receive any *WM_?BUTTONDOWN* or *WM_NC?BUTTONDOWN* messages. A method that demonstrates how to disable *WM_?BUTTONDOWN* side-effect for MDI Child windows appears below. The implementation of the method involves the interception of three messages by three message cracker functions.

```
static HWND   _hWndPrevChild = NULL;
```

```
       .
       .
       .

void Chart_MDIActivate(HWND hwnd, BOOL fActive, HWND hwndActivate,
    HWND hwndDeactivate) {
    if (fActive == FALSE) {
        // Child is being deactivated.
        // Reset the previous child so WM_MOUSEACTIVATE will work OK.
        _hWndPrevChild = NULL;
        return;
    }

    // Child is being activated.

    // Set handle of child being deactivated.
    _hWndPrevChild = hwndDeactivate;

    // If this child is being activated and no other child exists,
    // pretend that this child was the last activated child.
    if (_hWndPrevChild == NULL) _hWndPrevChild = hwnd;
        .
        .
        .
}
    .
    .
    .

int Chart_OnMouseActivate (HWND hwnd, HWND hwndTopLevel, UINT
    codeHitTest, UINT msg) {
    // User clicked the mouse of the Child window.
    // If the mouse is clicked in the window's client area and
    // the previously active child was NOT this child, the
    // mouse message should be eaten.
    if ((HTCLIENT == codeHitTest) && (hwnd != _hWndPrevChild))
```

```
      return(MA_ACTIVATEANDEAT);
    return(MA_ACTIVATE);
}


BOOL Chart_OnSetCursor (HWND hwnd, HWND hwndCursor, UINT codeHitTest,
    UINT msg) {
    // After an MDI Child becomes active, set the previously active
    // child to this window so that mouse messages will NOT be eaten.
    _hWndPrevChild = hwnd;
    return(FORWARD_WM_SETCURSOR(hwnd, hwndCursor,
        codeHitTest, msg, Chart_DefProc));
}
```

When an inactive MDI Child window is activated by a mouse click, Windows sends a series of messages to that window: *WM_MDIACTIVATE, WM_MOUSE-ACTIVATE*, and *WM_SETCURSOR*. The *WM_MDIACTIVATE* message notifies the *Chart_MDIActivate* function that the MDI Child window is being activated (*fActivate* is TRUE). The *hwndDeactivate* parameter contains the handle of the window that is being deactivated. The MDI Child saves this handle in a global static variable, *_hWndPrevChild*.

When the *WM_MOUSEACTIVATE* message is received, the *Chart_OnMouse-Activate* function is called. This function compares the value of *_hWndPrevChild* to the window handle that is processing the message. If the handles are different and the mouse was clicked in the MDI Child's client area (*HTCLIENT == code-HitTest*), the mouse message is eaten (*MA_ACTIVATEANDEAT* is returned). If either of these conditions is FALSE, the mouse message is not eaten and *MA_ACTIVATE* is returned.

Whether the MDI Child is activated by the mouse or by some other means, Windows sends a *WM_SETCURSOR* message after the MDI Child has been activated. The *_hWndPrevChild* variable is set to the handle of the newly activated window. This prevents future mouse messages from being eaten.

CHART.C (presented at the end of the chapter) demonstrates how mouse messages are eaten by displaying a dialog box whenever the window procedure receives a *WM_LBUTTONDOWN* message.

Status Bars

Many MDI applications have status bars. A status bar is a line of text usually consisting of statistical information about the document the user is working on. MDI.EXE demonstrates how to implement a status bar as part of the Frame window's client area. When the user chooses to display the status bar, the MDICLIENT is resized (by calling the *MoveWindow* function) so that its height does not cause the Frame's client area to be completely obscured.

The Frame window maintains a Boolean value in its window extra bytes that reflects the current state (on or off) of the status bar. When the Frame window is created, this value is initialized to TRUE:

```
BOOL Frame_OnCreate(HWND hwnd, CREATESTRUCT FAR* lpCreateStruct) {
    .
    .
    .
    SETWNDEB(hwnd, WNDEB, fStatusBarOn, TRUE);
    .
    .
}
```

This makes the status bar visible by default when the application is started. A complete description of the macros that store and retrieve class and window extra bytes can be found in Appendix B.

The application must know the dimensions of the status bar. The user-defined message *FW_GETSTATBARRECT* was created to make this information accessible. The Frame window's window procedure processes this message using the *Frame_OnGetStatBarRect* message cracker function as follows:

```
void Frame_OnGetStatBarRect (HWND hwnd, LPRECT lpRect) {
    HDC hDC; TEXTMETRIC tm;
    // Get the client area of the Frame window.
    GetClientRect(hwnd, lpRect);
```

```
   // If the status bar is OFF, set the status bar to have no height.
   if (! (BOOL) GETWNDEB(hwnd, WNDEB, fStatusBarOn)) {
      lpRect->top = lpRect->bottom;
      return;
   }


   // Change the dimensions so that the status bar is the height of
   // one line of text plus a small border.
   hDC = GetDC(hwnd);
   GetTextMetrics(hDC, &tm);
   ReleaseDC(hwnd, hDC);
   lpRect->top = lpRect->bottom - tm.tmHeight -
      GetSystemMetrics(SM_CYBORDER);
}
```

If the user has turned off the status bar, the rectangle will simply be a rectangle of zero height that spans the width of the Frame window's client area. If the status bar is turned on, the height of the bar is calculated as the height of a line of text plus the height of a window frame that cannot be sized. *GetSystemMetrics(SM_CYBORDER)* allows the application to draw a horizontal line that separates the MDICLIENT window from the status bar. Because this type of horizontal line is drawn so frequently, the *FW_DRAWSTATUSDIVIDE* message is defined so that the processing for drawing this line does not have to be duplicated in all MDI Child window procedures. The code for this message cracker function appears as follows:

```
int Frame_OnDrawStatusDivide (HWND hwnd, LPPAINTSTRUCT lpPaintStruct) {
   HPEN hPen;
   // Draw a line separating the status bar from the MDICLIENT window.
   int cyBorder = GetSystemMetrics(SM_CYBORDER);
   hPen = CreatePen(PS_SOLID, cyBorder, RGB(0, 0, 0));
   hPen = SelectObject(lpPaintStruct->hdc, hPen);
   MoveTo(lpPaintStruct->hdc, 0, lpPaintStruct->rcPaint.top);
   LineTo(lpPaintStruct->hdc, lpPaintStruct->rcPaint.right,
      lpPaintStruct->rcPaint.top);
```

```
hPen = SelectObject(lpPaintStruct->hdc, hPen);
DeleteObject(hPen);
return(cyBorder);
}
```

The most important thing to take note of is the use of *GetSystemMetrics (SM_CYBORDER)*. Because the application uses this value as the width of the dividing line instead of hard-coding a one- or two-pixel line, the dividing line should be visible on any monitor. This message cracker function returns the height of the non-sizeable border so that the calling procedure can take this value into account before it does any additional painting.

Drawing information in the status bar is simply a matter of intercepting the *WM_PAINT* message when it is sent to the Frame's window procedure. Because the only visible part of the Frame's client area is the status bar (the rest is obscure by the MDI Client window), this message indicates that the status bar needs to be repainted. Each MDI Child window class may wish to display different information in the status bar, so painting this information should be the responsibility of the MDI Child window. The processing for the paint message determines whether any MDI Child windows exist, then sends the user-defined *AC_PAINTSTATBAR* message to the active MDI Child window.

If an MDI Child does not exist, the Frame window can paint any information it desires in the status bar.

While a user is working in an MDI Child window, that Child window may wish to update the information in the status bar. It can do this by executing the following statements:

```
RECT rc;
.
.
.
FORWARD_FW_GETSTATBARRECT(GETFRAME(hwndMDIChild), &rc, SendMessage);
InvalidateRect(GETFRAME(hWndMDIChild), &rc, TRUE);
```

These statements inform Windows that the status-bar area of the Frame window needs repainting. However, some MDI Child windows update their status bars frequently. For example, Word for Windows' status bar shows the column containing the cursor. If the user is typing quickly, Word won't be able to keep up. When the column changes, Word invalidates the status bar's area but doesn't update it so that Windows won't send the *WM_PAINT* message to the Frame window until the queue holds no other messages. This has the effect of updating the status bar when the user has momentarily stopped typing.

If it is absolutely necessary for the status bar to be updated as changes occur, the MDI Child can add the following line after the code previously shown:

```
UpdateWindow(GETFRAME(hWndMDIChild));
```

Each Child window procedure is written to expect the *AC_PAINTSTATBAR* message. This message includes the handle to the device context that must be used for painting and a pointer to a *PAINTSTRUCT* structure initialized by the call to the *BeginPaint* function.

Menu Option Help

Because it is not always obvious to a user what a particular menu item does, some applications display help text at the bottom of the window as the user highlights menu options. This section discusses a method of adding menu help text to applications. Although the technique discussed here applies to MDI applications, a similar technique could also be used in non-MDI applications.

Menu option help is displayed in the area used by an application's status bar. If the user has elected to hide the status bar, the menu help text is not displayed. When the user highlights menu options, help text for the highlighted menu item is painted in the application's status bar. After the user has selected a menu option or exited from the menu system, the menu help text is replaced by the normal statistical information.

As the user navigates through the application's menu system, Windows sends *WM_MENUSELECT* messages to the window that owns the active menu. The prototype for the message cracker used to process *WM_MENUSELECT* messages looks like the following.

```
void Cls_OnMenuSelect(HWND hwnd, HMENU hmenu, int item, HMENU
menuPopup, UINT flags);
```

The *flags* parameter associated with this message cracker function is used to determine which type of item the user has highlighted. The following table lists the identifiers that may be *AND*ed with the *flags* parameter to determine the status of the highlighted menu item:

Identifier	Value	Description
MF_GRAYED	0x0001	The highlighted menu item is grayed.
MF_DISABLED	0x0002	The highlighted menu item is disabled.
MF_BITMAP	0x0004	The highlighted menu item is a bitmap.
MF_CHECKED	0x0008	The highlighted menu item is checked.
MF_POPUP	0x0010	The highlighted menu item is a pop-up menu and has no menu ID.
MF_OWNERDRAW	0x0100	The highlighted menu item is an owner-drawn item.
MF_SYSMENU	0x2000	The highlighted menu item is an item in the window's system menu or is the system menu's pop-up (if the *MF_POPUP* bit is on).
MF_MOUSESELECT	0x8000	The highlighted menu item was selected with the mouse.

Before deciding which help text to display, the window procedure processing the *WM_MENUSELECT* message must know if a menu item is highlighted or if a pop-up menu is highlighted. The window procedure performs a bitwise *AND* operation on the *flags* parameter and the *MF_POPUP* identifier. If the *MF_POPUP* bit is on, the user highlighted a pop-up menu and the *menuPopup* parameter is the menu handle of the highlighted menu. If the *MF_POPUP* bit is off, the user highlighted a menu item and the *item* parameter is its menu item ID.

The window procedure must also determine whether the highlighted item is part of the window's system menu. To do this, the procedure performs another bitwise

AND operation between the *flags* parameter and the *MF_SYSMENU* identifier. If the *MF_SYSMENU* bit is on, the user highlighted the window's system menu or an item in the window's system menu.

Now, it's time to add MDI Child windows to our discussion. When an MDI Child window is maximized, the Child's system menu is appended to the beginning of the Frame window's menu. Because the menu is part of the Frame's menu, highlighting options in the MDI Child's system menu causes *WM_MENUSELECT* messages to be sent to the Frame's window procedure. The *MF_SYSMENU* bit will be off because this menu is not the Frame window's system menu.

A *Restore Box* is appended to the end of the Frame's menu when the MDI Child window is maximized. This menu item is not a pop-up but a bitmap menu item. A user can enter the Frame's menu system and, using the right and left arrows, scroll through the menus until the Restore Box is the highlighted option. When this happens, Windows sends the *WM_MENUSELECT* message to the Frame's window procedure. The *flags* parameter to the message cracker will have the *MF_POPUP* and *MF_SYSMENU* bits turned off and the *MF_BITMAP* bit turned on.

When an MDI Child window is not maximized, the MDI Child's system menu is not part of the Frame's menu but is the system menu for the MDI Child window. When menu items are highlighted in the non-maximized MDI Child's system menu, the *WM_MENUSELECT* message is sent to the MDI Child's window procedure because it owns the active menu. In addition, since this menu is the Child's system menu, the *flags* parameter for this message will always have the *MF_SYSMENU* bit turned on.

Whenever a *WM_MENUSELECT* message is retrieved by a window procedure, the procedure must determine which help text to paint in the status bar. Let's examine the simplest situation first. When no MDI Child windows exist, all *WM_MENU-SELECT* messages are sent to the Frame's window procedure. The Frame window can use the parameters passed to the message cracker to determine which text should be displayed. The following template shows the skeleton code to set this up:

```
void Frame_OnMenuSelect(HWND hwnd, HMENU hmenu, int item,
    HMENU hmenuPopup, UINT flags) {
    switch (flags & (MF_POPUP | MF_SYSMENU)) {
```

```
    case 0:
        // Item is a menu item ID from a nonsystem menu.
        break;

    case MF_POPUP:
        // menuPopup is handle to pop-up menu.
        break;

    case MF_SYSMENU:
        // Item is menu item ID from system menu.
        break;

    case MF_POPUP | MF_SYSMENU:
        // menuPopup is handle to application's system menu.
        break;
}

.

.

.
```

In each case, the window procedure can examine the status of bits in the *flags* parameter to modify the help text displayed to the user. For example, if the user highlighted the "Copy" option in the Edit menu when this option is grayed (*flags & MF_GRAYED) != FALSE*), the help text could tell the user that an object in the window needs to be selected before this option can be chosen.

This is a good method to use when implementing menu help text in a non-MDI application, but in an MDI application some additional work is necessary. Because the menu in the Frame window is placed there by the active MDI Child, that Child should be responsible for determining which help text is displayed. However, since the menu is part of the Frame window and not the MDI Child, the *WM_MENUSE-LECT* message is sent to the Frame window for all highlighted menu options, except the non-maximized MDI Child's system menu.

When the MDI sample application's Frame window receives the *WM_MENU-SELECT* message, it determines whether an MDI Child exists and forwards the message to the MDI Child directly. The MDI Child's window procedure passes the message along to its *WM_MENUSELECT* message cracker. The following code fragment from FRAME.C shows how the Frame's window procedure processes the *WM_MENUSELECT* message:

```
switch (flags & (MF_POPUP | MF_SYSMENU)) {

   case 0:
      // Item is a menu item ID NOT on the application's system menu.

      if (hWndActiveMDIChild != NULL) {
         // An MDI Child exists.
         if (fMDIChildIsMaximized) {
            // If menu item is from the MDI Child's system menu,
            // set the MF_SYSMENU bit in the lParam parameter.
            wTemp = GetSubMenu(GetMenu(hWnd), 0);
            if (GetMenuState(wTemp, wParam, MF_BYCOMMAND) != -1)
               flags |= MF_SYSMENU;
         }

            // Make active MDI Child think it received the
            // WM_MENUSELECT message.
            FORWARD_WM_MENUSELECT(hWndActiveMDIChild, hmenu, item,
               hmenuPopup, flags, SendMessage);
            wTemp = 0;     // MDI Child handled the message.
            break;
         }
         wTemp = IDS_FRAMEMENUID + wParam;
         break;

   case MF_POPUP:
      // menuPopup is handle to pop-up menu.
      if (hWndActiveMDIChild != NULL) {
         // An MDI Child exists.
```

```
        if (fMDIChildIsMaximized) {
           // If pop-up menu is first top-level menu, it is
           // the MDI Child's system menu; set MF_SYSMENU flag.
           if (wParam == GetSubMenu(GetMenu(hWnd), 0))
              lParam |= MF_SYSMENU;
        }

        // Make active MDI Child think it received the
        // WM_MENUSELECT message.
        FORWARD_WM_MENUSELECT(hWndActiveMDIChild, hmenu, item,
           hmenuPopup, flags, SendMessage);
        wTemp = 0;    // MDI Child handled the message.
        break;
     }

     // Calculate the index of the top-level menu.
     hMenu = GetMenu(hWnd);
     wTemp = GetMenuItemCount(hMenu);
     while (wTemp--)
        if (GetSubMenu(hMenu, wTemp) == (HMENU) wParam) break;
     wTemp += IDS_FRAMEPOPUPID + 1;   // Jump over system menu.
     break;

  case MF_SYSMENU:
     // Item is menu item ID from system menu.
     wTemp = IDS_FRAMEMENUID + ((wParam & 0x0FFF) >> 4);
     break;

  case MF_POPUP | MF_SYSMENU:
     // menuPopup is handle to application's system menu.
     wTemp = IDS_FRAMEPOPUPID;
     break;
}
```

If the *MF_SYSMENU* bit is on, the *WM_MENUSELECT* message is for a menu item on the Frame's system menu and must be processed by the Frame. If the *MF_SYSMENU* bit is off, the *WM_MENUSELECT* message is passed to the active MDI Child window (if one exists). First, check to ensure that the MDI Child window is maximized. If so, and if the highlighted menu item is from the first pop-up menu of the Frame's window, the *MF_SYSMENU* bit is turned on before the message is sent to the MDI Child. This tells the MDI Child window that an option on the Child's system menu is highlighted.

By turning on the *MF_SYSMENU* bit, the MDI Child window can process *WM_MENUSELECT* messages just as the Frame window procedure does. The following table shows what the Frame's window procedure should expect to receive in the *flags* parameter for a *WM_MENUSELECT* message:

Highlighted item	MF_POPUP bit	MF_SYSMENU bit
Application's system menu item	Off	On
Application's system menu pop-up	On	On
Maximized MDI Child's system menu item	Off	Off
Maximized MDI Child's system menu pop-up	On	Off
Maximized MDI Child's restore box	Off	Off
Application's nonsystem menu item	Off	Off
Application's nonsystem menu pop-up	On	Off

The following table shows what an MDI Child window procedure should expect to receive in the *flags* parameter for a *WM_MENUSELECT* message:

Highlighted item	MF_POPUP bit	MF_SYSMENU bit
MDI Child's system menu item	Off	On
MDI Child's system menu pop-up	On	On
Frame's nonsystem menu item	Off	Off
Frame's nonsystem menu pop-up	On	Off

By examining the parameters to the *WM_MENUSELECT* message cracker functions, the Frame and MDI Child window procedures find a string-table identifier representing a line of help text in the MDI sample application's resource file. This will be used later when the help text needs to be displayed in the status bar.

If the *MF_POPUP* bit is turned on, the procedure must determine which pop-up menu is highlighted. This is done by the following loop:

```
hMenu = GetMenu(hWnd);
wTemp = GetMenuItemCount(hMenu);
while (wTemp-)
   if (GetSubMenu(hMenu, wTemp) == hmenuPopup) break;
```

At the end of this loop, *wTemp* will contain the zero-based index of the highlighted pop-up menu. If there are any menu items (not pop-up menus) in the Frame window's top-level menu, the loop will still work correctly. This is because the *GetSubMenu* function returns NULL if the item at the specified index is not a pop-up menu.

If the *hmenuPopup* parameter indicates a handle to a cascading menu, this loop will not locate it. To locate the handle of a cascading menu, use the menu item ID for the first option in the cascading menu and compare it to what the first item should be in that menu:

```
if (GetMenuItemID(hmenuPopup, 0) == IDM_FIRSTOPTIONINCASCADINGMENU) {
   // Pop-up menu is the cascading menu pop-up.
}
```

Now that we have determined the string-table ID for the help text, the window that received the *WM_MENUSELECT* message forwards the user-defined *FW_SET-MENUHELP* message to the Frame's window procedure:

```
FORWARD_FW_SETMENUHELP(hwnd, hwndSender, dwMenuDescCode, fn)
```

The first parameter is the handle of the window that you are forwarding the message to. This should always be the MDI application's Frame window. The second parameter, *hwndSender*, is the handle of the window that processed the *WM_MENU-SELECT* message. This is either the Frame window's handle or an MDI Child window's handle. The third parameter, *dwMenuDescCode*, is the menu help code. In this example application, the menu help codes are always string table ID values.

When the Frame window receives the *FW_SETMENUHELP* message, it saves the window handle and the menu help code in its extra bytes:

```
void Frame_OnSetMenuHelp (HWND hwnd, HWND hwndSender,
    DWORD dwMenuDescCode) {
    RECT rc;

    // Save the handle of the window sending the message.
    SETWNDEB(hwnd, WNDEB, hWndMenuHelp, hwndSender);

    // Save the menu help code that the window sent to.
    SETWNDEB(hwnd, WNDEB, dwMenuHelp, dwMenuDescCode);
    .
    .
    .

}
```

Displaying help text as the user highlights each menu option requires a lot of painting. Painting is a slow operation that degrades Windows' performance. To alleviate this problem, take advantage of the *WM_ENTERIDLE* message. This message is sent to a window procedure when a message was just processed by a menu or dialog box and no other messages are waiting in the queue.

For our discussion, this means that as long as the user holds down the arrow key, *WM_KEYDOWN* messages are appended to the queue and processed by the menu system. When the user releases the arrow key, Windows sends the *WM_ENTERIDLE* message to the window procedure. At this point, the help text for the last highlighted menu option should be painted.

When the MDI sample application's Frame window receives the *WM_ENTERIDLE* message, the *Frame_OnEnterIdle* message cracker function is called:

```
void Frame_OnEnterIdle(HWND hwnd, UINT source, HWND hwndSource) {
   RECT rc; PAINTSTRUCT ps;
   if (source != MSGF_MENU) return;

   // User has stopped scrolling through menu items.

   // If Menu help already displayed, nothing more to do.
   // This is signaled by hWndMenu help being 0xFFFF.
   if (GETWNDEB(hwnd, WNDEB, hWndMenuHelp) == 0xFFFF)
      return;

   // Display new menu help, invalidate the status bar.
   FORWARD_FW_GETSTATBARRECT(hwnd, &rc, SendMessage);
   InvalidateRect(hwnd, &rc, TRUE);
   // BeginPaint is OK because an invalid rectangle must exist because
   // of the call to InvalidateRect above. This causes the background
   // for the Frame's client area to be drawn correctly.
   BeginPaint(hwnd, &ps);

   // Set up the device context.
   SetBkMode(ps.hdc, TRANSPARENT);

   // Send message to window that last received a WM_MENUSELECT
   // message to tell it to paint the status bar with the
   // appropriate menu help text.
   FORWARD_AW_PAINTMENUHELP((HWND) GETWNDEB(hwnd, WNDEB,
      WndMenuHelp), &ps, SendMessage);

   EndPaint(hwnd, &ps);
   // Set flag notifying this message that the most recently selected
   // menu item has had its help text painted. This stops unsightly
   // screen flicker.
   SETWNDEB(hwnd, WNDEB, hWndMenuHelp, (HWND) 0xFFFF);
   return;
}
```

The *source* parameter is either *MSGF_DIALOGBOX* or *MSGF_MENU*. These identifiers reveal whether the user was just using a dialog box or the application's menu system.

This code tells Windows that the area occupied by the Frame's status bar needs to have its background and text repainted. *BeginPaint* and *EndPaint* are not usually called except in response to a *WM_PAINT* message. However, calling the *Begin-Paint* function here has the side effect of having Windows automatically send the *WM_ERASEBKGND* message to the Frame's window procedure to ensure that the background is drawn in the correct color. Once the device context gives us permission to write on the status-bar area of the Frame, the background mode is changed to *TRANSPARENT* so that painting the menu help text does not change the Frame's background color.

Finally, you're ready to paint the menu help text. The Frame window sends the user-defined *AW_PAINTMENUHELP* message to the window specified by the *hwnd-Sender* parameter when the Frame window last processed a *FW_SETMENUHELP* message. This window may be the Frame window or an MDI Child window. The code for processing the *AW_PAINTMENUHELP* message is almost identical in either case. Here's how an MDI Child processes the message:

```
void Child_OnPaintMenuHelp (HWND hwnd, LPPAINTSTRUCT lpPaintStruct) {
    char szString[150], szCaption[90], szBuf[150];
    // Message sent from Frame window to notify child that it should
    // paint the status bar text for the last highlighted menu item.

    // Ask the Frame window what the last selected menu ID was.
    // This value was sent to the frame by this window during the
    // processing for the WM_MENUSELECT message.
    WORD wTemp = FORWARD_FW_GETMENUHELP(GETFRAME(hwnd), SendMessage);

    // Draw the horizontal dividing line separating the status bar
    // from the MDICLIENT window.
    lpPaintStruct->rcPaint.top += (int)
        FORWARD_FW_DRAWSTATUSDIVIDE(GETFRAME(hwnd),
            lpPaintStruct, SendMessage);
```

```
// Construct the string that is to be displayed.
LoadString(_hInstance, wTemp, szString, sizeof(szString));
GetWindowText(hwnd, szCaption, sizeof(szCaption));
wsprintf(szBuf, szString, (LPSTR) szCaption);

// Paint the menu help text in the status bar.
TextOut(lpPaintStruct->hdc,
    0, lpPaintStruct->rcPaint.top, szBuf, lstrlen(szBuf));
}
```

Because a message can only pass *WORD* and *DWORD* parameters, the Frame window cannot pass the menu help code. Instead, the code that processes the *AW_PAINTMENUHELP* message must send the *FW_GETMENUHELP* message back to the Frame to retrieve the help code. The *FW_GETMENUHELP* message simply returns the value that was stored in the Frame window's window extra bytes the last time the *FW_SETMENUHELP* message was processed:

```
DWORD Frame_OnGetMenuHelp (HWND hwnd) {
    // Sent by the Frame or MDI Child when each
    // receives an AW_PAINTMENUHELP message.
    return(GETWNDEB(hwnd, WNDEB, dwMenuHelp));
}
```

Let's tie up some loose ends.

We've assumed that Windows sends the *WM_ENTERIDLE* message to the Frame's window procedure. This is not always true in an MDI application. If the user is scrolling through options and passes through a non-maximized MDI Child's system menu, Windows sends the *WM_ENTERIDLE* message to the MDI Child. The MDI Child window must tell the Frame window when it receives a *WM_ENTERIDLE* message:

```
void Child_OnEnterIdle(HWND hwnd, UINT source, HWND hwndSource) {
    // User stopped moving around in the help system, make the Frame
    // believe that it received this message directly.
```

```
    FORWARD_WM_ENTERIDLE(GETFRAME(hwnd), source, hwndSource, SendMessage);
}
```

Windows sends the *WM_ENTERIDLE* message when a message has been processed and the application's queue is empty. Let's say the user has opened a menu and its help text appears at the bottom of the Frame window. The user starts moving the mouse across the screen and then stops. This causes several *WM_MOUSEMOVE* messages to be sent to the window procedure. After the last one is processed, Windows sends a *WM_ENTERIDLE* message. Our procedure erases the status bar and repaints the help text. Erasing and redrawing the same text repeatedly causes an annoying flashing to occur. To prevent this flashing, add the following lines to the processing of the *WM_ENTERIDLE* message in the Frame's window procedure:

```
void Frame_OnEnterIdle(HWND hwnd, UINT source, HWND hwndSource) {
   .

   .

   .

   // If Menu help already displayed, nothing more to do.
   // This is signaled by hWndMenu help being 0xFFFF.
   if (GETWNDEB(hwnd, WNDEB, hWndMenuHelp) == 0xFFFF)
      return;

   .

   .

   .

   // Set flag notifying this message that the most recently selected
   // menu item has had its help text painted. This stops unsightly
   // screen flicker.
   SETWNDEB(hwnd, WNDEB, hWndMenuHelp, (HWND) 0xFFFF);
   return;
}
```

A final loose end: If the menu system is closed (because the user selected a menu item or pressed the Esc key), the area occupied by the status bar must be invalidated so Windows will send a *WM_PAINT* message to the Frame window and restore the statistical information. Fortunately, Windows notifies the window procedure that the menu system has been closed by sending the *WM_MENUSELECT* message with the *flags* parameter equal to negative one. The Frame and the MDI Children check for this and send a *FW_SETMENUHELP* message to the Frame window with *wParam* equal to null:

```
void Frame_OnMenuSelect(HWND hwnd, HMENU hmenu, int item,
   HMENU hmenuPopup, UINT flags) {
      .
      .
      .
   if (flags == (UINT) -1) {
      // User has stopped using the menu system.
      FORWARD_FW_SETMENUHELP(hwnd, NULL, NULL, SendMessage);
      return;
      .
      .
      .
}
```

When the Frame window gets this message, it executes the following code to invalidate the status-bar area:

```
void Frame_OnSetMenuHelp (HWND hwnd, HWND hwndSender,
   DWORD dwMenuDescCode) {
      .
      .
      .
   // When the Frame or MDI Child receives a WM_MENUSELECT message
   // specifying that the menu system is closed, the menu help should
   // disappear and be replaced by the proper information on the
   // status bar.
```

```
    if (hwndSender == NULL) {
        FORWARD_FW_GETSTATBARRECT(hwnd, &rc, SendMessage);
        // Force status bar to be updated.
        InvalidateRect(hwnd, &rc, TRUE);
    }
}
```

Custom Tiling

Almost all MDI applications contain a Window menu that allows the user to manipulate MDI Child windows. Usually the first options to appear in this menu are "Cascade" and "Tile." "Cascade" organizes MDI Child windows so that only the caption bar of each is visible, except for the active MDI Child, which is positioned on the top of the stack. The "Tile" option organizes the MDI Child windows side by side so none of the windows overlap and all of the area in the MDICLIENT window is occupied. The active MDI Child is the upper left window.

The window procedure for the MDICLIENT window contains all the code required to arrange the MDI Child windows. The *WM_MDICASCADE* and *WM_MDITILE* messages make the MDICLIENT window rearrange the MDI Children. The programmer does not have to write any additional code. A third message, *WM_MDIICONARRANGE*, causes the MDICLIENT window to arrange any MDI Children that have been reduced to icons. The MDICLIENT window organizes the icons so that they align at the bottom of the MDICLIENT window's area. Whenever the MDICLIENT receives a *WM_MDICASCADE* or *WM_MDITILE* message, the iconic MDI Children are automatically arranged and the non-iconic windows are positioned so that only the bottom row of icons is visible.

In Windows 3.0, the method of tiling implemented by the MDICLIENT window causes windows to be tiled vertically. That is, if two windows exist, tiling places the active one on the left and the inactive one on the right. In many applications, it would be better if a form of horizontal tiling were used. For example, Word for Windows tiles its MDI Children so that the active window is above the inactive window. Fewer lines of text are displayed, but each line is seen in its entirety.

Microsoft addresses this method of tiling in Windows 3.1 by giving meaning to the *wParam* parameter for a *WM_MDITILE* message. Either the *MDITILE_HOR-IZONTAL* or *MDITILE_VERTICAL* identifiers may be passed as the *wParam* parameter. Since *MDITILE_VERTICAL* identifier is defined as zero, backward compatibility is maintained for applications written prior to Windows 3.1. In addition to these two identifiers, a third identifier may be *OR*ed with one of these when you instruct the MDICLIENT window to tile the child windows, *MDITILE_SKIPDIS-ABLED*. This identifier tells the MDICLIENT window to ignore any disabled MDI Children when tiling the windows.

FRAME.C includes a function called *TileHorizontally* that shows how to design a custom tiling scheme for MDI Child windows. It takes two parameters, the first is the window handle of the MDICLIENT window, *hWndMDIClient,* and the second is a Boolean value, *fSkipDisabled,* which indicates whether disabled windows should be included in the tiling.

This function starts by calculating the area occupied by the MDICLIENT window. Assuming that all of the MDI Child windows will be completely contained within this window after tiling, the size of the MDICLIENT window without scroll bars must be calculated. This can be done by hiding the scroll bars before calling *GetClientRect*:

```
ShowScrollBar(hWndMDIClient, SB_BOTH, 0);
```

As with *WM_MDICASCADE* and *WM_MDITILE*, you want to arrange the iconic MDI Children too. Do this by sending the *WM_MDIICONARRANGE* message to the MDICLIENT window. It is important to do this after the scroll bars have been hidden and before adjusting the position of any of the other MDI Children. When MDI Children are iconic, the MDICLIENT window ensures that the other MDI Children are positioned so that the bottom row of icons is visible. This means that the usable area in the MDICLIENT window is smaller if any MDI Children are iconic. To calculate the amount of usable space, the iconic children must be arranged first and the y-coordinate that represents the top of the bottom row of icons must be calculated.

This is done by creating a loop that cycles through all the child windows of the MDICLIENT window:

```
int nTopOfBottomIconRow = 0, nMDIChildrenToTile = 0;
HWND hWndChild;
RECT rc;
```

.
.
.

```
// Get handle to first MDI Child window.
hWndChild = GetFirstChild(hWndMDIClient);
do {
    if (IsMinimized(hWndChild) && GetWindowOwner(hWndChild) == NULL) {
        // Window is iconic and window is NOT an icon's caption.

        // Get client area of the icon window.
        GetWindowRect(hWndChild, &rc);

        // rc.top is in screen coordinates.
        nTopOfBottomIconRow = max(nTopOfBottomIconRow, rc.top);
    }

    if (!IsMinimized(hWndChild) && GetWindowOwner(hWndChild) == NULL) {

        // If you should include all windows (even disabled) or
        // the window isn't disabled, increment the number of
        // children to tile.
        if (!fSkipDisabled || IsWindowEnabled(hWndChild))
            ++nMDIChildrenToTile;
    }
} while ((hWndChild = GetNextSibling(hWndChild)) != NULL);
```

When a window is minimized, Windows creates another window of a System Global class that displays the icon's caption. This window's parent and owner is the icon window. The non-minimized MDI Children will not have explicit owners; therefore, *GetWindowOwner(hWndChild)* returns NULL. The icon caption bar windows should not be taken into account when the loop is processing children of the MDICLIENT window.

The loop calculates the y-coordinate of the bottom row of icons by getting the window coordinates for each minimized window and setting *nTopOfBottomIcon-*

473

Row to the largest *y* value (*rc.top*). If the child window is to be included in the tiling, *nMDIChildrenToTile* is incremented by one. When the Children have been enumerated, *GetNextSibling(hWndChild)* returns NULL and the loop terminates.

Finally, the height of the usable area can be computed:

```
GetClientRect(hWndMDIClient, &rc);
if (nTopOfBottomIconRow) {
    Point.x = 0; Point.y = nTopOfBottomIconRow;
    ScreenToClient(hWndMDIClient, &Point);
    // Point.y contains top of bottom icon row in client coordinates.
    rc.bottom = Point.y;
}
```

If *nTopOfBottomIconRow* is not zero, the y-coordinate is converted to client coordinates and the usable area identified by the *rc* variable is updated to reflect the appropriate dimensions.

MDI Child windows can't be repositioned if any MDI Child is maximized. Here's the code that restores any maximized MDI Children:

```
hWndActiveMDIChild = GetActiveMDIChild(&fIsMDIChildMaximized);
if (fIsMDIChildMaximized)
    ShowWindow(hWndActiveMDIChild, SW_RESTORE);
```

The tiling algorithm positions the MDI Child windows on top of each other. However, if several MDI Children are open and tiled in this way, each of the windows will be extremely short. For this reason, the algorithm selects a desired minimum height for the MDI Child windows as five times the height of a caption bar:

```
nMinWndHeight = max(1, rc.bottom /
    (5 * GetSystemMetrics(SM_CYCAPTION)));
```

If the usable region in the MDICLIENT area is so short that one window does not fit, the windows will be tiled in one row. The number of rows and the height of each row that will appear in the MDICLIENT is calculated as follows:

```
nNumRows = min(nMDIChildrenToTile, nMinWndHeight);
nRowHeight = rc.bottom / nNumRows;
```

The tiling algorithm is designed so that each row has at least the sum of the number of windows divided by the number of rows of MDI Children. If the result of this division yields a remainder, the remaining MDI Children are distributed evenly among the rows closest to the bottom. This formula determines the number of MDI Children to be placed on each row:

```
nNumWndsOnRow = nOpenMDIChildren / nNumRows +
    (((nMDIChildrenToTIle % nNumRows) > (nNumRows - (nCrntRow + 1)))
    ? 1 : 0);
```

Now that the initial calculations have been done, the loop cycles through the rows and columns to tile the open MDI Children:

```
// Get the handle to the first MDI Child window.
hWndChild = GetFirstChild(hWndMDIClient);

// Prime the storage of positioning information.
hDWPWinPosInfo = BeginDeferWindowPos(nMDIChildrenToTile);

// Execute the loop for each row.
for (nCrntRow = 0; nCrntRow < nNumRows; nCrntRow++) {

    // Calculate the number of MDI Children that will appear on this row.
    nNumWndsOnRow = nMDIChildrenToTile / nNumRows +
        ((nMDIChildrenToTile % nNumRows >
        (nNumRows - (nCrntRow + 1))) ? 1 : 0);

    // Calculate the width of each of these children.
    nColWidth = rc.right / nNumWndsOnRow;
```

```
    // Fill each column with an MDI Child window.
    for (nCrntCol = 0; nCrntCol < nNumWndsOnRow; ) {

        if (IsMinimized(hWndChild) ||
            (GetWindowOwner(hWndChild) != NULL) ||
            (fSkipDisabled && !IsWindowEnabled(hWndChild)) {
            // Don't reposition if the window:
            // 1. is iconic
            // 2. has an owner (icon's caption)
            // 3. is disabled and caller wants to ignore disabled windows.
        } else {
            // Everything is OK, reposition the window.

            // Tell windows what the new position and
            // dimensions of this MDI Child should be.
            hDWPWinPosInfo = DeferWindowPos(hDWPWinPosInfo,
                hWndChild, NULL, nCrntCol * nColWidth,
                nCrntRow * nRowHeight, nColWidth,
                nRowHeight, SWP_NOACTIVATE | SWP_NOZORDER |
                SWP_NOCOPYBITS);

            // Go to the next column.
            nCrntCol++;
        }

        // Get handle to the next MDI Child window.
        hWndChild = GetNextSibling(hWndChild);
    }
}

// All of the positioning has been set. Now, tell Windows to update
// all of the windows at once.
EndDeferWindowPos(hDWPWinPosInfo);
```

The MDI Child windows are repositioned by making calls to *DeferWindow-Pos.*You must call *BeginDeferWindowPos* first. This function allocates a block of memory that holds the repositioning information set by calls to the *DeferWindowPos* function. The parameter passed to the *BeginDeferWindowPos* function specifies the number of windows to be repositioned. If the *DeferWindowPos* function is called more often than this number, Windows automatically increases the size of the memory block to contain the additional information. The new block of memory is returned by *DeferWindowPos.* After all the position information has been set, call *EndDeferWindowPos.* This function instructs Windows to repaint all the MDI Child windows at once.

It is possible to call *SetWindowPos* instead of *BeginDeferWindowPos, DeferWindowPos,* and *EndDeferWindowPos,* but this would cause an annoying amount of screen updating, and repositioning all the windows would take much longer.

When tiling occurs, the active MDI Child window should be positioned in the upper left corner of the MDICLIENT window. In the *TileHorizontally* function, this is done for us automatically. Whenever a window is active, it appears closest to the top of the window manager's list. Therefore, the call to *GetFirstChild(hWndMDIClient)* always returns the active MDI Child window. Since the tiling algorithm places the first child in the upper left corner, everything works fine.

Implementing a Ribbon

A ribbon is a set of controls that appears just under an MDI application's menu bar. It allows easy access to options that affect an area in an MDI Child window. For example, the ribbon in Word for Windows allows the user to alter paragraph and character attributes of text. Microsoft Excel and Project for Windows also use ribbons that allow the user to enter text or select miniature icons to perform operations.

Most applications let the user show or hide the ribbon. When the ribbon is hidden, more screen real estate is available for the MDI Child windows. The MDI sample application implements a ribbon using a modeless dialog box. The dialog-box procedure for the ribbon can be found in RIBBON.C. However, the dialog box is created in the *WinMain* function in MDI.C as a child of the Frame window. For a dialog box to be created as a child window, *WS_CHILD* must appear on the *STYLE* line in the template.

If you examine MDI.RC, you will notice that *WS_CLIPSIBLINGS* also appears on the *STYLE* line. This is necessary for Windows to update the screen correctly. Because the MDICLIENT window and the ribbon can occupy the same area of the screen, Windows might allow either window to paint over the other's area. The *WS_CLIPSIBLINGS* style prevents windows from painting areas occupied by their siblings. The MDICLIENT window is also created with the *WS_CLIPSIBLINGS* style.

Ribbons usually exist so that the user can alter characteristics of elements in an MDI Child window. But in Word for Windows the ribbon is used to change the formatting of the selected paragraph or text. In the MDI sample application, the ribbon is implemented as a dumb ribbon, meaning that it has no effect on the MDI Child windows.

The user turns the ribbon on and off by selecting the "Ribbon" option from the Options menu. When the Frame's window procedure receives this message in the *Frame_OnCommand* message cracker, it toggles the visible state of the ribbon and forwards the user-defined *FW_RESIZEMDICLIENT* message to the Frame window:

```
void Frame_OnCommand(HWND hwnd, int id, HWND hwndCtl, UINT codeNotify) {
    .
    .
    .

    case IDM_OPTIONSRIBBON:
        // Toggle the status of the ribbon, resize the MDICLIENT.
        ShowWindow(_hDlgRibbon,
            IsWindowVisible(_hDlgRibbon) ? SW_HIDE : SW_SHOW);
        FORWARD_FW_RESIZEMDICLIENT(hwnd, SendMessage);
        break;
    .
    .
    .
```

The *FW_RESIZEMDICLIENT* message is received by the Frame's window procedure whenever the user resizes the Frame window, toggles the status bar on or off, or toggles the ribbon on or off. This message calculates the new height and position of the MDICLIENT window:

```
void Frame_OnResizeMDIClient (HWND hwnd) {
   RECT rc, rcTemp;
   if (!IsWindow(_hWndMDIClient)) return;
   // Sent when the Frame window is resized or when the status bar
   // and ribbon are toggled.
   GetClientRect(hwnd, &rc);

   if (IsWindow(_hDlgRibbon) && IsWindowVisible(_hDlgRibbon))  {
      // Ribbon is displayed, adjust rectangle.
      GetClientRect(_hDlgRibbon, &rcTemp);
      rc.top += rcTemp.bottom;
      rc.bottom -= rcTemp.bottom;
   }

   // Get the dimensions of the status bar rectangle and adjust the
   // dimensions of the MDICLIENT window.
   FORWARD_FW_GETSTATBARRECT(hwnd, &rcTemp, SendMessage);
   rc.bottom -= rcTemp.bottom - rcTemp.top;
   MoveWindow(_hWndMDIClient, 0, rc.top, rc.right, rc.bottom, TRUE);
}
```

Once the user turns the ribbon on, it stays visible until the user explicitly turns it off. If the user closes all the MDI Child windows, the ribbon should be disabled and all of its controls should appear gray. You do this by having each MDI Child's window procedure post the *FW_MDICHILDDESTROY* message to the Frame window when the child processes the *WM_DESTROY* message. When the Frame window receives the *FW_MDICHILDDESTROY* message from the last MDI Child, it disables the ribbon dialog box:

```
void Frame_OnMDIChildDestroy (HWND hwnd) {
   // Message is posted by an MDI Child just before it is destroyed.

   HWND hWndActiveMDIChild = GetActiveMDIChild(NULL);
```

```
// If another MDI Child exists, nothing to do.
if (hWndActiveMDIChild != NULL) return;

.

.

.


// Disable the Ribbon.
EnableWindow(_hDlgRibbon, FALSE);
}
```

When the user selects "Open sheet" or "Open chart" from the File menu in the MDI sample application, the Frame window creates a new MDI Child window and enables the ribbon.

When a window is disabled, Windows won't send it mouse or keyboard messages. Children of the disabled window don't receive mouse or keyboard input either. This means that the ribbon's child controls don't receive input when the ribbon is disabled. However, when a child control is drawn, the control's window procedure determines if the *WS_DISABLE* style is on for the particular control. If this style is on, the control is drawn using grayed text. Although the child controls won't receive input, disabling the ribbon doesn't change the *WS_DISABLE* style bit for the controls. To make the controls paint themselves using gray text, the individual controls must be disabled by having the ribbon's dialog-box procedure process the *WM_ENABLE* message in the following way:

```
void Ribbon_OnEnable (HWND hwnd, BOOL fEnable) {
    // Make all child windows have the same status as the dialog box.
    HWND hwndCtl = GetFirstChild(hwnd);

    for (; hwndCtl != NULL; hwndCtl = GetNextSibling(hwndCtl))
        EnableWindow(hwndCtl, fEnable);
}
```

The value in *fEnable* for a *WM_ENABLE* message indicates whether the window is being enabled (*fEnable* is nonzero) or disabled (*fEnable* is zero). This loop simply makes all the children of the dialog box have the same state as the dialog box itself.

The *WM_PAINT* message is also intercepted in the ribbon's dialog-box procedure. This message is used to draw a dividing line between the dialog box and the MDICLIENT window. Like the dividing line drawn for the status bar, this line is painted with a pen that has a thickness of *GetSystemMetrics(SM_CYBORDER)*.

Child controls in a ribbon should retain focus for a short time. Once the user has selected the desired option, the control should set the focus back to the MDI application's Frame window. This allows the user to work fluidly with the document, perform some operation by selecting a control in the ribbon, and continue to work. The code fragment below shows how focus is set to the Frame window after a ribbon control has performed its operation:

```
void Ribbon_OnCommand (HWND hwnd, int id, HWND hwndCtl,
    UINT codeNotify) {
    // Make sure that focus is given back to the Frame after an
    // option is chosen by the user.

    switch (id) {
        case ID_FONT:
        case ID_SIZE:
            if (codeNotify != CBN_SELCHANGE) break;
            SetFocus(GetParent(hwnd));
            break;

        case ID_BOLD:
        case ID_ITALIC:
        case ID_UNDERLINE:
            if (codeNotify != BN_CLICKED) break;
            SetFocus(GetParent(hwnd));
            break;
```

```
      case IDOK:
      case IDCANCEL:
        SetFocus(GetParent(hwnd));
        break;
    }
  }
```

When the ribbon's dialog-box procedure receives the *WM_COMMAND* message, focus is sent back to the Frame window. The Frame window sets focus to the MDICLIENT window, and the MDICLIENT window sets focus to the active MDI Child window.

Some controls, like list boxes, combo boxes, and scroll bars, keep the input focus for a longer period than buttons so that a user can scroll through a list of choices. If the user is working with one of these controls in the ribbon, the Enter and Esc keys should set the focus back to the active MDI Child window. When either of these keys is pressed, Windows sends a *WM_COMMAND* message with *wParam* (*id* in the message cracker) set to *IDOK* or *IDCANCEL*. Windows sends these identifiers regardless of whether "OK" and "Cancel" buttons exist in the dialog box. The dialog-box procedure calls *SetFocus* when either of these events occur.

Closing an MDI Application

An MDI application allows the user to work with many documents at once. Because several windows are displayed, it's easy for the user to lose track of which documents have been updated and not saved. For this reason, it is important that an MDI application be forgiving and take extra precautions so that no work is accidentally destroyed. Of course, this is important for non-MDI applications as well.

An MDI application should see if any data could be lost when the user attempts one of the following actions:

- Closing an MDI Child window.
- Terminating the MDI application.
- Terminating the Windows session.

Most MDI Child windows maintain a Boolean value (called a *dirty flag*) in the window's extra bytes to indicate whether the document has been updated since it was last saved. Whenever an action takes place that changes the document, this value is set to TRUE. After the file has been successfully written to disk, the value is changed to FALSE.

Let's examine the situation where the user is terminating the Windows session first. When the user closes Program Manager, a system-modal message box is presented to verify that the Windows session should be terminated. If the user answers affirmatively, Windows sends the *WM_QUERYENDSESSION* message to all running applications. Each application has an opportunity to determine whether any data would be lost if the application were terminated and may prompt the user to take some action. If an application finds that the dirty flag is set, it presents a message box similar to the one in Figure 8-2.

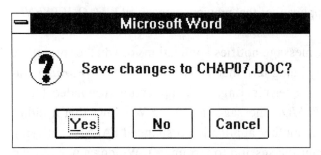

**Figure 8-2. Dialog box presented to user when application
terminates and documents have not been saved**

The caption of the message box should indicate the name of the application that is presenting it. Remember that every application is going to get a chance to present a message box, and the user may not remember which application a particular file belongs. The name of the file should also appear in the message box. In MDI applications, this message box may appear several times, once for every document window the user has opened. The options in the box allow the user to do one of the following.

Option	Description
Yes	Save the updated document. Continue terminating the Windows session.
No	Do not save the updated document. Continue terminating the Windows session.
Cancel	Do not save the updated document. Stop terminating the Windows session.

If the user presses the "Yes" or "No" button, the application returns TRUE in response to *WM_QUERYENDSESSION*. Windows sends the *WM_QUERY-ENDSESSION* message to the next application.

If the user selects "Cancel," the window procedure returns FALSE. Windows stops sending *WM_QUERYENDSESSION* messages and starts sending *WM_END-SESSION* messages to the applications that previously received *WM_QUERYEND-SESSION* messages.

The *WM_ENDSESSION* message notifies applications of whether or not the Windows session is actually being terminated. The value of the *wParam* parameter is TRUE if the session is terminating. If an application responded TRUE to the *WM_QUERYENDSESSION* message (notifying Windows that it didn't mind being terminated), but another application responded FALSE (notifying Windows that it did not want the session to terminate), Windows would send the *WM_ENDSESSION* message to the first application with the *wParam* parameter set to FALSE. If all applications returned TRUE, Windows would send the *WM_ENDSESSION* message with *wParam* set to TRUE and then terminate the Windows session.

For an MDI application, this processing should be extended so that when the MDI Frame window receives a *WM_QUERYENDSESSION* message, it sends a *AC_QUERYCLOSEMDICHILD* message to each of the MDI Child windows. Similarly, the Frame window forwards an *AC_MDICHILDENDSESSION* message to all MDI Children in response to a *WM_ENDSESSION* message.

In the MDI sample application, the code in the Frame's window procedure for sending the *AC_QUERYCLOSEMDICHILD* message to the MDI Children looks like the following:

```
BOOL Frame_OnQueryEndSession (HWND hwnd) {
   HWND hWndChildStop;

   // Assume that it is OK to end the session.
   BOOL fOkToTerminate = TRUE;


   // Get the handle of the first MDI Child.
   HWND hWndChild = GetFirstChild(_hWndMDIClient);

   // If no MDI Children exist, it is OK to terminate.
   if (hWndChild == NULL) return(fOkToTerminate);

   // Ask each child if it is OK to terminate.
   do {
      // Do not ask caption bars of iconic MDI Children.
      if (GetWindowOwner(hWndChild) != NULL) continue;

      fOkToTerminate =
         FORWARD_AC_QUERYCLOSEMDICHILD(hWndChild, _fSysModal,
            SendMessage);

      // If the MDI Child says that it is NOT OK, don't ask the
      // rest of the MDI Children.
      if (!fOkToTerminate) break;

   } while ((hWndChild = GetNextSibling(hWndChild)) != NULL);


   // If any MDI Child said NO, tell the other children that
   // the session is NOT being terminated.
   if (!fOkToTerminate) {
      hWndChildStop = hWndChild;
      hWndChild = GetFirstChild(_hWndMDIClient);
```

```
      do {
          // If this child is the one that said NO, stop.
          if (hWndChildStop == hWndChild) break;

          // Do not send to caption bars of iconic MDI Children.
          if (GetWindowOwner(hWndChild) != NULL) continue;

          // Tell child we are not ending the session (wParam is
          // FALSE).
          FORWARD_AC_MDICHILDENDSESSION(hWndChild, FALSE, SendMessage);
      } while ((hWndChild = GetNextSibling(hWndChild)) != NULL);
  }
  return(fOkToTerminate);
}
```

The first loop enumerates all the MDI Child windows and sends the *AC_QUERY-CLOSEMDICHILD* message to each. If all the MDI Children return TRUE, TRUE is returned to Windows and the next application gets the *WM_QUERYENDSESSION* message. If any of the MDI Children return FALSE, however, the loop is immediately stopped and a new loop is started. The second loop sends the *AC_MDI-CHILDENDSESSION* message (with the *fEnding* parameter set to FALSE) to each of the MDI Children that responded TRUE. When the loop completes, FALSE returns to Windows so the session will not be terminated.

The MDI Child window procedures for the Sheet and Chart classes process the *AC_QUERYCLOSEMDICHILD* message in the following way:

```
BOOL Child_OnQueryCloseMDIChild (HWND hwnd, BOOL fSysModal) {
    BOOL fOkToTerminate = TRUE; char szBuf[100];
    WORD wTemp;
    // Prompt user whether to save changes to this document.
    // Usually, a dirty flag (stored in the window's extra bytes)
    // is used to determine if it is necessary to ask this question.

    // Construct string including the document's name.
```

```
lstrcpy(szBuf, "Save changes to ");
wTemp = lstrlen(szBuf);
GetWindowText(hwnd, szBuf + wTemp, sizeof(szBuf) - wTemp);
lstrcat(szBuf, "?");

// Display message box to user. The message box should
// be system modal if the entire Windows session is being
// terminated. (wParam is FALSE).
wTemp = MessageBox(hwnd, szBuf, _szAppName,
    MB_ICONQUESTION | MB_YESNOCANCEL |
    (fSysModal ? MB_SYSTEMMODAL : MB_APPLMODAL));

switch (wTemp) {
    case IDYES:
        // Save the document and it's OK to quit.
        fOkToTerminate = TRUE;
        break;

    case IDNO:
        // Don't save the document and it's OK to quit.
        fOkToTerminate = TRUE;
        break;

    case IDCANCEL:
        // Don't save the document and it's NOT OK to quit.
        fOkToTerminate = FALSE;
        break;
    }
    return(fOkToTerminate);
}
```

The MDI sample application does not maintain a dirty flag for each of the created windows; therefore, the previous code always prompts the user to save the updated document to disk. You will also notice that the call to *MessageBox* tests the value of *fSysModal.* This parameter indicates whether a system modal or application modal dialog box should be displayed. Whenever Windows sends the *WM_QUERYEND-SESSION* message to the application, it means that the user is terminating the whole Windows session. In this case, each MDI Child window should show a system modal dialog box. The message box must be system modal so that the user cannot close Program Manager a second time. When the user is just terminating the MDI application, the MDI children show an application modal dialog box.

The Frame's window procedure notifies its *WM_QUERYENDSESSION* message cracker that the dialog boxes should be application modal by setting a global variable, *_fAppModal*, to TRUE when the Frame receives a *WM_CLOSE* message. The following code makes the application believe that the Windows session is terminating:

```
void Frame_OnClose (HWND hwnd) {
    BOOL fOkToTerminate;
    // Before closing the application, ask the MDI Children if it
    // is OK?
    // Set _fAppModal to TRUE so that system modal dialog boxes will
    // not be shown.
    _fAppModal = TRUE;
    fOkToTerminate = FORWARD_WM_QUERYENDSESSION(hwnd, SendMessage);
    _fAppModal = FALSE;
    if (fOkToTerminate) {
        FORWARD_WM_ENDSESSION(hwnd, TRUE, SendMessage);
        FORWARD_WM_CLOSE(hwnd, Frame_DefProc);
    }
}
```

Normally, the *DefFrameProc* function destroys the window when it processes a *WM_CLOSE* message. Therefore, if the result from sending the *WM_QUERYENDSESSION* message to the Frame window indicates that the application may be terminated, the *WM_CLOSE* message is forwarded to the Frame's default window procedure.

If any of the MDI Child windows return FALSE, the processing in the Frame's window procedure automatically sends the *AC_MDICHILDENDSESSION* message to all the MDI Children that returned TRUE. When these MDI Children receive the message, the *fEnding* parameter will be FALSE, indicating that the session is not closing after all. However, if the application is going to terminate, you must send the *WM_ENDSESSION* message to the Frame window so that the MDI Children will be notified that the application is, in fact, terminating by sending all the children *AC_MDICHILDENDSESSION* messages with the *fEnding* parameter set to TRUE. The processing of the *WM_ENDSESSION* message in the Frame's window procedure is shown below:

```
void Frame_OnEndSession(HWND hwnd, BOOL fEnding) {
    // Get handle of first MDI Child window.
    HWND hWndChild = GetFirstChild(_hWndMDIClient);

    // Tell each MDI Child whether or not the session is ending.
    while (hWndChild != NULL) {

        // Do not send to caption bars of iconic MDI Children.
        if (GetWindowOwner(hWndChild) == NULL)
            FORWARD_AC_MDICHILDENDSESSION(hWndChild, fEnding,
                SendMessage);

        hWndChild = GetNextSibling(hWndChild);
    }
}
```

Since none of the MDI Children have any processing to do when the *AC_MDICHILDENDSESSION* message is processed, they simply return:

```
void Child_OnMDIChildEndSession (HWND hwnd, BOOL fEnding) {
    // Do any last minute cleanup during this message.
}
```

So far, we have discussed two occasions when the application should test for possible data loss. The third occasion is when the user simply closes a single MDI

Child window. In this case, the window receives a *WM_CLOSE* message and processes it as follows:

```
void Child_OnClose (HWND hwnd) {
    // Make sure that it is OK to close this child window.
    BOOL fOkToTerminate =
        FORWARD_AC_QUERYCLOSEMDICHILD(hwnd, TRUE, SendMessage);
    if (fOkToTerminate) {
        FORWARD_AC_MDICHILDENDSESSION(hwnd, TRUE, SendMessage);
        FORWARD_WM_CLOSE(hwnd, Child_DefProc);
    }
}
```

The *AC_QUERYCLOSEMDICHILD* message is only sent to the MDI Child window that is being closed. The *fAppModal* parameter is TRUE, so an application modal message box appears instead of a system modal message box. If the user indicated that the MDI Child could be closed, the *AC_MDICHILDEND-SESSION* message is sent so the Child can do last-minute cleanup; the *DefMDIChildProc* function is allowed to process the *WM_CLOSE* message, destroying the Child window.

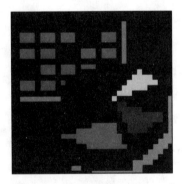

Figure 8-3. MDI.ICO

490

Figure 8-4. SHEET.ICO

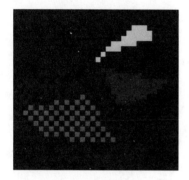

Figure 8-5. CHART.ICO

Listing 8-1. MAKEFILE for MDI application

```
#***************************************************************************
#Module name: MAKEFILE
#Programmer : Jeffrey M. Richter.
#***************************************************************************

PROG = MDI

MODEL = m
CFLAGS = -c -f- -WS -p -v -w -m$(MODEL) -I$(INCLUDEDIR)
LFLAGS = /P/v/n/m/s/L$(LIBDIR)
LIBS = CW$(MODEL) Import

MODULES = $(PROG).obj Frame.obj Sheet.obj Chart.obj Child.obj Ribbon.obj
```

```
ICONS   = $(PROG).ico
BITMAPS =
CURSORS =

$(PROG).Exe: $(MODULES) $(PROG).Def $(PROG).Res
    tlink $(LFLAGS) @&&!
COW$(MODEL) $(MODULES)
$(PROG), $(PROG), $(LIBS), $(PROG)
!
   rc -30 -T -i$(INCLUDEDIR) $(PROG).Res
   TDStrip -s $(PROG)

$(PROG).res: $(PROG).rc $(PROG).h $(RESOURCES)
```

Listing 8-2. MDI.H application header module

```
/*******************************************************************
Module name: MDI.H
Programmer : Jeffrey M. Richter & Elvira Peretsman.
*******************************************************************/

extern const HINSTANCE _cdecl _hInstance;
extern const HINSTANCE _cdecl _hPrev;

extern char   _szAppName[];    // The name of the application.
extern HACCEL _hAccelTable;    // Handle to active Accelerators.
extern HWND   _hWndMDIClient;  // Handle to MDICLIENT window.
extern HWND   _hDlgRibbon;     // Ribbon modeless dialog box.

ATOM WINAPI RegisterFrameWndClass (void);
BOOL WINAPI InitSheetWndClass (BOOL fInitialize);
BOOL WINAPI InitChartWndClass (BOOL fInitialize);
BOOL CALLBACK RibbonDlgProc (HWND hDlg, UINT uMsg, WPARAM wParam,
    LPARAM lParam);

#define GETFRAME(hWnd)  ((HWND) (GetParent(GetParent(hWnd))))

// User-defined Messages processed by Frame Window class.
#define FW_MDICHILDDESTROY    (WM_USER + 0)
/* void Cls_OnMDIChildDestroy (HWND hwnd) */
#define HANDLE_FW_MDICHILDDESTROY(hwnd, wParam, lParam, fn) \
    ((fn)((hwnd)), 0L)
#define FORWARD_FW_MDICHILDDESTROY(hwnd, fn) \
    (void)(fn)((hwnd), FW_MDICHILDDESTROY, (WPARAM)0, (LPARAM)0)
```

```
#define FW_RESIZEMDICLIENT    (WM_USER + 1)
/* void Cls_OnResizeMDIClient (HWND hwnd) */
#define HANDLE_FW_RESIZEMDICLIENT(hwnd, wParam, lParam, fn) \
    ((fn)((hwnd)), 0L)
#define FORWARD_FW_RESIZEMDICLIENT(hwnd, fn) \
    (void)(fn)((hwnd), FW_RESIZEMDICLIENT, (WPARAM)0, (LPARAM)0)


#define FW_GETSTATBARRECT     (WM_USER + 2)
/* void Cls_OnGetStatBarRect (HWND hwnd, LPRECT lpRect) */
#define HANDLE_FW_GETSTATBARRECT(hwnd, wParam, lParam, fn) \
    ((fn)((hwnd), (LPRECT)(lParam)), 0L)
#define FORWARD_FW_GETSTATBARRECT(hwnd, lpRect, fn) \
    (void)(fn)((hwnd), FW_GETSTATBARRECT, (WPARAM)0,
(LPARAM)(LPRECT)(lpRect))


#define FW_SETMENUHELP        (WM_USER + 3)
/* void Cls_OnSetMenuHelp (HWND hwnd, HWND hwndSender,
   DWORD dwMenuDescCode) */
#define HANDLE_FW_SETMENUHELP(hwnd, wParam, lParam, fn) \
    ((fn)((hwnd), (HWND)(wParam), (DWORD)(lParam)), 0L)
#define FORWARD_FW_SETMENUHELP(hwnd, hwndSender, dwMenuDescCode, fn) \
    (void)(fn)((hwnd), FW_SETMENUHELP, (WPARAM)(HWND)(hwndSender),
(LPARAM)(DWORD)(dwMenuDescCode))


#define FW_GETMENUHELP        (WM_USER + 4)
/* DWORD Cls_OnGetMenuHelp (HWND hwnd) */
#define HANDLE_FW_GETMENUHELP(hwnd, wParam, lParam, fn) \
    ((fn)((hwnd)))
#define FORWARD_FW_GETMENUHELP(hwnd, fn) \
    (DWORD)(fn)((hwnd), FW_GETMENUHELP, (WPARAM)0, (LPARAM)0)


#define FW_DRAWSTATUSDIVIDE   (WM_USER + 5)
/* int Cls_OnDrawStatusDivide (HWND hwnd, LPPAINTSTRUCT lpPaintStruct) */
#define HANDLE_FW_DRAWSTATUSDIVIDE(hwnd, wParam, lParam, fn) \
    ((fn)((hwnd), (LPPAINTSTRUCT)(lParam)))
#define FORWARD_FW_DRAWSTATUSDIVIDE(hwnd, lpPaintStruct, fn) \
    (int)(fn)((hwnd), FW_DRAWSTATUSDIVIDE, (WPARAM)0,
(LPARAM)(LPPAINTSTRUCT)(lpPaintStruct))


// User-defined Messages processed by all window classes.
#define AW_PAINTMENUHELP      (WM_USER + 100)
/* void Cls_OnPaintMenuHelp (HWND hwnd, LPPAINTSTRUCT lpPaintStruct) */
#define HANDLE_AW_PAINTMENUHELP(hwnd, wParam, lParam, fn) \
    ((fn)((hwnd), (LPPAINTSTRUCT)(lParam)), 0L)
#define FORWARD_AW_PAINTMENUHELP(hwnd, lpPaintStruct, fn) \
   (void)(fn)((hwnd), AW_PAINTMENUHELP, (WPARAM)0,
     (LPARAM)(LPPAINTSTRUCT)(lpPaintStruct))
```

```
// User-defined messages processed by all MDI Child window classes.

#define AC_PAINTSTATBAR        (WM_USER + 200)
/* void Cls_OnMDIChildPaintStatBar (HWND hwnd, HDC hDC,
   LPPAINTSTRUCT lpPaintStruct) */
#define HANDLE_AC_PAINTSTATBAR(hwnd, wParam, lParam, fn) \
    ((fn)((hwnd), (HDC)(wParam), (LPPAINTSTRUCT) lParam), 0L)
#define FORWARD_AC_PAINTSTATBAR(hwnd, hDC, lpPaintStruct, fn) \
    (void)(fn)((hwnd), AC_PAINTSTATBAR, (WPARAM)(HDC)(hDC),
(LPARAM)(LPPAINTSTRUCT)(lpPaintStruct))

#define AC_QUERYCLOSEMDICHILD (WM_USER + 201)
/* BOOL Cls_OnQueryCloseMDIChild (HWND hwnd, BOOL fSysModal) */
#define HANDLE_AC_QUERYCLOSEMDICHILD(hwnd, wParam, lParam, fn) \
    (BOOL)((fn)((hwnd), (BOOL)(wParam)))
#define FORWARD_AC_QUERYCLOSEMDICHILD(hwnd, fSysModal, fn) \
    (BOOL)(DWORD)(fn)((hwnd), AC_QUERYCLOSEMDICHILD, fSysModal, 0L)

#define AC_MDICHILDENDSESSION (WM_USER + 202)
/* void Cls_OnMDIChildEndSession (HWND hwnd, BOOL fEnding) */
#define HANDLE_AC_MDICHILDENDSESSION(hwnd, wParam, lParam, fn) \
    ((fn)((hwnd), (BOOL)(wParam)), 0L)
#define FORWARD_AC_MDICHILDENDSESSION(hwnd, fEnding, fn) \
    (void)(fn)((hwnd), AC_MDICHILDENDSESSION, (WPARAM)(BOOL)(fEnding), 0L)

void Child_OnClose (HWND hwnd);
BOOL Child_OnQueryCloseMDIChild (HWND hwnd, BOOL fSysModal);
void Child_OnMDIChildEndSession (HWND hwnd, BOOL fEnding);
void Child_OnDestroy(HWND hwnd);
void Child_OnEnterIdle(HWND hwnd, UINT source, HWND hwndSource);
void Child_OnCommand(HWND hwnd, int id, HWND hwndCtl, UINT codeNotify);
void Child_OnPaintMenuHelp (HWND hwnd, LPPAINTSTRUCT lpPaintStruct);

// FILE MENU
#define IDM_FILEOPENSHEET          101
#define IDM_FILEOPENCHART          102
#define IDM_FILESAVE               104
#define IDM_FILESAVEAS             105
#define IDM_FILEPRINT              106
#define IDM_FILEPRINTERSETUP       107
#define IDM_EXIT                   108

// EDIT MENU
#define IDM_EDITCUT                110
#define IDM_EDITCOPY               111
#define IDM_EDITPASTE              112
```

```
// SHEET MENU
#define IDM_SHEETOPTION            120

// CHART MENU
#define IDM_CHARTOPTION            130

// OPTIONS MENU
#define IDM_OPTIONSSTATUS          140
#define IDM_OPTIONSRIBBON          141

// HELP MENU
#define IDM_HELPINDEX              150
#define IDM_HELPKEYBOARD           151
#define IDM_HELPCOMMANDS           152
#define IDM_HELPPROCEDURES         153
#define IDM_HELPUSINGHELP          154

// WINDOW MENU
#define IDM_WINDOWTILEVERT         160
#define IDM_WINDOWTILEHORIZ        161
#define IDM_WINDOWCASCADE          162
#define IDM_WINDOWARRANGEICONS     163
#define IDM_WINDOWCHILD            164

//********************** Dialog-Box Identifiers **************************
#define ID_BOLD         105
#define ID_FONT         101
#define ID_FONTTEXT     102
#define ID_ITALIC       106
#define ID_SIZE         104
#define ID_SIZETEXT     103
#define ID_UNDERLINE    107


//********************** String Table Constants *************************
// String table used to fill the font and the size comboboxes in the
// Ribbon.
#define IDS_FONT         100
#define IDS_SIZE         200

// String table for Frame window's menu.
#define IDS_FRAMEPOPUPID   1000
#define IDS_FRAMEMENUID    2000

// String table for Sheet window's menu.
#define IDS_SHEETPOPUPID   3000
#define IDS_SHEETMENUID    4000
```

```
// String table for chart window's menu.
#define IDS_CHARTPOPUPID    5000
#define IDS_CHARTMENUID     6000

// String table for contents of status bar when no menu is open.
#define IDS_FRAMESTATUSBAR 7000
#define IDS_SHEETSTATUSBAR 7001
#define IDS_CHARTSTATUSBAR 7002

// Identifiers to help use string tables for menu help descriptions for
// menu items in the Application and MDI Child system menus.
#define IDM_SYSMENUSIZE         0x00  // ((SC_SIZE       & 0x0FFF) >> 4)
#define IDM_SYSMENUMOVE         0x01  // ((SC_MOVE       & 0x0FFF) >> 4)
#define IDM_SYSMENUMINIMIZE     0x02  // ((SC_MINIMIZE   & 0x0FFF) >> 4)
#define IDM_SYSMENUMAXIMIZE     0x03  // ((SC_MAXIMIZE   & 0x0FFF) >> 4)
#define IDM_SYSMENUNEXTWINDOW   0x04  // ((SC_NEXTWINDOW & 0x0FFF) >> 4)
#define IDM_SYSMENUCLOSE        0x06  // ((SC_CLOSE      & 0x0FFF) >> 4)
#define IDM_SYSMENURESTORE      0x12  // ((SC_RESTORE    & 0x0FFF) >> 4)
#define IDM_SYSMENUTASKLIST     0x13  // ((SC_TASKLIST   & 0x0FFF) >> 4)

void WINAPI ChangeMDIMenu (HWND hWndFrame, HWND hWndClient,
        HMENU hTopLevelMenu, WORD wMenuID);

HWND WINAPI CreateMDIChild (LPSTR szClassName, LPSTR szWindowName,
        DWORD dwStyle, short x, short y, short nWidth, short nHeight,
        HWND hWndMDIClient, HINSTANCE hInstance, LPARAM lParam);

//****** Macros for Using Window and Class Extra Bytes ***********
#define GETWNDEB(hWnd, Struct, Member) \
    ( \
      (sizeof(((Struct FAR *)0)->Member) == sizeof(LONG)) ? \
      ((LONG)GetWindowLong(hWnd, FIELDOFFSET(Struct, Member))) :\
      ((WORD)GetWindowWord(hWnd, FIELDOFFSET(Struct, Member))) \
    )

#define SETWNDEB(hWnd, Struct, Member, Value) \
    ( \
      (sizeof(((Struct FAR *)0)->Member) == sizeof(LONG)) ? \
      ((LONG)SetWindowLong(hWnd, FIELDOFFSET(Struct, Member), \
        (LONG)(Value))) : \
      ((WORD)SetWindowWord(hWnd, FIELDOFFSET(Struct, Member), \
        (WORD)(Value))) \
    )

#define GETCLSEB(hWnd, Struct, Member) \
    ( \
```

```
    (sizeof(((Struct FAR *)0)->Member) == sizeof(LONG)) ? \
    ((LONG)GetClassLong(hWnd, FIELDOFFSET(Struct, Member))) : \
    ((WORD)GetClassWord(hWnd, FIELDOFFSET(Struct, Member))) \
  )

#define SETCLSEB(hWnd, Struct, Member, Value) \
  ( \
    (sizeof(((Struct FAR *)0)->Member) == sizeof(LONG)) ? \
    ((LONG)SetClassLong(hWnd, FIELDOFFSET(Struct, Member), \
       (LONG)(Value))) : \
    ((WORD)SetClassWord(hWnd, FIELDOFFSET(Struct, Member), \
       (WORD)(Value))) \
  )
```

Listing 8-3. MDI.C application source module

```
/*********************************************************************
Module name: MDI.C
Programmer : Jeffrey M. Richter & Elvira Peretsman.
*********************************************************************/

// This module contains routines that initialize the
// MDI application as well as some help functions.

#include <windows.h>
#include <windowsx.h>

#include "mdi.h"

// Application global variables.
char     _szAppName[] = "MDI";   // The name of the application.
HACCEL   _hAccelTable = NULL;     // Handle to active Accelerators.
HWND     _hWndMDIClient = NULL;  // Handle to MDICLIENT window.
HWND     _hDlgRibbon = NULL;      // Ribbon modeless dialog box.

/*********************** Main Application Loop ***********************/
#pragma argsused
int WinMain (HINSTANCE hInstance, HINSTANCE hPrevInstance,
                 LPSTR lpszCmdLine, int nCmdShow) {
   MSG msg;
   HWND hWndFrame;

   if (hPrevInstance != NULL) {
      // Only allow one instance of the application to run.
      MessageBox(NULL, "MDI application is already running.",
```

```
            _szAppName, MB_OK | MB_ICONINFORMATION);
        return(0);
    }
    // Register the Frame window class.
    if (RegisterFrameWndClass() == NULL) return(0);

    // Initialize the MDI Child window classes.
    if (!InitSheetWndClass(TRUE)) return(0);
    if (!InitChartWndClass(TRUE)) return(0);

    // Create the Frame window.
    hWndFrame = CreateWindow("Frame", _szAppName,
        WS_OVERLAPPEDWINDOW | WS_CLIPCHILDREN | WS_MAXIMIZE |
        WS_VISIBLE | WS_MAXIMIZEBOX | WS_MINIMIZEBOX,
        CW_USEDEFAULT, nCmdShow, CW_USEDEFAULT, CW_USEDEFAULT,
        NULL, NULL, _hInstance, NULL);
    if (hWndFrame == NULL) return(0);

    // Create the Ribbon dialog box with Frame as owner.
    _hDlgRibbon = CreateDialog(_hInstance, "RIBBON", hWndFrame,
        (DLGPROC) RibbonDlgProc);
    if (_hDlgRibbon == NULL) return(0);

    while (GetMessage(&msg, NULL, 0, 0)) {
        if (!TranslateMDISysAccel(_hWndMDIClient, &msg)) {
            if (_hAccelTable == NULL || !TranslateAccelerator(
                hWndFrame, _hAccelTable, &msg)) {
                if (!IsDialogMessage(_hDlgRibbon, &msg)) {
                    TranslateMessage(&msg);
                    DispatchMessage(&msg);
                }
            }
        }
    }

    // De-initialize the MDI Child window classes.
    InitSheetWndClass(FALSE);
    InitChartWndClass(FALSE);

    return(msg.wParam);
}

// Function to make creating MDI Child as easy as creating
// any other kind of window.
HWND WINAPI CreateMDIChild (LPSTR szClassName,
    LPSTR szWindowName, DWORD dwStyle, short x, short y,
    short nWidth, short nHeight, HWND hWndMDIClient,
```

```
    HINSTANCE hInstance, LPARAM lParam) {

    MDICREATESTRUCT cs;

    cs.szClass = szClassName;
    cs.szTitle = szWindowName;
    cs.hOwner  = hInstance;
    cs.x       = x;
    cs.y       = y;
    cs.cx      = nWidth;
    cs.cy      = nHeight;
    cs.style   = dwStyle;
    cs.lParam  = lParam;

    return(FORWARD_WM_MDICREATE(hWndMDIClient, &cs, SendMessage));
}

// Function to change the menu in the Frame window whenever a
// new MDI Child becomes active.
void WINAPI ChangeMDIMenu (HWND hWndFrame, HWND hWndClient,
         HMENU hMenuNew, WORD wMenuID) {
   WORD wCount;
   HMENU hSubMenu = 0;

   // Get number of top-level menu items in the menu used by
   // the window being activated.
   wCount = GetMenuItemCount(hMenuNew);

   // Locate the POPUP menu that contains the menu option with
   // the 'wMenuID' identifier in it. This must be an ID
   // for an option in the new menu's "Window" pop-up menu.
   while (wCount) {
      hSubMenu = GetSubMenu(hMenuNew, wCount - 1);
      if ((int) GetMenuState(hSubMenu, wMenuID, MF_BYCOMMAND)
          != -1)
         break;
      wCount--;
   }

   // Tell the MDICLIENT window to set up the new menu.
   (void) FORWARD_WM_MDISETMENU(hWndClient,
      FALSE, hMenuNew, hSubMenu, SendMessage);
   DrawMenuBar(hWndFrame);
}
```

Listing 8-4. FRAME.C Frame window source module

```
/***********************************************************************
Module name: FRAME.C
Programmer : Jeffrey M. Richter & Elvira Peretsman.
***********************************************************************/

// This module contains routines for processing the MDI
// application's Frame window.

#define OEMRESOURCE
#include <windows.h>
#include <windowsx.h>

#include "mdi.h"

static char _szClassName[] = "Frame";
static BOOL _fAppModal = FALSE;

// Structure for use with Window Extra Bytes.
typedef struct {
    WORD   wNumSheets;      // Number of Sheet windows created.
    WORD   wNumCharts;      // Number of Chart windows created.
    HMENU  hMenu;           // Menu used when no MDI Children are active.
    BOOL   fStatusBarOn;    // Is the status bar showing.
    HWND   hWndMenuHelp;    // Window that last received a WM_MENUSELECT
                            // message.
    DWORD  dwMenuHelp;      // Menu help code placed here by hWndMenuHelp
                            // window.
} WNDEB;

void NEAR TileHorizontally (HWND hWndMDIClient, BOOL fSkipDisabled);

HWND GetActiveMDIChild (BOOL FAR *lpfIsMaximized) {
    DWORD dwTemp;

    if (lpfIsMaximized != NULL)
        *lpfIsMaximized = FALSE;

    if (!IsWindow(_hWndMDIClient)) return(NULL);

    // We cannot use a message cracker here because Microsoft
    // wrote it so that it does not return whether the MDI child
    // is maximized or not.
    dwTemp = SendMessage(_hWndMDIClient, WM_MDIGETACTIVE, 0, 0);
    if (lpfIsMaximized != NULL)
```

```
      *lpfIsMaximized = (HIWORD(dwTemp) == 1);
   return((HWND) LOWORD(dwTemp));
}


// Default procedure for the MDI application's Frame window.
LRESULT Frame_DefProc (HWND hwnd, UINT uMsg, WPARAM wParam, LPARAM lParam)
{
   return(DefFrameProc(hwnd, _hWndMDIClient, uMsg, wParam, lParam));
}


#pragma argsused
BOOL Frame_OnCreate (HWND hwnd, CREATESTRUCT FAR* lpCreateStruct) {
   CLIENTCREATESTRUCT ccs;

   // Initialize default values in the window extra bytes.
   HMENU hMenu = LoadMenu(_hInstance, _szClassName);
   SetMenu(hwnd, hMenu);
   SETWNDEB(hwnd, WNDEB, hMenu, hMenu);
   SETWNDEB(hwnd, WNDEB, fStatusBarOn, TRUE);

   // Create the MDICLIENT window as a child of the Frame.
   ccs.hWindowMenu = GetSubMenu(GetMenu(hwnd), 1);
   ccs.idFirstChild = IDM_WINDOWCHILD;

   _hWndMDIClient = CreateWindow("MDIClient", "",
      WS_CHILD | WS_CLIPCHILDREN | WS_VSCROLL | WS_HSCROLL |
      WS_VISIBLE | WS_CLIPSIBLINGS, 0, 0, 0, 0, hwnd, NULL,
      _hInstance, (LPSTR) (LPCLIENTCREATESTRUCT) &ccs);

   return(_hWndMDIClient != NULL);
}

void Frame_OnClose (HWND hwnd) {
   BOOL fOkToTerminate;

   // Before closing the application, ask the MDI Children
   // if it is OK?

   // Since this message occurs when the user explicitly closes
   // this application and NOT the whole system, have the MDI
   // Children display application modal windows instead of
   // system modal window.
   _fAppModal = TRUE;
   fOkToTerminate = FORWARD_WM_QUERYENDSESSION(hwnd, SendMessage);
   _fAppModal = FALSE;

   if (fOkToTerminate) {
```

501

```
        FORWARD_WM_ENDSESSION(hwnd, TRUE, SendMessage);
        FORWARD_WM_CLOSE(hwnd, Frame_DefProc);
    }
}


#pragma argsused
BOOL Frame_OnQueryEndSession (HWND hwnd) {
    HWND hWndChildStop;

    // Assume that it is OK to end the session.
    BOOL fOkToTerminate = TRUE;

    // Get the handle of the first MDI Child.
    HWND hWndChild = GetFirstChild(_hWndMDIClient);

    // If no MDI Children exist, it is OK to terminate.
    if (hWndChild == NULL) return(fOkToTerminate);

    // Ask each child if it is OK to terminate.
    do {
        // Do not ask caption bars of iconic MDI Children.
        if (GetWindowOwner(hWndChild) != NULL) continue;

        // _fAppModal defaults to FALSE. But it can be set
        // to TRUE during the WM_CLOSE processing.
        fOkToTerminate = FORWARD_AC_QUERYCLOSEMDICHILD(
            hWndChild, _fAppModal, SendMessage);

        // If the MDI Child says that it is NOT OK, don't
        // ask the rest of the MDI Children.
        if (!fOkToTerminate) break;

    } while ((hWndChild = GetNextSibling(hWndChild)) != NULL);

    // If any MDI Child said NO, tell the other children
    // that the session is NOT being terminated.
    if (!fOkToTerminate) {
        hWndChildStop = hWndChild;
        hWndChild = GetFirstChild(_hWndMDIClient);
        do {
            // If this child is the one that said NO, stop.
            if (hWndChildStop == hWndChild) break;

            // Do not send to caption bars of iconic MDI Children.
            if (GetWindowOwner(hWndChild) != NULL) continue;

            // Tell child you are not ending the session (wParam is FALSE).
```

```
            FORWARD_AC_MDICHILDENDSESSION(hWndChild, FALSE, SendMessage);

      } while ((hWndChild = GetNextSibling(hWndChild)) != NULL);
   }
   return(fOkToTerminate);
}


#pragma argsused
void Frame_OnEndSession(HWND hwnd, BOOL fEnding) {
   // Get handle of first MDI Child window.
   HWND hWndChild = GetFirstChild(_hWndMDIClient);

   // Tell each MDI Child whether or not the session is ending.
   while (hWndChild != NULL) {

      // Do not send to caption bars of iconic MDI Children.
      if (GetWindowOwner(hWndChild) == NULL)
         FORWARD_AC_MDICHILDENDSESSION(hWndChild, fEnding,
            SendMessage);

      hWndChild = GetNextSibling(hWndChild);
   }
}


void Frame_OnDestroy (HWND hwnd) {
   HMENU hMenu = (HMENU) GETWNDEB(hwnd, WNDEB, hMenu);

   if ((hMenu != NULL) && (hMenu != GetMenu(hwnd))) {
      // Select the Frame's default menu back into the window.
      // This way, it will be destroyed automatically by
      // DestroyWindow. The menus for any children will also NOT
      // be in use. So, when the children's de-initialization
      // code attempts to destroy their menus, they will be there
      // to destroy because the frame didn't accidentally
      // destroy it first.
      ChangeMDIMenu(hwnd, _hWndMDIClient,
         hMenu, IDM_WINDOWTILEVERT);
   }


   PostQuitMessage(0);
}

void Frame_OnSysCommand(HWND hwnd, UINT cmd, int x, int y) {
   // Set focus to frame window. This causes any comboboxes
   // in the ribbon to be closed.
   SetFocus(hwnd);
   FORWARD_WM_SYSCOMMAND(hwnd, cmd, x, y, Frame_DefProc);
```

```
}

void Frame_OnNCLButtonDown (HWND hwnd, BOOL fDoubleClick,
   int x, int y, UINT codeHitTest) {

   // Code to allow double-clicking the MDI Child's system
   // menu to close the MDI Child window.

   RECT rc;
   HBITMAP hBitmap;
   BITMAP Bitmap;
   POINT pt;
   BOOL fIsMDIChildMaximized;
   HWND hWndActiveMDIChild;

   // If user didn't double-click, do default processing.
   if (!fDoubleClick) goto DWP;

   // If mouse wasn't clicked in the application's menu,
   // do default processing.
   if (codeHitTest != HTMENU) goto DWP;

   // If the active child is not maximized,
   // do default processing.
   hWndActiveMDIChild = GetActiveMDIChild(&fIsMDIChildMaximized);
   if (!fIsMDIChildMaximized) goto DWP;

   // Get position and dimensions of the MDI Child's system
   // menu in the Frame's menu bar.

   // Get position and dimensions of the Frame window.
   GetWindowRect(hwnd, &rc);

   // Get handle to the "Close Box" bitmaps.
   hBitmap = LoadBitmap(NULL, MAKEINTRESOURCE(OBM_CLOSE));

   // Get dimensions of the bitmaps.
   GetObject(hBitmap, sizeof(BITMAP),
      (LPSTR) (LPBITMAP) &Bitmap);
   DeleteBitmap(hBitmap);  // Must delete predefined bitmaps.

   // Adjust the rectangle.
   rc.top += GetSystemMetrics(SM_CYCAPTION) +
      GetSystemMetrics(SM_CYFRAME);
   rc.bottom = rc.top + Bitmap.bmHeight;
   rc.left += GetSystemMetrics(SM_CXFRAME);
```

```
   // The "Close Box" bitmap includes the Application and
   // MDI Child Close boxes. So you only want half of the
   // bitmap's width.
   rc.right = rc.left + Bitmap.bmWidth / 2;

   // If the mouse cursor is within this rectangle, tell
   // the MDI Child window to close.
   pt.x = x;
   pt.y = y;
   #pragma warn -stv
   if (!PtInRect(&rc, pt)) goto DWP;
   #pragma warn .stv

   FORWARD_WM_SYSCOMMAND(hWndActiveMDIChild, SC_CLOSE, 0, 0, SendMessage);
   return;

DWP:
   FORWARD_WM_NCLBUTTONDOWN(hwnd, fDoubleClick, x, y, codeHitTest,
      Frame_DefProc);
}


#pragma argsused
void Frame_OnSize(HWND hwnd, UINT state, int cx, int cy) {
   // Force MDI Child window to be resized.
   FORWARD_FW_RESIZEMDICLIENT(hwnd, SendMessage);
}


void Frame_OnPaint(HWND hwnd) {
   PAINTSTRUCT ps; char szBuf[150];
   HWND hWndActiveMDIChild = GetActiveMDIChild(NULL);

   // Since the only visible portion of the Frame's client
   // area is the status bar when it is ON, this must mean
   // that the status bar needs to be repainted.

   // Set up the device context.
   BeginPaint(hwnd, &ps);
   FORWARD_FW_GETSTATBARRECT(hwnd, &ps.rcPaint, SendMessage);
   SetBkMode(ps.hdc, TRANSPARENT);

   // If an MDI Child exists, it updates the status bar.
   if (hWndActiveMDIChild) {
     FORWARD_AC_PAINTSTATBAR(hWndActiveMDIChild,
        ps.hdc, &ps, SendMessage);
   } else {
     // No MDI Child exists, the Frame updates the status bar.
     ps.rcPaint.top += FORWARD_FW_DRAWSTATUSDIVIDE(hwnd, &ps, SendMessage);
```

```
        LoadString(_hInstance, IDS_FRAMESTATUSBAR, szBuf, sizeof(szBuf));
        TextOut(ps.hdc, 0, ps.rcPaint.top, szBuf, lstrlen(szBuf));
    }
    EndPaint(hwnd, &ps);
}

void Frame_OnInitMenu(HWND hwnd, HMENU hMenu) {
    // The user has entered the menu system, set any options.
    CheckMenuItem(hMenu, IDM_OPTIONSSTATUS, MF_BYCOMMAND |
        (GETWNDEB(hwnd, WNDEB, fStatusBarOn)
        ? MF_CHECKED : MF_UNCHECKED));

    CheckMenuItem(hMenu, IDM_OPTIONSRIBBON, MF_BYCOMMAND |
        (IsWindowVisible(_hDlgRibbon)
        ? MF_CHECKED : MF_UNCHECKED));
}

void Frame_OnMenuSelect(HWND hwnd, HMENU hmenu, int item, HMENU hmenuPopup,
    UINT flags) {
    HMENU hMenu;
    BOOL fIsMDIChildMaximized;
    HWND hWndActiveMDIChild =
        GetActiveMDIChild(&fIsMDIChildMaximized);

    // If wTemp == 0 after switch, MDI Child handled the message.
    WORD wTemp = 0;

    if (flags == (UINT) -1) {
        // User has stopped using the menu system.
        FORWARD_FW_SETMENUHELP(hwnd, NULL, NULL, SendMessage);
        return;
    }

    switch (flags & (MF_POPUP | MF_SYSMENU)) {

        case 0:
            // "item" is a menu item ID.

            if (hWndActiveMDIChild != NULL) {
                // An MDI Child exists.
                if (fIsMDIChildMaximized) {

                    // If menu item from the MDI Child's system menu,
                    // set the MF_SYSMENU bit in the "flags" param.
                    wTemp = GetSubMenu(GetMenu(hwnd), 0);
                    if ((int) GetMenuState(wTemp, item, MF_BYCOMMAND) != -1)
                        flags |= MF_SYSMENU;
                }
```

```
        // Make active MDI Child think that it received
        // the WM_MENUSELECT message.
        FORWARD_WM_MENUSELECT(hWndActiveMDIChild, hmenu, item,
            hmenuPopup, flags, SendMessage);
        wTemp = 0;  // MDI Child handled the message.
        break;
    }

    wTemp = IDS_FRAMEMENUID + item;
    break;

case MF_POPUP:
    // "hmenuPopup" is handle to pop-up menu.

    if (hWndActiveMDIChild != NULL) {
        // An MDI Child exists.
        if (fIsMDIChildMaximized) {
            // If pop-up menu is first top-level menu, it is
            // the MDI Child's system menu, set the
            // MF_SYSMENU bit in the "flags" param.
            if (hmenuPopup == GetSubMenu(GetMenu(hwnd), 0))
                flags |= MF_SYSMENU;
        }

        // Make active MDI Child think that it received
        // the WM_MENUSELECT message.
        FORWARD_WM_MENUSELECT(hWndActiveMDIChild, hmenu, item,
            hmenuPopup, flags, SendMessage);
        wTemp = 0;  // MDI Child handled the message.
        break;
    }

    // Calculate the index of the top-level menu.
    hMenu = GetMenu(hwnd);
    wTemp = GetMenuItemCount(hMenu);
    while (wTemp—)
        if (GetSubMenu(hMenu, wTemp) == hmenuPopup)
            break;

    wTemp += IDS_FRAMEPOPUPID + 1; // Skip the system menu.
    break;

case MF_SYSMENU:
    // "item" is menu item ID from system menu.
    wTemp = IDS_FRAMEMENUID + ((item & 0x0FFF) >> 4);
    break;
```

```
      case MF_POPUP | MF_SYSMENU:
         wTemp = IDS_FRAMEPOPUPID;
         break;
   }

   // If message handled by MDI Child, nothing more to do.
   if (wTemp == 0) return;

   // Tell the Frame that the Frame window should display the
   // help text and the identifier for the help text.
   FORWARD_FW_SETMENUHELP(hwnd, hwnd, wTemp, SendMessage);
}

#pragma argsused
void Frame_OnEnterIdle(HWND hwnd, UINT source, HWND hwndSource) {
   RECT rc;
   PAINTSTRUCT ps;

   // If user is not using the menu system, get out.
   if (source != MSGF_MENU) return;

   // User has stopped scrolling through menu items.

   // If Menu help already displayed, nothing more to do.
   // This is signaled by hWndMenu help being 0xFFFF.
   if (GETWNDEB(hwnd, WNDEB, hWndMenuHelp) == 0xFFFF)
      return;

   // Display new menu help, invalidate the status bar.
   FORWARD_FW_GETSTATBARRECT(hwnd, &rc, SendMessage);
   InvalidateRect(hwnd, &rc, TRUE);

   // BeginPaint is OK because an invalid rectangle must exist
   // because of the call to InvalidateRect above. This causes
   // the background for the Frame's client area to be drawn.
   BeginPaint(hwnd, &ps);

   // Set up the device context.
   SetBkMode(ps.hdc, TRANSPARENT);

   // Send message to window that last received a WM_MENUSELECT
   // message to tell it to paint the status bar with the
   // appropriate menu help text.
   FORWARD_AW_PAINTMENUHELP((HWND) GETWNDEB(hwnd, WNDEB,
      hWndMenuHelp), &ps, SendMessage);
```

```
        EndPaint(hwnd, &ps);

        // Set flag notifying this message that the most recently
        // selected menu item has had its help text painted. This
        // stops unsightly screen flicker.
        SETWNDEB(hwnd, WNDEB, hWndMenuHelp, (HWND) 0xFFFF);
        return;
}


void Frame_OnCommand(HWND hwnd, int id, HWND hwndCtl, UINT codeNotify) {
        WORD wTemp;
        char szBuf[50];

        // If a child is being activated via the "Window" menu, let
        // the DefFrameProc handle it.
        if (id >= IDM_WINDOWCHILD) goto DWP;

        // Do default processing for any system commands (SC_*).
        if ((unsigned) id >= 0xF000u) goto DWP;

        switch (id) {

        case IDM_FILEOPENSHEET:
            // Get the # of sheets already created and increment by 1.
            wTemp = (WORD) GETWNDEB(hwnd, WNDEB, wNumSheets) + 1;
            SETWNDEB(hwnd, WNDEB, wNumSheets, wTemp);

            // The sheet's caption should display the sheet number.
            wsprintf(szBuf, "Sheet%d", wTemp);

            // Create the MDI Child window.
            CreateMDIChild("Sheet", szBuf, 0,
                CW_USEDEFAULT, CW_USEDEFAULT, CW_USEDEFAULT,
                CW_USEDEFAULT, _hWndMDIClient, _hInstance, 0);

            // Enable the ribbon if any children exist.
            EnableWindow(_hDlgRibbon, TRUE);
            break;

        case IDM_FILEOPENCHART:
            // Get the # of charts already created and increment by 1.
            wTemp = (WORD) GETWNDEB(hwnd, WNDEB, wNumCharts) + 1;
            SETWNDEB(hwnd, WNDEB, wNumCharts, wTemp);

            // The chart's caption should display the chart number.
            wsprintf(szBuf, "Chart%d", wTemp);
```

```
            // Create the MDI Child window.
            CreateMDIChild("Chart", szBuf, 0,
                CW_USEDEFAULT, CW_USEDEFAULT, CW_USEDEFAULT,
                CW_USEDEFAULT, _hWndMDIClient, _hInstance, 0);

            // Enable the ribbon if any children exist.
            EnableWindow(_hDlgRibbon, TRUE);
            break;

        case IDM_OPTIONSSTATUS:
            // Toggle the status of the status bar, resize the MDICLIENT.
            wTemp = !GETWNDEB(hwnd, WNDEB, fStatusBarOn);
            SETWNDEB(hwnd, WNDEB, fStatusBarOn, wTemp);
            FORWARD_FW_RESIZEMDICLIENT(hwnd, SendMessage);
            break;

        case IDM_OPTIONSRIBBON:
            // Toggle the status of the ribbon, resize the MDICLIENT.
            ShowWindow(_hDlgRibbon,
                IsWindowVisible(_hDlgRibbon) ? SW_HIDE : SW_SHOW);
            FORWARD_FW_RESIZEMDICLIENT(hwnd, SendMessage);
            break;

        case IDM_EXIT:
            FORWARD_WM_CLOSE(hwnd, SendMessage);
            break;

        case IDM_HELPINDEX:
        case IDM_HELPKEYBOARD:
        case IDM_HELPCOMMANDS:
        case IDM_HELPPROCEDURES:
        case IDM_HELPUSINGHELP:
            MessageBox(hwnd, "Option not implemented.", _szAppName, MB_OK);
            break;

        case IDM_WINDOWTILEHORIZ:
            // Call our own function to perform vertical tiling.
            TileHorizontally(_hWndMDIClient, TRUE);

            // In Windows 3.1, you could call:
            // (void) FORWARD_WM_MDITILE(_hWndMDIClient,
            //    MDITILE_HORIZONTAL, SendMessage);
            break;

        case IDM_WINDOWTILEVERT:
            // Let the MDICLIENT window do the repositioning.
            (void) FORWARD_WM_MDITILE(_hWndMDIClient,
```

```
                MDITILE_VERTICAL, SendMessage);
           break;

        case IDM_WINDOWCASCADE:
           // Let the MDICLIENT window do the repositioning.
           (void) FORWARD_WM_MDICASCADE(_hWndMDIClient, 0,
              SendMessage);
           break;

        case IDM_WINDOWARRANGEICONS:
           // Let the MDICLIENT window do the repositioning.
           FORWARD_WM_MDIICONARRANGE(_hWndMDIClient, SendMessage);
           break;

        default:
           // Menu options not processed by the Frame window must
           // be passed to the MDI Children for processing.
           FORWARD_WM_COMMAND(GetActiveMDIChild(NULL),
              id, hwndCtl, codeNotify, SendMessage);
           break;
        }
        return;

DWP:
     FORWARD_WM_COMMAND(hwnd, id, hwndCtl, codeNotify, Frame_DefProc);
}

void Frame_OnMDIChildDestroy (HWND hwnd) {
     // Message posted by MDI Child just before it is destroyed.

     HWND hWndActiveMDIChild = GetActiveMDIChild(NULL);

     // If another MDI Child exists, nothing to do.
     if (hWndActiveMDIChild != NULL) return;

     // Set the menu and accelerators to the Frame's defaults.
     ChangeMDIMenu(hwnd, _hWndMDIClient,
        (HMENU) GETWNDEB(hwnd, WNDEB, hMenu), IDM_WINDOWTILEVERT);
     _hAccelTable = NULL;

     // Force the status bar to be updated.
     InvalidateRect(hwnd, NULL, TRUE);

     // Disable the Ribbon.
     EnableWindow(_hDlgRibbon, FALSE);
}
```

```
void Frame_OnGetStatBarRect (HWND hwnd, LPRECT lpRect) {
    HDC hDC;
    TEXTMETRIC tm;

    // Get the client area of the Frame window.
    GetClientRect(hwnd, lpRect);

    // If the status bar is OFF, set status bar to have no height.
    if (! (BOOL) GETWNDEB(hwnd, WNDEB, fStatusBarOn)) {
        lpRect->top = lpRect->bottom;
        return;
    }

    // Change the dimensions so that the status bar is the
    // height of one line of text plus a small border.
    hDC = GetDC(hwnd);
    GetTextMetrics(hDC, &tm);
    ReleaseDC(hwnd, hDC);
    lpRect->top = lpRect->bottom - tm.tmHeight -
        GetSystemMetrics(SM_CYBORDER);
}

#pragma argsused
int Frame_OnDrawStatusDivide (HWND hwnd, LPPAINTSTRUCT lpPaintStruct) {
    HPEN hPen;

    // Draw a line separating the status bar from the MDICLIENT window.
    int cyBorder = GetSystemMetrics(SM_CYBORDER);
    hPen = CreatePen(PS_SOLID, cyBorder, RGB(0, 0, 0));
    hPen = SelectObject(lpPaintStruct->hdc, hPen);
    MoveTo(lpPaintStruct->hdc, 0, lpPaintStruct->rcPaint.top);
    LineTo(lpPaintStruct->hdc, lpPaintStruct->rcPaint.right,
        lpPaintStruct->rcPaint.top);
    hPen = SelectObject(lpPaintStruct->hdc, hPen);
    DeleteObject(hPen);
    return(cyBorder);
}

void Frame_OnResizeMDIClient (HWND hwnd) {
    RECT rc, rcTemp;

    if (!IsWindow(_hWndMDIClient)) return;

    // Sent when the Frame window is resized or when the
    // status bar and ribbon are toggled.
    GetClientRect(hwnd, &rc);
```

```
   if (IsWindow(_hDlgRibbon) && IsWindowVisible(_hDlgRibbon))  {
      // Ribbon is displayed, adjust rectangle.
      GetClientRect(_hDlgRibbon, &rcTemp);
      rc.top += rcTemp.bottom;
      rc.bottom -= rcTemp.bottom;
   }

   // Get the dimensions of the status bar rectangle and
   // adjust the dimensions of the MDICLIENT window.
   FORWARD_FW_GETSTATBARRECT(hwnd, &rcTemp, SendMessage);
   rc.bottom -= rcTemp.bottom - rcTemp.top;
   MoveWindow(_hWndMDIClient, 0, rc.top, rc.right,
      rc.bottom, TRUE);
}

void Frame_OnSetMenuHelp (HWND hwnd, HWND hwndSender, DWORD dwMenuDescCode) {
   RECT rc;

   // Called by the Frame and MDI Children whenever a
   // WM_MENUSELECT message is received.

   // Save the handle of the window sending the message.
   SETWNDEB(hwnd, WNDEB, hWndMenuHelp, hwndSender);

   // Save the menu help code that the window sent to.
   SETWNDEB(hwnd, WNDEB, dwMenuHelp, dwMenuDescCode);

   // When the Frame or MDI Child receives a WM_MENUSELECT message
   // specifying that the menu system is closed, the menu help
   // should disappear and be replaced by the proper information
   // on the status bar.

   if (hwndSender == NULL) {
      FORWARD_FW_GETSTATBARRECT(hwnd, &rc, SendMessage);
      // Force status bar to be updated.
      InvalidateRect(hwnd, &rc, TRUE);
   }
}

DWORD Frame_OnGetMenuHelp (HWND hwnd) {
   // Sent by the Frame or MDI Child when they
   // receive a AW_PAINTMENUHELP message.
   return(GETWNDEB(hwnd, WNDEB, dwMenuHelp));
}

void Frame_OnPaintMenuHelp (HWND hwnd, LPPAINTSTRUCT lpPaintStruct) {
   char szBuf[100];
```

```
    // Message sent from Frame to notify itself that it should
    // paint the status bar for the last highlighted menu item.

    // Ask the Frame window what the last selected menu ID was.
    // This value was sent to the frame by this window during the
    // processing for the WM_MENUSELECT message.
    DWORD dwMenuDescCode =
        FORWARD_FW_GETMENUHELP(hwnd, SendMessage);

    // Draw the horizontal dividing line separating the status
    // bar from the MDICLIENT window.
    lpPaintStruct->rcPaint.top += FORWARD_FW_DRAWSTATUSDIVIDE(
        hwnd, lpPaintStruct, SendMessage);

    // Construct the string that is to be displayed.
    LoadString(_hInstance, LOWORD(dwMenuDescCode),
        szBuf, sizeof(szBuf));

    // Paint the menu help text in the status bar.
    TextOut(lpPaintStruct->hdc, 0,
        lpPaintStruct->rcPaint.top, szBuf, lstrlen(szBuf));
}

LRESULT CALLBACK FrameWndProc (HWND hwnd, UINT uMsg, WPARAM wParam,
    LPARAM lParam) {
    switch (uMsg) {
        HANDLE_MSG(hwnd, WM_CREATE,            Frame_OnCreate);
        HANDLE_MSG(hwnd, WM_CLOSE,             Frame_OnClose);
        HANDLE_MSG(hwnd, WM_QUERYENDSESSION,   Frame_OnQueryEndSession);
        HANDLE_MSG(hwnd, WM_ENDSESSION,        Frame_OnEndSession);
        HANDLE_MSG(hwnd, WM_DESTROY,           Frame_OnDestroy);
        HANDLE_MSG(hwnd, WM_SYSCOMMAND,        Frame_OnSysCommand);
        HANDLE_MSG(hwnd, WM_NCLBUTTONDBLCLK,   Frame_OnNCLButtonDown);
        HANDLE_MSG(hwnd, WM_SIZE,              Frame_OnSize);
        HANDLE_MSG(hwnd, WM_PAINT,             Frame_OnPaint);
        HANDLE_MSG(hwnd, WM_INITMENU,          Frame_OnInitMenu);
        HANDLE_MSG(hwnd, WM_MENUSELECT,        Frame_OnMenuSelect);
        HANDLE_MSG(hwnd, WM_ENTERIDLE,         Frame_OnEnterIdle);
        HANDLE_MSG(hwnd, WM_COMMAND,           Frame_OnCommand);
        HANDLE_MSG(hwnd, FW_MDICHILDDESTROY,   Frame_OnMDIChildDestroy);
        HANDLE_MSG(hwnd, FW_GETSTATBARRECT,    Frame_OnGetStatBarRect);
        HANDLE_MSG(hwnd, FW_DRAWSTATUSDIVIDE,  Frame_OnDrawStatusDivide);
        HANDLE_MSG(hwnd, FW_RESIZEMDICLIENT,   Frame_OnResizeMDIClient);
        HANDLE_MSG(hwnd, FW_SETMENUHELP,       Frame_OnSetMenuHelp);
        HANDLE_MSG(hwnd, FW_GETMENUHELP,       Frame_OnGetMenuHelp);
        HANDLE_MSG(hwnd, AW_PAINTMENUHELP,     Frame_OnPaintMenuHelp);
```

```
    }
    return(DefFrameProc(hwnd, _hWndMDIClient, uMsg, wParam, lParam));
}

ATOM WINAPI RegisterFrameWndClass (void) {
    WNDCLASS wc;

    wc.style          = CS_HREDRAW | CS_VREDRAW;
    wc.lpfnWndProc    = FrameWndProc;
    wc.cbClsExtra     = 0;

    // Number of window extra bytes used by structure.
    wc.cbWndExtra     = sizeof(WNDEB);
    wc.hInstance      = _hInstance;
    wc.hIcon          = LoadIcon(_hInstance, _szClassName);
    wc.hCursor        = LoadCursor(NULL, IDC_ARROW);
    wc.hbrBackground  = COLOR_WINDOW + 1;
    wc.lpszMenuName   = NULL;
    wc.lpszClassName  = _szClassName;
    return(RegisterClass(&wc));
}

void NEAR TileHorizontally (HWND hWndMDIClient, BOOL fSkipDisabled) {
    int nNumWndsOnRow, nMDIChildrenToTile = 0;
    int nTopOfBottomIconRow = 0, nCrntCol, nColWidth, nCrntRow;
    int nNumRows, nRowHeight, nMinWndHeight;
    HWND hWndChild, hWndActiveMDIChild;
    BOOL fIsMDIChildMaximized;
    HDWP hDWPWinPosInfo;
    RECT rc;
    POINT Point;

    // Assume that scroll bars will be off after windows are tiled.
    // By forcing them off now, GetClientRect returns the
    // correct size.
    ShowScrollBar(hWndMDIClient, SB_BOTH, 0);

    // The WM_MDICASCADE and WM_MDITILE messages cause the icons
    // to be arranged. So you will too. In fact, this is
    // necessary to locate the top of the bottom icon row in the
    // next step of this function.
    FORWARD_WM_MDIICONARRANGE(hWndMDIClient, SendMessage);

    // Get handle to first MDI Child window.
    hWndChild = GetFirstChild(hWndMDIClient);
    do {
        if (IsMinimized(hWndChild) &&
```

```
      GetWindowOwner(hWndChild) == NULL) {
      // Window is iconic and window is NOT an icon's caption.

      // Get client area of the icon window.
      GetWindowRect(hWndChild, &rc);

      // rc.top is in screen coordinates.
      nTopOfBottomIconRow = max(nTopOfBottomIconRow, rc.top);
    }

  if (!IsMinimized(hWndChild) &&
      GetWindowOwner(hWndChild) == NULL) {

      // If you should include all windows (even disabled) or
      // the window isn't disabled, increment the # of
      // children to tile.
      if (!fSkipDisabled || IsWindowEnabled(hWndChild))
         ++nMDIChildrenToTile;
    }

} while ((hWndChild = GetNextSibling(hWndChild)) != NULL);

// There are no MDI Children to tile.
if (nMDIChildrenToTile == 0) return;

// Find height of usable client area for tiling.
GetClientRect(hWndMDIClient, &rc);

if (nTopOfBottomIconRow) {
   // At least one MDI Child is iconic.

   // Convert coordinates from screen to client.
   Point.x = 0; Point.y = nTopOfBottomIconRow;
   ScreenToClient(hWndMDIClient, &Point);
   // Point.y is top of bottom icon row in client coordinates.
   rc.bottom = Point.y;
}

// Restore the active MDI child if it's maximized.
hWndActiveMDIChild = GetActiveMDIChild(&fIsMDIChildMaximized);
if (fIsMDIChildMaximized)
   ShowWindow(hWndActiveMDIChild, SW_RESTORE);

// Calculate the minimum desired height of each MDI Child.
nMinWndHeight = max(1, rc.bottom /
   (5 * GetSystemMetrics(SM_CYCAPTION)));
```

```
// Calculate the number of rows that will be tiled.
nNumRows = min(nMDIChildrenToTile, nMinWndHeight);

// Calculate the height of each row.
nRowHeight = rc.bottom / nNumRows;

// Get the handle to the first MDI Child window.
hWndChild = GetFirstChild(hWndMDIClient);

// Prime the storage of positioning information.
hDWPWinPosInfo = BeginDeferWindowPos(nMDIChildrenToTile);

// Execute the loop for each row.
for (nCrntRow = 0; nCrntRow < nNumRows; nCrntRow++) {

   // Calculate the number of MDI Children that appear
   // on this row.
   nNumWndsOnRow = nMDIChildrenToTile / nNumRows +
      ((nMDIChildrenToTile % nNumRows >
      (nNumRows - (nCrntRow + 1))) ? 1 : 0);

   // Calculate the width of each of these children.
   nColWidth = rc.right / nNumWndsOnRow;

   // Fill each column with an MDI Child window.
   for (nCrntCol = 0; nCrntCol < nNumWndsOnRow; ) {

      if (IsMinimized(hWndChild) ||
         (GetWindowOwner(hWndChild) != NULL) ||
         (fSkipDisabled && !IsWindowEnabled(hWndChild))) {
         // Don't reposition if the window:
         // 1. is iconic
         // 2. has an owner (icon's caption)
         // 3. is disabled & caller wants to ignore
         //    diabled windows.
      } else {
         // Everything is OK, reposition the window.

         // Tell windows what the new position and
         // dimensions of this MDI Child should be.
         hDWPWinPosInfo = DeferWindowPos(hDWPWinPosInfo,
            hWndChild, NULL, nCrntCol * nColWidth,
            nCrntRow * nRowHeight, nColWidth,
            nRowHeight, SWP_NOACTIVATE | SWP_NOZORDER |
            SWP_NOCOPYBITS);

         // Go to the next column.
```

```
            nCrntCol++;
        }


        // Get handle to the next MDI Child window.
        hWndChild = GetNextSibling(hWndChild);
    }
  }

  // All of the positioning has been set. Now, tell Windows
  // to update all windows at once.
  EndDeferWindowPos(hDWPWinPosInfo);
}
```

Listing 8-5. RIBBON.C source module

```
/**************************************************************************
Module name: RIBBON.C
Programmer : Jeffrey M. Richter & Elvira Peretsman.
**************************************************************************/

// This module contains routines for processing the
// application's Ribbon modeless dialog box.

#include <windows.h>
#include <windowsx.h>

#include "mdi.h"

#pragma argsused
BOOL Ribbon_OnInitDialog (HWND hwnd, HWND hwndFocus, LPARAM lParam) {
   char szBuf[25];

   // Add strings to the font combobox.
   HWND hwndCtl = GetDlgItem(hwnd, ID_FONT);
   int i = IDS_FONT;
   while (LoadString(_hInstance, i++, szBuf, sizeof(szBuf)) != 0)
      (void) ComboBox_AddString(hwndCtl, szBuf);
   (void) ComboBox_SetCurSel(hwndCtl, 0);

   // Add strings to the fontsize combobox.
   hwndCtl = GetDlgItem(hwnd, ID_SIZE);
   i = IDS_SIZE;
   while (LoadString(_hInstance, i++, szBuf, sizeof(szBuf)) != 0)
      (void) ComboBox_AddString(hwndCtl, szBuf);
   (void) ComboBox_SetCurSel(hwndCtl, 0);
   return(TRUE);
```

```
}

void Ribbon_OnEnable (HWND hwnd, BOOL fEnable) {
   // Make all child windows have the same status as the dialog box.
   HWND hwndCtl = GetFirstChild(hwnd);

   for (; hwndCtl != NULL; hwndCtl = GetNextSibling(hwndCtl))
      EnableWindow(hwndCtl, fEnable);
}

void Ribbon_OnPaint (HWND hwnd) {
   PAINTSTRUCT ps;
   HPEN hPen;
   RECT rc;

   // Paint a horizontal dividing line between the Ribbon and the
   // MDICLIENT window.
   BeginPaint(hwnd, &ps);
   hPen = CreatePen(PS_SOLID, GetSystemMetrics(SM_CYBORDER),
      RGB(0, 0, 0));
   SelectObject(ps.hdc, hPen);
   GetClientRect(hwnd, &rc);
   MoveTo(ps.hdc, 0, rc.bottom - GetSystemMetrics(SM_CYBORDER));
   LineTo(ps.hdc, rc.right, rc.bottom - GetSystemMetrics(SM_CYBORDER));
   EndPaint(hwnd, &ps);
   DeleteObject(hPen);
}

#pragma argsused
void Ribbon_OnCommand (HWND hwnd, int id, HWND hwndCtl, UINT codeNotify) {
   // Make sure that focus is given back to the Frame after an
   // option is chosen by the user.
   switch (id) {
      case ID_FONT:
      case ID_SIZE:
         if (codeNotify != CBN_SELCHANGE) break;
         SetFocus(GetParent(hwnd));
         break;

      case ID_BOLD:
      case ID_ITALIC:
      case ID_UNDERLINE:
         if (codeNotify != BN_CLICKED) break;
         SetFocus(GetParent(hwnd));
         break;

      case IDOK:
```

```
      case IDCANCEL:
         SetFocus(GetParent(hwnd));
         break;
   }
}

BOOL CALLBACK RibbonDlgProc (HWND hDlg, UINT uMsg, WPARAM wParam, LPARAM
lParam) {
   LRESULT lResult = 0;

   switch (uMsg) {

      case WM_INITDIALOG:
         lResult = HANDLE_WM_INITDIALOG(hDlg, wParam, lParam,
            Ribbon_OnInitDialog);
         break;

      case WM_ENABLE:
         lResult = HANDLE_WM_ENABLE(hDlg, wParam, lParam,
            Ribbon_OnEnable);
         break;

      case WM_PAINT:
         lResult = HANDLE_WM_PAINT(hDlg, wParam, lParam,
            Ribbon_OnPaint);
         break;

      case WM_COMMAND:
         lResult = HANDLE_WM_COMMAND(hDlg, wParam, lParam,
            Ribbon_OnCommand);
         break;
   }
   return((BOOL) lResult);
}
```

Listing 8-6. SHEET.C MDI Child source module

```
/***********************************************************************
Module name: SHEET.C
Programmer : Jeffrey M. Richter & Elvira Peretsman.
***********************************************************************/

// This module contains routines for processing Sheet
// MDI Children windows.
```

```
#include <windows.h>
#include <windowsx.h>

#include "mdi.h"

static char   _szClassName[] = "Sheet";
static HMENU  _hMenu = NULL;
static HACCEL _hAccel = NULL;

LRESULT Sheet_DefProc (HWND hwnd, UINT uMsg, WPARAM wParam, LPARAM lParam) {
    return(DefMDIChildProc(hwnd, uMsg, wParam, lParam));
}

#pragma argsused
void Sheet_MDIActivate(HWND hwnd, BOOL fActive, HWND hwndActivate,
    HWND hwndDeactivate) {
    if (fActive == FALSE) return;

    // Child is being activated.

    // Set the menu bar and the accelerators to the appropriate ones
    // for this window class.
    ChangeMDIMenu(GETFRAME(hwnd), GetParent(hwnd),
        _hMenu, IDM_WINDOWTILEVERT);
    _hAccelTable = _hAccel;

    // For the status bar at the bottom of the Frame window to be
    // updated for this child's information.
    InvalidateRect(GETFRAME(hwnd), NULL, TRUE);
}

#pragma argsused
void Sheet_OnMenuSelect(HWND hwnd, HMENU hmenu, int item, HMENU hmenuPopup,
    UINT flags) {
    WORD wTemp; HMENU hMenu;
    // Normally, only MDI Child system menu options could appear
    // in this message. But the Frame window forces WM_MENUSELECT
    // messages to appear here whenever a menu selection occurs.

    if (flags == (UINT) -1) {
        // User has stopped using the menu system. Notify Frame window
        // so that the status bar will be invalidated.
        FORWARD_FW_SETMENUHELP(hwnd, NULL, NULL, SendMessage);
        return;
    }

    switch (flags & (MF_POPUP | MF_SYSMENU)) {
```

```
    case 0:
        // "item" is a menu item ID NOT on the Child's system menu.

        // If "item" is any of the MDI Children listed in the
        // "Window" menu, display the same help text.
        if ((item > IDM_WINDOWCHILD) && (item <= IDM_WINDOWCHILD + 9))
            item = IDM_WINDOWCHILD;

        // Tell the Frame that this window should display the help
        // text and the identifier for the help text.
        wTemp = IDS_SHEETMENUID + item;
        break;

    case MF_POPUP:
        // "hmenuPopup" is handle to popup menu.
        // Calculate the index of the top-level menu.
        hMenu = GetMenu(GETFRAME(hwnd));
        wTemp = GetMenuItemCount(hMenu);
        while (wTemp-)
            if (GetSubMenu(hMenu, wTemp) == hmenuPopup) break;
        wTemp += IDS_SHEETPOPUPID;
        if (!IsMaximized(hwnd)) wTemp++;
        break;

    case MF_SYSMENU:
        // "item" is menu item ID from MDI Child's system menu.
        wTemp = IDS_SHEETMENUID + ((item & 0x0FFF) >> 4);
        break;

    case MF_POPUP | MF_SYSMENU:
        // "hmenuPopup" is handle to MDI Child's system menu.
        wTemp = IDS_SHEETPOPUPID;
        break;
    }
    // Tell the Frame that this window should display the help
    // text and the identifier for the help text.
    FORWARD_FW_SETMENUHELP(GETFRAME(hwnd), hwnd, wTemp, SendMessage);
}

void Sheet_OnMDIChildPaintStatBar (HWND hwnd, HDC hDC,
    LPPAINTSTRUCT lpPaintStruct) {
    char szBuf[150];

    // Message sent by the Frame window when the status bar needs to
    // be repainted.
```

```
   // Construct status bar string for display.
   LoadString(_hInstance, IDS_SHEETSTATUSBAR, szBuf, sizeof(szBuf));

   // Draw the horizontal dividing line separating the status
   // bar from the MDICLIENT window.
   lpPaintStruct->rcPaint.top += FORWARD_FW_DRAWSTATUSDIVIDE(
      GETFRAME(hwnd), lpPaintStruct, SendMessage);

   // Paint the text in the status bar.
   TextOut(hDC, 0, lpPaintStruct->rcPaint.top,
      szBuf, lstrlen(szBuf));
}

LRESULT CALLBACK SheetProc (HWND hwnd, UINT uMsg, WPARAM wParam,
   LPARAM lParam) {
   switch (uMsg) {
      HANDLE_MSG(hwnd, WM_MDIACTIVATE,
         Sheet_MDIActivate);

      HANDLE_MSG(hwnd, WM_CLOSE,
         Child_OnClose);

      HANDLE_MSG(hwnd, AC_QUERYCLOSEMDICHILD,
         Child_OnQueryCloseMDIChild);

      HANDLE_MSG(hwnd, AC_MDICHILDENDSESSION,
         Child_OnMDIChildEndSession);

      HANDLE_MSG(hwnd, WM_DESTROY,
         Child_OnDestroy);

      HANDLE_MSG(hwnd, WM_MENUSELECT,
         Sheet_OnMenuSelect);

      HANDLE_MSG(hwnd, WM_ENTERIDLE,
         Child_OnEnterIdle);

      HANDLE_MSG(hwnd, WM_COMMAND,
         Child_OnCommand);

      HANDLE_MSG(hwnd, AC_PAINTSTATBAR,
         Sheet_OnMDIChildPaintStatBar);

      HANDLE_MSG(hwnd, AW_PAINTMENUHELP,
         Child_OnPaintMenuHelp);
   }
```

```
      return(DefMDIChildProc(hwnd, uMsg, wParam, lParam));
}


BOOL WINAPI InitSheetWndClass (BOOL fInitialize) {
   WNDCLASS wc;
   ATOM aClass;

   if (fInitialize) {
      if (_hPrev == NULL) {
         // Initialization that gets performed for the first instance.
         wc.style          = 0;
         wc.lpfnWndProc    = SheetProc;
         wc.cbClsExtra     = 0;
         wc.cbWndExtra     = 0;
         wc.hInstance      = _hInstance;
         wc.hIcon          = LoadIcon(_hInstance, _szClassName);
         wc.hCursor        = LoadCursor(NULL, IDC_ARROW);
         wc.hbrBackground  = COLOR_WINDOW + 1;
         wc.lpszMenuName   = NULL;
         wc.lpszClassName  = _szClassName;
         aClass = RegisterClass(&wc);
         if (aClass == NULL) return(FALSE);
      }
      // Initialization that gets performed for every instance.
      _hMenu = LoadMenu(_hInstance, _szClassName);
      _hAccel = LoadAccelerators(_hInstance, _szClassName);
   } else {
      // De-initializing the class.
      DestroyMenu(_hMenu);
   }
   return(TRUE);
}
```

Listing 8-7. CHART.C MDI Child window source module

```
/****************************************************************************
Module name: CHART.C
Programmer : Jeffrey M. Richter & Elvira Peretsman.
****************************************************************************/

// This module contains routines for prccessing Chart
// MDI Children windows.

#include <windows.h>
#include <windowsx.h>
```

```
#include "mdi.h"

static char    _szClassName[] = "Chart";
static HMENU   _hMenu = NULL;
static HACCEL  _hAccel = NULL;

// Used for mouse activation code.
static HWND    _hWndPrevChild = NULL;

// Default procedure for Chart MDI Children.
LRESULT Chart_DefProc (HWND hwnd, UINT uMsg, WPARAM wParam, LPARAM lParam) {
   return(DefMDIChildProc(hwnd, uMsg, wParam, lParam));
}

#pragma argsused
void Chart_MDIActivate(HWND hwnd, BOOL fActive, HWND hwndActivate,
   HWND hwndDeactivate) {
   if (fActive == FALSE) {
      // Child is being deactivated. Reset the previous child
      // so WM_MOUSEACTIVATE will work OK.
      _hWndPrevChild = NULL;
      return;
   }

   // Child is being activated.

   // Set handle of child being de-activated.
   _hWndPrevChild = hwndDeactivate;

   // If this child is being activated and no other child exists,
   // pretend that this child was the last activated child.
   if (_hWndPrevChild == NULL) _hWndPrevChild = hwnd;

   // Set the menu bar and the accelerators to the appropriate
   // ones for this window class.
   ChangeMDIMenu(GETFRAME(hwnd), GetParent(hwnd),
      _hMenu, IDM_WINDOWTILEVERT);
   _hAccelTable = _hAccel;

   // For the status bar at the bottom of the Frame window to
   // be updated for this child's information.
   InvalidateRect(GETFRAME(hwnd), NULL, TRUE);
}

#pragma argsused
void Chart_OnMenuSelect(HWND hwnd, HMENU hmenu, int item, HMENU hmenuPopup,
   UINT flags) {
```

```
WORD wTemp;
HMENU hMenu;

// Normally, only MDI Child system menu options could appear
// in this message. But the Frame window forces WM_MENUSELECT
// messages to appear here whenever a menu selection occurs.

if (flags == (UINT) -1) {
    // User has stopped using the menu system. Notify Frame
    // window so that the status bar will be invalidated.
    FORWARD_FW_SETMENUHELP(GETFRAME(hwnd), NULL, NULL,
        SendMessage);
    return;
}

switch (flags & (MF_POPUP | MF_SYSMENU)) {

    case 0:
        // "item" is a menu item ID NOT on the Child's system menu.

        // If "item" is any of the MDI Children listed in the
        // "Window" menu, display the same help text.
        if ((item > IDM_WINDOWCHILD) && (item <= IDM_WINDOWCHILD + 9))
            item = IDM_WINDOWCHILD;

        // Tell the Frame that this window should display the help
        // text and the identifier for the help text.
        wTemp = IDS_CHARTMENUID + item;
        break;

    case MF_POPUP:
        // "hmenuPopup" is handle to pop-up menu.
        // Calculate the index of the top-level menu.
        hMenu = GetMenu(GETFRAME(hwnd));
        wTemp = GetMenuItemCount(hMenu);
        while (wTemp-)
            if (GetSubMenu(hMenu, wTemp) == hmenuPopup) break;
        wTemp += IDS_CHARTPOPUPID;
        if (!IsMaximized(hwnd)) wTemp++;
        break;

    case MF_SYSMENU:
        // "item" is menu item ID from MDI Child's system menu.
        wTemp = IDS_CHARTMENUID + ((item & 0x0FFF) >> 4);
        break;

    case MF_POPUP | MF_SYSMENU:
```

```
        // "hmenuPopup" is handle to MDI Child's system menu.
        wTemp = IDS_CHARTPOPUPID;
        break;
    }

    // Tell the Frame that this window should display the help
    // text and the identifier for the help text.
    FORWARD_FW_SETMENUHELP(GETFRAME(hwnd), hwnd, wTemp, SendMessage);
}


void Chart_OnMDIChildPaintStatBar (HWND hwnd, HDC hDC,
    LPPAINTSTRUCT lpPaintStruct) {
    char szBuf[150];

    // Message sent by the Frame window when the status bar
    // needs to be repainted.

    // Construct status bar string for display.
    LoadString(_hInstance, IDS_SHEETSTATUSBAR, szBuf, sizeof(szBuf));

    // Draw the horizontal dividing line separating the status
    // bar from the MDICLIENT window.
    lpPaintStruct->rcPaint.top += FORWARD_FW_DRAWSTATUSDIVIDE(
        GETFRAME(hwnd), lpPaintStruct, SendMessage);

    // Paint the text in the status bar.
    TextOut(hDC, 0, lpPaintStruct->rcPaint.top,
        szBuf, lstrlen(szBuf));
}


#pragma argsused
int Chart_OnMouseActivate (HWND hwnd, HWND hwndTopLevel, UINT codeHitTest,
    UINT msg) {
    // User clicked the mouse of the Child window.
    // If the mouse is clicked in the window's client area and
    // the previously active child was NOT this child, the
    // mouse message should be eaten.
    if ((HTCLIENT == codeHitTest) && (hwnd != _hWndPrevChild))
        return(MA_ACTIVATEANDEAT);
    return(MA_ACTIVATE);
}


#pragma argsused
BOOL Chart_OnSetCursor (HWND hwnd, HWND hwndCursor, UINT codeHitTest,
    UINT msg) {
    // After an MDI Child becomes active, set the previously active
    // child to this window so that mouse messages will NOT be eaten.
```

```
    _hWndPrevChild = hwnd;
    return(FORWARD_WM_SETCURSOR(hwnd, hwndCursor,
        codeHitTest, msg, Chart_DefProc));
}


#pragma argsused
void Chart_OnLButtonDown (HWND hwnd, BOOL fDoubleClick, int x, int y,
    UINT keyFlags) {
    // Just to let you know when the WM_LBUTTONDOWN message is received.
    MessageBox(hwnd, "WM_LBUTTONDOWN", "Chart", MB_OK);
}

LRESULT CALLBACK ChartProc (HWND hwnd, UINT uMsg, WPARAM wParam,
    LPARAM lParam) {
    switch (uMsg) {
        HANDLE_MSG(hwnd, WM_MDIACTIVATE,
            Chart_MDIActivate);

        HANDLE_MSG(hwnd, WM_CLOSE,
            Child_OnClose);

        HANDLE_MSG(hwnd, AC_QUERYCLOSEMDICHILD,
            Child_OnQueryCloseMDIChild);

        HANDLE_MSG(hwnd, AC_MDICHILDENDSESSION,
            Child_OnMDIChildEndSession);

        HANDLE_MSG(hwnd, WM_DESTROY,
            Child_OnDestroy);

        HANDLE_MSG(hwnd, WM_MENUSELECT,
            Chart_OnMenuSelect);

        HANDLE_MSG(hwnd, WM_ENTERIDLE,
            Child_OnEnterIdle);

        HANDLE_MSG(hwnd, WM_COMMAND,
            Child_OnCommand);

        HANDLE_MSG(hwnd, AC_PAINTSTATBAR,
            Chart_OnMDIChildPaintStatBar);

        HANDLE_MSG(hwnd, AW_PAINTMENUHELP,
            Child_OnPaintMenuHelp);

        HANDLE_MSG(hwnd, WM_MOUSEACTIVATE,
            Chart_OnMouseActivate);
```

```
        HANDLE_MSG(hwnd, WM_SETCURSOR,
            Chart_OnSetCursor);

        HANDLE_MSG(hwnd, WM_LBUTTONDOWN,
            Chart_OnLButtonDown);
    }
    return(DefMDIChildProc(hwnd, uMsg, wParam, lParam));
}

BOOL WINAPI InitChartWndClass (BOOL fInitialize) {
    WNDCLASS wc;
    ATOM aClass;

    if (fInitialize) {
        if (_hPrev == NULL) {
            // Initialization that gets performed for the first instance.
            wc.style          = 0;
            wc.lpfnWndProc    = ChartProc;
            wc.cbClsExtra     = 0;
            wc.cbWndExtra     = 0;
            wc.hInstance      = _hInstance;
            wc.hIcon          = LoadIcon(_hInstance, _szClassName);
            wc.hCursor        = LoadCursor(NULL, IDC_ARROW);
            wc.hbrBackground  = COLOR_WINDOW + 1;
            wc.lpszMenuName   = NULL;
            wc.lpszClassName  = _szClassName;
            aClass = RegisterClass(&wc);
            if (aClass == NULL) return(FALSE);
        }
        // Initialization that gets performed for every instance.
        _hMenu = LoadMenu(_hInstance, _szClassName);
        _hAccel = LoadAccelerators(_hInstance, _szClassName);
    } else {
        // De-initializing the class.
        DestroyMenu(_hMenu);
    }
    return(TRUE);
}
```

Listing 8-8. CHILD.C source module

```
/***************************************************************************
Module name: CHILD.C
Programmer : Jeffrey M. Richter & Elvira Peretsman.
***************************************************************************/

// This module contains routines that are common to both
// Sheet and Chart MDI Child windows.

#include <windows.h>
#include <windowsx.h>

#include "mdi.h"

// Default procedure for all MDI Children.
LRESULT Child_DefProc (HWND hwnd, UINT uMsg, WPARAM wParam, LPARAM lParam)
{
    return(DefMDIChildProc(hwnd, uMsg, wParam, lParam));
}

void Child_OnClose (HWND hwnd) {
    // Make sure that it is OK to close this child window.
    BOOL fOkToTerminate =
        FORWARD_AC_QUERYCLOSEMDICHILD(hwnd, TRUE, SendMessage);

    if (fOkToTerminate) {
        FORWARD_AC_MDICHILDENDSESSION(hwnd, TRUE, SendMessage);
        FORWARD_WM_CLOSE(hwnd, Child_DefProc);
    }
}

BOOL Child_OnQueryCloseMDIChild (HWND hwnd, BOOL fAppModal) {
    BOOL fOkToTerminate = TRUE;
    char szBuf[100];
    WORD wTemp;

    // Prompt user whether to save changes to this document.
    // Usually, a dirty flag (stored in the window's extra bytes
    // is used to determine if it is necessary to ask this question).

    // Construct string including the document's name.
    lstrcpy(szBuf, "Save changes to ");
    wTemp = lstrlen(szBuf);
    GetWindowText(hwnd, szBuf + wTemp, sizeof(szBuf) - wTemp);
    lstrcat(szBuf, "?");
```

```
    // Display message box to user. The message box should
    // be system modal if the entire Windows session is being
    // terminated (fAppModal is FALSE).
    wTemp = MessageBox(hwnd, szBuf, _szAppName,
        MB_ICONQUESTION | MB_YESNOCANCEL |
        (fAppModal ? MB_APPLMODAL : MB_SYSTEMMODAL));

    switch (wTemp) {
        case IDYES:
            // Save the document and it's OK to quit.
            fOkToTerminate = TRUE;
            break;

        case IDNO:
            // Don't save the document and it's OK to quit.
            fOkToTerminate = TRUE;
            break;

        case IDCANCEL:
            // Don't save the document and it's NOT OK to quit.
            fOkToTerminate = FALSE;
            break;
    }
    return(fOkToTerminate);
}

#pragma argsused
void Child_OnMDIChildEndSession (HWND hwnd, BOOL fEnding) {
    // Do any last minute cleanup during this message.
}

void Child_OnDestroy(HWND hwnd) {
    // Notify the Frame window that a child has been destroyed
    // after the child is actually destroyed. (That's why you
    // use PostMessage instead of SendMessage here).
    FORWARD_FW_MDICHILDDESTROY(GETFRAME(hwnd), PostMessage);
    FORWARD_WM_DESTROY(hwnd, Child_DefProc);
}

void Child_OnEnterIdle(HWND hwnd, UINT source, HWND hwndSource) {
    // User stopped moving around in the help system, make the Frame
    // believe that it received this message directly.
    FORWARD_WM_ENTERIDLE(GETFRAME(hwnd), source, hwndSource, SendMessage);
}

#pragma argsused
```

```
void Child_OnCommand(HWND hwnd, int id, HWND hwndCtl, UINT codeNotify) {
   // Any menu options NOT processed by the Frame are
   // passed to the active child.
   MessageBox(hwnd, "Option not implemented.", _szAppName, MB_OK);
}

void Child_OnPaintMenuHelp (HWND hwnd, LPPAINTSTRUCT lpPaintStruct) {
   char szString[150], szCaption[90], szBuf[150];

   // Message sent from Frame window to notify child that it
   // should paint the status bar text for the last
   // highlighted menu item.

   // Ask the Frame window what the last selected menu ID was.
   // This value was sent to the frame by this window during
   // the processing for the WM_MENUSELECT message.
   WORD wTemp = FORWARD_FW_GETMENUHELP(GETFRAME(hwnd), SendMessage);

   // Draw the horizontal dividing line separating the status
   // bar from the MDICLIENT window.
   lpPaintStruct->rcPaint.top +=
      FORWARD_FW_DRAWSTATUSDIVIDE(GETFRAME(hwnd),
      lpPaintStruct, SendMessage);

   // Construct the string that is to be displayed.
   LoadString(_hInstance, wTemp, szString, sizeof(szString));
   GetWindowText(hwnd, szCaption, sizeof(szCaption));
   wsprintf(szBuf, szString, (LPSTR) szCaption);

   // Paint the menu help text in the status bar.
   TextOut(lpPaintStruct->hdc, 0,
      lpPaintStruct->rcPaint.top, szBuf, lstrlen(szBuf));
}
```

Listing 8-9. MDI.RC application resource file

```
/**************************************************************************
Module name: MDI.RC
Programmer : Jeffrey M. Richter & Elvira Peretsman.
**************************************************************************/

#include <windows.h>
#include "mdi.h"

Frame ICON MDI.ico
Sheet ICON Sheet.ico
```

```
Chart ICON Chart.ico


/************** Frame Menu Setup (No Open Documents) *********************/
Frame MENU
BEGIN
    POPUP "&File"
       BEGIN
       MENUITEM "Open &sheet",                    IDM_FILEOPENSHEET
       MENUITEM "Open &chart",                    IDM_FILEOPENCHART
       MENUITEM SEPARATOR
       MENUITEM "E&xit",                          IDM_EXIT
       END

    POPUP "&Help"
       BEGIN
       MENUITEM "&Index",                         IDM_HELPINDEX
       MENUITEM "&Keyboard",                      IDM_HELPKEYBOARD
       MENUITEM "&Commands",                      IDM_HELPCOMMANDS
       MENUITEM "&Procedures",                    IDM_HELPPROCEDURES
       MENUITEM "&Using Help",                    IDM_HELPUSINGHELP
       END
END

RIBBON DIALOG LOADONCALL MOVEABLE DISCARDABLE 0, 0, 600, 15
STYLE WS_CHILD | WS_CLIPSIBLINGS
BEGIN
    CONTROL "Font:", ID_FONTTEXT, "static", SS_RIGHT | WS_CHILD, 4, 2, 16, 8
    CONTROL "", ID_FONT, "combobox", CBS_DROPDOWNLIST | WS_VSCROLL |
        WS_TABSTOP | WS_CHILD, 21, 1, 48, 51
    CONTROL "Size:", ID_SIZETEXT, "static", SS_RIGHT | WS_CHILD, 74, 2, 16, 8
    CONTROL "", ID_SIZE, "combobox", CBS_DROPDOWNLIST | WS_VSCROLL |
        WS_TABSTOP | WS_CHILD, 91, 1, 48, 51
    CONTROL "Bold", ID_BOLD, "button", BS_AUTOCHECKBOX | WS_TABSTOP |
        WS_CHILD, 147, 1, 28, 12
    CONTROL "Italic", ID_ITALIC, "button", BS_AUTOCHECKBOX | WS_TABSTOP |
        WS_CHILD, 177, 1, 28, 12
     CONTROL "Underline", ID_UNDERLINE, "button", BS_AUTOCHECKBOX |
        WS_TABSTOP | WS_CHILD, 207, 1, 42, 12
END

// Menu help descriptions for Frame's top-level menu.
STRINGTABLE LOADONCALL MOVEABLE DISCARDABLE
BEGIN
    IDS_FRAMEPOPUPID + 0,
       "Move, size, or close the application window"
    IDS_FRAMEPOPUPID + 1,
       "Open, print or save documents; quit MDI Application"
```

```
    IDS_FRAMEPOPUPID + 2,    "Get help"
END


// Menu help descriptions for Frame's menu items.
STRINGTABLE LOADONCALL MOVEABLE DISCARDABLE
BEGIN
    IDS_FRAMEMENUID + IDM_SYSMENUSIZE,      "Changes window size"
    IDS_FRAMEMENUID + IDM_SYSMENUMOVE,      "Changes window position"
    IDS_FRAMEMENUID + IDM_SYSMENUMINIMIZE, "Reduces window to an icon"
    IDS_FRAMEMENUID + IDM_SYSMENUMAXIMIZE, "Enlarges the window to full size"
    IDS_FRAMEMENUID + IDM_SYSMENUCLOSE,
        "Quit MDI Application; prompts to save documents"
    IDS_FRAMEMENUID + IDM_SYSMENURESTORE,   "Restores window to normal size"
    IDS_FRAMEMENUID + IDM_SYSMENUTASKLIST, "Make another application active"
    IDS_FRAMEMENUID + IDM_FILEOPENSHEET,    "Open new sheet"
    IDS_FRAMEMENUID + IDM_FILEOPENCHART,    "Open new chart"
    IDS_FRAMEMENUID + IDM_EXIT,
        "Quit MDI Application; prompts to save documents"

    IDS_FRAMEMENUID + IDM_HELPINDEX,        "Lists Help topics"
    IDS_FRAMEMENUID + IDM_HELPKEYBOARD,     "Lists keys and their actions"
    IDS_FRAMEMENUID + IDM_HELPCOMMANDS,     "Lists help on commands"
    IDS_FRAMEMENUID + IDM_HELPPROCEDURES,  "Lists help on various procedures"
    IDS_FRAMEMENUID + IDM_HELPUSINGHELP,    "How to use the help system"
END

/*************************** Sheet Menu ********************************/
Sheet ACCELERATORS
BEGIN
    VK_DELETE,  IDM_EDITCUT,   VIRTKEY, SHIFT
    VK_INSERT,  IDM_EDITCOPY,  VIRTKEY, CONTROL
    VK_INSERT,  IDM_EDITPASTE, VIRTKEY, SHIFT
END

Sheet MENU
BEGIN
    POPUP "&File"
        BEGIN
        MENUITEM "Open &sheet",                 IDM_FILEOPENSHEET
        MENUITEM "Open &chart",                 IDM_FILEOPENCHART
        MENUITEM SEPARATOR
        MENUITEM "&Save",                       IDM_FILESAVE
        MENUITEM "Save &as...",                 IDM_FILESAVEAS
        MENUITEM SEPARATOR
        MENUITEM "&Print",                      IDM_FILEPRINT
        MENUITEM "P&rinter setup...",           IDM_FILEPRINTERSETUP
        MENUITEM SEPARATOR
        MENUITEM "E&xit",                       IDM_EXIT
```

```
        END

    POPUP "&Edit"
        BEGIN
        MENUITEM "Cu&t\tShift+Del",              IDM_EDITCUT
        MENUITEM "&Copy\tCtrl+Ins",              IDM_EDITCOPY
        MENUITEM "&Paste\tShift+Ins",            IDM_EDITPASTE
        END

    POPUP "&Sheet"
        BEGIN
        MENUITEM "Sheet option",                 IDM_SHEETOPTION
        END
    POPUP "&Options"
        BEGIN
        MENUITEM "&Status",                      IDM_OPTIONSSTATUS
        MENUITEM "&Ribbon",                      IDM_OPTIONSRIBBON
        END

    POPUP "&Window"
        BEGIN
        MENUITEM "Tile &vertically",             IDM_WINDOWTILEVERT
        MENUITEM "Tile &horizontally",           IDM_WINDOWTILEHORIZ
        MENUITEM "&Cascade",                     IDM_WINDOWCASCADE
        MENUITEM "&Arrange icons",               IDM_WINDOWARRANGEICONS
        END

    POPUP "&Help"
        BEGIN
        MENUITEM "&Index",                       IDM_HELPINDEX
        MENUITEM "&Keyboard",                    IDM_HELPKEYBOARD
        MENUITEM "&Commands",                    IDM_HELPCOMMANDS
        MENUITEM "&Procedures",                  IDM_HELPPROCEDURES
        MENUITEM "&Using Help",                  IDM_HELPUSINGHELP
        END
END

// Menu help descriptions for Sheet's top-level menu.
STRINGTABLE LOADONCALL MOVEABLE DISCARDABLE
BEGIN
    IDS_SHEETPOPUPID + 0,   "Move, size, or close the active sheet"
    IDS_SHEETPOPUPID + 1,
        "Upen, print or save the sheet; quit MDI Application"
    IDS_SHEETPOPUPID + 2,   "Cut, copy, and paste"
    IDS_SHEETPOPUPID + 3,   "Perform sheet specific operations"
    IDS_SHEETPOPUPID + 4,   "Toggle visibility of status bar and ribbon"
    IDS_SHEETPOPUPID + 5,   "Rearrange windows or activates specified window"
    IDS_SHEETPOPUPID + 6,   "Get help"
```

```
END

// Menu help descriptions for Sheet's menu items.
STRINGTABLE LOADONCALL MOVEABLE DISCARDABLE
BEGIN
    IDS_SHEETMENUID + IDM_SYSMENUSIZE,          "Changes sheet's size"
    IDS_SHEETMENUID + IDM_SYSMENUMOVE,          "Changes sheet's position"
    IDS_SHEETMENUID + IDM_SYSMENUMINIMIZE,      "Reduces sheet to an icon"
    IDS_SHEETMENUID + IDM_SYSMENUMAXIMIZE,      "Enlarges sheet to full size"
    IDS_SHEETMENUID + IDM_SYSMENUCLOSE,
        "Closes the sheet; prompts to save"
    IDS_SHEETMENUID + IDM_SYSMENURESTORE,       "Restores sheet to normal size"
    IDS_SHEETMENUID + IDM_SYSMENUNEXTWINDOW,
        "Switches to the next sheet or chart document"

    IDS_SHEETMENUID + IDM_FILEOPENSHEET,        "Open new sheet"
    IDS_SHEETMENUID + IDM_FILEOPENCHART,        "Open new chart"
    IDS_SHEETMENUID + IDM_FILESAVE,             "Save the active sheet (%s)"
    IDS_SHEETMENUID + IDM_FILESAVEAS,
        "Save the active sheet with a new name"
    IDS_SHEETMENUID + IDM_FILEPRINT,            "Print the active sheet (%s)"
    IDS_SHEETMENUID + IDM_FILEPRINTERSETUP,
        "Changes the printer and printing options"
    IDS_SHEETMENUID + IDM_EXIT,
        "Quit MDI Application; prompts to save documents"

    IDS_SHEETMENUID + IDM_EDITCUT,
        "Cuts the selection from %s and puts it on the Clipboard"
    IDS_SHEETMENUID + IDM_EDITCOPY,
        "Copies the selection from %s and puts it on the Clipboard"
    IDS_SHEETMENUID + IDM_EDITPASTE,
        "Inserts Clipboard contents into %s"

    IDS_SHEETMENUID + IDM_SHEETOPTION,
        "Perform some sheet related operation on %s"

    IDS_SHEETMENUID + IDM_OPTIONSSTATUS,        "Toggles the status bar on/off"
    IDS_SHEETMENUID + IDM_OPTIONSRIBBON,        "Toggles the ribbon on/off"

    IDS_SHEETMENUID + IDM_WINDOWTILEVERT,       "Tiles windows vertically"
    IDS_SHEETMENUID + IDM_WINDOWTILEHORIZ,      "Tiles windows horizontally"
    IDS_SHEETMENUID + IDM_WINDOWCASCADE,
        "Arranges windows in a cascading fashion"
    IDS_SHEETMENUID + IDM_WINDOWARRANGEICONS,   "Arranges iconic windows"

    IDS_SHEETMENUID + IDM_HELPINDEX,            "Lists Help topics"
    IDS_SHEETMENUID + IDM_HELPKEYBOARD,         "Lists keys and their actions"
    IDS_SHEETMENUID + IDM_HELPCOMMANDS,         "Lists help on commands"
```

```
    IDS_SHEETMENUID + IDM_HELPPROCEDURES,
        "Lists help on various procedures"
    IDS_SHEETMENUID + IDM_HELPUSINGHELP,         "How to use the help system"

    IDS_SHEETMENUID + IDM_WINDOWCHILD,
        "Switches to the window containing this document"
END


/***************************** Chart Menu *****************************/
Chart ACCELERATORS
BEGIN
    VK_DELETE,   IDM_EDITCUT,   VIRTKEY, SHIFT
    VK_INSERT,   IDM_EDITCOPY,  VIRTKEY, CONTROL
    VK_INSERT,   IDM_EDITPASTE, VIRTKEY, SHIFT
END


Chart MENU
BEGIN
    POPUP "&File"
        BEGIN
        MENUITEM "Open &sheet",                 IDM_FILEOPENSHEET
        MENUITEM "Open &chart",                 IDM_FILEOPENCHART
        MENUITEM SEPARATOR
        MENUITEM "&Save",                       IDM_FILESAVE
        MENUITEM "Save &as...",                 IDM_FILESAVEAS
        MENUITEM SEPARATOR
        MENUITEM "&Print",                      IDM_FILEPRINT
        MENUITEM "P&rinter setup",              IDM_FILEPRINTERSETUP
        MENUITEM SEPARATOR
        MENUITEM "E&xit",                       IDM_EXIT
        END

    POPUP "&Edit"
        BEGIN
        MENUITEM "Cu&t\tShift+Del",             IDM_EDITCUT
        MENUITEM "&Copy\tCtrl+Ins",             IDM_EDITCOPY
        MENUITEM "&Paste\tShift+Ins",           IDM_EDITPASTE
        END

    POPUP "&Chart"
        BEGIN
        MENUITEM "Chart option",                IDM_CHARTOPTION
        END

    POPUP "&Options"
        BEGIN
        MENUITEM "&Status",                     IDM_OPTIONSSTATUS
        MENUITEM "&Ribbon",                     IDM_OPTIONSRIBBON
```

```
            END

        POPUP "&Window"
            BEGIN
            MENUITEM "Tile &vertically",              IDM_WINDOWTILEVERT
            MENUITEM "Tile &horizontally",            IDM_WINDOWTILEHORIZ
            MENUITEM "&Cascade",                      IDM_WINDOWCASCADE
            MENUITEM "&Arrange icons",                IDM_WINDOWARRANGEICONS
            END

        POPUP "&Help"
            BEGIN
            MENUITEM "&Index",                        IDM_HELPINDEX
            MENUITEM "&Keyboard",                     IDM_HELPKEYBOARD
            MENUITEM "&Commands",                     IDM_HELPCOMMANDS
            MENUITEM "&Procedures",                   IDM_HELPPROCEDURES
            MENUITEM "&Using Help",                   IDM_HELPUSINGHELP
            END
    END

// Menu help descriptions for Chart's top-level menu.
STRINGTABLE LOADONCALL MOVEABLE DISCARDABLE
BEGIN
    IDS_CHARTPOPUPID + 0,    "Move, size, or close the active chart"
    IDS_CHARTPOPUPID + 1,
        "Open, print or save the chart; quit MDI Application"
    IDS_CHARTPOPUPID + 2,    "Cut, copy, and paste"
    IDS_CHARTPOPUPID + 3,    "Perform chart specific operations"
    IDS_CHARTPOPUPID + 4,    "Toggle visibility of status bar and ribbon"
    IDS_CHARTPOPUPID + 5,    "Rearrange windows or activates specified window"
    IDS_CHARTPOPUPID + 6,    "Get help"
END

// Menu help descriptions for Chart's menu items.
STRINGTABLE LOADONCALL MOVEABLE DISCARDABLE
BEGIN
    IDS_CHARTMENUID + IDM_SYSMENUSIZE,        "Changes chart's size"
    IDS_CHARTMENUID + IDM_SYSMENUMOVE,        "Changes chart's position"
    IDS_CHARTMENUID + IDM_SYSMENUMINIMIZE,    "Reduces chart to an icon"
    IDS_CHARTMENUID + IDM_SYSMENUMAXIMIZE,    "Enlarges chart to full size"
    IDS_CHARTMENUID + IDM_SYSMENUCLOSE,
        "Closes the chart; prompts to save"
    IDS_CHARTMENUID + IDM_SYSMENURESTORE,     "Restores chart to normal size"
    IDS_CHARTMENUID + IDM_SYSMENUNEXTWINDOW,
        "Switches to the next sheet or chart document"

    IDS_CHARTMENUID + IDM_FILEOPENSHEET,      "Open new sheet"
    IDS_CHARTMENUID + IDM_FILEOPENCHART,      "Open new chart"
```

```
    IDS_CHARTMENUID + IDM_FILESAVE,            "Save the active chart (%s)"
    IDS_CHARTMENUID + IDM_FILESAVEAS,
        "Save the active char with a new name"
    IDS_CHARTMENUID + IDM_FILEPRINT,           "Print the active chart (%s)"
    IDS_CHARTMENUID + IDM_FILEPRINTERSETUP,
        "Changes the printer and printing options"
    IDS_CHARTMENUID + IDM_EXIT,
        "Quit MDI Application; prompts to save documents"

    IDS_CHARTMENUID + IDM_EDITCUT,
        "Cuts the selection from %s and puts it on the Clipboard"
    IDS_CHARTMENUID + IDM_EDITCOPY,
        "Copies the selection from %s and puts it on the Clipboard"
    IDS_CHARTMENUID + IDM_EDITPASTE,
        "Inserts Clipboard contents into %s"

    IDS_CHARTMENUID + IDM_CHARTOPTION,
        "Perform some chart related operation on %s"

    IDS_CHARTMENUID + IDM_OPTIONSSTATUS,       "Toggles the status bar on/off"
    IDS_CHARTMENUID + IDM_OPTIONSRIBBON,       "Toggles the ribbon on/off"

    IDS_CHARTMENUID + IDM_WINDOWTILEVERT,      "Tiles windows vertically"
    IDS_CHARTMENUID + IDM_WINDOWTILEHORIZ,     "Tiles windows horizontally"
    IDS_CHARTMENUID + IDM_WINDOWCASCADE,
        "Arranges windows in a cascading fashion"
    IDS_CHARTMENUID + IDM_WINDOWARRANGEICONS, "Arranges iconic windows"

    IDS_CHARTMENUID + IDM_HELPINDEX,           "Lists Help topics"
    IDS_CHARTMENUID + IDM_HELPKEYBOARD,        "Lists keys and their actions"
    IDS_CHARTMENUID + IDM_HELPCOMMANDS,        "Lists help on commands"
    IDS_CHARTMENUID + IDM_HELPPROCEDURES,
        "Lists help on various procedures"
    IDS_CHARTMENUID + IDM_HELPUSINGHELP,       "How to use the help system"

    IDS_CHARTMENUID + IDM_WINDOWCHILD,
        "Switches to the window containing this document"
END

/*************** String tables to fill comboboxes in Ribbon *************/

STRINGTABLE LOADONCALL MOVEABLE DISCARDABLE
BEGIN
    IDS_FONT + 0, "Courier"
    IDS_FONT + 1, "Helv"
    IDS_FONT + 2, "Modern"
    IDS_FONT + 3, "Roman"
    IDS_FONT + 4, "Script"
```

```
    IDS_FONT + 5, "Symbol"
    IDS_FONT + 6, "System"
    IDS_FONT + 7, "Terminal"
END


STRINGTABLE LOADONCALL MOVEABLE DISCARDABLE
BEGIN
    IDS_SIZE + 0, "10"
    IDS_SIZE + 1, "12"
    IDS_SIZE + 2, "15"
    IDS_SIZE + 3, "18"
    IDS_SIZE + 4, "22"
    IDS_SIZE + 5, "28"
END
// Status bar statistics line for Frame and MDI Children windows.
STRINGTABLE LOADONCALL MOVEABLE DISCARDABLE
BEGIN
    IDS_FRAMESTATUSBAR,     "Frame status line"
    IDS_SHEETSTATUSBAR,     "Sheet status line"
    IDS_CHARTSTATUSBAR,     "Chart status line"
END
```

Listing 8-10. MDI.DEF application definitions file

```
; Module name: MDI.DEF
; Programmer : Jeffrey M. Richter & Elvira Peretsman.

NAME            MDI
DESCRIPTION     'MDI: Multiple Document Interface Sample Application'
STUB            'WinStub.exe'
EXETYPE         WINDOWS
DATA            MOVEABLE MULTIPLE PRELOAD
SEGMENTS
    _TEXT       MOVABLE DISCARDABLE PRELOAD
    _MDI        MOVABLE DISCARDABLE PRELOAD
    _Frame      MOVABLE DISCARDABLE PRELOAD
    _Sheet      MOVABLE DISCARDABLE LOADONCALL
    _Chart      MOVABLE DISCARDABLE LOADONCALL
    _Child      MOVABLE DISCARDABLE LOADONCALL
    _Ribbon     MOVABLE DISCARDABLE LOADONCALL
CODE            MOVEABLE DISCARDABLE
HEAPSIZE        1024
STACKSIZE       5120
```

CHAPTER 9

Implementing Drag-and-Drop

With the introduction of Windows 3.1, Microsoft has taken some big steps toward reaching its "Information at your Fingertips" objective. This objective allows computer users to concentrate more on getting their work done rather than having to understand and master the tools being used to complete that task. Certainly, one of the primary technologies created to help reach this objective is the concept of Object Linking and Embedding (OLE). This technology allows a user to select the host application that is best designed for the presentation of the data (for example, word processing, spreadsheet, or slide presentations). Once the host application has been decided, OLE allows the user to insert information into the host document in various forms by using other applications. For example, a user creating a document in a word processor can easily insert a chart created by a spreadsheet program into the document. When the user needs to edit or change this chart, the application best suited to process the work (in this case, the spreadsheet) is automatically invoked for the user. The user can then change the data and the new chart is replaced in the document. This technology lets someone use whatever tools he or she is most comfortable with to get a job done, and OLE helps by seamlessly (almost) integrating these operations into the host application.

It is more natural for a user to concentrate on data instead of the programs required to process data. In addition to OLE, Windows 3.1 offers another facility that allows users to think in this way. This technology is called *drag-and-drop*. Probably the easiest way to get the feel of drag-and-drop is by using the Windows' File Manager.

Many end users have not had an easy time understanding the file system of the MS-DOS operating system with its directory structures and hierarchies. The File Manager is meant to let users manipulate files productively and efficiently. The Windows Version 3.0 File Manager fell short of this goal, so it was rewritten for Windows 3.1. The new File Manager is so much better and faster that I even find myself using it more often than performing file operations from the DOS command line.

Without a doubt, the feature that makes the File Manager so easy to use is its drag-and-drop capabilities. Drag-and-drop simplifies several common tasks. First, you can copy and move files from one directory to another. Figure 9-1 shows the File Manager with the contents of the D:\DEMYSTS directory displayed in the right panel. To move the DEMSYST.DLL file from this directory to the VOYEUR directory, you simply select DEMYSTS.DLL with the mouse, drag the mouse cursor so that it is on top of the VOYEUR file folder icon in the left panel, and release the mouse button.

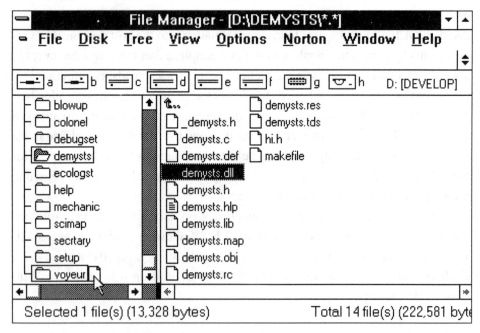

Figure 9-1. Copying D:\DEMYSTS\DEMYSTS.DLL to Voyeur directory by dragging

Wherever the mouse is when its button is released is where the file will be moved or copied. The File Manager assumes that you are copying a file if you position the mouse cursor over a target directory on a drive other than the source file's drive. It assumes that the file is to be moved if the mouse is positioned over a directory present on the same drive as the selected file.

As the mouse cursor is dragged over different areas of the screen, the File Manager alters the shape of the cursor. If the mouse is dragged over an area that doesn't accept files, File Manager changes the cursor to look like Figure 9-2. If the cursor is over a location that will cause the file to be moved, the cursor looks like Figure 9-3. If the file will be copied, the cursor looks like Figure 9-4. The plus sign in a cursor indicates that an additional file will be created.

Figure 9-2. **Figure 9-3.** **Figure 9-4.**

You can select several files at once using the Ctrl key and drag them all with the mouse. For multiple files, the cursors shown in Figures 9-5 and 9-6 are used.

Figure 9-5. **Figure 9-6.**

There is another drag-and-drop operation available from within the File Manager. Figure 9-7 shows a bitmap file being opened for editing by dropping it onto PBRUSH.EXE. When the mouse button is released, the File Manager constructs the following command line and then executes it:

```
C:\WINDOWS\PBRUSH.EXE C:\WINDOWS\FLOCK.BMP
```

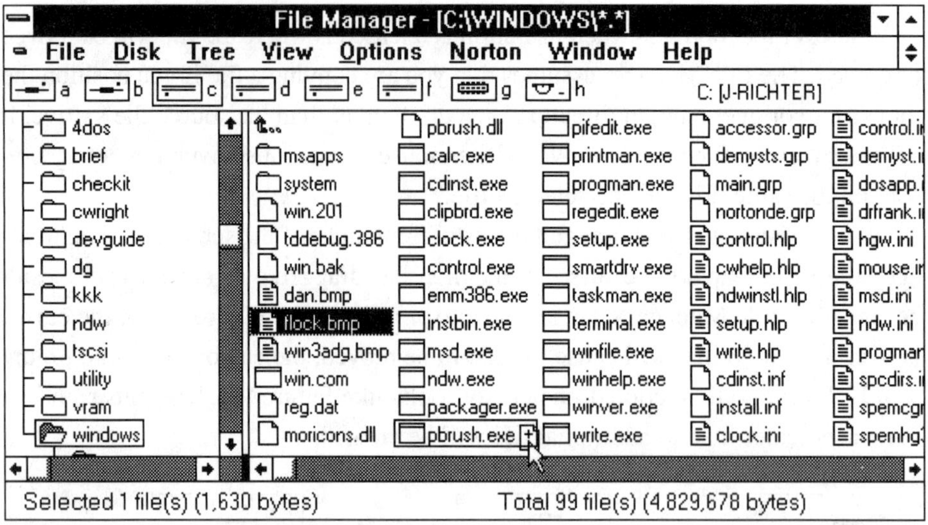

Figure 9-7. A bitmap file being opened for editing

Up till now, you have been dragging files from the File Manager to the File Manager. It is also possible to select files in the File Manager and to drag them outside the File Manager's window, dropping the files onto another application's window. When you drop files from the File Manager onto an application running as an icon, the application opens the file that was dropped onto it. For example, if Notepad is running as an icon and I drag the SETUP.INF file from the File Manager and drop it on top of Notepad's icon, Notepad's caption changes from "Notepad—(Untitled)" to "Notepad—SETUP.INF" to show that the file is the one currently being edited.

As you can see, this method of opening a file is extremely intuitive for a user. The user is concentrating on the data and not the tool that is required to process it. If the Print Manager were running, the user could have just as easily dropped the filename on top of it, causing the file to be printed instead of edited. If there were a spelling-checker application available, the user could just drop the filename on top of the spelling checker to have the document proofed for misspellings. This is the way users think—they are working on something and wish to perform different tasks on it. They do not want to load an editor (like Notepad) and edit several different files in succession.

In Figure 9-8, the ARCADE.BMP file was dragged from the File Manager and dropped into Write's client area. Write automatically created a "Package" for the dropped file and inserted the package into the document at the location of the caret. This package is an embedded or linked object that is identified by a bitmap or icon. Packages can be embedded only in applications that support the OLE client protocol. If a TXT file were dropped into Write instead, Write would display the icon for Notepad. You could also drag a WAV file into Write. Whenever the user double-clicks on this package, the Windows sound recorder activates and plays the recorded audio in the WAV file. As of Windows 3.1, Write is OLE-aware; Notepad isn't. If a BMP or WAV file is dropped into Notepad, Notepad simply tries to open the file as an ASCII test file—most likely with less-than-acceptable results.

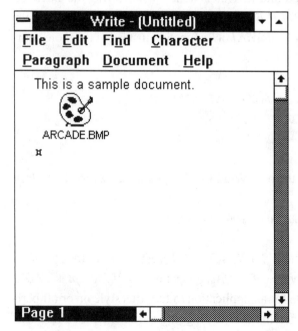

Figure 9-8. ARCADE.BMP embedded as a package in Write document

The icon chosen for an embedded package is determined by the association list for file extensions. The File Manager maintains a list of extensions and the pathnames of the programs that can operate on each file type. This list is nothing new to Windows and has been a part of it ever since the Windows 1.0 days. It allows the user to double-click on a data file from the File Manager or MS-DOS Executive (pre-Windows 3.0) to cause the proper application to execute and load the data file automatically. File extensions can be associated with applications from the Associate dialog box in the File Manager.

Becoming a Dropfile Client

Modifying your application so that it is a dropfile client is extremely easy. There are only four new Windows API functions, one new message, and one new window style. To use the new APIs, you must include the SHELLAPI.H file in your application's source modules. This file is included with the Windows 3.1 SDK.

To become a dropfile client, your application must first tell the File Manager that it can process filenames dropped into it. This is done by specifying the extended window style *WS_EX_ACCEPTFILES*. This style requires that you create your application's window using the *CreateWindowEx* function instead of the more common *CreateWindow* function:

```
hWnd = CreateWindowEx(WS_EX_ACCEPTFILES, "ClassName", "Caption",
    WS_OVERLAPPED, CW_USEDEFAULT, CW_USEDEFAULT, CW_USEDEFAULT,
    CW_USEDEFAULT, NULL, NULL, hInstance, 0);
```

Alternatively, you could use the new Windows 3.1 function, *DragAcceptFiles*:

```
void DragAcceptFiles(HWND hWnd, BOOL fAccept);
```

This function simply turns the *WS_EX_ACCEPTFILES* style for the specified window on or off, based on the value of the *fAccept* parameter. If *fAccept* is TRUE, the bit is turned on. It is possible for an application to turn this style on or off periodically while it is running. When the user is dragging a filename, the File Manager examines this style bit for the window that is directly under the mouse cursor. If the window does not have the *WS_EX_ACCEPTFILES* style on, the File Manager changes the cursor to appear as Figure 9-2. This informs the user that the filename cannot be dropped at the current location. If, on the other hand, the File Manager sees that the *WS_EX_ACCEPTFILES* style is on, it changes the cursor to look like Figure 9-4.

I mentioned earlier that multiple files can be selected in the File Manger for moving or copying. It is also possible to drag multiple files before dropping all of them on top of an application. This is useful if you wish to add several files to a group in the Program Manager. You could simply select all the filenames, drag them over the desktop and drop them onto the desired group window. The Program Manager knows how to process several filenames dropped onto it at once and simply retrieves all of the icons for the dropped filenames and displays them in the group window. In the case where the user is dragging multiple filenames, the File Manager changes the mouse cursor to appear as Figure 9-6.

Sometimes, it is necessary for a drag-and-drop client application to call the *Drag-AcceptFiles* function periodically. If an application is printing a file, it should call *DragAcceptFiles* and pass FALSE as the *fAccept* parameter so that the user cannot drop any filenames into the application before printing completed. Once the document completes printing, the application calls *DragAcceptFiles* again with *fAccept* set as TRUE so that filenames can again be dropped.

How it Works

When the user drags one or more filenames and releases the mouse button, the File Manager allocates a global block of memory and fills it with the list of filenames that the user selected. Actually, each file's full path is inserted into the block instead of just the file's name. The File Manager then posts a *WM_DROPFILES* message to the window that was under the mouse cursor when the user released the mouse button. The *wParam* parameter of this message indicates the handle to this block of memory containing the selected file's pathnames. The *lParam* parameter for this message is not used.

Once this message has been received, the application calls the *DragQueryFile* function to process the memory block:

```
WORD DragQueryFile(HDROP hDrop, WORD wFileNum, LPSTR lpszFile,
    WORD wMaxFileSize);
```

The *hDrop* parameter indicates the memory handle containing the list of pathnames that have been dropped into the window. This handle was passed as the *wParam* parameter for the *WM_DROPFILES* message. The *wFileNum* parameter indicates which pathname should be retrieved from the memory block. This value can be between zero and the number of pathnames dropped minus one. If the value is -1, *DragQueryFile* returns the total number of pathnames contained in the memory block.

When *DragQueryFile* is used to request an individual pathname, the *lpszFile* parameter gives the location of a buffer where the indicated pathname should be copied. The *wMaxFileSize* parameter is the maximum number of bytes that can be copied into this buffer. After copying the pathname, *DragQueryFile* returns the number of bytes actually copied into the buffer.

It is possible to determine the length of an individual entry's pathname by specifying NULL as the *lpszFile* parameter to this function. When you do this, *DragQueryFile* returns the length of the specified pathname.

The following code fragment from a dropfile client's window procedure demonstrates how all of the dropped pathnames could be added to a "ListBox" control:

```
case WM_DROPFILES:
// Get the number of pathnames that have been dropped.
wNumFilesDropped = DragQueryFile((HDROP) wParam, -1, NULL, 0);

// Get the handle to the list box and empty it.
hWndLB = GetDlgItem(hWnd, ID_LISTBOX);
ListBox_ResetContent(hWndLB);

// Add each pathname to the list box.
for (x = 0 ; x < wNumFilesDropped; x++) {

   // Get the number of bytes required by the file's full pathname.
   wPathnameSize = DragQueryFile((HDROP) wParam, x, NULL, 0);

   // Allocate memory to contain full pathname and zero byte.
   npszFile = (NPSTR) LocalAlloc(LPTR, wPathnameSize += 1);

   // If not enough memory, skip this one.
   if (npszFile == NULL) continue;
```

```
    // Copy the pathname into the buffer and add to list box.
    DragQueryFile((HDROP) wParam, x, npszFile, wPathnameSize);
    ListBox_AddString(hWndLB, npszFile);

    LocalFree(npszFile);
}

// Free the memory block containing the dropped-file information.
DragFinish((HDROP) wParam);
break;
```

After the *WM_DROPFILES* messages have been processed, the memory block containing all of the pathnames must be freed via a call to *DragFinish*. This function's only parameter is the handle to the memory block containing the list of dropped pathnames. If you do not call *DragFinish,* the memory block will not be freed until the application that allocated the block (in this case, the File Manager) is terminated. If the user does several drag-and-drop operations, extra memory is unnecessarily used.

In addition to the list of pathnames contained in the memory block, the File Manager also adds other information that may be useful to the dropfile client application. This information can be obtained by calling the *DragQueryPoint* function:

```
BOOL DragQueryPoint(HDROP hDrop, LPPOINT lpPoint)
```

As always, the *hDrop* parameter is the handle to the memory block while the *lpPoint* parameter is the address to a *POINT* data structure. *DragQueryPoint* copies the coordinates of the mouse cursor when the files were dropped into the *lpPoint* buffer. The x- and y-values in the *POINT* structure are relative to the client area of the window receiving the *WM_DROPFILES* message. The *DragQueryPoint* function also returns TRUE if the mouse cursor were in the client area of the window or FALSE if it were outside the client area.

An application can use this information to determine how to process the dropped pathnames. For example, Write opens a file if it is dropped on its non-client area (such as its title bar) and inserts the file as a package into the current document if it is dropped in Write's client area.

Sometimes, it does not make sense for an application to have more than one pathname dropped into it. To use Write again as an example, when multiple files are dropped onto Write's non-client area, Write simply ignores the request to open a file. But when multiple files are dropped onto Write's client area, Write inserts all of the files as packages into the current document. Whether your application uses the dropped pathnames or not, the block of memory must still be freed by calling *DragFinish*.

BurnIt

BurnIt is a small Windows application that demonstrates a useful example of a dropfile client. When it is invoked, it simply runs as a small icon at the bottom of the screen. While it is running, you can select any number of filenames from the File Manager and drop them into BurnIt's fireplace. When these filenames are dropped, BurnIt will delete all of the files.

BurnIt registers a window class and then creates an instance of this class in the minimized state. It does so by specifying the *WS_MINIMIZE* style in the call to *CreateWindowEx*. Of course, since this window allows filenames to be dropped onto it, the *WS_EX_ACCEPTFILES* style is also specified in this call.

So that BurnIt always runs as an icon that can never be restored or maximized, the following code is added to its window procedure:

```
case WM_QUERYOPEN:
    // Don't allow this application to be opened. It only runs
    // as an icon.
    lResult = FALSE;
    break;
```

Whenever Windows is about to restore or maximize an iconic window, it sends the *WM_QUERYOPEN* message to that window's window procedure. If the window procedure responds by returning FALSE, Windows will not open the window.

When I use the File Manager, I always maximize it. The problem with this, of course, is that the File Manager completely obscures the BurnIt icon, prohibiting my use of it. Fortunately, Windows 3.1 offers a solution to this problem. Windows 3.1, supplies two z-orders that a window can be placed in. The new z-order is called the topmost z-order and is discussed more in Chapter 1. Windows placed in the topmost z-order are closer to the user than windows not in the topmost z-order. By placing the BurnIt window in the topmost z-order, it will always appear on top of the File Manager window, even when the File Manager is maximized (see Figure 9-9).

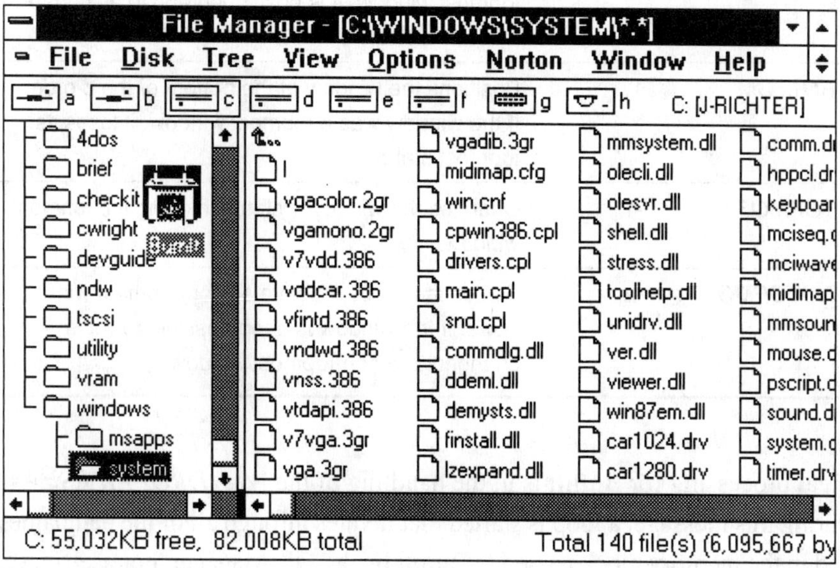

Figure 9-9. BurnIt window placed in the topmost z-order remains visible even when File Manager is the active application

The *SetWindowPos* function has been enhanced in Windows 3.1 to support moving windows into and out of the topmost z-order. In the BurnIt program, the code to place the window in the topmost z-order can be found in the processing of the *WM_CREATE* message in the *BurnItWndProc* function:

```
case WM_CREATE:
SetWindowPos(hWnd, HWND_TOPMOST, 0, 0, 0, 0,
    SWP_NOMOVE | SWP_NOSIZE);
```

When calling *SetWindowPos*, the second parameter indicates which window should immediately precede your window (the first parameter) in the z-order. However, you can specify any of the following identifiers instead:

WINDOWS.H identifier	Value	Meaning
HWND_TOP	NULL	If the window is a topmost window, it is positioned above all topmost windows. If the window is a non-topmost window, it is positioned above all non-topmost windows.
HWND_BOTTOM	1	Positions the window at the bottom of the z-order. If the window was a topmost window, it loses its topmost status.
HWND_TOPMOST	-1	Changes the window's status, making it a topmost window.
HWND_NOTOPMOST	-2	Places the window above all non-topmost windows. If the window is a topmost window it is changed to a non-topmost window.

The real processing for BurnIt is in the handling of the *WM_DROPFILES* message. During this message, a loop is started that iterates through all of the pathnames contained in the memory block passed to BurnIt by the File Manager. For each entry, the full pathname is copied to a local block of memory by using the *DragQueryFile* function; then the pathname is passed to the *OpenFile* function:

```
OpenFile(npszPathName, &of, OF_DELETE);
```

This call to *OpenFile* tells Windows to delete the file indicated by the *npszPathName* parameter. When the loop has cycled through every pathname, the *DragFinish* function is called so that the memory block is freed.

Adding drag-and-drop capabilities to your own applications is very easy and can be done with only a few lines of code.

Listing 9-1. BURNIT.C

```
/*******************************************************************
Module name: BURNIT.C
Programmer : Jeffrey M. Richter.
Description: Dropfile Client Sample Application.
*******************************************************************/

#include <windows.h>
#include <shellapi.h>

extern HINSTANCE _cdecl _hInstance;

//*********** Prototypes for Local Functions ********************
LRESULT CALLBACK BurnItWndProc (HWND hWnd, UINT uMsg,
   WPARAM wParam, LPARAM lParam);

//****************** Global Variables ************************
char _szAppName[] = "BurnIt";

#define BURNICONS       2
#define FLAREICONS      3
#define MAX_ICONS       (BURNICONS + FLAREICONS)

#define ICON_First      100

HICON hIconList[MAX_ICONS];
int _nIconNum;          // Index into hIcons of last displaced icon.
BOOL _fFlaring = FALSE;

#pragma argsused
int WinMain (HINSTANCE hInstance, HINSTANCE hPrevInstance,
                  LPSTR lpszCmdLine, int nCmdShow) {
   MSG msg;
   HWND hWnd;
   WNDCLASS wc;

   if (hPrevInstance != NULL) {
      // If instance of BurnIt is already running, bring it to
      // top and terminate this instance.
      BringWindowToTop(FindWindow(_szAppName, _szAppName));
      return(0);
   }

   wc.style        = 0;
   wc.lpfnWndProc  = (WNDPROC) BurnItWndProc;
```

```
    wc.cbClsExtra    = wc.cbWndExtra = 0;
    wc.hInstance     = hInstance;
    wc.hIcon         = NULL;
    wc.hCursor       = LoadCursor(NULL, IDC_ARROW);
    wc.hbrBackground = NULL;
    wc.lpszMenuName  = NULL;
    wc.lpszClassName = _szAppName;
    if (!RegisterClass(&wc)) return(0);

    // Create the Frame window.
    hWnd = CreateWindowEx(WS_EX_ACCEPTFILES, _szAppName,
        _szAppName, WS_OVERLAPPED | WS_VISIBLE | WS_CAPTION |
        WS_SYSMENU, CW_USEDEFAULT, SW_MINIMIZE, CW_USEDEFAULT,
        CW_USEDEFAULT, NULL, NULL, hInstance, NULL);
    if (hWnd == NULL) return(0);

    while (GetMessage(&msg, NULL, 0, 0)) {
        DispatchMessage(&msg);
    }

    return(msg.wParam);
}

LRESULT CALLBACK BurnItWndProc (HWND hWnd, UINT uMsg,
    WPARAM wParam, LPARAM lParam) {

    BOOL fCallOrigProc = FALSE;
    LRESULT lResult = 0;
    WORD wFilesDropped, wSize;
    NPSTR npszPathName;
    OFSTRUCT of;
    HDC hDC;
    WORD x;

    switch (uMsg) {

        case WM_CREATE:
            // Place BurnIt in the topmost z-order.
            SetWindowPos(hWnd, HWND_TOPMOST,
                0, 0, 0, 0, SWP_NOMOVE | SWP_NOSIZE);

            // Start a timer for icon animation.
            SetTimer(hWnd, 1, 250, NULL);

            // Get the handles for all the icons that
            // you are cycling through.
            for (x = 0; x < MAX_ICONS; x++) {
```

```
        hIconList[x] = LoadIcon(_hInstance,
            MAKEINTRESOURCE(ICON_First + x));
    }
    break;

case WM_DESTROY:
    KillTimer(hWnd, 1);
    PostQuitMessage(0);
    break;

case WM_QUERYOPEN:
    // Don't allow this applcation to be opened.
    // It only runs as an icon.
    lResult = FALSE;
    break;

case WM_TIMER:
    // Show the next icon in the sequence.
    x = _nIconNum + 1;
    x = x % (int) (_fFlaring ? MAX_ICONS : BURNICONS);
    if (x == 0)
        _fFlaring = 0; // Reset to burning only.
    _nIconNum = x;

    hDC = GetDC(hWnd);
    DrawIcon(hDC, 0, 0, hIconList[x]);
    ReleaseDC(hWnd, hDC);
    break;

case WM_DROPFILES:
    _fFlaring = TRUE; // Stoke the fire!

    // Get the number of pathnames that
    // are being dropped on us.
    wFilesDropped =
        DragQueryFile((HDROP) wParam, -1, NULL, 0);

    while (wFilesDropped- > 0) {

        // Get the length of the the pathname.
        wSize = DragQueryFile((HDROP) wParam,
            wFilesDropped, NULL, 0) + 1;
        // Allocate a block of memory
        // large enough for the pathname.
        npszPathName = (NPSTR) LocalAlloc(LMEM_FIXED, wSize);
        if (npszPathName == NULL)  // Insufficient memory.
            continue;
```

```
            // Copy the pathname into our local buffer.
            DragQueryFile((HDROP) wParam, wFilesDropped,
                npszPathName, wSize);

            // Delete this file.
            OpenFile(npszPathName, &of, OF_DELETE);

            LocalFree((HLOCAL) npszPathName);
        }

        // Free the memory block containing the pathnames.
        DragFinish((HDROP) wParam);
        break;

    default:
        fCallOrigProc = TRUE;
        break;
    }
    if (fCallOrigProc)
        lResult = DefWindowProc(hWnd, uMsg, wParam, lParam);

    return(lResult);
}
```

Listing 9-2. BURNIT.DEF

```
; Module name: BURNIT.DEF
; Programmer : Jeffrey M. Richter.

NAME            BURNIT
DESCRIPTION     'BurnIt: Dropfile Client Sample Application'
STUB            'WinStub.exe'
EXETYPE         WINDOWS
DATA            MOVEABLE MULTIPLE PRELOAD
CODE            MOVEABLE DISCARDABLE PRELOAD
HEAPSIZE        2048
STACKSIZE       5120
```

Listing 9-3. BURNIT.RC

```
/********************************************************************
Module name: BURNIT.RC
Programmer : Jeffrey M. Richter.
********************************************************************/

#include <windows.h>

100 ICON MOVEABLE DISCARDABLE BurnIt1.ico
101 ICON MOVEABLE DISCARDABLE BurnIt2.ico
102 ICON MOVEABLE DISCARDABLE BurnIt3.ico
103 ICON MOVEABLE DISCARDABLE BurnIt4.ico
104 ICON MOVEABLE DISCARDABLE BurnIt3.ico
```

Listing 9-4. MAKEFILE

```
#********************************************************************
#Module name: MAKEFILE
#Programmer : Jeffrey M. Richter.
#********************************************************************

!include "..\builtins.jmr"

PROG = BurnIt

MODEL = s
CFLAGS = -P-c -c -f- -WS -p -v -w -m$(MODEL) -I$(INCLUDEDIR)
LFLAGS = /P/v/n/m/s/L$(LIBDIR)
LIBS = CW$(MODEL) Import

MODULES = $(PROG).obj

ICONS   = $(PROG)1.ico $(PROG)2.ico $(PROG)3.ico $(PROG)4.ico
BITMAPS =
CURSORS =

$(PROG).Exe: $(MODULES) $(PROG).Def $(PROG).Res
     tlink $(LFLAGS) @&&!
COW$(MODEL) $(MODULES)
$(PROG), $(PROG), $(LIBS), $(PROG)
!
   rc -31 -T $(PROG).Res
   TDStrip -s $(PROG)

$(PROG).res: $(PROG).rc $(RESOURCES)
```

Becoming A Dropfile Server

You may have noticed that up to now, the only way that applications can have pathnames dropped on them is when the user initiates the drag-and-drop sequence from the File Manager. The reason for this is because the Windows' File Manager is the only dropfile server application that comes with Windows 3.1. In fact, Microsoft has not documented or published any of the data structures or functions so that you can write your own dropfile server applications.

I decided to investigate the four *Dragxxx* API functions and determine what they exactly do. I have also investigated the structure of the memory block that is created by the File Manager and passed to a window procedure via the *wParam* parameter for the *WM_DROPFILES* message. Having done all this work, I would like to share my findings, so that you can create a dropfile server application.

But before I explain what I found, I'd like to emphasize that it's officially undocumented. Anything you use from this section you *use at your own risk*. Any of the functions' internals or the structure of the memory clock discussed here may change in future versions of Windows, possibly breaking your code.

Let's begin with the internal data structure:

```
typedef struct {
    WORD wSize;             // Number of bytes in this structure
    POINT ptMousePos;       // Mouse position.
    BOOL fInNonClientArea;  // TRUE if mouse was in client area.
    // Pathnames begin after structure; each one zero-terminated.
    // Zero-length pathname used to indicate the end.
} DROPFILESTRUCT, FAR *LPDROPFILESTRUCT;
```

This is the structure that is created by the File Manager when the user drops pathnames into a window. After allocating a memory block large enough to hold this structure, the *wSize* member is initialized to the number of bytes in the structure:

```
lpDropFileStruct->wSize = sizeof(DROPFILESTRUCT);
```

The *ptMousePos* member is set to the x- and y-coordinates of the mouse when it was released (these coordinates are relative to the client area of the window under the mouse cursor). The *fInNonClientArea* member is set to TRUE if the mouse was in the windows non-client area when the button was released. Following this structure in the memory block is the full pathname for each of the filenames that was selected in the File Manager. Each pathname is terminated with a zero byte and an extra zero byte after the last pathname indicates the end of the entire list. For example, the complete block of memory containing two pathnames (D:\DROPFILE\ARTICLE.DOC and C:\WINDOWS\CALC.EXE) would look like Figure 9-10.

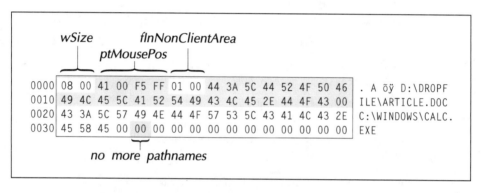

Figure 9-10. Memory block containing DROPFILESTRUCT and two full pathnames

To implement a dropfile server, your application must create a memory block containing the structure described above. I have written two functions to help you do this. The first function, *DragInitBlock*, allocates a global block of memory large enough to contain the *DRAGFILESTRUCT* structure and initializes its three data members. The handle to this memory block returns by the function or NULL if an error occurs.

You'll notice that the global memory block is allocated using the *GMEM_SHARE* flag. If you examine this flag in the WINDOWS.H file, you'll notice that it has the same value as the *GMEM_DDESHARE* flag. This flag indicates to Windows that the application that allocated this memory block is not necessarily the same application going to use it. Actually, when running Windows 3.0 and 3.1 in protected mode, memory blocks created by one application are not protected from another application. Because of this, it really isn't necessary to specify the *GMEM_SHARE* flag. The *GMEM_SHARE* flag is also used to make a module an owner of a memory block instead of a task. This is discussed in more detail in Chapter 6 and has little to do with dragging and dropping files.

```
HDROP DragInitBlock (LPPOINT lpptMousePos, BOOL fInNonClientArea) {
    HDROP hDrop;
    LPDROPFILESTRUCT lpDropFileStruct;

    // GMEM_SHARE must be specified because the block will
    // be accessed by another application.
    hDrop = GlobalAlloc(GMEM_SHARE | GMEM_MOVEABLE | GMEM_ZEROINIT,
            sizeof(DROPFILESTRUCT) + 1);

    // If unsuccessful, return NULL.
    if (hDrop == NULL) return(hDrop);

    // Lock block and initialize the data members.
    lpDropFileStruct = (LPDROPFILESTRUCT) GlobalLock(hDrop);
    lpDropFileStruct->wSize = sizeof(DROPFILESTRUCT);
    lpDropFileStruct->ptMousePos = *lpptMousePos;
    lpDropFileStruct->fInNonClientArea = fInNonClientArea;
    GlobalUnlock(hDrop);
    return(hDrop);
}
```

The second function, *DragAppendFile*, can be called repeatedly to append new pathnames to the memory block:

```
HDROP DragAppendFile (HDROP hDrop, LPCSTR szPathname) {
    LPDROPFILESTRUCT lpDropFileStruct;
    LPCSTR lpCrnt;
    WORD wSize;

    lpDropFileStruct = (LPDROPFILESTRUCT) GlobalLock(hDrop);
```

```
// Point to first pathname in list.
lpCrnt = (LPSTR) lpDropFileStruct + lpDropFileStruct->wSize;

// Search for a pathname where first byte is a zero byte.
while (*lpCrnt) {   // While the first character of path
                    // is nonzero.
   while (*lpCrnt) lpCrnt++;   // Skip to zero byte.
   lpCrnt++;
}

// Calculate current size of block.
wSize = (WORD) (lpCrnt - (LPSTR) lpDropFileStruct + 1);
GlobalUnlock(hDrop);

// Increase block size to accommodate new pathname being appended.
hDrop = GlobalReAlloc(hDrop, wSize + lstrlen(szPathname) + 1,
   GMEM_MOVEABLE | GMEM_ZEROINIT | GMEM_SHARE);

// Return NULL if insufficient memory.
if (hDrop == NULL) return(hMem);

lpDropFileStruct = (LPDROPFILESTRUCT) GlobalLock(hDrop);
// Append the pathname to the block.
lstrcpy((LPSTR) lpDropFileStruct + wSize - 1, szPathname);
GlobalUnlock(hDrop);
return(hDrop);   // Return the new handle to the block.
}
```

The first parameter to this function is the handle to the memory block created by a call to *DragInitBlock* or a previous call to *DragAppendFile*. *DragAppendFile* then locks the block and counts the number of bytes that are currently being used in it. The block is then enlarged by calling *GlobalReAlloc* so it will be large enough to contain all the block's current data plus the new pathname being appended. If this is successful, the new pathname is copied onto the end of the block and the new global memory handle is returned.

After all of the pathnames are appended to the block with *DragAppendFile*, the window under the mouse cursor can process the dropped pathnames. This is done by having the dropfile server post a *WM_DROPFILES* message to the dropfile client, passing the memory handle returned from *DragAppendFile* as the *wParam* parameter. It is important to use *PostMessage* instead of *SendMessage* here so that Windows does not enter a deadlock situation. To understand this, let's examine the following situation:

When filenames are dropped on a Program Manager group, the Program Manager adds icons to the group window. If a filename is dropped that does not represent an executable program or a file whose extension has an association, the Program Manager displays a message box (Figure 9-11).

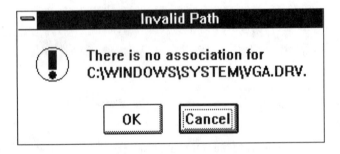

Figure 9-11. Message box from Program Manager

For the Program Manager to become the active task (so that it can present the message box), Windows must make the dropfile server yield control. Windows does this by posting messages into the dropfile server's queue. If the dropfile server sends the *WM_DROPFILES* message by calling *SendMessage* instead of *PostMessage*, it will be unable to process any messages that have accumulated in its queue. This puts Windows in a deadlock situation: It must take control away from the active task but that task is unable to give it up because it is waiting for *SendMessage* to return. This situation is discussed in greater detail in Chapter 6.

The code below demonstrates how to drop two files (XYZ.TXT and ABC.WRI) onto the Print Manager. It is assumed that the Print Manager is running:

```
HDROP hDrop, hDropT;

// Create the initial block telling the Print Manager that the
// mouse was clicked in its left-top corner of its client area.
hDrop = DragInitBlock(&MAKEPOINT(0), FALSE);
if (hDrop == NULL) break;

// Append the two files to the memory block.
hDropT = DragAppendFile(hDrop, "C:\\WINDOWS\\XYZ.TXT");
if (hDropT != NULL) hDrop = hDropT;
hDropT = DragAppendFile(hDrop, "C:\\WINDOWS\\ABC.WRI");
if (hDropT != NULL) hDrop = hDropT;

PostMessage(FindWindow("PrintManager", NULL), WM_DROPFILES, hDrop, 0);
// When the message returns, do NOT free the block. It is freed by
// the window receiving the WM_DROPFILES message.
```

Sample Dropfile Server

DROPFILE.EXE demonstrates how to create a dropfile server application. When executing the application, first select the filename(s) you wish to drag with the "Select files!" menu option. This causes a "File open" dialog box to appear. This is one of the common dialog boxes that Microsoft created and put in the COMMDLG.DLL file distributed with Windows 3.1. Unlike most "File open" dialog boxes, I allow the user to select multiple files. This is done by specifying the *OFN_ALLOWMULTISELECT* flag when initializing the *Flags* member of the *OPENFILENAME* structure.

When the user presses the "OK" button in this dialog, the *GetOpenFileName* function fills the *szAllFilenames* buffer with a string having the form:

```
"Path File1 File 2 File 3 ..."
```

For example, if I select the Calculator, Notepad, and Recorder filenames from the WINDOWS directory on Drive C, the *szAllFilenames* buffer would look like this:

```
C:\WINDOWS CALC.EXE NOTEPAD.EXE RECORDER.EXE\0
```

Once this string is returned, the number of filenames in the string can be determined by counting the number of spaces. This is done in the program by sending the user-defined message *FW_GETNUMFILENAMES* to the dropfile server's window procedure. The number of filenames that have been selected for dropping is displayed in the application's caption bar.

You initiate dropping pathnames by holding down the left mouse button in the client area of the Dropfile's window. When this happens, Windows sends a *WM_LBUTTONDOWN* message to its window's window procedure. This is where all of the code for the dragging and dropping process is. The first step is to track the mouse position and change the shape of the cursor as it passes over different windows on the screen. The window under the mouse is determined by placing a call to the *WindowFromPoint* function. If this function returns the handle to a valid window, you must then check to see if the *WS_EX_ACCEPTFILES* style bit is turned on for that window:

```
fOkToDrop = IsWindow(hWndPotentialClient);
if (fOkToDrop)
    fOkToDrop = fOkToDrop &&
        (GetWindowLong(hWndPotentialClient, GWL_EXSTYLE) & WS_EX_TOPMOST);
```

If the window is invalid or the *WS_EX_ACCEPTFILES* style is off, you change the shape of the cursor to look like Figure 9-2. On the other hand, if the window is valid and the *WS_EX_ACCEPTFILES* style is on, you determine the shape of the cursor by how many filenames have been selected to be dropped. If one filename is selected, the cursor is changed to appear as Figure 9-4; for more than one, the cursor is changed to appear as Figure 9-6. To save myself the trouble of drawing these cursors, I used Borland's Resource Workshop to extract the *dropping-not-allowed* cursor from USER.EXE and the single-file and multiple-file cursors from the File Manager (WINFILE.EXE).

The *do/while* loop causes the mouse cursor to change repeatedly until the user releases the mouse button. Passing *VK_LBUTTON* to *GetAsyncKeyState* tests for mouse button release.

When the mouse button is released, the dropfile memory block is created, initialized, and the full pathname for each of the files that had originally been selected by the user is appended to it.

For initialization, you simply convert the mouse position from screen coordinates to client coordinates and then determine if the mouse cursor was in the client area of the window or not. The first task is done by simply calling the *Screen-ToClient* function.

The second is accomplished by sending the *WM_NCHITTEST* message to the dropfile client window. When the client's window procedure receives this message, it examines the coordinates passed in the *lParam* parameter and determines the part of the window that is at this location. For example, the return value will indicate *HTCAPTION* if the coordinate is somewhere in the window's caption or *HTSYSMENU* if the coordinate is in the area occupied by the window's system menu. For a dropfile server application, you just need to see if the coordinate is in the client area of the window or its non-client area. The return value from sending the *WM_NCHITTEST* message will be *HTCLIENT* if the coordinate is in the window's client area. Any other return value indicates a coordinate in the window's non-client area.

Armed with the initialization information, you can call the *DragInitBlock* function to allocate the dropfile memory block and initialize it. Assuming that all went well (a valid memory handle was returned), you can loop through all the filenames selected by the user, construct a full pathname for each, and append each one to the memory block by calling *DragAppendFile*. After all of the pathnames have been appended, the *WM_DROPFILES* message (with the handle to the dropfile memory block as the *wParam* parameter) can be posted (not sent) to the dropfile client window. Remember, the dropfile server must not free this memory because it will be freed by the dropfile client when it is done with it.

Listing 9-5. DROPFILE.C

```
/*******************************************************************
Module name: DROPFILE.C
Programmer : Jeffrey M. Richter.
Description: Dropfile Server Sample Application.
*******************************************************************/

#include <windows.h>
#include <shellapi.h>
#include <commdlg.h>
#include <string.h>

#include "Dropfile.h"

//*********** Prototypes for File Open Utility Function **********
WORD GetSinglePathName (LPCSTR szFileOpenStr, WORD wIndex,
   LPSTR szPathName, WORD wMaxLen);

//********* Prototypes for Dropfile Server Functions ************
HDROP DragCreateFiles (LPPOINT lpptMousePos,
   BOOL fInNonClientArea);
HDROP DragAppendFile (HDROP hDrop, LPCSTR szPathname);

//***************** Prototypes for Local Functions **************
LRESULT CALLBACK WndProc (HWND hWnd, UINT Msg,
   WPARAM wParam, LPARAM lParam);
#define UM_UPDATECAPTION   (WM_USER + 0)

//********************** Global Variables ********************
char _szAppName[] = "Drop File Server";
extern _cdecl HINSTANCE _hInstance;

#pragma argsused
int WinMain (HINSTANCE hInstance, HINSTANCE hPrevInstance,
   LPSTR lpszCmdLine, int nCmdShow) {

   MSG msg;
   HWND hWnd;
   WNDCLASS wc;

   if (hPrevInstance == NULL) {
      wc.style = 0;
      wc.lpfnWndProc = (WNDPROC) WndProc;
      wc.cbClsExtra = wc.cbWndExtra = 0;
      _hInstance = wc.hInstance = hInstance;
```

```
        wc.hIcon = LoadIcon(hInstance, "DropFile");
        wc.hCursor = LoadCursor(NULL, IDC_UPARROW);
        wc.hbrBackground = COLOR_GRAYTEXT + 1;
        wc.lpszMenuName = "DROPFILE";
        wc.lpszClassName = _szAppName;
        if (!RegisterClass(&wc)) return(0);
    }

    // Create the Frame window.
    // The WS_EXACCEPTFILES style is not needed for
    // server-only applications.
    hWnd = CreateWindow(_szAppName, _szAppName,
        WS_OVERLAPPED | WS_VISIBLE | WS_CAPTION | WS_THICKFRAME |
        WS_SYSMENU | WS_MINIMIZEBOX | WS_MAXIMIZEBOX,
        CW_USEDEFAULT, nCmdShow,
        GetSystemMetrics(SM_CXSCREEN) / 2,   // 1/2-screen width.
        GetSystemMetrics(SM_CYSCREEN) / 8,   // 1/8-screen height.
        NULL, NULL, hInstance, NULL);
    if (hWnd == NULL) return(0);

    while (GetMessage(&msg, NULL, 0, 0)) {
        TranslateMessage(&msg);
        DispatchMessage(&msg);
    }
    return(msg.wParam);
}

LRESULT CALLBACK WndProc (HWND hWnd, UINT Msg,
    WPARAM wParam, LPARAM lParam) {

    static char szAllFileNames[1000] = { 0 };
    HCURSOR hCrsrDrpNotAllow, hCrsrDrpSingle, hCrsrDrpMultiple;
    char szBuf[100], szDropPathName[200];
    BOOL fCallDefProc = FALSE, fInNonClientArea, fOkToDrop;
    LONG lResult = 0;
    POINT ptMousePos;
    WORD x, wNumFiles;
    HWND hWndSubject;
    HDROP hDrop, hDropT;
    OPENFILENAME ofn;

    switch (Msg) {
        case WM_CREATE:
            SendMessage(hWnd, UM_UPDATECAPTION, 0, 0);
            break;

        case WM_DESTROY:
```

```
        // Terminate the application.
        PostQuitMessage(0);
        break;

    case WM_COMMAND:
        if (wParam != IDM_FILESELECT) {
            fCallDefProc = TRUE;
            break;
        }

        // Initialize structure for calling the "Open File"
        // common dialog.
        _fmemset(&ofn, 0, sizeof(ofn));
        ofn.lStructSize = sizeof(ofn);
        ofn.hwndOwner = hWnd;
        ofn.lpstrFilter = "All files\0*.*\0";
        ofn.Flags = OFN_ALLOWMULTISELECT | OFN_FILEMUSTEXIST |
            OFN_HIDEREADONLY;

        // Set up the buffer to receive the selected file(s).
        szAllFileNames[0] = 0;
        ofn.lpstrFile = szAllFileNames;
        ofn.nMaxFile = sizeof(szAllFileNames);

        if (GetOpenFileName(&ofn))
            wNumFiles =
                GetSinglePathName(szAllFileNames, -1, NULL, 0);
        else wNumFiles = 0;
        SendMessage(hWnd, UM_UPDATECAPTION, wNumFiles, 0);
        break;

    case UM_UPDATECAPTION:
        // Update the window's caption to reflect the # of
        // selected files.
        wsprintf(szBuf, "%s - %d file(s) to drop",
            (LPSTR) _szAppName, wParam);
        SetWindowText(hWnd, szBuf);
        break;

    case WM_LBUTTONDOWN:
        // User has initiated the drag-and-drop sequence.

        // Make sure that there are some selected
        // files to be dropped.
        wNumFiles =
            GetSinglePathName(szAllFileNames, -1, NULL, 0);
        if (wNumFiles == 0) {
```

```
      MessageBox(hWnd, "No files to drop.",
         _szAppName, MB_OK);
      break;
   }

   // Get the handles to the cursors
   // that will be shown to the user.
   hCrsrDrpNotAllow =
      LoadCursor(_hInstance, "DRPFIL_NOTALLOWED");
   hCrsrDrpSingle   =
      LoadCursor(_hInstance, "DRPFIL_SINGLE");
   hCrsrDrpMultiple =
      LoadCursor(_hInstance, "DRPFIL_MULTIPLE");

   // Loop for determining the dropfile client window.
   SetCapture(hWnd);
   do {
      MSG Msg;
      while (PeekMessage(&Msg, NULL, NULL, NULL, PM_REMOVE))
         DispatchMessage(&Msg);

      // Get cursor position and window under the cursor.
      GetCursorPos(&ptMousePos);
      hWndSubject = WindowFromPoint(ptMousePos);

      if (!IsWindow(hWndSubject) ||
            !(GetWindowLong(hWndSubject, GWL_EXSTYLE) &
            WS_EX_ACCEPTFILES)) {
         fOkToDrop = FALSE;
         SetCursor(hCrsrDrpNotAllow);
      } else {
         fOkToDrop = TRUE;
         SetCursor((wNumFiles > 1)
            ? hCrsrDrpMultiple : hCrsrDrpSingle);
      }

      // Terminate loop when mouse button is released.
   } while (GetAsyncKeyState(VK_LBUTTON) & 0x8000);
   ReleaseCapture();

   // Free the loaded cursors from memory.
   DestroyCursor(hCrsrDrpNotAllow);
   DestroyCursor(hCrsrDrpSingle);
   DestroyCursor(hCrsrDrpMultiple);

   if (!fOkToDrop) break;
```

```
// Is the cursor in the window's non-client area?
fInNonClientArea = (HTCLIENT !=
   SendMessage(hWndSubject, WM_NCHITTEST, 0,
      MAKELPARAM(ptMousePos.x, ptMousePos.y)));

// Create dropfile memory block and initialize it.
ScreenToClient(hWndSubject, &ptMousePos);
hDrop = DragCreateFiles(&ptMousePos, fInNonClientArea);
if (hDrop == NULL) {
   MessageBox(hWnd,
      "Insufficient memory to dropfile(s).",
      _szAppName, MB_OK);
   break;
}

// Append each full pathname to
// the dropfile memory block.
for (x = 0; x < wNumFiles; x++) {
   GetSinglePathName(szAllFileNames, x,
      szDropPathName, sizeof(szDropPathName));

   // Append pathname to end of dropfile memory block.
   hDropT = DragAppendFile(hDrop, szDropPathName);

   if (hDropT == NULL) {
      MessageBox(hWnd,
         "Insufficient memory to dropfile(s).",
         _szAppName, MB_OK);
      GlobalFree(hDrop);
      hDrop = NULL;
      break;   // Terminate while loop.
   } else {
      hDrop = hDropT;
   }
}

if (hDrop != NULL) {
   // All pathnames appended successfully; post
   // the message to the dropfile client window.
   PostMessage(hWndSubject, WM_DROPFILES, hDrop, 0L);

   // Clear our own state.
   szAllFileNames[0] = 0;
   SendMessage(hWnd, UM_UPDATECAPTION, 0, 0);

   // Don't free the memory; the dropfile
   // client will do it.
```

```
            }
         break;

      default:
         fCallDefProc = TRUE;
         break;
   }

   if (fCallDefProc)
      lResult = DefWindowProc(hWnd, Msg, wParam, lParam);

   return(lResult);
}

/*************************************************************************/
/*********************                      *********************/
/********************* File Open Utility Function *********************/
/*********************                      *********************/
/*************************************************************************/

WORD GetSinglePathName (LPCSTR szFileOpenStr, WORD wIndex,
   LPSTR szPathName, WORD wMaxLen) {

   WORD wNumFiles = 0, x, y;
   LPCSTR p = szFileOpenStr, q;
   char szBuf[200];

   // Initialize the buffer by clearing it.
   _fmemset(szBuf, 0, sizeof(szBuf));

   // Calculate the number of files in szFileOpenStr.
   while (*p) {
      if (*p == ' ') wNumFiles++;
      p++;
   }

   // If a single file was selected, there are no spaces. But you
   // should return that one file exists.
   if ((wNumFiles == 0) && (p != szFileOpenStr))
      wNumFiles = 1;

   // If the user only wants the number of files, return that.
   if ((int) wIndex == -1)
      return(wNumFiles);

   // User requested more files than exist.
   if (wIndex > wNumFiles)
```

```
        return(0);

    // *** Construct the full pathname of the requested string.***
    if ((wIndex == 0) && (wNumFiles == 1)) {
        _fstrncpy(szBuf, szFileOpenStr, wMaxLen);
    } else {
        // Copy the path portion of the string into a temporary buffer.
        x = (WORD) ((p = _fstrchr(szFileOpenStr, ' ')) - szFileOpenStr);
        _fstrncpy(szBuf, szFileOpenStr, x);

        // Append a backslash if necessary.
        if (*(p - 1) != '\\') {
            szBuf[x] = '\\';
            x++;
        }

        for (y = 0; y < wIndex; y++) {
            p++;  // Increment past the space; 'p' points to proper filename.
            while (*p != ' ') p++;
        }
        p++;  // Increment past the space; 'p' points to proper filename.

        // Find the end of the filename.
        q = _fstrchr(p, '-');

        if (q != NULL) {
            // Copy the filename into the temporary buffer.
            _fstrncpy(&szBuf[x], p, (WORD) (q - p));
        } else {
            // Copy the filename (remainder of string) into the temporary
            // buffer.
            _fstrcpy(&szBuf[x], p);
        }
    }

    if (szPathName != NULL) {
        // If the user passed an address, copy the string into its buffer.
        _fstrncpy(szPathName, szBuf, wMaxLen);
        szPathName[wMaxLen - 1] = 0;  // Force zero-termination.
    }

    return(lstrlen(szBuf)); // Returns length of string.
}
```

```
//****************************************************************
//*******************                     *****************
//***************** Dropfile Server Functions  *****************
//*******************                     *****************
//****************************************************************


typedef struct {
    WORD  wSize;                // Size of data structure.
    POINT ptMousePos;           // Position of mouse cursor.
    BOOL  fInNonClientArea;     // Was the mouse in the
                                // window's non-client area?
} DROPFILESTRUCT, FAR *LPDROPFILESTRUCT;

HDROP DragCreateFiles (LPPOINT lpptMousePos,
    BOOL fInNonClientArea) {

    HGLOBAL hDrop;
    LPDROPFILESTRUCT lpDropFileStruct;

    // GMEM_SHARE must be specified because the block will
    // be passed to another application.
    hDrop = GlobalAlloc(GMEM_SHARE | GMEM_MOVEABLE |
        GMEM_ZEROINIT, sizeof(DROPFILESTRUCT) + 1);

    // If unsuccessful, return NULL.
    if (hDrop == NULL) return(hDrop);

    // Lock block and initialize the data members.
    lpDropFileStruct = (LPDROPFILESTRUCT) GlobalLock(hDrop);
    lpDropFileStruct->wSize = sizeof(DROPFILESTRUCT);
    lpDropFileStruct->ptMousePos = *lpptMousePos;
    lpDropFileStruct->fInNonClientArea = fInNonClientArea;
    GlobalUnlock(hDrop);
    return(hDrop);
}

HDROP DragAppendFile (HGLOBAL hDrop, LPCSTR szPathname) {
    LPDROPFILESTRUCT lpDropFileStruct;
    LPCSTR lpCrnt;
    WORD wSize;

    lpDropFileStruct = (LPDROPFILESTRUCT) GlobalLock(hDrop);

    // Point to first pathname in list.
    lpCrnt = (LPSTR) lpDropFileStruct + lpDropFileStruct->wSize;

    // Search for a pathname where first byte is a zero byte.
```

```
   while (*lpCrnt) {   // While the first character of path is nonzero,
      while (*lpCrnt) lpCrnt++;    // skip to zero byte.
      lpCrnt++;
   }

   // Calculate current size of block.
   wSize = (WORD) (lpCrnt - (LPSTR) lpDropFileStruct + 1);
   GlobalUnlock(hDrop);

   // Increase block size to accommodate
   // the new pathname being appended.
   hDrop = GlobalReAlloc(hDrop, wSize + lstrlen(szPathname) + 1,
      GMEM_MOVEABLE | GMEM_ZEROINIT | GMEM_SHARE);

   // Return NULL if insufficient memory.
   if (hDrop == NULL) return(hDrop);

   lpDropFileStruct = (LPDROPFILESTRUCT) GlobalLock(hDrop);
   // Append the pathname to the block.
   lstrcpy((LPSTR) lpDropFileStruct + wSize - 1, szPathname);
   GlobalUnlock(hDrop);
   return(hDrop); // Return the new handle to the block.
}
```

Listing 9-6. DROPFILE.DEF

```
; Module name: DROPFILE.DEF
; Programmer : Jeffrey M. Richter.

NAME             DROPFILE
DESCRIPTION      'Dropfile Server Sample Application'
STUB             'WinStub.exe'
EXETYPE          WINDOWS
DATA             MOVEABLE MULTIPLE PRELOAD
CODE             MOVEABLE DISCARDABLE PRELOAD
HEAPSIZE         2048
STACKSIZE        10240
```

Listing 9-7. DROPFILE.H

```
//*****************************************************************
Module name: DROPFILE.H
Programmer : Jeffrey M. Richter.
Description: Dropfile Server Sample Application Header File.
*****************************************************************/


#define IDM_FILESELECT   100
```

Listing 9-8. DROPFILE.RC

```
/*****************************************************************
Module name: DROPFILE.RC
Programmer : Jeffrey M. Richter.
*****************************************************************/

#include "Dropfile.h"

DropFile ICON Dropfile.ico

DRPFIL_NOTALLOWED CURSOR "df-notok.cur"
DRPFIL_SINGLE     CURSOR "df-singl.cur"
DRPFIL_MULTIPLE   CURSOR "df-multi.cur"

DROPFILE MENU
BEGIN
   MENUITEM   "&Select files!",   IDM_FILESELECT
END
```

Listing 9-9. MAKEFILE

```
#*****************************************************************
#Module name: MAKEFILE
#Programmer : Jeffrey M. Richter.
#*****************************************************************

!include "..\builtins.jmr"

PROG = Dropfile

MODEL = s
```

```
CFLAGS = -P-c -c -f- -WS -p -v -w -m$(MODEL) -I$(INCLUDEDIR)
LFLAGS = /P/v/n/m/s/L$(LIBDIR)
LIBS = CW$(MODEL) Import

MODULES = $(PROG).obj

ICONS   = $(PROG).ico
BITMAPS =
CURSORS =

$(PROG).Exe: $(MODULES) $(PROG).Def $(PROG).Res
     tlink $(LFLAGS) @&&!
COW$(MODEL) $(MODULES)
$(PROG), $(PROG), $(LIBS), $(PROG)
!
   rc -31 -T $(PROG).Res
   TDStrip -s $(PROG)

$(PROG).res: $(PROG).rc $(RESOURCES)
```

Other Uses for Drag-and-Drop

The drag-and-drop metaphor can be extended to allow users to work more efficiently with the applications you develop. For example, look at how Word for Windows Version 2.0 has changed the way people use word processors by allowing users
to select a region of text so that it can be dragged and dropped into a new location in
users' documents. Similarly, Excel Version 4.0 allows users to select a range of cells
in spreadsheets so that they can be moved or copied to other locations. Adding this
type of capability is fairly easy given the data structure and functions discussed above.
In addition, all of the dragging and dropping takes place inside one application; you
do not need to rely on a standard protocol to which other applications must adhere.
Because of this, the code could be implemented so as not to break in future versions
of Windows. A rough outline of actions to take include:

1. Create your own user-defined message, something like *WM_DROPTEXT*,
   instead of *WM_DROPFILES*.

2. Create your own *DragInitBlock* function that has the same parameters as my
   DragInitBlock function with any additional information. For example, to move

text, you might include a starting address in the file for the text that is to be moved and the number of characters. For a spreadsheet, you might specify a range of cells.

3. Process the *WM_LBUTTONDOWN* message in any way that is particular to your situation. For example, you could change the cursor to your own desired shape as the user passes over different regions of your application's window.

4. Once you receive your own user-defined message indicating the data has been dropped, perform whatever actions you desire and free the memory block.

Where do we go from Here?

The drag-and-drop technology implemented in Windows 3.1 is both simple and incredibly useful. It's something that almost every Windows-based application should add to its feature list. Of course, the biggest obstacle hindering the acceptance of drag-and-drop is that Microsoft has not created an official specification explaining how applications can become dropfile servers. With the growing number of Windows shell replacement programs available today, each should be able to "compete" with Microsoft's File Manager by having drag-and-drop support.

Drag-and-drop technology is still in its infancy and could use some fine adjustments. For instance: The ability for a potential dropfile client window to notify the File Manager if multiple filenames can be dropped or a way to specify if files can be dropped in the application's client area, non-client area, or both. It would also be nice if there were a way for an application to specify the shape of the mouse cursor as the mouse is moved over the window. With this enhancement, the application could indicate to the user the type of action that would be performed if the filename were to be dropped in a specific location.

While there are still many things that Microsoft could add to Windows for supporting drag-and-drop technology across applications, the seeds have been planted in Windows 3.1. This is a technology that will certainly have an impact on how users work with and feel about computers.

This chapter is based upon Jeffrey Richter's "Drop Everything: How to Make Your Application Accept and Source Drag-and-Drop Files," *Microsoft Systems Journal*, May/June, 1992 (Volume 7, No. 3).

CHAPTER 10

Installing Commercial Applications

When your application is complete, you will need to organize the files so they can be distributed. Most applications are distributed on floppy disks and contain an installation or setup program. The setup program introduces the application, prompts the user for any information that is required before installation can begin, and copies the files from the distribution disks onto the user's drive.

With all the new applications being developed for Windows everyday, the need for a smooth and easy way for users to install the software is becoming more and more important. This chapter begins with some ideas as to how a setup program should be designed. It then discusses and explains how to use many of the new features, enhancements, and dynamic-link libraries that Microsoft has added to Windows 3.1. At the end of the chapter, the sample program, SETUP.EXE, demonstrates the concepts discussed and uses many of the Windows 3.1 DLLs. You may distribute this program with your own software.

Designing a Setup Program

The setup program usually gives the user a first impression of the software. For this reason, the program should be easy to use, should ask very few questions, and should get the user up and running as quickly as possible. Until recently, Windows applications were installed with DOS-based rather than Windows-based setup programs. I recommend that you use a Windows-based setup program because it has the same interface as all other Windows applications, making it easier for the user.

To execute the installation program, the user should only be required to insert the first distribution disk into the desired floppy drive, select "Run..." from the Program Manager's File menu, and type *A:\SETUP*. The setup program should not require command-line parameters. If the user can fine-tune the installation procedure, the setup program should prompt the user with dialog boxes once it is running.

Keep in mind that the setup program is being executed from a floppy disk. This means that disk operations execute more slowly than if they were being performed from the hard drive. The mouse cursor should be turned into an hourglass while any lengthy operations are executing. In addition, progress meters should be displayed to inform the user of the current operation's status. The SETUP.EXE program presented in this chapter uses the Meter custom child control discussed in Chapter 4. As files are copied from the floppy to the hard disk, the Meter custom child control is updated.

A setup program should always keep the user abreast of the installation process by presenting windows that report which operations are being performed. These windows should always appear in a consistent location on the monitor. The first window should welcome the user to the installation program. This window contains the name of the application being installed. It lets the user enter a destination directory where the application's files will be placed. If the application software requires several directories, they should be created as subdirectories of the destination directory. Any windows that contain questions for the user should be accompanied by a reasonable default value.

When the user has entered the desired destination directory, the setup program should immediately verify that there is enough available disk space to hold the files that need to be copied. If the desired drive does not contain sufficient disk space, the user should be notified of the new application's space requirements and how much space is available on the desired drive. At this point, the user can easily delete unneeded files using the File Manager. The File Manager could also be used to determine if there is another drive that has sufficient free space to install the application.

Once the setup program has started copying files, the user should be interrupted only to insert new distribution disks. If the software package allows the user to select portions of an application to install, the user should be able to choose those options before the setup program begins copying files. For example, if the application comes with an online tutorial or filter DLLs that allow the user to convert data from one application to another, the user should be able to decide whether the tutorial should be installed and which conversion DLLs are to be installed in the beginning of the installation process.

Sometimes the setup program needs to ask the user questions that require some knowledge of the application. You should write a help file for users to access with the Windows help engine during the installation process. The.HLP file supplied with your application can include descriptions of installation options and define terms that have specific meaning for your application.

Now that all the installation options have been specified, the setup program can begin copying files. The files on the distribution floppies should be organized so that a minimum of disk swapping is necessary. Of course, the placement of files depends on the distribution media. A user who is installing your application from low-density 3.5-inch disks will need to perform more swapping than a user installing from high-density 3.5-inch disks.

The SETUP.EXE program presented in this chapter allows you to create a SETUP.INF file that contains the layout of files on the distribution disks. This lets you support different media simply by modifying SETUP.INF.

Another way to speed installation that has many advantages is to perform data compression on the distributed files. Fewer floppies are required, making packaging less expensive to produce. Fewer floppies also means fewer disk swaps during installation. And since the compressed files are smaller than their decompressed counterparts, less data is read from the floppy for each file. The time necessary to decompress files is relatively short, speeding the installation process.

The only disadvantage to compressing files is that a user cannot go directly to a distribution disk and copy a desired file from the disk to the hard drive. If this would be desirable with your application, supply an additional program for the user or document some procedure that the user could follow. For example, the README.TXT file included with Windows states that individual files may be copied and decompressed using the supplied EXPAND.EXE utility.

Finally, the setup program can add a new program group to the Windows Program Manager. This new program group should contain a program item for each of the executable files that have been installed. The setup program can now display a window to the user stating that the installation has been completed successfully.

Many applications use initialization files for saving information between invocations. An application should not use the WIN.INI file to save information about itself, rather the application should create a private profile file for its own use. There are several good reasons for doing this. If every application used WIN.INI, the file would become extremely large. The larger this file gets, the longer it takes to retrieve information from it. Second, if a new version of Windows becomes available, installing the new version may destroy the current WIN.INI file and all the information saved in it.

The best way to create an initialization file is to have your application do it instead of the setup program. When your application is first invoked, have it check for the existence of the initialization file and if it does not exist, create it with reasonable default values. If this file should somehow be destroyed, the file can be re-created simply by having the user execute the application. If re-creating the file is necessary, all of the user's settings have been lost. A message box should be displayed notifying the user that the application must be configured again.

Microsoft's Setup Program Support

Microsoft has done a number of things in Windows 3.1 to help the developer get the software from the distribution floppies onto the user's hard disk. The biggest thing that they have done is to supply a complete installation program called the *Setup Toolkit for Windows*. This toolkit allows a company to produce scripts using the BASIC programming language, which are then interpreted by the program. This is such a comprehensive toolkit that the Windows' SDK ships with a manual dedicated to explaining how to use it. One of the drawbacks of using the toolkit is that you are required to ship many of its own files the distribution diskettes. While Microsoft's licensing agreement allows you to do this, the needed files can require somewhere in the neighborhood of 200K to 400K of floppy disk space. If your application is large or has many components that the user can pick and choose from, I highly recommend using the Setup Toolkit. If, on the other hand, your application is relatively small, it will be much easier for you to create your own setup program rather than learning the ins and outs of Microsoft's Setup Toolkit.

Another alternative is to use the setup program presented at the end of this chapter. This program may be ideal for your needs as is, or it may be modified to create *your* perfect setup program.

Gone are the days when an application consisted of one executable file and a README.TXT file on a single diskette. Today's applications are monstrous beasts that frequently consist of literally hundreds of files, including program files, tutorial files, conversion filter files, some data files, help files, utility programs and their respective files—the list goes on and on. For some applications, placing all of these files on diskettes requires somewhere in the neighborhood of 10 floppies or more. Once, I purchased a computer game that required seventeen 720K 3.5 inch floppies due to all the graphic images and sound files.

Not only does this increase the cost of packaging a product but it is also annoying for the end user to have to sit by the computer and constantly swap one disk after another into the drive. Probably the best way to solve this problem is to fit all the data on a CD-ROM. This disk can hold up to 680 megabytes of data, is easy to master, inexpensive reproduce, and less susceptible to media errors. As a bonus for the company producing the software, CD-ROMs are much more difficult for end users to duplicate, cutting down the occurrences of pirated software. Unfortunately, CD-ROM drives are still slow and expensive (although their prices have dropped dramatically). For this reason, many users don't own them. Until both of these situations are remedied, software publishers must continue to distribute their products on floppies.

However, all is not lost. Data compression has become extremely popular. By compressing the files before placing them on the distribution diskettes, a savings of maybe 50 percent or more can be realized. This cuts down on the number of floppies used to distribute a product, thereby cutting the number of disk swaps that a user must perform.

The tool that you will need to compress the files is COMPRESS.EXE. This program comes with the Windows' SDK and is not supplied with the Windows run time. Unlike most other SDK programs, COMPRESS.EXE is actually a DOS application rather than a Windows application. You invoke COMPRESS with one of the following command lines:

```
COMPRESS [-r] Source Destination
COMPRESS  r Source [Destination]
```

The -r switch instructs COMPRESS to automatically rename the source file. It does this by simply appending an underscore to the end of the file's extension. If the file extension is already three characters long, the last character is changed to an underscore. For example, compressing WINDOWS.H creates WINDOWS.H_ and compressing GDI.EXE creates GDI.EX_. The *Source* parameter indicates the source files or filespec (for example, *.exe) of the files that are to be compressed. The *Destination* parameter indicates destination name or path where the compressed files are to be placed. If you use the -r switch and specify a destination, the *Destination* must represent a path, not a file.

The complementary tool to COMPRESS.EXE is EXPAND.EXE. Like COMPRESS.EXE, EXPAND.EXE is a DOS application rather than a Windows application. You invoke EXPAND with one of the following command lines:

```
EXPAND [-r] Source Destination
EXPAND -r Source [Destination]
```

The -r switch instructs EXPAND to automatically rename the destination file back to its original name. The other two parameters are identical to those of the COMPRESS utility.

Since you want to write your setup program to be a Windows application, don't use EXPAND.EXE. Instead, use the new LZEXPAND.DLL dynamic-link library. This library contains a number of functions for decompressing and copying files. It contains no functions to compress files; use COMPRESS.EXE to compress your files. The prototypes for all of these functions can be found in the LZEXPAND.H file included with the Windows' SDK.

Basically, there are two ways to use the functions in this library. Use the first method when you want to copy or decompress a single file. The following code, for example, shows the steps necessary to copy or decompress a single file:

```
OFSTRUCT ofSrc, ofDst;
HFILE hFileSrc, hFileDst;
char szSrcFileName[128] = "A:\\SOURCE.DA_", szDstFileName[128];

// Open the source file.
hFileSrc = LZOpenFile(szSrcFileName, &ofSrc, OF_READ);

// Get the original name of the file.
```

```
GetExpandedName(szSrcFileName, szDstFileName);

// Create the destination file.
hFileDst = LZOpenFile(szDstFileName, &ofDst, OF_CREATE);

// Copy or decompress the file.
LZCopy(hFileSrc, hFileDst);

// Close the files.
LZClose(hFileSrc);
LZClose(hFileDst);
```

In the previous example, the first call to *LZOpenFile* tells the LZExpand library that you are going to open a file. This prototype for *LZOpenFile* is identical to that of *OpenFile*. In fact, the functions do almost the same thing except that the *LZOpenFile* function also allocates a block of memory as a buffer. This buffer is used by the copying and decompression algorithms so that file transfers proceed quickly.

Once you have opened the source file, the destination file must also be opened. But before doing this, determine the name that this file should have. This is done by calling the *GetExpandedName* function. The first parameter to this function is the pathname of a source file and the second parameter is the address to a buffer that receives the file's original name. *GetExpandedName* can return the original name of the file if the source file is not compressed or if the file was originally compressed by calling COMPRESS with the -r switch. In the first case, *GetExpandedName* simply returns the same name as the source file. If *GetExpandedName* is successful, it returns TRUE. Now that you have the destination file's name, you can open it by placing a second call to *LZOpenFile*.

Copying and decompressing the data is as easy as calling *LZCopy*. This function takes two parameters, the file handles of both the source and destination files. When this function is called, it first determines if the source file is compressed. If it isn't, *LZCopy* just copies the data from the source file to the destination file. If the source file is compressed, *LZCopy* decompresses the file as it copies it automatically. *LZCopy* returns the number of bytes in the destination file if it is successful or a negative value indicating the error. After the file has been copied/decompressed, the calls to *LZClose* close the files and free the buffers associated with each.

Earlier, I mentioned that there are two ways to work with the LZExpand library. Use the second method when copying several files at once. The following code fragment demonstrates this:

```
char *szSrcFileNames[] = {"FILE.DA_", "README.TX_", "XYZ.EX_"};
char szDstFileName[128];
OFSTRUCT ofSrc, ofDst;
HFILE hFileSrc, hFileDst;
int i;

// Allocate internal buffers.
LZStart();

// Open, copy, and close the files.
for (i = 0; i < (sizeof(szSrcFileNames) / sizeof(szSrcFileNames[0]));
i++) {
    hFileSrc = LZOpenFile(szSrcFileNames[i], &ofSrc, OF_READ);

    // Get the original name of the file.
    GetExpandedName(szSrcFileName[i], szDstFileName);

    hFileDst = LZOpenFile(szDstFileName, &ofDst, OF_CREATE);
    CopyLZFile(hFileSrc, hFileDst);
    LZClose(hFileSrc);
    LZClose(hFileDst);
}

// Free the internal buffers.
LZDone();
```

This code is almost identical to the code fragment discussed earlier. The difference here is that *LZStart* is called at the beginning. This function allocates all of the necessary buffers for doing multiple file copies. If the function is unable to allocate the buffers, it returns the value *LZERROR_GLOBALLOC* (defined in LZEXPAND.H). After allocating the space necessary, the previous procedure opens the source file, determines the destination file's name, creates the destination file, and calls *CopyLZFile* to copy/decompress the file. Notice that you call *CopyLZ-File* instead of *LZCopy*. The difference is that *CopyLZFile* knows to use the buffers allocated by the call to *LZStart*. After all of the copying is done, the call to *LZDone* at the end of the fragment frees the buffers.

Of course, you could use the first method for copying multiple files but this second method is much faster because the LZExpand library doesn't have to allocate and free buffers over and over again for each file.

The LZExpand library includes some additional functions that let you have more control over the copying/decompression process. Most of these functions are used internally by the functions previously discussed. Since these functions are rarely used, I will not discuss them here. More information can be found about them in the Windows' SDK documentation.

The main purpose of the EXPAND.EXE utility is to let the user decompress an individual file from your distribution diskettes. Usually, the documentation that accompanies your application gives instructions on how to do this. Remember, EXPAND.EXE is distributed with the Windows run time. This means that you do not have to distribute the program yourself because the user is certain to have it.

Version Control

The bulk of Windows has always been composed of three main dynamic-link libraries: USER.EXE, GDI.EXE, and KERNEL.EXE. These DLLs are responsible for managing Windows' user interface, graphical device interface, and memory management respectively. When going from Windows 3.0 to 3.1, Microsoft added many new features, such as a multimedia device interface, object linking and embedding (OLE), a formal dynamic data exchange interface, shell application support, and developer tool support. Instead of implementing the code that encompasses each of these additional features into USER, GDI, or KERNEL, Microsoft created separate dynamic-link libraries to handle each of these tasks. For example, the multimedia device interface is contained in the MMSYSTEM.DLL library, and the OLE interface is split among the two OLECLI.DLL and OLESVR.DLL libraries.

If you are developing an application that supports OLE, the code in your application makes calls to the functions contained in one or both of the OLE DLLs. There is one problem, however. Since these DLLs were not present in Windows 3.0, your application now requires the libraries be distributed with Windows 3.1 or later. If your potential end users have Windows 3.0, they will be forced to upgrade to Windows 3.1 before they can reap the benefits of your application. But since the OLE support is in DLLs, why not distribute both the OLECLI.DLL and OLESVR.DLL files with your application. Then when users install your application, these DLLs are also installed and users can use your application while running Windows 3.0.

Well, this is what Microsoft expects you to do. Microsoft's licensing agreement to the software developer allows the developer to ship any of the DLLs listed below with your product (royalty free):

DLL name	Description
COMMDLG.DLL	Common dialog-box library
DDEML.DLL	Dynamic-data exchange library
LZEXPAND.DLL	Lempel-Zev file expansion (decompression) library
OLECLI.DLL	Object linking and embedding client library
OLESVR.DLL	Object linking and embedding server library
PENWIN.DLL	Pen windows library
SHELL.DLL	Shell application library
STRESS.DLL	Application stress-testing library
TOOLHELP.DLL	Developer tools library
VER.DLL	Version checking library
WINMEM32.DLL	32-bit memory support library

Now, let's look at a possible scenario. An end user goes to the computer store and buys a copy of your software to run on his or her machine, which currently has Windows 3.0 installed. Since your software uses many of the new Windows 3.1

features, you distribute the COMMDLG.DLL library with it. When the user installs your product, the COMMDLG.DLL library is copied to the Windows' system directory on the user's hard disk. One month later, the user goes to the store and buys another software package from a different company. This package also distributes the COMMDLG.DLL library. When the user goes to install this new package, what should happen with the COMMDLG.DLL library?

Should the new file be installed over the original? Should the new product's setup program sense that a copy of COMMDLG.DLL already exists and not copy its own version of the file? Often, the language-dependent parts of an application are contained in DLLs. For example, there are actually 11 versions of the COMMDLG.DLL library; each one for a different language. If the new product being installed has a version that's in a different language, how can the setup program determine this and what should it do about it?

I will answer these questions in a moment but before I do, let's look at another situation. Suppose that in a month Microsoft finds a serious bug in the DDEML.DLL library. Normally, this bug would not be fixed until the next version of Windows becomes available. But now, because the dynamic-data exchange code resides in its own DLL, Microsoft can fix the bug, create a new DDEML.DLL library and release it to the public. This is great! Windows is such a large system that normally we would have to wait maybe a year or more before the next release but now, there can be updates with bug fixes or even new features released as necessary.

Of course, this presents the setup program with a new problem. Let's say that Microsoft does release a new DDEML.DLL with some new features and you want to take advantage of these new features in the next release of your application. So, you distribute the new DDEML.DLL library on your distribution diskettes. Now, let's say a user goes to the store and buys your application. When the user gets home, he or she installs it into his or her Windows 3.1 system. Windows 3.1 already has a DDEML.DLL library; should yours be installed anyway? Let's say that you do install your library. A week later, the user buys another program and installs this new one. This new one has been sitting on the store's shelf for three months and contains the DDEML.DLL library that originally shipped with Windows 3.1. This version does not have the new features in it that your application requires to run. If the new application's setup program copies the new DDEML.DLL library on top of yours, the user will no longer be able to run your application. Your company will be getting customer support calls even though it was the other company's setup program that caused the problem.

As you can see, there are a lot of questions that need answering. The solution to all of these problems lies in a new resource, *VERSIONINFO*. This resource is placed in each of your executable's or DLL's resource files (RC), just like any other icon, cursor, dialog box, or string table resource. A sample of what the resource looks like appears as follows:

```
#include <ver.h>
    .

    .

    .

VS_VERSION_INFO          VERSIONINFO
FILEVERSION              1, 0
PRODUCTVERSION           1, 0
FILEFLAGSMASK            VS_FFI_FILEFLAGSMASK
FILEFLAGS                (VS_FF_PRERELEASE | VS_FF_DEBUG)
FILEOS                   VOS_DOS_WINDOWS16
FILETYPE                 VFT_APP
FILESUBTYPE              VFT2_UNKNOWN
BEGIN
   BLOCK "VarFileInfo"
   BEGIN
      VALUE "Translation", 0x0409, 1252
   END

   BLOCK "StringFileInfo"
   BEGIN
      BLOCK "040904E4"
      BEGIN
      VALUE "CompanyName",     "My company name goes here.\0"
      VALUE "FileDescription", "Description of file goes here.\0"
      VALUE "FileVersion",     "1.00\0"
      VALUE "InternalName",    "Internal name\0"
```

```
    VALUE "LegalCopyright",  "Copyright (c) 1992 ABC.\0"
    VALUE "LegalTrademarks", "XYZ is a trademark of ABC company.\0"
    VALUE "ProductName",     "Product name goes here.\0"
    VALUE "ProductVersion",  "1.00\0"
  END
 END
END
```

You'll notice that the file VER.H is included at the top. This is very important because it contains several identifiers that are used within the *VERSIONINFO* block. The first part of the resource (from *FILEVERSION* to *FILESUBTYPE*) contains fixed-length binary information. The following table describes the meaning of these fields:

Field	Description
FILEVERSION	Specifies the file's version number. It consists of four 16-bit integers. If you specify less than four, the resource compiler pads the remaining integers with zero. For example, you could state a version as "3,10,0,61" to represent version 3.10.0.61.
PRODUCTVERSION	Specifies the product's version for which this file is distributed. It consists of four 16-bit integers just like the *FILEVERSION* field.
FILEFLAGSMASK	Specifies which bits in the *FILEFLAGS* field are valid. This value should always be *VS_FFI_FILEFLAGSMASK* (defined in VER.H to have a value of 0x0000003FL).
FILEFLAGS	A set of flags (from VER.H) that are *OR*ed together. Below is the list of possible flags: *VS_FF_DEBUG* *VS_FF_INFOINFERRED,* *VS_FF_PATCHED* *VS_FF_PRERELEASE,* *VS_FF_PRIVATEBUILD* *VS_FF_SPECIALBUILD.*
FILEOS	Specifies the operating system for which the file was designed. Below is the list of possible identifiers from VER.H: *VOS_UNKNOWN* *VOS_DOS* *VOS_NT* *VOS_WINDOWS16* *VOS_WINDOWS32* *VOS_DOS_WINDOWS16* *VOS_DOS_WINDOWS32* *VOS_NT_WINDOWS32.*

Field	Description
FILETYPE	Specifies the type of file. Below is the list of possible identifiers from VER.H: *VFT_UNKNOWN* *VFT_APP* *VFT_DLL* *VFT_DRV* *VFT_FONT* *VFT_VXD* *VFT_STATIC_LIB*
FILESUBTYPE	Specifies the sub type of the file. If the file type is not *VFT_DRV, VFT_FONT,* or *VFT_VXD,* this field should be set to *VFT2_UNKNOWN.* If the file type is *VFT_DRV,* this field must be one of the following identifiers: *VFT2_UNKNOWN* *VFT2_DRV_COMM* *VFT2_DRV_PRINTER* *VFT2_DRV_KEYBOARD* *VFT2_DRV_LANGAUGE* *VFT2_DRV_DISPLAY* *VFT2_DRV_MOUSE* *VFT2_DRV_NETWORK* *VFT2_DRV_SYSTEM* *VFT2_DRV_INSTALLABLE* *VFT2_DRV_SOUND* If the file type is *VFT_FONT,* this field must be one of the following identifiers: *VFT2_UNKNOWN* *VFT2_FONT_RASTER* *VFT2_FONT_VECTOR* *VFT2_FONT_TRUETYPE.* If the file type is *VFT_VXD,* this field must be the virtual device identifier included in the virtual-device control block.

Following the fixed-length portion of the *VERSIONINFO* resource is the variable-length portion. This section is divided into two subsections, *VarFileInfo* and *StringFileInfo*.

The *VarFileInfo* section describes the variable information part of the resource. Currently, there is only one type of variable information, *Translation*. This section describes which languages are supported by the file. Following the string "Translation," is a sequence of number pairs. In the *VERSIONINFO* resource shown previously, the first number in the pair, 0x0409, indicates the language for which a *StringFileInfo* section exists. The following table shows the list of languages that are currently recognized by Windows:

Language ID	Language
0x0401	Arabic
0x0402	Bulgarian
0x0403	Catalan
0x0404	Traditional Chinese
0x0405	Czech
0x0406	Danish
0x0407	German
0x0408	Greek
0x0409	U.S. English
0x040A	Castilian Spanish
0x040B	Finnish
0x040C	French
0x040D	Hebrew
0x040E	Hungarian
0x040F	Icelandic
0x0410	Italian
0x0411	Japanese
0x0412	Korean
0x0413	Dutch
0x0414	Norwegian-Bokmål
0x0415	Polish
0x0416	Brazilian Portuguese
0x0417	Rhaeto-Romanic
0x0418	Romanian
0x0419	Russian
0x041A	Croato-Serbian (Latin)
0x041B	Slovak
0x041C	Albanian
0x041D	Swedish
0x041E	Thai
0x041F	Turkish
0x0420	Urdu

Language ID	Language
0x0421	Bahasa
0x0804	Simplified Chinese
0x0807	Swiss German
0x0809	U.K. English
0x080A	Mexican Spanish
0x080C	Belgian French
0x0810	Swiss Italian
0x0813	Belgian Dutch
0x0814	Norwegian-Nynorsk
0x0816	Portuguese
0x081A	Serbo-Croatian (Cyrillic)
0x0C0C	Canadian French
0x100C	Swiss French

The second number in the pair, 1252, indicates the character set for which the *StringFileInfo* section exists. The following table shows the list of character sets that are currently recognized by Windows:

0	7-bit ASCII
932	Windows, Japan (Shift - JIS X-0208)
949	Windows, Korea (Shift - KSC 5601)
950	Windows, Taiwan (GB5)
1200	Unicode
1250	Windows, Latin-2 (Eastern European)
1251	Windows, Cyrillic
1252	Windows, Multilingual
1253	Windows, Greek
1254	Windows, Turkish
1255	Windows, Hebrew
1256	Windows, Arabic

If you wanted to include additional string information for other languages and/or character sets, you would just add another pair to the "Translation" field in the resource. For example, to add the Greek language and Greek character set, the line would look like this:

```
VALUE "Translation", 0x0409, 1252, 0x0408, 1253
```

Notice that the string "Translation" only appears once in the *VarFileInfo* subsection and that language and character set information is always added in pairs.

Following the *VarFileInfo* subsection is the *StringFileInfo* subsection. This section consists of zero-terminated strings that describe information about the file. The *StringFileInfo* subsection can be divided into multiple blocks, one for each language and character set specified in the *VarFileInfo* section. Referring to the *VERSION-INFO* resource shown earlier, there is only one block, identified by the string "040904E4." The first four characters of this string ("0409") come from the hexadecimal value for the language (0x0409 is U.S. English). The last four characters ("04E4") come from the hexadecimal value for the character set. In this case, the character ID 1252 decimal is 04E4 in hexadecimal, representing the Windows Multilingual character set.

Within this block is the string information for the file. To keep this section as flexible as possible, Microsoft choose to identify each of the possible fields with a string name. This is the name that appears immediately to the right of the *VALUE* keyword. Currently, there are 12 recognized fields. The following table lists them:

String name	Req'd	Description
"Comments"	N	Additional information for diagnostic purposes.
"CompanyName"	Y	Company that produced the file.
"FileDescription"	Y	File description to be presented to users.
"FileVersion"	Y	Version number for the file.
"InternalName"	Y	Internal name for file.
"LegalCopyright"	N	Copyright notices for file.
"LegalTrademarks"	N	Any trademarks that apply to the file.

String name	Req'd	Description
"OriginalFilename"	Y	Original name of file in case user renames it.
"PrivateBuild"	*	Explains what makes this build private.
"ProductName"	Y	Name of product for which file is distributed.
"ProductVersion"	Y	Version of product for which file is distributed.
"SpecialBuild"	*	Explains what makes this build special.

When creating a string block, it is not necessary to use all of the string fields that are shown above. The "Req'd" column indicates whether that string field must appear or not. Two of the entries, *PrivateBuild* and *SpecialBuild*, are required if their respective bits have been turned on in the *FILEFLAGS* field contained in the fixed-length section. The order in which any of these strings appear, as well as its case, is insignificant.

When creating the string block, it is important that you explicitly place a zero-byte at the end of each string, for example:

```
VALUE "CompanyName", "The Q Foundation.\0"
```

Notice the "\0" after the period. You must do this yourself because, unlike the C compiler that places a zero byte automatically at the end of every string, the resource compiler does not do this.

When this *VERSIONINFO* resource is compiled by the resource compiler, the resource compiler concatenates all the information into a large block of memory. When your setup program needs to check the version information for a file already installed on the user's hard disk and a file that is on your distribution floppies, all you have to do is read their respective resources into memory and compare their contents.

The VER.DLL library, supplied with Windows 3.1, includes a number of functions that read resource information from a file and places it in a memory block. There are also functions that parse the information contained in the memory block so you don't have to. The prototypes for these functions are in the VER.H file supplied with the Windows' SDK.

When an application wants to load the version information resource into memory it first calls the *GetFileVersionInfoSize* function:

```
DWORD GetFileVersionInfoSize(LPCSTR lpszFileName, DWORD FAR *lpdwHandle);
```

The first parameter is the path name of the file that is expected to contain a *VERSIONINFO* resource. The second parameter is a pointer to a double-word variable that will receive a handle to the resource information. This function returns the number of bytes required to hold the file's resource information. If the file couldn't be found or does not contain any resource information, *GetFileVersionInfoSize* returns NULL.

Once you have the size required to hold the resource information, call *GlobalAlloc* to allocate a block of memory large enough to hold the data and then call *GetFileVersionInfo*:

```
BOOL GetFileVersionInfo(LPCSTR lpszFileName, DWORD dwHandle,
    DWORD cbBuf, void FAR *lpvData);
```

This function actually loads the *VERSIONINFO* resource into the memory block that you previously allocated. The first parameter is the path name of the file from which you wish to retrieve the version information. The second parameter is the handle that was filled by the call to *GetFileVersionInfoSize*. This handle may be NULL; in which case, *GetFileVersionInfo* searches through the file to locate the version information. Using the value returned from *GetFileVersionInfoSize* makes the locating of this information much faster. The third parameter specifies the size of the buffer that is available to hold the version information. It should be at least the size returned by the previous call to *GetFileVersionInfoSize*, or *GetFileVersionInfo* will truncate the information. The last parameter is the memory address of the block that is to be filled with the version information. If the data is loaded successfully, *GetFileVersionInfo* returns a nonzero value. Otherwise, zero is returned, indicating the file did not exist or that the handle was invalid.

Once the version information is contained in our memory block, you can use the *VerQueryValue* function to retrieve the various pieces of information it contains. *VerQueryValue* has the following prototype:

```
BOOL VerQueryValue (const void FAR *lpvBlock, LPCSTR lpszSubBlock,
    VOID FAR * FAR *lplpBuffer, UINT FAR *lpcb);
```

The first parameter is the memory address to the block containing the version information. This is the same address that was passed as the last parameter to *Get-FileVersionInfo*. The second parameter, *lpszSubBlock*, is a pointer to a zero-terminated string that represents the information that you are requesting. This will be discussed in more detail later.

The third parameter is a pointer to a void pointer. When *VerQueryValue* is called, it searches through the memory block for the information that you request. If it successfully locates that information, *VerQueryValue* fills the void pointer with the address of the located information within the memory block. You can then use this address to access the data required. The last parameter, *lpcb*, is a pointer to an unsigned integer that *VerQueryValue* will fill with the length of the data value that it found. For example, if you asked *VerQueryValue* to locate the "CompanyName" information and the string stored there was "ABC," *VerQueryValue* would fill the integer that *lpcb* pointed to with the number four (three letters plus a zero byte).

VerQueryValue returns nonzero if it found the requested information. Otherwise it returns zero, indicating that the requested information did not exist or that the contents of the memory block was invalid.

Now, let's come back to the second parameter, *lpszSubBlock*. The string that's passed can have one of three forms. The first form is a string that contains nothing but a backslash ("\"). For example, if you call *VerQueryValue* like this:

```
VS_FIXEDFILEINFO FAR *lpVSFixedFileInfo;
UINT uLen;
.

.

.
VerQueryValue(lpVerInfo, "\\", &lpVSFixedFileInfo, &uLen);
```

VerQueryInfo locates the fixed-length portion of the version resource information and fills the *lpVSFixedFileInfo* pointer with the address of where that data is in the memory block. The data is in the form of a *VS_FIXEDFILEINFO* structure (defined in VER.H):

```
typedef struct tagVS_FIXEDFILEINFO {
    DWORD   dwSignature;        // e.g. 0xfeef04bd
    DWORD   dwStrucVersion;     // e.g. 0x00000042 = "0.42"
    DWORD   dwFileVersionMS;    // e.g. 0x00030075 = "3.75"
    DWORD   dwFileVersionLS;    // e.g. 0x00000031 = "0.31"
    DWORD   dwProductVersionMS; // e.g. 0x00030010 = "3.10"
    DWORD   dwProductVersionLS; // e.g. 0x00000031 = "0.31"
    DWORD   dwFileFlagsMask;    // 0x3F for Windows 3.1
    DWORD   dwFileFlags;        // e.g. VS_FF_DEBUG | VS_FF_PRERELEASE
    DWORD   dwFileOS;           // e.g. VOS_DOS_WINDOWS16
    DWORD   dwFileType;         // e.g. VFT_DRIVER
    DWORD   dwFileSubtype;      // e.g. VFT2_DRV_KEYBOARD
    DWORD   dwFileDateMS;       // e.g. 0
    DWORD   dwFileDateLS;       // e.g. 0
} VS_FIXEDFILEINFO;
```

The first two members of this structure, *dwSignature* and *dwStructVersion,* are set by the resource compiler when the resource is compiled. They are used so that the version control functions know that they are working on a data block, which contains version information, by checking the data block's *dwSigniture* member. So that the functions themselves can support future versions of this structure they also check the *dwStrucVersion* member. The last two members in this structure, *dwFileDateMS* and *dwFileDateLS,* are also set by the resource compiler. The current version of the resource compiler always sets these members to zero. All of the remaining members in the structure have a one-to-one correspondence with the fields in the *VERSIONINFO* resource.

Once *VerQueryValue* has filled in the *lpVSFixedFileInfo* variable with the address of this structure, you can reference any structure member to obtain various pieces of information about the file. If you wanted to determine if the file contained debugging information, for example, do this:

```
BOOL fHasDebugInfo = (lpVSFixedFileInfo->dwFileFlags & VS_FF_DEBUG);
```

The second form of calling *VerQueryValue* is when the *lpszSubBlock* parameter points to a string that contains "\VarFileInfo\Translation." For example, if you call *VerQueryValue* like this:

```
DWORD FAR *lpdwTranslationInfo;
UINT uLen, uLangID, uCharSetID;
    .

    .

    .
VerQueryValue(lpVerInfo, "\\VarFileInfo\\Translation",
    (VOID FAR * FAR *) &lpdwTranslationInfo, &uLen);

uLangId = LOWORD(*lpdwTranslationInfo);
uCharSetId = HIWORD(*lpdwTranslationInfo);
```

VerQueryValue will locate the Translation subsection within the *VarFileInfo* section of the version information resource and return a pointer to it in the *lpdwTranslationInfo* variable. When *VerQueryValue* returns, *lpdwTranslationInfo* will point to the list of language/character-set pairs. The low word of each pair contains the language identifier and the high word contains the character set ID. The *uLen* variable is filled with the number of bytes in the Translation section when *VerQueryValue* returns. Dividing this value by four gives you the number of translation pairs in the version resource.

If you want to display the language information to the user as a string, you can use the *VerLanguageName* function:

```
UINT VerLanguageName (UINT uLang, LPSTR lpszLang, UINT cbLang);
```

This function accepts as its first parameter a language ID as retrieved from the Translation section in a version resource. It then fills a string buffer pointed to by the *lpszLang* parameter with a zero-terminated string that identifies the language. The last parameter is the maximum length of the buffer. If a language ID value of

0x0414 is passed as the *uLang* parameter, for example, the *lpszLang* buffer will be filled with "Norwegian-Bokmål." If a language ID is passed to this function that is not recognized, *VerLanguageName* will fill the buffer with the string "Unknown language." It is important to note that this function returns the length of the string copied into the buffer. In the case of an unknown language ID, the function returns the length of the "Unknown language" string and does not indicate an error.

The last form of calling *VerQueryValue* is when the *lpszSubBlock* parameter points to a string that contains "\StringFileInfo\Lang-CharSet\StringName." This form requests that *VerQueryValue* locate a language-specific string from a block in the StringFileInfo section of the version resource. The Lang-CharSet part is a concatenation of a language and character-set identifier pair found in the translation table by a previous call to *VerQueryValue*. The Lang-CharSet part must be specified as a hexadecimal string. The last part of the string, StringName, identifies one of the predefined strings shown in an earlier table. For example, if you call *VerQueryValue* like this:

```
DWORD FAR *lpdwTranslationInfo;
UINT uLen, uLangID, uCharSetID;
char szStringFileInfo[50];
LPCSTR szCompanyName;
  .
  .
  .
VerQueryValue(lpVerInfo, "\\VarFileInfo\\Translation",
  (VOID FAR * FAR *) &lpdwTranslationInfo, &uLen);

uLangId = LOWORD(*lpdwTranslationInfo);
uCharSetId = HIWORD(*lpdwTranslationInfo);
  .
  .
  .
wsprintf(szStringFileInfo, "\\StringFileInfo\\%04x%04x\\CompanyName",
  uLangID, uCharSetID);
VerQueryValue(lpVerInfo, szStringFileInfo, (VOID FAR* FAR *)
  &szCompanyName, &uLen);
```

VerQueryInfo locates the "CompanyName" string within the language block identified by the first translation pair and return a pointer to it in the *szCompany-Name* variable.

Putting Version Control and Decompression Together

By now, you have all the information necessary to build a setup program. It should be written something like this:

1. For each file on the distribution diskettes, test if it already exists on the user's hard drive.
2. If it doesn't exist, copy the file and return to Step 1 to process the next file.
3. If a file with the same name does exist, load the resource information from both files into memory using *GetFileVersionInfoSize* and *GetFileVersionInfo*.
4. Compare all of the fields in the resource blocks using the *VerQueryValue* function and compare the time stamps of the files.
5. If any version values or the time stamps differ, present a dialog box requesting that the user decide which action to take. If the user says install the file, copy the new one to the hard disk using the LZExpand functions. Otherwise, skip this file and return to Step 1 for the next file.

Well, this is a lot of work, and I left out some important issues. For instance, if you are installing one of the Windows 3.1 redistributable files, you should determine where that file will be placed and where an existing one can be found. This is usually the user's system directory (for example, C:\WINDOWS\SYSTEM), if the user is running a personal version of Windows. Or, it could be the user's Windows' directory (such as C:\WINDOWS), if the user is running Windows on a network.

Another problem is that the file on the diskette could be compressed. If it is, you cannot call *GetFileVersionInfoSize*, *GetFileVersionInfo*, *VerQueryValue*, and so on because these functions only operate on decompressed files. You would have to decompress the files by copying them to a place on the hard disk, giving them a temporary name. Then you can call these functions to retrieve the version information. If the setup program determines that the file should not be copied, it will delete the temporary file. If the file should be copied, the original file (if it exists) will be deleted and then the temporary file can be renamed.

Because this is a good amount of work that every setup program would have to do, Microsoft added two additional functions into the VER.DLL library, *VerFindFile* and *VerInstallFile*. The first function, *VerFindFile*, is used to locate the correct path on the user's hard disk for installing the file. The second function, *VerInstallFile*, actually performs the work of installing the file. Let's begin by discussing *VerFindFile:*

```
UINT VerFindFile (UINT flags, LPCSTR lpszFilename, LPCSTR lpszWinDir,
LPCSTR lpszAppDir, LPSTR lpszCurDir, UINT FAR *lpuCurDirLen,
LPSTR lpszDestDir, UINT FAR * lpuDestDirLen);
```

This function searches the user's hard disk for an existing file with the same name as the file you are attempting to install. Let's hold off on the discussion of the *flags* parameter until we have discussed the other parameters.

VerFindFile searches for a file whose name is identified by the *lpszFilename* parameter. The *lpszWinDir* parameter identifies the Windows directory. Microsoft includes static-link versions of the VER library in the files VER*x*.LIB, where *x* indicates the desired memory model. These files are for use by DOS-based setup programs that I do not recommend you create. Because Windows may not be running when a DOS-based setup program executes, the VER*x*.LIB functions cannot determine where the Windows directory is. For this reason, the directory must be passed as the *lpszWinDir* parameter when *VerFindFile* is called. This parameter is ignored by the dynamic-link version of the VER.DLL library and should always be passed as NULL.

The *lpszAppDir* parameter indicates the directory on the user's hard disk where the product is being installed. Given this information, *VerFindFile* scans the user's hard disk in search of an already existing file. If *VerFindFile* locates an existing file, it copies the full path (not including the filename) into the buffer pointed to by the *lpszCurDir* parameter. Before calling *VerFindFile*, the *lpuCurDirLen* parameter must point to an unsigned integer variable that contains the maximum length of the buffer pointed to by *lpszCurDir*. When *VerFindFile* returns, this variable will contain the length of the string that was copied into this buffer.

While scanning the user's hard disk, *VerFindFile* determines the most suitable directory for the file to be placed. *VerFindFile* fills the buffer pointed to by the *lpszDestDir* parameter with this path. Like the *lpuCurDirLen* parameter, the *lpuD-estDirLen* parameter must point to an unsigned integer that contains the maximum length of the buffer pointed to by the *lpszDestDir* parameter. The *lpszDest-Dir* parameter is also filled with the length of the path copied to this buffer when *VerFindFile* returns. Most of the time, this path in the *lpszDestDir* buffer will be the same as the one identified by the *lpszAppDir* parameter. However, it may be different, depending on the *flags* parameter.

When calling *VerFindFile*, the *flags* parameter can be either zero or *VFFF_ISSHAREDFILE* (defined in VER.H). This flag tells *VerFindFile* if the file you are attempting to install is a file that is likely to be shared by different products. All of the Windows 3.1 redistributable files should be considered shared files because it is likely that several applications will need them. If your company produces several products that make use of a single DLL, this file also should be considered sharable. When *VerFindFile* sees the *VFFF_ISSHAREDFILE* flag specified, it will look in the Windows and system directories for the file. If the flag is not specified, *VerFindFile* only looks in the destination directory (specified by the *lpszAppDir* parameter).

The value that *VerFindFile* returns is an unsigned integer where each bit identifies the status of the file. This value can be *AND*ed with the following values:

Identifier in VER.H	Description
VFF_BUFFTOOSMALL	At least one of the buffers identified by the *lpszCurDir* or *lpszDestDir* parameters was too small to hold the copied path.
VFF_CURNEDEST	Indicates that a file with the same name already exists and is not in the recommended destination directory identified by the *lpszAppDir* parameter.
VFF_FILEINUSE	Indicates that a file with the same name already exists and is currently being used by an application.

The current version of VER.DLL has a bug in it. This bug causes the *VFF_CURNEDEST* bit to be turned on even when the file is in the recommended destination directory. In order to really know if the *VFF_CURNEDEST* flag is accurately set, you must test the contents of the *lpszCurDir* buffer. If this buffer is empty (the first byte is zero), then the flag is set incorrectly. The following code shows the proper way to test if a file is in the recommended destination directory:

```
char lpszCurDir[_MAX_PATH];
.

.

.

uVFFResult = VerFindFile(..., lpszCurDir,...);
if ((uVFFResult & VFF_CURNEDEST) && (lpszCurDir[0] != 0)) {
    // The file is really not in the recommended directory.
} else {
    // The file is in the recommended directory.
}
```

Figure 10-1. Attempting to install a file when a file with the same name currently exists in another directory

If the setup program determines that the current directory is not the same as the destination directory, the setup program should notify the user by presenting a dialog box (Figure 10-1) allowing the user to decide which action should take place. The following table shows what actions will be presented to the user and how the setup program will respond:

605

User action	Setup's response
Install the new file and destroy the preexisting file.	Call *VerInstallFile* (see the discussion of *VerInstallFile* later in this chapter for more information).
Install the new file and keep the preexisting file (assumes that files are in different directories).	Call *VerInstallFile* and pass *VIFF_DONTDELETEOLD* in the flags parameter.
Replace the existing file with the new file.	Copy the contents of the *lpszCurDir* buffer into the *lpszDestDir* buffer before calling *VerInstallFile*.

The *VFF_FILEINUSE* flag indicates that an existing file has been found and that it is currently being used. If this is the case, it will be impossible for the setup program to delete this file or to replace it with the file on the distribution diskettes. Normally, the setup program will notify the user of this situation (Figure 10-2), allow the user to terminate any applications that may be using the file and attempt to call *VerFindFile* again. In some cases, the user will be unable to free the file. For example, the Windows 3.1 Program Manager uses the SHELL.DLL library and the only way to install a new version of SHELL.DLL would be to terminate the Program Manager, which would terminate Windows as well.

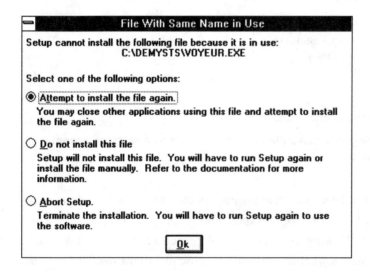

Figure 10-2. Setup program notifying user that a file cannot be deleted or replaced

In this case, the user may have to manually install the file. Directions for file installation, usually found in the product's documentation, should explain how to use the EXPAND.EXE utility to decompress the file from the floppy onto the hard disk.

Microsoft handles this with its Setup Toolkit for Windows; the toolkit copies the new SHELL.DLL library to a temporary directory. Microsoft's Setup Toolkit also creates a DOS batch file containing commands to copy the file to the Windows directory. When the setup program completes, it notifies the user that the installation is not quite finished and that the user will have to restart Windows to complete the installation. When the user selects restart, the Setup Toolkit calls the *ExitWindowsExec* function to run this batch file. This causes the necessary files to be moved to the Windows system directory. After this is done, the batch file is destroyed and Windows is restarted—this time using the new SHELL.DLL library.

After the *VerFindFile* has returned, you're ready to actually install the file on the user's hard disk. This is done by calling *VerInstallFile*:

```
DWORD VerInstallFile(UINT flags, LPCSTR lpszSrcFilename,
    LPCSTR lpszDestFilename, LPCSTR lpszSrcDir, LPCSTR lpszDestDir,
    LPCSTR lpszCurDir, LPSTR lpszTmpFile, UINT FAR *lpwTmpFileLen);
```

This function does a lot of work. First, it copies the file from the installation diskette to the hard disk, decompressing it if necessary by using the functions in the LZExpand library. The path and filename of the file on the installation diskette are identified by the *lpszSrcDir* and *lpszSrcFilename* parameters respectively. The file is then copied/decompressed to the directory identified by the *lpszDestDir* parameter. However, when the file is copied, it is given a temporary name rather than the name identified by the *lpszDstFilename* parameter. The reason for this is that this function also does version information comparisons. If it copied the file over with the same name, it destroys the original and would not be able to check its version resource.

After the new file has been copied, *VerInstallFile* compares the version information of the newly installed file with the currently existing file. Since it is possible that the existing file is in a directory other than where the new file has just been copied, you have to tell *VerInstallFile* just where the existing file is. This is the responsibility of the *lpszCurDir* parameter.

If the *VerInstallFile* determines that a file with the same name doesn't exist, it simply renames the temporary file to the filename specified by the *lpszDestFile-name* parameter and returns—the installation was successful. If the new file and the preexisting files were in different directories, *VerInstallFile* deletes the preexisting file by default. This behavior can be overridden by passing *VIFF_DONT-DELETEOLD* in the *flags* parameter.

If, on the other hand, *VerInstallFile* determines that the files differ, *VerInstall-File* returns and notifies the setup program what the status of the installation is. The value that *VerInstallFile* returns is an unsigned long where each bit identifies the status of the file. This value can be *AND*ed with the following values:

Identifier in VER.H	Description
VIF_TEMPFILE	Indicates that *VerInstallFile* created the temporary file but did not destroy the file before returning. The setup program must destroy this file itself.
VIF_MISMATCH	Indicates that the new and preexisting files differ in one or more attributes.
VIF_SRCOLD	Indicates that the file to install is older than the preexisting file.
VIF_DIFFLANG	Indicates that the new and preexisting files have different languages.
VIF_DIFFCODEPG	Indicates that the new file requires a code page that cannot be displayed by the currently running version of Windows.
VIF_DIFFTYPE	Indicates that the new file has a different type, subtype, or operating system than the preexisting file.
VIF_WRITEPROT	Indicates that the preexisting file is write-protected. The setup program can turn off this read-only bit for this file before continuing with the installation.
VIF_FILEINUSE	Indicates that the preexisting file is currently in use and cannot be deleted.
VIF_OUTOFSPACE	Indicates that *VerInstallFile* cannot create the temporary file due to insufficient disk space on the destination drive.

Identifier in VER.H	Description
VIF_ACCESSVIOLATION	Indicates that a create, delete, or rename operation failed due to an access violation.
VIF_SHARINGVIOLATION	Indicates that a create, delete, or rename operation failed due to a sharing violation.
VIF_CANNOTCREATE	Indicates that the function cannot create the temporary file. Another flag may be set, giving more detailed information.
VIF_CANNOTDELETE	Indicates that the function cannot delete the destination file or the existing version of the file. Another flag may be set, giving more detailed information.
VIF_CANNOTRENAME	Indicates that the function cannot rename the temporary file but already deleted the destination file.
VIF_OUTOFMEMORY	Indicates that the function cannot complete the requested operation due to insufficient memory.
VIF_CANNOTREADSRC	Indicates that the function cannot read the source file.
VIF_CANNOTREADDST	Indicates that the function cannot read the destination (existing) file.
VIF_BUFFTOOSMALL	The buffer identified by the *lpszTmpFile* parameter was too small to hold the name of the temporary file.

Many of the flags above indicate that a fatal error has occurred and that the file cannot be installed. If any of these flags are set, it probably means that the remainder of the installation will fail as well. The fatal flags are: *VIF_CANNOTCREATE*, *VIF_CANNOTDELETE*, *VIF_CANNOTRENAME*, *VIF_OUTOFSPACE*, *VIF_ACCESSVIOLATION*, *VIF_SHARINGVIOLATION*, *VIF_OUTOFMEMORY*, and *VIF_CANNOTREADDST*.

Two flags, *VIF_FILEINUSE* and *VIF_WRITEPROT,* can be handled in a special manner. If the *VIF_FILEINUSE* flag is set, you can prompt the user to terminate other applications that might be using the file and attempt the call to *VerInstallFile* again. For the *VIF_WRITEPROT* flag, you can alter the read-only bit of the destination file, call *VerInstallFile* again to have the installation of the new file continue, and turn the read-only bit on for the new file. The other alternative is to just notify the user that an error occurred and allow the user to manually install the files later.

The *VIF_CANNOTREADSRC* flag indicates that the source file could not be found. This is usually an indication that the user must swap disks. When a setup program sees this flag, it displays a dialog box notifying the user which diskette must be inserted so that the next file can be copied. After the user swaps diskettes and presses the "OK" button, the setup program calls *VerInstallFile* again.

Most of the remaining flags indicate that the new and preexisting files differ in one way or another. These flags are: *VIF_MISMATCH*, *VIF_SRCOLD*, *VIF_DIF-FLANG*, *VIF_DIFFCODEPG*, and *VIF_DIFFTYPE*. When the setup program determines that one of these flags is set, it notifies the user by displaying a dialog box (Figure 10-3) containing all the version information for the new file as well as the preexisting file. It does this, of course, by using the *GetFileVersion-InfoSize*, *GetFileVersionInfo*, *VerQueryValue*, and *VerLanguageName* functions discussed earlier in this chapter. The full pathname of the new file can be obtained by using the buffers pointed to by the *lpszDestDir* and *lpszTmpFile* parameters. The existing file's full pathname can be acquired by using the buffers pointed to by the *lpszCurDir* and *lpszDestFilename* parameters.

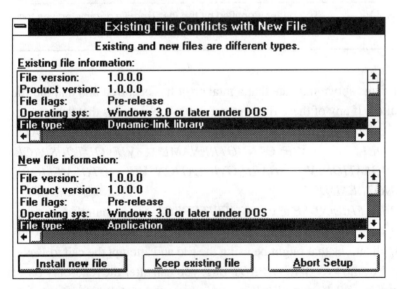

Figure 10-3. Setup program notifies user that the existing and new files have conflicting version information

The user can then decide in the dialog box whether to keep the preexisting file or to install the new file, destroying the preexisting one. If the user chooses to keep the preexisting file, the setup program should construct a buffer containing the full path of the temporary file by using the *lpszDestDir* and *lpszTmpFile* parameters. It should then call the *OpenFile* function and pass it the *OF_DELETE* flag so that the temporary file is deleted.

If the user decided to force the installation of the new file, the setup program should call *VerInstallFile* a second time. However, this time, *VIFF_FORCEINSTALL* should be ORed into the flags parameter to the function. This instructs *VerInstallFile* to copy the file even though it mismatches the information in the preexisting file.

Special Considerations for Setup Programs

There is one big problem when designing a setup program that keeps returning to haunt you again and again. This problem is that the setup program is executed from a diskette which may be switched during the installation. This means that Windows won't be able to load a program segment or resource from the executable file after the setup process has started. To ensure that the code is always available, make sure that the *PRELOAD* and *NONDISCARDABLE* flags are specified in the setup programs' definitions (.DEF) file. If the setup application uses any DLLs, the code segments in them must include the *PRELOAD*, *NONDISCARDABLE*, and *FIXED* flags. The *FIXED* flag is necessary because Windows will not make a DLL's code segment nondiscardable without it.

All the resources (icons, dialog boxes, string tables, and so on) must be marked as *PRELOAD* and *FIXED*. Windows treats all resources as discardable unless they have the *FIXED* flag specified. In addition, any resources in the setup program must be referenced by number. Many applications use the following method to declare an icon in the application's resource file:

```
Setup            ICON SETUP.ICO
```

Then the application references the icon with the following syntax:

```
LoadIcon(hInstance, "Setup");
```

When you declare resources this way, Windows creates a *NameTable* in memory. The *NameTable* is a list of all the resource's string names. When the application references a resource by name, Windows must scan the *NameTable* for the desired string and determine where the resource is in the executable file. The problem is that Windows always creates an application's *NameTable* in a discardable block of memory and reloads the table from the executable file when it is needed. This is unsatisfactory for a setup program. You must access resources differently. Here's how you can declare and access an icon.

First, in a header file that is included by both the application and the resource file, define an identifier that represents the icon:

```
#define ICON_SETUP        1
```

Declare the icon in the application's resource file:

```
ICON_SETUP          ICON            SETUP.ICO
```

The application then references the icon using the following syntax:

```
LoadIcon(hInstance, MAKEINTRESOURCE(ICON_SETUP));
```

This method of accessing resources is better because it requires less disk and memory space. It's also faster than the first approach.

When SETUP.EXE is first executed, a dialog-box template (*DLG_INSERT-DISK*) is loaded into memory. This dialog box is the one that asks the user to insert the next diskette to continue the installation. When it's time for the second disk, Windows locks the memory block containing the template and creates the *DLG_INSERTDISK* dialog box. Windows then unlocks and frees the memory block containing the dialog-box template. When it's time to prompt the user to swap disks again, Windows must reload *DLG_INSERTDISK* from the SETUP.EXE file. However, Windows no longer has access to this file because it is on the first disk. This causes SETUP.EXE to fail.

The work around: The memory block containing *DLG_INSERTDISK* must be locked before it is used to create the dialog box. The lock prevents Windows from freeing the block after the dialog box is created. Windows will always be able to find the dialog-box template in memory. This additional lock must be done for all of the dialog boxes used by the setup program.

The code for locking the memory blocks containing all of setup's dialog-box templates is in the *LockResources* function in the SETUP.CPP source module:

```
void LockResources (void) {
    HRSRC hResDlg;
    HGLOBAL hGlblRes;
    int nDlg, nIcon;

    for (nDlg = DLG_FIRST; nDlg <= DLG_LAST; nDlg++) {
        // Get the resource handle of the dialog box from the executable
        // file.
        hResDlg = FindResource(_hInstance, MAKEINTRESOURCE(nDlg), RT_DIALOG);

        // Get the memory handle of the dialog box in memory.
        // The block is already in memory because the dialog
        // box is marked as PRELOAD FIXED.
        hGlblRes = LoadResource(_hInstance, hResDlg);

        // Force the memory block to be locked down. This
        // prohibits Windows from discarding the dialog-box
        // template from memory.
        LockResource(hGlblRes);
    }

    for (nIcon = ICN_FIRST; nIcon <= ICN_LAST; nIcon++) {
        LoadIcon(_hInstance, MAKEINTRESOURCE(nIcon));
    }
}
```

FindResource searches through the module associated with the *_hInstance* parameter. The second parameter is the name of the resource. If the resource is identified by a numeric value, the *MAKEINTRESOURCE* macro (defined in WINDOWS.H) should be used as above. If the resource is identified by name, the name may be used as the second parameter. The third parameter indicates the type of resource *FindResource* should attempt to locate. The table below shows the values that can be used:

Value (defined in WINDOWS.H)	Meaning
RT_ACCELERATOR	Accelerator table resource
RT_BITMAP	Bitmap resource
RT_DIALOG	Dialog-box template resource
RT_FONT	Font resource
RT_FONTDIR	Font directory resource
RT_MENU	Menu resource
RT_RCDATA	User-defined resource

Since all of the IDs from *DLG_FIRST* through *DLG_LAST* identify dialog-box templates, *RT_DIALOG* is used.

The value returned by *FindResource* is a handle that identifies the resource's location in the executable file. If the resource cannot be found, NULL is returned.

Now that you have the location of the resource in the executable file, call *LoadResource* to allocate a memory handle for the dialog-box template. Windows won't load a resource until *LockResource* is called. In the case of SETUP.EXE, the dialog-box templates are already in memory because all the templates have the *PRELOAD* and *FIXED* flags specified in SETUP.RC. *LoadResource* ascertains this and returns the handle of the existing memory block.

Finally, call *LockResource*. This forces Windows to place a lock on the memory block. As long as at least one lock is outstanding, Windows will not free the memory.

When a STATIC control is used in a dialog box to display an icon, the icon is discarded when the control is destroyed. The next time that the dialog box is created, Windows will search for the icon and determine that it must be reloaded from the executable file. This is the same problem as the dialog-box template issue and is solved in a similar way. At the bottom of the previous *LockResources* function, a loop is executed that cycles through each of the icons used by the program. For each icon, the call to *LoadIcon* simply increments the lock count on the memory block containing the icon.

Resources are shared among different instances of the same application. If two instances of an application load the same icon into memory, *LoadIcon* returns the same value to both applications. The advantage is that memory is conserved when several instances of the application are running. However, this method can cause some problems for the software developer. Let's look at one possible scenario:

Application APP.EXE contains a dialog-box template marked *PRELOAD* and *FIXED*. When this application is executed, Windows creates a memory block for the dialog-box template and loads the template into memory. At this point, APP.EXE has *not* created a dialog box based on this template.

The user now executes a second instance of APP.EXE. When this second instance is loaded, Windows sees that the dialog-box template is already in memory and does not create another memory block. The two instances will share the block of memory containing the template.

Now, the second instance of APP.EXE creates a dialog box based on the template. Windows creates the dialog box, unlocks the memory block containing the template, and frees the block. When the first instance of APP.EXE needs to create the dialog box, the template will not be in memory and Windows must reload it from the APP.EXE file on disk.

This could be quite a problem. If APP.EXE requires that a particular resource (a dialog-box template, in this example) be in memory, the program will most likely fail. Guaranteeing that a particular resource resides in memory requires that the resource have at least one outstanding lock before it's used. This is accomplished by using the *FindResource*, *LoadResource*, and *LockResource* functions, as demonstrated earlier.

The Setup Application

The application discussed in this section is a complete setup program that can be used without modification to install your own applications. The program reads and analyzes a SETUP.INF file (Listing 10-1) that contains information describing how the files are laid out on the distribution floppy disks. To prepare an application for distribution, simply change this file to reflect information about your program. SETUP.EXE also shows how to use the Meter custom child control presented in Chapter 4.

The SETUP.INF File

SETUP.INF describes how files are arranged on the distribution disks. This file, located on this book's companion disk, describes the directories and files necessary to compile and link all the sample applications presented throughout the book.

Listing 10-1. SETUP.INF setup information file

```
;SETUP.INF for Windows 3.1: A Developer's Guide.
;Copyright (c) 1992 by Jeffrey M. Richter - All rights reserved.

[App]
;Application global information
AppName=Windows 3.1: A Developer's Guide
DefDir=C:\DevGuide
SpaceNeeded=1024
DefPMGroup=DevGuide.GRP, A Developer's Guide
ShowSubDirCreateStats=Y

[Disks]
;List of diskettes needed to install the product and the name
;of each diskette.
1=Disk1: Chapters 1 through 10

[SrcDirs]
;Lists of directories from root of source drive/directory where
;source files can be found.
 1=Misc
 2=Voyeur.01
 3=PMRest.02
 4=NoAlpha.02
 5=DlgTech.03
 6=Meter.04
```

```
 7=Spin.04
 8=CustCntl.04
 9=PrntDemo.05
10=ScrnBlnk.07
11=Echo.07
12=MDI.08
13=BurnIt.09
14=DropFile.09
15=Setup.10


[DstDirs]
;Lists of directories from root of destination drive/directory
;where destination files will be placed.
 1=.
 2=Voyeur.01
 3=PMRest.02
 4=NoAlpha.02
 5=DlgTech.03
 6=Meter.04
 7=Spin.04
 8=CustCntl.04
 9=PrntDemo.05
10=ScrnBlnk.07
11=Echo.07
12=MDI.08
13=BurnIt.09
14=DropFile.09
15=Setup.10
```

```
[Files]
;Description,                    Src(Dsk-Dir:Name),   Dst(Dir:Name),   Shared
;———————————————                 ——————————————————   ————————————     ——————
Builtins.JMR,                    1-1:Builtins.JMR,    1:Builtins.JMR,    N

Voyeur.01: Voyeur.Exe,           1-2:voyeur.exe,      2:voyeur.exe,      N
Voyeur.01: Voyeur.C,             1-2:voyeur.c,        2:voyeur.c,        N
Voyeur.01: Voyeur.H,             1-2:voyeur.h,        2:voyeur.h,        N
Voyeur.01: Voyeur.Rc,            1-2:voyeur.rc,       2:voyeur.rc,       N
Voyeur.01: Voyeur.Def,           1-2:voyeur.def,      2:voyeur.def,      N
Voyeur.01: Voyeur.Ico,           1-2:voyeur.ico,      2:voyeur.ico,      N
Voyeur.01: Eyes.Cur,             1-2:eyes.cur,        2:eyes.cur,        N
Voyeur.01: Makefile,             1-2:makefile,        2:makefile,        N

PMRest.02: PMRest.Exe,           1-3:pmrest.exe,      3:pmrest.exe,      N
PMRest.02: PMRest.C,             1-3:pmrest.c,        3:pmrest.c,        N
PMRest.02: PMRest.Rc,            1-3:pmrest.rc,       3:pmrest.rc,       N
PMRest.02: PMRest.Def,           1-3:pmrest.def,      3:pmrest.def,      N
PMRest.02: PMRest.Ico,           1-3:pmrest.ico,      3:pmrest.ico,      N
```

617

```
PMRest.02: Makefile,          1-3:makefile,        3:makefile,         N

NoAlpha.03: NoAlpha.Exe,      1-4:noalpha.exe,     4:noalpha.exe,      N
NoAlpha.03: NoAlpha.C,        1-4:noalpha.c,       4:noalpha.c,        N
NoAlpha.03: NoAlpha.H,        1-4:noalpha.h,       4:noalpha.h,        N
NoAlpha.03: SuperCls.C,       1-4:supercls.c,      4:supercls.c,       N
NoAlpha.03: SuperCls.H,       1-4:supercls.h,      4:supercls.h,       N
NoAlpha.03: NoAlpha.Rc,       1-4:noalpha.rc,      4:noalpha.rc,       N
NoAlpha.03: NoAlpha.Def,      1-4:noalpha.def,     4:noalpha.def,      N
NoAlpha.03: NoAlpha.Ico,      1-4:noalpha.ico,     4:noalpha.ico,      N
NoAlpha.03: Makefile,         1-4:makefile,        4:makefile,         N

DlgTech.03: DlgTech.Exe,      1-5:dlgtech.exe,     5:dlgtech.exe,      N
DlgTech.03: DlgTech.C,        1-5:dlgtech.c,       5:dlgtech.c,        N
DlgTech.03: DlgTech.H,        1-5:dlgtech.h,       5:dlgtech.h,        N
DlgTech.03: DlgTech.Rc,       1-5:dlgtech.rc,      5:dlgtech.rc,       N
DlgTech.03: DlgTech.Def,      1-5:dlgtech.def,     5:dlgtech.def,      N
DlgTech.03: DlgTech.Ico,      1-5:dlgtech.ico,     5:dlgtech.ico,      N
DlgTech.03: Makefile,         1-5:makefile,        5:makefile,         N
DlgTech.03: Dlg-Opts.C,       1-5:dlg-opts.c,      5:dlg-opts.c,       N
DlgTech.03: Dlg-Opts.H,       1-5:dlg-opts.h,      5:dlg-opts.h,       N
DlgTech.03: Dlg-Mdls.C,       1-5:dlg-mdls.c,      5:dlg-mdls.c,       N
DlgTech.03: Dlg-Mdls.H,       1-5:dlg-mdls.h,      5:dlg-mdls.h,       N
DlgTech.03: Dlg-Dyna.C,       1-5:dlg-dyna.c,      5:dlg-dyna.c,       N
DlgTech.03: Dlg-Dyna.H,       1-5:dlg-dyna.h,      5:dlg-dyna.h,       N
DlgTech.03: Dlg-Mode.C,       1-5:dlg-mode.c,      5:dlg-mode.c,       N
DlgTech.03: Dlg-Mode.H,       1-5:dlg-mode.h,      5:dlg-mode.h,       N

Meter.04: Meter.C,            1-6:meter.c,         6:meter.c,          N
Meter.04: Meter.H,            1-6:meter.h,         6:meter.h,          N
Meter.04: MeterDlg.C,         1-6:meterdlg.c,      6:meterdlg.c,       N
Meter.04: Meter.Rc,           1-6:meter.rc,        6:meter.rc,         N
Meter.04: Meter.Def,          1-6:meter.def,       6:meter.def,        N
Meter.04: Cntl-DE.C,          1-6:cntl-de.c,       6:cntl-de.c,        N
Meter.04: Cntl-DE.H,          1-6:cntl-de.h,       6:cntl-de.h,        N
Meter.04: Makefile,           1-6:makefile,        6:makefile,         N

Spin.04: Spin.C,              1-7:spin.c,          7:spin.c,           N
Spin.04: Spin.H,              1-7:spin.h,          7:spin.h,           N
Spin.04: SpinDlg.C,           1-7:spindlg.c,       7:spindlg.c,        N
Spin.04: Spin.Rc,             1-7:spin.rc,         7:spin.rc,          N
Spin.04: Spin.Def,            1-7:spin.def,        7:spin.def,         N
Spin.04: Cntl-DE.C,           1-7:cntl-de.c,       7:cntl-de.c,        N
Spin.04: Cntl-DE.H,           1-7:cntl-de.h,       7:cntl-de.h,        N
Spin.04: Makefile,            1-7:makefile,        7:makefile,         N

CustCntl.04: CustCntl.Exe,    1-8:custcntl.exe,    8:custcntl.exe,     N
CustCntl.04: CustCntl.C,      1-8:custcntl.c,      8:custcntl.c,       N
```

```
CustCntl.04: CustCntl.H,       1-8:custcntl.h,       8:custcntl.h,       N
CustCntl.04: CustCntl.Def,     1-8:custcntl.def,     8:custcntl.def,     N
CustCntl.04: CustCntl.Rc,      1-8:custcntl.rc,      8:custcntl.rc,      N
CustCntl.04: CustCntl.Ico,     1-8:custcntl.ico,     8:custcntl.ico,     N
CustCntl.04: Makefile,         1-8:makefile,         8:makefile,         N
CustCntl.04: Meter.Dll,        1-8:meter.dll,        8:meter.dll,        N
CustCntl.04: Spin.Dll,         1-8:spin.dll,         8:spin.dll,         N

PrntDemo.05: PrntDemo.Exe,     1-9:prntdemo.exe,     9:prntdemo.exe,     N
PrntDemo.05: PrntDemo.C,       1-9:prntdemo.c,       9:prntdemo.c,       N
PrntDemo.05: PrntDemo.H,       1-9:prntdemo.h,       9:prntdemo.h,       N
PrntDemo.05: PrntDemo.Def,     1-9:prntdemo.def,     9:prntdemo.def,     N
PrntDemo.05: PrntDemo.Rc,      1-9:prntdemo.rc,      9:prntdemo.rc,      N
PrntDemo.05: PrntDemo.Ico,     1-9:prntdemo.ico,     9:prntdemo.ico,     N
PrntDemo.05: Makefile,         1-9:makefile,         9:makefile,         N

ScrnBlnk.07: ScrnBlnk.Exe,     1-10:scrnblnk.exe,    10:scrnblnk.exe,    N
ScrnBlnk.07: ScrnBlnk.C,       1-10:scrnblnk.c,      10:scrnblnk.c,      N
ScrnBlnk.07: ScrnBlnk.H,       1-10:scrnblnk.h,      10:scrnblnk.h,      N
ScrnBlnk.07: ScrnBlnk.Def,     1-10:scrnblnk.def,    10:scrnblnk.def,    N
ScrnBlnk.07: ScrnBlnk.Rc,      1-10:scrnblnk.rc,     10:scrnblnk.rc,     N
ScrnBlnk.07: ScrnBlnk.Ico,     1-10:scrnblnk.ico,    10:scrnblnk.ico,    N
ScrnBlnk.07: Makefile,         1-10:makefile,        10:makefile,        N
ScrnBlnk.07: SBDll.Dll,        1-10:sbdll.dll,       10:sbdll.dll,       N
ScrnBlnk.07: SBDll.C,          1-10:sbdll.c,         10:sbdll.c,         N
ScrnBlnk.07: SBDll.Def,        1-10:sbdll.def,       10:sbdll.def,       N
ScrnBlnk.07: SBDll.Lib,        1-10:sbdll.lib,       10:sbdll.lib,       N
ScrnBlnk.07: SBDll.Rc,         1-10:sbdll.rc,        10:sbdll.rc,        N
ScrnBlnk.07: SBDll.Mkf,        1-10:sbdll.mkf,       10:sbdll.mkf,       N

Echo.07: Echo.C,               1-11:echo.c,          11:echo.c,          N
Echo.07: Echo.Def,             1-11:echo.def,        11:echo.def,        N
Echo.07: Echo.Exe,             1-11:echo.exe,        11:echo.exe,        N
Echo.07: Echo.H,               1-11:echo.h,          11:echo.h,          N
Echo.07: Echo.Ico,             1-11:echo.ico,        11:echo.ico,        N
Echo.07: Echo.Rc,              1-11:echo.rc,         11:echo.rc,         N
Echo.07: Makefile,             1-11:makefile,        11:makefile,        N
Echo.07: Record.C,             1-11:record.c,        11:record.c,        N
Echo.07: Record.Def,           1-11:record.def,      11:record.def,      N
Echo.07: Record.Dll,           1-11:record.dll,      11:record.dll,      N
Echo.07: Record.H,             1-11:record.h,        11:record.h,        N
Echo.07: Record.Lib,           1-11:record.lib,      11:record.lib,      N
Echo.07: Record.Mkf,           1-11:record.mkf,      11:record.mkf,      N
Echo.07: Record.Rc,            1-11:record.rc,       11:record.rc,       N

MDI.08: MDI.Exe,               1-12:mdi.exe,         12:mdi.exe,         N
MDI.08: MDI.C,                 1-12:mdi.c,           12:mdi.c,           N
MDI.08: MDI.H,                 1-12:mdi.h,           12:mdi.h,           N
```

```
MDI.08: Ribbon.C,          1-12:ribbon.c,      12:ribbon.c,      N
MDI.08: Frame.C,           1-12:frame.c,       12:frame.c,       N
MDI.08: Child.C,           1-12:child.c,       12:child.c,       N
MDI.08: Sheet.C,           1-12:sheet.c,       12:sheet.c,       N
MDI.08: Chart.C,           1-12:chart.c,       12:chart.c,       N
MDI.08: MDI.Def,           1-12:mdi.def,       12:mdi.def,       N
MDI.08: MDI.Rc,            1-12:mdi.rc,        12:mdi.rc,        N
MDI.08: MDI.Ico,           1-12:mdi.ico,       12:mdi.ico,       N
MDI.08: Sheet.Ico,         1-12:sheet.ico,     12:sheet.ico,     N
MDI.08: Chart.Ico,         1-12:chart.ico,     12:chart.ico,     N

Burnit.09: BurnIt.Exe,     1-13:burnit.exe,    13:burnit.exe,    N
Burnit.09: BurnIt.C,       1-13:burnit.c,      13:burnit.c,      N
Burnit.09: BurnIt.Def,     1-13:burnit.def,    13:burnit.def,    N
Burnit.09: BurnIt.Rc,      1-13:burnit.rc,     13:burnit.rc,     N
Burnit.09: BurnIt1.Ico,    1-13:burnit1.ico,   13:burnit1.ico,   N
Burnit.09: BurnIt2.Ico,    1-13:burnit2.ico,   13:burnit2.ico,   N
Burnit.09: BurnIt3.Ico,    1-13:burnit3.ico,   13:burnit3.ico,   N
Burnit.09: BurnIt4.Ico,    1-13:burnit4.ico,   13:burnit4.ico,   N
Burnit.09: Makefile,       1-13:makefile,      13:makefile,      N

DropFile.09: DropFile.Exe, 1-14:dropfile.exe,  14:dropfile.exe,  N
DropFile.09: DropFile.C,   1-14:dropfile.c,    14:dropfile.c,    N
DropFile.09: DropFile.H,   1-14:dropfile.h,    14:dropfile.h,    N
DropFile.09: DropFile.Def, 1-14:dropfile.def,  14:dropfile.def,  N
DropFile.09: DropFile.Rc,  1-14:dropfile.rc,   14:dropfile.rc,   N
DropFile.09: DropFile.Ico, 1-14:dropfile.ico,  14:dropfile.ico,  N
DropFile.09: DF-NotOK.Cur, 1-14:df-notok.cur,  14:df-notok.cur,  N
DropFile.09: DF-Singl.Cur, 1-14:df-singl.cur,  14:df-singl.cur,  N
DropFile.09: DF-Multi.Cur, 1-14:df-multi.cur,  14:df-multi.cur,  N
DropFile.09: Makefile,     1-14:makefile,      14:makefile,      N

Setup.10: Disk.Ico,        1-15:disk.ico,      15:disk.ico,      N
Setup.10: Makefile,        1-15:makefile,      15:makefile,      N
Setup.10: Setup.Cpp,       1-15:setup.cpp,     15:setup.cpp,     N
Setup.10: Setup.Def,       1-15:setup.def,     15:setup.def,     N
Setup.10: Setup.Exe,       1-15:setup.exe,     15:setup.exe,     N
Setup.10: Setup.H,         1-15:setup.h,       15:setup.h,       N
Setup.10: Setup.Ico,       1-15:setup.ico,     15:setup.ico,     N
Setup.10: Setup.Inf,       1-15:setup.inf,     15:setup.inf,     N
Setup.10: Setup.Rc,        1-15:setup.rc,      15:setup.rc,      N
Setup.10: SetupDlg.Cpp,    1-15:setupdlg.cpp,  15:setupdlg.cpp,  N
Setup.10: SetupInf.Cpp,    1-15:setupinf.cpp,  15:setupinf.cpp,  N
Setup.10: SetupInf.H,      1-15:setupinf.h,    15:setupinf.h,    N
Setup.10: SetupPM.Cpp.,    1-15:setuppm.cpp,   15:setuppm.cpp,   N
```

```
[PM Info]
;DstFileName  AppDesc                 (Icon #)
;───────────  ───────────────         ────────
VOYEUR.EXE,   Voyeur
PMREST.EXE,   PM Restore
NOALPHA.EXE,  NoAlpha
DLGTECH.EXE,  Dialog Techniques
CUSTCNTL.EXE, Custom Controls
PRNTDEMO.EXE, Print Demo
SCRNBLNK.EXE, Screen Blanker
ECHO.EXE,     Echo
MDI.EXE,      MDI
BURNIT.EXE,   Burn It!
DROPFILE.EXE, Drop-file Server
SETUP.EXE,    Setup
[End]
```

Any blank lines or lines beginning with a semicolon are not parsed by the setup program. The sections appearing in the SETUP.INF file are discussed in the following paragraphs.

The *[App]* section. This section contains information that is global to the application being installed. The following table discusses each of the fields in this section.

Field	Description
AppName	Specifies the name of the program that is being installed. The name appears in the caption of every dialog box.
DefDir	Specifies the default destination directory. The user is allowed to select a different drive or directory.
SpaceNeeded	Specifies the amount of hard disk space required to contain the files that will be installed. The value is specified in kilobytes.
DefPMGroup	Specifies the name of the program group that will be created in Program Manager at the end of the installation.
ShowSubDirCreateStats	Specifies whether the setup program will display a statistics box while it is creating the directory structure on the hard drive. Since the installation of the sample application in this book requires about 15 directories be created, I turn this flag on. Most applications will only create up to three directories, if this is your situation, set this flag to N.

The *[Disks]* section. This section tells setup how many disks are in the distribution package and the name of each disk. Each line consists of a number, an equal sign, and the name of a distribution disk. The numbers are used only internally to let setup determine where to locate a particular file. The numbers are arbitrary: They needn't start at one and they needn't be contiguous.

When setup cannot find a file, a dialog box requests that the user insert the appropriate disk. The name of this disk is retrieved from the *[Disks]* section.

The *[SrcDirs]* section. This section lists all the subdirectories from the root where files may appear on the distribution diskette. Each line consists of a number, an equal sign, and the subdirectory's path. The number is for internal use only. Setup uses this information to determine which directory on the distribution disk contains the file to be copied. The path is always relative to the source path, which can be changed by the user when the "Insert diskette" dialog box appears.

The *[DstDirs]* section. This section lists all the subdirectories setup should create on the user's hard disk. Each line consists of a number, an equal sign, and the subdirectory's path. The number is for internal use only. Setup uses this information to determine which directory the installed file should be copied to. The path is always relative to the destination path chosen by the user when the setup program first starts.

If setup is about to create a subdirectory and notices that it already exists, an error does not occur; setup simply tries to create the next subdirectory in the list. It tries to create subdirectories in the order in which they appear in the *[DstDirs]* section. If you need to create subdirectories that are more than one level deep, make sure the subdirectories closer to the root are listed first. If you need to create a D:\DESTDIR\LEVEL1\LEVEL2 directory, for example, SETUP.INF must list the entries in the following order:

```
[DstDirs]
    .
    .
    .
6=LEVEL1
7=LEVEL1\LEVEL2
```

The *[Files]* section. This section notifies setup of the files that need to be installed. Each line in this section consists of four fields separated by commas:

Field	Description
File description	This text is displayed in the Progress dialog box as setup copies the file.
Source file	This field is divided into three parts. The first part is a number that identifies the disk in the *[Disks]* section where the file can be found. If setup cannot locate the file, it displays a dialog box prompting the user to insert this disk. The second part must be separated from the first by a hyphen and indicates the directory in the *[SrcDirs]* section where the file can be found. Setup attempts to look for the file in this directory relative to the installation drive's root directory. The last part, separated from the previous part by a colon, indicates the name of the file as it appears on the distribution diskette. If the file is compressed, it usually has an underscore as the last character of its extension whereas its corresponding destination filename will not have the underscore. For the sample application's, distributed with this book, I chose not to compress any of the files. This makes it much easier for you to access any of the information. You can run the programs directly off the floppy or examine the source code in an editor without decompressing the files first.
Destination file	This field is divided into two parts. The first part indicates the directory in the *[DstDirs]* section where the file should be copied. The last part, separated from the first by a colon, indicates the name of the file as it should appear on the user's hard disk.
Sharable	This field tells setup if the file is a sharable file. If it is, setup uses the *VFFF_ISSHAREDFILE* flag when calling the *VerFindFile* function. This makes the function check for the file in the Windows and system directories to determine where the file should be installed.

The *[PM Info]* section. This section tells setup which application files should be added to the newly created group in Program Manager. The group's name is specified by the *DefPMGroup* line that appears in the *[App]* section of the SETUP.INF file. Each line in the *[PM Info]* section consists of three fields separated by commas:

WINDOWS 3.1: A DEVELOPER'S GUIDE

Field	Description
File name	This is the file that will be invoked when the user chooses this icon from Program Manager. Every time setup successfully copies a file, it records the path of the file. When setup adds this program to the group, it uses the recorded path information and constructs the complete path name using the destination directory and subdirectory specified for the file. Program Manager uses this path name to access the program. Because the complete path is specified, there is no need for setup to modify the *PATH=* line in the users AUTOEXEC.BAT file.
File description	This is the text Program Manager will display under the icon for the newly installed application.
Icon number	This is an optional field. By default, Program Manager will display the first icon that appears in the executable file. If you specify a value in this field, setup will instruct Program Manager to use a different icon from the file. If the value is zero, the first icon is used; if the value is one, the second icon is used, and so on.

The *[End]* section. This must be the last section. When setup parses the line containing *[End]*, the SETUP.INF file is closed and setup's Welcome window is presented. Any text appearing after this line is ignored.

SETUPINF.CPP and SETUPINF.H contain all the code to process the SETUP.INF file. The most important C++ class that is defined is the *SETUPINFO* class. This class is responsible for reading the file, parsing the information, and retrieving the various pieces as the main program needs it. Originally, the setup program was written using standard C. But as I was redesigning this section from the first edition, it became more and more clear that this area was extremely well suited to C++ code. If the structure of the SETUP.INF file should change in the future or if you want to change it, the modifications should be fairly simple and localized to the SETUPINF.CPP and SETUPINF.H files. Aside from this section, the remainder of the code is in standard C.

Since the setup program can only operate on one SETUP.INF file at a time, a global *SETUPINFO* object is created and made external to all modules, including the SETUPINF.H file. This is done by placing the following line at the bottom of the SETUPINF.H file:

```
extern SETUPINFO _SetupInfo;
```

When any part of the program needs information contained in the _SetupInfo_ object, it simply calls one of the member functions for that object. For example, telling setup to load and parse the SETUP.INF file is as easy as calling:

```
_SetupInfo.InitSetupInfo(szSetupInfoPathName);
```

When setup needs to know how many destination directories were specified, it calls:

```
_SetupInfo.GetNumDstDirs();
```

These functions plus all the others for retrieving information about the SETUP.INF file can be found in the class definition for the *SETUPINFO* class in the SETUPINF.H file.

The setup program makes extensive use of the VER.DLL and the LZEX-PAND.DLL libraries supplied with Windows 3.1. Actually, setup doesn't use the LZEXPAND.DLL directly; the VER.DLL library requires it. Since setup may be executing on a machine running Windows 3.0 instead of Windows 3.1, setup can't assume that these two libraries will be available. No problem, setup will just use the VER.DLL and LZEXPAND.DLL files on the diskette, right? Wrong! There is a problem. Microsoft didn't mark all the code segments and resources as *NONDIS-CARDABLE* in these two libraries. If setup tries to use these libraries and the disk is swapped, setup will crash. It seems to me that Microsoft should have anticipated this situation and made everything nondiscardable.

This was an interesting problem to solve—here's how it was done. I wanted to come up with the easiest way possible to solve this problem and was thinking of different ways of preloading and locking the code segments and resources in memory. I soon gave up because every method I thought of always seemed too kludgy. I resorted to copying the files to the user's hard disk and using them from there.

For this discussion, let's assume that the VER.DLL library has been compressed and placed on the diskette with the filename VER.DL_. Let's also assume that the LZEXPAND.DLL library has been placed on the distribution diskette with the name LZEXPAND.DLX. Note that the LZEXPAND.DLX file is *not* compressed, only renamed. There is something else that setup does; it does not directly call any of the functions in either of these two libraries. This is important. If setup made a direct call to *VerInstallFile*, for instance, the linker knows that this function is in VER.DLL. When setup is executed, Windows automatically loads VER.DLL into memory. Since VER.DLL uses functions in LZEXPAND.DLL, Windows also loads LZEXPAND.DLL into memory. All this takes place long before setup's *WinMain* function is called. To guarantee that these libraries will not be implicitly loaded, setup does not call any of the functions in these libraries directly. You'll see how setup calls these functions shortly.

Now, when setup executes, it calls the *PrepareSetup* function in SETUP.CPP to copy the VER.DLL and LZEXPAND.DLL files. Here's how setup does it.

The first thing that *PrepareSetup* does is check to see if the user already has a version of VER.DLL available for use:

```
HINSTANCE PrepareSetup (LPCSTR szSrcDir) {
    .

    .

    .

    UINT uPrevErrMode = SetErrorMode(SEM_NOOPENFILEERRORBOX);
    HINSTANCE hInstLib = LoadLibrary("VER.DLL");
    SetErrorMode(uPrevErrMode);
    if (hInstLib >= HINSTANCE_ERROR)
        goto GetVerFuncAddresses;

    .

    .

    .
```

The previous code calls *LoadLibrary* to explicitly load the VER.DLL file into memory. There is no chance that this attempts to load the copy on the floppy because it is compressed and its filename is VER.DL_. The only VER.DLL file that can be loaded is the one that exists on the user's hard disk. If *LoadLibrary* locates the VER.DLL file, *LoadLibrary* returns the data-instance handle of this library and *PrepareSetup* jumps to the *GetVerFuncAddress* label at the bottom of this function.

Let me pause for a moment. I know that some of you are shaking your heads in embarrassment for me and my use of the *goto*. While it's true that I generally do not recommend using *goto*s, they can be used to improve code readability and understandability. Since this is the case with the *goto* used, I stand behind it! So there! Having said this, let's go on...

Notice the previous call to *SetErrorMode*. When *LoadLibrary* attempts to load a library and does not find it, Windows displays a system modal dialog box informing the user that a library was requested and could not be found. The user then must dismiss the dialog box. You don't really want to bother the user with this—just take care of it in the code. Calling *SetErrorMode* and passing it the value *SEM_NOOPEN-FILEERRORBOX*, forces Windows not to display the dialog box. The return value from *SetErrorMode* is its previous state. This value is saved and restored after the call to *LoadLibrary*.

Now that you know the user does not have a copy of VER.DLL available for use, you can also assume that the user doesn't have a copy of LZEXPAND.DLL. So, you must copy/decompress the LZExpand and Ver library files to the user's hard disk. The easiest way to do this is using the LZEXPAND.DLX files on the distribution diskette. Since the user probably doesn't have a LZEXPAND.DLX file anywhere and because *LoadLibrary* always looks for files in the directory where the executable was run before checking the Windows system directories, the call to *LoadLibrary* below causes your LZExpand library to be loaded:

```
char szOurLZExpand[] = "LZExpand.DLx";
char szBuf[MAXPATH], szDstDir[MAXPATH];
   .


   .


   .

hInstLib = LoadLibrary(szOurLZExpand);
if (hInstLib < HINSTANCE_ERROR) return(hInstLib);
```

If for some reason the library cannot be loaded, *PrepareSetup* returns the error value. But if the library loaded successfully, you must now get the address of the functions needed to copy and decompress the files:

```
// Prototypes and declaration of LZExpand functions.
int   (LZAPI* LZStart)(void);
void  (LZAPI* LZDone)(void);
HFILE (LZAPI* LZOpenFile)(LPCSTR, OFSTRUCT FAR *, UINT);
LONG  (LZAPI* CopyLZFile)(HFILE, HFILE);
void ·(LZAPI* LZClose)(HFILE);

// Get address of all these functions.
* ((FARPROC *) &LZStart)    = GetProcAddress(hInstLib, "LZStart");
* ((FARPROC *) &LZDone)     = GetProcAddress(hInstLib, "LZDone");
* ((FARPROC *) &LZOpenFile) = GetProcAddress(hInstLib, "LZOpenFile");
* ((FARPROC *) &CopyLZFile) = GetProcAddress(hInstLib, "CopyLZFile");
* ((FARPROC *) &LZClose)    = GetProcAddress(hInstLib, "LZClose");
```

All of the previous calls to *GetProcAddress* request that Windows return the address of the specified function. The first parameter indicates the data-instance handle of the library; in this case, LZEXPAND.DLX. The second parameter indicates the name of the function of which you want the address. *GetProcAddress* is prototyped as returning a *FARPROC*, but none of the LZExpand functions are of type *FARPROC*. So, if you tried to compile the following line:

```
CopyLZFile = GetProcAddress(hInstLib, "CopyLZFile");
```

the compiler would generate an error. To avoid this error, I performed the casting as shown above. The only reason for the casting is to defeat the compiler error.

You now need to decide where these libraries should be copied. If the user is running a personal copy of Windows, the files should be copied into the Windows' system directory. However, if the user is running a networking version of Windows, the files should be copied to the user's personal Windows directory. There is no function in Windows that tells you if the user is running a personal copy or a networked copy. I solved this problem with the following code:

```
GetSystemDirectory(szDstDir, sizeof(szDstDir));
if (GetDriveType(szDstDir[0] - 'A') == DRIVE_REMOTE) {
```

```
    // User is running a shared copy of Windows.
    GetWindowsDirectory(szDstDir, sizeof(szDstDir));
}
```

First, I get the full path of the Windows' system directory. If this is a networked version of Windows, this directory resides on the network server. I test for this by calling *GetDriveType* and passing the drive letter of the system path. Actually, *GetDriveType* expects a zero for Drive A, a one for Drive B, and so on. I have to subtract the binary equivalent of the letter "A" from the Windows' system drive. If *GetDriveType* returns *DRIVE_REMOTE*, the system directory is on a network server. For a personal copy of Windows, *GetDriveType* returns *DRIVE_FIXED*, indicating that the system directory is on the user's hard drive.

If the *GetDriveType* returns *DRIVE_REMOTE*, I call *GetWindowsDirectory* to load the path of the user's personal Windows directory into the *szDstDir* buffer. Now that I know where the files are going, I use the LZ functions to copy/decompress them:

```
OFSTRUCT ofSrc, ofDst; HFILE hFileSrc, hFileDst;

LZStart();// Initialize the LZExpand library.
wsprintf(szBuf, "%s%s", szSrcDir, szOurLZExpand);
hFileSrc = LZOpenFile(szBuf, &ofSrc, OF_READ);

wsprintf(szBuf, "%s\\LZExpand.DLL", szDstDir);
hFileDst = LZOpenFile(szBuf, &ofDst, OF_CREATE);


CopyLZFile(hFileSrc, hFileDst);
LZClose(hFileSrc); LZClose(hFileDst);

wsprintf(szBuf, "%sVER.DL_", szSrcDir);
hFileSrc = LZOpenFile(szBuf, &ofSrc, OF_READ);

wsprintf(szBuf, "%s\\Ver.DLL", szDstDir);
hFileDst = LZOpenFile(szBuf, &ofDst, OF_CREATE);
```

```
CopyLZFile(hFileSrc, hFileDst);
LZClose(hFileSrc); LZClose(hFileDst);

LZDone();
```

After the files have been placed on the hard drive, tell setup to stop using the LZEXPAND.DLX library from the floppy and to start using the libraries from the hard drive:

```
FreeLibrary(hInstLib);    // Free our LZEXPAND.DLL.

// Load the copied VER.DLL from the hard disk.
hInstLib = LoadLibrary("VER.DLL");
if (hInstLib < HINSTANCE_ERROR) return(hInstLib);

GetVerFuncAddresses:
    // Get the address of all VER.DLL functions.
    *((FARPROC *) &_VerFindFile) =
       GetProcAddress(hInstLib, "VerFindFile");
    *((FARPROC *) &_VerInstallFile) =
       GetProcAddress(hInstLib, "VerInstallFile");
    *((FARPROC *) &_GetFileVersionInfoSize) =
       GetProcAddress(hInstLib, GetFileVersionInfoSize");
    *((FARPROC *) &_GetFileVersionInfo) =
       GetProcAddress(hInstLib, GetFileVersionInfo");
    *((FARPROC *) &_VerLanguageName) =
       GetProcAddress(hInstLib, VerLanguageName");
    *((FARPROC *) &_VerQueryValue) =
       GetProcAddress(hInstLib, "VerQueryValue");
    return(hInstLib);
}
```

If everything goes as planned, the addresses of the version control functions are obtained by calling *GetProcAddress* for each one and storing the results in global variables. Any code in the setup program that needs to call one of these functions, does so by using the global variable. Finally, *PrepareSetup* returns the data-instance handle of the VER.DLL library. Since this library is explicitly loaded, it must be explicitly freed by setup before it terminates. Setup passes this handle to *FreeLibrary* just before it terminates.

SETUP.CPP and SETUPDLG.CPP contain all the code for user prompts and dialog boxes. None of the code in these modules should be new to you by now.

Dynamic Data Exchange with Program Manager

SETUPPM.CPP adds the new program group and files to Program Manager. This is accomplished via a dynamic data exchange (DDE) conversation with Program Manager. Chapter 17 of the *Microsoft's Windows' SDK Programmer's Reference*, Volume 1, contains a description of what commands may be sent to Program Manager. The following table describes each command:

Command	Description
CreateGroup	Instructs Program Manager to create a new group window.
AddItem	Instructs Program Manager to add a new program item to the active group.
ReplaceItem	Instructs Program Manager to delete an item and record its position. The next item added (by using *AddItem*) will be placed at this position.
DeleteGroup	Instructs Program Manager to delete a group, including its contents and associated data file.
ShowGroup	Instructs Program Manager to alter the appearance of a group window. (A window may be maximized, minimized, or restored.)
Reload	Instruct Program Manager to remove and reload an existing group.
ExitProgman	Instructs Program Manager to terminate and (optionally) save its current state.

The first step is to initiate a DDE conversation. This is most easily managed by creating a window class whose job is to handle DDE communications. Setup registers a window class called DDEClient for this purpose.

A program starts a DDE conversation by informing all running applications that it wants to communicate with a particular application about a particular topic. Setup wishes to communicate with PROGMAN, and the topic is also PROGMAN. The following is how setup initiates the DDE conversation with Program Manager:

```
char szProgMan[] = "PROGMAN";
.

.

.

// Create the Application and Topic atoms.
aApp = GlobalAddAtom(szProgMan);
aTopic = GlobalAddAtom(szProgMan);

// Initiate a conversation with Program Manager.
// The last parameter contains the Application and Topic atoms.
hWndDDEClient = CreateWindow("DDEClient", "", 0, 0, 0, 0, 0,
    NULL, NULL, hInstance, (LPSTR) MAKELONG(aApp, aTopic));

// Delete the Application and Topic atoms.
GlobalDeleteAtom(aApp);
GlobalDeleteAtom(aTopic);

if (hWndDDEClient == NULL) {
    // If the DDE conversation could not be initiated, the
    // "DDEClient" would not allow itself to be created.
    // This causes NULL to be returned from CreateWindow above.
    return(FALSE);
}
```

When Windows tries to create a DDEClient window, the *WM_CREATE* message is sent to the window procedure. The code to process this message is shown below:

```
case WM_CREATE:
    SendMessage(HWND_BROADCAST, WM_DDE_INITIATE, hWnd,
```

```
        (LONG) ((LPCREATESTRUCT) lParam)->lpCreateParams);
    if (GETWNDEB(hWnd, WNDEB, hWndServer) != NULL)
        break;

    // A conversation was not established.
    // Attempt to execute the desired application.
    GlobalGetAtomName(LOWORD(
        (LONG) ((LPCREATESTRUCT) lParam)->lpCreateParams),
        szBuf, sizeof(szBuf));
    WinExec(szBuf, SW_RESTORE);

    SendMessage(-1, WM_DDE_INITIATE, hWnd,
        (LONG) ((LPCREATESTRUCT) lParam)->lpCreateParams);

    if (GETWNDEB(hWnd, WNDEB, hWndServer) == NULL)
        lResult = -1;
    break;
```

If a running application matches the specification and knows how to talk about the topic, it will send a *WM_DDE_ACK* message to the DDEClient window. The DDEClient window processes *WM_DDE_ACK* as follows:

```
case WM_DDE_ACK:
    if (hWndServer == NULL) {
        // No conversation initiated; WM_DDE_ACK must be from
        // a potential server that just received my
        // WM_DDE_INITIATE message.
        SETWNDEB(hWnd, WNDEB, hWndServer, (HWND) wParam);
        break;
    }

    // WM_DDE_ACK message received from a potential Server
    // but you already established a conversation with
    // another Server. Tell this potential Server that you do not wish
```

```
// to continue your conversation with it.
PostMessage((HWND) wParam, WM_DDE_TERMINATE, hWnd, 0);
break;
```

When a DDEClient window is created, two extra window bytes are reserved. These store the window handle of the server. They are NULL if a conversation is not established. The window extra bytes are accessed with *GETWNDEB* and *SETWNDEB*, as explained in Appendix B.

After all the potential servers have responded to our broadcast, *WM_CREATE* checks the contents of the extra bytes to see if a conversation has been started. If not, it may be because Program Manager isn't running; so, the DDEClient window attempts to execute Program Manager by calling *WinExec*. The process of trying to initiate a DDE conversation is started again. If a conversation is not established this time, the *WM_CREATE* message returns -1 so that the window is not created and Windows returns a NULL window handle to the application to notify it that a conversation could not be established.

Sending Commands to Program Manager

Setup uses code like the following to send commands to Program Manager:

```
// Create the PM Group box.
_SetupInfo.GetPMGroupInfo(szPMGroupFileName, szPMGroup);
wsprintf(szCmd, "[CreateGroup(%s%s%s)]", (LPSTR) szPMGroup,
    (LPSTR) (*szPMGroupFileName == 0 ? "" : ","),
    (LPSTR) szPMGroupFileName);

// Allocate a block of memory large enough to contain the
// desired command. Memory blocks used in DDE conversations
// must be created with the GMEM_DDESHARE flag.
hGlbl = GlobalAlloc(GMEM_MOVEABLE | GMEM_DDESHARE, lstrlen(szCmd) + 1);

// Copy the command into the memory block.
lpCommand = GlobalLock(hGlbl);
lstrcpy(lpCommand, szCmd);
```

```
GlobalUnlock(hGlbl);

// Tell the DDEClient window that you wish it to send the command to
// the server.
fOk = (BOOL) SendMessage(hWndDDEClient, WM_DDECLIENT_EXECUTE, 0, MAKE-
LONG(0, hGlbl));

// A DDE server does not free a memory block used in a
// WM_DDE_EXECUTE message; so, you must do it.
GlobalFree(hGlbl);
```

This code creates the command string to be sent and allocates a block of memory large enough to contain the string. The block of memory must be allocated using the *GMEM_DDESHARE* flag. The command string is then copied into the memory block. Setup sends the user-defined message, *WM_DDECLIENT_EXECUTE*, to the DDEClient window that is communicating with Program Manager. The result will be TRUE or FALSE, indicating whether Program Manager successfully processed the command.

A DDEClient window sends a *WM_DDE_EXECUTE* message to its server when it wants the server to process commands. Here's how the DDEClient window procedure processes *WM_DDECLIENT_EXECUTE*:

```
case WM_DDECLIENT_EXECUTE:
    // This message was sent to this window from the
    // Setup Application. The lParam parameter contains
    // the handle of the memory containing the commands
    // to be executed by the Server.

    // Verify that a conversation started and
    // hasn't terminated.
    if (hWndServer == NULL) break;

    PostMessage(hWndServer, WM_DDE_EXECUTE, hWnd, lParam);
```

```
// Wait for response from the Server.
GetMessage(&Msg, hWnd, WM_DDE_ACK, WM_DDE_ACK);

// Return whether the command was
// acknowledged successfully.
wParam = LOWORD(Msg.lParam);
lResult = ((DDEACK *) &wParam)->fAck;
break;
```

This code first ensures that neither application has terminated the DDE conversation. The *WM_DDE_EXECUTE* message is then posted to Program Manager's window, and the DDEClient window waits for Program Manager to respond by calling *GetMessage* and telling it to wait for *WM_DDE_ACK*. When *WM_DDE_ACK* is retrieved from the application's queue, the low-order word of the *lParam* parameter contains a *DDEACK* bit-field structure. This structure is declared in the DDE.H file included with the Windows' SDK:

```
typedef struct {
    unsigned bAppReturnCode:8;
    unsigned reserved:6,
    unsigned fBusy:1,
    unsigned fAck:1;
} DDEACK;
```

The *fAck* member of this structure indicates whether the message was processed successfully (*fAck* is nonzero) or not (*fAck* is zero).

Terminating the DDE Conversation

After setup has sent all the commands to Program Manager, it is no longer necessary to continue the conversation. Setup terminates the DDE conversation by destroying the DDEClient window:

```
DestroyWindow(hWndDDEClient);
```

The processing of the *WM_DESTROY* message in the DDEClient's window procedure is shown as follows:

```
case WM_DESTROY:
    PostMessage(hWndServer, WM_DDE_TERMINATE, hWnd, 0);
    SETWNDEB(hWnd, WNDEB, hWndServer, NULL);
    // From now on, do not send a WM_DDE_ACK message to the
    // server in response to any messages sent from the Server.
    break;
```

This code posts the *WM_DDE_TERMINATE* message to the Server window, informing it that you wish to terminate the conversation. Then set the extra bytes in the DDEClient window to NULL, indicating that a conversation is no longer active.

Figure 10-4. SETUP.ICO

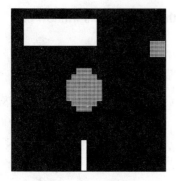

Figure 10-5. DISK.ICO

Listing 10-2. MAKEFILE for setup application

```
#*******************************************************************
#Module name: MAKEFILE
#Programmer : Jeffrey M. Richter.
#*******************************************************************

!include "..\builtins.jmr"

PROG = Setup

MODEL = 1
CFLAGS = -P-c -c -f- -WS -p -v -w -m$(MODEL) -I$(INCLUDEDIR)
LFLAGS = /P/v/n/m/s/L$(LIBDIR)
LIBS = CW$(MODEL) Import

MODULES = $(PROG).obj SetupInf.obj SetupDlg.obj SetupPM.obj

ICONS   = $(PROG).ico Disk.ico
BITMAPS =
CURSORS =

$(PROG).Exe: $(MODULES) $(PROG).Def $(PROG).Res
     tlink $(LFLAGS) @&&!
COW$(MODEL) $(MODULES)
$(PROG), $(PROG), $(LIBS), $(PROG)
!
   rc -30 -T $(PROG).Res
   TDStrip -s $(PROG)

$(PROG).res: $(PROG).rc $(PROG).h $(RESOURCES)
```

Listing 10-3. SETUP.CPP application source module

```c
/*******************************************************************
Module name: SETUP.C
Programmer : Jeffrey M. Richter.
*******************************************************************/

#include <windows.h>
#include <windowsx.h>
#include <ver.h>
#include <lzexpand.h>
#include <dos.h>
#include <dir.h>
#include <direct.h>
#include <io.h>
#include <string.h>
#include "Setup.H"
#include "SetupInf.H"
#include "..\Meter.04\Meter.h"

BOOL WINAPI CreateDstDirTree (HWND hDlgStatus);
BOOL WINAPI CopyAllFiles (HWND hDlgStatus);
BOOL WINAPI CreatePMInfo (HINSTANCE hInstance);
#define WasCancelled(hDlg) \
    (!IsWindowEnabled(GetDlgItem(hDlg, IDCANCEL)))

HINSTANCE PrepareSetup (LPCSTR szSrcDir);

char _szAppName[] = "Setup";
char _szSrcDir[MAXDIR] = "x:\\"; // Where SETUP.EXE was run from.
char _szDstDir[MAXDIR];

HINSTANCE _hInstVer = NULL;    // Handle of VER.DLL library.

UINT (WINAPI *_VerFindFile)(UINT, LPCSTR, LPCSTR, LPCSTR,
    LPSTR, UINT FAR*, LPSTR, UINT FAR*);

DWORD (WINAPI* _VerInstallFile)(UINT, LPCSTR, LPCSTR, LPCSTR,
    LPCSTR, LPCSTR, LPSTR, UINT FAR*);

DWORD (WINAPI* _GetFileVersionInfoSize)(LPCSTR, DWORD FAR *);

BOOL  (WINAPI* _GetFileVersionInfo)
    (LPCSTR, DWORD, DWORD, void FAR*);

UINT  (WINAPI* _VerLanguageName)(UINT, LPSTR, UINT);
BOOL  (WINAPI* _VerQueryValue)
    (const void FAR*, LPCSTR, void FAR* FAR*, UINT FAR*);
```

```
#pragma argsused
extern "C" int WinMain (HINSTANCE hInstance,
   HINSTANCE hPrevInstance, LPSTR lpszCmdLine, int nCmdShow) {
   int nResult;
   HWND hDlgStatus, hWndSignOn;
   DWORD dwDiskSpaceNeeded, dwFreeDiskSpace;
   struct dfree DiskFreeSpace;
   char szBuf[100];
   HINSTANCE hInstMeter = NULL;
   SETUPINFO::ISIERROR ISIError;

   // Don't let another instance of this application execute.
   if (hPrevInstance != NULL) return(0);

   // Prepare the DDE Client window class.
   if (!RegisterDDEClient(hInstance))
      goto Cleanup;

   // Initialize the default source path so that it uses the same
   // drive that the SETUP.EXE application was executed from.
   GetModuleFileName(hInstance, _szSrcDir, sizeof(_szSrcDir));
   *(_fstrrchr(_szSrcDir, '\\') + 1) = 0;

   // Sign-on window while initializing.
   hWndSignOn = CreateDialog(hInstance,
      MAKEINTRESOURCE(DLG_INITIALIZE),
      NULL, (DLGPROC) InitDlgProc);

   hInstMeter = LoadLibrary("Meter.DLL");
   if (hInstMeter < HINSTANCE_ERROR)
      goto Cleanup;

   _hInstVer = PrepareSetup(_szSrcDir);
   if (_hInstVer < HINSTANCE_ERROR) {
      MsgBox(hInstance, NULL, IDS_CANNOTINIT, _szAppName,
         MB_OK | MB_ICONINFORMATION);
      goto Cleanup;
   }

   // Read the SETUP.INF file into memory.
   wsprintf(szBuf, "%s%sSETUP.INF", _szSrcDir,
      ((*(_fstrrchr(_szSrcDir, '\\') + 1) == 0) ? "" : "\\"));

   ISIError = _SetupInfo.InitSetupInfo(szBuf);
   // Remove sign-on window after initialization.
   if (IsWindow(hWndSignOn))
      DestroyWindow(hWndSignOn);
```

```
if (ISIError != SETUPINFO::ISI_NOERROR) {
   MsgBox(hInstance, NULL,
      (ISIError == SETUPINFO::ISI_NOMEM)
      ? IDS_NOMEMORY : IDS_NOSETUPINFOFILE, _szAppName,
         MB_ICONINFORMATION | MB_OK | MB_TASKMODAL, szBuf);
   goto Cleanup;
}

// Get the amount of memory (in K) needed for the installation.
dwDiskSpaceNeeded = _SetupInfo.GetDstDiskSpaceNeeded();

// Create the Status dialog box.
hDlgStatus = CreateDialog(hInstance,
   MAKEINTRESOURCE(DLG_STATUS), NULL, (DLGPROC) StatusDlgProc);

do {
   // Welcome user and prompt for destination directory.
   nResult = DialogBox(hInstance,
      MAKEINTRESOURCE(DLG_WELCOME), NULL,
      (DLGPROC) WelcomeDlgProc);
   if (nResult == IDCANCEL) break;

   // Check if there is sufficient disk space on
   // the destination drive.
   getdfree(_szDstDir[0] - 'A' + 1, &DiskFreeSpace);
   dwFreeDiskSpace = ((DWORD) DiskFreeSpace.df_avail *
                      (DWORD) DiskFreeSpace.df_sclus *
                      (DWORD) DiskFreeSpace.df_bsec) / 1024UL;

   if (dwFreeDiskSpace < dwDiskSpaceNeeded) {
      MsgBox(hInstance, NULL, IDS_NODISKSPACE, _szAppName,
         MB_OK | MB_ICONINFORMATION | MB_TASKMODAL,
         _szDstDir[0], dwFreeDiskSpace, dwDiskSpaceNeeded);
      continue;
   }

   // Try to create the destination directory tree.
   nResult = CreateDstDirTree(hDlgStatus);

   if (nResult == FALSE) {
      // If the directory tree cannot be created,
      // force loop to repeat.
      dwFreeDiskSpace = 0;
   }

} while (dwFreeDiskSpace < dwDiskSpaceNeeded);

if (nResult == IDCANCEL) {
   DestroyWindow(hDlgStatus);
```

```
      goto Cleanup;
   }

   // Make the destination directory the current directory.
   _chdrive(_szDstDir[0] - 'A' + 1);
   chdir(_szDstDir);
   // Try to copy the files.
   ShowWindow(hDlgStatus, SW_SHOW);
   UpdateWindow(hDlgStatus);
   nResult = CopyAllFiles(hDlgStatus);
   ShowWindow(hDlgStatus, SW_HIDE);
   FreeLibrary(_hInstVer);

   // Clean up the things that you no longer need.
   DestroyWindow(hDlgStatus);

   if (nResult == FALSE) {
      // Installation not complete.
      MsgBox(hInstance, NULL, IDS_SETUPNOGOOD, _szAppName,
         MB_OK | MB_ICONINFORMATION | MB_TASKMODAL);
      goto Cleanup;
   }

   MsgBox(hInstance, NULL,
      CreatePMInfo(hInstance) ? IDS_PMADDOK : IDS_PMADDNOGOOD,
      _szAppName, MB_OK | MB_ICONINFORMATION | MB_TASKMODAL);

   Cleanup:
   if (hInstMeter >= HINSTANCE_ERROR)
      FreeLibrary(hInstMeter);
   if (_hInstVer >= HINSTANCE_ERROR)
      FreeLibrary(_hInstVer);
   return(0);
}

// Returns the hInstance for VER.DLL on hard disk.
HINSTANCE PrepareSetup (LPCSTR szSrcDir) {
   HINSTANCE hInstLib;
   char szOurLZExpand[] = "LZExpand.DLx";
   char szBuf[MAXPATH], szDstDir[MAXPATH];

   // Check for the existence of the VER.DLL and LZEXPAND.DLL
   // files on the user's system. If they are on the user's
   // hard disk, let's use them. If not, let's copy them from
   // the floppy to the hard disk.
   UINT uPrevErrMode = SetErrorMode(SEM_NOOPENFILEERRORBOX);
   hInstLib = LoadLibrary("VER.DLL");
   SetErrorMode(uPrevErrMode);
```

```
if (hInstLib >= HINSTANCE_ERROR)
   goto GetVerFuncAddresses;

// User does not have VER.DLL installed on his or her hard disk.
// The user doesn't have a VER.DLL file or a LZEXPAND.DLL
// file since VER.DLL requires LZEXPAND.DLL.

// Load our LZEXPAND.DLL file from our floppy.
hInstLib = LoadLibrary(szOurLZExpand);
if (hInstLib < HINSTANCE_ERROR) return(hInstLib);

int   (LZAPI* LZStart)(void);
void  (LZAPI* LZDone)(void);
HFILE (LZAPI* LZOpenFile)(LPCSTR, OFSTRUCT FAR *, UINT);
LONG  (LZAPI* CopyLZFile)(HFILE, HFILE);
void  (LZAPI* LZClose)(HFILE);

* ((FARPROC *) &LZStart)   =
   GetProcAddress(hInstLib, "LZStart");
* ((FARPROC *) &LZDone)    =
   GetProcAddress(hInstLib, "LZDone");
* ((FARPROC *) &LZOpenFile) =
   GetProcAddress(hInstLib, "LZOpenFile");
* ((FARPROC *) &CopyLZFile) =
   GetProcAddress(hInstLib, "CopyLZFile");
* ((FARPROC *) &LZClose)   =
   GetProcAddress(hInstLib, "LZClose");

GetSystemDirectory(szDstDir, sizeof(szDstDir));
if (GetDriveType(szDstDir[0] - 'A') == DRIVE_REMOTE) {
   // User is running a shared copy of Windows.
   GetWindowsDirectory(szDstDir, sizeof(szDstDir));
}

OFSTRUCT ofSrc, ofDst; HFILE hFileSrc, hFileDst;

LZStart();  // Initialize the LZExpand library.
wsprintf(szBuf, "%s%s", szSrcDir, szOurLZExpand);
hFileSrc = LZOpenFile(szBuf, &ofSrc, OF_READ);

wsprintf(szBuf, "%s\\LZExpand.DLL", szDstDir);
hFileDst = LZOpenFile(szBuf, &ofDst, OF_CREATE);

// Error check.
CopyLZFile(hFileSrc, hFileDst);
LZClose(hFileSrc); LZClose(hFileDst);

wsprintf(szBuf, "%sVER.DL_", szSrcDir);
hFileSrc = LZOpenFile(szBuf, &ofSrc, OF_READ);
```

```
   wsprintf(szBuf, "%s\\Ver.DLL", szDstDir);
   hFileDst = LZOpenFile(szBuf, &ofDst, OF_CREATE);
   // Error check.
   CopyLZFile(hFileSrc, hFileDst);
   LZClose(hFileSrc); LZClose(hFileDst);

   LZDone();
   FreeLibrary(hInstLib);   // Free our LZEXPAND.DLL.

   // Load the copied VER.DLL from the hard disk.
   hInstLib = LoadLibrary("VER.DLL");
   if (hInstLib < HINSTANCE_ERROR) return(hInstLib);

GetVerFuncAddresses:
   // Get the address of all VER.DLL functions.
   *((FARPROC *) &_VerFindFile) =
      GetProcAddress(hInstLib, "VerFindFile");
   *((FARPROC *) &_VerInstallFile) =
      GetProcAddress(hInstLib, "VerInstallFile");
   *((FARPROC *) &_GetFileVersionInfoSize) =
      GetProcAddress(hInstLib, "GetFileVersionInfoSize");
   *((FARPROC *) &_GetFileVersionInfo) =
      GetProcAddress(hInstLib, "GetFileVersionInfo");
   *((FARPROC *) &_VerLanguageName) =
      GetProcAddress(hInstLib, "VerLanguageName");
   *((FARPROC *) &_VerQueryValue) =
      GetProcAddress(hInstLib, "VerQueryValue");
   return(hInstLib);
}

// **** Functions for creating the destination directory tree.****
BOOL WINAPI CreateDstDirTree (HWND hDlgStatus) {
   int nResult, nMaxDirs, nDirNum;
   char szBuf[MAXDIR]; MSG Msg;

   ShowWindow(hDlgStatus,
      _SetupInfo.ShowSubDirCreateStats() ? SW_SHOW : SW_HIDE);
   UpdateWindow(hDlgStatus);
   SetDlgItemText(hDlgStatus, ID_STATLINE1,
      "Creating destination directory tree...");
   nMaxDirs = _SetupInfo.GetNumDstDirs();
   SendDlgItemMessage(hDlgStatus, ID_METER,
      MM_SETPARTSCOMPLETE, 0, 0);
   SendDlgItemMessage(hDlgStatus, ID_METER,
      MM_SETPARTSINJOB, nMaxDirs + 1, 0);
   SetDlgItemText(hDlgStatus, ID_STATLINE2, _szDstDir);

   // Create the destination directory.
   nResult = chdir(_szDstDir);
```

```
      if (nResult != 0) {
         nResult = mkdir(_szDstDir);
         if (nResult != 0) {
            MsgBox(_hInstance, hDlgStatus, IDS_CANTMAKEDIR,
               _szAppName, MB_ICONINFORMATION | MB_OK, _szDstDir);
            ShowWindow(hDlgStatus, SW_HIDE);
            return(FALSE);
         } else chdir(_szDstDir);
      }
   SendDlgItemMessage(hDlgStatus, ID_METER,
      MM_SETPARTSCOMPLETE, 1, 0);

   // Create any subdirectories under the destination directory.
   for (nDirNum = 0; nDirNum < nMaxDirs; nDirNum++) {
      // Let other applications execute.
      while (PeekMessage(&Msg, NULL, NULL, NULL, PM_REMOVE)) {
         TranslateMessage(&Msg);
         DispatchMessage(&Msg);
      }

      if (WasCancelled(hDlgStatus)) {
         nResult = IDCANCEL;
         break;
      }

      wsprintf(szBuf, "%s%s", _szDstDir,
         ((*(_fstrrchr(_szDstDir, '\\') + 1) == 0) ? "" : "\\"));
      _SetupInfo.GetDstDir(nDirNum, _fstrchr(szBuf, 0));
      SetDlgItemText(hDlgStatus, ID_STATLINE2, szBuf);

      nResult = chdir(szBuf);
      if (nResult != 0) {
         nResult = mkdir(szBuf);
         if (nResult != 0) {
            MsgBox(_hInstance, hDlgStatus, IDS_CANTMAKEDIR,
               _szAppName, MB_ICONINFORMATION | MB_OK, szBuf);
            nResult = IDCANCEL;
            break;
         } else chdir(szBuf);
      }
      nResult = IDOK;
      SendDlgItemMessage(hDlgStatus, ID_METER,
         MM_SETPARTSCOMPLETE, nDirNum + 2, 0);
   }
   ShowWindow(hDlgStatus, SW_HIDE);
   return(nResult != IDCANCEL);
}
```

```
// *************** Functions for Copying Files ******************

#define PTIF_INSTALLTHISFILE          0
#define PTIF_ABORTSETUP               1
#define PTIF_SKIPTHISFILE             2
#define PTIF_REPLACEEXISTINGFILE      3
#define PTIF_DONTERASEEXISTINGFILE    4
#define PTIF_INTERNALERROR            5

UINT WINAPI PrepareToInstallFile (HWND hWnd, UINT uFlags,
    LPCSTR szDstFileName, LPCSTR szAppDir, LPSTR szCurDir,
    UINT FAR* lpuCurDirLen, LPSTR szDestDir,
    UINT FAR* lpuDestDirLen, LPCSTR szSrcDir,
    LPCSTR szSrcFileName);

#define IF_INSTALLEDOK                0
#define IF_ABORTSETUP                 1
#define IF_SKIPTHISFILE               2
#define IF_CHANGEDISK                 3
UINT WINAPI InstallFile (HWND hWnd, UINT uFlags,
    LPCSTR szSrcFileName, LPCSTR szDestFileName, LPCSTR szSrcDir,
    LPCSTR szDestDir, LPCSTR szCurDir, LPSTR szTmpFile,
    UINT FAR* lpuTmpFileLen);

void LockResources (void) {
    HRSRC hResDlg;
    HGLOBAL hGlblRes;
    int nDlg, nIcon;

    for (nDlg = DLG_FIRST; nDlg <= DLG_LAST; nDlg++) {
        // Get the resource handle of the dialog box from
        // the executable file.
        hResDlg = FindResource(_hInstance,
            MAKEINTRESOURCE(nDlg), RT_DIALOG);

        // Get the memory handle of the dialog box in memory.
        // The block is already in memory because the dialog
        // box is marked as PRELOAD FIXED.
        hGlblRes = LoadResource(_hInstance, hResDlg);

        // Force the memory block to be locked down. This
        // prohibits Windows from discarding the dialog-box
        // template from memory.
        LockResource(hGlblRes);
    }

    for (nIcon = ICN_FIRST; nIcon <= ICN_LAST; nIcon++) {
        LoadIcon(_hInstance, MAKEINTRESOURCE(nIcon));
    }
```

```
    }

// Returns FALSE if setup must be terminated.
BOOL WINAPI CopyAllFiles (HWND hDlgStatus) {
    int nMaxFiles, nFileNum;
    char szSrcDir[MAXPATH];
    char szFileDesc[MAXFILEDESC], szSrcDiskDesc[MAXDISKDESC];
    char szSrcFilePath[MAXPATH], szSrcFileName[MAXPATH];
    char szDstFilePath[MAXPATH], szDstFileName[MAXPATH];
    char szCurDir[MAXPATH], szDstDir[MAXPATH], szTmpFile[MAXPATH];
    UINT uCurDirLen, uDstDirLen, uTmpFileLen;
    DWORD x;
    MSG Msg;
    BOOL fSharable;

    LockResources();

    SetDlgItemText(hDlgStatus, ID_STATLINE1, "Copying files...");
    nMaxFiles = _SetupInfo.GetNumFilestoInstall();
    SendDlgItemMessage(hDlgStatus, ID_METER,
        MM_SETPARTSCOMPLETE, 0, 0);
    SendDlgItemMessage(hDlgStatus, ID_METER,
        MM_SETPARTSINJOB, nMaxFiles, 0);

    for (nFileNum = 0; nFileNum < nMaxFiles; nFileNum++) {
Retry:
        // Let other applications execute.
        while (PeekMessage(&Msg, NULL, NULL, NULL, PM_REMOVE)) {
            TranslateMessage(&Msg); DispatchMessage(&Msg);
        }
        if (WasCancelled(hDlgStatus)) // Terminate setup.
            return(FALSE);

        _SetupInfo.GetFileInstallInfo(nFileNum,
            szSrcDiskDesc, szFileDesc,
            szSrcFilePath, szSrcFileName,
            szDstFilePath, szDstFileName, &fSharable);
        SetDlgItemText(hDlgStatus, ID_STATLINE2, szFileDesc);

        if (!lstrcmp(szSrcFilePath, "."))
            lstrcpy(szSrcDir, _szSrcDir);
        else
            wsprintf(szSrcDir, "%s%s%s", _szSrcDir,
                ((*(_lstrrchr(_szSrcDir, '\\') + 1) == 0)
                ? "" : "\\"), szSrcFilePath);
        if (!lstrcmp(szDstFilePath, "."))
            lstrcpy(szDstDir, _szDstDir);
        else
            wsprintf(szDstDir, "%s%s%s", _szDstDir,
```

```
         ((*(_fstrrchr(_szDstDir, '\\') + 1) == 0)
         ? "" : "\\"), szDstFilePath);

uCurDirLen  = sizeof(szCurDir);
uDstDirLen = sizeof(szDstDir);
uTmpFileLen = sizeof(szTmpFile);

x = PrepareToInstallFile(hDlgStatus,
   fSharable ? VFFF_ISSHAREDFILE : 0,
   szDstFileName, szDstDir, szCurDir, &uCurDirLen,
   szDstDir, &uDstDirLen, szSrcDir, szSrcFileName);
if (x == PTIF_ABORTSETUP)    return(FALSE);  // Abort setup.
if (x == PTIF_INTERNALERROR) return(FALSE);  // Abort setup.
if (x == PTIF_SKIPTHISFILE)  continue;

UINT uVIFFlags = 0;

if (x == PTIF_DONTERASEEXISTINGFILE)
   uVIFFlags |= VIFF_DONTDELETEOLD;

if (x == PTIF_REPLACEEXISTINGFILE)
   lstrcpy(szDstDir, szCurDir);

// Attempt to install the file.
x = InstallFile(hDlgStatus, uVIFFlags, szSrcFileName,
   szDstFileName, szSrcDir, szDstDir, szCurDir,
   szTmpFile, &uTmpFileLen);
if (x == IF_ABORTSETUP)    return(FALSE);
if (x == IF_SKIPTHISFILE) continue;
if (x == IF_INSTALLEDOK)
   _SetupInfo.SetFileDstDir(nFileNum, szDstDir);

if (x == IF_CHANGEDISK) {
   // Normally, Windows would have discarded the dialog-box
   // template from memory after the dialog box had been
   // created. By forcing the memory block to be locked by
   // the call to LockResource() above, the template will
   // NOT be discarded. If the template were discarded,
   // the next time this dialog box needed to be created,
   // Windows would load the template from the
   // executable file. However, the SETUP.EXE file is
   // probably not on the diskette that is currently in the
   // drive. This would cause the program to crash.
   x = DialogBoxParam(_hInstance,
      MAKEINTRESOURCE(DLG_INSERTDISK), hDlgStatus,
      (DLGPROC) InsertDiskDlgProc,
      (LONG) (LPSTR) szSrcDiskDesc);
   if (x == IDCANCEL) return(FALSE);
   if (x == IDOK) {
```

```
            // The dialog box already copied the new directory
            // into the _szSrcDir buffer. Attempt to install
            // the file again.
            goto Retry;
         }
      }

      SendDlgItemMessage(hDlgStatus, ID_METER,
         MM_SETPARTSCOMPLETE, nFileNum + 1, 0);
   }
   // We'll let Windows worry about unlocking the resources
   // when setup terminates.
   return(TRUE);  // Setup went to completion.
}


// **************** Miscellaneous Function ********************
int _cdecl MsgBox (HINSTANCE hInstance, HWND hWnd, WORD wID,
   LPCSTR szCaption, WORD wType, ...) {
   char szResString[200], szText[200];
   void FAR *VarArgList = (WORD FAR *) &wType + 1;
   LoadString(hInstance, wID, szResString,
      sizeof(szResString) - 1);
   wvsprintf(szText, szResString, (LPSTR) VarArgList);
   return(MessageBox(hWnd, szText, szCaption, wType));
}


#define CFTS_CANTOPENFILE1    0
#define CFTS_CANTOPENFILE2    1
#define CFTS_FILE1ISNEWER     2
#define CFTS_FILE1ISOLDER     3
#define CFTS_FILESARESAME     4

int CompareFileTimeStamps (LPCSTR szPath1, LPCSTR szPath2) {
   struct ftime ftime1, ftime2;
   OFSTRUCT of;

   HFILE hFile = OpenFile(szPath1, &of, OF_READ);
   if (hFile == -1) return(CFTS_CANTOPENFILE1);
   getftime(hFile, &ftime1);
   _lclose(hFile);

   hFile = OpenFile(szPath2, &of, OF_READ);
   if (hFile == -1) return(CFTS_CANTOPENFILE2);
   getftime(hFile, &ftime2);
   _lclose(hFile);

   int x = ftime1.ft_year - ftime2.ft_year;
   if (x != 0)
      return((x > 0) ? CFTS_FILE1ISNEWER : CFTS_FILE1ISOLDER);
```

```
    x = ftime1.ft_month - ftime2.ft_month;
    if (x != 0)
        return((x > 0) ? CFTS_FILE1ISNEWER : CFTS_FILE1ISOLDER);

    x = ftime1.ft_day - ftime2.ft_day;
    if (x != 0)
        return((x > 0) ? CFTS_FILE1ISNEWER : CFTS_FILE1ISOLDER);

    x = ftime1.ft_hour - ftime2.ft_hour;
    if (x != 0)
        return((x > 0) ? CFTS_FILE1ISNEWER : CFTS_FILE1ISOLDER);

    x = ftime1.ft_min - ftime2.ft_min;
    if (x != 0)
        return((x > 0) ? CFTS_FILE1ISNEWER : CFTS_FILE1ISOLDER);

    x = ftime1.ft_tsec - ftime2.ft_tsec;
    if (x != 0)
        return((x > 0) ? CFTS_FILE1ISNEWER : CFTS_FILE1ISOLDER);

    return(CFTS_FILESARESAME);
}

UINT WINAPI PrepareToInstallFile (HWND hWnd, UINT uFlags,
    LPCSTR szDstFileName, LPCSTR szAppDir, LPSTR szCurDir,
    UINT FAR* lpuCurDirLen, LPSTR szDestDir,
    UINT FAR* lpuDestDirLen, LPCSTR szSrcDir,
    LPCSTR szSrcFileName) {

    char szBuf[100];
    UINT x;

Retry:
    UINT uVFFResult = _VerFindFile(uFlags, szDstFileName,
        NULL, szAppDir, szCurDir, lpuCurDirLen, szDestDir,
        lpuDestDirLen);

    if (uVFFResult & VFF_FILEINUSE) {
        char szSrcPath[MAXPATH];

        wsprintf(szSrcPath, "%s%s%s", szSrcDir,
            ((szSrcDir[lstrlen(szSrcDir) - 1] == '\\') ? "" : "\\"),
            szSrcFileName);

        wsprintf(szBuf, "%s%s%s", szCurDir,
            ((szCurDir[lstrlen(szCurDir) - 1] == '\\') ? "" : "\\"),
            szDstFileName);
```

```
        x = CompareFileTimeStamps(szSrcPath, szBuf);
        if (CFTS_FILESARESAME != x) {
            x = DialogBoxParam(_hInstance,
                MAKEINTRESOURCE(DLG_FILEINUSE), hWnd,
                (DLGPROC) FileInUseDlgProc, (LPARAM) szBuf);
            if (x == IDABORT) return(PTIF_ABORTSETUP);
            if (x == IDRETRY) goto Retry;
        }
        return(PTIF_SKIPTHISFILE); // x == IDIGNORE
    }

    if ((uVFFResult & VFF_CURNEDEST) && (szCurDir[0] != 0)) {
        CURNEDESTSTRUCT CurNEDestStruct;
        lstrcpy(CurNEDestStruct.szDstFileName, szDstFileName);
        lstrcpy(CurNEDestStruct.szDstDir, szDestDir);
        lstrcpy(CurNEDestStruct.szCurDir, szCurDir);
        x = DialogBoxParam(_hInstance,
            MAKEINTRESOURCE(DLG_CURNEDEST), hWnd,
            (DLGPROC) CurNEDestDlgProc, (LPARAM) &CurNEDestStruct);
        if (x == ID_INSTALLANDDELETE)
            return(PTIF_INSTALLTHISFILE);
        if (x == ID_INSTALLANDKEEP)
            return(PTIF_DONTERASEEXISTINGFILE);
        if (x == ID_REPLACEEXISTING)
            return(PTIF_REPLACEEXISTINGFILE);
        if (x == ID_SKIPINSTALL)
            return(PTIF_SKIPTHISFILE);
        if (x == ID_ABORTINSTALL)
            return(PTIF_ABORTSETUP);
    }

    if (uVFFResult & VFF_BUFFTOOSMALL)
        return(PTIF_INTERNALERROR);

    // Everything was successful.
    return(PTIF_INSTALLTHISFILE);
}
UINT WINAPI InstallFile (HWND hWnd, UINT uFlags,
    LPCSTR szSrcFileName, LPCSTR szDestFileName, LPCSTR szSrcDir,
    LPCSTR szDestDir, LPCSTR szCurDir, LPSTR szTmpFile,
    UINT FAR* lpuTmpFileLen) {

    char szBuf[100];
    UINT x;
    OFSTRUCT of;

Retry:
    DWORD dwVIFResult = _VerInstallFile(uFlags, szSrcFileName,
        szDestFileName, szSrcDir, szDestDir, szCurDir, szTmpFile,
```

```
    lpuTmpFileLen);
wsprintf(szBuf, "%s%s%s", szCurDir,
    ((szCurDir[lstrlen(szCurDir) - 1] == '\\') ? "" : "\\"),
    szDestFileName);

// Check if an unrecoverable error occurred.
// Errors are listed in least critical to most critical order.
x = 0;
if (dwVIFResult & VIF_CANNOTCREATE)
    x = IDS_CANNOTCREATE;

if (dwVIFResult & VIF_CANNOTDELETE)
    x = IDS_CANNOTDELETE;

if (dwVIFResult & VIF_CANNOTRENAME)
    x = IDS_CANNOTRENAME;

if (dwVIFResult & VIF_OUTOFSPACE)
    x = IDS_OUTOFSPACE;

if (dwVIFResult & VIF_ACCESSVIOLATION)
    x = IDS_ACCESSVIOLATION;

if (dwVIFResult & VIF_SHARINGVIOLATION)
    x = IDS_SHARINGVIOLATION;

if (dwVIFResult & VIF_FILEINUSE)
    x = IDS_FILEINUSE;

if (dwVIFResult & VIF_OUTOFMEMORY)
    x = IDS_OUTOFMEMORY;

if (dwVIFResult & VIF_CANNOTREADDST)
    x = IDS_CANNOTREADDST;

if (dwVIFResult & VIF_WRITEPROT)
    x = IDS_WRITEPROT;

if (x != 0) {
    x = MsgBox(_hInstance, hWnd, x, _szAppName,
        MB_ICONQUESTION | MB_ABORTRETRYIGNORE, szBuf);

    // If the temporary file was created, delete it.
    if (dwVIFResult & VIF_TEMPFILE) {
        wsprintf(szBuf, "%s%s%s", szDestDir,
            ((szDestDir[lstrlen(szDestDir) - 1] == '\\')
            ? "" : "\\"), szDestFileName);
        OpenFile(szBuf, &of, OF_DELETE);
    }
```

```
   if (x == IDRETRY)
      goto Retry;

   if (x == IDIGNORE)
      return(IF_SKIPTHISFILE);

   if (x == IDABORT)
      return(IF_ABORTSETUP);
}

if (dwVIFResult & VIF_CANNOTREADSRC)
   return(IF_CHANGEDISK);

// An unrecoverable error did NOT occur.
if (dwVIFResult & (VIF_MISMATCH | VIF_SRCOLD | VIF_DIFFLANG |
   VIF_DIFFCODEPG | VIF_DIFFTYPE)) {

   MISMATCHSTRUCT MismatchStruct;

   wsprintf(MismatchStruct.szExistingPath, "%s%s%s", szCurDir,
      ((szCurDir[lstrlen(szCurDir) - 1] == '\\') ? "" : "\\"),
      szDestFileName);

   wsprintf(MismatchStruct.szTmpPath, "%s%s%s", szDestDir,
      ((szDestDir[lstrlen(szDestDir) - 1] == '\\')
      ? "" : "\\"), szTmpFile);

   wsprintf(MismatchStruct.szSrcPath, "%s%s%s", szSrcDir,
      ((szSrcDir[lstrlen(szSrcDir) - 1] == '\\')
      ? "" : "\\"), szSrcFileName);

   MismatchStruct.dwVIFResult = dwVIFResult;
   x = DialogBoxParam(_hInstance,
      MAKEINTRESOURCE(DLG_MISMATCH), hWnd,
      (DLGPROC) MismatchDlgProc, (LPARAM) &MismatchStruct);
   if (x == IDYES) {
      // Force the installation.
      uFlags |= VIFF_FORCEINSTALL;
      goto Retry;
   }

   // You are not installing this file; delete the temporary file.
   if (dwVIFResult & VIF_TEMPFILE) {
      wsprintf(szBuf, "%s\\%s", szDestDir, szTmpFile);
      OpenFile(szBuf, &of, OF_DELETE);
   }

   if (x == IDNO)
      return(IF_SKIPTHISFILE);
```

```
    if (x == IDABORT)
        return(IF_ABORTSETUP);
  }
  return(IF_INSTALLEDOK);
}
```

Listing 10-4. SETUP.DEF application definitions file

```
; Module name: SETUP.DEF
; Programmer : Jeffrey M. Richter.

NAME          SETUP
DESCRIPTION 'Setup: Window Application installation Application'
STUB          'WinStub.exe'
EXETYPE       WINDOWS
;Segments must be NONDISCARDABLE so that Windows will not
;attempt to load a segment after the user has swapped diskettes.
CODE          MOVEABLE PRELOAD NONDISCARDABLE
DATA          MOVEABLE MULTIPLE PRELOAD
HEAPSIZE    1024
STACKSIZE   5120
```

Listing 10-5. SETUP.H application header module

```
/****************************************************************
Module name: SETUP.H
Programmer : Jeffrey M. Richter.
****************************************************************/

// Defines used by the SETUP program.
#define MAXPATH       80
#define MAXDRIVE       3
#define MAXDIR        66
#define MAXFILE        9
#define MAXEXT         5
#define MAXFILENAME  (MAXFILE + MAXEXT)

#define ARRAY_LEN(Array)  (sizeof(Array) / sizeof(Array[0]))
#define min(a,b)    (((a) < (b)) ? (a) : (b))
#define max(a,b)    (((a) > (b)) ? (a) : (b))

extern char _szAppName[];
extern const cdecl HINSTANCE _hInstance;
```

```
extern char _szSrcDir[MAXDIR];
extern char _szDstDir[MAXDIR];

extern HINSTANCE _hInstVer;    // Handle of VER.DLL library.
extern UINT (WINAPI *_VerFindFile)(UINT, LPCSTR, LPCSTR, LPCSTR,
   LPSTR, UINT FAR*, LPSTR, UINT FAR*);
extern DWORD (WINAPI* _VerInstallFile)(UINT, LPCSTR, LPCSTR,
   LPCSTR, LPCSTR, LPCSTR, LPSTR, UINT FAR*);
extern DWORD (WINAPI* _GetFileVersionInfoSize)
   (LPCSTR, DWORD FAR *);
extern BOOL  (WINAPI* _GetFileVersionInfo)
   (LPCSTR, DWORD, DWORD, void FAR*);
extern UINT  (WINAPI* _VerLanguageName)(UINT, LPSTR, UINT);
extern BOOL  (WINAPI* _VerQueryValue)
   (const void FAR*, LPCSTR, void FAR* FAR*, UINT FAR*);

// Prototypes for various functions.
BOOL WINAPI RegisterDDEClient (HINSTANCE hInstance);
BOOL CALLBACK InitDlgProc (HWND hDlg, UINT uMsg,
   WPARAM wParam, LPARAM lParam);
BOOL CALLBACK WelcomeDlgProc (HWND hDlg, UINT uMsg,
   WPARAM wParam, LPARAM lParam);
BOOL CALLBACK StatusDlgProc (HWND hDlg, UINT uMsg,
   WPARAM wParam, LPARAM lParam);
BOOL CALLBACK InsertDiskDlgProc (HWND hDlg, UINT uMsg,
   WPARAM wParam, LPARAM lParam);
BOOL CALLBACK FileInUseDlgProc (HWND hDlg, UINT uMsg,
   WPARAM wParam, LPARAM lParam);

typedef struct {
   char szExistingPath[MAXPATH], szSrcPath[MAXPATH];
   char szTmpPath[MAXPATH];
   DWORD dwVIFResult;
} MISMATCHSTRUCT, FAR *LPMISMATCHSTRUCT;
BOOL CALLBACK MismatchDlgProc (HWND hDlg, UINT uMsg,
   WPARAM wParam, LPARAM lParam);

typedef struct {
   char szDstFileName[MAXPATH], szDstDir[MAXPATH];
   char szCurDir[MAXPATH];
} CURNEDESTSTRUCT, FAR *LPCURNEDESTSTRUCT;
BOOL CALLBACK CurNEDestDlgProc (HWND hDlg, UINT uMsg,
   WPARAM wParam, LPARAM lParam);

int _cdecl MsgBox (HINSTANCE hInstance, HWND hWnd, WORD wID,
   LPCSTR szCaption, WORD wType, ...);

// Defines for use with SETUP's string table.
#define IDS_CANNOTINIT         1001
```

```
#define IDS_NOMEMORY          1002
#define IDS_NOSETUPINFOFILE   1003
#define IDS_NODISKSPACE       1004
#define IDS_SETUPNOGOOD       1005
#define IDS_PMADDOK           1006
#define IDS_PMADDNOGOOD       1007
#define IDS_CANTMAKEDIR       1008
#define IDS_QUERYABORT        1009
#define IDS_FILEINUSE         1010
#define IDS_UNRECOVERABLE     1011
#define IDS_OUTOFSPACE        1012
#define IDS_ACCESSVIOLATION   1013
#define IDS_SHARINGVIOLATION  1014
#define IDS_CANNOTCREATE      1015
#define IDS_CANNOTDELETE      1016
#define IDS_CANNOTRENAME      1017
#define IDS_OUTOFMEMORY       1018
#define IDS_CANNOTREADSRC     1019
#define IDS_CANNOTREADDST     1020
#define IDS_WRITEPROT         1021
#define IDS_MISMATCH          1022
#define IDS_SRCOLD            1023
#define IDS_DIFFLANG          1024
#define IDS_DIFFCODEPG        1025
#define IDS_DIFFTYPE          1026


//***** Macros for Using Window and Class Extra Bytes ************

#define GETWNDEB(hWnd, Struct, Member) \
    ( \
        (sizeof(((Struct FAR *)0)->Member) == sizeof(LONG)) ? \
        ((LONG)GetWindowLong(hWnd, FIELDOFFSET(Struct, Member))) :\
        ((WORD)GetWindowWord(hWnd, FIELDOFFSET(Struct, Member))) \
    )

#define SETWNDEB(hWnd, Struct, Member, Value) \
    ( \
        (sizeof(((Struct FAR *)0)->Member) == sizeof(LONG)) ? \
        ((LONG)SetWindowLong(hWnd, FIELDOFFSET(Struct, Member), \
            (LONG)(Value))) : \
        ((WORD)SetWindowWord(hWnd, FIELDOFFSET(Struct, Member), \
            (WORD)(Value))) \
    )

#define GETCLSEB(hWnd, Struct, Member) \
    ( \
        (sizeof(((Struct FAR *)0)->Member) == sizeof(LONG)) ? \
        ((LONG)GetClassLong(hWnd, FIELDOFFSET(Struct, Member))) : \
        ((WORD)GetClassWord(hWnd, FIELDOFFSET(Struct, Member))) \
```

```
    )

#define SETCLSEB(hWnd, Struct, Member, Value) \
    ( \
        (sizeof((((Struct FAR *)0)->Member) == sizeof(LONG)) ? \
        ((LONG)SetClassLong(hWnd, FIELDOFFSET(Struct, Member), \
            (LONG)(Value))) : \
        ((WORD)SetClassWord(hWnd, FIELDOFFSET(Struct, Member), \
            (WORD)(Value))) \
    )

//************* Identifiers Used in Dialog Boxes ****************
#define DLG_FIRST           1
#define DLG_INITIALIZE      1
#define DLG_WELCOME         2
#define DLG_INSERTDISK      3
#define DLG_STATUS          4
#define DLG_CURNEDEST       5
#define DLG_FILEINUSE       6
#define DLG_MISMATCH        7
#define DLG_LAST            7
#define ICN_FIRST           10
#define ICN_SETUP           10
#define ICN_DISK            11
#define ICN_LAST            11

#define ID_METER            100
#define ID_DESTPATH         101
#define ID_DISKNAME         102
#define ID_STATLINE1        103
#define ID_STATLINE2        104
#define ID_SRCPATH          105

// Identifiers for CURNEDEST dialog box.
#define ID_DSTFILENAME      100
#define ID_DSTDIR           101
#define ID_CURDIR           102
#define ID_INSTALLANDDELETE 103
#define ID_INSTALLANDKEEP   104
#define ID_REPLACEEXISTING  105
#define ID_SKIPINSTALL      106
#define ID_ABORTINSTALL     107

// Identifiers for FILEINUSE dialog box.
#define ID_FILENAMEINUSE    100
    // Also uses IDRETRY, IDABORT, IDIGNORE, and IDOK.

// Identifiers for DLG_MISMATCH dialog box.
#define ID_VERMISMATCHTEXT  100
```

```
#define ID_VERINFOEXISTING     101
#define ID_VERINFONEW          102
    // Also uses IDOK, IDCANCEL, and IDABORT.
```

Listing 10-6. SETUP.RC application resource file. Note that the strings are broken here to accommodate the narrow page width and would not normally break.

```
/************************************************************************
Module name: SETUP.RC
Programmer : Jeffrey M. Richter.
*************************************************************************/

#include <windows.h>
#include <ver.h>
#include "setup.h"

ICN_SETUP     ICON      PRELOAD FIXED Setup.Ico
ICN_DISK      ICON      PRELOAD FIXED Disk.Ico

STRINGTABLE PRELOAD FIXED
BEGIN
IDS_CANNOTINIT,
    "Cannot initialize Setup."
IDS_NOMEMORY,
    "Insufficient memory to run Setup. Close some applications and try
again."
IDS_NOSETUPINFOFILE,
    "The %s file cannot be found. Please verify the distribution diskette."
IDS_NODISKSPACE,
    "Drive %c: contains %ldK of free disk space. Setup requires a minimum of
%ldK. Please select another drive."
IDS_SETUPNOGOOD,
    "The software has not been successfully installed. You must run Setup
again before using the software."
IDS_PMADDOK,
    "Setup has installed the software successfully and added the applica-
tion(s) to the Program Manager."
IDS_PMADDNOGOOD,
    "Setup has installed the software successfully but could not add the
application(s) to the Program Manager."
IDS_CANTMAKEDIR,
    "The %s directory cannot be created. Enter another directory or try
another drive."
IDS_QUERYABORT,
    "Setup has not completed installing the software. Are you sure you want
to cancel?"
```

```
IDS_FILEINUSE,
    "%s is in use."
IDS_OUTOFSPACE,
    "Insufficient space on destination drive."
IDS_ACCESSVIOLATION,
    "An access violation occurred."
IDS_SHARINGVIOLATION,
    "A sharing violation occurred."
IDS_CANNOTCREATE,
    "The new file could not be created on the destination drive."
IDS_CANNOTDELETE,
    "The existing file or temporary file could not be deleted."
IDS_CANNOTRENAME,
    "The temporary file cannot be renamed."
IDS_OUTOFMEMORY,
    "Insufficient memory to install file."
IDS_CANNOTREADSRC,
    "The source file cannot be read."
IDS_CANNOTREADDST,
    "The existing file cannot be read."
IDS_WRITEPROT,
    "The existing file is write protected."
IDS_MISMATCH,
    "Existing file and new file mismatch."
IDS_SRCOLD,
    "The new file is older than the existing file."
IDS_DIFFLANG,
    "Existing and new files are different languages."
IDS_DIFFCODEPG,
    "Existing and new files are different code pages."
IDS_DIFFTYPE,
    "Existing and new files are different types."
END


DLG_INITIALIZE DIALOG PRELOAD FIXED 0, 0, 192, 33
STYLE DS_MODALFRAME | WS_POPUP | WS_VISIBLE
FONT 6, "Helv"
BEGIN
    CONTROL "Initializing Setup\nPlease wait...",
        -1, "static", SS_CENTER | SS_NOPREFIX | WS_CHILD |
        WS_VISIBLE, 8, 8, 180, 20
END

DLG_WELCOME DIALOG PRELOAD FIXED 0, 0, 192, 100
CAPTION "Caption"
FONT 6, "Helv"
STYLE WS_BORDER | WS_CAPTION | WS_DLGFRAME | WS_SYSMENU |
    DS_MODALFRAME | WS_POPUP
BEGIN
```

```
    CONTROL "Setup will install this application into the following direc-
tory, which it will create on your hard disk.", -1, "static", SS_LEFT |
WS_CHILD, 8, 8, 180, 20
    CONTROL "If you want to install the application in a different directory
and/or drive. Type the name of the directory below:", -1, "static", SS_LEFT
| WS_CHILD, 8, 32, 180, 28
    CONTROL "Copy to:", -1, "static",
        SS_LEFT | WS_CHILD, 32, 60, 32, 12
    CONTROL "", ID_DESTPATH, "edit", ES_AUTOHSCROLL | ES_LEFT |
        ES_UPPERCASE | WS_BORDER | WS_TABSTOP | WS_CHILD,
        64, 60, 84, 12
    CONTROL "&Ok", IDOK, "button", BS_DEFPUSHBUTTON |
        WS_TABSTOP | WS_CHILD, 48, 80, 32, 16
    CONTROL "&Cancel", IDCANCEL, "button", BS_PUSHBUTTON |
        WS_TABSTOP | WS_CHILD, 108, 80, 32, 16
END

DLG_INSERTDISK DIALOG PRELOAD FIXED 0, 0, 192, 72
CAPTION "Caption"
FONT 6, "Helv"
STYLE WS_BORDER | WS_CAPTION | WS_DLGFRAME | WS_SYSMENU |
    DS_MODALFRAME | WS_POPUP
BEGIN
    CONTROL "#11", -1, "static", SS_ICON | WS_CHILD, 4, 4, 16, 16
    CONTROL "Setup needs the following disk:", -1, "static",
        SS_LEFT | WS_CHILD, 40, 4, 112, 8
    CONTROL "Application Diskette", ID_DISKNAME, "static",
        SS_LEFT | WS_CHILD, 40, 12, 112, 12
    CONTROL "", ID_SRCPATH, "edit", ES_LEFT | ES_UPPERCASE |
        WS_BORDER | WS_TABSTOP | WS_CHILD, 16, 32, 160, 12
    CONTROL "&Ok", IDOK, "button", BS_DEFPUSHBUTTON | WS_TABSTOP |
        WS_CHILD, 48, 52, 32, 16
    CONTROL "&Cancel", IDCANCEL, "button", BS_PUSHBUTTON |
        WS_TABSTOP | WS_CHILD, 112, 52, 32, 16
END

DLG_STATUS DIALOG PRELOAD FIXED 0, 0, 188, 68
CAPTION "Caption"
FONT 6, "Helv"
STYLE DS_MODALFRAME | WS_POPUP | WS_CAPTION | WS_SYSMENU
BEGIN
    CONTROL "", ID_STATLINE1, "static", SS_LEFT | WS_CHILD,
        4, 4, 144, 12
    CONTROL "", ID_STATLINE2, "static", SS_LEFT | WS_CHILD,
        4, 16, 144, 12
    CONTROL "", ID_METER, "meter", WS_BORDER | WS_CHILD,
        16, 28, 156, 12
    CONTROL "&Cancel", IDCANCEL, "button", BS_DEFPUSHBUTTON |
        WS_TABSTOP | WS_CHILD, 76, 48, 32, 16
```

```
END


DLG_CURNEDEST DIALOG PRELOAD FIXED 18, 18, 170, 162
CAPTION "Caption"
FONT 6, "helv"
STYLE DS_MODALFRAME | WS_POPUP | WS_VISIBLE |
    WS_CAPTION | WS_SYSMENU
BEGIN
    CONTROL "Attempted to install the file:", -1, "STATIC",
        SS_LEFT | WS_CHILD | WS_VISIBLE | WS_GROUP, 4, 4, 160, 12
    CONTROL "FILENAME.EXT", ID_DSTFILENAME, "STATIC", SS_CENTER |
        SS_NOPREFIX | WS_CHILD | WS_VISIBLE | WS_GROUP,
        4, 16, 164, 12
    CONTROL "in this directory:", -1, "STATIC", SS_LEFT |
        WS_CHILD | WS_VISIBLE | WS_GROUP, 4, 28, 160, 12
    CONTROL "D:/DESIRED/PATH", ID_DSTDIR, "STATIC", SS_CENTER |
        SS_NOPREFIX | WS_CHILD | WS_VISIBLE | WS_GROUP, 4, 39, 164, 12
    CONTROL "but, it currently exists in:", -1, "STATIC",
        SS_LEFT | WS_CHILD | WS_VISIBLE | WS_GROUP, 4, 52, 160, 12
    CONTROL "D:/EXISTING/PATH", ID_CURDIR, "STATIC", SS_CENTER |
        SS_NOPREFIX | WS_CHILD | WS_VISIBLE | WS_GROUP,
        4, 63, 164, 12
    CONTROL "Install the new file and &delete the existing file",
        ID_INSTALLANDDELETE, "BUTTON", BS_AUTORADIOBUTTON |
        WS_CHILD | WS_VISIBLE | WS_TABSTOP, 4, 80, 164, 12
    CONTROL "Install the new file and &keep the existing file",
        ID_INSTALLANDKEEP, "BUTTON", BS_AUTORADIOBUTTON |
        WS_CHILD | WS_VISIBLE | WS_TABSTOP, 4, 92, 164, 12
    CONTROL "&Replace existing file with new file",
        ID_REPLACEEXISTING, "BUTTON", BS_AUTORADIOBUTTON |
        WS_CHILD | WS_VISIBLE | WS_TABSTOP, 4, 104, 164, 12
    CONTROL "Do &not install the new file", ID_SKIPINSTALL,
        "BUTTON", BS_AUTORADIOBUTTON | WS_CHILD | WS_VISIBLE |
        WS_TABSTOP, 4, 116, 156, 12
    CONTROL "&Abort the installation", ID_ABORTINSTALL, "BUTTON",
        BS_AUTORADIOBUTTON | WS_CHILD | WS_VISIBLE | WS_TABSTOP,
        4, 128, 100, 12
    CONTROL "&Ok", IDOK, "BUTTON", BS_DEFPUSHBUTTON | WS_CHILD |
        WS_VISIBLE | WS_TABSTOP, 64, 144, 32, 14
END


DLG_FILEINUSE DIALOG PRELOAD FIXED 18, 18, 245, 174
CAPTION "Caption"
FONT 6, "helv"
STYLE DS_MODALFRAME | WS_POPUP | WS_CAPTION | WS_SYSMENU
BEGIN
    CONTROL "Setup cannot install the following file because it is in use:",
-1, "STATIC", SS_LEFT | WS_CHILD | WS_VISIBLE | WS_GROUP, 4, 4, 228, 8
    CONTROL "D:/DIRECTORY/PATH/FILENAME.EXT", ID_FILENAMEINUSE,
```

```
        "STATIC", SS_CENTER | SS_NOPREFIX | WS_CHILD |
        WS_VISIBLE | WS_GROUP, 4, 12, 235, 12
    CONTROL "Select one of the following options:", -1, "STATIC",
        SS_LEFT | WS_CHILD | WS_VISIBLE | WS_GROUP, 4, 32, 188, 12
    CONTROL "A&ttempt to install the file again.", IDRETRY,
        "BUTTON", BS_AUTORADIOBUTTON | WS_CHILD | WS_VISIBLE |
        WS_TABSTOP, 4, 44, 200, 12
    CONTROL "You may close other applications using this file and attempt to
install the file again.", -1, "STATIC", SS_LEFT | WS_CHILD | WS_VISIBLE,
12, 57, 228, 16
    CONTROL "&Do not install this file", IDIGNORE, "BUTTON",
        BS_AUTORADIOBUTTON | WS_CHILD | WS_VISIBLE | WS_TABSTOP,
        4, 80, 216, 12
    CONTROL "Setup will not install this file.  You will have to run Setup
again or install the file manually.  Refer to the documentation for more
information.", -1, "STATIC", SS_LEFT | WS_CHILD | WS_VISIBLE, 12, 93, 228, 24
    CONTROL "&Abort Setup.", IDABORT, "BUTTON",
        BS_AUTORADIOBUTTON | WS_CHILD | WS_VISIBLE | WS_TABSTOP,
        4, 124, 96, 12
    CONTROL "Terminate the installation.  You will have to run Setup again
to use the software.", -1, "STATIC", SS_LEFT | WS_CHILD | WS_VISIBLE, 12,
137, 228, 16
    CONTROL "&Ok", IDOK, "BUTTON", BS_DEFPUSHBUTTON | WS_CHILD |
        WS_VISIBLE | WS_GROUP | WS_TABSTOP, 108, 156, 28, 14
END

DLG_MISMATCH DIALOG PRELOAD FIXED 6, 16, 244, 164
CAPTION "Caption"
FONT 6, "helv"
STYLE DS_MODALFRAME | WS_POPUP | WS_CAPTION | WS_SYSMENU
BEGIN
    CONTROL "Why the mismatch occurred goes here",
        ID_VERMISMATCHTEXT, "STATIC", SS_CENTER | WS_CHILD |
        WS_VISIBLE | WS_GROUP, 4, 3, 236, 12
    CONTROL "&Existing file information:", -1, "STATIC",
        SS_LEFT | WS_CHILD | WS_VISIBLE | WS_GROUP, 4, 14, 108, 8
    CONTROL "", ID_VERINFOEXISTING, "LISTBOX", LBS_NOTIFY |
        LBS_USETABSTOPS | WS_CHILD | WS_VISIBLE | WS_BORDER |
        WS_VSCROLL | WS_HSCROLL | WS_GROUP | WS_TABSTOP,
        4, 24, 236, 52
    CONTROL "&New file information:", -1, "STATIC", SS_LEFT |
        WS_CHILD | WS_VISIBLE | WS_GROUP, 4, 80, 108, 8
    CONTROL "", ID_VERINFONEW, "LISTBOX", LBS_NOTIFY |
        LBS_USETABSTOPS | WS_CHILD | WS_VISIBLE | WS_BORDER |
        WS_VSCROLL | WS_HSCROLL | WS_GROUP | WS_TABSTOP,
        4, 92, 236, 52
    CONTROL "&Install new file", IDYES, "BUTTON",
        BS_DEFPUSHBUTTON | WS_CHILD | WS_VISIBLE | WS_TABSTOP,
        4, 148, 72, 12
```

```
    CONTROL "&Keep existing file", IDNO, "BUTTON",
        BS_PUSHBUTTON | WS_CHILD | WS_VISIBLE | WS_TABSTOP,
        86, 148, 72, 12
    CONTROL "&Abort Setup", IDABORT, "BUTTON", BS_PUSHBUTTON |
        WS_CHILD | WS_VISIBLE | WS_TABSTOP, 168, 148, 72, 12
END


// The version information resource
VS_VERSION_INFO          VERSIONINFO
FILEVERSION              2, 0
PRODUCTVERSION           2, 0
FILEFLAGSMASK            VS_FFI_FILEFLAGSMASK
FILEFLAGS                0
FILEOS                   VOS_DOS_WINDOWS16
FILETYPE                 VFT_APP
FILESUBTYPE              VFT2_UNKNOWN
BEGIN
    BLOCK "VarFileInfo"
    BEGIN
        VALUE "Translation", 0x409, 1252
    END


    BLOCK "StringFileInfo"
    BEGIN
        BLOCK "040904E4"
        BEGIN
//          VALUE "Comments",         "\0"
            VALUE "CompanyName",      "Jeffrey M. Richter\0"
            VALUE "FileDescription",  "Setup: Application Installer Program\0"
            VALUE "FileVersion",      "2.00\0"
            VALUE "InternalName",     "SETUP.EXE\0"
            VALUE "LegalCopyright",   "Copyright \251 1992 Jeffrey Richter\0"
//          VALUE "LegalTrademarks",  "\0"
            VALUE "OriginalFilename", "SETUP.EXE\0"
//          VALUE "PrivateBuild",     "\0"
            VALUE "ProductName",      "Windows 3.1: A Developer's Guide\0"
            VALUE "ProductVersion",   "2.00\0"
//          VALUE "SpecialBuild",     "\0"
        END
    END
END
```

Listing 10-7. SETUPDLG.CPP dialog-box source module

```c
/******************************************************************
Module name: SETUPDLG.C
Programmer : Jeffrey M. Richter.
******************************************************************/

#include <windows.h>
#include <windowsx.h>
#include <Ver.h>
#include <StdLib.h>
#include "..\Meter.04\Meter.H"
#include "Setup.h"
#include "SetupInf.h"

void PrepareDialogBox (HWND hWnd, BOOL fBeep) {
   RECT rc; char szBuf[MAXAPPNAME];
   GetWindowRect(hWnd, &rc);
   SetWindowPos(hWnd, NULL,
      (GetSystemMetrics(SM_CXSCREEN) - (rc.right - rc.left)) / 2,
      (GetSystemMetrics(SM_CYSCREEN) - (rc.bottom - rc.top)) / 3,
      0, 0, SWP_NOSIZE | SWP_NOZORDER);

   // Place the correct title in the dialog-box caption.
   _SetupInfo.GetAppName(szBuf);
   SetWindowText(hWnd, szBuf);
   if (fBeep) MessageBeep(0);
}

WORD WINAPI GetCheckedRadioBtn (HWND hDlg, WORD wStartId,
   WORD wEndId) {
   for (; wStartId <= wEndId; wStartId++) {
      if (IsDlgButtonChecked(hDlg, wStartId)) return(wStartId);
   }
   return(-1);
}

// ******************************************************************
// Setup's initializing screen.
#pragma argsused
BOOL CALLBACK InitDlgProc (HWND hDlg, UINT uMsg,
   WPARAM wParam, LPARAM lParam) {

   BOOL fProcessed = TRUE;

   switch (uMsg) {
      case WM_INITDIALOG:
         PrepareDialogBox(hDlg, FALSE);
```

```
            UpdateWindow(hDlg);
            break;

        default:
            fProcessed = FALSE;
            break;
    }
    return(fProcessed);
}

// ****************************************************************
// Initial sign on screen. Asks user for destination directory.
BOOL CALLBACK WelcomeDlgProc (HWND hDlg, UINT uMsg,
    WPARAM wParam, LPARAM lParam) {

    BOOL fProcessed = TRUE;
    char szBuf[MAXDIR];
    OFSTRUCT ofStruct;

    switch (uMsg) {
        case WM_INITDIALOG:
            PrepareDialogBox(hDlg, FALSE);

            _SetupInfo.GetDefaultDstDir(szBuf);
            SetDlgItemText(hDlg, ID_DESTPATH, szBuf);
            Edit_LimitText(GetDlgItem(hDlg, ID_DESTPATH),
                sizeof(szBuf));
            break;

        case WM_COMMAND:
            switch (wParam) {
                case ID_DESTPATH:
                    EnableWindow(GetDlgItem(hDlg, IDOK),
                        Edit_LineLength(LOWORD(lParam), 0) > 0);
                    break;

                case IDOK:
                    GetDlgItemText(hDlg, ID_DESTPATH,
                        szBuf, sizeof(szBuf));
                    OpenFile(szBuf, &ofStruct, OF_PARSE);
                    lstrcpy(_szDstDir, (LPSTR) ofStruct.szPathName);
                    // Do IDCANCEL case.

                case IDCANCEL:
                    EndDialog(hDlg, wParam);
                    break;
            }
            break;
```

```
    default:
        fProcessed = FALSE;
        break;
    }
    return(fProcessed);
}


// ********************************************************************
// Displays copying status. Allows user to cancel setup.
#pragma argsused
BOOL CALLBACK StatusDlgProc (HWND hDlg, UINT uMsg,
    WPARAM wParam, LPARAM lParam) {

    BOOL fProcessed = TRUE;
    int nResult;

    switch (uMsg) {
        case WM_INITDIALOG:
            PrepareDialogBox(hDlg, FALSE);
            break;

        case WM_SHOWWINDOW:
            fProcessed = FALSE;
            if (!wParam) break;
            EnableWindow(GetDlgItem(hDlg, IDCANCEL), TRUE);
            SetDlgItemText(hDlg, ID_STATLINE1, "");
            SetDlgItemText(hDlg, ID_STATLINE2, "");
            SendDlgItemMessage(hDlg, ID_METER,
                MM_SETPARTSCOMPLETE, 0, 0);
            SendDlgItemMessage(hDlg, ID_METER,
                MM_SETPARTSINJOB, 0, 0);
            break;

        case WM_COMMAND:
            switch (wParam) {
                case IDOK:
                    // User presses ENTER. DO IDCANCEL case.

                case IDCANCEL:
                    nResult = MsgBox(_hInstance, hDlg, IDS_QUERYABORT,
                        _szAppName, MB_ICONQUESTION | MB_YESNO);
                    if (nResult == IDYES)
                        EnableWindow(GetDlgItem(hDlg, IDCANCEL), FALSE);
                    break;
                }
            break;

        default:
            fProcessed = FALSE;
```

```
            break;
    }
    return(fProcessed);
}

// ****************************************************************
// Prompts user to insert a different diskette.
BOOL CALLBACK InsertDiskDlgProc (HWND hDlg, UINT uMsg,
    WPARAM wParam, LPARAM lParam) {

    BOOL fProcessed = TRUE;
    int nResult;

    switch (uMsg) {
        case WM_INITDIALOG:
            PrepareDialogBox(hDlg, TRUE);

            // lParam is address of diskette description.
            // Throw away the data segment and use the new one.
            // This is in case the data segment has moved.
            SetDlgItemText(hDlg, ID_DISKNAME, (LPSTR) lParam);
            SetDlgItemText(hDlg, ID_SRCPATH, _szSrcDir);
            Edit_LimitText(GetDlgItem(hDlg, ID_SRCPATH),
                sizeof(_szSrcDir));
            break;

        case WM_COMMAND:
            switch (wParam) {
                case ID_SRCPATH:
                    EnableWindow(GetDlgItem(hDlg, IDOK),
                        Edit_LineLength(LOWORD(lParam), 0) > 0);
                    break;

                case IDOK:
                    GetDlgItemText(hDlg, ID_SRCPATH,
                        _szSrcDir, sizeof(_szSrcDir));
                    EndDialog(hDlg, wParam);
                    break;

                case IDCANCEL:
                    nResult = MsgBox(_hInstance, hDlg, IDS_QUERYABORT,
                        _szAppName, MB_ICONQUESTION | MB_YESNO);
                    if (nResult == IDNO) break;
                    EndDialog(hDlg, wParam);
                    break;
            }
            break;

        default:
```

```
            fProcessed = FALSE;
            break;
    }
    return(fProcessed);
}

// ****************************************************************
BOOL CALLBACK CurNEDestDlgProc (HWND hDlg, UINT uMsg,
    WPARAM wParam, LPARAM lParam) {

    BOOL fProcessed = TRUE;
    LPCURNEDESTSTRUCT lpCurNEDestStruct;
    UINT x;
    int nResult;

    switch (uMsg) {
        case WM_INITDIALOG:
            PrepareDialogBox(hDlg, TRUE);

            lpCurNEDestStruct = (LPCURNEDESTSTRUCT) lParam;
            SetDlgItemText(hDlg, ID_DSTFILENAME,
                lpCurNEDestStruct->szDstFileName);
            SetDlgItemText(hDlg, ID_DSTDIR,
                lpCurNEDestStruct->szDstDir);
            SetDlgItemText(hDlg, ID_CURDIR,
                lpCurNEDestStruct->szCurDir);
            CheckRadioButton(hDlg, ID_INSTALLANDDELETE,
                ID_ABORTINSTALL, ID_INSTALLANDDELETE);
            break;

        case WM_COMMAND:
            if (wParam != IDOK) break;
            x = GetCheckedRadioBtn(hDlg,
                ID_INSTALLANDDELETE, ID_ABORTINSTALL);
            if (x == ID_ABORTINSTALL) {
                nResult = MsgBox(_hInstance, hDlg, IDS_QUERYABORT,
                    _szAppName, MB_ICONQUESTION | MB_YESNO);
                if (nResult == IDNO) break;
            }
            EndDialog(hDlg, x);
            break;

        default: fProcessed = FALSE; break;
    }
    return(fProcessed);
}

// ****************************************************************
BOOL CALLBACK FileInUseDlgProc (HWND hDlg, UINT uMsg,
```

```
      WPARAM wParam, LPARAM lParam) {

   BOOL fProcessed = TRUE;
   UINT x;
   int nResult;

   switch (uMsg) {
      case WM_INITDIALOG:
         PrepareDialogBox(hDlg, TRUE);
         SetDlgItemText(hDlg, ID_FILENAMEINUSE, (LPSTR) lParam);
         CheckRadioButton(hDlg, IDABORT, IDIGNORE, IDRETRY);
         break;

      case WM_COMMAND:
         if (wParam != IDOK) break;
         x = GetCheckedRadioBtn(hDlg, IDABORT, IDIGNORE);
         if (x == IDABORT) {
            nResult = MsgBox(_hInstance, hDlg, IDS_QUERYABORT,
               _szAppName, MB_ICONQUESTION | MB_YESNO);
            if (nResult == IDNO) break;
         }
         EndDialog(hDlg, x);
         break;

      default: fProcessed = FALSE; break;
   }
   return(fProcessed);
}

// ****************************************************************
char _szUnknown[] = "Unknown";

enum VERFILEFIXFIELD {
   VF_FF_FILEVER, VF_FF_PRODVER, VF_FF_FILEFLAGS,
   VF_FF_OPSYS, VF_FF_FILETYPE
};

char *szVerFileFixedField[] = {
   "File version",
   "Product version",
   "File flags",
   "Operating sys",
   "File type"
};

enum VERFILEVARFIELD {
   VF_VF_COMMENTS, VF_VF_COMPANY, VF_VF_DESC, VF_VF_FILEVER,
   VF_VF_INTERNALNAME, VF_VF_COPYRIGHT, VF_VF_TRADEMARKS,
   VF_VF_ORIGNAME, VF_VF_PRVTBLD, VF_VF_PRODNAME, VF_VF_PRODVER,
```

669

```
    VF_VF_SPECIALBLD
};

char *szVerFileVarField[][2] = {
    { "Comments",         "Comments"        },
    { "Company",          "CompanyName"     },
    { "Description",      "FileDescription" },
    { "File version",     "FileVersion"     },
    { "Internal name",    "InternalName"    },
    { "Copyright",        "LegalCopyright"  },
    { "Trademarks",       "LegalTrademarks" },
    { "Original name",    "OriginalFilename"},
    { "Private build",    "PrivateBuild"    },
    { "Product name",     "ProductName"     },
    { "Product version",  "ProductVersion"  },
    { "Special build",    "SpecialBuild"    }
};

static BOOL NEAR GetVerInfo (LPCSTR szPathname, HWND hwndLB) {
    LPSTR szFileType, szFileSubtype, p, q;
    void FAR *lpVerInfo;
    VS_FIXEDFILEINFO FAR *lpVSFixedFileInfo;
    UINT uLen, x, uMaxFieldLen = 0;
    DWORD dwVerInfoSize, dwHandle;
    HGLOBAL hGlbl;
    char szBuf[100], szVXDID[10];
    HDC hDC;
    HFONT hFont;

    ListBox_ResetContent(hwndLB);
    dwVerInfoSize = _GetFileVersionInfoSize(szPathname, &dwHandle);
    if (dwVerInfoSize == 0) // No version information exists.
        return(FALSE);

    hGlbl = GlobalAlloc(GMEM_MOVEABLE, dwVerInfoSize);
    if (hGlbl == NULL)
        return(FALSE);

    lpVerInfo = GlobalLock(hGlbl);
    x = _GetFileVersionInfo(szPathname, dwHandle,
        dwVerInfoSize, lpVerInfo);
    if (x == 0) {
        // Couldn't get the version information for some reason.
        GlobalUnlock(hGlbl);
        GlobalFree(hGlbl);
        return(FALSE);
    }

    // Find the address of the VS_FIXEDFILEINFO structure.
```

```
if (!_VerQueryValue(lpVerInfo, "\\",
    (void FAR * FAR *) &lpVSFixedFileInfo, &uLen) ||
    (uLen == 0)) {
  // VS_FIXEDFILEINFO structure is not available.
  ListBox_AddString(hwndLB,
      "Version information is not available.");
  GlobalUnlock(hGlbl);
  GlobalFree(hGlbl);
  return(FALSE);
}

SetWindowRedraw(hwndLB, FALSE);
hDC = GetDC(hwndLB);
hFont = GetWindowFont(hwndLB);
if (hFont != NULL)
  SelectObject(hDC, hFont);

// Cycle through all the members in VS_FIXEDFILEINFO.
for (x = 0; x < ARRAY_LEN(szVerFileFixedField); x++) {
  p = szBuf +
      wsprintf(szBuf, "%s:\t", szVerFileFixedField[x]);

  uMaxFieldLen = max(uMaxFieldLen, LOWORD(
      GetTextExtent(hDC, szBuf, (int) (p - szBuf) - 1)));

  switch (x) {
  case VF_FF_FILEVER:
    wsprintf(p, "%d.%d.%d.%d",
        HIWORD(lpVSFixedFileInfo->dwFileVersionMS),
        LOWORD(lpVSFixedFileInfo->dwFileVersionMS),
        HIWORD(lpVSFixedFileInfo->dwFileVersionLS),
        LOWORD(lpVSFixedFileInfo->dwFileVersionLS));
    break;

  case VF_FF_PRODVER:
    wsprintf(p, "%d.%d.%d.%d",
        HIWORD(lpVSFixedFileInfo->dwProductVersionMS),
        LOWORD(lpVSFixedFileInfo->dwProductVersionMS),
        HIWORD(lpVSFixedFileInfo->dwProductVersionLS),
        LOWORD(lpVSFixedFileInfo->dwProductVersionLS));
    break;

  case VF_FF_FILEFLAGS:
    DWORD dwNum = lpVSFixedFileInfo->dwFileFlags;
    if (dwNum & VS_FF_DEBUG)
      lstrcat(p, "Debug ");
    if (dwNum & VS_FF_PRERELEASE)
      lstrcat(p, "Pre-release ");
    if (dwNum & VS_FF_PATCHED)
```

671

```
            lstrcat(p, "Patched ");
        if (dwNum & VS_FF_PRIVATEBUILD)
            lstrcat(p, "Private ");
        if (dwNum & VS_FF_INFOINFERRED)
            lstrcat(p, "Info ");
        if (dwNum & VS_FF_SPECIALBUILD)
            lstrcat(p, "Special ");
        if (dwNum == 0)
            lstrcat(p, "No flags");
        break;

    case VF_FF_OPSYS:
        switch (lpVSFixedFileInfo->dwFileOS) {
            case VOS_DOS:
                q = "DOS"; break;
            case VOS_DOS_WINDOWS16:
                q = "Windows 3.0 or later under DOS"; break;
            case VOS_DOS_WINDOWS32:
                q = "Windows-32 under DOS"; break;
            case VOS_OS216:
                q = "OS/2-16"; break;
            case VOS_OS216_PM16:
                q = "OS/2-16 PM-16"; break;
            case VOS_OS232:
                q = "OS/2-32"; break;
            case VOS_OS232_PM32:
                q = "OS/2-32 PM-32"; break;
            case VOS_NT:
                q = "Windows NT"; break;
            case VOS_NT_WINDOWS32:
                q = "Windows-32 under Windows-NT"; break;
            case VOS_UNKNOWN:
                default: q = _szUnknown; break;
        }
        lstrcat(p, q); break;

    case VF_FF_FILETYPE:
        szFileSubtype = NULL;
        switch (lpVSFixedFileInfo->dwFileType) {
        case VFT_UNKNOWN: default:
            szFileType = _szUnknown; break;
        case VFT_APP:
            szFileType = "Application"; break;
        case VFT_DLL:
            szFileType = "Dynamic-link library"; break;
        case VFT_DRV:
            szFileType = "Device driver";
            switch (lpVSFixedFileInfo->dwFileSubtype) {
            case VFT2_UNKNOWN:
```

```
        default: szFileSubtype = _szUnknown; break;
    case VFT2_DRV_PRINTER:
        szFileSubtype = "Printer"; break;
    case VFT2_DRV_KEYBOARD:
        szFileSubtype = "Keyboard"; break;
    case VFT2_DRV_LANGUAGE:
        szFileSubtype = "Language"; break;
    case VFT2_DRV_DISPLAY:
        szFileSubtype = "Display"; break;
    case VFT2_DRV_MOUSE:
        szFileSubtype = "Mouse"; break;
    case VFT2_DRV_NETWORK:
        szFileSubtype = "Network"; break;
    case VFT2_DRV_SYSTEM:
        szFileSubtype = "System"; break;
    case VFT2_DRV_INSTALLABLE:
        szFileSubtype = "Installable"; break;
    case VFT2_DRV_SOUND:
        szFileSubtype = "Sound"; break;
    case VFT2_DRV_COMM:
        szFileSubtype = "Communication"; break;
    }
    break;

case VFT_FONT:
    szFileType = "Font";
    switch (lpVSFixedFileInfo->dwFileSubtype) {
    case VFT2_UNKNOWN: default:
        szFileSubtype = _szUnknown; break;
    case VFT2_FONT_RASTER:
        szFileSubtype = "Raster"; break;
    case VFT2_FONT_VECTOR:
        szFileSubtype = "Vector"; break;
    case VFT2_FONT_TRUETYPE:
        szFileSubtype = "TrueType"; break;
    }
    break;

case VFT_VXD:
    szFileType = "Virtual device";
    ltoa(lpVSFixedFileInfo->dwFileSubtype,
        szFileSubtype = szVXDID, 10);
    break;

case VFT_STATIC_LIB:
    szFileType = "Static-link library"; break;
} // Switch (lpVSFixedFileInfo->dwFileType).

wsprintf(p, "%s%s%s%s", szFileType,
```

```
            ((szFileSubtype == NULL) ? "" : " ("),
            ((szFileSubtype == NULL) ? "" : szFileSubtype),
            ((szFileSubtype == NULL) ? "" : ")"));
    }  // Switch.
    ListBox_AddString(hwndLB, szBuf);
}  // for

// Variable file Version information.

// Use the first translation Langauge-CharSet pair.

_VerQueryValue(lpVerInfo, "\\VarFileInfo\\Translation",
    (VOID FAR * FAR *) &p, &x);

char szStringName[50];
DWORD dwTranslation = * ((DWORD FAR *) p);
WORD wRootLen = wsprintf(szStringName,
    "\\StringFileInfo\\%04x%04x\\",
    LOWORD(dwTranslation), HIWORD(dwTranslation));

p = szBuf + wsprintf(szBuf, "Language:\t");
_VerLanguageName(LOWORD(dwTranslation), p,
    (UINT) (sizeof(szBuf) - (p - szBuf)));
ListBox_AddString(hwndLB, szBuf);

// Cycle through all the StringNames.
for (x = 0; x < ARRAY_LEN(szVerFileVarField); x++) {
    p = szBuf +
        wsprintf(szBuf, "%s:\t", szVerFileVarField[x][0]);

    uMaxFieldLen = max(uMaxFieldLen, LOWORD(
        GetTextExtent(hDC, szBuf, (int) (p - szBuf) - 1)));

    lstrcat(szStringName, szVerFileVarField[x][1]);
    WORD wStringLen;
    if (!_VerQueryValue(lpVerInfo, szStringName,
        (VOID FAR * FAR *) &p, (UINT FAR *) &wStringLen) ||
        (wStringLen == 0))
        lstrcat(szBuf, _szUnknown);
    else lstrcat(szBuf, p);
    ListBox_AddString(hwndLB, szBuf);

    // Be sure to reset to zero so that you can contact.
    szStringName[wRootLen] = 0;
}
ReleaseDC(hwndLB, hDC);

RECT rc;
SetRect(&rc, 4, 8, 0, 0);
```

```
      MapDialogRect(GetParent(hwndLB), &rc);
      x = 6 + ((uMaxFieldLen * 4) / rc.left);
      ListBox_SetTabStops(hwndLB, 1, &x);

      ListBox_SetHorizontalExtent(hwndLB,
         2 * GetSystemMetrics(SM_CXSCREEN));
      SetWindowRedraw(hwndLB, TRUE);
      InvalidateRect(hwndLB, NULL, TRUE);

      GlobalUnlock(hGlbl);
      GlobalFree(hGlbl);
      return(TRUE);
   }

static LRESULT ListBoxSubclass (HWND hWnd, UINT uMsg,
   WPARAM wParam, LPARAM lParam) {

   if ((uMsg == WM_HSCROLL) || (uMsg == WM_VSCROLL))
      FORWARD_WM_COMMAND(GetParent(hWnd), GetWindowID(hWnd),
         hWnd, LBN_SELCHANGE, PostMessage);

   return(CallWindowProc((FARPROC)
      GetClassLong(hWnd, GCL_WNDPROC), hWnd, uMsg,
      wParam, lParam));
   }

BOOL CALLBACK MismatchDlgProc (HWND hDlg, UINT uMsg,
   WPARAM wParam, LPARAM lParam) {

   BOOL fProcessed = TRUE;
   LPMISMATCHSTRUCT lpMismatchStruct;
   char szBuf[100];
   WORD x;
   int nResult;

   switch (uMsg) {
      case WM_INITDIALOG:
         PrepareDialogBox(hDlg, TRUE);

         lpMismatchStruct = (LPMISMATCHSTRUCT) lParam;

         // Tell the user why there is a file conflict.
         DWORD dwVIFResult = lpMismatchStruct->dwVIFResult;
         x = 0;
         if (dwVIFResult & VIF_MISMATCH)   x = IDS_MISMATCH;
         if (dwVIFResult & VIF_SRCOLD)     x = IDS_SRCOLD;
         if (dwVIFResult & VIF_DIFFLANG)   x = IDS_DIFFLANG;
         if (dwVIFResult & VIF_DIFFCODEPG) x = IDS_DIFFCODEPG;
         if (dwVIFResult & VIF_DIFFTYPE)   x = IDS_DIFFTYPE;
```

```
        LoadString(_hInstance, x, szBuf, sizeof(szBuf));
        SetDlgItemText(hDlg, ID_VERMISMATCHTEXT, szBuf);

        GetVerInfo(lpMismatchStruct->szExistingPath,
            GetDlgItem(hDlg, ID_VERINFOEXISTING));

        GetVerInfo(lpMismatchStruct->szTmpPath,
            GetDlgItem(hDlg, ID_VERINFONEW));

        SubclassWindow(GetDlgItem(hDlg, ID_VERINFOEXISTING),
            ListBoxSubclass);
        SubclassWindow(GetDlgItem(hDlg, ID_VERINFONEW),
            ListBoxSubclass);
        break;

    case WM_COMMAND:
        switch (wParam) {
            case IDABORT:
                nResult = MsgBox(_hInstance, hDlg, IDS_QUERYABORT,
                    _szAppName, MB_ICONQUESTION | MB_YESNO);
                if (nResult == IDNO) break;
                EndDialog(hDlg, wParam);
                break;
            case IDYES: case IDNO:
                EndDialog(hDlg, wParam);
                break;

            case ID_VERINFOEXISTING:
            case ID_VERINFONEW:
                if (HIWORD(lParam) != LBN_SELCHANGE) break;
                HWND hWndOtherLB = GetDlgItem(hDlg,
                    ((wParam == ID_VERINFONEW)
                    ? ID_VERINFOEXISTING : ID_VERINFONEW));

                x = ListBox_GetCurSel(LOWORD(lParam));
                if (x != ListBox_GetCurSel(hWndOtherLB))
                    ListBox_SetCurSel(hWndOtherLB, x);

                x = ListBox_GetTopIndex(LOWORD(lParam));
                if (x != ListBox_GetTopIndex(hWndOtherLB))
                    ListBox_SetTopIndex(hWndOtherLB, x);
                break;
        }
        break;

    default: fProcessed = FALSE; break;
    }
    return(fProcessed);
}
```

Listing 10-8. SETUPINF.CPP file-handling source module

```c
/*************************************************************************
Module name: SETUPINF.C
Programmer : Jeffrey M. Richter.
*************************************************************************/

#include <windows.h>
#include <string.h>
#include <stdlib.h>
#include "Setup.H"
#include "SetupInf.H"

SETUPINFO _SetupInfo;    // The global setup information.

#define MAXSETUPINFOSIZE    20480
#define MAXAPPDESC          50
#define MAXPARSELINELEN     100

#define ARRAY_LEN(Array)    (sizeof(Array) / sizeof(Array[0]))

static WORD NEAR latoi (LPSTR szString) {
   WORD wNum = 0;
   while (*szString >= '0' && *szString <= '9')
      wNum = (wNum * 10) + (*szString++ - '0');
   return(wNum);
}

static LPSTR NEAR StripEndBlanks (LPSTR szString) {
   LPSTR p = szString, q = szString;

   while (*p == ' ' || *p == '\t') p++;
   while (*p) *szString++ = *p++;
   *szString- = 0;
   while (szString >= q && (*szString == ' ' || *szString == '\t'))
      *szString- = 0;
   return(q);
}


//************************************************************************

class DISKINFO {
   UINT uNum;
   char szDesc[MAXDISKDESC];
   public:
   DISKINFO (LPSTR szLine);
   void GetDesc (LPSTR szDesc) const
      { lstrcpy(szDesc, this->szDesc); }
```

```
    UINT GetNum (void) const { return(uNum); }
};

DISKINFO::DISKINFO (LPSTR szLine) {
   LPSTR szData;
   if ((szData = _fstrchr(szLine, '=')) != NULL) *szData++ = 0;
   uNum = latoi(szLine);
   lstrcpy(szDesc, szData);
}

//***********************************************************************

class DIRINFO {
   UINT uNum;
   char szPath[_MAX_PATH];
   public:
   DIRINFO (LPSTR szLine);
   void GetPath (LPSTR szPath) const
       { lstrcpy(szPath, this->szPath); }
   UINT GetNum (void) const { return(uNum); }
};

DIRINFO::DIRINFO (LPSTR szLine) {
   LPSTR szData;
   if ((szData = _fstrchr(szLine, '=')) != NULL) *szData++ = 0;
   uNum = latoi(szLine);
   lstrcpy(szPath, szData);
}

//***********************************************************************

class FILEINFO {
   char szDesc[MAXDIRDESC];
   UINT uSrcDiskette;
   UINT uSrcDir;
   char szSrcName[MAXFILENAME];
   UINT uDstDir;
   char szDstName[MAXFILENAME];
   BOOL fSharable;
   char szDstDir[_MAX_PATH];  // Where file was installed
   public:
   FILEINFO (LPSTR szLine);

   UINT GetSrcDiskNum (void) const
       { return(uSrcDiskette); }

   UINT GetSrcDirNum (void) const
       { return(uSrcDir); }
```

```
    UINT GetDstDirNum (void) const
        { return(uDstDir); }

    BOOL GetFileInfo (LPSTR szDesc, LPSTR szSrcFileName,
        LPSTR szDstFileName) const {
        lstrcpy(szDesc, this->szDesc);
        lstrcpy(szSrcFileName, szSrcName);
        lstrcpy(szDstFileName, szDstName);
        return(fSharable);
    }

    BOOL DoesDstFileNameMatch (LPCSTR szDstFileName) const
        { return(lstrcmpi(szDstFileName, szDstName) == 0); }

    void SetDstDir (LPCSTR szDstDir)
        { lstrcpy(this->szDstDir, szDstDir); }

    void GetDstDir (LPSTR szDstDir) const
        { lstrcpy(szDstDir, this->szDstDir); }

};

FILEINFO::FILEINFO (LPSTR szLine) {
    LPSTR p = _fstrchr(szLine, ','), q;
    *p++ = 0;
    lstrcpy(szDesc, szLine);
    uSrcDiskette = latoi(StripEndBlanks(p));
    uSrcDir = latoi(p = StripEndBlanks(_fstrchr(p, '-') + 1));
    p = StripEndBlanks(_fstrchr(p, ':') + 1);
    q = _fstrchr(p, ','); *q = 0;
    lstrcpy(szSrcName, p);
    p = StripEndBlanks(p = q + 1);   // Point to 1st char of DstName
    uDstDir = latoi(p);
    p = StripEndBlanks(p = _fstrchr(p, ':') + 1);
    q = _fstrchr(p, ','); *q = 0;
    lstrcpy(szDstName, p);
    p = StripEndBlanks(p = q + 1);   // Point to 1st char of Sharable
    fSharable = ((*p == 'Y') || (*p == 'y'));
    szDstDir[0] = 0;
}


//*************************************************************************

class PMINFO {
    char szDstFileName[MAXFILENAME];
    char szAppDesc[MAXAPPDESC];
    UINT uIconNum;
    public:
    PMINFO (LPSTR szLine);
```

```
   UINT GetPMItemInfo (LPSTR szAppDesc, LPSTR szDstFileName) const;
};

PMINFO::PMINFO (LPSTR szLine) {
   LPSTR p = _fstrchr(szLine, ','), q;
   *p++ = 0;
   lstrcpy(szDstFileName, szLine);
   p = StripEndBlanks(p);  // Point to 1st char of AppDesc
   lstrcpy(szAppDesc, p);
   q = _fstrchr(p, ',');
   if (q == NULL) uIconNum = 0;
   else {
      p = StripEndBlanks(q + 1); // Point to 1st char of Icon #
      uIconNum = latoi(p);
   }
}

UINT PMINFO::GetPMItemInfo (LPSTR szAppDesc, LPSTR szDstFileName) const {
   lstrcpy(szAppDesc, this->szAppDesc);
   lstrcpy(szDstFileName, this->szDstFileName);
   return(uIconNum);
}
//************************************************************************

// -1 if an error occurs: File has no destination path (file wasn't
// installed).
UINT SETUPINFO::GetPMItemInfo (UINT uPMItemNum, LPSTR szAppDesc,
   LPSTR szDstFilePath) const {
   char szDstFileName[MAXFILENAME];

   UINT uIconNum =
      PMFiles[uPMItemNum]->GetPMItemInfo(szAppDesc, szDstFileName);
   // Find the destination filename in the file list.
   for (UINT x = 0; x < uNumFiles; x++)
      if (Files[x]->DoesDstFileNameMatch(szDstFileName)) break;

   if (x == uNumFiles) return(-1);  // Error in SETUP.INF, file not found.
   Files[x]->GetDstDir(szDstFilePath);
   if (szDstFilePath[0] == 0) return(-1);
   if (szDstFilePath[lstrlen(szDstFilePath) - 1] != '\\')
      lstrcat(szDstFilePath, "\\");
   lstrcat(szDstFilePath, szDstFileName);
   return(uIconNum);
}

void SETUPINFO::GetFileInstallInfo (UINT uFileNum,
   LPSTR szSrcDiskDesc, LPSTR szFileDesc,
   LPSTR szSrcFilePath, LPSTR szSrcFileName,
   LPSTR szDstFilePath, LPSTR szDstFileName, BOOL FAR *fSharable) const {
```

```
      FindDiskFromNum(Files[uFileNum]->
         GetSrcDiskNum())->GetDesc(szSrcDiskDesc);
      FindSrcDirFromNum(Files[uFileNum]->
         GetSrcDirNum())->GetPath(szSrcFilePath);
      FindDstDirFromNum(Files[uFileNum]->
         GetDstDirNum())->GetPath(szDstFilePath);
      *fSharable = Files[uFileNum]->
         GetFileInfo(szFileDesc, szSrcFileName, szDstFileName);
   }

DISKINFO *SETUPINFO::FindDiskFromNum (UINT uNum) const {
   UINT x;
   for (x = 0; x < uNumDisks; x++)
      if (Disks[x]->GetNum() == uNum) return(Disks[x]);
   return(NULL);
}

DIRINFO *SETUPINFO::FindSrcDirFromNum (UINT uNum) const {
   UINT x;
   for (x = 0; x < uNumSrcDirs; x++)
      if (SrcDirs[x]->GetNum() == uNum) return(SrcDirs[x]);
   return(NULL);
}

DIRINFO *SETUPINFO::FindDstDirFromNum (UINT uNum) const {
   UINT x;
   for (x = 0; x < uNumDstDirs; x++)
      if (DstDirs[x]->GetNum() == uNum) return(DstDirs[x]);
   return(NULL);
}

SETUPINFO::SETUPINFO (void) {
   ReadState = RS_UNDEFINED;
   szAppName[0] = 0;
   szDefaultDstDir[0] = 0;
   uSpaceNeeded = 0;
   szPMGrpFileName[0] = 0;
   szPMGrpName[0] = 0;
   fShowSubDirCreateStats = FALSE;

   uNumDisks = uNumSrcDirs = uNumDstDirs = uNumFiles = uNumPMFiles = 0;
   UINT x;
   for (x = 0; x < ARRAY_LEN(Disks);   x++) Disks[x]   = NULL;
   for (x = 0; x < ARRAY_LEN(SrcDirs); x++) SrcDirs[x] = NULL;
   for (x = 0; x < ARRAY_LEN(DstDirs); x++) DstDirs[x] = NULL;
   for (x = 0; x < ARRAY_LEN(Files);   x++) Files[x]   = NULL;
   for (x = 0; x < ARRAY_LEN(PMFiles); x++) PMFiles[x] = NULL;
}
```

```
SETUPINFO::~SETUPINFO (void) {
   ReadState = RS_UNDEFINED;
   szAppName[0] = 0;
   szDefaultDstDir[0] = 0;
   uSpaceNeeded = 0;
   szPMGrpFileName[0] = 0;
   szPMGrpName[0] = 0;
   fShowSubDirCreateStats = FALSE;

   UINT x;
   for (x = 0; x < uNumDisks; x++) delete Disks[x];
   for (x = 0; x < uNumSrcDirs; x++) delete SrcDirs[x];
   for (x = 0; x < uNumDstDirs; x++) delete DstDirs[x];
   for (x = 0; x < uNumFiles;   x++) delete Files[x];
   for (x = 0; x < uNumPMFiles; x++) delete PMFiles[x];
   uNumDisks = uNumSrcDirs = uNumDstDirs = uNumFiles = uNumPMFiles = 0;
}

void SETUPINFO::GetDstDir (UINT uDirNum, LPSTR szDstDir) const
   { DstDirs[uDirNum]->GetPath(szDstDir); }

void SETUPINFO::SetFileDstDir (UINT uFileNum, LPCSTR szDstDir) {
   Files[uFileNum]->SetDstDir(szDstDir);
}

SETUPINFO::ISIERROR SETUPINFO::InitSetupInfo (LPSTR szSetupInfoPathName) {
   HGLOBAL hGlbl;
   BOOL fOk;
   LPSTR p;

   hGlbl = GlobalAlloc(GMEM_MOVEABLE | GMEM_ZEROINIT, MAXSETUPINFOSIZE);
   if (hGlbl == NULL) return(ISI_NOMEM);

   OFSTRUCT of;
   HFILE hFile = OpenFile(szSetupInfoPathName, &of, OF_READ);
   if (hFile == -1) {
      GlobalFree(hGlbl);
      return(ISI_FILENOTFOUND);
   }
   p = GlobalLock(hGlbl);
   // Put a terminating zero byte at the end of the buffer.
   *(p + _lread(hFile, p, MAXSETUPINFOSIZE)) = 0;
   _lclose(hFile);
   fOk = ReadSetupInfo(p);
   GlobalUnlock(hGlbl);
   GlobalFree(hGlbl);
   return(fOk ? ISI_NOERROR : ISI_CANTPARSE);
}
```

682

```c
// Set the cursor to an hourglass before this call is made.
BOOL SETUPINFO::ReadSetupInfo (char FAR * lpSetupInfo) {
   char szLine[MAXPARSELINELEN];
   LPSTR p, szData;

   while (ReadState != RS_TERMINATE) {

      // Read next line from data buffer.
      p = _fstrchr(lpSetupInfo, '\r');
      if (p != NULL) *p = 0;
      lstrcpy(szLine, lpSetupInfo);
      if (p != NULL) lpSetupInfo = p + 2;

      // Remove leading white-space.
      StripEndBlanks(szLine);

      // Check if the state has changed.
      if (*szLine == '[') {
         ReadState = RS_UNDEFINED;

         if (!lstrcmpi(szLine, "[End]"))     ReadState = RS_TERMINATE;
         if (!lstrcmpi(szLine, "[App]"))     ReadState = RS_APPLICATION;
         if (!lstrcmpi(szLine, "[Disks]"))   ReadState = RS_DISKS;
         if (!lstrcmpi(szLine, "[SrcDirs]")) ReadState = RS_SRCDIRS;
         if (!lstrcmpi(szLine, "[DstDirs]")) ReadState = RS_DSTDIRS;
         if (!lstrcmpi(szLine, "[Files]"))   ReadState = RS_FILES;
         if (!lstrcmpi(szLine, "[PM Info]")) ReadState = RS_PMINFO;

         if (ReadState == RS_UNDEFINED) {
            // Unrecognized section in SETUP.INF file.
            return(FALSE); // Parse was not successful.
         }
         continue;
      }

      // Line is part of the current state.
      if (*szLine == ';') continue;   // Is it a comment?
      if (*szLine == 0) continue;     // Is it blank?

      switch (ReadState) {
         case RS_UNDEFINED: break;
         case RS_TERMINATE: break;
         case RS_APPLICATION:

            if ((szData = _fstrchr(szLine, '=')) != NULL) *szData++ = 0;
            // szLine is start of line to equal sign ('=').
            // szData is remainder of line after equal sign ('=').

            if (!lstrcmpi(szLine, "AppName")) lstrcpy(szAppName, szData);
```

```
          if (!lstrcmpi(szLine, "DefDir"))  lstrcpy(szDefaultDstDir,
             szData);
          if (!lstrcmpi(szLine, "SpaceNeeded")) uSpaceNeeded =
             latoi(szData);
          if (!lstrcmpi(szLine, "DefPMGroup")) {
             p = _fstrchr(szData, ','); *p = 0;
             lstrcpy(szPMGrpFileName, StripEndBlanks(szData));
             lstrcpy(szPMGrpName, StripEndBlanks(p + 1));
          }
          if (!lstrcmpi(szLine, "ShowSubDirCreateStats"))
             fShowSubDirCreateStats =
                ((*szData == 'Y') || (*szData == 'y'));
          break;

       case RS_DISKS:
          Disks[uNumDisks++] = new DISKINFO(szLine); break;

       case RS_SRCDIRS:
          SrcDirs[uNumSrcDirs++] = new DIRINFO(szLine); break;

       case RS_DSTDIRS:
          DstDirs[uNumDstDirs++] = new DIRINFO(szLine); break;

       case RS_FILES:
          Files[uNumFiles++] = new FILEINFO(szLine); break;

       case RS_PMINFO:
          PMFiles[uNumPMFiles++] = new PMINFO(szLine); break;
    }
 }
 return(TRUE);  // Parse was successful.
}
```

Listing 10-9. SETUPINF.H file-handling header

```
/***************************************************************
Module name: SETUPINF.H
Programmer : Jeffrey M. Richter.
***************************************************************/

// Defines used by the SETUP program.
#define MAXDISKDESC     50
#define MAXDIRDESC      30
#define MAXFILEDESC     50
#define MAXPMDESC       30
#define MAXAPPNAME      40
```

```
#define MAXDISKS      15
#define MAXDIRS       25
#define MAXFILES      250
#define MAXPMFILES    20

class DISKINFO;
class DIRINFO;
class FILEINFO;
class PMINFO;

class SETUPINFO {
    typedef enum {
        RS_UNDEFINED, RS_APPLICATION, RS_DISKS, RS_SRCDIRS,
        RS_DSTDIRS, RS_FILES, RS_PMINFO, RS_TERMINATE
    } READSTATE;
    READSTATE ReadState;

    char      szAppName[MAXAPPNAME];
    char      szDefaultDstDir[MAXDIR];
    UINT      uSpaceNeeded;
    char      szPMGrpFileName[MAXFILENAME];
    char      szPMGrpName[MAXPMDESC];
    BOOL      fShowSubDirCreateStats;
    UINT      uNumDisks, uNumSrcDirs, uNumDstDirs;
    UINT      uNumFiles, uNumPMFiles;
    DISKINFO *Disks[MAXDISKS];
    DIRINFO  *SrcDirs[MAXDIRS];
    DIRINFO  *DstDirs[MAXDIRS];
    FILEINFO *Files[MAXFILES];
    PMINFO   *PMFiles[MAXPMFILES];

    DISKINFO *FindDiskFromNum (UINT uNum) const;
    DIRINFO  *FindSrcDirFromNum (UINT uNum) const;
    DIRINFO  *FindDstDirFromNum (UINT uNum) const;
    BOOL ReadSetupInfo (char FAR *lpSetupInfo);

    public:
    SETUPINFO (void);

    ~SETUPINFO (void);

    typedef enum {
        ISI_NOERROR, ISI_NOMEM, ISI_FILENOTFOUND, ISI_CANTPARSE
    } ISIERROR;

    ISIERROR InitSetupInfo (LPSTR szSetupInfoPathName);

    void GetAppName (LPSTR szAppName) const
```

```
        { lstrcpy(szAppName, this->szAppName); }

    BOOL ShowSubDirCreateStats (void) const
        { return(fShowSubDirCreateStats); }

    void GetDefaultDstDir (LPSTR szDefaultDstDir) const
        { lstrcpy(szDefaultDstDir, this->szDefaultDstDir); }

    UINT GetDstDiskSpaceNeeded (void) const
        { return(uSpaceNeeded); }

    UINT GetNumDstDirs (void) const
        { return(uNumDstDirs); }

    void GetDstDir (UINT uDirNum, LPSTR szDstDir) const;

    void GetPMGroupInfo (LPSTR szGrpFileName, LPSTR szPMGrpName)
        const {
        lstrcpy(szGrpFileName, this->szPMGrpFileName);
        lstrcpy(szPMGrpName, this->szPMGrpName);
    }

    UINT GetPMItemNum (void) const
        { return(uNumPMFiles); }

    UINT GetPMItemInfo (UINT uPMItemNum, LPSTR szAppDesc,
        LPSTR szDstFileName) const;

    UINT GetNumFilestoInstall (void) const
        { return(uNumFiles); }

    void GetFileInstallInfo (UINT uFileNum,
        LPSTR szSrcDiskDesc, LPSTR szFileDesc,
        LPSTR szSrcFilePath, LPSTR szSrcFileName,
        LPSTR szDstFilePath, LPSTR szDstFileName,
        BOOL FAR *fSharable) const;

    void SetFileDstDir (UINT uFileNum, LPCSTR szDstDir);
};

extern SETUPINFO _SetupInfo;
```

Listing 10-10. SETUPPM.CPP Program Manager DDE conversation

```
/*********************************************************************
Module name: SETUPPM.C
Programmer : Jeffrey M. Richter.
*********************************************************************/

#include <windows.h>
#include <dde.h>
#include <stdlib.h>
#include <string.h>
#include "Setup.h"
#include "SetupInf.h"

char _szClassName[] = "DDEClient";

typedef struct {
   HWND hWndServer;
} WNDEB;

#define WM_DDECLIENT_EXECUTE  (WM_USER + 0)

LPARAM CALLBACK DDEClientWndProc (HWND hWnd, UINT wMsg,
   WPARAM wParam, LPARAM lParam) {

   LRESULT lResult = 0;
   BOOL fCallDefProc = FALSE;
   HWND hWndServer = (HWND) GETWNDEB(hWnd, WNDEB, hWndServer);
   char szBuf[100]; MSG Msg;

   switch (wMsg) {

      case WM_CREATE:
         SendMessage(-1, WM_DDE_INITIATE, hWnd,
            (LONG) ((LPCREATESTRUCT) lParam)->lpCreateParams);

         if (GETWNDEB(hWnd, WNDEB, hWndServer) != NULL)
            break;

         // A conversation was not able to be established.
         // Attempt to execute the desired application.
         GlobalGetAtomName(LOWORD(
            (LONG) ((LPCREATESTRUCT) lParam)->lpCreateParams),
            szBuf, sizeof(szBuf));
         WinExec(szBuf, SW_RESTORE);

         SendMessage(-1, WM_DDE_INITIATE, hWnd,
            (LONG) ((LPCREATESTRUCT) lParam)->lpCreateParams);
```

```
      if (GETWNDEB(hWnd, WNDEB, hWndServer) == NULL)
          lResult = -1;

      break;

case WM_DESTROY:
      PostMessage(hWndServer, WM_DDE_TERMINATE, hWnd, 0);
      SETWNDEB(hWnd, WNDEB, hWndServer, NULL);
      // From now on, do not send a WM_DDE_ACK message to the
      // server in response to any messages sent from the
      // server.
      break;

case WM_DDE_DATA:
      if (hWndServer != (HWND) wParam) {
          // Conversation not initiated with this server or
          // server sent after you have terminated the
          // conversation.
          if (HIWORD(lParam) != NULL) {
              // Data handle is not. If it were NULL, a link
              // was set using the WM_DDE_ADVISE message.
              GlobalFree(HIWORD(lParam));
          }
          GlobalDeleteAtom(LOWORD(lParam));
      }
      break;

case WM_DDECLIENT_EXECUTE:
      // This message was sent to this window from the
      // setup application. The lParam parameter contains
      // the handle of the memory containing the commands
      // to be executed by the server.

      // Verify that a conversation was started and
      // hasn't been terminated.
      if (hWndServer == NULL) break;

      PostMessage(hWndServer, WM_DDE_EXECUTE, hWnd, lParam);

      // Wait for response from the server.
      GetMessage(&Msg, hWnd, WM_DDE_ACK, WM_DDE_ACK);

      // Return whether the command was
      // acknowledged successfully.
      wParam = LOWORD(Msg.lParam);
      lResult = ((DDEACK *) &wParam)->fAck;
      break;
```

```
        case WM_DDE_TERMINATE:
            if (hWndServer == NULL) break;
            // The server has terminated the conversation.
            // You must post the WM_DDE_TERMINATE message back to
            // the server.
            PostMessage(hWndServer, WM_DDE_TERMINATE, hWnd, 0);
            SETWNDEB(hWnd, WNDEB, hWndServer, (HWND) NULL);
            break;

        case WM_DDE_ACK:
            if (hWndServer == NULL) {
                // No conversation initiated, WM_DDE_ACK must be from
                // a potential server that just received
                // WM_DDE_INITIATE message.
                SETWNDEB(hWnd, WNDEB, hWndServer, (HWND) wParam);
                break;
            }

            // WM_DDE_ACK message received from a potential server
            // but already established a conversation with
            // another server. Tell the server that you do not wish
            // to continue conversation with it.
            PostMessage((HWND) wParam, WM_DDE_TERMINATE, hWnd, 0);
            break;

        default:
            fCallDefProc = TRUE;
        break;
    }

    if (fCallDefProc)
        lResult = DefWindowProc(hWnd, wMsg, wParam, lParam);

    return(lResult);
}

BOOL WINAPI RegisterDDEClient (HINSTANCE hInstance) {
    WNDCLASS wc;
    wc.style = 0;
    wc.cbClsExtra = 0;
    wc.cbWndExtra = sizeof(WNDEB);
    wc.lpfnWndProc = DDEClientWndProc;
    wc.hInstance = hInstance;
    wc.hIcon = NULL;
    wc.hCursor = NULL;
    wc.hbrBackground = NULL;
    wc.lpszMenuName = NULL;
    wc.lpszClassName = _szClassName;
    return(RegisterClass(&wc));
```

```
}

// **** Functions for Adding Files to the Program Manager ********

BOOL WINAPI CreatePMInfo (HINSTANCE hInstance) {
    int nPMProg, nMaxPMProgs;
    UINT uTemp;
    BOOL fOk;
    char szPMGroup[_MAX_PATH], szPMGroupFileName[_MAX_PATH];
    char szPMProgPath[_MAX_PATH], szPMProgDesc[MAXPMDESC];
    char szCmd[200], szProgMan[] = "PROGMAN";
    HWND hWndDDEClient, hWndPM;
    ATOM aApp, aTopic;
    HGLOBAL hGlbl; LPSTR lpCommand;

    // Initiate a conversation with the Program Manager.
    aApp = GlobalAddAtom(szProgMan);
    aTopic = GlobalAddAtom(szProgMan);
    hWndDDEClient = CreateWindow("DDEClient", "", 0, 0, 0, 0, 0,
        NULL, NULL, hInstance, (LPSTR) MAKELONG(aApp, aTopic));
    GlobalDeleteAtom(aApp);
    GlobalDeleteAtom(aTopic);

    if (hWndDDEClient == NULL) {
        // Conversation could not be initiated.
        return(FALSE);
    }

    // Notice that I use the FindWindow function here. I can not
    // use the window handle of the DDE server window because the
    // Program Manager could acknowledge DDE conversation by
    // creating a "DDEServer" window.
    hWndPM = FindWindow(szProgMan, NULL);
    if (!IsWindow(hWndPM))  // Program Manager cannot be found.
        return(FALSE);

    // Force the Program Manager to open so that the user can
    // see which group and applications you are adding.
    ShowWindow(hWndPM, SW_RESTORE);

    // Disable the Program Manager so that the user
    // can't work with it while you are doing your stuff.
    EnableWindow(hWndPM, FALSE);

    // Create the PM group box.
    _SetupInfo.GetPMGroupInfo(szPMGroupFileName, szPMGroup);
    wsprintf(szCmd, "[CreateGroup(%s%s%s)]",
        (LPSTR) szPMGroup,
        (LPSTR) (*szPMGroupFileName == 0 ? "" : ","),
```

```
        (LPSTR) szPMGroupFileName);

    hGlbl = GlobalAlloc(GMEM_MOVEABLE | GMEM_DDESHARE,
        lstrlen(szCmd) + 1);
    lpCommand = GlobalLock(hGlbl);
    lstrcpy(lpCommand, szCmd);
    GlobalUnlock(hGlbl);

    fOk = (BOOL) SendMessage(hWndDDEClient,
        WM_DDECLIENT_EXECUTE, 0, MAKELONG(0, hGlbl));
    GlobalFree(hGlbl);

    // Add the individual PM files to the group box.
    nMaxPMProgs = _SetupInfo.GetPMItemNum();
    for (nPMProg = 0; fOk && (nPMProg < nMaxPMProgs); nPMProg++) {
        uTemp = _SetupInfo.GetPMItemInfo(nPMProg,
            szPMProgDesc, szPMProgPath);
        if (uTemp == (UINT) -1) // File cannot be added to group.
            continue;

        // Add the new file to the already created PM group.
        // Syntax: AddItem(CmdLine, Name, IconPath, Icon Index,
        //                  xPos, yPos, DefDir, HotKey, fMinimize)
        wsprintf(szCmd, "[AddItem(%s,%s)]",
            szPMProgPath, szPMProgDesc, uTemp);
        hGlbl = GlobalAlloc(GMEM_MOVEABLE | GMEM_DDESHARE,
            lstrlen(szCmd) + 1);
        lpCommand = GlobalLock(hGlbl);
        lstrcpy(lpCommand, szCmd);
        GlobalUnlock(hGlbl);

        fOk = (BOOL) SendMessage(hWndDDEClient,
            WM_DDECLIENT_EXECUTE, 0, MAKELONG(0, hGlbl));
        GlobalFree(hGlbl);
    }
    // Terminate the DDE conversation with the Program Manager.
    DestroyWindow(hWndDDEClient);
    EnableWindow(hWndPM, TRUE);
    return(fOk);
}
```

APPENDIX A

Determining the Stack Size Required by an Application

All of our applications need to allocate a stack in the program's data segment. But, how many of us really know how much stack space our application needs? Every application specifies the size of the stack required in the application's definitions file by specifying a value for the *STACKSIZE* statement. If you allocate a stack that is too small, you introduce hard-to-find bugs into our program or even an **Unrecoverable Application Error**. A stack that is too big will be "stealing" valuable memory from your application's local heap. With the structure and the two functions described below, you no longer have to guess how much stack space your application needs.

At the start of every application's data segment (address DS:0000), is a 16 byte data structure that Windows uses to manage your application's data segment:

```
typedef struct {
   BYTE bReserved[6];
   BYTE NEAR *npbLocalHeap;
   BYTE NEAR *npbAtomTable;
   BYTE NEAR *npbStackTop;
   BYTE NEAR *npbStackMin;
   BYTE NEAR *npbStackBtm;
} LOCALHEAPINFO, NEAR *NPLOCALHEAPINFO;
```

693

In this structure, all of the near pointers indicate offsets into the data segment where the associated information is located. For example, the *npbStackTop* and *npbStackBtm* pointers specify offsets into the data segment where the top and bottom of the stack area is located. You can use this information to write functions that directly manipulate and access the stack.

The first function, *StackPrepare*, fills the stack from the top up to the current position of the stack pointer (SP) with the value 0x88.

```
void WINAPI StackPrepare (void) {
    BYTE NEAR *npbStackTop =
            ((NPLOCALHEAPINFO) 0x0000)->npbStackTop;
    BYTE NEAR *npbStackNow;
    _asm MOV npbStackNow, SP;
    npbStackNow -= 2;
    while (npbStackTop < npbStackNow)
            *npbStackTop++ = 0x88;
}
```

Once the stack has been prepared, the *StackReport* function can be called to determine how much of the stack has ever been used. This function starts at the top of the stack and searches for the first byte that is not a 0x88. Once it has this offset, you can subtract it from the offset of the stack bottom giving the number of bytes of the stack that have been used.

```
WORD WINAPI StackReport (void) {
    BYTE NEAR *npbStackTop =
            ((NPLOCALHEAPINFO) 0x0000)->npbStackTop;
    while (*npbStackTop == 0x88)
            npbStackTop++;
    return(((NPLOCALHEAPINFO) 0x0000)->npbStackBtm -
                npbStackTop);
}
```

DETERMINING AN APPLICATION'S REQUIRED STACK SIZE

To determine how much stack space your application needs do the following:

1. Add these function to your program
2. Call the *StackPrep*are function as soon as your *WinMain* function starts
3. Call the *StackReport* function just before your *WinMain* function ends

For example, your *WinMain* function might look like this:

```
int WinMain (HINSTANCE hInstCurrent, HINSTANCE hInstPrev,
   LPSTR lpCmdLine, int nCmdShow) {
   char szBuf[50];
   MSG msg;
   StackPrepare();
   ...
   while (GetMessage(&msg, NULL, 0, 0)) {
      TranslateMessage(&msg);
      DispatchMessage(&msg);
   }
   ...
   wsprintf(szBuf, "Stack used = %u\n\r", StackReport());
   OutputDebugString(szBuf);
}
```

Now, you can run your application a number of times and perform different actions with each invocation. After each run, record the largest amount of stack space that has been used. This value is the minimum value that you must specify for the *STACKSIZE* statement in your module-definitions file. However, you should make the number somewhat larger so that you have room for your application to grow and in case you missed a path that the user might cause your program to execute through.

Accessing Class and Window Extra Bytes

This appendix introduces macros that give Windows developers a convenient method for storing and retrieving data associated with class and window extra bytes. For a complete description of how class and window extra bytes are used, refer to Chapter 1.

To use these macros to access a window's extra bytes, the application must declare a data structure listing the elements to be stored and their types. Each element should be a two- or four-byte entity. For example, a window class that needs to store a window handle and a *DWORD* value would declare a structure like this:

```
typedef struct {
    HWND hWndChild;
    DWORD dwLastEventTime;
} WNDEXTRABYTES;
```

When the application is initializing the *WNDCLASS* structure to pass to *RegisterClass*, the *cbWndExtra* member of this structure should be initialized as follows:

```
WndClass.cbWndExtra = sizeof(WNDEXTRABYTES);
```

This guarantees that the proper number of extra bytes is always allocated. If the programmer later adds, deletes, or changes the type of a member, the *sizeof* operator returns the proper length of the structure when the module is recompiled.

Storing information in the window's extra bytes is accomplished like this:

```
SETWNDEB(hWnd, WNDEXTRABYTES, dwLastEventTime, GetTickCount());
```

The *SETWNDEB* macro is shown as follows:

```
#define SETWNDEB(hWnd, Struct, Member, Value) \
   ( \
      (sizeof(((Struct FAR *)0)->Member) == sizeof(LONG)) ? \
      ((LONG)SetWindowLong(hWnd, FIELDOFFSET(Struct, Member), \
         (LONG)(Value))) : \
      ((WORD)SetWindowWord(hWnd, FIELDOFFSET(Struct, Member), \
         (WORD)(Value))) \
   )
```

This macro causes the compiler to determine whether the *SetWindowWord* or *SetWindowLong* function should be called, based on the size of the member being passed. In the previous example, the *SetWindowLong* function will be called because the *dwLastEventTime* member of the *WNDEXTRABYTES* structure is the same size as a *DWORD*.

A member's offset into the structure is the same as its offset into the window's extra bytes. Therefore, the offset is also automatically determined at compile time. If members of the structure are added, deleted, moved, or changed, recompiling the module automatically generates the correct offsets.

Values stored in the window's extra bytes are retrieved by the *GETWNDEB* macro:

```
#define GETWNDEB(hWnd, Struct, Member) \
   ( \
      (sizeof(((Struct FAR *)0)->Member) == sizeof(LONG)) ? \
      ((LONG)GetWindowLong(hWnd, FIELDOFFSET(Struct, Member))) :\
      ((WORD)GetWindowWord(hWnd, FIELDOFFSET(Struct, Member))) \
   )
```

This macro is similar to *SETWNDEB* except that it calls *GetWindowWord* or *GetWindowLong* and doesn't require an additional parameter specifying a new value.

To extend this method to work with class extra bytes, the application must declare another data structure containing the elements to be stored in the class extra bytes:

```
typedef struct {
    .
    .
    .
} CLSEXTRABYTES;
```

You then modify the function that initializes the *WNDCLASS* structure by adding the following line:

```
WndClass.cbClsExtra = sizeof(CLSEXTRABYTES);
```

To store and retrieve data in the class extra bytes, use the following macros:

```
#define SETCLSEB(hWnd, Struct, Member, Value) \
    ( \
        (sizeof(((Struct FAR *)0)->Member) == sizeof(LONG)) ?  \
        ((LONG)SetClassLong(hWnd, FIELDOFFSET(Struct, Member), \
            (LONG)(Value))) : \
        ((WORD)SetClassWord(hWnd, FIELDOFFSET(Struct, Member), \
            (WORD)(Value))) \
    )


#define GETCLSEB(hWnd, Struct, Member) \
    ( \
        (sizeof(((Struct FAR *)0)->Member) == sizeof(LONG)) ? \
        ((LONG)GetClassLong(hWnd, FIELDOFFSET(Struct, Member))) : \
        ((WORD)GetClassWord(hWnd, FIELDOFFSET(Struct, Member))) \
    )
```

These are identical to *SETWNDEB* and *GETWNDEB* except that they call *SetClassWord, SetClassLong, GetClassWord*, and *GetClassLong*.

All of these macros reference *FIELDOFFSET*. This macro is located in the WINDOWS.H file included with the Window's SDK:

```
#define FIELDOFFSET(type, field) /
    ((int)(&((type NEAR*)1)->field)-1)
```

The *FIELDOFFSET* macro assumes that there is a data structure of type at memory address one. It then references the specified member (*field*) of the structure (*type*), and returns the memory address where this member is located.

The BUILTINS.JMR File

    All of the MAKEFILEs used to create the sample applications in this book include the BUILTINS.JMR file (see Listing C-1). This file contains the rules that describe how the various source code files should be compiled. In addition, the directory paths for the include files and libraries are also specified in this file. If your include and library paths are not D:\BC\INCLUDE and D:\BC\LIB respectively, just change the INCLUDEDIR and LIBDIR lines in BUILTINS.JMR and all of the sample applications should compile and link correctly.

Listing C-1. The BUILTINS.JMR file

```
#************************************************************************
#Module name: BUILTINS.JMR
#Programmer : Jeffrey M. Richter.
#Description: MAKE macros/rules used to create Windows applications & DLLs
#************************************************************************

.autodepend

INCLUDEDIR = D:\BC\Include
LIBDIR = D:\BC\Lib

MODEL = m

RESOURCES = $(ICONS) $(BITMAPS) $(CURSORS)

.c.obj:
```

```
        bcc $(CFLAGS) $(DEFINES) {$< }

.cpp.obj:
        bcc $(CFLAGS) $(DEFINES) {$< }

.asm.obj:
        tasm $(AFLAGS) $<

.rc.res:
        rc -r $(DEFINES) -I$(INCLUDEDIR) $<
```

Index

A

About Program Manager help
  menu 74
AC message prefix 445
AC_MDICHILDENDSESSION
  484, 486, 488, 489, 490
AC_PAINTSTATBAR 456, 457
AC_QUERYCLOSEMDICHILD
  484, 486, 490
Add control button 130
Add>> push button 296
AddControlType 260, 261
AddDlgControl 150, 151, 153
AddItem 631
Advanced Power Management
  Specification Guide 357
AnyAppsRunning 81, 84
APP.EXE 615
Application global class 4
Application local class 5
Applications Programming
  Interface (API) 126, 546
AppName 621
AppWndProc 139
ARCADE.BMP 545
Arrange Icons window menu 73-74
ARTICLE.DOC 559
ASCII text file 545
Atoi 138
Auto Arrange options menu 73
AW message prefix 445
AW_PAINTMENUHELP 467, 468
AX register 77, 79

B

base class 93
BASIC programming language 582
Batteries 357
BC_BINNAMES 321
BeginDeferWindowPos 477
BeginPaint 227, 241, 351, 467
BkColor 228
BLACK_BRUSH 241
BlnkWndProc 400

BM_GETCHECK 270
BM_SETSTYLE 68
BMP file 545
BN_CLICKED 108, 137
Borland
  C++ compiler 78, 367
  Resource Workshop 214, 255
  WinSight 73
BringWindowToTop 37
BS_DEFPUSHBUTTON 15
BuildDynamicDlgBox 148, 149, 151
BUILTINS.JMR 701
Burnit 550
BURNIT.C 553
BURNIT.DEF 556
BURNIT.RC 557
BurnitWndProc 551
BUTTON system global class
  15, 25
  base class 93
  dialog box 164
  styles specific to 215
  undocumented message 68

C

C compiler 596
C++ 81
C++ compiler 78, 367
C/C++ compiler 78, 367
CALC.EXE 344, 345, 559
CalcClassByteIndex 104
CalcWindowByteIndex 104
CallDeviceModeFunc 306
CallMsgFilter 381, 383, 384
CallNextHookEx 363, 372, 374, 398
CallWindowProc
  address of Program Manager 75
  AX register 78, 79
  message to original window
    procedure 93
  normal operations for a
    message 67
CALLWNDPROC 374
Cascade option 471

Cascade window menu 74
cbClsAdditional 103
cbClsExtra
  class extra byte values 103
  default attributes and behavior 8
  increasing values 95
  RegisterNoAlphaWndClass 105
  RegisterSuperClass 100, 101
cbMaxCopy 312
CBT_ACTIVATESTRUCT 392
CBT_CREATEWND 160, 392, 394
CBTACTIVATESTRUCT 393
CBTProc 160
cbWndExtra 16, 697
  custom child controls 222
  default attributes and behavior 8
  increasing values 95
  RegisterNoAlphaWndClass 105
  RegisterSuperClass 100, 101
CD-ROM 583
Change Tab order button 128, 129
ChangeableArea 157, 165, 168
Character sets 594
CHART.C 445, 453, 524
Chart_MIDActivate 453
Chart_OnMouseActivate 453
Child controls 4
ChildWindowFromPoint 36
Class styles 42
Class type class style 7
Class*DlgFn* 258
Class*Flags* 258
Class*Info* 258
Class*Style* 258
Class*WndFn* 258
Class*Word* 8
ClientToScreen 36
Clock help menu 34
CNTL-DE.C 255, 258, 263, 268,
  280
CNTL-DE.H 255, 258, 284
CNTL-DE.OBJ 255
Code implementation 156
Color 38
COLOR_ACTIVECAPTION 451

COLOR_BTNFACE 240, 241
COLOR_BTNSHADOW 240
COLOR_BTNTEXT 240
COM1 299
COM2 299
COM3 299
COM4 299
COMBOBOX system global class 15, 25
  base class 93
  dialog box 164
  Software Development Kit 63
  uppercase characters 66
COMMDLG.DLL 295, 563, 588, 589
COMMDLG.H 324
Common Dialog-Box Library 323
COMPRESS.EXE 583
Compressing files 581, 583
Computer-based training (CBT) 391
Contents help menu 74
Control Panel 125, 213, 227, 237, 245
CONTROL system global class 97
CONTROL.INF 296, 298
ControlClassName 257
ControlID 257
ControlInfo 260, 261
ControlStyles 257
ControlText 257
Copy file menu 73
CreateDC 319, 320, 322, 330
CreateDialog 15, 29, 31, 159
CreateDialogIndirect 31, 144, 149, 154
CreateDialogIndirectParam 31, 144
CreateDialogParam 31, 142
CreateDlgTemplate 150, 153
CreateGroup 631
CreateModalLessDlgBox 139, 141, 142
CreatePen 39
CreatePrinterDC 330, 334
CREATESTRUCT 101, 146, 160
CreateWindow 12, 27, 76, 101
  Class Information 343
  custom control 287
  dwStyle 215
  dynamic dialog box 146
  filter function call 160
  Meter control 220
  SetWindowPos 130

subclassing 78
system global class 4
WS_EX_ACCEPTFILES 546
CreateWindowEx 12, 16, 164
  Class Information 343
  custom control 287
  dwStyle 215
  Meter control 220
  system global class 4
  WS_EX_ACCEPTFILES 546
  WS_MINIMIZE 550
CS_BYTEALIGNCLIENT 7
CS_BYTEALIGNWINDOW 7
CS_CLASSDC 7
CS_DBLCLKS 7
CS_GLOBALCLASS 5, 7, 222
CS_HREDRAW 7, 222
CS_KEYCVTWINDOW 7
CS_NOCLOSE 7
CS_NOKEYCVT 7
CS_OWNDC 7
CS_PARENTDC 7
CS_SAVEBITS 7
CS_VREDRAW 7, 222
CTLCOLOR_BTN 228
CTLCOLOR_DLG 228
CTLCOLOR_EDIT 228
CTLCOLOR_LISTBOX 228
CTLCOLOR_SCROLLBAR 228
CTLCOLOR_STATIC 228
CTLINFO 259, 260
CTLSTYLE 263
CTLSTYLEDLG 264
CtlStyleLock 267
CtlStyleUnlock 267
CTLTYPES 260
Ctrl key 543
CUSTCNTL.C 287
CUSTCNTL.DEF 292
CUSTCNTL.EXE 285
CUSTCNTL.H 258
CUSTCNTL.RC 292
CUTSTCNTL.H 292
CW_USEDEFAULT 27

D

Data-instance handle 341
Date/Time option 237, 245
DC_BINS 321
DC_COPIES 321
DC_DRIVER 321

DC_DUPLEX 321
DC_ENUMRESOLUTIONS 321
DC_EXTRA 321, 322
DC_FIELDS 321
DC_FILEDEPENDENCIES 321
DC_MAXEXTENT 321
DC_MINEXTENT 321
DC_ORIENTATION 321
DC_PAPERNAMES 321
DC_PAPERS 321
DC_PAPERSIZE 321
DC_SIZE 321
DC_TRUETYPE 321
DC_VERSION 321
DDE.H 636
DDEClient 631, 632
DDEML.DLL 588, 589
DEBUGHOOKINFO 397, 398
Default area 132
Default area control 132
Default Printer dialog box 301
DefDir 621
DeferWindowPos 477
DefFrameProc 449, 488
DefFramProc 437
DefHookProc 363
DefMDIChildProc 441, 448, 490
DefPMGroup 621, 623
DefWindowProc 98, 401
  default window procedure 7
  passing messages 22
  processing messages 23
  SubclassWindow 67
  superclassing 93
  WM_CTLCOLOR 228
  WM_ERASEBKGND 223
  WM_NCCREATE 12
  WM_SYSCOMMAND 35
Delete file menu 73
DeleteDC 320
DeleteGroup 631
DEMYSTS.DLL 542
Desktop option 237
DestroyControlsInChangeableArea 165, 169
DestroyModalLessDlgBox 142
DestroyWindow 142, 160
Developer tool support 587
Device context 40
Device driver 300
Device Not Selected timeout 300, 301

DeviceCapabilities 320, 321, 322
DeviceMode 304, 305, 306, 312, 313
DEVMODE 306, 308
DEVNAMES 330
Dialog-box templates 157
Dialog Editor 214, 255, 271
DIALOG system global class 15, 25
DialogBox 15, 31
    dialog box procedure 77
    MakeProcInstance 78
    modalless dialog box function
        equivalent 140
    ModalLessDialogBox 142
    SetParent 159
DialogBoxIndirect 31, 144, 154
DialogBoxIndirectParam 31, 138,
    144
DialogBoxParam 31, 138, 140,
    142, 266
Dirty flag 483
Disk swapping 581
DispatchMessage 359
Distribution floppy disks 581
DLG-DYNA.C 126, 148, 149, 185
DLG-DYNA.H 126, 194
DLG-MDLS.C 126, 142, 182
DLG-MDLS.H 126, 141, 142, 184
DLG-MODE.C 126, 161
DLG-MODE.H 126
DLG-OPTS.C 126, 132, 133
DLG-OPTS.H 126, 132, 181
DLG_FIRST 614
DLG_INSERTDISK 612, 613
DLG_LAST 614
DLG_WANTALLKEYS 224
DLGC_BUTTON 224
DLGC_DEFPUSHBUTTON 224
DLGC_HASSETSEL 224
DLGC_RADIOBUTTON 224
DLGC_STATIC 224
DLGC_UNDEFPUSHBUTTON 224
DLGC_WANTALLKEYS 224
DLGC_WANTARROWS 224
DLGC_WANTCHARS 224
DLGC_WANTMESSAGE 224
DLGC_WANTTAB 224
DLGITEMTEMPLATE 145
    AddDlgControl 151
    building templates in memory
        144
    CreateDlgTemplate memory
        allocation 153

CreateWindow 146
    MergeControlsIntoDlg 163
DLGOPTS.C 178
DLGTECH.C 126, 128, 171
DLGTECH.DEF 212
DLGTECH.EXE 126
DLGTECH.H 177
DLGTECH.RC 127, 207
DLGTEMPLATE
    CreateDlgTemplate 150
    DS_SETFONT 145
    MergeControlsIntoDlg 163
    Windows Programmer's
        Reference 144
DM_COLOR 309, 317
DM_COPIES 309
DM_COPY 315, 317
DM_DEFAULTSOURCE 309
DM_DUPLEX 309
DM_MODIFY 315, 317
DM_ORIENTATION 309
DM_PAPERLENGTH 309
DM_PAPERSIZE 309
DM_PAPERWIDTH 309
DM_PRINTQUALITY 309
DM_PROMPT 315, 317, 318
DM_SCALE 309
DM_TTOPTION 309
DM_UPDATE 315, 317, 318
DM_YRESOLUTION 309
DMBIN_AUTO 311
DMBIN_CASSETTE 311
DMBIN_ENVELOPE 311
DMBIN_ENVMANUAL 311
DMBIN_LARGECAPACITY 311
DMBIN_LARGEFMT 311
DMBIN_LOWER 311
DMBIN_MANUAL 311
DMBIN_MIDDLE 311
DMBIN_ONLYONE 310
DMBIN_SMALLFMT 311
DMBIN_TRACTOR 311
DMBIN_UPPER 310
dmColor 308, 311
DMCOLOR_COLOR 311
DMCOLOR_MONOCHROME 311
dmCopies 308, 310, 316, 317
dmDefaultSource 308, 310
dmDeviceName 308, 313
dmDriverExtra 308, 317
dmDriverSpec 308
dmDriverVersion 308, 317

DMDUP_HORIZONTAL 311
DMDUP_SIMPLEX 311
DMDUP_VERTICAL 311
dmDuplex 308, 311
dmFields 308, 309, 316, 317
dmOrientation 308, 309, 316, 317
DMPAPER_10X14 309
DMPAPER_11X17 309
DMPAPER_A3 309
DMPAPER_A4 309
DMPAPER_A4SMALL 309
DMPAPER_A5 309
DMPAPER_B4 309
DMPAPER_B5 309
DMPAPER_CSHEET 310
DMPAPER_DSHEET 310
DMPAPER_ENV_10 309
DMPAPER_ENV_11 310
DMPAPER_ENV_12 310
DMPAPER_ENV_14 310
DMPAPER_ENV_9 309
DMPAPER_ENV_B4 310
DMPAPER_ENV_B5 310
DMPAPER_ENV_B6 310
DMPAPER_ENV_C3 310
DMPAPER_ENV_C4 310
DMPAPER_ENV_C5 310
DMPAPER_ENV_C6 310
DMPAPER_ENV_C65 310
DMPAPER_ENV_DL 310
DMPAPER_ENV_ITALY 310
DMPAPER_ENV_MONARCH 310
DMPAPER_ENV_PERSONAL 310
DMPAPER_ESHEET 310
DMPAPER_EXECUTIVE 309
DMPAPER_FANFOLD_LGL
    _GERMAN 310
DMPAPER_FANFOLD_STD
    _GERMAN 310
DMPAPER_FANFOLD_US 310
DMPAPER_FOLIO 309
DMPAPER_LEDGER 309
DMPAPER_LEGAL 309
DMPAPER_LETTER 309
DMPAPER_LETTERSMALL 309
DMPAPER_NOTE 309
DMPAPER_QUARTO 309
DMPAPER_STATEMENT 309
DMPAPER_TABLOID 309
dmPaperLength 308, 310
dmPaperSize 308, 309
dmPaperWidth 308, 310

dmPrintQuality 308, 311
DMRES_DRAFT 311
DMRES_HIGH 311
DMRES_LOW 311
DMRES_MEDIUM 311
dmScale 308, 310
dmSize 308
dmSpecVersion 308
DMTT_BITMAP 311
DMTT_DOWNLOAD 311
DMTT_SUBDEV 311
dmTTOption 308, 311
dmYResolution 308, 311
do...while loop 244
DoneAddingControls 153
Drag-and-drop technology 541, 549, 577
DragAcceptFiles 546, 547
DragAppendFile 560, 561, 565
DRAGFILESTRUCT 559
DragFinish 549, 552
DragInitBlock 559, 561, 565
DragQueryFile 547, 548, 552
DragQueryPoint 549
Dragxx API 558
DrawWindowFrame 37, 38
DRIVE_FIXED 629
DRIVE_REMOTE 629
Driver filename 298
DROPFILE.C 566
DROPFILE.DEF 574
DROPFILE.EXE 563
DROPFILE.H 575
DROPFILE.RC 575
Dropping-not-allowed cursor 564
DS register
   message sent to dialog box 77
   pushing upon calling window procedure 76
   SS register 367
   task switching 75
DS_SETFONT 145, 150, 153
dtCaptionText 153
dtClassName 153
dtilClass 153
dtilCX 164
dtilCY 164
dtilData 146, 153
dtilItemCount 153
dtilInfo 146
dtilText 153
dtilX 164

dtilY 164
dtItemCount 154
dtMenuName 153
dwEventTime 245
dwExtraInfo 379
dwFileDateLS 599
dwFileDateMS 599
dwFlags 270
dwLastEventTime 698
dwMenuDescCode 465
DWORD 42, 239, 697
dwSignature 599
dwStructVersion 599
dwStyle 215, 261, 263, 269
Dynamic dialog box 126
Dynamic link library (DLL) 3, 77, 78, 214, 364
Dynamic modeless demo option 148

E

Echo sample application 415
ECHO.C 421
ECHO.DEF 426
ECHO.H 426
ECHO.RC 426
EDIT control 64
EDIT system global class 15, 25, 63, 164
EDIT windows 12
EndDeferWindowPos 477
EndDialog 109, 140, 141, 143, 270
EndModalLessDlgBox 140, 141, 142, 143
EndPaint 351, 467
EnumChildProc 166
EnumChildWindows 160, 165
EnumFontFamilies 320
EnumFonts 320
EnumProps 20
EnumWindows 81, 84
EPSON9.DRV 298
EPT 299
ETO_CLIPPED 230, 231
ETO_OPAQUE 230
EVENTMSG 352
Exit Windows file menu 73
ExitDeviceMode 314, 315
ExitProgram 631
EXPAND.EXE 581, 584, 587, 606
Expanded memory (EMS) 346
Extended window styles 42

Extra bytes list box 41
ExtTextOut 229, 230

F

fAck 636
fAppModal 490
FAR function 93
FARPROC 628
fCallDefProc 139
fCallNexHookProc 420
fCallOrigProc 83
fDoubleClick 449
fEnable 481
fEnding 486, 489
FIELDOFFSET 699, 700
FILE 299
File Manager 541, 580
FILEFLAGMASK 591
FILEFLAGS 591, 596
FILEOS 591
FILESUBTYPE 592
FILETYPE 592
FILEVERSION 591
FileVersionInfo 598
Filter-function chain 370
FilterFunc 369
FindResource 162, 614, 615
FindWindow 70, 72
FIXED 611, 614
Flags member 326
flnNonClientArea 559
FloodFill 241
fModeless 149
FONTINFO 144, 145, 153, 163
FORWARD_WM_COMMAND 216
fpDlgProc 167
fPlaying 418
Frame dialog 157
FRAME.C 445, 461, 500
Frame_OnCommand 478
Frame_OnEnterIdle 465
Frame_OnGetStatBarRect 454
Frame_OnNCLButtonClick 449
Frame_OnNCLButtonDown 446
fRecording 418
FreeLibrary 286, 306, 631
FreeProcInstance 75, 77, 78, 79
fShowDefAreaOnly 135, 136
fSkipDisabled 472
fSysModal 488
fuFlags 358

FW message prefix 445
FW_DRAWSTATUSDIVIDE 455
FW_GETMENUHELP 468
FW_GETNUMFILENAMES 564
FW_GETSTATBARRECT 454
FW_RESIZEMDICLIENT 478
FW_SETMENUHELP 464, 465, 467, 470
fwCapability 321
FWMDICHILDDESTROY 479
fwMode 315, 316, 317

G
GCL_MENUNAME 11
GCL_WNDPROC 11
GCW_ATOM 8, 11
GCW_CBCLSEXTRA 11
GCW_CBWNDEXTRA 11
GCW_CDWNDEXTRA 41
GCW_HANDLE 11
GCW_HBRBACKGROUND 11
GCW_HCURSOR 11
GCW_HINSTANCE 8, 343
GCW_HMODULE 11, 343, 344
GCW_MODULE 8
GCW_STYLE 11
GDI function 302
GDI.EXE 584
General Protection Violation 160
GetActiveWindow 451
GetAsyncKeyState 244, 565
GetBCWndProc 104, 108
GetCapture 35
GetClassByte 41
GetClassInfo
   display information 40
   register new superclass 100
   RegisterNoAlphaWndClass 105
   superclassing 93
   window properties 20
   WNDCLASS 10
GetClassLong 10, 11, 104, 699
GetClassName 17, 40
GetClassWord
   atom value 8
   extra byte reference 104
   Extra bytes list box 41
   GCW_HMODULE 343, 344
   retrieving class structure members 10

stack size 699
WINDOWS.H identfiers 11
GetClientRect 472
GetCurrentTask
   PM Restore 70, 84
   task-instance handle 347
   task-specific hook 368
   WH_KEYBOARD 419
GetCurrentTime 352
GetCursorPos 246
GetDC 39
GetDeviceCaps 320
GetDriveType 629
GetEnvironment 313, 319, 322
GetExpandedName 585
GetFileVersionInfo 597, 602, 610
GetFileVersionInfoSize 597, 602, 610
GetFirstChild 477
GetIDString 266, 267
GetLastEventTime 401
GetMessage 636
   EVENTMSG 354
   GetQueueStatus 359
   retrieve a message 353
   TranslateMessage 350
   WH_CALLWNDPROC 375
   WH_GETMESSAGE 365
   WH_HARDWARE 366
   window message queue 231
   WinMain 83
GetMessageExtraInfo 379
GetMessagePos 359
GetModuleFileName
   executable file 40, 41
   hModuleHook 397
   Voyeur 344
GetNextDlgTabItem 129
GetNextSibling 474
GetNumTasks 347
GetOpenFilename 563
GetParent 267
GetProcAddress 306, 314, 367, 628, 630
GetProp 20, 143, 267
GetQueueStatus 359
GetSCClassLong 104
GetSCClassWord 104
GetSCWindowLong 104
GetSCWindowWord 104
GetStringId 267

GetSubMenu 464
GetSysColor 240
GetSystemMetrics 455, 456, 481
GetTextExtent 29
GetTickCount 244, 352
GetVerFuncAddress 626
GetWindowDC 39
GetWindowFont 165
GetWindowLong 698
   extended styles 34
   retrieving individual structure members 17
   SetClassInfo 41
   style information 16
GetWindowOwner 473
GetWindowRect 41, 449
GetWindowsdirectory 629
GetWindowTask 347, 368
GetWindowText 41
GetWindowWord 17, 41, 227, 698
GETWNDEB 634, 698, 699
Global memory blocks 346
Global Protection Violation 348
Global variable 215
GlobalAlloc 346, 347, 597
GlobalFree 14, 146, 148
GlobalLock 148, 346
GlobalReAlloc 153
GlobalSize 153
GlobalUnlock 148, 346
GMEM_DDESHARE 346, 347, 559, 635
GMEM_SHARE 347, 559
Group Windows window menu 74
GWL_EXSTYLE 17
GWL_STYLE 17
GWL_WNDPROC 17
GWW_HINSTANCE 17, 41, 344
GWW_HWNDPARENT 17
GWW_ID 17

H
Handle to a device context (HDC) 29
hardware_event 379
HARDWAREHOOKSTRUCT 379
hbrBackground
   BeginPaint 241
   Meter control 223
   RegisterControlClass 239

SCRNBLNKPOPUP 401
WNDCLASS member 8, 97
HC_ACTION
  JrnlRecHookFunc 417
  KybdHookFunc 420
  message to window 374
  MSG structure 375
  WH_CALLWNDPROC 373
  WH_DEBUG 397
  WH_HARDWARE 379
  WH_JOURNALRECORD 384, 385
  WH_KEYBOARD 376
  WH_MOUSE 378
HC_GETNEXT 386, 388
HC_NOREMOVE 376, 378, 379
HC_SKIP 386
HC_SYSMODALOFF 384, 385, 386, 417
HC_SYSMODALON 384, 385, 386, 417
HCBT_ACTIVATE 392, 393
HCBT_CLICKSKIPPED 393, 394
HCBT_CREATEWND 160, 392, 394
HCBT_DESTROYWND 392
HCBT_KEYBOARD 395
HCBT_KEYSKIPPED 393, 395, 396
HCBT_MINMAX 392
HCBT_MOVESIZE 392
HCBT_QS 393, 396
HCBT_SETFOCUS 392
HCBT_SYSCOMMAND 392
hCursor 8, 97
hDC 326
hDevMode 325, 330
hDevNames 326, 330
hdlg 161
hDriver 315
hDrop 547, 549
HELP_QUIT 420
hFont 165
hGlblCtlStyle 263, 264
hGlobal 14
hHook 373
HIBYTE 41
hIcon 8, 97
hInst 367
hInstance 3, 6
  AX register 78
  CreateWindow 76

dialog-box template 161
module handle and data
  instance handle 8
NoAlpha 105
PRINTDLG 327
superclassing 93
WinMain 342
HINSTANCE handle 341, 344
HINSTANCE_ERROR 306
hinstCurrent 367
hkPrc 367
hmenuPopup 464
HMODULE 341, 344
hModuleHook 397
How to Use Help help menu 74
HPPLOT.DRV 315
hPrevInstance 70, 342
hPrintTemplate 327
hrsrcDialog 162
hSetupTemplate 328
HSHELL_ACTIVATESHELL-
  WINDOW 390
HSHELL_WINDOWCREATED
  390, 391
HSHELL_WINDOWDESTROYED
  390, 391
HTASK 341, 368
HTCAPTION 565
HTCLIENT 453, 565
HTMENU 449
HTSYSMENU 565
HW_MOUSE 395
hWnd
  CallWindowProc 67
  ExitDeviceMode 315
  GetCapture 36
  MOUSEHOOKSTRUCT 378
  MSG structure 349
  WH_CALLWNDPROC 374
HWND_BOTTOM 34, 552
HWND_NOTOPMOST 34, 552
HWND_TOP 34, 552
HWND_TOPMOST 34, 552
hWndActive 393
hwndDeactivate 453
hwndInsertAfter 394
hWndLastSubject 32, 37
hWndMDIClient 472
hwndParent 161, 394
hWndPrevChild 165
hwndSender 465

I
ID_NAME 129
ID_NAMETEXT 129
ID_OVER25 129
IDCANCEL 270, 316, 482
idHook 365
IDM_PEERINTOWINDOW 35
IDM_PMRESTORABOUT 83
IDM_PMRESTOREREMOVE 83
IDOK 270, 316, 482
INFO window 24
INFO.C 24
INFO.H 24
Information at Your Fingertips
  Objective 541
Input conversion class style 7
Installed Printers list box 298, 301
InstallJrnlHook 398
InvalidateRect 41, 226, 231, 245, 350
InvalidateRgn 350
io.device 296
IsTask 347
IsWindowEnabled 226
IsWindowVisible 401

J
JournalRecordProc 385
JrnlPlybkHookFunc 415
JrnlRecHookFunc 415, 417

K
KERNEL.EXE 587
Keyboard interface 156
KeyboardProc 363
KybdHookFunc 419, 420

L
Landscape mode 295
Language support 593, 594
LB_DELETESTRING 216
LB_ERR 216
LB_SETTABSTOPS 30
LBN_SELCHANGE 168
LBS_USETABSTOPS 29
lCustData 327
LibEntry 6, 285
LIBENTRY.ASM 285
LibMain 221, 239, 257, 285, 367

List of Printers list box 298
LISTBOX system global class 15, 25
  dialog box 164
  dropfile client window 548
  Microsoft Windows' Software Development Kit (SDK) 63
  styles specific to 215
  windows requiring alteration 97
LoadAccelerator 162
LoadBitmap 162, 449
LoadCursor 162
LoadFont 145
LoadIcon 162, 615
LoadLibrary 285, 306, 626
LoadMenu 162
LoadResource 614, 615
LOBYTE 41
LockResource 164, 613, 614
lParam 22, 67, 216
lpCreateParams 101, 146
lpDevMode 319, 322
lpdmInput 316, 318
lpdmOutput 317
lpdwTranslationInfo 600
lpEventMsg 387
lpfnIdToStr 264, 266, 267, 269
lpfnPrintHook 327
lpfnSCWndProc 102
lpfnSetupHook 327
lpfnStrToId 264, 269
lpfnWndProc 3, 6, 7
  address of procedure 63
  RegisterNoAlphaWndClass 105
  RegisterSuperClass 100, 101
  value in base class window procedure 93
lpInitData 322
lpOutput 321
lpPoint 549
lpSetupTemplateName 327
lpszAppDir 604
lpszClassName 3, 6, 93, 105
lpszCurDir 603, 604, 605, 607, 610
lpszDestDir 603, 605, 607, 610
lpszDestFilename 608, 610
lpszDevice 315, 319
lpszDriver 319
lpszDstFilename 607
lpszFile 548
lpszFilename 603
lpszMenuName 8

lpszPort 315, 319, 321
lpszSrcDir 607
lpszSrcFilename 607
lpszSubBlock 598, 600, 601
lpszTmpFile 610
lpszWinDir 603
LPT1 299
LPT1.DOS 299
LPT2 299
LPT2.DOS 299
LPT3 299
lpuCurDirLen 603, 604
lpuDestDirLen 604
lpvEnviron 313, 322
lpVSFixedFileInfo 598, 599
lpzMenuName 97
lStructSize 325
LZClose 586
LZCopy 585, 587
LZDone 587
LZERROR.GLOBALLOC 587
LZExpand library 586, 587, 602
LZEXPAND.DLL 584, 625, 627
LZEXPAND.DLX 626, 628, 630
LZEXPAND.H 587
LZFile 587
LZFinish 587
LZOpenFile 585
LZStart 586, 587

M

MA_ACTIVATE 451
MA_ACTIVATEANDEAT 451, 453
MA_NOACTIVATEANDEAT 451
MA_NOACTIVE 451
MAKEINTRESOURCE 10, 162, 614
MakeProcInstance 75
  dialog box procedure 77
  function prologues 78
  hkPrc 367
  procedural instance and use of 75
  Program Manager data segment 79
MapDialogRect 30, 130
MDI Child windows 437
MDI Child's Close Box 446, 449, 450
MDI.C 444, 477, 497
MDI.DEF 540

MDI.EXE 454
MDI.H 445, 492
MDI.RC 478, 532
MDICLIENT 437, 454, 455
MDICLIENT system global class 15, 25
MDITILE_HORIZONTAL 471
MDITILE_SKIPDISABLED 472
MDITILE_VERTICAL 471, 472
Memory 218
MergeControlsIntoDlg 161, 163, 165
Message 67
Message cracker 22
MessageBeep 107
MessageBox 108, 361, 487
Meter 213, 218, 580
METER.C 232
METER.DEF 231, 278
METER.H 228, 232
METER.RC 278
METERDLG.C 271, 276
MeterWndFn 224, 226
MF_BITMAP 458, 459
MF_CHECKED 458
MF_DISABLED 458
MF_GRAYED 458
MF_MOUSESELECT 458
MF_OWNERDRAW 458
MF_POPUP 458, 459, 463, 464
MF_SYSMENU 458, 459, 463
Microsoft
  C/C++ compiler 78, 367
  Dialog Editor 214, 255, 271
  Excel 131, 477
  Project for Windows 477
  SDK Programmer's Reference 374, 376, 378
  Spy 73, 373
  Windows Programmer's Reference 7, 22, 325, 328
  Windows Software Development Kit (SDK) 63, 125, 255, 312
  Word for Windows 131, 450, 471
  Word for Windows 2.0 154
Minimize on Use option 68
Minimize on Use options menu 73
MM_GETPARTSCOMPLETE 219, 220, 226, 231
MM_GETPARTSINJOB 219, 220, 226, 231

MM_SETPARTSCOMPLETE 219, 220, 231
MM_SETPARTSINJOB 219, 231
MMSYSTEM.DLL 587
Modal dialog 156
Modal dialog box 20, 138
Modalless dialog box 126, 138
ModalLessDlgBox 140, 141, 142, 143
ModalLessDlgProc 142
Mode selection dialog box 126
Modeless dialog box 35, 40, 156
ModeSelDlgProc 167, 170
Module-instance handle 341
ModuleFindHandle 397
More Windows window menu 74
Mouse cursor 25
Mouse interface 156
MOUSEHOOKSTRUCT 378, 393
Move file menu 73
MoveWindow 27, 454
MS-DOS 542
MS-DOS Executive 546
MS_CHANGEAWAY 170
MSG_CHANGEAWAY 169
MSGF_DIALOGBOX 380, 381, 467
MSGF_MENU 380, 467
MSGF_NEXTMENU 381
MSGF_NEXTWINDOW 381
MSGF_SCROLLBAR 381
MSGF_USER 383
Multilingual character set 595
Multimedia device interface 587
Multiple 437

N

Name-mangling 81
NameTable 612
nAveCharHeight 30
nAveCharWidth 30
nCode 369, 372, 383
nCopies 327
NEC Pinwriter P6 303, 331
NEC24PIN.DRV 298
New file menu 73
NEWLISTBOX system global class 97
nExitCode 349
nFromPage 327
nIndex 104

nMaxPage 327
nMaxTextLen 31
nMDIChildrenToTile 474
nMinPage 327
NoAlpha 99
NOALPHA.C 99, 109
NOALPHA.DEF 117
NOALPHA.EXE 99
NOALPHA.H 116
NOALPHA.RC 116
NoAlphaApp 105
NoAlphaWndProc 106
NONDISCARDABLE 611, 625
Notepad 243, 544
npbStackBtm 694
npbStackTop 694
npszPathName 552
nResult 143
nToPage 327
nTopOfBottomIconRow 473, 474
NullPort 313

O

Object Linking and Embedding (OLE) 541, 587
OBM_CLOSE 449
OF_DELETE 611
OFN_ALLOWMULTISELECT 563
OLECLI.DLL 587, 588
OLESVR.DLL 587 588
Open Custom option 255
Open file menu 73
OpenFile 552, 585, 611
OPENFILENAME 563
Options>> dialog box 125, 135
OptionsDlgProc 133, 135
Out of timers! message 243

P

Package, creating 545
Painting class style 7
PAINTSTRUCT 457
Paper orientation 302
Paper size 302
PASCAL 93
PBRUSH.DLL 345
PBRUSH.EXE 345, 543
PD_ALLPAGES 328
PD_COLLATE 328
PD_COLLATECOPIES 328

PD_DISABLEPRINTTOFILE 328
PD_ENABLEPRINTHOOK 328
PD_ENABLEPRINTTEMPLATE 328
PD_ENABLEPRINTTEMPLATE-HANDLE 328
PD_ENABLESETUPHOOK 328
PD_ENABLESETUPTEMPLATE 329
PD_ENABLESETUPTEMPLATE–HANDLE 329
PD_HIDEPRINTTOFILE 329
PD_NOPAGENUMS 329
PD_NOSELECTION 329
PD_NOWARNING 329
PD_PAGENUMS 329
PD_PRINTSETUP 329
PD_PRINTTOFILE 329
PD_RETURNDC 329
PD_RETURNDEFAULT 329
PD_RETURNIC 330
PD_SELECTION 330
PD_SHOWHELP 330
PD_USEDEVMODECOPIES 330
PeekMessage
    EVENTMSG 354
    message queue 231
    retrieve a message 353
    TranslateMessage 350
    WH_CALLWNDPROC 375
    WH_GETMESSAGE 365
    WH_HARDWARE 366
PENWIN.DLL 588
Performance overhead 218
Plus sign in a cursor 543
PM_NOREMOVE 355, 376, 378, 379
PM_NOYIELD 355
PM_REMOVE 355
PMREST.C 85
PMREST.DEF 81, 91
PMREST.EXE 84
PMREST.RC 91
PMSubClass 75, 84
POINT 549
*POP*ing 76
PostAppMessage 83, 349
PostMessage 349, 562
PostQuitMessage 349, 355
PRELOAD 611, 614
PrepareSetup 626, 627, 631
Print Manager 544

Print Setup Command dialog box 323
PRINT.C 334
PRINT.DEF 340
PRINT.H 306, 307, 315
PRINT.RC 340
PRINTDEMO.C 331
PRINTDLG 324
Printer technology 302
Printers dialog box 295, 300
PrivateBuild 596
PROC_OLDDEVICEMODE 306
PRODUCTVERSION 591
PROGMAN class name 71
PROGMAN.EXE 345
Program Manager 26, 69
Program Manager Restore (PM Restore) 68, 78, 350
Properties file menu 73
Protected mode 75
PS_INSIDEFRAME 39
PSCRIPT.DRV 298
Pseudo-dialog box 167, 170
PtInRect 246, 450
ptMousePos 558
*PUSH*ing 76

Q

QS_KEY 358
QS_MOUSE 358
QS_MOUSEBUTTON 358
QS_MOUSEMOVE 358
QS_PAINT 359
QS_POSTMESSAGE 359
QS_SENDMESSAGE 359
QS_TIMER 359

R

rc.left 449
rc.top 449, 474
README.TXT 581, 582
REC_ACTIVE 416
REC_INACTIVE 416
REC_NOEVENTS 416
REC_NOMEMORY 416, 417
REC_OK 416, 417
REC_SYSMODALON 416, 417
REC_TOOMANY 416
RECORD.C 428

RECORD.DEF 435
RECORD.H 435
RECORD.MKF 436
Recorder application 375
Recorder function 415
Rectangle 39
RegisterClass 3
    application local class 6
    extra bytes 697
    Meter control 221
    sequence of events 8
    subclassing 63
    superclassing 97
    system global class 4
RegisterControlClass 221, 239
Registering a class 3
RegisterMsgFilterCode 383
RegisterNoAlphaWndClass 105
RegisterSuperClass 99, 101, 105
RegisterWindowMessage 23, 25, 383
    adding user messages 98
    internal messages 68
    message value conflicts 105
    ValidRange and *SetRange* 106
Reload 631
Remove Custom option 256
RemoveProp 20, 143
ReplaceItem 631
ReplyMessage 360
ResetDC 319
Resolution, horizontal or vertical 302
RIBBON.C 477
RM_STARTPLAY 416
RM_STARTRECORD 416
RM_STOPPLAY 416
RM_STOPRECORD 416
RT_ACCELERATOR 162, 614
RT_BITMAP 162, 614
RT_CURSOR 162
RT_DIALOG 162, 614
RT_FONT 162, 614
RT_FONTDIR 162, 614
RT_ICON 162
RT_MENU 162, 614
RT_RCDATA 162, 614
RT_STRING 162
Run file menu 73

S

Save Settings on Exit options menu 73
SBDLL.C 398, 412
SBDLL.DEF 414
SBDLL.MKF 414
SBDLL.RC 414
SC_CLOSE 450
SC_HOTKEY 392
Scaling information 298
ScreenToClient 565
SCRNBLNK.C 403
SCRNBLNK.DEF 411
SCRNBLNK.EXE 398
SCRNBLNK.H 410
SCRNBLNK.RC 411
SCRNBLNKPOPUP 398, 400
Scroll bar, initializing values 12
SCROLLBAR system global class 15, 25, 164
Search for Help on help menu 74
Segmented architecture 75
SEM_NOOPENFILEERRORBOX 627
SendDlgItemMessage 220, 270
SendMessage
    active tasks 345
    DeviceMode 312
    DragAppendFile 562
    MDI Child window 450
    Meter 220
    SetDlgMsgResult 218
    WH_CALLWNDPROC 365, 373, 375
    WM_DEVMODECHANGE 314, 318
Set As Default Printer button 301
SetCapture 35
SetClassInfo
    filling dialog box 37
    modeless dialog box 40
    SetWindowInfo 41
SetClassLong 11, 101, 104, 699
SetClassWord 11, 101, 104, 699
SetDlgItemText 267
SetDlgMsgResult 217
SetEnvironment 312, 314, 318, 322
SetErrorMode 627
SetFocus 108, 129, 348, 482
SetIdValue 268, 269
SetMessageQueue 348

SetParent 160
SetProp 20
SetRange message 105, 106
SetSCClassLong 104
SetSCClassWord 104
SetSCWindowLong 104
SetSCWindowWord 104, 106
SetStyleOff 137
SetStyleOn 137
SetTextColor 228
SetTimer 351
Setup program 213
Setup Toolkit for Windows 582
SETUP.CPP 613, 626, 631, 639
SETUP.DEF 654
SETUP.EXE 579, 580, 612, 616
SETUP.H 654
SETUP.INF 544, 581, 616, 624
SETUP.RC 614, 658
SETUPDLG.CPP 631, 664
SETUPINF.CPP 624, 677
SETUPINF.H 624, 684
SETUPINFO 624
SETUPM.CPP 631
SETUPPM.CPP 687
SetWindowInfo 37, 41
SetWindowLong
   changing members 19
   stack size 698
   SubclassWindow 67
   superclassing 97
   WS_EX_TOPMOST 34
SetWindowPos 33, 34
   Burnit 552
   dialog-box technique 125
   moving windows 551
   restoring window to original
      size 138
   window manager list 130
   z-order correction 165
SetWindowsHookEx 419
   event and type of hook 369
   filter function in DLL 367
   hHook 373
   hook installation 365
   returning handle of filter
      function 371
SetWindowText 137
SetWindowWord 19, 231, 698
SETWNDEB 634, 699
SHEET.C 445, 520
SHELL.DLL 588, 606

SHELLAPI.H 546
ShowArea 135
ShowGroup 631
ShowStyleDlg 263, 264, 265
ShowSubDirCreateStats 621
ShowWindow 70, 81, 401
Sound recorder 545
Source code 63
SpaceNeeded 621
SpecialBuild 596
Spin button 213
Spin Button control 236
Spin Button Style dialog box 266
SPIN class 5
SPIN.C 239, 245, 249
SPIN.DEF 248
SPIN.H 237, 238, 245, 248
SPIN.RC 274
SPINDLG.C 271
SpinDlgFn 266
SpinFlags 270
SpinInfo 259
SpinStyle 262
SPNDLG.C 270
SPNM_GETCRNTVALUE 238
SPNM_GETRANGE 238
SPNM_SCROLLVALUE 238
   event time 244
   message from spin button
      window 238
   scrolling sping button 245
   storing the triangle 248
   TrianglePresses 243
SPNM_SETCRNTVALUE 238, 247
SPNM_SETRANGE 238
SPNN_VALUECHANGE 239, 248
SPNS_WRAP 237, 246, 267, 270
SS register 76, 78, 367
SS_BLACKRECT 137
SS_CENTER 15
SS_LEFT 137
StackPrepare 694, 695
StackReport 694, 695
STACKSIZE 693, 695
Standard menu item 35
STATIC system global class 15,
   25, 157, 164
Static variable 215
Static windows 41
STRESS.DLL 588
StringFileInfo 592, 594, 595
Style member 7

Style of a window 14
STYLELIST 42
Styles option 257
Subclassing versus superclassing
   97, 98
SubclassWindow 67
Superclassing versus subclassing
   97, 98
SUPERCLS.C 99, 104, 108, 118
SUPERCLS.H 122
SUPERCLSINIT 100
SuperClsInitWndProc 101, 102
Switch-case construct 107
SWP_NOMOVE 35
SWP_NOSIZE 35
SWPDlgProc 128, 129
System Application Architecture
   Common User Access
   Advanced Interface Design
   Guide 236
System global child control classes
   213
System global class 4, 76, 346, 473
System queue 351
SYSTEM.INI 69
szAllFilenames 564
szClass 263
szDescr 261
szDlgTemplate 161, 167
szDstDir 629
szId 269
SZMODALLESSSHOWMSG 141,
   142
szModeName 167
szString 270

T

TA_CENTER 230
Tab key 127, 128, 156
Task switching 75
Task-instance handle 341
Task-specific hooks 368
TI microLaser PS35 302, 331
Tile option 471
Tile window menu 74
TileHorizontally 472, 477
Tiling algorithm 474
Time delay between scrolling
   events 244
TImicroLaser PS35 304
TOOLHELP.DLL 347, 397, 588

TranslateMessage 350
Transmission Retry timeout 300, 301
TrianglePresses 243

U

uChangeAwayMsg 167
uIDChangeableArea 161, 165
uLen 600
uMsg 67, 374
uMsgFilterFirst 354
uMsgFilterLast 354
UnhookWindowsHookEx 373, 386, 419
Unrecoverable Application Error 693
UnregisterClass 3, 223, 286
Up-arrow cursor 12
UpdateWindow 231, 350
USER.EXE 344, 346, 564, 587

V

ValidateRect 350
ValidateRgn 350
ValidRange message 105, 106
VarFileInfo 592, 595
VER.DLL
    bug 604
    copying to hard disk 627
    developer package 588
    resource information 596
    setup program 625
    *VER.DL_* 625
    VerFindFile and *VerInstallFile* 603
VER.H 591, 596, 599, 604, 608
VerFindFile 603, 604, 606
VerInstallFile 603, 605, 607, 611
VerLanguageName 601, 610
VerQueryInfo 600
VerQueryValue
    lpszSubBlock 600, 601
    resource blocks 602
    retrieve memory block information 597
    VER.H 610
    void pointer 598
VERSIONINFO 590, 592, 595
VFF_BUFFTOOSMALL 604
VFF_CURNEDEST 604

VFF_FILEINUSE 604, 605
VFFF_ISSHAREDFILE 604
VFT2_DRV_COMM 592
VFT2_DRV_DISPLAY 592
VFT2_DRV_INSTALLABLE 592
VFT2_DRV_KEYBOARD 592
VFT2_DRV_LANGUAGE 592
VFT2_DRV_MOUSE 592
VFT2_DRV_NETWORK 592
VFT2_DRV_PRINTER 592
VFT2_DRV_SOUND 592
VFT2_DRV_SYSTEM 592
VFT2_FONT_RASTER 592
VFT2_FONT_TRUETYPE 592
VFT2_FONT_VECTOR 592
VFT2_UNKNOWN 592
VFT_APP 592
VFT_DLL 592
VFT_DRV 592
VFT_FONT 592
VFT_STATIC_LIB 592
VFT_UNKNOWN 592
VFT_VXD 592
VIF_ACCESSVIOLATION 609
VIF_BUFFTOOSMALL 609
VIF_CANNOTCREATE 609
VIF_CANNOTDELETE 609
VIF_CANNOTREADDST 609
VIF_CANNOTREADSRC 609, 610
VIF_CANNOTRENAME 609
VIF_DIFFCODEPG 608, 610
VIF_DIFFLANG 608, 610
VIF_DIFFTYPE 608, 610
VIF_FILEINUSE 608
VIF_MISMATCH 608, 610
VIF_OUTOFMEMORY 609
VIF_OUTOFSPACE 608
VIF_SHARINGVIOLATION 609
VIF_SRCOLD 608, 610
VIF_TEMPFILE 608
VIF_WRITEPROT 608, 609
VIFF_DONTDELETEOLD 605, 608
VIFF_FORCEINSTALL 611
VK_LBUTTON 244, 565
VM_VKEYTOITEM 217
VOS_DOS 591
VOS_DOS_WINDOWS16 591
VOS_DOS_WINDOWS32 591
VOS_NT 591
VOS_NT_WINDOW32 591
VOS_UNKNOWN 591

VOS_WINDOWS16 591
VOS_WINDOWS32 591
Voyeur 25, 542
    About box 27
    dialog box 125
    Drop back and peer 27, 33
    Peer into window 26, 32, 343
    Program manager window handle 71
VOYEUR.C 44
VOYEUR.H 58
VOYEUR.RC 27, 59
VoyeurAppWndProc 27, 29, 32
VoyeurDlgProc 29
VS_FF_DEBUG 591
VS_FF_INFOINFERRED 591
VS_FF_PATCHED 591
VS_FF_PRERELEASE 591
VS_FF_PRIVATEBUILD 591
VS_FF_SPECIALBUILD 591
VS_FFI_FILEFLAGSMASK 591
VS_FIXEDFILEINFO 599

W

WaitMessage 231, 357
WAV file 545
wCtlTypes 260
wFileNum 547
WH_CALLWNDPROC
    description 365
    installation 374
    keystroke conversion 377
    performance of Windows 375
    Spy 373
WH_CBT 395
    computer-based training 391
    description 366
WH_DEBUG 366, 396, 397, 398
WH_GETMESSAGE 365, 373, 375, 377
WH_HARDWARE 366, 379
WH_JOURNALPLAYBACK
    adding macro 384
    description 366
    HCBT_CLICKSKIPPED 394
    HCBT_KEYSKIPPED 396
    system scope installation 368
    WH_CBT 391
WH_JOURNALRECORD
    adding macro 384
    description 366

EVENTMSG 385
SCRNBLNK.EXE 398
system scope installation 368
WH_KEYBOARD
  CallNextHookEx 420
  description 365
  Echo application 415, 418
  filter function 370, 372
  HCBT_KEYSKIPPED 395
  messages to application 377
  Recorder application 375
  task scope 369
WH_MOUSE 365, 377, 395
WH_MSGFILTER
  control message 383
  description 366
  dialog-box message 380
  lParam 381
  WH_SYSMSGFILTER priority
    368
WH_SHELL 366, 390, 391
WH_SYSMSGFILTER
  CallMsgFilter 383, 384
  description 366
  dialog-box message 380
  lParam 381
  system scope installation 368
wHeight 261
wHitTestCode 378
WIN.INI
  application file information
    581, 582
  ports section 298
  PrintersPorts section 300
  system startup 72
Window
  aborting the creation 13
  caption 12
  class 3
  handle 67
  internal representation of the
    structure 17
  manager's list 33
  procedure address 64
  styles 42
WindowFromPoint 36, 564
Windows
  Control Panel 213, 227, 237,
    245
  DDK documentation 312
  Help 33, 34
  NT 79, 368

Programmer's Reference 129,
  144
SDK Programmer's Reference
  363
Tutorial help menu 74
Windows exit procedure (WEP)
  223, 257, 258
WINDOWS.H
  class structure elements 10
  class-specific messages 24
  compressing files 584
  dialog-box templates 144
  extended window styles 16
  FIELDOFFSET 699
  GMEM_SHARE 559
  HANDLE 341
  MSGF_USER 383
  structures and data types 363
  system global class 15
  user messages 68
  value definitions 614
  WM_USER 239
WINDOWSX.H 22
  FORWARD_WM_COMMAND
    216
  MDI application 445
  SubclassWindow 67
WinExec 634
WINFILE.EXE 564
WinHelp 418, 420
WinMain
  data-instance handler 341
  DLGTECH.C 126
  GetMessage 83
  hInst 367
  hInstance 6, 93
  MDI.C 477
  stack space 695
WINMEM32.DLL 588
WM_?BUTTONDOWN 451
WM_ACTIVATEAPP 69, 80
WM_BLBUTTONDOWN 450
WM_BUTTONDOWN 242, 243,
  378
WM_BUTTONUP 378
WM_CHAR 66, 107, 350
WM_CHARTOITEM 217
WM_CLOSE 139, 488, 490
WM_COMMAND
  Dialog Editor 268
  FORWARD_WM_COMMAND
    217

menu option 73
notification codes 216, 239
ribbon dialog box 482
superclass window procedure
  97
WM_COMPAREITEM 217
WM_CREATE 14, 27, 139
  broadcast response 634
  BurnitWndProc 551
  creating a window 98
  DDEClient 632
  dynamic dialog box 146
  HCBT_CREATEWND 394
  initializing extra words 107
  MDI 437
  printer setup demonstration 332
  screen-blanker utility 398
  superclassing 102
  SuperClsInitWndProc 101
WM_CTLCOLOR 217, 228, 240
WM_DDE_ACK 633, 636
WM_DDE_EXECUTE 635, 636
WM_DDE_TERMINATE 637
WM_DDECLIENT_EXECUTE 635
WM_DESTROY 14, 229, 420, 479,
  637
WM_DEVMODECHANGE 313,
  314, 318
WM_DROPFILES
  Burnit 552
  DragAppendFile 562, 565
  DragFinish 549
  Dropfile client 547
  Dropfile server 558
  user-defined messages 576
WM_DROPTEXT 576
WM_ENABLE 224, 226, 480, 481
WM_ENDSESSION 489
WM_ENTERIDLE 465, 468, 469
WM_ERASEBKGND 223, 401, 467
WM_GETDLGCODE 224
WM_GETFONT 224, 225
WM_GETMINMAXINFO 101
WM_INITDIALOG 29, 97, 108
  CreateModalLessDlgBox 141
  creating brushes 229
  CtlStyleLock 267
  modeless dialog box 138
  ModeSelDlgProc 167
  OptionsDlgProc 135
  pseudo-dialog box 169, 170
  ShowArea 136

SpinDlgFn 266
zero value as response to
    message 217
WM_KEYDOWN 350, 365, 393,
    420, 465
WM_KEYUP 365
WM_KILLFOCUS 348
WM_LBUTTONDBLCLK 35
WM_LBUTTONDOWN 35, 246,
    453, 564, 577
WM_LBUTTONUP 35
WM_MDIACTIVATE 453
WM_MDICASCADE 471, 472
WM_MDIICONARRANGE 471,
    472
WM_MDITILE 471, 472
WM_MENUSELECT
    Frame window 460
    hwndSender 465
    MDI Child's system menu 459
    menu options 457
    message cracker 461, 464
    MF_SYSMENU 463
    value and description 458
WM_MOUSEACTIVATE 450, 451,
    453
WM_MOUSEFIRST 354
WM_MOUSELAST 354
WM_MOUSEMOVE 35
    dialog box 35
    lParam value 36
    system queue 352
    WM_ENTERIDLE 469
    wParam 378
WM_NC?BUTTONDOWN 451
WM_NCCALCSIZE 101
WM_NCCREATE 12, 13
    creating a window 98
    dynamic dialog box 146
    HCBT_CREATEWND 394
    superclassing 102
    SuperClsInitWndProc 101
WM_NCDESTROY 101, 102
WM_NCHITTEST 378, 449, 565
WM_NCLBUTTONDBLCLK 446
WM_NCPAINT 35
WM_PAINT
    GetMessage 350
    GetQueueStatus 359
    IsWindowEnabled 226
    message queue 353
    Meter 223, 226

SCRNBLNKPOPUP 402
Spin button 240
status bar 456
Voyeur 35
WM_POWER 357
WM_QUERYDRAGICON 217
WM_QUERYENDSESSION 483,
    484, 486, 488
WM_QUERYOPEN 398, 550
WM_QUEUESYNC 396
WM_QUIT 83, 349, 355
WM_SETCRNTVALUE 247
WM_SETCURSOR 38, 453
WM_SETFOCUS 348
WM_SETFONT 224, 225
WM_SETREDRAW 41
WM_SYSCHAR 350
WM_SYSCOMMAND 32, 35, 73,
    450
WM_SYSKEYDOWN 350
WM_TIMER
    application queue 353
    BlnkWndProc 400
    SCRNBLNKPOPUP 402
    SetTimer 351
    WM_BUTTONDOWN 243
WM_USER 23, 239
wMaxFileSize 548
wMaxString 270
WNDCLASS 40
    creating a window class 3
    extra bytes 20
    hbrBackground 239, 401
    RegisterClass 343, 697
    RegisterControlClass 221
    subclassing 63
    superclassing 93
    system global class 4
WNDEXTRABYTES 698
wNumEvents 387
WORD 239
wParam 22, 29, 67, 69, 216
WS_BORDER 14, 15, 215
WS_CAPTION 14, 15, 43
WS_CHILD 14, 28, 130, 451, 477
WS_CLIPCHILDREN 14
WS_CLIPSIBLINGS 14, 478
WS_DISABLE 480
WS_DISABLED 14
WS_DLGFRAME 14
WS_EX_ACCEPTFILES 16, 546,
    550, 564

WS_EX_DLGMODALFRAME 16
WS_EX_NOPARENTNOTIFY 16
WS_EX_TOPMOST 16, 33, 400
WS_EX_TRANSPARENT 16
WS_GROUP 14, 15, 43
WS_HSCROLL 14
WS_MAXIMIZE 14
WS_MAXIMIZEBOX 14, 15, 43
WS_MINIMIZE 14, 550
WS_MINIMIZEBOX 14, 15, 43
WS_OVERLAPPED 14
WS_POPUP 14, 28, 215, 400
WS_SYSCOMMAND 28
WS_SYSMENU 14
WS_TABSTOP
    CreateWindow 130
    GetNextDlgTabItem 129
    Tab key 135
    Voyeur 43
    WINDOWS.H identifier 14, 15
WS_THICKFRAME 14
WS_VISIBLE 14, 215
WS_VSCROLL 14
WSHELL_ACTIVATESHELL-
    WINDOW 391
wSize 558
wType 261
wWidth 261

X

xDLGPROC 167

Z

Z-order 33, 551

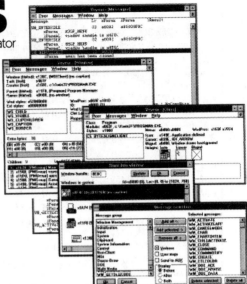

Tell us what you think and we'll send you a free M&T Books catalog

It is our goal at M&T Books to produce the best technical books available. But you can help us make our books even better by letting us know what you think about this particular title. Please take a moment to fill out this card and mail it to us. Your opinion is appreciated.

Tell us about yourself

Name _____

Company _____

Address _____

City _____

State/Zip _____

Title of this book?

_____

Where did you purchase this book?

☐ Bookstore
☐ Catalog
☐ Direct Mail
☐ Magazine Ad
☐ Postcard Pack
☐ Other

Why did you choose this book?

☐ Recommended
☐ Read book review
☐ Read ad/catalog copy
☐ Responded to a special offer
☐ M&T Books' reputation
☐ Price
☐ Nice Cover

How would you rate the overall content of this book?

☐ Excellent
☐ Good
☐ Fair
☐ Poor

Why?

_____

_____

What chapters did you find valuable?

_____

_____

_____

What did you find least useful?

_____

_____

_____

What topic(s) would you add to future editions of this book?

_____

_____

_____

What other titles would you like to see M&T Books publish?

_____

_____

_____

Which format do you prefer for the optional disk?

☐ 5.25"   ☐ 3.5"

Any other comments?

_____

_____

_____

☐ Check here for
M&T Books Catalog

M&T BOOKS

2764

BUSINESS REPLY MAIL

FIRST CLASS MAIL PERMIT 2660 SAN MATEO, CA

POSTAGE WILL BE PAID BY ADDRESSEE

M&T BOOKS

411 Borel Avenue, Suite 100
San Mateo, CA 94402-9885

PLEASE FOLD ALONG LINE AND STAPLE OR TAPE CLOSED